SHAKE DOWN THE THUNDER

Also by Murray Sperber

Literature and Politics

And I Remember Spain:
Writers in the Spanish Civil War

Arthur Koestler:
A Collection of Essays

College Sports Inc.:
The Athletic Department vs
the University

SHAKE DOWN
THE THUNDER

The Creation of Notre Dame Football

MURRAY SPERBER

HENRY HOLT AND COMPANY / NEW YORK

Henry Holt and Company, Inc.
Publishers since 1866
115 West 18th Street
New York, New York 10011

Henry Holt® is a registered
trademark of Henry Holt and Company, Inc.

Published in Canada by Fitzhenry & Whiteside Ltd.,
195 Allstate Parkway, Markham, Ontario L3R 4T8.

Library of Congress Cataloging-in-Publication Data
Sperber, Murray.
Shake down the thunder: the creation of Notre Dame football/
Murray Sperber.—1st ed.
p.   cm.
Includes bibliographical references (p.   ) and index.
1. University of Notre Dame—Football—History.   2. Notre Dame
Fighting Irish (Football team)—History.   I. Title.
GV958.N6S64   1993
796.332'63'0977289—dc20   93-27979
                                                                CIP

ISBN 0-8050-1874-3

Henry Holt books are available for special promotions and
premiums. For details contact: Director, Special Markets.

First Edition—1993

Designed by Katy Riegel

Printed in the United States of America
All first editions are printed on acid-free paper. ∞

1   3   5   7   9   10   8   6   4   2

All photographs courtesy of Notre Dame Archives.

Contents

Preface

"Every time I read a story about either one of them [Knute Rockne and Frank Leahy], I get sick to my stomach . . . [and that movie] they did on Rock. Sheer garbage! That's what that one was. The stories about both of them are absolutely stuffed with mistakes. I can't understand why a newspaperman with nothing else to do but drink and go to football games can't occasionally check a fact. One man makes a mistake in print and the thing is repeated for fifty years."

> —Father Frank Cavanaugh, C.S.C. priest at Notre Dame,
> quoted in Wells Twombley,
> *Shake Down the Thunder: The Critical Biography of*
> *Notre Dame's Frank Leahy*

The title of my book originates in a series of 1960s conversations with the late Wells Twombley in a San Francisco bar across from Kezar Stadium, then the home of the 49ers. I lived nearby and often dropped in for a beer; Twombley and other sportswriters would gather in the Kezar Lounge after covering 49ers' practice. I often talked to Twombley about my alma mater, Purdue, and its annual games with Notre Dame, and I recall him saying that a great title for a book about N.D. would be a line from the school's "Victory March"—"Shake down the thunder."

He interpreted the line directly—the football wrath that the Fighting Irish have often brought down upon their opponents. Because at the time I was working on a Ph.D. in English literature, I argued for a double meaning: *the University of Notre Dame, with its famous football team, had shaken down the thunder and brought the procreating rain of fame and fortune to the school but also a destructive storm to its academic side* —that is, a hard-to-erase reputation as a "football factory." We debated this during quite a number of meetings and over many drinks.

In 1974, Wells Twombley published *Shake Down the Thunder,* his excellent biography of Frank Leahy. Sadly, he died a few years later. Thus I see the title of my book as both applicable to my work—my interpretation of the phrase informed the narrative—and an homage to a witty writer and long-ago conversations in a bar in San Francisco.

Before I went to Notre Dame to do research there, some of my colleagues at Indiana University warned me that I would receive a very cool reception, if I was welcomed at all. They based their predictions on an uninformed stereotype of the Catholic school. The opposite proved true: the people who run present-day Notre Dame were uniformly helpful, patient, and accommodating, spending many hours of their time to facilitate my work. Moreover, they permitted me to roam about the university and to ask any question of anyone—administrators, faculty, staff, and students—whom I encountered.

In the course of my wanderings, in a sub-basement of the Hesburgh Library, I happened upon some old wooden and cardboard boxes containing the office files of the Notre Dame athletic department for the years 1909 through 1934. I was amazed to discover that these papers included the daily correspondence of Knute Rockne, approximately 14,500 items, and that most of these documents had never been examined before. Reading them was like entering a world that I hardly knew existed—one so contrary to the legends and books about American college sports and Knute Rockne that I was startled by the discrepancy between the myths and the actual historical records in my hands.

Much of my book is based on these papers, but their existence also seems an apt symbol for the University of Notre Dame and its historical dilemma—the tension between its athletic prominence and its academic aspirations. Notre Dame authorities had kept the athletic department files because they understood the importance of Fighting Irish football in their school's history; however, they did not want to overemphasize sports, even to the point of cataloging these important papers. Many universities long ago discarded their athletic department records; others, such as the University of Michigan, felt secure enough in their academic standing to place their sports files in their main archives and to itemize them thoroughly. Notre Dame had both retained the papers and shoved them almost out of sight.

To help me with my project, the University of Notre Dame Archives negotiated the transfer of the materials from the University libraries, then processed the papers and placed them in their permanent collection. In addition, head archivist Wendy Schlereth allowed me to follow the paper trails begun in the athletic department folders—letters and memos leading to the Golden Dome, the Notre Dame administration building. She opened the files of the school's past presidents and vice presidents—over sixty thousand items—and permitted me to study their handling of the intercollegiate athletic program. Again, a previously unknown world opened—the complex tangle of religious and academic demands, financial pressures, and public relations in which these administrators worked. Because these men believed in tight-lipped secrecy, outsiders have not been aware of the crucial role they played in determining the nature of Fighting Irish sports.

The willingness to open the administrative papers to a researcher from another university is also a symbol of the current status of the University of Notre Dame. In the past, in its more parochial phase, the school would not have done this. But now, as a major research institution, it welcomes scholars studying many different subjects, including its own history and that of its famous football team. Furthermore, Notre Dame accepts the fact that objective scholars might find material reflecting negatively on its past and that they can reveal this information in their published research. Such is the nature of serious scholarship: disclosing the truth is more important than perpetuating comforting legends.

In defining itself as a research university and coming to terms with its fabled sports history, Notre Dame finally transcends its "football factory" image and builds its reputation as a major academic institution.

Acknowledgments

Many people helped me with this book. Foremost were my friend and agent John Wright and my sympathetic editor Bill Strachan. John is that rare person who returns phone calls promptly and also leaves long messages about the angst and joys of loving the New York Rangers and the Wagner Ring; Bill always keeps the writing temperature cool, edits politely but incisively, and truly believes in his authors. Special thanks also to Paul Strohm for his encouragement throughout the project, to Ken Johnston for sharing his knowledge of writing during coffee breaks in the library, and to Judd Kahn for advising me to focus on my work and not burden my friends by talking about it.

In the last twenty-five years I have done research in many university archives on this continent and abroad. In all of that time, I have never encountered more helpful and conscientious archivists than at the University of Notre Dame: I must thank them collectively and individually. Head archivist Wendy Clauson Schlereth always displayed wit and understanding in the face of exceedingly complicated and time-consuming requests—she made this project possible and helped me complete it on schedule. Associate archivist Peter Lysy, with brilliant detective powers and an insatiable perfectionism, brought order to the chaos of the Rockne papers. Charles Lamb, in charge of the UNDA graphics collection, found many vivid pictures for me and enabled the photographs in this book to transcend the usual clichéd depictions of Rockne and his era. I must also thank archivists Jennifer Webber, Wm.

Kevin Cawley, and Beth Ingle for their help; in addition, Bernie Terry was always cheerful on the telephone and willing to track down errant packages, and Sharon Sumpter learned to read my handwriting and filled every photocopy order perfectly.

I am also grateful to Jethrow Kyles, formerly with the University of Notre Dame, for allowing me access to the sub-basement of the Hesburgh Library, to his assistant at the time, Barb Pietraszewski, and to the staff in the Special Collections department, Laura Fuderer, Rita Erskine, and Marilyn Bierwagen. The Notre Dame athletic department was also helpful, particularly A.D. Dick Rosenthal, S.I.D. John Heisler, former associate S.I.D. Jim Daves, and assistant Rose Pietrzak. Larry Weaver, collector of Notre Dame anecdotes, patiently answered many questions about his alma mater during lengthy telephone calls, and John Kryk, author of a forthcoming book about the Michigan–Notre Dame series, generously shared some of his research with me.

At my own school—Indiana University, Bloomington—many persons aided me. In the Main Library, the help of Ann Bristow, head of the Reference department, her extraordinary assistant Dave Frasier—an expert on everything from axe murderers to Russ Meyer films—and assistant Frank Quinn was invaluable; in Interlibrary Loan, Rhonda Stone was always willing to track down obscure newspapers; and in Microfilm Services, Marty Sorury and Diana Hanson did their best to reproduce difficult films. In the English department, I received assistance from Reba Amerson, June Hacker, Mary Lou Jones, Linda Richardson, Anita Schaad, Casey Smith, Donna Stanger, and Penny Toliver; and moral support came from Indiana University faculty members Dianna Gray, Susan Gubar, Ray Hedin, Sheila and Peter Lindenbaum, Tim Long, Lew Miller, Scott Sanders, Lee Sterrenburg, Mary Jo Weaver, and Cary Wolfe. Special thanks to Don Gray, who directed me through the complexity of religious terminology, David Nordloh, who solved various computer problems, and research assistants Devin Werthem and Wayne Achterberg.

At my publisher, Henry Holt and Company, many people helped with this book and my previous one and I appreciate the time and effort they extended on my behalf: Greg Hamlin, Lottchen Shivers, Alison Juram, Darcy Tromanhauser, John Jusino, and Lisa Goldberg; and formerly with Holt, Mark Levine, Pam Duevel, and Susan Gilbert, as well as freelancers Toni Werbell, Bill Parkhurst, and Ravin Korothy.

I am also very grateful to the more than one hundred persons whom I interviewed for this book. Whether they spoke on or off the record, they were invariably generous with their time and comments. I was able to fit only a small fraction of their words and names into the final text but they all greatly contributed to my knowledge of Notre Dame and college sports and I thank them.

Finally, I am forever indebted to my father, Lawrence, my wife, Aneta, my daughter, GiGi, and my foster daughters, Jayme and Logan, for their constant patience and understanding, and to my late son Oliver, who was so inspiring in life and whose memory kept me company during the long hours in the library and in front of the computer. Ollie taught me the difference between the trivial and the important, how sports should be fun and games. To treat sports with deadly seriousness is to ruin them and to profane the realities of life and death.

Introduction

"Half the world loves Notre Dame and the other half seems to hate us.
. . . I couldn't begin to tell you where it all started but I can tell you
that there aren't many people unemotional and objective about us."

—Notre Dame Associate Vice President
Richard W. Conklin in an interview, March 12, 1991

Shake Down the Thunder: The Creation of Notre Dame Football is *not* a
Notre Dame football book. Most of those works are clearly partisan,
either cheering for "old Notre Dame" or denouncing the Fighting Irish
and their school. *Shake Down the Thunder* analyzes America's love-and-
hate affair with Notre Dame football, explores the origins of the phenomenon—the era of rabid anti-Catholicism in which Knute Rockne's teams
achieved national prominence—and explains how Notre Dame football
victories became a source of pride and group esteem for millions of
Catholics as well as a target of scorn and distrust by other Americans.

Many Notre Dame football books retell N.D. game stories and offer
the minutiae of the contests. *Shake Down the Thunder* is an explanation
of how and why the games occurred, the rise of big-time college sport,
the press and public that fed upon it, and the critics who tried to control
and reform it. In addition, this book focuses on what none of the Fighting
Irish football books mention—the complicated political and personal relations between and among administrators of Notre Dame; athletic de-

partment personnel; the school's faculty, students, and alumni; and the dealings with the outside world, especially the press, the sports public, and the educational establishment.

The history of Notre Dame football is enveloped in myths. With the triumphs of the team in New York City in the 1920s—an era of "Gee-Whiz" journalism—such influential writers as Grantland Rice began to describe the players and coaches in fantastic and unreal terms. They created legends and falsehoods about the Fighting Irish and Knute Rockne for naive readers. The coach's tragic death in 1931 solidified this process. Rather than considering Rockne as his friends and enemies knew him in life—an extremely smart man in a ruthless profession who built winning teams step-by-step, sometimes breaking rules, always seeing the world realistically—the writers transformed him into a saint. Hagiography turned a fascinating individual into a lifeless symbol of all possible virtues; then the film *Knute Rockne—All American* set the image in concrete.

The men who ran the University of Notre Dame during Rockne's lifetime and subsequent decades, with a reticence natural to their training and profession, went along with the historical amnesia. Many of the priests had clashed with the coach, fighting him for control of the increasingly important Notre Dame football program, refusing to allow it and him to overwhelm their religious and academic aspirations for their beloved school. But with his death, they were able to gain total control of the N.D. athletic department and saw no point in publicly remembering old quarrels.

Out of their silence came the myth of "The Seamless Whole," still cherished by some football fans: by good chance a genius football coach came along and everyone at the school happily cooperated with him and together they built a wonderful thing. History, daily life, does not work this way; for example, sentimentalists like to attribute the origin of the Notre Dame–USC series to Bonnie Rockne—because the coach's wife liked the wife of a USC official, she persuaded her husband to agree to the first game. This story, retold as recently as the ABC-TV broadcast of the 1992 USC–Notre Dame encounter, ignores the reality of how the Notre Dame faculty athletic board and coach scheduled games in the 1920s, the complicated negotiations among these men as well as with administrators of other schools, and the huge amounts of money at stake. ABC announcer Keith Jackson seemed to enjoy the little-woman-behind-the-Great-Man anecdote because it implies an innocent and charming past to college football—the opposite of the reality. In fact, in late 1925, Rockne wrote a friend about how the first Notre Dame–USC game was scheduled: "The Southern California officials came to South Bend and offered the authorities such a fluttering guarantee that they could not turn it down." No record exists in the Notre Dame Archives of the Southern Cal guarantee. However, the Trojans' athletic department manager of the time suggested that it was as high as $100,000 (over $10 million in 1990 dollars), and for Rockne to call it "fluttering"—1920s slang for a large financial risk—puts it above the standard guarantees of the period and into the high range.

Each generation sees the past through its own lens, and to many Americans in the 1990s, Knute Rockne will not seem important for his long-forgotten backfield "shift" but for his professional innovations. He was the prototype of the big-time college coach, not only in his ability to promote his team and himself but, as his business papers reveal, in his development of new commercial areas for college coaches, including summer camps and multifaceted endorsements. Rockne was the first great entrepreneurial coach, and he brought permanent change to his profession, setting the money standard for his successors.

In the same way, Notre Dame's successful football program started a financial fever and a central myth of college sports. In the 1920s, Fighting Irish football began to produce significant revenue for the university's educational and building funds, and later helped N.D. survive the Great Depression. This success also sparked one of the most pernicious illusions in American culture—that college sports generates substantial profits for schools with big-time teams and that these dollars aid academic endeavors. In fact, at most institutions with major sports programs, beginning with the Big Ten in the 1920s, athletic departments have always kept and spent all of their revenue and have run deficits. Thus, unlike Notre Dame, most universities have always lost money on their intercollegiate athletic programs.

In the 1920s, however, many colleges and universities watched the on-field and box office success of Fighting Irish football and tried to imitate it. Schools launched major athletic programs and justified the enormous cost by arguing that they too would achieve national fame and a sizable fortune. No school duplicated N.D.'s success, and many, especially if they built large stadiums, encountered severe financial problems.

The immutable fact is that *no imitator could match Notre Dame's unique formula:* a rich athletic culture, fan identification based on ethnicity and religion, an innovative and charismatic coach, a phenomenal won-lost record, powerful media allies, an immense number of supporters throughout the country, and most important of all, *the invention of the formula.* The Fighting Irish were there first; in the harsh world of college sports, imitation mainly produces runners-up and red ink.

Notre Dame's experience with great football success contradicts one of the other major myths about college sports—that it produces wonderful publicity for the schools involved. At best, the publicity is a two-edged sword, and in Notre Dame's case, although it drew attention to the institution and built fan support, much of the press coverage was negative and tarred the school with a "football factory" image that took generations to erase.

In our era, the public dispute about the function of intercollegiate athletics within the university continues, and proponents as well as critics of college sports repeat many arguments first offered years ago. Notre Dame football has long been at the epicenter of the controversy. The story of its creation should enlighten all persons interested in college sports—this dazzling, perplexing, and uniquely American phenomenon—and lower the temperature but increase the light on the ongoing debate.

I

"What Though the Odds
Be Great or Small"
1789–1918

1

L'Universite de Notre Dame du Lac and the Nineteenth Century

"Many [Catholic] institutions were founded where there was no significant Catholic population and were immediately foredoomed. Others, however, such as the University of Notre Dame, managed to survive their wilderness locale, although at least one high-level Notre Dame administrator . . . remarked that he regretted that Father Sorin hadn't settled a bit closer to Chicago."

> —Father Andrew Greeley, Emeritus Professor of Sociology, the University of Arizona

The first Catholic university in America was Georgetown. From its founding in 1789 to the year after World War I, another 170 Catholic institutions of higher education opened, but only 67 of these schools survive today. The University of Notre Dame du Lac in Indiana not only survived but went on to become, in Greeley's words, "the most famous, and in some ways, the best, of the [Catholic] universities." Notre Dame's triumph was connected to the history of Roman Catholics in the United States and to American higher education; to understand the story of Notre Dame, it is necessary to examine the world from which it emerged.

Before 1800, few Catholics settled in the United States. A small number of English Catholic families made it to Maryland, and some French and Quebecois lived on the frontier of the Western Reserve and along the

3

Mississippi River. Then, beginning in the 1830s with the famines in Ireland, and in the 1840s with the political turmoil on the European continent, large numbers of Irish and German Catholic immigrants started to come to America. In the second half of the century, many of their compatriots joined them, along with increasing numbers of coreligionists from Italy and Eastern Europe. Catholics began to form a sizable and distinct minority within a Protestant and often hostile culture—political parties like the so-called "Know-Nothings," determined to "Drive the Papists Out," were a nativist reaction to this immigration.

When the size of the American Catholic community reached critical mass and could sustain its own institutions, an internal debate over integration or separation began. The "liberals" argued for accommodation with the Protestant majority and attendance by Catholic children at public schools. The "conservatives," however, won the debate and, at the Third Plenary Council of Bishops at Baltimore in 1884, they began to implement the Catholic parochial school system. The bishops' edict required separate and complete schooling for every baptized child, and according to the eminent Catholic writer Garry Wills, it "meant a poor body of immigrants would have to make great sacrifices to build their own schools. It meant that . . . the problem of building, equipping, and operating this church-school complex formed a body of priests who advanced toward their monsignorate, their bishopric, by virtue of business skill . . . [they] adopted the businessman's 'no-nonsense' ways and practicality . . . [their] anti-intellectualism—defensive at first, and self-justifying—became in time self-congratulatory." Thus the bishops' Baltimore edict not only established a primary and secondary school system but shaped Catholic colleges and universities.

Ironically, across town from the bishops' meeting, Johns Hopkins University was changing the nature of American higher education. Founded in 1876 upon the German university model, Johns Hopkins introduced graduate education and the Ph.D. degree to this country. Its commitment to research, in the humanities as well as in science, challenged the divinity school and classical studies curriculum of the established American colleges. Johns Hopkins's faculty and graduate students sought truth through rigorous research and soon converted many leading educators to their method. In 1888, when John D. Rockefeller endowed the University of Chicago, its first president announced: "It is proposed in this institution to make the work of investigation primary, the work of giving instruction secondary."

Thus the vanguard of American higher education was proceeding in the opposite direction from the Catholic schools. Not only were there no Catholic laymen with the money of a Rockefeller, Stanford, or Carnegie to endow and financially stabilize a university, but intellectually, Johns Hopkins, Chicago, and like-minded places were moving from curricula of received "truths" to research methods that abolished the beliefs of the time. These new systems of inquiry were anathema to the Catholic church in America and in Rome, but an activist minority within the priesthood, including Father James Burns, a future president of Notre Dame, were intrigued by them.

In this period, the new state universities also plunged into the mainstream of American higher education. In the Midwest, the universities of Michigan, Illinois, and Minnesota grew in size and importance as the wealth of their states increased, and recently established land-grant schools like Wisconsin and Purdue gained prominence. A number of these institutions, to raise and insure their own academic standards, pioneered in the certification of high school students and attempted to set up a coherent college admission process. Catholic colleges were out of step on these issues, and for this reason, major Midwestern state universities, along with Northwestern and Chicago, shunned schools like Notre Dame when they formed the nucleus of the Western Conference.

"[In the nineteenth century] no young man or boy was turned away who wished to attend Notre Dame and who could, by one means or another (cash, labor, barter), pay some sort of tuition for his support. There were no entrance requirements, and students were simply placed wherever they seemed to fit into the curriculum. Students arrived and departed at odd times during the year, as did their professors."

—Thomas Schlereth, historian
of the University of Notre Dame

Historically, religious orders founded and staffed Catholic colleges and universities. The Society of Jesus began the practice in Europe and continued it in America by establishing Georgetown (1789), Xavier (1831), Fordham (1841), Boston College (1863), Marquette (1881), and many other schools, including all those named for the founder of the Jesuits, Saint Ignatius Loyola. In the nineteenth century, other Catholic orders began institutions that survive today—the Christian Brothers founded La Salle, Manhattan College, and Saint Mary's in California; the Vincentians began De Paul and Saint John's in New York; the Franciscans founded Saint Bonaventure—and many schools that vanished long ago.

All of these orders, as well as the Dominicans (Providence College) and Augustinians (Villanova) have long histories within the Catholic church. The University of Notre Dame is unusual in that its founding order, the C.S.C. (*Congregatio a Sancta Cruce*), was a small French group begun only in 1820 and not recognized by Rome until 1857. (The English translation of *Congregatio a Sancta Cruce* is "Congregation of the Holy Cross"; however, the University of Holy Cross in Massachusetts is not a C.S.C. but a Jesuit school.)

One of the C.S.C.'s early adherents was a young French priest, Edward Sorin. In 1841, the order sent him and six brothers to its American frontier diocese headquartered in Vincennes, Indiana. Sorin wanted to start a college, and after his abortive attempt to do so in the Vincennes region, his religious superior offered him a tract of land owned by the order on the northern border of the diocese, near the village of South Bend.

On November 26, 1842, Sorin and a few companions, near a small lake on the C.S.C. property, founded the school that he grandly called L'Universite de Notre Dame du Lac. Sorin may have envisioned the Université de Paris, near the famed Notre Dame Cathedral in his native France, but his immediate objective was to build a school for all willing students, particularly of primary and secondary school age, and to give them a Catholic education.

Father Sorin, like many people on the American frontier, was both a visionary and an entrepreneur. He wanted his project to be independent and self-sustaining, and to that end he built farms, stables, a bakery, and other support structures. For both independence and public relations— so that his school would exist as a place on the map—he had Notre Dame, Indiana, established as a separate post office and himself appointed postmaster. Sorin tried numerous schemes to raise money, including sending some brothers and laymen to the California gold rush in 1850 (they were unsuccessful and a number did not come back), but his main source of revenue was the tuition paid, in any form offered, by his students.

At the time of the American Civil War, Notre Dame's primary and secondary schools—the Minim and Junior departments—attracted a steady number of youngsters. The Senior Department resembled other Catholic colleges of the period but had less than a dozen students. The faculty were mainly C.S.C. priests, and one of them, Father William Corby, later gained fame as a chaplain for the Union Army's Irish Brigade. (A statue of Corby giving the troops absolution before the Battle of Gettysburg commemorates his war work. Corby has his right arm raised straight up as if signaling a football referee—Notre Dame students have long called the statue "Fair Catch Corby.")

To build the Senior Department, and because of his practical nature, Sorin departed from an exclusive Catholic curriculum—with its emphasis on church text and argument as well as ancient languages—and introduced a science course in 1865 as well as the first law (1869) and engineering (1873) courses in American Catholic higher education. Notre Dame became increasingly different from contemporary Catholic schools, especially the Jesuit institutions, and its distinctiveness reflected the pragmatism of Midwest life.

With improved rail transportation, the school—situated within a day's ride from the growing Catholic populations of Milwaukee, Chicago, Toledo, Cleveland, and Detroit—became a logical place to send Catholic youths for part or all of their formal education. The majority of these boys were of Irish or German descent, and a number stayed on at Notre Dame to enter the C.S.C. seminary and become priests. Sorin is reported to have disliked the Irish because they were "not obedient by nature," but increasingly, they came to dominate the ranks of the C.S.C. clergy and supply most of Notre Dame's faculty and administration.

Sorin, however, remained intractably French in culture and often traveled to his homeland as well as to Quebec. From the French nineteenth-century revival of the cult of the Virgin Mary, he imported many items of Marian devotion to his school. In addition to its name, and the gilding of the dome of the main building as well as the statue of the Virgin Mary on its top, he had a replica of the Grotto of Our Lady of Lourdes built on campus (he had visited the original in 1876). Inevitably, when college football teams and their supporters began adopting signature colors, Notre Dame took those historically associated with the Virgin Mary—blue and gold.

From Sorin also comes the Notre Dame tradition of young leaders. Only twenty-eight when he founded the school, he named a succession of young men to run the institution in his absences and retirement. To this day, all Notre Dame presidents have been in their thirties or forties when they assumed office. In addition, because for much of its history the vice presidency of the school was the usual preparation for the top job, these key Notre Dame officials were often in their late twenties or early thirties when they became second in command. (This tradition also explains the relative youth of many Notre Dame head football coaches: Rockne was twenty-nine when appointed, Leahy thirty-three, and Parseghian forty.

The record holder was Terry Brennan at twenty-five; his appointment at such a young age baffled many journalists and sports fans, but it made sense within Notre Dame's unique history.)

Sorin's last great act came after the fire of 1879. Of uncertain origin, the blaze destroyed the six-story Main Building—the core of the school —and many ancillary structures. The *South Bend Tribune* headlined THE UNIVERSITY OF NOTRE DAME IN ASHES and estimated the loss at a "fifth of a million dollars." Sorin, in Montreal at the time, hurried back to his school. He arrived to find a smoldering, desolate scene and a despondent group of students and faculty. One of the latter described Sorin's reaction: "He walked around the ruins and those who followed him were confounded by his attitude. Instead of bending, he stiffened . . . after looking over the destruction of his life's work, [he] spoke . . . the most sublime words I have ever listened to. There was absolute faith, confidence, resolution in his very look and pose, 'If it were ALL gone, I should not give up.' "

Sorin galvanized his followers to action and he supervised the rebuilding of Notre Dame; all histories of the school refer to this incident as a primary source of the "indomitable Notre Dame spirit." Fire destroyed other institutions in the nineteenth century, and many of them, including some Catholic schools, did not rebuild. Notre Dame did, in large part, because of the perseverance and resourcefulness of its founder. Notre Dame historian Thomas Schlereth sums up Father Edward Sorin well: "master entrepreneur, gambler, diplomat, legerdemain, adventurer, man of faith."

2

The Origins of
Notre Dame's Athletic Culture

"In 1873, football seemed sufficiently ridiculous to prompt a classic remark of President Andrew D. White of Cornell. In response to a challenge from thirty players of the University of Michigan who wanted to
arrange a game in Cleveland [against Cornell], President White telegraphed: 'I will not permit thirty men to travel four hundred miles
merely to agitate a bag of wind.'"

—Frederick Rudolph,
historian of American higher education

In nineteenth-century America, the most popular sport was prizefighting.
Only after the Civil War did baseball and, at the end of the century,
college football begin to compete in crowds and newspaper attention
with boxing. The bare-knuckle version was particularly popular and, because of its brutality, mainly attracted desperate and hungry athletes,
among them immigrant Irishmen. The newspapers of the day and the
original sports weekly, the *National Police Gazette*, headlined the exploits
of the Irish-American champions and challengers and helped create the
first American sports hero, John L. Sullivan, heavyweight champion from
1882 to 1892, eventually defeated by his compatriot Jim Corbett.

The fame of these Irish-American fighters is the probable source of
the Notre Dame nickname, "Fightin' Irish," but because nineteenth-
century boxing was attached to a drinking, gambling, brawling, and
disreputable subculture, the priests who ran the university did not

encourage or even condone the nickname until well into the twentieth century.

A more important contribution of nineteenth-century Irish-American culture to Notre Dame was baseball—and, less directly, football. In Ireland, after the abortive 1860s Fenian revolts against British rule, the nationalists created the Gaelic Athletic Association. Scorning all British sports, the group promoted Gaelic games; its branches and imitators in America translated the Fenian mandate into opposition to cricket—popular in many eastern cities—and sponsorship of the emerging American sport of baseball. Irish-American support of baseball became so strong that in the first decades of professional leagues, at least one third of the players and a majority of managers were of Irish descent—for example, the five Delahanty brothers, Willie Keeler, and John McGraw—and they were also influential in contemporary baseball lore, such as "Casey at the Bat."

Since Notre Dame had many Irish-American students, baseball was the most popular sport at the school, and Notre Dame had a team as early as 1867. From those first squads and during the following decades, many players went on to the professional leagues, including the famous Adrian "Cap" Anson, player-manager of the Chicago Cubs for many years.

The Irish nationalists' opposition to British association football (soccer) and rugby also played a role in the evolution of American football. In its original forms, college football closely resembled the British sports, but it soon evolved into a distinctive American game. Some of its early stars, like James Hogan of Yale, came from the Irish-American milieu; they also saw nothing wrong in accepting payment, like boxers, for engaging in a brutal sport.

The Ivy schools, particularly Yale, Harvard, and Princeton, systematized the game in the 1880s, and Walter Camp of Yale devised many of the playing rules, became the first regular coach, and promoted the sport through such inventions as the All-America team. By the 1890s, the annual Thanksgiving game in New York City between Princeton and Yale attracted crowds as large as forty thousand people and generated sizable profits for the schools. In 1892, one of the initial actions of the first president of the University of Chicago was to hire a famous Yale player, Amos Alonzo Stagg, to found a football team at the new school.

From the beginning of college football, winning was important, and at many institutions, particularly where the students and/or alumni controlled the team, it became paramount. Among the standard ways to win were "proselyting" (recruiting) and hiring "tramp athletes" for the football season. A generation later, the Carnegie Foundation looked back at the 1890s and complained, "The practice of dressing up the butcher's boy, the iron molder, the boilermaker, or even a bond salesman, in football clothing . . . was more than merely scandalous," it corrupted many educational institutions.

The lack of standard college admission procedures and playing eligibility rules created hopscotch transfers of athletes from school to school as well as playing careers that extended well beyond four years. The famed Fielding Yost was a lineman for West Virginia University in 1896 when he "transferred" to Lafayette for its crucial game against Penn. After helping Lafayette win, Yost returned to West Virginia. A few years later, when he became coach at Michigan, Yost brought in many "tramp players" as well as the graduate coach of Stanford to star on his first Wolverine squad.

One of the enduring myths about intercollegiate athletics is that they were originally innocent and pure. In reality, because they began during the highly corrupt era in American sports that culminated in the Black Sox scandal of 1919, and because they were connected to the brawling and gambling sports subculture, dishonesty and unethical practices marked their first period. The large football schools in the East and in the Western Conference were particularly adept at pioneering new forms of fraud and hypocrisy. In these shark-infested waters, the men in charge of Notre Dame football had to learn to swim.

> "There was small interest aroused in last Saturday's [home Notre Dame] contest with Lake Forest. No doubt was entertained as to the outcome of the game and those that went to see it, were there mostly out of curiosity."
>
> —*Notre Dame Scholastic,* Fall 1899

The Catholic school entered college football relatively late and never engaged in the flagrant abuses of the sport's early days. Notre Dame's first intercollegiate game occurred in 1887 when some University of Michigan students came to the campus, gave a teaching demonstration of the sport, challenged the locals to a contest, and won 8–0. Michigan returned the following spring to beat the home team twice. In 1889, Notre Dame triumphed over Northwestern in a one-game season and then stopped playing the sport for two years.

Yet Notre Dame was fertile ground for college football, and as the school yearbook of 1906 proclaimed, in the last decades of the nineteenth century "the various branches of sports grew continually here, and today there is probably no college in the country in which the students as a whole take such an active part in athletics." Because Notre Dame housed large numbers of boys in geographic isolation, it encouraged athletics as physical exercise and diversion. In addition, the school's emphasis on a "democratic masculine atmosphere . . . provided an ideal athletic climate."

Unlike that of many Catholic institutions, Notre Dame's masculine democracy was very ecumenical. Father Sorin had always welcomed Protestants and Jews to Notre Dame, and although non-Catholics never numbered over 20 percent of the students, their attendance helped the school financially and built positive relations with the Protestant and Jewish communities of the region. The priests required the Catholic boys to attend daily religious services but exempted the Protestants and Jews. As a result of this ecumenical attitude, Protestants such as Knute Rockne and George Gipp later came to the school.

In 1896, the arrival of another non-Catholic, Frank Hering, began Notre Dame's first serious interest in college football. Hering had quarterbacked two of Stagg's Chicago teams and also coached at Bucknell. He came to Notre Dame to study law and to run its football team. Adding Chicago, Purdue, and Indiana to the schedule, Hering's teams lost to these major opponents but beat smaller schools like Albion, Beloit, and DePauw.

Hering's football scheduling was, in part, the result of a decision by the Notre Dame president, Father Andrew Morrissey. Unhappy with the financial losses resulting from intercollegiate athletics and preferring a large intramural program, Morrissey considered dropping the varsity teams. He relented when an aide pointed out that "intercollegiate sports [especially baseball] attracted a great number of students to Notre Dame." He decided to try to have it both ways—keep the varsity teams and proceed with the construction of a large indoor gymnasium.

After the 1898 season, Hering left coaching for law and business. Notre Dame, like most schools at the time, did not employ a football coach on a full-time or regular basis. The player-captain was still important in organizing the squad and directing on-field play, and after Hering, Notre Dame continued with a variety of player-captains and part-time coaches.

"Are you out for the [football] Varsity? If not, why not? Do you realize that Notre Dame needs every good man within her bounds. Come out and boost the team, swell the numbers, make the competition fiercer

. . . If you have any muscle, any ginger, any fighting blood, anything that goes to make up a man, get out and show it."

—The *Notre Dame Scholastic*'s appeal to undergraduates, 1906

At the turn of the century, Notre Dame football was an informal, student-based game, but it contained the seeds of its big-time future. The 1899 season began with a contest against Englewood High School of Chicago, and the anonymous author of the game story in the student weekly, the *Notre Dame Scholastic*, did not even mention the final score (the newspapers reported it as 29–5 for N.D.). A month later, because of heavy rains, the Northwestern game was moved from Cartier Field, the regular football terrain, to the grounds behind Brownson Hall. But the contest in Chicago against Stagg's powerhouse showed the potential seriousness—and deadliness—of the sport: although Notre Dame lost 23–6, it claimed a moral victory because, according to the *Scholastic*, "When time was called . . . the men representing the windy city were barely able to walk to their training quarters on account of the quick and many mass-plays sent against their line." (A few years later, President Theodore Roosevelt demanded a change in the rules of college football to outlaw the flying wedge and other deadly mass-plays.)

The most important away game of the 1899 season was against Michigan, and the Notre Dame student paper reported that "at Ann Arbor on Wednesday . . . the merchants of the town who closed their places of business and went with a thousand or more students out to Regent's Field were not disappointed"—at the spectacle or at the fact that Michigan won 12–0.

Notre Dame was not able to attract as many people for its biggest home game of the season, but the victory over Indiana "was a gala-day for the [student] rooters. . . . They had a system in their work for the first time. Each hall came well supplied with songs and yells and cheered themselves hoarse long before the game was finished."

Also on the schedule in 1899 was Lake Forest (N.D. beat them 38–0), and during the following years, Notre Dame continued to play this school as well as Beloit, DePauw, Knox, Wabash, and similar institutions. In fact, these were Notre Dame's natural opponents: residential campuses with male student bodies approximately the same size as its own. However, as the 1899 victories over Northwestern and Indiana, the close loss to Michigan, and a tie against Purdue indicate, Notre Dame's true athletic peers were the much wealthier private and state institutions with much larger student bodies.

In the following decades, when college football developed into two tiers—the rich Have schools and the small Have-Nots—and the latter remained with or fell back to an informal, student-based version of the sport, why did Notre Dame, still poor and with a small student body, go on to win national championships and field many of the most powerful teams in college football history?

A number of key individuals, especially Jesse Harper and Knute Rockne, played crucial roles in Notre Dame's initial football glory, but they were able to succeed, in large part, because of the school's unique culture of athleticism: Notre Dame's ability to harness and focus the majority of its students into sports endeavors and, once its athletic success became well-known, to attract like-minded and athletically talented boys to the campus.

By 1900, Notre Dame's culture of athleticism was in place, and although the school was not on a direct line to national championships, it was on course. Ironically, during the first decades of the twentieth century, the main obstacles to N.D.'s sports success came not on the football field but in administration offices. The growing conservatism of Catholic higher education and the liberalism of American universities presented Notre Dame with unexpected predicaments and insults, most of them involving intercollegiate athletics.

3

Catholic versus American Higher Education

"At the beginning of the twentieth century Catholic colleges were small, in constant financial difficulty, academically inferior, static in educational philosophy, traditional in curriculum and pedagogy, rigid in discipline and student life, clerical in faculty and administration, and isolated almost completely from the mainstream of American higher education."

— Father Andrew Greeley, Emeritus Professor of Sociology, the University of Arizona

Although turn-of-the-century Notre Dame was different from most Catholic schools, it still fit within the boundaries of Father Greeley's description. Part of the problem for American Catholic colleges was Rome's increasing rejection of modern thought and science. The climax of the papal campaign came in 1907 when Pope Pius X formally condemned modernism and ordered Catholic schools not to hire "anyone who in any way is found to be tainted by modernism."

Unlike more prominent Catholic universities of the period, Notre Dame was not in the direct papal loop. Most teaching orders had their leaders in Rome, but the superiors of the C.S.C. were in France and within the Golden Dome—the C.S.C. Superior of the American Province also served as president of Notre Dame. Moreover, the school claimed one of the leading Catholic liberal intellectuals of the period, Father John A. Zahm.

Nevertheless, Notre Dame, like all American Catholic schools at this time, saw its primary mission as molding student character through religious training. Because, at the turn of the century, about six hundred Notre Dame students were in the Minim or Junior departments and only about two hundred were in the university program, the priests who ran the school and taught a majority of the classes considered the moral education of their charges more important than their intellectual development. Father Zahm complained that "Notre Dame ought to be one of the first educational institutions in the land, whereas it is in reality nothing more than a large boarding school for elementary students."

The nature of N.D.'s parochial education, as well as the imperative of keeping the school financially afloat, resulted in an open admissions policy. The priests welcomed any boy of any age who sought Catholic training and could pay in cash or labor. They also accepted non-Catholics who wanted a basic education in a religious environment.

However, with the ascendancy of Father John W. Cavanaugh to the presidency in 1906, the school slowly began to change. Cavanaugh, influenced by Zahm, began to emphasize the university program and to attract more students to it. Yet admission standards remained loose. Knute Rockne arrived in 1910 from Chicago with enough money to pay for his college tuition but no secondary school diploma (he had dropped out of high school and worked in a post office for three years). Rockne came because of Notre Dame's athletic culture (he excelled at sports, especially track) and the school's reputation as a "poor boy's" institution, a place where students with little money but a willingness to work for their tuition, room, and board could succeed.

In the second decade of the century, the school admitted increasing numbers of collegians and began to shrink the Minim and Junior departments. In addition, more teachers with doctorates joined the faculty (their degrees were mainly from Catholic University in Washington). New courses were added to the college curriculum, including such practical disciplines as journalism (the school, in line with its ecumenical tradition, also accepted a Chair of Journalism from a Jewish benefactor, Max Pam). But for all these changes, Notre Dame, like all Catholic schools of the period, was still far from the mainstream of American higher education and increasingly distant from its regional competitors.

"[Elective courses] permitted the professor to indulge his interests and the students to follow theirs; [they] encouraged the accumulation of knowledge and welcomed into the world of learning subjects that had been forbidden through an ill-considered belief that the ancients knew everything worth knowing."

—Frederick Rudolph,
historian of American higher education

One of the major innovations in turn-of-the-century American higher education, the one that drew a clear line between the static past and the dynamic future, was the adoption of the elective principle. Promoted by President Charles Eliot of Harvard, elective courses freed the curriculum —and faculty and students—from the weight of the past and allowed researchers to pursue their intellectual interests. Elective courses grew into new disciplines such as sociology and spawned professors such as Thorstein Veblen, who questioned the very premises of American society and Western capitalism.

Among the most enthusiastic adherents of the elective principle and its research imperative were the new universities of the Midwest, particularly Chicago, Michigan, and Wisconsin. By the turn of the century, they were awarding Ph.D.'s and sponsoring faculty on the frontiers of their fields; indeed, Frederick Jackson Turner, at Wisconsin, was redefining the word *frontier* and the way Americans regarded their past.

At these schools, the content of courses, those required as well as elective, was becoming radically different from the curriculum of Catholic institutions and would remain so for many years. (Father Burns, when president of Notre Dame in the early 1920s, tried to introduce Harvard-style elective courses but failed; Father Hesburgh succeeded only in the 1960s.) In addition, the faculty members at the modern universities were becoming a totally different species from their colleagues, laity as well as clergy, at the Catholic schools. This new phenomenon went by the name of "Academic Man," and at the vanguard schools, he began to replace the teacherly "Mr. Chips" types. "Academic Man" was committed to research and was more loyal to his work and his new professional societies and journals than he was to any particular school. Moreover, because the new professors needed freedom in which to pursue their research, especially if they questioned the received opinions and pieties of American society, they began to demand guarantees to insulate their work from the disapproval of school administrators, trustees, alumni, and powerful citizens. Thus tenure—guaranteed freedom of inquiry and speech for the professoriate—began.

Catholic schools, with their emphasis on moral and religious training, were light-years from accepting either "Academic Man" or tenure. (At Notre Dame, "Academic Man" began to appear in the 1930s but only formed a majority of faculty in the 1970s; tenure came in the 1950s.) Notre Dame's priest-teachers placed pedagogy far ahead of research. One student who entered in 1919 commented that "student-teacher relationships are strong at Notre Dame [because] the priests have no boys of their own." Also, some of the lay faculty were "bachelor-dons," single males who lived in the residence halls, like many of the priests, and were devoted to teaching and mentoring their charges.

Thus, when "Academic Men" from the new universities of the Midwest met Notre Dame priests or lay teachers, the two groups came from places geographically near but continents apart intellectually. In fact, they rarely met, but the few times they did the result was argument and bitter feelings. These occasions often concerned intercollegiate athletics.

> "[When the Western Conference rejected Notre Dame's application for admission, Vice President] Father Thomas Crumley, chairman of the athletic board at the time, was adamant in defense of Notre Dame's standards. He lost the battle, but announced that it had been 'fought on theological rather than athletic grounds.' "
>
> —James Armstrong,
> first director of the Notre Dame Alumni Association

In the early days of college football, when students and/or alumni ran the teams, the faculty had no interest in the operation or governance of the sport. However, the growing emphasis on winning, which sparked multifaceted cheating, alarmed faculty members at many schools. First at Princeton and then at other Ivy universities, the faculty began to set up "athletic boards of control" to monitor the activities of the students, alumni, and coaches who ran the teams. These boards succeeded when backed by the president and the trustees of the school; otherwise they were paper tigers.

By the 1890s, most major midwestern universities had faculty boards, but because each school set its own athletic rules, conflicts between institutions frequently occurred. In 1895–1896, the presidents of the universities of Chicago, Minnesota, Wisconsin, Illinois, Northwestern, Purdue, and Michigan established the Western Conference to construct a uniform code of intercollegiate sports rules. They insisted that each member's "Committee on College Athletics" control its school's teams, and they also set up a supercommittee of faculty representatives from each institution to make new regulations and to run the conference's business.

They named the organization the Intercollegiate Conference of Faculty Representatives, but the press and public preferred geographic or numeric nicknames. Many educators, especially at these schools, hailed the launching and structure of the Western Conference as a major step toward the reform of the college sports scene.

Notre Dame immediately applied for admission to the conference but was rejected on the grounds that its university division was not large or serious enough and also because of its vague player eligibility rules. In 1897, N.D. amended its "Athletic Constitution" to allow only *"bona fide* students taking the full course of studies" to play on its intercollegiate teams and also to limit playing eligibility to six years, four as an undergraduate and two "post graduate." This was in line with Western Conference rules but still did not gain the Catholic school entrance.

In the next few years, the conference took in Indiana and Iowa and became known as the Big Nine, but in 1908, Michigan withdrew over a rules dispute. Notre Dame applied again and was rejected, prompting Father Crumley's remark about the battle being "theological rather than athletic."

Father Crumley was correct, but in more than one sense: the Western Conference representatives not only showed contempt for Catholic higher education, with its emphasis on religious training and open admissions, they also scorned the idea that the N.D. faculty board could control intercollegiate sports at its school when, in the "theological" world in which it existed, it had limited power. However, the conference representatives failed to realize that Notre Dame's hierarchical system worked well for the school and insulated it from many of the athletic abuses that harmed their own institutions.

In 1906–1907, the president of Michigan proposed a series of conference reforms to tighten player eligibility rules, but the Wolverine football coach, Fielding Yost, urged the school's trustees to reject the changes. The trustees agreed to overrule the president and they also replaced the reformers on the school's athletic committee with faculty amenable to the trustees' will. Then, in 1908, the trustees pulled Michigan out of the Big Nine.

Notre Dame did not have trustees or any board to whom its president reported. The C.S.C. owned and ran the school, and from this small religious order came the priests who occupied N.D.'s key administrative and faculty positions. Open conflict between the C.S.C., the president (who was also the provincial superior of the order), and the faculty athletic board was not possible, nor could a football coach divide and humiliate the Notre Dame president and faculty as Yost did at Michigan.

The conference representatives also misunderstood the basic nature of Notre Dame's athletic board of control. According to the school's "Athletic Constitution," the university vice president, the second most powerful figure at N.D., was chair of the board and directly controlled the athletic department. Unlike the conference schools, where often the faculty committee and the central administrators did not possess real power over the athletic department, at Notre Dame the vice president made all major decisions about athletics and also directly supervised the revenues and expenses of that department. The N.D. hierarchical system offended the midwestern faculty representatives' sense of themselves as new "Academic Men" but it was the authentic product of the Catholic school and, in many ways, more effective than the faculty boards at their institutions.

The Western Conference's 1908 rejection set in motion the future of Notre Dame athletics. Instead of the Catholic school's modifying its system to please the conference universities, their rebuff forced Notre Dame to pursue an independent course and to continue its unique way of running its intercollegiate athletics program.

4

The Origin of
"The Notre Dame Victory March"

When the Varsity wins out,
E'en the bookworm has to shout,
There's such magic in victory ath-a-letic.

—From a poem in the 1909
Notre Dame yearbook, *The Dome*

A key ingredient in the Notre Dame story, one so obvious that it is surprising how many of the histories fail to note it, is that from the turn of the century on, Notre Dame's intercollegiate teams generally won— not only with increasing ease in football but also in baseball and track. Ring Lardner wrote that the Western Conference "unanimously voted not to admit the Catholics" because "the big nine" (lowercase scorn intended) "carefully studied Notre Dame's gridiron and baseball records."

In their publications, Notre Dame students hailed each victory, and when their team triumphed over important foes like Michigan in 1909 and Army in 1913, they reached new heights of praise for the players and for themselves. After the undefeated 1913 season, the poem "The Peerless Squad of the Gold and Blue" consumed the entire front page of the *Scholastic* and many more pages within. The student poets shared Notre Dame's culture of athleticism. According to one eyewitness, there were "no eggheads" at Notre Dame at this time, and "if there were grinds and bookworms . . . they were integrated with the whole academic and ath-letic community." One authentic student intellectual was George N. Shuster, class of 1915 (he later became the president of Hunter College and a leading Catholic liberal). But even Shuster's religious poetry re-flected the athletic ethos: "At games robust and bold, / We know thou art our patron, / O Lady robed in gold."

A major reason for Notre Dame's homogeneous culture was its geo-graphic isolation. Unlike most of the schools in the Western Conference, where the university was in the middle of the town or city (Ann Arbor, Madison, Chicago, and Minneapolis, for example), Notre Dame was two miles north of the city of South Bend and surrounded by its own forest, cemetery, and farms. A popular N.D. expression stated: "The mile of land between the university and the city of South Bend is the most valuable property Notre Dame has." And beyond Notre Dame's mile was the mile of South Bend's outskirts.

The Catholic school was also different from those midwestern univer-sities that were somewhat isolated from the nearest town; for example, Purdue. Unlike them, Notre Dame would not allow social fraternities (the church opposed American secret societies), whereas at schools with Greek organizations, fraternities formed a separate center of social life, entertainment, and excitement. Moreover, throughout the Western Con-ference, fraternities played an important—and often uncontrolled—role in the recruiting, housing, and paying of intercollegiate athletes. (The conference admitted Ohio State in 1912 as a ninth member and added that school's frat system and rabid fans to its problems.)

In addition, unlike the Big Nine universities, Notre Dame would not admit female students. Saint Mary's, the women's college run by the C.S.C., was small and, although not as distant from the Notre Dame campus as South Bend, a long walk away. The C.S.C. priests and nuns had very strict rules about unsupervised visits to Saint Mary's, and they enforced the regulations by expelling offenders. Notre Dame students tended to ignore Saint Mary's women and see themselves as, to quote one of them, part of a "traditionally he-man institution." A popular cheer was: "He's a man. / Who's a man? / ——— [the name of the "man"] / Rah, rah, rah. / He's a Notre Dame man."

From the late nineteenth century on, Notre Dame men were divided into residence halls mainly according to class year. Each hall had its own sports teams, and interhall competition was at the center of campus life. For the fall football season of 1912, the student weekly noted, "Organiza-tion has been the keynote in interhall circles during the past week. . . .

Unusually large squads have been out every day and are fast rounding into shape . . . well over half of the student body will suit up for league play." The student publications devoted much space to interhall sports and helped turn the winners of the interhall competitions into campus celebrities. When outside reporters visited the school to cover the increasingly successful varsity teams, they were surprised at the extent of the interhall leagues and began calling them "Notre Dame's minor leagues." Because the Minims and Preparatory departments also had teams, some of Notre Dame's opponents charged that the varsity coaches trained athletes for up to ten years before suiting them up for intercollegiate sports.

In fact, only a small number of university students so distinguished themselves in interhall play that they moved on to the varsity, and in the twentieth century, only one, Norm Barry, began in the Minims and made it to first string of the school team. But the halls were crucial in creating the athletic culture in which the intercollegiate teams thrived. The halls focused Notre Dame students on athletics and made them ardent supporters of the varsity.

As early as 1901, the *South Bend Tribune* reported that, for the football game against Indiana for the unofficial state title, "rooter preparations are on a strong scale. Every student will be there whether he likes it or not and take part in organized cheering." As the team became more successful during the first decades of the century, the student fans grew more enthusiastic and better organized. Each hall had its own cheers, pennants, and flags. Cheerleaders, who originally were self-appointed, soon became hall sponsored, and by 1910 there was a special squad for the entire school.

In the same way, the cheering rituals expanded from the football games themselves to pep rallies on the eve of contests—and then, from 1913 on, when the team went on major trips, to huge "send-off" and "welcome back" sessions at the railroad station.

Sometimes the pep rallies were to impress and/or intimidate the opposition. In 1913, the *Scholastic* reported on the eve of the home game against South Dakota: "Just to show the Dakota lads how things are done at Notre Dame . . . 'Nig' Kane called his rooters together in the big gym Friday evening and went through the cheers with them."

This event "proved the greatest demonstration of 'pep' " in years but was topped by the rally for the first Army game a few weeks later. Early on the morning the team departed for West Point, all of the students left their halls and walked to the railroad depot for a prolonged cheering session. Only a few days later, when the victorious team returned, an even larger crowd greeted them, including many priests on the faculty and from the nearby C.S.C. seminary.

But the crowds did not turn out only for victories. The following year, when the team returned from a 28–0 shellacking at Yale, *The Dome* reported: "A thousand fellows shrieking, shouting and cheering, swarmed about the old Lake Shore Station . . . It was a surprise to the team . . . And it was a finer exemplification of the true Notre Dame spirit [than if] the fortunes of war had been reversed."

The Dome for 1915–1916 also showed the head cheerleader, Joe Gargan, in action (Gargan later became Joseph P. Kennedy's brother-in-law and factotum). *The Dome* praised Gargan's hard work and it trumpeted, "The real secret of Notre Dame's success lies in the spirit behind her teams. . . . Because the men out on the field are not only the representatives of [our] school, but also [our] friends and associates, the Notre Dame rooter has imbibed the spirit of our teams: he never quits."

> Cheer, cheer for old Notre Dame,
> Wake up the echoes cheering her name,
> Send a volley cheer on high,
> Shake down the thunder from the sky.
> What though the odds be great or small,
> Old Notre Dame will win over all,
> While her loyal sons are marching,
> Onward to Victory.
>
> —Chorus of "The Notre Dame Victory March"

Even sports fans with an aversion to Notre Dame, like football analyst Beano Cook, admit that its "Victory March" is one of the "greatest things about college football." Cook says, "When the 'Victory March' starts and the team comes out of the tunnel, it's kind of like hearing the National Anthem when you're in a foreign country." In fact, so many Americans can recognize "The Notre Dame Victory March" that it is considered one of the nation's four best known songs—along with the "Star-Spangled Banner," "God Bless America," and "White Christmas."

The origins of the "Victory March" and its initial popularity at Notre Dame belong to the first decades of this century and are a product of the school's culture of athleticism. The standard attribution for the song is "Music by Michael J. Shea (N.D. class of '04) and words by John F. Shea (N.D. class of '06)." In the 1910s on the Notre Dame campus, the "Victory March" was coequal with a number of popular fight songs and

cheers, but then, in the 1920s, with the tempo rearranged by band director Joseph Casasanta, it began to gain its preeminent position.

The histories of Notre Dame differ on the song's exact genesis: One
story has the Shea brothers visiting the campus as alumni in 1908 and
hammering out the words and lyrics on a piano in Sorin Hall; another has
Michael returning from seminary to the family home in Holyoke, Massachusetts, and composing the song with his younger brother, John. Most
of the stories have one element in common—they were told many years
after the event by the surviving brother, John. (Michael died in 1940.)

No one disputes that Michael Shea wrote the music. A talented musi-
cian, he later became an organist at Saint Patrick's Cathedral in New
York and a teacher of ecclesiastical chants. In a 1930s letter, he admitted
that he was "greatly surprised at the success attained" by the march
because he considered it "very amateurish."

John Shea, after graduating from Notre Dame, went back to his
hometown and spent much of his working life in Massachusetts politics,
including stints as chairman of his local board of public works and as a
state senator. In his later years, he often told the story of the origins of
the march—except he kept changing important details about where and
when it was written. However, one part of John's narrative never varied:
his brother had written the music and he had penned the words. John
also copyrighted the march under his own name.

Ascertaining the exact authorship of the verses and chorus of the
"Victory March" is now impossible; however, the *Notre Dame Scholastic*
for the years when the Shea brothers were N.D. students undercuts
John's stories and the standard attributions. The *Scholastic* provides evidence that Michael Shea not only wrote the music but also many of the
words. The older brother always gave the younger some credit for the
lyrics; after Michael's death, John seems to have taken more.

Michael was an accomplished poet, and the *Scholastic* contains many
of his verses, including the class poem for his graduation year. At times,
his student poetry foreshadows lines of the "Victory March." In one
poem, he writes, "Where new-born echoes never die," and in the class
poem, "Life's trumpet notes to each one call." Another poem contains
the couplet "A quarter of life's journey done, / Victories still must be
fought and won."

On the other hand, the few verses by John in the *Scholastic* tend
toward the lugubrious, with lines such as "Still bright and unfading are
the faces of yore, / And brightest and dearest, my sweet Elinore." John
was clearly a less talented and productive poet than his older brother.

Because the Sheas did not keep the manuscript of the "Victory

March," who wrote what will forever remain in doubt. Possibly they collaborated in one of the ways that John later related, more probably Michael wrote the music *and* most of the lyrics and John suggested word changes. But the origins of the song do not concern the millions of people who, every Saturday when Notre Dame plays football, respond fervently to the "Victory March" and sing every line of the chorus (few fans know the accompanying two verses). The march has become an important part of the Notre Dame mystique and one of America's most famous cultural artifacts. When Michael Shea died, his eulogist noted: "He, more than any other student of his time, caught in his soul that indefinable but inspirational something that has become celebrated all through the nation and . . . characterized as 'The Spirit of Notre Dame.'"

5

Notre Dame Sports: 1900–1912

"By the time Knute Rockne showed up at Notre Dame, the Gold and Blue baseball teams had won 145 games while losing 40 in more formidable competition than early football teams encountered."

—Chet Grant, former Notre Dame athlete, coach, and sports historian

At the turn of the century, the most important intercollegiate sport at Notre Dame was baseball. Reflecting both the long-standing Irish-American love of the game and baseball's growing popularity, Notre Dame played most of the regional schools and usually beat them. The Notre Dame baseball team was so good that, in 1902, it had a series of exhibition matches against Charlie Comiskey's White Sox, and in the following years it took on the Chicago Cubs as well as top minor league teams from the American Association and the International League.

Many Notre Dame players from this era went on to the major leagues, including star pitchers George Cutshaw and Cy Williams, as well as Roger Bresnaham (the inventor of the catcher's shin guards) and Frank "Shag" Shaughnessy (the originator of the baseball play-off system). Many of these athletes also played varsity football, but they considered baseball their main sport and pursued it professionally (pro football did not yet exist in a viable form).

In fact, a major controversy in intercollegiate athletics at this time concerned college athletes who earned money by participating in summer professional or semipro baseball leagues. Every year, more and more incidents occurred, and the college authorities tried to outlaw the practice. The issue became very public in 1913 when Jim Thorpe was stripped of his Olympic medals for having played summer baseball as a collegian.

Notre Dame was not immune to the summer baseball problem. A 1910 letter by football coach Frank "Shorty" Longman discussed the pending "case" of his quarterback, Don Hamilton, who had played pro baseball for Louisville of the American Association. The coach wondered whether Vice President Crumley, head of the athletic board, would rule Hamilton ineligible for the coming football season. Longman added: "Nine out of ten college players are playing somewhere in the summer all over and I will be glad when the colleges come out in favor of it." The colleges never did and Hamilton did not suit up for the 1910 football season—Father Crumley ruled him ineligible.

NOTRE DAME 142—AMERICAN COLLEGE OF MEDICINE AND SURGERY 0

The halves were to have been twenty-five and twenty [minutes], but the last half was only eight minutes long, as the "doctors" must eat before catching their train. And anyway, the score suited them as it stood.

—Item in the *Notre Dame Scholastic,* 1905

Notre Dame football during the first decade of the century still resembled its 1890s origins. Many games were played against club teams like the one from the American College of Medicine and Surgery, and even a few against high school squads. In 1901, the school opened the season against the South Bend Athletic Club, and Pat O'Dea, the Notre Dame coach, played for the opposition!

Throughout the decade, Notre Dame head coaches were part-timers who showed up for the season and sometimes returned for a following year but often did not. The position was so ephemeral at times that the coach now listed in the histories of Notre Dame football for 1902–1903, James F. Farragher, is a ghost. For these years, playing captain Louis "Red" Salmon ran the team without a coach. (Apparently, in the 1930s, when N.D. publicists began compiling the history of Notre Dame football, no one could ascertain who had coached in 1902 and 1903. Because Farragher had played on the team at the turn of the century and was a popular policeman on the Notre Dame campus in the 1930s, the publicists inscribed his name on one of the most prestigious lists in American sports—head football coach at Notre Dame.)

These early years do contain foreshadowings of Notre Dame's football future. In 1903, the school played Northwestern at the American League Ball Grounds in Chicago, the first of many games during later decades at major stadiums in that city. In 1904, the football team traveled to the University of Kansas in Lawrence, marking the first Notre Dame trip beyond the Mississippi. For the rest of the decade, however, the squad journeyed no farther than Pittsburgh.

Because football at Notre Dame was still student based, the player-captains trained the team, the student managers did the scheduling and finances, and the vice president supervised the operation (the position of N.D. athletic director did yet not exist). Part-time coaches like Salmon in 1904 and McGlew in 1905 contributed what they could to the team. Students were enthusiastic, particularly when their squad played Western Conference schools, and disappointed when it could not beat Indiana and Purdue for bragging rights in the state. After the mediocre 1905 season—5–4, including bad losses to the in-state rivals—the *Notre Dame Scholastic* announced: "The time has come when Notre Dame should take her old rank in the football world. The rank she had when Fortin and Farragher and Farley were [playing] here; the rank she had when Salmon, the invincible, tore through [the opposition]."

This invocation to the glorious past, this demand to "Wake up the Echoes," would become a recurring mantra during future low periods in Notre Dame football history, but the 1906 version is particularly ironic because it invokes some less than glorious players. However, the desire to win was already strong at Notre Dame and the athletic culture to sustain winning teams existed—hence the student frustration at losing.

In the spring of 1906, the athletic board, under Father Crumley, tried to solve this problem by hiring an excellent coach from the East, Thomas Barry, a former star and coach at Brown University. Barry put together 6–1 and 6–0–1 seasons, including victories over Purdue. After the 1907 season, he told the *Scholastic* that he was moving west to practice law, but he soon turned up coaching at Wisconsin. For 1908, Victor M. Place came from Dartmouth and directed the team to an 8–1 record (the only loss was at Michigan), but he left after the season. With the arrival of Shorty Longman in 1909 the football situation began to stabilize, and with the victory that year over Michigan, Notre Dame made its first bid for national recognition.

"My last year as a player at Notre Dame was 1906. I then joined the school's faculty as a physics and mathematics professor in '09 and served as an assistant football coach. It was a poor school in those days. Most of the coaches were volunteers, ex-players, even some priests."

—Allan Dwan, prolific Hollywood film director
from 1911 to 1958

Allan Dwan was an assistant to Frank "Shorty" Longman, a tough, bombastic man who had played for Fielding Yost at Michigan. In 1909, Longman owned a photography supplies shop in Ann Arbor and agreed to come to Notre Dame for the football season. His hiring was fortuitous, not for his talent as a coach—by all accounts, he was mediocre—but because he temporarily extricated the school from a scheduling bind.

Along with the 1908 rejection of Notre Dame by the Western Conference had come a refusal by its members, including Purdue and Indiana, to schedule football and baseball games against the Catholic school. Major midwestern opponents became hard to find, but because Michigan, having dropped out of the conference, was in a similar predicament and Longman had worked with Yost, the N.D. coach was able to reschedule that school and add Michigan Agricultural (now Michigan State) as well as Olivet College in Michigan to the 1909 slate. He also helped arrange the team's first trip to Pitt.

Longman's moves came at a propitious moment for the Notre Dame athletic community and its football ambitions because the president of the school, Father John W. Cavanaugh, was willing to solve the scheduling dilemma by having the team play only small local colleges. However, the on-field success of the 1909 squad, especially the 11–3 victory over the Wolverines, dampened Cavanaugh's deemphasis sentiments.

Before the game in Ann Arbor, a Detroit journalist wrote, "Notre Dame has the crust to think they can beat Michigan." Indeed, Yost's teams, especially his point-a-minute squads, had dominated midwestern football for almost a decade, and the 1909 version did not expect a small Catholic school to upset it. But, on the day, the individual brilliance of the Notre Dame running backs and N.D.'s recovery of two onside kicks defeated the Wolverines.

When the Notre Dame students learned about the win over Michigan, they celebrated with a huge bonfire, speeches by student leaders and priests on the faculty, and round after round of school songs and cheers. The *Scholastic* played up the small-parochial-school-versus-state-university-giant angle, and one issue illustrated the theme with David and Goliath drawings. The weekly also ran extensive excerpts from mid-western and New York papers about the fine play of the "Catholics," as many sportswriters called the team, enabling N.D. readers to bask in the media attention.

Adding to Notre Dame's triumph and Michigan's embarrassment was Walter Camp's attendance at the game and his praise for N.D.'s running attack. Yost was irate, and he later told the press that he regarded the match as merely an exhibition: "We went into the game caring little whether we won or lost." This infuriated Notre Dame rooters and ex-posed Yost to sharp jibes from midwestern sportswriters, which in turn contributed to Yost's long antipathy toward Notre Dame.

As often happens after an important victory, the following week, ac-cording to the *Scholastic,* "the largest crowd seen at a football game at Notre Dame in years" turned out. The team did not disappoint them, beating Miami of Ohio 46–0, and the next week, Wabash 38–0, bringing its record to 7–0.

Going into the final game of the season against Marquette, some of the South Bend and Chicago sportswriters hailed Notre Dame not only as "Champions of the West" but of the whole nation. One Chicago writer argued that because Michigan had beaten Syracuse by a bigger score than Yale had downed the Orangemen, and Notre Dame had defeated Michigan, the Gold and Blue deserved to be national champs. "Of course," he warned, "the East, according to its custom, will calmly claim the championship of the entire country for Yale."

Notre Dame made this debate moot by tying Marquette in its final game, 0–0. Yet the Notre Dame students claimed the "Championship of the West" and devoted almost an entire issue of the *Scholastic* to paeans to the team and its "rooter-clans." The poem on the front cover an-nounced, "Football simply owned the college." (One article inside was signed with the initials "J. F. O'H."—it was written by student John F. O'Hara, who later, as the school's prefect of religion and then its vice president and president, played a crucial role in building Notre Dame football.)

After the season, the students held a large banquet for the varsity. The yearbook pictures of the regular students and the official photograph of the team reveal an interesting contrast. The students tend to have puffy young faces whereas the players seem older and stare out with the hard eyes of Irish immigrants (and the majority have Irish names). The coach, Shorty Longman, sits in an ill-fitting suit with a too-small bowler on his head, his face thin, his eyes mean, his demeanor like a ticket-of-leave man released from a British prison. The team photo is a reminder that football then, as it is now, was a violent sport played by men willing to inflict and accept pain.

In fact, the Notre Dame players were beginning to be a different breed from the regular Notre Dame students. Longman recruited some of his own athletes, and the 1909 team had players from twelve states. The eligibility of two of them would cause a major incident with Michigan in 1910 and lead to severe scheduling problems as well as further isolation of the Catholic school.

"The Wolverines did more damage to themselves than to the Catholics . . . worst of all, it gives Notre Dame leverage for a boast that Michigan is afraid of the big eleven from South Bend."

—A *Detroit News* report on Michigan's
cancellation of its 1910 game with Notre Dame

During the summer of 1910, Longman wrote a long letter from Ann Arbor to James Hope, the student manager of Notre Dame athletics, about prospects for the coming year. Longman was pleased with his "proselyting"—among his recruits was star quarterback Charles "Gus" Dorais, Rockne's future roommate—and the coach listed prospects from a variety of places outside the state of Indiana, including three men from Spokane, Washington.

Longman added that he wished "something could be done" for Dorais and another recruit "for they are good men and we sure need them." Longman's wishes were answered when President John W. Cavanaugh told him to have Dorais send an N.D. alum in Chicago "a request for aid in getting through Notre Dame, with an expression of a willingness to be useful in any service the university may need for him." This arrangement did not violate any rules and was much more modest than the "packages" awarded to prime prospects by most big-time football programs at this time.

Because of Notre Dame's new football fame, its administrators soon learned firsthand about the cutthroat world of recruiting when poachers from other institutions showed up on campus. According to right end Joe Collins, "the entire [1909] team was offered the proposition to go to Princeton . . . they [the Ivy school] were willing to spend a lot of money"; star running back Pete Vaughan and lineman Luke Kelly took the offer and a few of their teammates went to other schools. Collins characterized the Princeton package as "typical of what the big fellows have done for years and will continue to do for years to come," and said that a leader of the Western Conference like Chicago "offends just as regular as the next fellow."

Unfortunately for Notre Dame, most of the "big fellows" would not schedule them and the 1910 opponent list was lean, with only Michigan, the Michigan (State) Aggies, and Marquette providing real competition.

For the November match in Ann Arbor, Notre Dame planned to transport the entire undergraduate student body to the game. This was "a contest toward which both sides have been looking for exactly a year," announced the *Detroit News,* but "on the eve of the first whistle," Fielding Yost canceled the game. The Michigan coach claimed that two Notre Dame players, Dimmick and Philbrook, had played football for Whitman College in the state of Washington and then had entered Notre Dame as freshmen, embarking on full playing careers at N.D. Yost had a point: these athletes had played for Whitman; were in their twenties— Dimmick had been a cowboy in Argentina before playing college football; and, in fact, had come to Notre Dame with a third Whitman "footballer" named Mathews. However, Notre Dame was correct in its counteraccusation that two Michigan starters had played for previous schools and had used up their four years of eligibility. The Notre Dame authorities were particularly upset at Yost's waiting until the last minute to protest and cancel.

But the game was gone and then the season was lost, especially after an N.D. defeat at the Michigan Aggies and a tie at Marquette. The six-game schedule was the most abbreviated in twentieth-century Notre Dame football history (except for the six games played during the war year 1918) and, in part, cost Longman his job.

The next summer, James Hope, in summing up his time as student athletic manager, wrote to Father Matthew J. Walsh, the new vice president of N.D.: "We apparently are in a bad rut and it will take some hard work to put things back on the old standing." Michigan and the Michigan Aggies had joined the Big Nine's boycott of Notre Dame, and as a result, the 1911 schedule had a preponderance of games against Catholic schools. "From a financial standpoint," Hope did not like playing them; not only did such games attract small crowds but Marquette, in the spring of 1911, had welched on a guarantee for a canceled baseball game. Hope explained his "impudence" in calling upon "such a good Catholic institution for the payment of a forfeiture," but he wanted to try to balance the athletic department's books.

He also advised Father Walsh: "We must all keep our eye out for good athletes in all lines and be careful in our choice [because] the standing of our men is going to be watched for the next few years." His one bit of optimism concerned the new football coach, Jack Marks from Dartmouth: "I hear he is a good coach in every respect."

Marks was good, and his 1911 squad squashed five soft teams by a total of 218 points to 6; however, against two tough opponents, Pittsburgh and Marquette, they played to scoreless ties. The latter contest sparked an interesting exchange of letters between Marquette officials and the new Notre Dame student manager, John P. Murphy. In trying to agree on referees for the contest, Murphy had rejected Walter Eckersall of the *Chicago Tribune* as "partial" against Notre Dame. The Marquette manager replied that because Eckersall was the "authority on football for the most powerful paper in the West, [and gave] excellent newspaper accounts before and after the games" that he refereed, and also because he chose the All-Western teams, it was "certainly to both our interests" to employ him as a game official. Marquette went ahead and hired Eckersall; Murphy was incensed and complained to Father Walsh. Throughout the episode, the N.D. student manager did not seem to understand how this system worked—athletic directors and coaches routinely employed journalists as game officials and expected positive "news" articles in return. (A few years later, Jesse Harper turned Eckersall to Notre Dame's advantage, and in the 1920s, Rockne established a close personal and professional relationship with the Chicago referee-journalist.)

The 1911 football season was a failure not only in terms of the schedule but also financially. The home contests against Ohio Northern, Saint Viator, Butler, Loyola of Chicago, and Saint Bonaventure netted successive sums of $99, $34, $66, $137, and $86.20. The final figure for the football season was a $2,367 loss. By the end of the academic year in June 1912, with losses of $9,024 in other intercollegiate sports as well as coaches' salaries of $1,480, the total loss was $12,872. This was partially offset by $6,400 from student athletic fees, making the net deficit for 1911–1912 for the athletic department $6,472, but the school could not afford this loss.

This grim situation prompted Notre Dame to try to break out of its scheduling straitjacket and arrange some profitable games for 1912. The student manager wrote Glenn "Pop" Warner, the coach of the Carlisle Indians, suggesting a match in the "White Sox ball park" in Chicago and promising: "Our hundreds of [Chicago] alumni . . . would devote all their energy to making such a game a great success." Warner, coming off a season when Jim Thorpe had led Carlisle to new records, rejected

N.D.'s offer and instead scheduled games against Army, Penn, and other eastern powers. (Warner was one of the great buccaneer coaches of the era, openly paying and lavishly housing his "Athletic Boys," scheduling long money-making tours for his team, personally pocketing part of the game receipts, and betting heavily on his own and other games. A congressional investigation in 1914–1915 ended his Carlisle career, but he went on to further fame and fortune at Pitt and Stanford.)

The Notre Dame 1912 schedule turned out weaker than the previous year's, with tiny Adrian College of Michigan and even smaller Morris Harvey of West Virginia added to some of 1911's undistinguished opponents. The N.D. student manager did place the Marquette game in Comiskey Park, but he did not promote it well and failed to make much of a profit.

Jack Marks coached the team to a 7–0 record and introduced a forerunner of the Notre Dame box formation as well as a few passing plays. The students tried to generate some enthusiasm, but only the victory over Wabash and the 69–0 whomping of Marquette excited them. They also trumpeted quarterback Dorais, fullback Eichenlaub, and left end Knute Rockne as All-America candidates. Walter Camp, who chose the team, ignored the Notre Dame players. A student wit in the *Scholastic* captured the school's frustration with its football fortunes in a satire on how Walter Camp selected his squad: "My plan is just pick Harvard first / And then pick good old Yale. / With five of crimson, six of blue, / It seems the only way, / To pick the best of East and West / For All-Amerikay."

Notre Dame football was at a crucial juncture. President John W. Cavanaugh was still willing to go small-time, and the financial loss after this season (1912) against minor opponents ($463) made that a viable option. But, in its history, Notre Dame athletics had grown steadily, and the students and the increasing number of alumni, as well as many priests within the C.S.C. community, strongly opposed shrinking the football program. Thus, in early December of 1912, Cavanaugh made a fateful decision: he hired Notre Dame's first full-time coach and athletic director, Jesse Harper, for a salary, including bonuses, of approximately $5,000 a year.

Harper, a Protestant, had learned football under Stagg at Chicago and was one of the new breed of professional athletic administrators.

Harper signed to coach varsity football and baseball and to run the business of the athletic department, thus ending the student manager system at N.D. The school knew Harper well—for the previous four years he had coached the Wabash College team in their games against Notre Dame. His "Little Giants" never beat N.D., but they usually played them tough, losing the 1911 game by only 6–3.

When Notre Dame hired Harper, his first priority was clear: to extricate the Catholic school from the scheduling box into which its midwestern foes had placed it and, in so doing, regularize the athletic department's finances. Father Joseph Burke, later Notre Dame's treasurer, wrote to Harper: "The athletic management here for some time has been far from satisfactory and we are looking forward to the time when we will be relieved of a great deal of worry."

Because of Harper's connections with Stagg and other Western Conference coaches, N.D. officials particularly hoped that their new athletic director could break the impasse with the Big Nine. Harper was unable to accomplish this, but he soon managed something better—games against the eastern athletic powers. Ironically, his means of doing it came first in baseball, not football.

6

Jesse Harper: 1913 and the First Army Game

ROCKNE AND DORAIS [*on the beach*]

DORAIS: [*Reading this morning's* Tribune] Notre Dame's playing Army this fall.

[*Rockne stops in great surprise to stare excitedly at his roommate.*]

ROCKNE: Army!? When? Where?

DORAIS: At West Point—in November.

—From the film *Knute Rockne—All American*

One of the most dramatic sequences in the Hollywood version of Rockne's life is the buildup to the 1913 contest with Army and the game itself. The movie, however, is a fantasy; the reality of Rockne's life was much messier, more complicated, and infinitely more interesting. In the film, for example, the scheduling of the first game at West Point seems to fall from the sky and land on the beach. The N.D. boys grab it and thereupon invent the forward pass to beat the eastern champs. In historical fact, the origins of the contest began in the 1908 rejection of Notre Dame by the Western Conference and the Catholic school's decision to send its baseball team on an eastern road trip the following year, then more extensive eastern swings during subsequent seasons. Not only did this extricate Notre Dame baseball from Big Nine exclusion but the 1912 trip east generated over $2,500 in revenue and a profit of $861.

For the spring of 1913, the Notre Dame student manager arranged another long baseball tour to the East Coast, including games at the

Naval Academy, Fordham, and most significantly, at West Point. Correspondence with that school had begun in the fall of 1912. Thus, when
Jesse Harper began sending out letters seeking football games for the
1913 season, he logically mailed one to West Point.

Some sports historians claim that Army wrote Notre Dame first, but
Harper's correspondence files clearly show that he initiated contact in his
letter of December 18, 1912, and that the Army manager of athletics
telegraphed back his agreement to a game.

A more interesting question than who wrote whom first is why was
Army so quick to schedule its first game in a decade against a non-eastern
opponent? The immediate explanation was that, after the 1912 season,
Yale decided to discontinue its series with West Point and suddenly Army
had an opening on its 1913 calendar for November 1. The more important reason was that Army, because it flaunted standard eligibility rules,
had become a pariah in intercollegiate athletics. West Point recruited
players who had completed entire undergraduate careers at other schools
and enrolled them for up to four more years of college sports. Army
argued that its men needed the extra time to be trained as officers but
the Naval Academy neither made this claim nor used this eligibility trick.

The history of Elmer Oliphant illustrates West Point's system. "Ollie"
competed for Purdue for three years, from 1911 through 1913, attaining
All-America status, then played at West Point from 1914 through 1917,
adding to his All-America honors. Even when the United States went to
war in 1916, Oliphant played on, continuing to help lead the Cadets to
football victories.

But Jesse Harper was not squeamish about Army's peculiar views on
playing eligibility and he immediately agreed to the contest, with a visitor's guarantee to Notre Dame of $1,000. By March 1913, Harper had
completed his schedule for the fall; after the Army game, his team would
play at Penn State and then go to Saint Louis University and on to the
University of Texas at Austin. This was the most extensive series of road
football games in Notre Dame history up to this time. As Harper later
explained: "Well, Lord, I was forced to get a national schedule. . . . I
had to go someplace where I could get some ball games."

N.D. Vice President Walsh congratulated Harper on putting together
"the best football schedule that Notre Dame ever had," and said that
"from a financial point of view it seems that you should make out very
well both on your trips and home games." Walsh also noted on March 25,
1913: "You may reach [football] Captain Rockne by addressing Mr.
Knute Rockne, Corby Hall, Notre Dame, Indiana." Harper was completing his contract at Wabash and, no doubt, he wrote to Captain Rockne—

thus the latter learned about the fall schedule well before the summer at the beach.

> DORAIS: Don't be a sap, Rock. The Army will outweigh us twenty pounds to the man. We couldn't lick 'em if we took a shotgun along.
> ROCKNE: All right—we'll *take* a shotgun. . . . We're going to *pass* the Army, Gus—we're going to pass 'em dizzy!
> DORAIS: Rock—if that works it'll make history!

> —From the film *Knute Rockne—All American*

The 1913 football season started with home games against Ohio Northern, South Dakota, and tiny Alma College of Michigan. Notre Dame overwhelmed these opponents and practiced its passing attack. Unfortunately, in the opener, according to a student reporter, Rockne "was tackled hard around the waist which tore a floating rib from the cartilage. The doughty captain stayed in the game until" the end of the first half. Notre Dame players and fans accepted the violence of football and even enjoyed such tongue-in-cheek items in the *Scholastic* as: "GRID-IRON GOSSIP . . . Darwin's Original football squad met Barnum's Pets in a gridiron-warmer on Cartier Field last Saturday before the big battle. Results—six dead; seventeen wounded."

Much of the brutality was a result of the hammering ground attacks and ferocious line combat popular in football at the time. Walter Camp believed that this was the essence of the game, and only over his objections did the Rules Committee of the IAA (the forerunner of the NCAA) liberalize the forward pass regulations in 1910 and, two years later, increase the number of downs to four.

Coaches at schools that could not attract bruising runners and hefty linemen began to experiment with forward passing. Jesse Harper's players at Wabash were more "Little" than "Giants," and he proudly stated: "I used the forward pass a great deal at Wabash before going to Notre Dame. In fact, Wabash was the first team to use intentional grounding." And, in 1913, according to an N.D. assistant coach, "Mr. Harper devoted much time to the development of the forward pass combination of Dorais to Rockne." Jesse Harper never claimed to have invented the forward pass; that honor belonged to Eddie Cochems, coach of Saint Louis University from 1906 to 1908. (The *Saint Louis Post-Dispatch* sports editor during those years later wrote: "The Rockne-Dorais glamour story had wide circulation but Cochems' players were throwing 50 yard forward pass strikes when Dorais and Rockne were high school sophomores.")

What Harper demonstrated on the playing field at West Point in 1913 was that the forward pass could spread out the defense, allowing a more varied attack. Instead of the defense being able to pack the line, blunt the running plays, and slug it out until the physically strongest team won, Notre Dame proved against Army that an efficient passing attack—it completed fourteen out of seventeen for over two hundred yards—would allow faster, lighter teams to score.

Contrary to legend, Notre Dame's first visit to West Point did not revolutionize football—teams were slow to adopt the forward pass as a central part of their offense. Coaches still favored a pounding running attack and they employed the pass mainly as a diversionary or desperation tactic. Even Harper preferred to rely on such fullbacks as the bullish Ray Eichenlaub to carry most of the Notre Dame attack (he scored two touchdowns and gained over one hundred yards in the first Army game). The final ironic footnote to the movie myth is that Knute Rockne, as a coach, used the pass sparingly. He frequently said: "The sweetest thing in football is a completed pass—but the sourest is an intercepted pass. The pass is like a lot of dangerous things in life . . . if it cannot be controlled, it's wisest to stay away from it before it ruins you."

> "Nowhere in football's annals has there ever been a team more obscure than the one which arrived at West Point on November 1 of 1913 to play the cadets."
>
> —Delos Lovelace, *Rockne of Notre Dame*

During its history, Notre Dame football has sparked many legends, and the first victory over Army generated more than most. Lovelace wrote his version only eighteen years after the event and almost a decade before the Hollywood enshrining of the "obscure school" myth. In reality, Notre Dame in 1913 was well-known, and the newspaper accounts of the game acknowledged the "Catholics" as a major midwestern football force.

Most contemporary sportswriters did not see this game or the N.D. team in the singular, unique light that subsequent legend cast over them. One Chicago reporter compared Notre Dame's "overwhelming victory over Army" to Michigan's "equally decisive drubbing of Syracuse" on the same day, and wondered which was the best team, along with the Michigan Aggies and Chicago, in the Midwest.

Harper, however, immediately took the team away from the Midwest for other intersectional matches. The week after Army, Notre Dame beat Penn State, and later in the month went west for a game against Saint Louis University and then directly to Texas for a Thanksgiving game in Austin. For the Texas trip, Harper, worried about dysentery in the local water, took bottled water from Notre Dame. (Rockne is often credited as being the first coach to do this, but as with so many of his so-called inventions, he merely repeated or improved upon what Harper had done.)

Notre Dame easily won the Saint Louis and Texas games, and at the end of the season was well represented on Walter Eckersall's All-Western team as well as on Ring Lardner's "Wake of the News" squad. Walter Camp even noticed the star players by naming fullback Eichenlaub to his second All-America team and Rockne to his third squad.

Notre Dame students were ecstatic with the team's success, and the *Scholastic* printed page after page of laudatory comments by midwestern and eastern papers on the Catholic school's football prowess. This provided interesting news and a service for the Notre Dame community— students and faculty did not have access to most of these papers—and a collective ego booster. Whatever inferiority feelings Notre Damers experienced because of the ostracism by the Big Nine were assuaged by the long commentaries in the most important journals in the country. The midwestern universities might consider the Catholic school invisible but the national media validated Notre Dame's existence.

The newspapers, however, mainly commented on the football team, its coach and players; rarely was any other aspect of the school mentioned. Moreover, the publicity from football had another negative aspect —some papers ran unsubstantiated rumors about N.D.'s football program. A nationally syndicated article summed up: "Whether justly or not, Notre Dame has been looked at askance by what would seem its natural rivals [the Big Nine], and innuendoes concerning its players have brought heated replies from the athletic authorities at the Catholic institution."

Yet, because of the press, Catholics beyond the Midwest were beginning to notice Notre Dame and enjoy its football success. Their reaction was muted at first but became a roar a decade later. According to one historian, the victory over Army in 1913 was "the greatest single miracle in the history of Catholic higher education" because it began the transformation of Notre Dame "into a household word."

Of more immediate importance to N.D. President Cavanaugh and Vice President Walsh in 1913 was the fact that for the first time in the school's history, the football program, even with the expensive road trips, showed a profit ($1,364); at the end of the 1913–1914 academic year, the athletic department, helped out by student athletic fees, was close to the black.

In December 1913, because of the growth of the student body and to insure stable future athletic revenues, the N.D. administration decided to apply again for Western Conference membership. In preparation, to bring its football program in line with Big Nine regulations, it ended freshman eligibility and tightened other rules. Jesse Harper told the press that N.D. "is the logical successor to Michigan," still outside the group. But at its annual meeting, the conference, led by Chicago and Minnesota, rebuffed the Catholic institution. Its representatives argued that Notre Dame's athletic success indicated lack of faculty control and systematic cheating, thus, according to an N.D. reporter, "we were deemed 'undesirable' by the athletic trust of the Middle West." As in future N.D. disputes with the Big Nine, the conference men acted on the basis of rumors, refusing to ascertain the truth—in fact, Notre Dame ran a cleaner athletic program than most of their schools, and because it had a small, disorganized alumni, it was not burdened by "old grad" and booster interference with its football team, as was the case at the Big Nine schools and Michigan.

Many sportswriters as well as N.D. student journalists explained the turndown only in terms of Notre Dame's athletic prowess, *The Dome* commenting, "It is easy to understand why Northwestern and Indiana— teams that would end last in our interhall race—objected, but why Chicago and Minnesota, with pretensions to Western Championships demurred" makes no sense. But the professional prejudices of the conference's "Academic Men" as well as the growing anti-Catholicism of midwestern state legislatures were more important factors. The N.D. administrators involved in this and previous applications to the conference, Fathers Crumley and Walsh, attributed their school's "lack of success . . . [first of all] to religious prejudice."

Again, at a crucial juncture in the creation of Notre Dame football, a rejection by the Western Conference forced the Catholic institution to remain independent and to look beyond its geographic region. In 1913, the veto by the Big Nine determined the future national character of Notre Dame football and was more significant than the victory at West Point.

7

Jesse Harper: 1914 and the Finances of College Football

"I certainly will be on hand for the Carlisle game and it should be a great attraction up here. I wrote Father Walsh in regard to the other matter. I wrote him the same day I received the money. . . ."

—Walter Eckersall, *Chicago Tribune*
writer and football referee,
to Jesse Harper, March 30, 1914

After the successful 1913 season, Harper immediately started work on the next year's schedule. He wrote to West Point suggesting a 1914 game and received a warm but cagey reply. The officer in charge of athletics began by stating: "The Army is very proud to call Notre Dame its friend," but then pointed out that "our funds are limited" in providing guarantees for visitors. West Point did not charge admission to its home games ("our athletics are financed solely by subscriptions from officers and cadets"), and "proceeds from the sale of tickets for the Army-Navy game [in a neutral stadium]" went "to charity." However, Harper wanted the game and accepted the same $1,000 guarantee he had obtained in 1913.

He also approached Yale University and assented to a $700 guarantee from them even though he knew, because of its large stadium in New Haven, that Yale would make a sizable profit from the contest. But, for the Notre Dame athletic director, the plan was to build the schedule with big-name opponents, and Yale was the top bulldog of the era. Harper also

arranged an eastern game at Syracuse and a western one against South
Dakota in Sioux Falls. Because Cartier Field at Notre Dame was small
and could not attract major opponents, he scheduled only three home
games—Alma, Rose Polytechnical, and Haskell Indians (a small government school in Lawrence, Kansas).

Harper's main money-making scheme for 1914 was to play the famous Carlisle Indians in Chicago. Glenn "Pop" Warner, their coach and
athletic director, was agreeable but demanded half the gate. Harper accepted and then asked Amos Alonzo Stagg if the teams could stage the
game at the University of Chicago's field. Stagg replied that his "Board of
Trustees were opposed. . . . No reasons were given." Harper must have
guessed the reason—the Big Nine's dislike of Notre Dame as well as its
disapproval of the Indian institution.

In fact, Carlisle was more of a trade school than a college and its
admission and eligibility rules deviated far from the norm. Moreover,
Pop Warner had a well-earned reputation for deceptive practices. By
1914, the Indian school had become an outcast in college sports, but as
with the Army, Notre Dame was willing to play all opponents, especially
if the games could improve its schedule and football revenue.

After Stagg's refusal, Harper turned to Charlie Comiskey and placed
the contest at the south side ballpark. The Notre Dame athletic director's
next step was to line up publicity agents and referees for the game. At the
time, the two roles were often bundled together, with the most important
football journalists obtaining the most lucrative refereeing jobs as well as
extra money for promoting the contest in the press. The sportswriter-
referee would place the publicity items in his own paper and with colleagues on other journals. The public was oblivious to the practice and
read the puff pieces as straight news. Paul Gallico, one of the few honest
sportswriters of the era, argued that the real villains were the publishers
who paid their journalists poorly and "permitted this kind of [promo-
tional] swill to appear on their pages." Fight promoters and baseball team
owners often used newspaper reporters as secret publicists, but college
coaches took the deception to a new low by also employing them as
referees.

Harper first contacted Walter Eckersall, the *Chicago Tribune*'s football expert (and a former All-America player) to referee and promote.
Eckersall replied: "The fee you stated in your letter . . . is perfectly
satisfactory to me." (Harper had suggested "Eck" for the Army game in
1913 but West Point officials had vetoed him.) The N.D. athletic director
also lined up Otto Engel from the *Chicago Tribune*'s sports department
as "head linesman" for the Haskell Indians game at Notre Dame.

Harper, however, needed a large crowd for the Carlisle game and he knew that Eckersall was too important to do all of the publicity work. Thus, he wrote to the sports editor of the *Chicago Tribune,* Harvey Woodruff, asking "what kind of publicity man McEvoy of the [Chicago] *Record-Herald* would make." Woodruff recommended McEvoy highly; Harper thanked him and sent along fourteen complimentary tickets to the Carlisle game for Woodruff's personal use.

Once McEvoy was hired, Harper barraged him with ideas on how to promote the event: "Write up the game as the big game in Chicago on that date . . . write it up from the standpoint of the possibilities of a spectacular game. . . . I think a picture of Glenn Warner would go well . . . write up that we are running a special train and practically all the students of Notre Dame will be on hand."

In addition, Harper sent complimentary tickets to writers and sports editors on other Chicago papers; for example, Lambert Sullivan of the *Chicago Daily News* received eight along with the request for a "little article some evening this week, preferably about Thursday, on the game."

The Notre Dame athletic director was both innovative and indefatigable in promoting his first big Chicago game. He sent a form letter and game posters to depot masters at major railroad stations throughout the Midwest, asking them to place "several posters of the game in conspicuous places." He also wrote a letter to Notre Dame alumni pointing out that "this is the biggest game ever pulled off in the West by Notre Dame" and imploring them to "make every effort to attend."

To render the game more attractive to spectators, Harper decided to have the players wear numbers, and he wrote Carlisle asking for a list of their players and the numerals that Warner would assign them. (Rockne is often credited with this innovation but he merely copied what he observed as Harper's assistant coach.) Notre Dame had no trouble supplying its team list and numbers but Carlisle's was more problematic. As Rockne later explained, the Indian institutions tended to move players around, "changing legal names to Indian names as they switched schools . . . The famous back, Emil Hauser of Haskell, became Chief Waseka at Carlisle, etc." In this way, Warner had his best players suit up for many more than the standard four years. In due course, the roster arrived from Carlisle—and along with names, numbers, position, weight, and age came information on "Tribe" and "Trade": for example, Hawk Eagle was a twenty-one-year-old, 163-pound tackle from the Sioux tribe, and a mason by trade.

In the end, all of Harper's hard work paid off and the game drew an estimated twelve thousand spectators, allowing Notre Dame and Pop Warner to split the $10,175 gate—the settlement statement listing Carlisle's share as specifically "Paid to Glenn Warner." However, the Indians put on a mediocre show, N.D. massacring them 48–6 (the congressional investigation into Warner's corrupt practices had begun and the Department of the Interior was winding down his Carlisle program). After the game, the Notre Dame athletic director also sent checks to sportswriters Walter Eckersall and J. P. McEvoy for their services.

"I must say that at present I am quite shaky in regard to the outcome of the Notre Dame–Yale game. Our team is not developing as it should. Right now I feel rather shaky about any bets."

—Jesse Harper to a friend, September 29, 1914

Notre Dame's most important game of the 1914 season was at Yale, and Harper received requests from friends and acquaintances for inside information on his team. During this era, large amounts of money were bet on college football and professional baseball, and gamblers constantly sought an edge. Before important games, college coaches were besieged by bettors. Out of this sporting culture came an increasing number of fixed contests and, within a few years, the Black Sox scandal.

Harper also had to contend with gambling problems in South Bend. At the time, significant sums were wagered on semipro football games, especially matches between the teams of rival towns. In 1914, when the South Bend Silver Edges, assembled by Knute Rockne, upset the Fort Wayne Friars and the loss cleaned out the latter's fans, they retaliated by publicly accusing the South Bend team of using five "ringers" from Notre Dame. The school investigated and suspended Harper's athletes, but this did not deter collegians at Notre Dame and elsewhere from playing semipro football on the side and betting on themselves (this practice continued well into the 1920s). Moreover, for college games, it was traditional for each team's players to pool their money and put the two sums into a winner-take-all pot; the Notre Dame and Army squads long did this with a neutral party holding the cash during the game.

The students at Notre Dame also supported their varsity by placing bets at the South Bend pool parlors, especially Hullie & Mike's and Jimmy the Goat's. For the Yale game, they composed a song to their team that included the couplet "We're going to bet our coat, / That you'll get Yale's goat."

In the event, Yale, using Canadian-style rugby passes, demolished

N.D. 28–0. The *Boston Post* reported: "The score was one of the upsets of the season. Betting made Notre Dame almost equal to Yale till the game started." The *Scholastic* was in shock: "It is a new and strange thing to chronicle a Notre Dame defeat in football." However, a few weeks later, the *Scholastic* had to report on N.D.'s loss to Army, 20–7. Trying to explain how his team had fumbled away the game, the student reporter gasped: "There must be something in the effete Eastern atmosphere conducive to nervousness." In fact, Notre Dame had encountered two excellent and powerful teams, both adept at ball control. Army, led by Charlie Daly, a five-time All-American at Harvard and at West Point, baffled Harper's players all afternoon.

The match the following week against Carlisle in Chicago relieved N.D.'s agony, and the soothing postgame words of Walter Eckersall in the *Chicago Tribune* added a touch of unreality to the season: "Although defeated by the Army and Yale, it was apparent yesterday [against Carlisle] that Notre Dame did not have the breaks of luck in the eastern combats."

But Jesse Harper and Vice President Matthew Walsh were realists and knew that, in future years, their team had to play better football and against better teams than Carlisle. Harper immediately began work on a national schedule for 1915 but mainly received turndowns. Particularly painful were the rejections in late 1914 by Yale and Michigan for games the following autumn. Both schools were polite and full of excuses, but except for the Army annual, Harper had a bare cupboard for 1915. He wrote Syracuse about playing Notre Dame in Chicago because "Carlisle made such a poor showing that the people were not interested in seeing them again," but the game never came off.

During this period, Harper also made his most serious error in scheduling. The business manager of the Polo Grounds in New York suggested a Notre Dame game in that stadium for 1915, pointing out that "the publicity which would accrue to your college through a New York game would be greater than through all the rest of the games which you play during the season. Practically every daily paper in the United States carries an account of the games played in New York."

Harper was interested but wanted exact financial figures on previous college games in the New York stadium. The Polo Grounds management provided them, but because the profits were less than what Notre Dame had made in Chicago against Carlisle, Harper refused. However, the New York people argued that if Notre Dame played a major eastern opponent and scheduled the game when such local teams as Princeton were on the road, the Catholic school could do terrifically well. This argument failed to persuade Harper.

His assistant, Knute Rockne, observed his boss's scheduling maneuvers and learned from this blunder—exactly ten years later, as N.D. coach and athletic director, he helped move the Notre Dame–Army game to the Polo Grounds and the receipts as well as the publicity were phenomenal, far beyond Jesse Harper's limited dreams.

For 1915, the Notre Dame A.D. ended up looking west and southwest, and he constructed his most difficult "road warrior" schedule. Games against Nebraska, Creighton, Texas, and Rice, as well as the trip to West Point, were the highlights, with the five road games coming in a thirty-five-day period. Money was a key consideration.

For the 1914 season, football revenue had doubled from the previous year to more than $16,000; however, expenses had also more than doubled and profit was only $2,047. When the coaches' salaries of $5,026 were factored in, football was still not a money-maker for Notre Dame and only student fees were keeping the athletic department close to the black. In this situation, the school had to accept the away-game guarantees and hope for a break in the Big Nine boycott.

8

Jesse Harper: 1915–1917 and the Job of Athletic Director

"Will you be good enough to let me know before the end of the week the name of the man whom you consider your best lineman. . . .

The information I want from you of course will be treated confidentially and will not be used for publication as coming from you."

—Frank G. Menke,
sports editor of the *International News Service*,
in a letter to Jesse Harper, November 15, 1915

Part of Harper's job was to cooperate with the press, even though journalists' methods were often corrupt and corrupting. Harper immediately answered the request from the *International News Service* (the Hearst wire service) with an effusive recommendation of his captain, Freeman Fitzgerald, and he added praise for his quarterback, Stan Cofall. The Notre Dame A.D. also had to go along with the maneuvers of the *Chicago Tribune*'s Walter Eckersall and other reporter-referees. In writing the athletic director of the Haskell Institute concerning refs for their 1915 game, Harper noted that Eckersall "is not entirely reliable. Sometimes he will take another game" after agreeing to ours. But Harper accepted the system and for the Haskell game backed up Eckersall with Otto Engel, also from the *Chicago Tribune* sports department.

The 1915 road warrior schedule started badly with a 20–19 defeat in

Lincoln, Nebraska, but the team came back by beating Army 7–0 at West Point. Creighton at Omaha was not a problem, nor were Texas and Rice. The *Austin American* proudly pointed out that, even though the final score was 36–7, "Texas was the second team of the season to score on the Catholics." In fact, in compiling a 7–1 record, Notre Dame outscored its opponents 230–29.

Harper had built Notre Dame into a formidable football machine, in part by setting up an excellent recruiting system. He kept tabs on the best prospects in the Midwest and offered them, as Chet Grant, one of his early recruits, explained, a Notre Dame "athletic scholarship"—a guaranteed job on campus to pay all N.D. bills. Harper also effectively used his current and past players as scouts. In January 1915, at the urging of Gus Dorais, he wrote to Dudley Pearson, a high school star in Chippewa Falls, Wisconsin (Dorais's hometown), about coming to Notre Dame. After negotiating with Pearson for a few months, he wrote him: "I had a talk with Father Walsh, Vice-President of the University . . . [and] I am sure you can count on being one of the fortunate men to receive work." The freshman athletes mainly worked in the dining halls, and in later years, if they made the varsity, they obtained less demanding and more lucrative jobs.

Pearson came to Notre Dame, played freshman football, and was on the varsity from 1917 to 1919. He was a waiter in his freshman hall, but by his senior year, as a backup quarterback, he held the profitable concession of selling student excursion tickets to away games. According to N.D. publications, "Old Jinx Injury" curtailed Dud's playing time, but his off-the-field career was highly successful.

On occasion, a high school star solicited Harper—a 205-pound fullback from Iowa wrote, "Let me know what sort of a proposition you may give me." Harper tended to turn aside the unsolicited inquiries, but he did pursue the highly recommended ones like Earl "Curly" Lambeau of Green Bay, Wisconsin. In his initial letter to Lambeau, he urged him to visit the campus and he talked up the advantages of Notre Dame, where "without doubt we have the most democratic student body you can find. There are no secret societies, no organizations which have a tendency to draw a small number of students together at the expense of the rest."

Lambeau replied that he was impressed with Notre Dame but "there is one drawback. I am not fixed very well financially and I would like to know what is the best you can do for me." Harper, with clear instructions from Vice President Walsh about no free rides, replied, "If you are willing to work I will be very glad to help you. If you are not willing to work and, in addition, looking for an offer [of a free ride], I assure you, you will have to consider some other institution." Lambeau came to Notre Dame for two years, playing on the varsity in 1918, but then went into professional football, where he helped start the Green Bay Packers.

Because of the corrupt state of college football at this time, Notre Dame's control of its football recruiting was unusual. Heartley "Hunk" Anderson, a future N.D. head coach, noted: "The only money spent by coaches for proselyting in Harper's day . . . was a quarter for a shot of booze in the pool hall while the coach looked over the clientele. If he found a 200-pounder who knew how to spell and sign his name, he was recruited." This description particularly applied to such swashbucklers as Glenn "Pop" Warner during his years at Pitt (1915–1923), and his "proselyting" tours of the coal-mining towns of western Pennsylvania.

Inevitably, as Notre Dame achieved greater on-field success, rumors about Harper's recruiting spread through the Midwest, often peddled by sportswriters friendly to N.D. opponents. In 1916, when a Nebraska reporter complained to Harper that during N.D.'s visit to Lincoln "certain players and members of your party . . . were putting pressure, religious and otherwise, to induce one of our Nebraska freshman players to leave Nebraska and go to Notre Dame," the Notre Dame coach uncharacteristically lost his temper. He told the reporter that he had never poached college players; in fact, whenever athletes at other schools approached him, he immediately informed their coaches, and during his years at N.D., he had accepted only two transfers. Moreover, the fact that the Nebraska freshman was a Catholic was immaterial—"I never saw a school so free of religious prejudices as Notre Dame. I feel I am in a position to know as I am a Protestant."

Ironically, until this letter from the Lincoln reporter, Harper had received only positive mail from Nebraska, including a feeler about coaching there. After N.D.'s visit the previous year, the Nebraska manager of athletics asked Harper if he were interested in coaching the Cornhuskers even though he "understood that you are under contract and that you are getting a monster salary now. How about it?" Harper, showing the same personal code that made him honor his Wabash contract until its very last day, replied that he was "still under contract at Notre Dame . . . hence it would be impossible for me to consider Nebraska even if you should want me."

"I suppose you know all about the case between Father Cavanaugh and
I. . . . Now, Coach, suppose you get some of the ball players to see
Father Walsh and have him intercede. I am sure that I can get back if
some of them intercede."

—Joseph "Chief" Meyer
in a letter to Harper, March 2, 1915

Athletes in the first decades of this century, as now, tended to drop
out of school for academic and/or disciplinary, not financial, reasons, and
Harper had his share of problem cases while he was athletic director at
Notre Dame. In the spring of 1915, one of his star baseball players,
Joseph "Chief" Meyer, departed. Meyer wrote Harper, pleading with
him to get him back into school, the ball player adding, in a foreshad-
owing of future events, that "Rock ought to know a way to go about this
case." Later, as A.D., Rockne used various maneuvers to get athletes
back into school, but in 1915, neither Rockne nor Harper could do anything for Meyer, and he sat out the year (he did return the following
season and starred on the baseball team in 1916–1917 before going on to
a minor league playing and managing career).

A more pleasant task for Harper was to write letters of recommendation for his graduating athletes. As Notre Dame gained fame in football,
its players applied for high school as well as college coaching jobs.
Harper was always generous in his recommendations; for his star end,
Mal Elward, he wrote about the athlete's intelligent play and added: "He
is a very clean man morally and very seldom smokes and does not drink
at all." Harper's most fulsome praise was for his center, Hugh O'Donnell:
"Never have I known a man who has a finer character. He has a wonderful disposition and at the same time has a great deal of energy and
aggressiveness." A few years later, O'Donnell, whose nickname was
"Pepper," entered the C.S.C. seminary, eventually becoming N.D. president from 1940 to 1946.

For a non-Catholic, Jesse Harper had a deep understanding of Notre
Dame's strengths and its culture of athleticism. But Harper, in his dealings with various schools, could not convince them of N.D.'s virtues, even
its acceptability as an opponent. For the 1916 season, he sent out many
requests for games but only Army replied enthusiastically. Other eastern
and midwestern football schools were not interested in playing "the
Catholics." Harvard was particularly insulting—Harper wrote a number
of full and polite letters to the Crimson's manager of athletics, only to

receive this short telegram: "REGRET COACHES CONSIDER GAME SUGGESTED INADVISABLE."

In the end, for 1916, Harper put very few attractive games on Notre Dame's schedule; only the perennial with Army and the second visit to Nebraska were definite pluses. Harper did bring back the Michigan Aggies after a six-year hiatus, but he had to fill out Notre Dame's dance card with Case Tech, South Dakota, Western Reserve, Wabash, Alma College, and the inevitable Haskell Indians—the latter three schools being willing to visit Cartier Field and accept the meager visitor's guarantee.

"Alfred Morales, the self-proclaimed King of the Mexicans, attempted a flying tackle along the sidelines in a 1916 game. He missed the runner but hit a parked car and broke his collarbone."

—Larry Weaver and Mike Bonifer,
collectors of Notre Dame football anecdotes

Although the Notre Dame administration kept promising Harper that it would add more permanent seats to Cartier Field, N.D. home games remained informal and unprofitable affairs. Because of their annual athletic fee, students were admitted for free, and South Bend townspeople were more interested in their semipro teams playing in local parks than in the collegians north of the city. Those South Benders who came to Cartier Field often parked their cars alongside the field and sat in them observing the game—hence Alfred Morales's accident.

Notre Dame opened the 1916 season at home against Case Tech of Cleveland. The following week it visited Case's neighbor, Western Reserve. Harper's team beat these two schools—eventually to merge as one —by identical 48–0 shutouts. Then, after a 26–0 whomping of the Haskell Indians, Notre Dame entertained Wabash College. Chet Grant, an N.D. player at the time, later described how assistant coach Knute Rockne gave the pregame talk and, "gradually working himself into a frenzy," announced that the Wabash head man had "called you dirty Catholics" and was "out to get the dirty Catholics." The players—"Catholic and Protestant and non-denominational alike"—started growling, and when Rockne ended with "Knock 'em down. Knock 'em down so they stay down. Hit 'em! Kill 'em! *Crucify 'em . . . Let's go,*" the N.D. team rushed onto the field and felled the "Little Giants" 60–0. (The previous year, Rockne had failed to obtain the head coaching job at Wabash and, no doubt, now wanted to show up the successful applicant.)

Possibly Rockne had gotten the squad too high for a weak opponent or the result had made them overconfident, because against Army the following Saturday, N.D. was flat. Army won, 30–10, in one of N.D.'s worst defeats in the series. Some reporters criticized Harper's coaching, particularly his failure to remove his quarterback, Stan Cofall, from the contest after the latter sustained a concussion and was wobbly on his feet. In this single-platoon era, Army used Cofall's incapacity to take charge of the game, aiming much of its offense into his zone.

The loss at West Point also combined with the usual $1,000 visitor's guarantee, and until the final game in Nebraska, the season was a financial flop for N.D. The Nebraska manager had predicted "a crowd of 15,000 providing both teams have a good record to that date," and fortunately, both squads entered the Thanksgiving Day contest with 7–1 records. Notre Dame won easily, 20–0, and received close to $6,500 for the visit. This allowed the N.D. athletic department in 1915–1916 to make a $644 profit in football. But the total department deficit for the year was $5,500, with student fees again covering it.

With the entry of the United States into World War I in late 1916, intercollegiate athletics went into a holding pattern. The government imposed restrictions on travel and also set up an enlistment system urging college-age men to join the armed forces.

Harper, as Notre Dame athletic director and head coach, made do as best he could, and in 1917, pointed for the rematch at West Point. Although Notre Dame and Army were depleted due to enlistments, his team managed a 7–2 victory, mainly on the fine running of first-year varsity player George Gipp. Because of the Cofall incident the previous year, Harper had purchased new and better helmets for the team, but he was rapped by a New York newspaper because "Notre Dame has been fooling 'em this year with helmets made to look like a football," opponents often tackling an N.D. helmet instead of the ball.

The 1917 schedule was similar to the previous year's but this time, instead of beating Nebraska, N.D. lost 7–0. Harper's team did triumph over the Michigan Aggies and a new eastern opponent, Washington and Jefferson. Harper's major breakthrough came with the scheduling of a game against a Big Nine school—Wisconsin.

After the visit to Madison, the *Scholastic* reminded its readers that "Notre Dame has not played a [Western] Conference eleven since 1908," and although "Yale has her Bulldog . . . and other schools have their various ferocious animals," including the Wisconsin badger, "they are welcome to the whole irrational kingdom as long as Notre Dame has her 'fight'n Irish.' " This early appearance of the nickname in print supported the *Scholastic*'s theme that all Notre Damers should hail the team's hard-fought 0–0 tie at Wisconsin.

Harper ended the season with a 6–1–1 record, including three easy home victories where Notre Dame outscored its opponents 108–0. In five short years, he had achieved a football record of 34–5–1 (86.3 percent), and he had taken football receipts from the $3,800 range when he arrived in 1913 to a high of $16,600 before wartime restrictions. Most important, he not only taught his assistant, Knute Rockne, how to build winning teams but, with the long road trips and games in big-city stadiums, showed him how to pan for future football gold.

9

Jesse Harper's Assistant:
Knute Rockne

CALLAHAN [*the fictitious president of N.D.*]: Doctor Nieuwland wants you to stay here at Notre Dame and help him teach chemistry. The job doesn't pay very much to start, but Nieuwland has great hopes for you later on.

ROCKNE [*after accepting the offer*]: Oh, just one more thing, Father—You don't have any objection to my just sort of helping Harper with the football team this fall, do you?

NIEUWLAND [*angrily*]: Yes! You're *through* with football. Get that into your head once and for all!

ROCKNE [*pleading*]: But it won't take much time, Father, and the extra money will be a great help to me.

—From the film *Knute Rockne—All American*

As with so many of the myths surrounding the famous Notre Dame coach, Rockne-as-Potential-Scientist has been polished to a high gloss, particularly by the Hollywood film on his life and by subsequent biographers. The origins of the fable belong more to the psychological than the factual realm. During the 1939–1940 production of the film, for complicated personal reasons, Rockne's widow demanded that the movie studio construct a fictitious portrait of her husband's academic career. Because she had veto power over the project, the studio, Warner Brothers, complied with her request.

That Rockne was an extremely bright man and that he graduated magna cum laude from Notre Dame in 1914, with honors in pharmacy, is indisputable. However, the film's portrayal of him as a baccalaureate at a crucial crossroads of his life, choosing between becoming a famous scientist or a football coach, is contrary to the historical record. Jesse Harper, when informed about the film scenes on Rockne's hiring, remarked, "Rock was hired at Notre Dame primarily as the head track coach and assistant football coach. Father John Cavanaugh [N.D. president] decided to have him teach chemistry [in the prep school] because he would not have enough to do assisting in football and coaching track. What a change in [Rockne in] twenty-seven years."

Knute Rockne loved sports. It was the passion of his life and the impetus for his attending Notre Dame—some of his high school track teammates convinced him to join them on the N.D. track-and-field squad. He had played sandlot football in Chicago but track was his first love.

The initial impression that Rockne, from the rough-and-tumble Logan Square area of Chicago, made on his freshman roommate at N.D., Charles "Gus" Dorais, was as a "not very genteel character . . . a very rugged character." Rockne had saved some money from working three years in a post office but he needed more to stay in college. According to Dorais, he initially earned it by such ventures as boxing at "smokers in South Bend and . . . Kalamazoo" under the nom de guerre of Frankie Brown.

Once Rockne discovered his talent for football, he picked up extra money by playing in semipro and professional games on Sundays. The IAA (forerunner of the NCAA) frowned on this practice, but many collegians engaged in it, usually under false names; one of Rockne's semipro opponents later recalled one Sunday during pregame warm-ups: "I couldn't mistake that kisser of his when I saw it. I yelled 'Rock!' and he turned around and came back to me and said, 'How are you? Look, between you and me, my name is Jones, okay?' And that was it."

During this era in the Midwest, with pro football increasingly popular, collegiate players hopscotched about, earning extra money by playing for various town teams. A generation later, an Ohio man reminisced to Father John W. Cavanaugh about how, in 1912, he had met Rockne on a train and the N.D. junior had "confided that he was on his way to Canton [Ohio] to play in a professional game," one of the contests "where he encountered Jim Thorpe" on the opposing crew.

During his undergraduate days at Notre Dame, Rockne also played and coached semipro football in South Bend. He particularly liked coaching and, according to reliable witnesses, "was sought out by the local teams to do what he could do best—coach." He supplemented his jobs at Notre Dame—as a senior, he had the "pool table concession" in his dormitory—with the $10 to $25 he took home after each game (payments varied according to game receipts).

One of his linemen on the South Bend Silver Edge team recalled that "Rockne looked for speed, quickness, and guts in his players. Most coaches in those days were impressed with size and went for big men." Rockne taught techniques that stressed agility and leverage as opposed to brute force. He was also quick to learn from his opponents' successes, and in 1914, after Yale beat N.D. with lateral passes, the *South Bend Tribune* noted: "Knute Rockne has been giving the Silver Edge squad some strenuous workouts this week, including drill in fancy plays he picked up at Yale."

Jesse Harper also recognized Rockne's potential as a coach. The University of Chicago grad had installed the offensive "shift" that he had learned from his mentor, Amos Alonzo Stagg, and in 1913, Harper noticed that "in the course of the development of the backfield shift," captain Rockne "worked out some very good ideas in regard to the ends shifting with the backfield." Harper hired him as his assistant for the 1914 season, putting together a financial package for Rockne of about $1,000 a year from football, track (as N.D. head coach), and teaching chemistry part-time.

During this period, because Notre Dame did not have graduate students but needed instructors to teach lower level classes as well as classes in the Minims and Junior departments, it hired part-timers from the local community as well as its own recent graduates. Rockne's deal was typical of the situation of many N.D. employees; teaching chemistry in the prep school did not signify his potential greatness as a scientist—it only indicated his willingness to work hard and for little pay.

Harper allowed Rockne free rein in training the players and encouraged him to run long, hard practices, repeating offensive plays and defensive formations until they were as perfect as possible. Harper was generous in praising Rockne's abilities, and after their first coaching season together, he tried to obtain a better job for his assistant. To the athletic director at Kansas, Harper wrote: "I cannot recommend this man too highly. . . . I dislike very much to have him leave, but feel that he can better himself."

President John W. Cavanaugh also wrote a letter of recommendation to Kansas for Rockne, commenting upon his "qualifications as a foot-ball expert" and his high moral character but never mentioning his potential as a great chemist.

Harper continued to try to obtain a head coaching position for his protégé in 1915. To his friends at Wabash, he wrote, "I think he has the making of the best coach of any young fellow I have ever known." And to Iowa State: "Mr. Rockne has a couple of other propositions but prefers your position."

Whether Harper was accurate about the "other propositions" or just trying to hype his candidate is unclear. However, he kept his assistant at Notre Dame, obtaining a raise for him to $1,500. Rockne also continued to earn money on the side by coaching teams in South Bend and playing semipro football in Ohio, especially after the Notre Dame season ended. An old N.D. teammate, Bill Kelleher, joined him and other Notre Dame men, "Jones, Dorais, Fitzgerald, Joe Collins . . . [on the] Massilon Tigers."

Rockne enjoyed this masculine, roustabout world, particularly the games against former teammates and rivals: "['Cap'] Edwards and [Don] Hamilton were against us for Canton, [Ray] Eichenlaub was against us for Toledo." An important part of the pro football scene at the time was the wagering on games and the sporting subculture in pool halls like Hullie & Mike's in South Bend and its equivalents in cities and towns throughout the Midwest. Rockne participated in this subculture—he frequently ate lunch at Hullie & Mike's—and probably bet on his own and other pro games. According to Chet Grant, a player on the 1916 team and a future N.D. assistant coach and football historian, Rockne also bet on at least one college game:

> On this occasion [the visit to Nebraska, in 1916, with Harper away], Rock assumed full charge [of the team]. . . . Rock is supposed to have wagered that we would score more points in any one period than Nebraska would score in the entire game. He ran the game, certainly, upon that principle.
>
> When we entered the fourth period, the score was 18–0 in our favor, but his bet was still a heavy risk because we had distributed our scoring among three periods, six points to the period. One Nebraska touchdown in the final period followed by a kicked goal would have cost him his money. . . . To protect his bet, Rock held out from the final quarter his less experienced quarterbacks in the fear that they might, in their exuberance to make a showing . . . fumble.

Instead of traveling with the team to Lincoln, Nebraska, Jesse Harper had gone to the Western Conference's annual meeting in Chicago in the hope of improving relations with those schools and possibly scheduling a game against a conference opponent (he managed to land Wisconsin for the following year).

With Rockne in charge, the team won easily, but according to Grant's expert testimony, the assistant coach wanted something more for his time and money—a winning wager. Grant concluded: "The foregoing is meant to illustrate *the ruthless side* of Rockne when under pressure," and it was precisely that side of her husband's personality, as well as the sporting culture in which it thrived, that Bonnie Rockne detested and later wanted expunged from the record.

However, Knute Rockne's "ruthless side" allowed him to prosper in a very corrupt and cutthroat world—college coaching. He did not invent the world into which he ventured, first as a player and then as an assistant coach, but because he was extremely intelligent, cunning, and competitive, he was able to become, within a decade, the most important football coach in America. He learned to swim with sharks, including Pop Warner, and not bleed.

A key ingredient in Rockne's success was his willingness to push the rules to the limit. As a collegian, he had played semipro football on the side, and as a semipro coach in South Bend, he had slipped in some N.D. "ringers" for his squads. This system was in place when he began playing and coaching and he liked to explore its boundaries.

In the same way, he questioned the football tactics of the era and probed them for weaknesses. As an assistant coach, he scorned "behemoth" players and stressed agility. As a young head coach, his version of the quick "shift" brought great success to his early 1920s teams; when rival coaches ganged up to change the playing rules to cripple his offense, "every [anti-Rockne] rule that was made," according to Jesse Harper's later testimony, "Rockne turned to his advantage and improved the effectiveness of the shift."

The same qualities of mind that enabled him, in 1916, to coach N.D. to a far larger score over Nebraska than Harper ever achieved against the Cornhuskers also allowed Rockne to make and win his bet on the game. To pretend that his "ruthless side" did not exist, as his widow and various hagiographers attempted, is to misunderstand his success and the era in which he achieved it.

"Rockne had served as Assistant Football Coach to Harper and as Track Coach for four years simultaneously when he was appointed to succeed

Harper in 1918. Notre Dame had already won a place of distinction among the colleges and [as N.D. president] I was then in a position to know that many well known coaches offered to take up the work [as head football coach and A.D.] of Harper."

—Father John W. Cavanaugh, 1931

From the beginning of his work with Harper, Rockne's importance to the N.D. football program was recognized by the school's administrators and students, the *Scholastic* often coupling his name with Harper's as co-coaches. After the Nebraska game in 1915, the paper wrote, "Again we congratulate Coaches Harper and Rockne upon the splendid showing of our team," and the yearbook also gave them equal billing. Harper was not jealous of the attention Rockne received and he continued to work harmoniously with him through the next few years. Moreover, after 1915, because Notre Dame excluded first-year players from the varsity and set up a freshman team, Harper needed his assistant to supervise that program in addition to his other duties.

By 1917, Rockne was married, had young children, and wanted to improve himself financially and professionally. He sought outside offers but Notre Dame worked hard to keep him. In February, the *South Bend News-Times* headlined "ROCKNE TO STAY AT NOTRE DAME" and reported that a new agreement "dispels the fears of students who have known of the efforts of several other schools to obtain the services of the Hoosier coach." Nevertheless, the outside offers continued—Rockne doing nothing to discourage them—and after the 1917 season, he verbally accepted the head coaching job at Michigan State. His departure from Notre Dame soon became moot because, in early 1918, Harper quit as coach and athletic director to return to his family's ranch in Kansas and Rockne was promoted to the top position. As Father John W. Cavanaugh later stated, many other coaches applied for the positions but the school recognized Rockne's special talents and chose him.

"I'm going to tell you why I left Notre Dame [in 1918]. It wasn't because of the school or anything else; I had a marvelous relationship, but I could see the handwriting on the wall. I could see the pressure by the alumni to do nothing but win, win, win. . . . You do not have any easy games [there]."

—Jesse Harper's standard explanation for leaving N.D. in 1918, quoted here by his son

For a coach and athletic director who scheduled tiny Alma College four years in a row, beating them by a total of 196–0, and feasted on other small schools, the line about "no easy games" rings rather false. Moreover, because Notre Dame did not have a functioning alumni association during this period, his contention about pressure from them is also thin. In reality, Jesse Harper left Notre Dame in 1918 because the opportunity to return to the family ranch in Kansas (a relative who ran the ranch had died unexpectedly) seemed far more attractive to him than remaining at N.D. and within intercollegiate athletics.

Harper's decision to resign was based, in part, on his feelings of uncertainty about the future of college sports. With America's participation in World War I there was already talk of canceling the 1918 football season, and many universities, including Notre Dame, were experiencing difficulty funding their academic programs, never mind their college sports sideline. Harper's family owned the thirty-thousand-acre Ranch of the Alamos in Kansas, with thirteen hundred head of cattle and a number of producing oil wells. Beef prices were increasing and the sky was the only limit on oil. Thus, Jesse Harper decided to leave intercollegiate athletics in the hope of making a lot more money in ranching than he could imagine earning as a coach and A.D. at Notre Dame or elsewhere.

In addition, Harper was frustrated because he had not fulfilled his original mandate from the N.D. administration—he had not appreciably improved relations with the Western Conference. The group was now the Big Ten—Michigan had reentered in 1917—and Fielding Yost had joined the implacable opposition to the Catholic school. At the end of that year, Harper had written to individual faculty representatives about Notre Dame's prospects for admission and had received sharp rebuffs. The Catholic school was as far from entering the Western Conference as when Harper had promised to knock on the door in 1913.

Thus, in the spring of 1918, going to the Ranch of the Alamos made perfect sense to Jesse Harper. Unfortunately for him, he guessed wrong: he failed to foresee the financial problems in beef and oil in the 1920s and, more important, the golden postwar future of college sports and Notre Dame's preeminent role in it. His young, ultra-ambitious assistant had a better sense of that future, and when it arrived, Rockne was able to seize fame and fortune for himself and for Notre Dame. (By the mid-1920s, in his letters to Rockne, Harper admitted his mistake—his ranch was losing money and he wanted to get back into college sports but, even with his protégé's help, he could not obtain a coaching job.)

––––––

The transition at Notre Dame from Harper to Rockne was noted enthusiastically by the *Scholastic:* the move gave "assurance that the high standard of Notre Dame athletics will not be lowered by the change of directors. Rockne, as no other man, seems ideally fitted for the directorship of athletics at his Alma Mater"; and the student paper correctly predicted: "Rockne will be quite as successful at the head of the athletic department as he has been as an assistant. He has the will to succeed, and his energy and enthusiasm are common knowledge." The yearbook, *The Dome*, was even more clairvoyant; it concluded its paean to Rockne with, "His popularity is in its infancy."

II

Shaking Down
the Thunder
1918–1931

10

Catholic versus American Higher Education in the 1920s

"The accrediting movement [in higher education] reflected trends in American academic culture toward a more rational, disciplined, and professional approach to education, one in harmony with spreading middle class values of merit and competence."

—Father William P. Leahy, S.J.,
historian of Catholic higher education

After World War I, with expanding prosperity and a more complex economy, higher education became more central to American life. In 1920, colleges and universities enrolled about 600,000 students, the majority of whom attended public universities because of their low fees and professional and business training.

Catholic schools, especially in the Midwest, were caught between their traditional role as custodians of the faith and the demand of the rising Catholic middle class for preparation of their children for better-paying jobs. Most parochial colleges were unable to accommodate these conflicting pressures, and increasing numbers of Catholics began attending state universities.

Complicating the problems of the Catholic schools was the growing power of the accrediting agencies. As higher education became more research oriented and run by "Academic Men," the certification of curricula and degrees became more important. Accreditation groups investigated schools and, using strict criteria, certified a college or university as providing a meaningful education and degree. The North Central Association in the Midwest, because of its backing by the Western Conference universities, became the most powerful accreditation agency in the country.

In 1920, the main criteria for this association, based upon the enrollment of the school, were a minimum number of faculty members with Ph.D.s, a minimum number of books and periodicals in the library, regular admission procedures, standard curricula, and a healthy endowment. Most Catholic schools could not meet the minimums and, as significantly, did not care to—they considered the accreditation criteria to be based on values alien to their religious purposes and they resented any secular agency telling them how to run their parochial institutions.

As it had been so often in its previous seventy-five years, Notre Dame was out of step with its coreligionists, and at this crucial juncture in its history—the end of World War I and Father John W. Cavanaugh's long presidency—it turned to a man who could not only satisfy the tough North Central Association but also move the school toward the mainstream of American higher education.

In 1919, Father James A. Burns became the first president of Notre Dame with a Ph.D. (from Catholic University in Washington, D.C.) and with knowledge of major secular universities (he had also attended Cornell and Harvard). Unlike most administrators of Catholic colleges in this period, as well as many past presidents of his own institution, Burns did not look inward. He had a clear vision of the role of Catholic schools within American education—he had written his Ph.D. dissertation and a number of books on the subject—and he stated: "One of my great ambitions is to make Notre Dame the 'Yale of the West.' "

In 1920, Burns's primary task was to satisfy the North Central Association's demand that Notre Dame meet basic standards, including "a productive endowment of not less than $200,000." In fact, the school had almost no endowment, and Burns set out to build one quickly. This decision marked a major break with Notre Dame's history of independence and self-reliance but the new president felt that he had to accommodate the accrediting agency. (Many Catholic schools chose to ignore the accreditation process and later paid dearly, including bankruptcy for some, for their detachment.)

To raise money, Burns turned to the national foundations and he found them sympathetic—but at a price. The General Education Board of the Rockefeller Foundation was willing to help Notre Dame but insisted that the school phase out its elementary and prep school divisions, that it set up a board of lay trustees to administer its endowment, and that it not use any of the endowment income "for specifically theological instruction." When Burns agreed, the Rockefeller Foundation pledged $250,000, contingent upon N.D.'s raising $750,000 on its own within two years. Significantly, Notre Dame received the largest grant this foundation gave to higher education at this time and was the only Catholic school on the recipient list.

Once Burns set in motion the fund-raising machine, there was no turning back to the old, prewar Notre Dame. He next called upon the Carnegie Foundation. They were willing to give $75,000 but insisted that the bulk of the money go toward improving faculty salaries. The Carnegie Foundation, like the Rockefeller, also sent investigators to examine the school and made other demands based on their findings.

The Notre Dame president then formed the promised board of lay trustees and asked them for help in fund-raising; they were willing to donate personally and to raise money but they wanted some input into the running of the university (this was truer of the alumni members than nonalums).

Beyond the board of lay trustees, Burns and Vice President Matthew Walsh organized the school's alumni into a network of clubs and, in 1922, set up a functioning alumni association and magazine. Inevitably, the appeal for alumni contributions often connected to Notre Dame's culture of athleticism: Father John McGuin, Burns's main assistant in the fund-raising drive, liked to compare the campaign to football, terming it "one of the biggest games in N.D.'s career . . . and to win that game will require all the fighting spirit characteristic of Notre Dame football." Coach Rockne also participated in the campaign and always used sports metaphors in his speeches; in addition, the football team frequently appeared at fund-raising rallies.

As a result of these and other efforts in the early 1920s, Notre Dame alumni and friends gave over $310,000 to the endowment fund and the school raised another $250,000 from the citizens of South Bend (to please a prominent group of them in 1920, Burns readmitted George Gipp to the school). The Knights of Columbus of the state of Indiana pledged $50,000, the Notre Dame students $27,000, and miscellaneous contributors $77,000, putting the total over $750,000 and securing the $250,000 from the Rockefeller Foundation.

In his brief term as president (1919–1922), Father James Burns took the school from a debt of $73,000 and no appreciable endowment to the absence of debt and a million-dollar endowment. He then became president emeritus to continue his fund-raising work and provincial superior of the C.S.C. to supervise the order's American activities.

> "You can look around here now [N.D. in the 1990s] and see what Father Walsh did in the 1920s. He built the 'collegiate gothic' lower quadrangle, east-west quadrangle, the law school, the dining hall, alumni hall. He transformed this campus from its muddy boarding-school look to a beautiful college. He did all that and the football money certainly helped."
>
> —Current Notre Dame Associate Vice President
> Richard W. Conklin

President Burns put Notre Dame on a sound financial basis and his successor, Father Matthew Walsh, decided to spend the school's excess revenue on a building campaign. Walsh presided over the construction of seven major new structures. Thus, Notre Dame in the 1920s, unlike many Catholic schools, was a stable, expanding institution—but it was still far from being a mainstream university.

In 1926, President Walsh was informed that although the school collected a $10 annual "library and entertainment fee" from every student, it was spending only "$2.56 per student" for books, periodicals, and binding, well below the $5 minimum expenditure recommended by the accrediting agencies. Walsh wanted to rectify this situation—he knew that his school could not claim academic seriousness or begin to grant graduate degrees without a decent library—but, with his building campaign under way, he had no way of obtaining the money to reach the recommended library expenditure.

An equally strong criticism of Notre Dame came from alumnus and faculty member George Shuster. In a famous 1925 article in the Catholic magazine *America,* he bemoaned the failure of Catholic colleges and universities, including his own, to produce "a single great literary man or writer . . . a scientist who has made an original contribution . . . an [important] historian [or] economist." Shuster concluded: "If we are honest, we must admit that during [the last] seventy-five years . . . we have had no influence on the general culture of America."

Because he was a philosopher and a lover of high art, Shuster did not consider sports a significant part of "the general culture of America." If he had, he could not have ignored Knute Rockne and his football teams or the impact the Notre Dame coach and players were having on the country. For, in the 1920s, Notre Dame's contribution to America did not come in the arts or sciences or from its commerce or law colleges but from its "culture of athleticism."

11

The Growth of the Athletic Culture

"Out in the midwest Knute Rockne was advising professors who found students apathetic to their lectures to 'make your classes as interesting as football.'"

—Quoted by James Wechsler,
social critic and historian

Notre Dame survived World War I and the loss of hundreds of students and potential students to the military by obtaining a Student Army Training Corps (S.A.T.C.) unit from the government for its campus. Instead of tuition revenue from undergraduates, the 700 or so student-soldiers brought in money to keep the school functioning. Many regular N.D. students enrolled in the S.A.T.C. unit—they jokingly called it "Safe At The College"—and after demobilization, most of the undergraduates in the S.A.T.C. and some of the other student-soldiers remained on campus. This swelled the school's enrollment to over 1,000 for the first time in its history.

The enrollment momentum continued through the 1920s and peaked at 3,227 undergraduates in 1930. During the decade, the total number of students in American higher education increased significantly, but at Notre Dame it tripled—the jump at N.D. was even more dramatic when compared to the 575 undergraduates enrolled at the outbreak of World War I. The Catholic school attracted students for a number of reasons:

many parochial high school teachers throughout the country, because they belonged to the C.S.C. order or attended on-campus summer sessions at Notre Dame, recommended the university to their pupils; a growing number of alumni sent their sons and talked up their alma mater in their home communities; and the fame of the winning football teams reinforced the affection of the clergy and alumni for N.D. and also spawned new supporters of the school, many of whom had sons and grandsons.

Students and their parents were also attracted to Notre Dame because of its low fees. Unlike the skyrocketing rates at private colleges and universities, N.D.'s charges compared favorably to the state universities and were below those of most Catholic schools. In 1920, tuition cost $120 a year, board in the commons dining room $350, and rooms from $30 per year in the open dormitories—where the freshman athletes were usually housed—to $110 in the "Gold Coast" suites in Walsh Hall. Other fees, including laundry, totaled about $40 a year. By 1931, the fees had kept pace with inflation but had not increased beyond that.

Notre Dame's 1920s growth was also helped by its open admissions policy. All that an applicant needed for entrance were fifteen high school academic units; character references, preferably from his parish priest and/or parochial school principal; and the money to pay the fees or a willingness to work them off at N.D. Non-Catholics (about 10 percent of the student body) were usually recommended by Notre Dame alumni or, if athletes, by former N.D. players or friends of Rockne. Although the accrediting agencies and foundations frowned upon this open-door policy, Notre Dame argued that its mandate from the C.S.C. prevented it from turning away any young man who wanted a college education in a Catholic environment.

As enrollment grew, Presidents Burns and Walsh tried to institute admission standards based on high school grades but they made no attempt to close the "special admit" loophole. According to a C.S.C. historian: "Pressures from alumni, the athletic department, benefactors, and [others] . . . forced the acceptance of 'special' cases," and these exceptions to the rules were so numerous that they made entrance regulations almost meaningless. Rockne was particularly adept at securing special admits for prime football prospects, often after the application date was long past and sometimes even after school had begun in September. (Similarly, coaches in the Big Ten had no difficulty obtaining admission for their recruits—some of the public universities automatically admitted all in-state high school graduates.)

In this period, Notre Dame, like most private schools, placed announcements in newspapers and magazines soliciting applications. In its standard ad, N.D. boasted that its curriculum was "of the same grade as that of the most highly endowed colleges or the best state universities." Undoubtedly, faculty at Western Conference schools dismissed this claim, but the North Central Association vouched for the improved N.D. courses, particularly in its Colleges of Commerce, Engineering, Science, Architecture, and Law.

In 1923–1924, Notre Dame also started a School of Education. It consisted of three departments—Secondary Education, Boy Guidance, and Physical Education—and the main focus of Phys Ed was sports courses as well as the training of future gym teachers and athletic coaches. The University of Wisconsin had pioneered a Phys Ed major in 1910, and between 1919 and 1923, five other Western Conference schools followed; at these institutions as well as at Notre Dame, Physical Education was split between the serious educators and the intercollegiate athletic coaches. In 1928, Rockne described the situation from the coaches' point of view:

> Most physical educators I know are insanely jealous of coaches—they are not interested in mass competitive games [but in recreation]. To them physical education has mainly to do with tibia, clavicle and the gluteus maximus. Their stock in trade is kinesiology, anthropometry, and group-consciousness. Remove their vocabulary and they have nothing left.

On the other hand, the educators accused the coaches of lacking academic training, of teaching "joke" courses in their particular sports, of allowing varsity athletes to take their classes for easy grades, and of keeping the "jocks" in school as P.E. majors. By the end of the 1920s in the Western Conference, only the University of Chicago refused to sanction a Phys Ed major—the other members sheltered a majority of their coaches and athletes beneath this academically leaky umbrella.

Observing his Big Ten rivals, Knute Rockne asked Notre Dame to appoint him "Professor of Physical Education," to put him in charge of various P.E. courses, and to allow his players to take his classes. For a number of years he had given informal noontime lectures on football to his athletes and all interested students; now he wanted N.D. to institutionalize his teaching of sports. Notre Dame agreed to some of his requests but because the Catholic institution would not change or shorten its extensive list of required, nonmajor courses, his athletes, unlike their Big Ten counterparts, could not avoid most of the difficult classes at their school.

Rockne had no training in Phys Ed and mocked those with degrees in the subject, telling a former player who had acquired several, "I don't believe your degrees in Physical Education are going to get you anywhere. There are two kinds of men in athletic work, men [like myself] who have been too busy doing things to get a degree and the man who can't do anything, hence hasn't anything but degrees to get him anywhere." Nevertheless, although he condemned "this bunk about having a lot of degrees behind your name," he insisted upon a full listing in the *Notre Dame* [Academic] *Bulletin* as a Professor of Physical Education, with his B.S. degree after his name, and he always used his academic title in the advertising for his summer coaching schools around the country.

No syllabi exist for his P.E. courses at Notre Dame, but the head of the school's Department of Physical Education in the 1920s, Father Vincent Mooney, complained to the president of the university in 1929 about the football coach's work in "Required Physical Education for All Freshmen": "Under Mr. Rockne and [his assistant] Mr. DuBois this required program was a farce. Two Colleges in the University voted to abandon the idea [of requiring their majors to take it]. We [Mooney and assistants] took it over and today under Mr. Masterson's supervision, the program is well balanced and the entire project is meeting with complete satisfaction despite limited facilities."

Like most faculty members and administrators at Notre Dame, Father Mooney was fond of Rockne personally—he had prepared him for his conversion to Catholicism—and he admired his football coaching and enthusiastically supported the team. But Mooney was of the new breed of N.D. faculty who also wanted to push the school into the academic mainstream (in this same letter, he discussed his ambitions for a Ph.D. degree and his desire to "make a real contribution to the field of Physical Education some day"). Mooney wanted Rockne to remain a football coach and not poach on his academic territory; throughout the Midwest, other P.E. specialists voiced similar grievances about predatory intercollegiate athletic coaches at their schools.

Finally, Father Mooney's complaint about Rockne characterized many of the disputes between the N.D. faculty and the famous football coach throughout the 1920s. On one side were men determined to improve Notre Dame academically, on the other was a football coach attempting to manipulate the educational system for his own ends.

"The interhall system cropped up naturally at Notre Dame because students, living away from the large amusement centers and with little to occupy their minds outside of scholastic and religious exercises, welcomed a chance to participate in athletics and develop themselves physically. A group spirit was formed by the various rivalries of the halls . . . almost everyone in school participated in one [sports] activity or another."

—Eugene "Scrapiron" Young,
a Notre Dame student in the mid-1920s

American Catholic schools in this period, for financial reasons and also because many were commuter colleges, tended to discourage intramural athletics. Notre Dame was an exception—it had steadily built up its sports facilities and, in the 1920s, had at least 80 percent of its students in interhall competition (and another 10 percent on varsity teams). At other schools, including Catholic ones, usually about fifty to seventy students tried out for varsity football; when Rockne held spring practice, a minimum of three hundred hopefuls appeared. Moreover, many of Rockne's rejects could have started at other schools, and when the N.D. reserve teams, freshman squad, and residence hall units played small-college varsities, they usually beat them.

The interhall football schedule for 1920–1921 listed six teams of about forty players per squad and seven weekends of competition leading to play-offs and a championship game. By the mid 1920s, as on-campus enrollment grew, Scrapiron Young bragged: "Twelve and fourteen team leagues were formed during the appropriate season for every sport." In addition, the best interhall teams played away games against regional colleges and amateur clubs. By this era, the student-captain-as-coach tradition had ended and the teams were run by more knowledgeable mentors —usually young priests living in the halls, some of whom, like Hugh "Pepper" O'Donnell, had won varsity monograms (letters).

After the football season, the hall athletes played hockey, basketball, and other winter sports; in the spring, outdoor track and baseball occupied their attention. Without exaggerating, Rockne could boast to a college president in 1928: "We have the best intramural program of any school in America with the exception of West Point and Annapolis" (where intramurals were part of the officer training regimen).

The N.D. intramural athletes were not jealous of the varsity players; they respected them and regarded them as role models. One student, arriving on campus in 1923, described how "the varsity athletes set the customs and unwritten rules," especially on dress and conduct.

Most of Rockne's early recruits came from working-class backgrounds and felt comfortable within Notre Dame's traditional "masculine democracy," especially its deemphasis on family origins, fancy clothes, and luxurious living accommodations. In turn, the football players appreciated the regular students' athleticism: Harry Stuhldreher, quarterback of the Four Horsemen, exclaimed, "Thank God, we have the type of boy at Notre Dame who prefers physical activity to drugstore athletics" (that is, sipping sodas with coeds).

The players acquired their ideas and lines from Rockne, and according to one of his first press assistants, Francis Wallace, the coach "fought any intrusion against masculine habits and outlook" at Notre Dame. Wallace related how, in 1922, the school's debating coach suggested that his team be awarded varsity letters; when Rockne learned of this, "he came into his office, pink-faced with outrage, [and] decided the way to scotch it was by ridicule." The football coach and press aide "kicked out a story" in which they "dressed the debaters in ruffles and laces, and had them go at each other in fierce formations." They published the piece in the *Scholastic* and the N.D. students laughed the debating coach's idea into oblivion.

The Notre Dame of the 1920s was a completely formed and self-contained world with an athletic culture that not only included the students but also lay faculty members, administrators, and priests. A majority of these men were N.D. graduates and shared the current students' enthusiasm for participatory and spectator sports. Thus Notre Dame had a homogeneity unknown at the large institutions of the Western Conference or even at the private schools of the East.

"Once while I was visiting a new university I was importuned by students (as an ancient who should know) to 'suggest some traditions to start.' . . .

Traditions are never started. They exist and grow strong long before anyone discovers them. . . . [For example] the old songs sung by generations of happy students without any thought of 'starting a tradition.'"

—President John W. Cavanaugh of Notre Dame

By the 1920s, Notre Dame's athletic culture had produced a number of authentic traditions, including the "Victory March" and the football team's nickname, "Fighting Irish." Cavanaugh was correct in stating that no one can consciously begin a tradition, but Notre Dame was fortunate in having talented individuals who helped its traditions along. In this era, Francis Wallace popularized the Fighting Irish nickname, and band director Joseph Casasanta gave the "Victory March" its famous tempo and also composed songs and cheers that the students adopted. In addition, Casasanta collaborated with an N.D. professor of architecture on two cheers—"Hike, Notre Dame" and "Down the Line"—that have endured at the school.

In the 1920s, the lay faculty and the priests became increasingly enthusiastic about football and attended most home games as well as pep rallies. Rockne proudly stated that "the school is alive with school spirit. Where you have an indifferent faculty and a listless student body, you'll have failure on the athletic field." As examples, he liked to point to the losing football records at Northwestern and Chicago, institutions where faculty members were "more interested in academics than athletics" and the students in "tea dances" and fraternity parties. He loved his school's total enthusiasm for sports and considered it an important ingredient in producing winning teams.

At N.D., school spirit was enhanced by the election of cheerleaders and the "cheer king," and once in office, they directed their fellows and other N.D. supporters in a variety of activities, particularly halftime shows and pregame "pep meetings." In addition, for away games in the Midwest, the Notre Dame students often rented railroad cars and traveled to the contest en masse. After a game against Indiana University at Indianapolis in 1919, the *Scholastic* bragged: "We out-yelled the Indiana crowd [and] . . . Our cheerleaders outclassed theirs and our rooters, though outnumbered two to one, showed that they had a vocal power second to none in the state."

For road games beyond the Midwest, the students installed a special telegraph wire in the campus gym and received play-by-play reports. The *Scholastic* noted that for the wire reports on the 1919 Nebraska game, the "occasion will be enlivened by a band, songs, stunts, and cheers." Almost every Notre Dame undergraduate came to the gym for the telegraphed away games, and the crowd cheered each successful N.D. play as if they were watching at Cartier Field.

In the 1920s, the wire system was improved by the Gridgraphie, an electronic scoreboard that reported each play and, in its most refined form, used a light for each player and illustrated individual plays. By the mid-1920s, the best Gridgraphie in northern Indiana was owned by Hullie & Mike's cigar store, restaurant, pool hall, and poker parlor in South Bend. For Notre Dame away games, they placed their Gridgraphie over the entrance, and the students as well as other N.D. fans filled the street outside, following the action and cheering for their heroes.

As Rockne's teams won increasing numbers of games and national championships, the *Scholastic* filled with more and more pages of praise for the squad and its players. Poems and articles with titles like "How They Did It," "To the Men of the Team," and "He's a Man" proliferated. The 1921 *Dome* yearbook was dedicated to Rockne—the first time the dedicatee was not a C.S.C. priest—and throughout the 1920s, the yearbook expanded its coverage of athletics, and the football team in particular, as well as the events surrounding the games.

The *Dome* photos for the Rockne years provide a clear record of how Notre Dame football grew from an informal Saturday afternoon outing at rickety Cartier Field, with about 4,000 in attendance, to a national phenomenon, with huge crowds in New York and Los Angeles and, in the most stunning pictures of all, the 120,000-plus fans at the games in Soldier Field in Chicago in the late 1920s.

The books on Notre Dame football attribute this amazing growth almost solely to the genius of Knute Rockne. Without question, the N.D. coach built and directed the winning teams, but as the history of the school reveals, he could not have succeeded without the growth of Notre Dame's unique athletic culture.

12

The Origin of the "Fighting Irish" Nickname

" 'O'Reilly, why doesn't Notre Dame have a mascot?'
'Just never got around to it . . .'
'Well—Yale has a bulldog, Princeton a tiger, we [USC] have a horse
—why don't you try a pig? I should think Paddy's Pig would be a good
symbol for the Irish. Then there's the old rhyme:
They kept the pig in the parlor,
And that was Irish too.' "

—Francis Wallace,
O'Reilly of Notre Dame, 1931

This exchange in a novel about college sports in the 1920s catches the
prejudices that many Americans of the time held toward citizens of Irish-
Catholic descent. However, unlike other immigrant groups who tried to
submerge their ethnicity into the American melting pot and considered
such terms as "Polack" and "Bohunk" insults, Irish Catholics gloried in
many of their nicknames, particularly the one given to the Notre Dame
football team: the "Fighting Irish."

Like other traditions at the school, the origins of the Notre Dame
nickname are both obvious and obscure. As previously noted, the many
Irish boxers and champions in the popular nineteenth-century sport of
prizefighting, coupled with N.D.'s preponderance of students, faculty,
and administrators of Irish-Catholic descent, is the most probable source.
But the first use of the term is not definite.

One history of Notre Dame football quotes an old alumnus remembering the Northwestern students yelling "Kill those Fighting Irish" during the 1889 game. Other histories claim that halfback Pete Vaughan, during halftime of the 1909 struggle with Michigan, looked around at his mainly Irish-American teammates and spit out, "What's the matter with you guys. You're all Irish and you're not fighting!" Both tales, however, depend on the memory of the teller and, if accepted, reflect glory on that person.

More authentic than these questionable anecdotes are the early uses of the term in the press: the 1904 *Scholastic* mentions that in the loss at Wisconsin, "the plucky fight of our boys won the applause of the crowd, who rooted for the 'game Irishmen' all during [the contest]"; in its coverage of the 1909 victory over Michigan, the *Detroit Free Press* reported: "Eleven fighting Irishmen wrecked the Yost machine this afternoon. These sons of Erin individually and collectively representing the University of Notre Dame . . ."; and by 1914, *The Dome* lauded the "traditional Irish fight of the Notre Dame" players and students.

During the first decades of N.D. football history, however, the midwestern press usually called the team the "Catholics," or, if strongly anti-Notre Dame, "Papists," "Horrible Hibernians," "Dumb Micks," and "Dirty Irish"—fans of opposing squads often yelled the last two insults. N.D. student publications carefully avoided these terms and usually referred to their players as the "Gold and Blue," the "Notre Damers," "Warriors," and occasionally, the "Irish."

From 1913 on, because of the team's annual trips east and its other travels, Chicago journalists began tagging them the "Ramblers" and the "Nomads." The New York newspapers, however, preferred "Hoosiers," and in the early 1920s, the *New York Daily News* tried "Hoosier Harps" (considering its Irish working-class readership, no insult was intended).

Like everyone living in Indiana, Rockne was frequently asked about the origin of the word *Hoosier.* He usually replied with an anecdote that also illustrated the toughness of Notre Dame football: "After every game the [N.D.] coach goes over the field, picks up what he finds, and asks his team, '*Whose ear* is this?' Hence Hoosier."

For many years, Notre Dame administrators disapproved of the "Catholic" and "Irish" nicknames. President Burns wrote that the terms are "discountenanced by the authorities of the University" but because often their "usage is in a playful spirit, no offense being intended, this makes it the harder to deal with the matter effectively." Even on his own campus, students increasingly used the "Fighting Irish" nickname; in the 1919 *Scholastic*, an alum's letter complaining that the "sobriquet" was foolish because so many of Notre Dame's players were not of Irish descent sparked an intense defense of the term. Student letter writers attacked the grad on two main points: over half of the varsity letter winners and team captains during "the last thirty years [were] men whose names strongly indicate Gaelic stock"; and "you don't have to be from Ireland to be Irish." The latter argument carried the day, and the disgruntled alum was advised to "cultivate some of that 'fighting Irish spirit' and . . . [stop] grumbling because Notre Dame is not called the Polish Falcon or the Spanish Omelette."

During the same month as this controversy, the future president of the Irish Republic, Eamon De Valera, visited the school and was hailed by the administrators and students. President Burns announced that Notre Dame was proud to be "the first university in the country to establish a branch of the Friends of Irish Freedom." De Valera's visit applied momentum to the "Fighting Irish" nickname, and the *Scholastic* began employing it in game accounts; after the victory over Army, the student reporter wrote that the "game unmistakably rebranded the Notre Dame warriors as 'The Fighting Irish.' "

In 1920, Rockne hired the first of his student press agents, Arch Ward (later the longtime sports editor of the *Chicago Tribune*), and Ward, taking his cue from his fellow students, used "Fighting Irish" in his dispatches to the *South Bend Tribune* and other newspapers. However, it was Ward's successor in the student press job, Francis Wallace, who played the key role in popularizing the nickname.

During his years with Rockne, Wallace continued using "Fighting Irish" or variations on it. After graduating in 1923, he became a sportswriter in New York and noticed that some papers in that city had started calling the team "Rockne's Ramblers," "Rockne's Rovers," the "Rambling Irish," and the "Wandering Irish." For Wallace and the N.D. authorities, these terms were pejorative, implying that the Catholic school was a "football factory" and that its players were always on the road, never in class. The Notre Dame administrators detested these nicknames and wanted to discourage them.

Wallace tried to create an acceptable alternative—nonethnic and nonnomadic—and came up with the "Blue Comets," based on the team's blue uniforms and quick offense. He soon saw that this name, "like most synthetic [traditions], didn't catch on," and he decided in 1925, while working on the *New York Post,* to refer to the team as the "Fighting Irish."

Other New York reporters picked up on this but tended to use only "Irish"; for example, in the Army victory over N.D. in 1926, the Kaydet runners came "crashing into the 'Irish' vanguard or slanting off the 'Irish' tackles" (*New York World*).

In 1927, Wallace moved to the mass circulation *New York Daily News* and disseminated "Fighting Irish" to a huge audience. The wire services then began employing the term and, that same year, when the editor of the *World* wrote to the Golden Dome about the official Notre Dame position on the nickname, President Walsh decided to put the school's imprimatur on "Fighting Irish."

Walsh acted mainly to short-circuit the increasing popularity of "Ramblers," "Nomads," and their variants (in fact, it took many years for these nicknames, as well as "Catholics" and "Hoosiers," to disappear). His 1927 reply to Herbert Bayard Swope, the influential editor of the *New York World*, permanently set Notre Dame's policy:

> The University authorities are in no way averse to the name "Fighting Irish" as applied to our athletic teams. . . . It seems to embody the kind of spirit that we like to see carried into effect by the various organizations that represent us on the athletic field. I sincerely hope that we may always be worthy of the ideals embodied in the term "Fighting Irish."

N.D. players of non-Irish descent also approved of the nickname. For Harry Stuhldreher, of German ancestry, it represented the team's "fighting, competitive spirit," and he liked to quote Rockne's retort to reporters who listed all the non-Irish players on the roster—"They're all Irish to me. They have the Irish spirit and that's all that counts." (Of Rockne's approximately 340 varsity monogram winners, almost half had Irish family names.)

In the early 1920s, the students' fondness for the nickname also led to Notre Dame's first mascot—an Irish terrier called Tipperary Terence. In 1923, the Toledo alumni club gave the dog to N.D. and encouraged the cheerleaders to parade him at home games. Other Irish terriers succeeded Terence, and the one in 1933, named Clashmore Mike, learned various performing tricks. This dog and his successors of the same name patrolled the N.D. sideline for many years, eventually being retired as the school's mascot in 1966. A small yelping dog—no matter what its connection to Ireland—seemed inappropriate as the Notre Dame mascot, and again, a too conscious attempt at establishing a tradition failed.

In the modern era, with Notre Dame fully in the mainstream of American higher education and its faculty, students, and alumni totally integrated into American life, the Catholic school's affection for its Irish heritage has increased, possibly in reaction to the loss of its ethnic connections in other areas. Instead of the Irish terrier, the school mascot is the "Leprechaun."

The N.D. version of the Irish folklore character is a five-foot-tall, redheaded-and-bearded student dressed in a cutaway green suit and Irish country hat (he is chosen annually at student tryouts). The Leprechaun, brandishing a shillelagh, aggressively leads cheers, interacts with the N.D. fans, and is supposed to bring magical powers and good luck to the teams. Although there is an artificial quality to his appearance and frenzy, most N.D. rooters seem to accept him, and he will probably remain as the school's mascot for the foreseeable future.

A second connection to Notre Dame's heritage is the dropping of the final letter of the gerund in the team's nickname. To render its pronunciation closer to nineteenth century Irish-American speech, "Fightin" is now the official spelling.

An alternative nickname, one popular during the Leahy and Parseghian eras, was the "University of Notre Game." Like the many terms for N.D. teams during Rockne's time, it has disappeared, but a few old nicknames continue or have come back with a different meaning or form. At the turn of the century, the *Scholastic* sometimes called the football team the "Domers." This dropped out of use for many years but then returned as an insiders' nickname—contemporary N.D. students and alumni call themselves "Domers." Another old Notre Dame term, the "Gold and Blue," has been reversed to the current "Blue and Gold." Only the popular abbreviation "N.D." continues intact from its beginning in the nineteenth century, a tradition so old, simple, and effective that its future is secure.

In the evolution of the University of Notre Dame from a "poor boys' school" to its present "upscale and affluent" state, Fighting Irish football played a crucial part. The first seventy-five years of the school's existence —1842 to 1917—laid the foundation for the institution, but when Knute Rockne took over the athletic department in 1918, Notre Dame was still poor and, because of World War I, the young coach had to build his football program from the ground up.

13

Rockne at Ground Zero: 1918–1919

"Rockne, I think, would have been successful as a football coach had he never seen Notre Dame. I believe Notre Dame would have won many notable football victories without Rockne. The degree of the greatness they would have attained apart, we don't know, of course; but we do know that together they mounted to the highest place."

—Chet Grant, former Notre Dame player, coach,
  and sports historian, in a letter to Father John W. Cavanaugh, 1931

When Knute Rockne took over as athletic director and head football coach in 1918, the Notre Dame sports cupboard was not bare, but because of wartime difficulties, it was understocked. Harper had left an incomplete football schedule for 1918 as well as low guarantees for the arranged contests. In addition, because the Catholic school was in financial difficulty at the time, the administration offered the new coach only $3,500 in salary, about $1,500 less than they had paid Harper, and they did not hire an assistant for him. The Notre Dame authorities also insisted that Rockne give up playing semipro football in Ohio. (During the following years, he snuck off for an occasional Sunday game and, in one of them, again played against Jim Thorpe; Rockne was out of shape and the great runner flattened him.)

For the 1918 football season, the Notre Dame financial situation was so tight that the new head coach lacked an adequate supply of uniforms, equipment, and even tape. Though Rockne also had to act as his own trainer, he believed that his greatest problem was the scarcity of experienced players. So many members of the 1917 team had entered the army that he was left with a mixed group of freshmen—allowed to play on the varsity until the war ended—and a few athletes who remained on campus. Fortunately, the latter group included team captain Pete Bahan and star halfback George Gipp.

Notre Dame's 1918 football situation was not unique. Many athletic departments were experiencing similar financial and recruiting problems, and some, including Harvard, Yale, and Princeton, had suspended their varsity programs for the duration of the war. Although Rockne and many other football coaches bemoaned the apparent shrinkage in college sports, not all athletic administrators shared their feelings.

The *New York Times* headlined an article on the 1917–1918 NCAA convention with "WAR CONDITIONS REFORM [INTERCOLLEGIATE ATHLETIC] ACTIVITIES AND BRING ABOUT SPORT FOR SPORT'S SAKE"; NCAA delegates, mainly faculty representatives, approved of the current deemphasis and voiced "the unanimous opinion [that] after the war there will be no return to the commercialized systems," including no financial inducements for college athletes.

Rockne was more prescient than the NCAA delegates and, in 1918, managed to put together N.D. "athletic scholarships"—free tuition, room, and board—for such excellent athletic prospects as Gipp's hometown friends Heartley "Hunk" Anderson and Fred "Ojay" Larson. The recruits had to work in the dining hall but, as Anderson explained, "Those who were out for a varsity sport-in-season qualified for training table and were exempted from slinging hash until the season concluded. Since I participated in all sports [football, hockey, basketball, track, and baseball], I continued on the training table and wasn't doing much work as a busboy."

With linemen such as Anderson and Larson, and Gipp leading the offense, Rockne's 1918 team had talent but limited experience. The opening game against Case Tech of Cleveland was an easy win for Notre Dame, but the home contest against Great Lakes Naval Station of Chicago ended in a 7–7 tie. On the military team were such semipros as George Halas and Paddy Driscoll.

The government's wartime restrictions on travel brought about the cancellation of the Army game at West Point and put other holes in the N.D. schedule. Rockne filled one by arranging a game at Wabash the day before the contest; according to the *Scholastic*, the players "were up at four o'clock Saturday morning and left on the 'Vandalia' at five. They got breakfast in Logansport," arrived for the contest in Crawfordsville, Indiana, around lunchtime, and feasted on the "Little Giants," 67–7.

Then the Spanish flu epidemic broke out, canceling the match against Washington and Jefferson and moving the Nebraska trip to late November. In mid-November, the team was allowed to make the short hop to East Lansing, Michigan, to play the Michigan State Aggies. The student reporter covering the game complained that "the field was a quagmire of mud" and the play exceptionally violent; among other N.D. casualties, "Gipp was taken out in the third quarter because of a rupture of a blood vessel in his face and other injuries." Final score: Michigan State 13, Notre Dame 7.

The travel restrictions had one salutary effect on N.D.'s 1918 schedule. Purdue University, only 107 miles from South Bend, agreed to host Notre Dame. This marked a scheduling breakthrough with a Western Conference school and the resumption of play after an eleven-year hiatus against one of N.D.'s most logical opponents. Rockne was able to build upon this contest and book games with the Boilermakers during the next five years.

Against Purdue in 1918, Gipp had his best afternoon of the season, and with the 26–6 victory, Notre Dame claimed the football "supremacy of the state." Unfortunately for Rockne, although the crowd was estimated at seven thousand, he had been unable to obtain a pregame guarantee and took home a profit of only $358.

The war ended on November 11, 1918, and the Notre Dame team was permitted to travel to Nebraska for a Thanksgiving Day contest. As in previous years, this match provided N.D. with its most nourishing financial meal of the season, $4,080 in payout. The fans were not disappointed with the 0–0 tie because, according to one reporter: "Mud alone, stickier and more treacherous than in Flanders, saved Nebraska from defeat." Gipp and the other N.D. runners were unable to cut away from defenders or, at times, to keep their footing.

Thus Rockne's first season as head football coach concluded with a less than glorious 3–1–2 record, and six months later, his first year as athletic director ended with equally meager numbers—"Athletic Expenses" approaching $17,000 versus "Gate & Guarantee Receipts" of less than half that amount. Only the $9,006 received from the sale of N.D. student tickets pushed the final figures into the black—a profit of $234.

The *Scholastic* summed up Rockne's initial campaign with: "Never in the history of football at Notre Dame has a coach opened his season under such discouraging difficulties as 'Rock.' " After reviewing the year's frustrations, the student paper predicted: "Under him victories will come." Notre Dame did not have long to wait—in 1919, he produced a perfect 9–0–0 season.

Dear Rockne,
    Your letter of July 31 [1919] received. I have held that date, Oct. 11, open for Notre Dame [and] will be pleased to work as an official that day . . . either referee or umpire.
    About Sept. 1, I plan to write a general football story about all the college teams of the state . . . [and] about some of the best players who will be back at each school. If you can send me a letter giving me some of this information, I will be pleased to give your team special mention.

Very truly yours,

Heze Clark,
Indiana Daily Times

For the 1919 football season, Rockne did not inherit any games from Harper's regime but he received the legacy of Western Conference animosity as well as the difficulty of attracting major opponents to N.D.'s small Cartier Field. In addition, as the letter from sportswriter Heze Clark reveals, Rockne, like his coaching colleagues, was heir to a corrupt system. From his years with Harper, he knew that either he worked the scheduling/officiating/press system to his advantage or it would be turned against him.

Rockne's first priority was to obtain Big Ten games and he succeeded in setting up road contests against in-state rivals Purdue and Indiana University. The other conference members were not interested in playing Notre Dame, and the *Detroit Free Press* commented that the Catholic school's attempts "to enter that more or less holy of holies, the Western Conference" were always "snubbed" even though "everything the Big 10 requires within its circle is obligatory at the South Bend institution."

Rockne also attempted to woo the Big Ten by attending its annual coaches' meeting in Chicago; because some preliminary scheduling occurred here, he hoped "to sneak in on a game." However, unlike the "Academic Men" of the conference, his coaching colleagues were less concerned with Notre Dame's educational standards than its football team's abilities. Rockne saw the problem clearly—his squad "was too pow-

erful to be a set-up" but didn't have enough "prestige to make it an attraction." He later admitted, "I don't blame them for not putting me on their
schedules. If I were in their shoes, I would have done the same thing."

Rockne, like Harper before him, had to look elsewhere for games.
Army was pleased to schedule the N.D. visit to West Point, but because
of postwar inflation, its usual $1,000 guarantee would probably not cover
the 1919 travel costs. A small Iowa college named Morningside, with
ambitions to enter big-time football, invited N.D. for a Thanksgiving Day
game and offered a $2,500 guarantee. And Nebraska wanted Notre
Dame to return and promised the usual fifty-fifty split of gate receipts
from the almost certain ten thousand–plus crowd. Rockne accepted all
three away games, Army for the prestige and the others for the money.

The trip to Nebraska would be the fifth in a row for N.D. and it under-
scored Rockne's most serious scheduling problem—Notre Dame lacked
an adequate stadium and home attendance at Cartier Field was low,
generally a few thousand per game, with the majority of those seats sold
to the N.D. community at discount rates. In 1918, the school hosted only
one game on campus, and for 1919, Rockne could arrange home contests
only against small midwestern colleges. Because of these scheduling
problems as well as his desire to upgrade the entire football program, in
1919, Rockne decided to try to transform Cartier Field from a small
grounds to a stadium.

Before the football season began, he wrote a form letter to prominent
local citizens—"men who will promote any plan to boost South Bend"—
pointing out the "very effective manner" in which the Notre Dame football team "advertises the city of South Bend" and the unfortunate fact
that it could play only "the best teams in the country—away from home."
He then promised to bring major opponents to Notre Dame in future
years if the local citizens would support that year's squad by buying
season athletic tickets for $5 each.

His plan was simple. By increasing home attendance and game receipts, he hoped to prevail upon the N.D. administrators to enlarge
Cartier; if they agreed, he could offer decent guarantees to big-time
visitors and also establish home-and-home series with them. Moreover,
with a decent home field, he would no longer have to go hat-in-hand to
the Big Ten coaches; he could negotiate with them as a football equal,
and if they refused to deal, he could easily build a schedule against other
big-time opponents.

The president of the Studebaker Automobile Corporation, headquartered in South Bend, took one hundred season tickets for his company and other local boosters responded well to the campaign. Throughout the summer of 1919, Rockne continued his personal efforts, often strolling around downtown South Bend with his pockets full of tickets, distributing them to newsstands, cigar shops, and luncheon counters, as well as peddling them to individuals. He repeated his personal ticket-selling campaign during the next few years and, combined with the success of his teams, he made Notre Dame football popular in South Bend. (His willingness to mix with the "locals" also set a precedent in the city against which all subsequent N.D. football coaches have been measured.)

After setting up a nine-game campaign for 1919, Rockne went about obtaining officials for the contests at Notre Dame. Traditionally, the coach of the home team hired and paid the referee, umpire, and linesmen—this was another reason Rockne wanted more home games. The visiting coach could suggest officials and, if he had enough clout, could insist on one or two; he could also veto any member of the crew, but because newspapermen-officials gave a bad press to coaches who vetoed them, these refusals rarely occurred. In any individual game, the officials tended to favor the team of the coach who could do them the most good —that is, hire them regularly and provide good copy. In this system, the most successful coaches—those with winning teams and secure jobs— thrived. Coaches of losing squads, especially those who had to play mainly road games, saw the on-field calls relentlessly go against them and their coaching careers enter downward spirals. Knute Rockne understood this system perfectly and his comprehension added to his determination to produce winning teams.

In addition to the sportswriters, some nonjournalists (often traveling salesmen) worked as game officials. Frequently these men attached themselves to particular coaches and depended upon them for a certain number of games per season. Usually the nonjournalists were even more biased for the home team than the newspapermen, and the mark of an important visiting coach was his ability to prevent his opponent from hiring "pet" officials. As Rockne's professional stature grew, his veto powers over his opponents' choices increased, as did his own list of favorite referees, umpires, and linesmen.

Like his mentor, Jesse Harper, Rockne cultivated the most important sportswriter-officials in the Midwest. At the top of the list was Walter Eckersall of the *Chicago Tribune,* and the young Notre Dame coach corresponded with "Eck" regularly, passing on inside information as well as invitations to officiate N.D. games. In 1919, Eckersall learned that Rockne was negotiating with Andy Smith, the coach of the University of California, for a game, and the journalist wrote the N.D. coach, "Although it is rather early and you have not yet decided, I wish you would bear me in mind as an official for such a game if arranged."

The contest against Berkeley never occurred, but Rockne hired Eckersall for the 1919 home opener against Kalamazoo (N.D. won by only 14–0) and a number of other matches. In a letter after the opener, the Chicago writer advised the Notre Dame coach to "get your backs to time their shifts more. They were badly off last Saturday and were in motion nearly every time." Of course, Eckersall did not whistle an infraction on every N.D. offensive play; he preferred to tell his new "friend" about the problem after the contest.

Throughout the 1919 season, their correspondence continued, and in mid-November, Eckersall wrote: "The time is getting pretty close where I will have to select an All-Western team and I wish you would slip me your candid opinions of your best men. I don't care to overlook any of them." Rockne's reply to "Eck" is lost, but there were four N.D. players on Eckersall's *Chicago Tribune* All-Western teams.

Rockne also worked well with other reporter-referees, and his first full year of hiring officials and massaging press egos was a success. Chet Grant always maintained that the great coach "was a finder, not a founder. His forte was the genius to make the most of what he found." This insight certainly applied to Rockne's handling of the corrupt journalist-as-game-official system in place at the time; characteristically, he quickly mastered what he came upon and, in later years, manipulated it to his great advantage.

Another corrupt college football system with which he had to deal was the recruiting of athletes, and he became extremely adept at this too.

September 20, 1919

Dear Mr. Rockney [*sic*]:
    Talking with Stanley Cofall and Jack Whalen today I was advised to write you in regard to a young athlete. . . . His name is Art Rooney, A.A.U. champion lightweight boxer, who is also a splendid prospect in

football. He is a halfback. . . . The purpose of this letter is to learn if you can handle him at Notre Dame, either in the varsity or one of the prep teams. He would require his expenses.

Sincerely Yours,

Richard Guy
Sporting Editor
The Pittsburgh Leader

By September 1919, Rockne was so well stocked with football talent that he routinely turned down potential recruits like Art Rooney (the future founder of the Pittsburgh Steelers). In fact, because of the abundance of excellent players on campus, the N.D. coach ordered some first-stringers from the 1918 squad, like Ojay Larson, to sit out the season with the reserves (Rockne "red-shirted" athletes long before the practice became common), and he also did not renew a number of athletic scholarships, including "Curly" Lambeau's.

The N.D. coach obtained his 1919 varsity from three main sources: the core of Harper's 1917 team, with such stars as "Slip" Madigan back from the military (most had played on service teams); Rockne's own scouting of service teams, which turned up men like "Buck" Shaw and George Trafton; and the return of the best 1918 players, including Gipp and Hunk Anderson. In addition, normal "proselyting" produced, according to the *Scholastic*, "the largest freshman team that ever reported . . . over sixty yearlings [that] included a wealth of fine material recruited from the preparatory and high schools."

Rockne's recruiting of secondary school athletes was still fairly primitive. He depended on former N.D. players, students, and personal friends to search for football talent in their home areas and to tell him about their discoveries. Stanley Cofall, the N.D. quarterback in 1915–1916, prompted the recommendation of Art Rooney and other prospects. Alumni like John Shea (of N.D. "Victory March" fame) also scouted; in 1919, Shea turned up Arthur "Hec" Garvey in his home town of Mount Holyoke, Massachusetts, and sent him on to Notre Dame (Garvey played two years on the varsity and then left after moonlighting with the Green Bay Packers).

If the N.D. coach could not obtain athletic scholarships that included on-campus jobs for his recruits—and in 1919 he had filled all of these—he had Notre Dame alumni sponsor them. Paul Castner, an outstanding multisport athlete of the early 1920s, related how, before entering N.D.

in 1919, he visited the Chicago office of Tom Shaughnessy, an alum in that city. From Shaughnessy he received "an athletic scholarship . . . [that] covered four years of free board, room and tuition. The only expense I would have was clothes, books, and transportation back [home] to St. Paul during vacations."

The problem with such "free rides" is that the NCAA and the Western Conference now banned them and the N.D. administration frowned upon them. But, in 1919, Rockne was impatient to win and willing to cut corners to do so, especially when he learned that rival coaches, particularly in the Big Ten, were awarding athletic scholarships through many different subterfuges.

> "Claims are made . . . that [the semipro Rockford] Grands, for the greater part, were made up of University regulars [from a school, N.D.] disputing the University championship of the middle west with Illinois."
>
> —The *Rockford* (Illinois) *Register Gazette,*
> November 24, 1919

During all periods of intercollegiate sports history, when college athletes are supposed to be amateurs but, in fact, receive various kinds of payments for their athletic services, they usually see nothing wrong in accepting further payments from sources within and outside of the university. In the post–World War I era, many college athletes wanted to earn extra money, particularly for doing what the schools paid them to do —play sports.

Semipro football was increasingly popular and collegians often suited up on Sunday for town teams. Because Notre Dame had some of the best players in the Midwest, inevitably some were recruited to play semipro ball. Rockne knew about but disliked the Sunday excursions—players sometimes returned so banged up that he could not use them in N.D. games—but he could not control the off-campus activities of his 1919 team, dominated by the war vets and Gipp.

According to the most reliable history of semipro football in the Midwest, "about half of the 1919 Notre Dame team . . . played for the [Rockford, Illinois] Grands. This squad was led by George Gipp and 'Slip' Madigan." The players earned as much as "a couple of hundred" dollars per game and used the Notre Dame offensive system and signals. After the Grands beat their arch-rival, Rockford A.C.C., the local paper commented that "the smooth-working Grand backfield" (Gipp and his running mates), "no ordinary bunch of gridiron talent," provided "some

of the niftiest football that has been seen on the local field in many
a day!"

Because towns like Rockford wanted to host the best football possible, the team promoters and game officials went along with the collegians' claims that their names were Smith, Brown, and Jones. The local
newspapers participated in the charade, nodding and winking between
the lines of the game accounts. And most college coaches looked the
other way—until a player became too open about his Sunday excursions
or an embarrassing incident occurred.

In 1919, George Trafton, already twenty-three years old and a war
vet, played under his own name for various semipro teams and publicly
defied Rockne to stop him (Red Grange termed Trafton "the toughest,
meanest, most ornery critter alive"). The Notre Dame coach valued
Trafton's football talent—he later became a star with the Chicago Bears
—but Rockne had no choice but to ask him to give up semipro ball or
leave school. Trafton departed. A former N.D. player, Charlie Bachman,
wrote the coach: "I think you made a wise move in the Trafton case. It
will make the right impression where it counts [with the semipro promot-
ers], and will keep the other boys at school in line."

Of all of Rockne's players, the postwar athletes were the most difficult
for him to discipline. Many were war vets, and because of crowded housing conditions at N.D., a number lived off-campus in South Bend. As a
young ambitious coach who wanted to win immediately, he was willing to
overlook some player transgressions, especially those committed by his
star, George Gipp. But Rockne was relieved when the hard cases like
George Trafton and the free spirits like Slip Madigan left Notre Dame
voluntarily or through graduation and the other vets moved through and
out of the N.D. system.

The postwar players were an anomaly at Notre Dame and, in the eyes
of many priests in the community, provided bad examples for the regular
students. When the authoritarian Father John O'Hara became prefect of
religion in 1921, he demanded that no student, including the athletes, be
allowed to live off-campus. Rockne backed this proposal.

Yet, a decade later, the N.D. coach admitted that he'd had a "soft
spot" for the war vets, who did not lose a game in their first two seasons
under him. Characteristically, he continued to help them in any way he
could, including writing a strong letter of recommendation for a coaching
position for the still-wild George Trafton but telling him privately, "If you
ever find yourself and get settled down, you've got a lot of ability to put a
job over. But you've got to quit being a fool. You are old enough to
realize that poise and balance are necessary."

"With such a number of 'old heads' to pick from, the [football] coaches
can devote less attention to the elementary training and can give the
huskies such a session of hard and fast preliminary work as no Notre
Dame squad has yet received."

—"Football Prospects" for 1919, *The Scholastic*

The opening of football practice for the 1919 season was far different
from the first sessions of the previous year. Not only did Rockne have an
abundance of excellent players but the N.D. administrators allowed him
to hire Gus Dorais, his old friend and teammate, as a full-time assistant.

The Notre Dame community was pleased with the nine-game schedule and the fact that college football had returned from its wartime dol-
drums. Enthusiasm about their team's prospects was so high that,
according to the student paper, "four or five hundred [people] are out
every day to witness the workouts."

The opening game, however, disappointed the estimated five thousand fans at Cartier Field. Against "an aggregation of 'gritty' gridders
from Kalamazoo College," N.D. could not score in the first half and
managed only a 14–0 win. Dorais ran the team in the absence of Rockne,
away scouting Nebraska, and for that reason, Walter Eckersall wrote the
N.D. coach the following week. The referee-journalist was direct: "Your
team did not play good football last Saturday as Dorais has probably told
you." Then "Eck" provided the N.D. coach with a critique of the squad's
problems.

Rockne had his team ready for their next match, a home encounter
versus Mount Union of Ohio. The crowd was down by a thousand from
the opener, but N.D. was up for a 60–7 victory. The winning momentum
continued the next week in Nebraska; Notre Dame brought home a
hard-fought 14–7 win and a profit of $3,515. Next came an excursion to
Indianapolis to face the Indiana University team. A trainload of N.D.
students bolstered the Notre Dame alumni in the stands, and in the mud,
their team won 16–3, returning a profit of $2,538.

The following week, the squad traveled to West Point, and although
the Army guarantee did not cover expenses, Notre Dame continued to
build its football reputation with a come-from-behind 12–9 victory. This
game, marking the resumption of the annual series, was an occasion for
the Notre Dame eastern alumni and friends to gather. Many came on a
special train from New York City, and the N.D. student reporter noted:
"Seven hundred [fans] in the east stand wore the gold and blue and

greeted every successful play with the thunderous 'N.D.U.' [cheer]. Of these, some were graduates, some had hoped to be, others are going to be, some were just friends, and many just friends of friends of Notre Dame."

Within a few years the number of fans in the stands cheering the Fighting Irish against Army would increase from seven hundred to fifty thousand; the fervor of the Notre Dame alumni present in 1919 and the enthusiasm of the nonalumni were a portent of this amazing future. When Rockne glanced up at them from the sideline, when he mingled with them before and after the game, he must have noted their passion, and in the 1920s, when he agreed to play Army in New York, he knew how to make their commitment work for him and Notre Dame.

The fan enthusiasm for the team and its winning momentum continued the next week at Cartier Field against the Michigan Aggies. A record crowd of almost six thousand, including many South Bend people as well as fans from Michigan, packed the bleachers and the standing-room areas. N.D. won 13–0 and the *Scholastic*, in an editorial titled "A Stadium for Notre Dame," rhapsodized over the event, the size of the crowd, the cheering, the marching bands, and how they all "provided those picturesque and romantic incidentals so necessary to a 'big' football game." The editorial concluded with a direct paraphrase of Rockne's position at the time: "And why cannot Notre Dame bring the greatest teams of East and West to a new Cartier Field? In other words, let's have a stadium for Notre Dame."

Midwestern sportswriters were also beginning to note the prowess of the 1919 team, and the next game, at Purdue, was billed as the title match for "the undisputed championship of Indiana." The *Lafayette* (Indiana) *Journal* warned Purdue fans: "It's Rockne's aim to run the score as high as possible so as to secure a rating among teams of the Western Conference." But the N.D. coach did not prepare his squad of war vets with one of his famous pep talks, explaining, "When I tried to key them up during the week for the weekend game, they just laughed. I couldn't fool 'em."

Rockne drilled the players in his offensive and defensive formations and, on Saturday, pointed them toward the field. Against Purdue, the "Irish," led by Gipp's running and passing, rolled over the Boilermakers 33–13, beating them by more points than any of their conference foes managed and signaling the Big Ten coaches that there was football "prestige" to be gained by taking on the Catholic school.

The following week, with a victory over Morningside in an Iowa snowstorm, Notre Dame claimed the "Championship of the West." This concluded a 9–0–0 season, and some writers also supported N.D. for the national championship. Parke Davis, a former coach, selected the team as co-champions with Illinois in his national poll; however, at the end of the year, most of the other polls had Harvard, with a 9–0–1 record, including a Rose Bowl victory, on top. Unfortunately for Notre Dame, the majority of eastern journalists still believed that Ivy football was America's best.

Rockne was disappointed about not winning a unanimous national championship. Nevertheless, he felt that he was building for the future, installing a football system that would produce winning teams and, if he succeeded, undisputed national titles. But not all of his battles were against other schools; some occurred within the Golden Dome at Notre Dame.

> Dear Rock,
>   I have been waiting a long time for an answer to my last letter and finally came to the conclusion that you had forgotten my address, so decided to write you again so that you would know I am still on earth even if I am buried out on the prairies of western Kansas.
>
>   —Jesse Harper to Rockne, 1919

When Rockne finally resumed the correspondence with his mentor, they mainly discussed the coach's low salary from N.D. and his other problems with the school's administrators. At this point in his relations with the men running Notre Dame, Rockne could not argue from strength, but as in his dealings with his coaching opponents and the newspapermen-referees, he always sought a way to win.

Harper's advice, after the 9–0–0 season, was to "strike [President] Burns for a raise except for the fact that you have a three-year contract to fulfill." Harper suggested some strategies for his former assistant; for example, point out to Burns that because of the "high cost of living . . . a $3,500 salary is not worth nearly as much now as when you signed the contract."

Father Burns did raise Rockne's salary to $5,000 a year, with the possibility that bonuses could move it higher. Whether the rhetorical arguments and/or the 1919 winning record persuaded the N.D. president is not known, but that same year, Rockne discovered an even more valuable lever for future negotiations—the outside offer. He had asked Harper about the availability of other coaching jobs but his mentor knew of only one (Kansas); however, after the 1919 season, unsolicited inquiries started coming to Rockne's office at Notre Dame, including one from Cornell. Though only a few outside inquiries arrived in 1919, in subsequent years they came in large numbers—often with Rockne's prompting —and he increasingly used them for leverage in his disputes with the Notre Dame administration.

In Harper's final letter to Rockne in 1919, he congratulated his protégé on the "financial report" on the football season. Revenues had increased to a bit above $17,500, and the coach claimed a profit of $3,509. However, six months later, the final "Athletic Report" for 1919–1920— with salaries and the debits from other varsity sports factored in—revealed that the athletic department had lost money. Again, only the mandatory student athletic fees, $11,663, up because of the increased N.D. enrollment, turned the loss into a $657 profit.

But Rockne, like generations of athletic directors and coaches after him, had a plan: he would spend more money to make more money. Unlike most of his imitators, he was able to make his plan work.

14

Rockne's Rocket—First Version: 1920

"I feel that Mr. Lee [Northwestern athletic director] needs one more big game to strengthen an otherwise weak schedule. . . . I talked him out of the idea of playing an eastern game, so this leaves Notre Dame and Nebraska, the only other schools without games on this date."

—Charlie Bachman to Rockne, December 1919

At the conclusion of the 1919 season, the N.D. football coach put on his athletic director's hat and began working on the next season's schedule. As always, his priority was to play Big Ten teams and he had no problem rescheduling Indiana and Purdue; with the latter, Rockne brought off a major coup—he got the Boilermakers to agree to come to Notre Dame. He then talked the N.D. administration into enlarging Cartier Field and proclaiming the Purdue visit the first "Homecoming" game for Notre Dame alumni.

Rockne had another breakthrough with a Big Ten school when he arranged a game with Northwestern. That university's A.D. and faculty representative were reluctant to schedule the Catholic school, but Rockne was aided by a "mole" in their athletic department—Charlie Bachman, a former N.D. player, coaching at the Illinois school. Throughout the negotiations, "Bach" gave the N.D. head man inside information on the situation, enabling Rockne to close the deal in January 1920.

The away games at Army and Nebraska almost arranged themselves, as did the contest against the Michigan Aggies. But the N.D. coach wanted another eastern road game and he wrote to Harvard; the national champions replied frostily that "it would seem to us inadvisable to play Notre Dame next year." Adding insult, Harvard scheduled a 1920 game against tiny Valparaiso College, only seventy-nine miles from South Bend. Because he wanted to beat "Valpo" by more points than Harvard would, Rockne also put that school on his 1920 schedule—the only time N.D. ever played Valparaiso in football.

Rockne's overture to Harvard sparked a policy debate in the Golden Dome—how many road games, especially to the East Coast, should the football team undertake? President Burns wanted to limit the schedule to the Army game in the East and Nebraska in the West. Rockne enlisted the students in the campaign but Burns remained firm, writing: "Two long Eastern trips would make too deep and serious a disarrangement of class work for the young men concerned to permit our allowing this."

As a result of Burns's position, Rockne had to turn down attractive offers from Syracuse in the East and the University of Texas in the Southwest. Syracuse had even suggested a contest in one of the stadiums in New York City (these venues were becoming popular for college teams; the Polo Grounds had long hosted the Army-Navy game).

Rockne completed his 1920 schedule with home games against Kalamazoo College and Western Michigan. But some small schools were balking at playing Notre Dame; Wabash politely begged off, stating that it did not "care to meet" a long list of "championship teams," including N.D., next fall.

One group of schools did want to play Notre Dame—its Catholic colleagues. Proposals for games on almost any terms came from such institutions as Saint Mary's of California, Georgetown, and Marquette, but Rockne was not interested in scheduling Catholic schools. He felt that these games would split the loyalty of the growing number of nonalumni Notre Dame rooters and that he had nothing to gain by winning—everyone expected N.D. to beat the Catholic competition—but he had football prestige to lose if his team were defeated.

In late 1919, the president of the Marquette Athletic Association complained to Rockne, "I thought, from your letters, that the game [for 1920] was assured, so I held up my schedule to accommodate you." The N.D. athletic director was to blame; he was often evasive in his schedule making—juggling a number of possibilities while he held out for the best ones—and he also did not like to explain to Catholic schools why he would not play them.

The Marquette official would not be denied and he took his com-

plaint to the Golden Dome. As a result he obtained a Notre Dame road
game for 1921 and the enmity of Rockne. The N.D. coach, with increasing power through the 1920s, refused to play Marquette again; the 1921
contest was the last football game between the schools.

> "Notre Dame's 'Homecoming' is an assured success. The reserve seat
> shortage and the 'last minute' rush is our only concern. See that you
> apply early and get a place to sit down. Mail your letter, with check
> enclosed, to K. K. Rockne, Athletic Director, Notre Dame, Indiana."
>
> —Special announcement in the September 1919
> issue of *The Scholastic*

Rockne believed in amassing large numbers of talented players. For
1920, he had many of the stars of the previous team back, including
George Gipp, Buck Shaw, and Hunk Anderson, as well as talented freshmen and reserves moving up to the varsity. He also acquired assorted
players like quarterback Chet Grant, who had wandered in and out of
Notre Dame for almost a decade ("When I came back, I was twenty-
eight and played my last game when I was twenty-nine"). Grant marveled
that, in 1920, "we had two distinct teams with which to wage our campaign, and for the first time in Notre Dame history—probably in collegiate football history—two elevens operated almost entirely as separate
units."

Close to five thousand fans attended the opening game at Cartier
Field and saw the home team demolish Kalamazoo, 39–0. The *Scholastic*
reported: "The work of Gipp and Barry was beautiful to watch. Each
pierced the Kalamazoo defense at will for long gains." The following
week, the "Celery City Gridders" of Western Michigan visited N.D. and
were crunched, 42–0.

Then the season became serious with a visit to Nebraska. Before a
large homecoming crowd in Lincoln, many spectators taunting the N.D.
contingent with anti-Catholic insults, Notre Dame slowly pulled ahead,
16–7. Late in the final quarter, Rockne sent in Chet Grant with instructions to sit on the ball and the lead.

The reserve QB had never dealt with Gipp "under fire" before, and
the star immediately demanded the ball. Simultaneously, Norm Barry,
another backfielder, said, "Let me have it." Then, according to Grant,
"Hunk Anderson, a miner lad from Gipp's hometown who fairly wor-
shipped the great halfback, turned around and growled, 'Let George
have it.'" Grant decided to take it himself, grounding the ball.

Gipp then wanted the quarterback to let him attempt a pass; Grant refused, explaining, "No, I'm here with instructions to play it safe." Gipp replied, "Listen, I've got friends in South Bend who've bet we'll win by two touchdowns. We've got to pass." Grant allowed Gipp to throw a pass—it failed—and then the QB followed Rockne's instructions for the 16–7 win. Gipp did not hold grudges, and after the game, he bought Grant a drink.

Back at Notre Dame, the expansion of Cartier Field continued, and an estimated eight thousand fans came to the following week's contest against Valparaiso. The "gold and blue warriors" won, 28–3, thus meeting Rockne's goal of a larger score against "Valpo" than Harvard obtained, 21–0.

Next came the annual trip to West Point and a struggle against a very strong Army team. Walter French, a former Rutgers All-American, led the Kaydets and for much of the afternoon he matched George Gipp's offensive thrusts. At halftime, Army led 17–14, and Rockne was so frustrated by the Kaydets' attack that in the locker room, according to Chet Grant, the N.D. coach began yelling at right end Eddie Anderson:

"Eddie, where the hell were you on French's runs?"

Eddie begins to explain, "It wasn't my fault, Rock." BANG. Rock blows up. I had never seen him in such a rage. I thought he was going to sock Eddie.

"Shut up, Anderson," he shouted. "Don't talk back to me. You go back in there and play football."

If Eddie had not subsided, Rock undoubtedly would have socked [him], or burst.

Just before leaving the locker room, the N.D. coach dispensed some loud advice to his team: "Go after them! Go after them! Knock 'em down. Tear 'em apart. Knock 'em down so they stay down!"

In the second half, Gipp prevailed, leading N.D. to a 27–17 victory. Ring Lardner wrote that at key moments Notre Dame had one offensive play: "Line up, pass the ball to Gipp, and let him use his own judgment."

The *New York Times* reporter was less analytic, leading with a typical patch of purple prose: "A lithe-limbed Hoosier football player named George Gipp galloped wild through the Army on the plains here this afternoon, giving a performance which was more like an antelope than a human being."

Rockne was pleased at the large number of sportswriters who came up the Hudson from New York City to cover the game. Most of them joined the laudatory chorus for the "Gipp-led Wonder Men," as did many

Chicago and midwestern journalists. The praise, reported at length in the *Scholastic*, carried the Notre Dame community through the following week and the preparations for the school's first Homecoming game. Cartier Field could now hold twelve thousand people, and extra sideline boxes—at $18 each—were sold for the match against Purdue.

The event was a great success: "a tremendous crowd that surged into every nook and cranny of Cartier Field" cheered the team's easy 28–0 victory over the Boilermakers and acclaimed such former N.D. football heroes as Louis "Red" Salmon and Ray Eichenlaub. Rockne did not invent the Homecoming game—it began at eastern colleges at least a decade earlier—but the Notre Dame coach had the idea of tapping into the increasingly enthusiastic N.D. alumni and bringing large numbers of them back to campus to fill the enlarged grounds. In addition, by summoning past football heroes for Homecoming, he greatly contributed to the school's awareness and pride about its sports past.

The following week, N.D. met the Indiana University Hoosiers in Indianapolis. The game was a slugfest. In the first quarter, the IU defense continuously gang-tackled Gipp, dislocating his shoulder and putting him on the sidelines. However, according to an N.D. reserve player, Rockne himself "bound up his [Gipp's] injured arm, taped it from shoulder to wrist, and sent him" back into the game "to ram the ball across the line for our first touchdown and to participate in the glory of the second and winning score," 13–10.

Notre Dame was becoming a road attraction—fourteen thousand spectators filled the Indianapolis park—and by the following Tuesday the *Chicago Tribune* headlined "MOST OF TICKETS GONE FOR [NORTHWESTERN] PURPLE CLASH WITH N.D." for the next Saturday. Rockne had sent out a form letter asking Notre Dame alumni in the Chicago area to attend, and in addition, the N.D. authorities were pleased that various "dignitaries of the Catholic church of the Chicago district have been invited . . . [and] Thousands of Catholics and other thousands of non-Catholics will go to the game." Walter Eckersall of the *Chicago Tribune* promoted the contest with such articles as "N.D. WILL BRING CORKING ATTACK TO PURPLE FIELD."

The result was a crowd of over twenty thousand on a wet, cold day. Gipp was already ill with the infection that would kill him, and his coach kept him out of the game until the fourth quarter. Although N.D. had a comfortable lead, Rockne gave in to the fans' shouts for Gipp to play and inserted him into the lineup. He helped N.D. add two touchdowns for a final score of 33–7. (This game proved to Rockne that Notre Dame could attract large numbers of spectators in Chicago and prompted him to schedule future N.D. contests in Soldier Field, resulting in crowds five and six times the size of the 1920 one.)

Gipp did not suit up for the finale at Michigan State Agricultural but was not needed in the easy 25–0 win. Nevertheless, his season achievements earned him consensus All-America honors—the first across-the-board All-American at Notre Dame—and the plaudits of such eastern sportswriters as Grantland Rice. Rockne also began to receive recognition: from the Army head coach's comment, "Mr. Rockne is among the very best coaches in the country," to the N.D. students' hyperbolic "the greatest coach of all times."

Unfortunately for Rockne, the 1920 team, although playing a harder schedule than the 1919 squad, did not capture the unanimous national championship. The first of Andy Smith's "Wonder Teams" at California won a number of polls, and Notre Dame managed only a number-one spot—tied with Princeton—in Parke Davis's rating. Rockne wanted a postseason trip to the West Coast to play California in the Rose Bowl but was frustrated when the Big Ten's best team, Ohio State, received the invitation.

Less frustrating were the attendance and financial figures from the 1920 football season. The previous year, Notre Dame had played before approximately 56,500 people, 16,500 of them at home. In 1920, almost 90,000 people paid to see Rockne's team, 28,500 for home games. Receipts from football had jumped to $34,000 and although expenses had increased to almost $19,500, the profit was $14,591. Even subtracting Rockne's salary of $5,000 and his assistant's salary of $2,500, the football profit was still over $7,000.

By the end of the 1920–1921 academic year, other varsity sports had lost $9,900, but the money from student fees, $12,556, more than covered that debit. Again, the students saved the athletic department from red ink, but Rockne's expansion plan also seemed to be paying off. The Notre Dame administrators must have thought so because they rewarded him with a year-end $1,000 bonus.

One of the most positive figures in the 1920–1921 "Athletics Financial Report" concerned the money earned from "Season tickets [sold in] South Bend"—$1,420. A historian of pro football in the Midwest points to 1920 as the year that the "downfall of professional football in South Bend began"—attendance dropped as "the local pro fans began to identify themselves with Notre Dame."

The year also marked the end of the first phase of Rockne's coaching and athletic director's career. He had moved Notre Dame football from its depleted wartime state of 1918 to national recognition in 1920. Most important, he had poised N.D. football for its amazing takeoff later in the decade. Much of the credit for the successful year was due to George Gipp, who died on December 14, 1920.

15

George Gipp's Five Seasons at Notre Dame

"[After high school] Gipp spent much time at Jimmy O'Brien's Pool Room, which was three blocks from his house on Hecla Street [in Laurium, Michigan]. . . . For money, Gipp would drive the cab on weekends, ferrying copper miners to and from the bars and the local house of prostitution."

—George Gekas, northern Michigan native and Gipp biographer

George Gipp grew up in the rough mining area of Upper Peninsula Michigan, one of eight children. His father was a carpenter and laborer—not a Congregationalist minister, as Rockne later claimed—and although Gipp attended Calumet High School, he did not graduate. For three years after high school, he worked on his pool game, drove a taxi, and played various outdoor sports, especially semipro baseball.

One of Gipp's baseball friends, Wilbur "Dolly" Gray, had been an outstanding catcher on the Notre Dame varsity under Jesse Harper in 1913–1914, and Gray told his old coach about Gipp. Harper offered the player a baseball scholarship—a job at N.D. to pay his way. Thus, in March 1916, Gipp sought academic admission to Notre Dame.

Father Matthew Schumacher, Director of Studies, replied on behalf of N.D., pointing out that Gipp did not have enough high school units to enter "in full standing" but that he could make up the deficiencies during his first year or in summer school. Schumacher admitted him as "a conditioned Freshman."

The twenty-one-year-old Gipp arrived at Notre Dame in September 1916 and discovered that his job as a waiter in Brownson Hall covered only his room and board bills; he would have to pay out-of-pocket for his books, supplies, fees, and other expenses. Gipp immediately embarked on what one of his fellow students called "his own private job plan"—earning money by playing pool and cards in downtown South Bend. He was so skillful a gambler that he quit his job waiting on tables after one semester and eventually moved out of the dormitories, living the rest of his N.D. years in the luxurious Oliver Hotel in South Bend, home to various affluent citizens, commercial travelers, and high-stakes billiard, pool, and poker games.

From the beginning of his Notre Dame career, Gipp's phenomenal athletic ability was apparent. On October 7, 1916, in a freshman football game against Western State Normal of Michigan, he kicked a sixty-two-yard field goal. Rockne later explained to John Heisman that "Gipp had never played football previous to this year but had an unusual knack of being able to kick long distance naturally." Moreover, Gipp's sixty-two-yarder was not a wind-aided soccer-style kick but an old-fashioned drop-kick into the wind.

Rockne's *Autobiography* depicts his emotions upon discovering this athlete: "I felt the thrill that comes to every coach when he knows it is his fate and his responsibility to handle unusual greatness—the perfect performer who comes rarely more than once in a generation." (The memoir was originally published in *Collier's* magazine in 1930 and for the Gipp section, the illustrations included a drawing of a pool player at night—Gipp's pool hustling, well-known to contemporaries, had not yet been sanitized by the Ronald Reagan film portrayal.)

Like most college coaches with exceptionally talented but wayward athletes, Rockne's method of handling Gipp was to humor and protect him. When Rockne took over the varsity in 1918, as Gipp's play became more spectacular and indispensable to Notre Dame's attack, the coach increasingly ignored his star's life-style, rationalized his transgressions, and fought to keep him in school and eligible for football.

Like many college athletes, because his time and energy went into sports and extracurricular activity, Gipp showed very little interest in academics. The transcript of his Notre Dame academic record reveals that for two of his four full school years (he died during his fifth), he received no grades whatsoever. In his sophomore year, he did not arrive on campus until October 14—missing the first two football games, including a key contest against Wisconsin—and then he dropped out of N.D. in November after breaking his leg in the Morningside contest. The following year, he also arrived late and although he played varsity football, his transcript for the 1918–1919 academic year is blank. Robert Burns, a history professor at Notre Dame who has studied this period of the school's past, says that "Gipp rarely went to class, not at all his last year. He was in a different major every year to take the easy courses. This was before President Burns tightened the curriculum."

On March 8, 1920, Notre Dame expelled him. According to his teammate and hometown friend Hunk Anderson, Gipp was "kicked out . . . for too many class cuts," but immediately "there were at least six major universities in contact with George trying to lure him to their schools in spite of his scholastic predicaments." Among the coaches and institutions bidding for Gipp were Fielding Yost of the University of Michigan, Pop Warner of Pittsburgh, the West Point athletic department (prodded by Superintendent Douglas MacArthur), and the University of Detroit (a Catholic school). Meanwhile, Gipp remained in South Bend, living and gambling in the Oliver Hotel and also working as a "house player" at Hullie & Mike's.

Rockne never wrote about the 1920 recruiting battle for his star player, but considering his competitive nature, he must have hated the prospect of losing Gipp to such rivals as Yost or Warner. He began lobbying within the university for Gipp's readmission and also in downtown South Bend; soon, eighty prominent citizens sent a petition to President Burns requesting that "you and your associates . . . give serious consideration to raising the ban against Gipp." The civic leaders, most of whom supported the expansion of Cartier Field as well as the university's fundraising campaign, pointedly added, "Increasingly South Bend is taking pride in the splendid accomplishments of Notre Dame. The most spectacular of these are, of course, your victories upon the athletic field. Here Gipp has been truly worthy of the University."

Father Burns, for all of his academic seriousness, could not remain immune to such pressure, and on April 29, 1920, he reinstated Gipp. Later in the 1920s, with the media spotlight upon Notre Dame football and accusations that Rockne was running a "wide-open" program, the N.D. coach and his press assistants tried to bury the facts of Gipp's readmission beneath layers of legend. In one tale, the faculty readmitted him after a grueling oral exam; in another, President Burns himself administered the tough oral examination. Current N.D. history professor

Robert Burns terms these stories "total fabrications—Father Burns saw himself as the first true academic president of Notre Dame, the first one with an advanced degree, and there is no way that he would have gone along with a special examination for Gipp or any other student in that situation. But he was a pragmatist and bowed to the pressure and simply allowed Gipp back in school."

The readmission flap—indeed, Gipp's entire career and life-style—only became important in historical retrospect. When President Burns acted in April 1920, no doubt he hoped and even assumed that the incident would soon be forgotten. He had no way of knowing that within nine months George Gipp would become Notre Dame's first consensus All-American, would die, and then, twenty years later, would be sanctified in a Hollywood film. Moreover, Father Burns and his contemporaries could not anticipate—and would have found incredible—the fact that the actor portraying Gipp would go on to become president of the United States and use his association with the role as his rallying cry: "Win One for the Gipper."

During George Gipp's lifetime, no one suggested that he was a future candidate for political office, much less for American sainthood. To those who knew him, he was an extraordinary athlete, a high-stakes and high-living gambler, and very far from a regular college student.

YOU HAVE BEEN RECOMMENDED FOR APPOINTMENT TO UNITED STATES MILITARY ACADEMY. . . . PLEASE WIRE ME COLLECT WHETHER OR NOT YOU WILL CONSIDER ACCEPTANCE.

> Captain Philip Hayes,
> Charge of A.A.A. [Army Athletic Association]
>
> —Telegram to George Gipp, July 27, 1920

The fallout from Gipp's brief expulsion from Notre Dame continued long after he was readmitted in late April (he played baseball for N.D. in May). Not only did West Point pursue him through the summer but Michigan stayed in the hunt and managed to snatch his favorite pass target, N.D. end Bernie Kirk. During the late summer of 1920, Gipp spent time on the Ann Arbor campus and then moved on to the University of Detroit, where his N.D. teammate Pete Bahan had transferred. Considering Gipp's penchant for cash and the corruption in college football at the time, probably the offers from Michigan and Detroit included various sums of money.

In the end, Rockne went to Michigan and convinced Gipp to return to Notre Dame. The Scholastic, in its September 1920 "Pigskin Prospects," crowed, "It would be sheer nonsense to wonder at Rockne's broad smiles of assurance and contentment these days with Gipp cavorting around the backfield."

But the player was back at Notre Dame on his own terms, and he resumed living at the Oliver Hotel and also playing semipro football. One of the South Bend pros recalled that Gipp "had practically nothing to do with the Notre Damers after he had finished . . . practice there." Moreover, according to his N.D. teammate, Chet Grant: "Throughout the season, he did not appear for more than two or three practices a week, at the outside." However, the N.D. "players did not seem to resent it"; they respected Gipp's athletic talents and also knew that their coach "had implicit confidence in him, permitted him indulgences which granted to another would have wrecked team morale." Rockne "was sufficiently sold on him to let him get away with murder."

Chet Grant maintained that "Gipp was a gambler, off and on the field"; in the famous Army game of 1920, at one point

> Gipp punched the man who tackled him. Seeing that an official had witnessed the act, he rolled over like a flash and began groaning as if he had been injured by the tackler, thus enlisting a sympathy which caused the official to overlook an infraction which could have been interpreted as slugging, which is punishable by removal of the offender from the game.

Off the field, the N.D. football star had become "South Bend's undisputed king of pocket and three-cushion billiards" and earned a sizable income by taking on all comers. The *South Bend Tribune* wrote up his pool playing exploits but did not discuss his more serious card sharking.

According to his friend Hunk Anderson, Gipp was an "exceptional poker player," and if the games in South Bend were too "quiet," he would "journey down to nearby towns and clean up in poker. Elkhart, Indiana, had a tidy railroad payroll earned by the citizenry and George would usually make their paydays his paydays."

Gipp called himself "the finest free-lance gambler ever to attend Notre Dame." He did not confine himself to games of chance but, as was the custom of the time in college football, bet on his team as well as his own game performances. For the 1920 contest against Indiana, he searched Indianapolis for someone to bet against N.D. and, in the end, mainly wagered that he personally would outscore the Big Ten team, thus contributing to his willingness to return to action with a dislocated shoulder.

That year at West Point, Gipp and Hunk Anderson organized the
Notre Dame team's share of the betting pool, raising $2,100 (the price of
a new house in South Bend at the time). Army came up with a similar
amount, and a local shoemaker held the winner-take-all purse. At halftime, Notre Dame was losing and, according to eyewitnesses, Rockne,
"after naming the return lineup and giving specific and dynamic injunction to each man," turned to Gipp leaning against a wall, smoking a
cigarette. He yelled, "What about you, Gipp? I don't suppose you have
any interest in this game?"

"Look, Rock," Gipp replied, "I got four hundred dollars [of my own
money] bet on this game, and I'm not about to blow it."

Gipp had a spectacular second half, leading Notre Dame to a 28–17
victory.

In the film *Knute Rockne—All American*, the Notre Dame coach,
declaiming against the evils of betting on football, throws some shady
gamblers out of the N.D. locker room. Other biographies of Rockne
portray him as totally unaware of his players' gambling. In fact, considering his fondness for Hullie & Mike's, his inside information on pro and
college football, and the money wagered on matches, as well as his
knowledge about his team, Knute Rockne had to know about his players'
betting habits. Because winning was so important to him, and losing a
star athlete like Gipp was so counterproductive to winning, the coach
went along with the players' gambling as long as he obtained his desired
result—football victories.

> "When I was a kid in the 1920s, I used to hawk newspapers in downtown
> South Bend. The story in the pool halls from Gipp's pals was that George
> got so drunk one night, he passed out in the snow and they found him
> the next morning. That's how he got the pneumonia that killed him."
>
> —Moe Aranson, a lifelong South Bend resident

During his life, many stories adhered to George Gipp; after his death,
they increased geometrically and their focal point was no longer around
to confirm or deny them. Moe Aranson stresses that he never met Gipp
and merely repeats an often-told South Bend tale. However, Grover Malone, an N.D. player in the late teens, offered an eyewitness explanation
for Gipp's fatal illness: after the Indiana game in 1920, Gipp visited him
in Chicago and they "went on a rip-roaring three-day drunk." When
Malone finally put his friend on the train back to South Bend, he noticed

that he was coughing. By the following Saturday in Evanston, Gipp's cough was much worse and Rockne kept him out of most of the Northwestern game.

Whether Gipp's fatal illness was pneumonia, infected tonsils, strep throat, or possibly a combination of all three, he was hospitalized in late November 1920 and slowly deteriorated until he died on December 14. His final hours sparked the two most controversial stories about his life: his deathbed conversion to Catholicism and his supposed last words.

Like many Notre Dame athletes, including Rockne, George Gipp was not born Catholic. In his years at N.D., he had not shown much interest in religion, but during his final illness, he discussed Catholicism with various priests. After his death, Presidents Burns and Walsh both affirmed that, according to their investigations, Gipp had definitely wanted to become a Catholic.

Gipp's family, however, were low-church Protestant and his mother was quite religious; she was also with him continuously during his last weeks in the hospital. At the end, with death inevitable and Gipp semiconscious, a C.S.C. priest, Father Pat Haggerty, gave him "conditional baptism and conditional absolution," explaining that "the conversion was one of interpreted intention as distinguished from concrete expression."

Eyewitnesses, particularly his mother and two siblings present, disputed the conversion, his sister writing to Gipp's fiancée that "we could deny it openly" but that that would mainly hurt his friends at N.D., and anyway, George would say, " 'Oh, let them [Notre Dame] go ahead' " with it. " 'Kid them along. It makes no difference to me.' "

Father John O'Hara administered the last rites of the church to Gipp and later wrote about his "martyrdom." By the time of Rockne's *Autobiography* in 1930, after his own conversion to Catholicism, Gipp's "embrace of the faith" was an important part of his legend and the coach's memoir treated it as such. Although Gipp's mother always disputed the event, the story had been launched, and it maintained a momentum of its own.

In 1940, for Warner Brothers' *Knute Rockne—All American*, the director wanted to include the conversion, describing it as "the anointing of Gipp by Father Callahan," the fictitious president of Notre Dame, "the prayers to be read in Latin, which is the same scene as in *The Fighting 69th*"—Warners' hit movie of the time—"when Father Duffy anointed Jimmy Cagney." When informed of this plan, a high N.D. official replied, "My first reaction is that this scene might cause some antagonism in northern Michigan" among Gipp's family and friends. But the filmmakers shot a visual version of Gipp's deathbed transformation—thus the event departed the realm of the conjectural and became "real" for millions of Americans.

The authenticity of Gipp's last words to Rockne is even more difficult to ascertain. In 1920, Rockne never mentioned the "Win One for the Gipper" request—no one called Gipp by that nickname, nor did he ever use it for himself. Moreover, Rockne was not at the deathbed; he did visit his player in the hospital during his final weeks but he was rarely alone with him.

The N.D. coach first told the story of Gipp's request in November 1928, almost eight years after the death, in the locker room at halftime of the Notre Dame–Army contest in New York. The story belongs to the narrative of those events and the context of Rockne's highly dramatic and sometimes fabricated locker room talks as well as to his desire to salvage his worst season by beating Army.

■ ■ ■

"We have decided to send you the enclosed check for three hundred and fifty dollars. This . . . is made necessary by Mr. Rockne's statement made in the presence of both of us that it was possible that he had committed himself in some way [to requesting your services for George Gipp] but had no definite recollection of so doing."

—Notre Dame President Matthew Walsh
to Dr. C. H. Johnson, January 1923

Reverberations from Gipp's death continued for many years at Notre Dame. The immediate effect of his passing was dismay and genuine grief in the N.D. community. Father Arthur Hope, a C.S.C. priest, wrote: "Neither the death [in 1921 of former president] Father Morrissey nor of [the famous] Father Zahm affected the students. But the death of George Gipp was another matter." The *Scholastic* was filled with long eulogies to the departed football hero as well as lengthy tributes from newspapers around the country to the recently named All-American. By the time the *Dome* appeared in late spring 1921, the Gipp myth had detached from reality. The yearbook's statement began, "Gipp came to Notre Dame not primarily for athletics" and escalated to "following the classic contest at West Point [in 1920], they called him Lochinvar of the West, and held him a demi-god of Football."

In 1921, however, Notre Dame administrators were less concerned about Gipp's legend than settling his medical and funeral expenses. Rockne and Gipp's family had summoned various doctors to attend him, including a specialist from Chicago, and these men had sent their bills to the Golden Dome. Father Burns felt that the family should pay a share, but when it became apparent that Rockne had juggled the physicians the way he did athletic directors during schedule making—promising whatever seemed most expedient at the moment—Notre Dame agreed to settle all accounts, over $4,500 worth.

The funeral dispute was more public and vicious. In the years after Gipp's death, Fielding Yost of Michigan claimed that N.D. had refused to pay anything toward the funeral and had stuck the family with a huge bill. Eventually the story reached the East Coast and Grantland Rice's column in the *New York Herald-Tribune*. Notre Dame officials patiently refuted it with the facts—they and Gipp's classmates had paid for the train expenses to northern Michigan and most of the funeral bill—but privately Rockne denounced Yost's slander, attributing it to the Michigan coach's anti-Catholicism and anti–Notre Dame feelings. The dispute became significant in 1926 when it affected N.D.'s renewed application to the Big Ten.

During the 1920s, Rockne received occasional inquiries about Gipp. Typical of them was a letter from a football fan in New Jersey asking "whom you consider the best football player of the following three: Gipp, Thorpe, or Grange." The Notre Dame coach replied, as he always did to this and similar questions, and with total sincerity, "I consider Gipp superior to either Jim Thorpe or Grange."

16

The Rocket Crashes—Rockne's Miraculous Escape: 1921

Dear Rock,

I have your letter of the 20th [of December 1920]. Am printing your [1921] schedule tomorrow and will follow up with several stories during the week.

I certainly thank you for taking an interest in my officiating. . . . I doubt if [Walter] Camp will attend the Army–Notre Dame game. For that reason I especially would like to officiate that particular contest as I probably will meet him prior to the N.D.–Rutgers game [a few days later]. You understand? This is strictly *confidential*.

If it would be possible for you to swing me in [as a game official] on the N.D.–Rutgers game I could remain in the east. . . .

With best wishes for a great season in 1921 and urging you to pass along plenty of N.D. dope, I am,

Sincerely,

Harry Costello
The Detroit News

During the month of Gipp's death in 1920, Rockne had to work on his football schedule for the following year. He attended the Big Ten coaches' meeting in Chicago and, in addition to lining up the usual games with Purdue and Indiana, came away with a contest at Iowa. Then, in his negotiations on the Army annual, a new element entered.

Major Philip Hayes, in charge of the Army Athletic Association, wired

Rockne in early December that a contest between the schools in the Polo Grounds in New York "will be [the] greatest drawing card of all games" (college matches in the forty-thousand-seat stadium had done well in 1920). Rockne was amenable but Hayes's superiors at West Point were not ready to move the Army–N.D. game—the annual with Navy, held at the Polo Grounds since 1913, drew capacity crowds, and they worried about undermining their own feature attraction.

Rockne, however, immediately approached Rutgers University about a New York City game—they had played Nebraska at the Polo Grounds in 1920—and on December 19, he received an offer, including a $5,000 guarantee, from their athletic department for the contest. Negotiations proceeded quickly, and soon the match was set for Election Day 1921, three days after the Army contest at West Point.

The Notre Dame A.D. also scheduled Nebraska but, in a major breakthrough, had them agree to visit Indiana for the first time. To complete his lineup, Rockne rounded up some of the usual patsies—Kalamazoo, DePauw, and the Haskell Indians—and accepted the semitough Michigan State Aggies and Marquette. For the first time, the Fighting Irish would travel east for two games. Also, they would play an eleven game season, two more than any preceding Notre Dame team.

After setting his schedule, Rockne worked on his officiating assignments; he now had enough clout that in addition to hiring the entire crew for home games, he could "work in" one or two officials for most road matches. The standard fee for a journalist-referee was $50 to $75 per game—the monthly pay range for most sportswriters at the time—plus expenses. Walter Eckersall of the *Chicago Tribune* agreed to do a number of N.D. contests; for the Rutgers match in New York, he received $75 plus $135.99 in expenses (his round-trip ticket from Chicago as well as all hotel, food, and incidental costs were picked up; newspapers went along with this practice, in part, because it allowed them to receive on-the-scene coverage and avoid travel expenses).

As Rockne's correspondence with Harry Costello of the *Detroit News* indicates, the N.D. coach wanted to enlarge his stable of newspapermen-referees. Journalists like Costello were more than willing to trade quid pro quos with coaches: Costello pushed himself for the Army–Notre Dame assignment by promising to put in a good word with Walter Camp for Rockne's All-America team candidates.

The N.D. coach agreed to "work in" the Detroit newspaperman for the Army game but not for Rutgers—the New York plum went to Eckersall and various eastern officials (during the summer of 1921, one of them was indicted in a financial scandal for "notorious malfeasance"). But Costello, whose pushiness was typical of the journalist-referees, then sought an N.D. home game—"I am open for the 24th of September"—and offered the following inducement: "The trip will serve dual purpose," officiating and reporting, "as I want to get a story on your outfit for syndicate stuff throughout the middle west." In his final sentence, he added, "If you can possibly land me [also] in the [Notre Dame versus] Nebraska game I will have four intersectional games to cover."

Dealing with players, even uncontrollable ones like George Gipp, must have been easier for Rockne and the other coaches of this era than feeding the greed of these newspapermen–game officials.

TO THE 'OLD BOYS':

To the grads and former students of Notre Dame, who have listened with tense nerves and pulses running high to the results of the annual N.D.–Nebraska game in the club rooms, newspaper shops and telegraph offices, year after year:

We are sorry but we can't let you carry on in that well-worn fashion any longer. On October 27 the Nebraska football team will perform on our campus for the first time. Your place will be . . . on the sidelines at Cartier Field.

—From the Notre Dame 1921 Homecoming announcement

In the fall of 1921, with the enlargement of Cartier Field and the best home schedule in its history, Notre Dame football became the sports focus of northern Indiana. The local papers expanded their coverage and student publicists like Francis Wallace fed them daily items. Profiles of the star players increased, and speculation about coming games as well as betting information—by how many points N.D. was favored or underdog —proliferated.

The Notre Dame coach liked to begin a football campaign with two home games against easy opponents. In 1921, before eight thousand fans for each contest, his squad ran over Kalamazoo, 56–0, and a week later beat up DePauw, 57–10. The team then traveled to Iowa City to meet a strong Hawkeye eleven. The Fighting Irish, as the student paper now regularly called the team, had won twenty straight games, and the players did not believe that a Big Ten starting unit featuring a majority of native Iowans as well as a helmetless black tackle (Duke Slater) could beat them. The Hawkeyes, however, scored ten points in the opening quarter and, with Slater dominating line play, managed a 10–7 victory.

Rockne was angry at himself and at his team for underestimating the opposition and for not being able to come back from the first quarter deficit. According to Chet Grant, who quarterbacked in this contest, "Rock had taunted the Big Ten for years in order to grab this date with Iowa and the set-back was a bitter dose, particularly in view of our over-confidence. He went into a rage, which was only settled [after the game] by a walk around the field in the company of a friend."

The coach made the players so ashamed of losing that, according to his press assistant, the next morning in Chicago when the N.D. squad changed train stations, "we split up into small groups as we walked along the streets. We didn't want people to identify us as that Notre Dame team that had lost a football game."

Rockne's wrath continued through a week of hard practices, and the following Saturday in Lafayette, Indiana, the team fell upon a weak Purdue crew, beating them 33–0. Within a three-minute span, Hunk Anderson, who always played with barely controlled fury, blocked two attempted punts and converted them into touchdowns.

The intensity continued for the next home game, the Nebraska visit. In a Homecoming weekend much more elaborate than the previous year's, the Notre Dame students and alumni created an atmosphere where the players felt that they had to avenge the Iowa defeat and beat the visiting Cornhuskers. Before a record crowd of fourteen thousand, they held Nebraska to three first downs and fifty-four yards offense, winning 7–0.

Next came the game with Indiana in Indianapolis. The N.D. coach still wanted blood from a Big Ten team and, in a lengthy pregame speech, reminded his players how IU "had *laid* for Gipp the year before, had bruised him unnecessarily" with vicious gang-tackling, "perhaps—had hastened his death." Chet Grant, listening to this talk, admitted that even though he "was twenty-nine years old" and "had never had any particular affection for George Gipp," Rockne "filled me with the will to do his will and the confidence that I could do it." (Significantly, although the N.D. coach really wanted to win this game and pulled out the oratorical stops in his locker room speech, he never mentioned Gipp's supposed deathbed request, further evidence that he created it for the crucial Army game in 1928.) Against Indiana, before ten thousand rain-soaked fans, the Fighting Irish responded to their coach's speech and demolished the Hoosiers, 28–7.

Rockne hoped for larger crowds for the following week in the East. The *Scholastic* headlined "ROUND THE WORLD IN EIGHT DAYS," and pointed out that N.D. would play three teams—Army, Rutgers, and the Haskell

Indians at home—within eight days; this "trip of 1,800 miles represents the full enormity of Rockne's gamble."

For this year's meeting, Army built extra wooden stands at West Point and welcomed special excursion trains from Manhattan—the result was a record crowd of twenty thousand to see Notre Dame easily beat the Cadets, 28–0. Three days later, however, the Irish debut in the Polo Grounds was disappointing. The New York papers did not build up the contest—Ivy teams were their main football preoccupation—and only twelve thousand came to see N.D. pummel Rutgers, 48–0.

The *New York Times* noted that "the much-heralded Notre Dame attack . . . was being unveiled in New York for the first time in many years" (the *Times* did not realize that this was the debut game). After subtracting the various game expenses, including the Polo Grounds' hefty percentage, N.D. received $5,000. Combined with Army's paltry $1,500 payout and the high travel expenses, the profit from the eastern trip was only $2,378.

But the Rutgers game was important to Rockne and to his plans for future contests in New York. For the first time, he had tapped into the city's Notre Dame alumni and, learning from the too ad hoc manner in which he and they worked in 1921, he determined that in future years he would harness their enthusiasm and start promoting the New York game much earlier.

A key player in his plans was Joe Byrne, Jr., the son of an important N.D. alum and an energetic recent grad who knew his way around Tammany Hall and Wall Street. Byrne wrote Rockne after the 1921 eastern trip: "If you could hear the compliments" in Irish-American circles "heaped upon yourself and the team, you could appreciate what a joy it is to be from Notre Dame."

But Byrne also mentioned the cloud forming over the N.D. coach: "Father Walsh and Father McGinn are still here in New York and I certainly have given them an ear full regarding your case." Byrne wanted to balance what the N.D. administrators, trying to raise money for the $750,000 endowment campaign, encountered as they visited the offices of major foundations and corporations—questions concerning Notre Dame's commitment to education as opposed to its seriousness about playing big-time football.

Back in Indiana, President Burns's mail contained similar queries. A prominent Iowan wondered whether the N.D. football players were real students; President Jessup of the University of Iowa had told her that "Notre Dame players were not required to pass their examinations or have any certain number of credits in order to be eligible to play—that a fellow could stay on five or six years and if you asked [the N.D. authorities] why he hadn't passed his examinations and finished, the reply would be, 'Oh, he's a Football Player.' "

Father Burns replied at length, stating that his school's academic standards for football players "conform strictly to the regulations of the Western Intercollegiate Conference." He also enclosed a letter from "the Chairman of our Faculty Athletic Board" validating the eligibility of the N.D. players who made the Iowa trip. But behind the necessary public display, President Burns must have remembered the Gipp case and also worried about some of the unruly characters on Rockne's current squad.

The 1921 team returned from the East to wallop the Haskell Indians, 42–7. Only five thousand fans came to Cartier, proving that minor opponents could not fill the expanded facility and that such contests could lose money (almost $1,600). Even Rockne was a no-show, traveling that day to Milwaukee to scout the next week's adversary, Marquette. The *Milwaukee Telegram* reported that as the N.D. coach "stood in line at the box office, the manager of the Marquette team recognized him. 'Hello there, Rockne. You don't have to buy a ticket. Come in as my guest.' " And he escorted the N.D. coach to the press box.

Rockne's scouting probably helped Notre Dame beat its fellow Catholic school, 21–7, the following Saturday in Milwaukee (in the second half, Pat O'Brien, later to portray the coach in *Knute Rockne—All American*, came on as a sub for Marquette). N.D. finished the season a week later by smashing the Michigan Aggies, 48–0, before a record home crowd of fifteen thousand at Cartier.

This game seemed to mark the triumphant end to a very successful schedule—ten victories and, for the first time, over 100,000 fans paying to see the Fighting Irish. The net profit for N.D. in 1921 from intercollegiate football was $14,875, enough to cover the athletic department deficit, including Rockne's salary. In addition, after the season, letters and press reports from the West Coast indicated the possibility of an invitation to the Rose Bowl in Pasadena and one more excellent payday.

In the next few weeks, however, Rockne's "Rocket" sputtered in midair, and with the revelation that eight of his men had played in an Illinois pro game on Thanksgiving Day and four others in Wisconsin soon after, it crashed, foreclosing a postseason appearance and a possible national championship.

"The game . . . was played in Taylorville, Ill., Nov. 27, 1921. The opposing team included several Notre Dame players in its line-up. The
team on which the [University of] Illinois players performed won by a 9
to 0 score, Sternaman kicking three field goals.

The fact that a number of college players took part in the contest
soon became rather generally known and resulted in reports that 'Illinois
had defeated Notre Dame.'"

—Associated Press report, January 28, 1922

Because college players had moonlighted in pro football for many
years, when Frank Seyfrit, an N.D. reserve from Carlinville, Illinois, approached seven of his teammates about playing for his hometown team
during the Thanksgiving break, none of them considered the offer—$200
each and expenses—inappropriate or even unusual. It also did not bother
them that for the game against arch-rival Taylorville, Carlinville team
officials planned a betting coup with the N.D. players as their secret
weapon.

Throughout the month of November, Carlinville citizens raised an
increasing amount of money for a winner-take-all pot with their rival
town. To obtain more cash, they told local lenders about the participation
of the Notre Dame players; soon most of Carlinville wanted a piece of
the "sure thing" bet. Inevitably, the Taylorville people heard about the
plan. Their team manager responded by hiring nine starters from the
University of Illinois's Big Ten squad. As Thanksgiving approached, the
Taylorville side matched their opponents' money, and the pot grew to an
astounding $100,000. The event became the talk of the midwestern gam-
bling world and many professional bettors got in on the action.

For the game, the Notre Dame contingent did not bring along a
quarterback; instead Eddie Anderson, an end, ran the offense and the
Carlinville attack fizzled, failing to score. Taylorville had better field position for most of the afternoon and won on three field goals by Illinois All-
American Joey Sternaman. Its backers left the football grounds with all of
the money, boasting as they went.

Immediately, information about the game and its collegiate participants reached Chicago reporters but they decided to sit on the story. It
was not in their self-interests as journalists–football officials and journalists–football publicists to anger the college coaching fraternity with ex-
posés; in addition, some Chicago sportswriters closed their typewriters
because they genuinely liked and did not want to embarrass Rockne or
the popular Illinois coach, Bob Zuppke. But, like the 1919 Black Sox
scandal, the Carlinville-Taylorville story was too big to disappear and, like

the baseball fix, lived underground for a time, slowly slouching toward daylight.

According to the Taylorville coach, Rockne first treated his players' holiday venture offhandedly; he "knew about it two days after the game" and he "kidded his athletes because they got a trimming in the game." The N.D. coach subsequently claimed that he first learned about his players' excursion when the Associated Press broke the story months later and he threatened to sue the Taylorville coach and all others who contended otherwise (no lawsuits were ever filed).

Rockne's claims of ignorance and innocence strain credibility: his keen intelligence, his vast knowledge of college and pro football, his contacts with the gambling crowd at Hullie & Mike's, his growing network of journalist friends, and most important of all, the small size of the Notre Dame football program and his close relationships with his players (there were only twenty-two lettermen on this squad) point to the probability that he knew about the Carlinville-Taylorville game either before it occurred or soon after. Assuming that he carried around the knowledge of the Illinois game, hoping that it would remain private, he must have been dismayed to next learn that three of his best athletes had suited up for the Green Bay Packers' 1921 season finale in Milwaukee. This game was too public and the league, the direct forerunner of the NFL, already too important for sportswriters to ignore the appearance of Hunk Anderson, Ojay Larson, and Hec Garvey.

Newspaper reports of the Milwaukee game soon reached South Bend, and the Notre Dame administration, urged on by Father William Carey, an activist on the Faculty Board of Control of Athletics, moved promptly, barring the athletes from further participation in N.D. varsity sports and withdrawing their monograms (varsity letters). In addition, Father Carey began campaigning for greater powers for the board over the athletic department.

Next, one of the gems on Rockne's 1922 schedule, a game against the University of Wisconsin—the first with this Big Ten school during his regime—cracked, the conference school backing out of the agreement.

The N.D. coach's world seemed to be fragmenting—after completing a highly successful 10–1 season and beginning negotiations with the Rose Bowl for an appearance on New Year's Day, he seemed to have lost control of his athletes and had even lost the confidence of some of the N.D. faculty. Then the Rose Bowl bid evaporated, a key member of the Pasadena committee informing him that the host team, Cal-Berkeley, amid the stories of "the professionalism of some of your players," had "proscribed" Notre Dame, refusing to play against Rockne's squad.

But the N.D. coach saw life as a football game—a hard, mean struggle—and he loved to come up with winning strategies, especially in tight
situations. His players' transgressions had thrown him on the defensive,
thus he decided on an offensive ploy, a plan to negate his real and potential critics, particularly at Notre Dame, as well as possible curbs on his
power over the N.D. athletic department. If his offense worked, he might
even turn a dire situation to his advantage. Rockne's game strategies were
often daring; his off-the-field ones no less so.

> "I noticed in the Chicago papers that Northwestern is trying to interest
> you in their football situation. Such publicity can do no harm, but by all
> means don't take them seriously. There is only one man who can coach a
> Northwestern team and do what they expect him to, and he isn't on
> earth."
>
> —Letter to Rockne from Charlie Bachman, December 9, 1921

While in New York in November, Rockne had complained to Joe
Byrne, Jr., about his low salary at N.D. and how he was not fully appreciated by the school. Byrne passed on the comments to various N.D. administrators and also "enlightened" them with "the fact that there are at
least six colleges here in the East who want [Rockne] as Coach." Indeed,
Rockne's reputation as a coach who produced winners was growing, and
earlier in 1921 he had received a number of unsolicited letters asking
whether he was interested in applying for various head coaching berths.
Then, in late November, Colgate University, a power in eastern football,
inquired about his availability, and alumni of Northwestern University
also sounded him out about moving to their alma mater.

These offers formed the basis of his offense. During the first weekend
in December, he went to Chicago for the annual Big Ten coaches' meeting and spent time with Walter Eckersall of the *Chicago Tribune* as well
as with some Northwestern alumni. Shortly after, Eckersall's sports section published an exclusive report that "the Notre Dame mentor [was]
considering" the soon-to-be-vacant head coaching job at Northwestern.
This maneuver, like Rockne's best football plays, scored a quick touchdown: Byron Kanaley, the most important N.D. alum in Chicago and a
member of President Burns's first board of lay trustees, telegraphed the
coach: "NOTRE DAME MEN GREATLY DISTURBED OVER REPORTS IN TODAY'S PAPER.
ANGUS MCDONALD AND I TALKED SITUATION OVER THOROUGHLY . . . EVERY NO-
TRE DAME MAN IN THE COUNTRY SINCERELY HOPES YOU STAY WITH US."

That same day, Kanaley also sent a special-delivery letter to President
Burns. He and McDonald, an important N.D. alum and a top executive

of the Southern Pacific Railroad, argued that "it is the unanimous opinion of all Notre Dame men that every reasonable effort should be made to keep him [Rockne] at our school," Kanaley adding, "My own suggestion would be a new five-year contract at an increased salary."

The next day more telegrams arrived for Rockne, prompted by the *Chicago Tribune* report: from Iowa State—"WHAT SALARY WOULD YOU CON-SIDER—NAME YOUR OWN TERMS"; and from the University of Cincinnati—"WOULD YOU CONSIDER POSITION AS FOOTBALL COACH." The coach's offensive strategy had lit up the scoreboard, shifting attention from charges about his "out of control" football program to speculation—and fear among N.D. supporters—that he would leave his school.

Minnesota soon joined conference rival Northwestern in the court-ship: "ST. PAUL AND MINNEAPOLIS ALUMNI WANT YOU AS MINNESOTA COACH. WOULD YOU CONSIDER POST? TERMS? ATHLETIC DIRECTORSHIP [ALSO] OPEN HERE. WIRE COLLECT AS EARLY AS POSSIBLE." On December 21, one of the Rockne's friends informed Minnesota that the coach was "seriously considering" Northwestern and "has been offered [$12,000] just to handle football." A day later, the president of the University of Minnesota invited the coach for an on-campus interview.

Before the New Year, however, President Burns short-circuited the outside offers by signing Rockne to a long-term contract with an increase in pay. The N.D. administration—in the midst of the school's most important fund-raising drive, pressured by overwhelming alumni support for the popular coach, and as yet unaware of the Carlinville-Taylorville affair—considered this the best course of action. Nevertheless, Rockne's faculty opponents, led by Father Carey, did not concede defeat, seeing the signing only as a "time-out" in their struggle to gain control of the athletic department.

Was Rockne's strategy merely a ploy to protect himself at Notre Dame and to obtain more security and pay, or would he have actually accepted an outside offer? Schools like Iowa State and Cincinnati, with thin ath-letic traditions, would not have attracted him, but if he had not liked the Notre Dame proposal, the opportunity to coach in the Big Ten might have proved irresistible. Probably he would have refused Northwestern, called at the time "the graveyard of coaches," and gone to Minnesota, his Scandinavian heritage fitting the school and state nicely. When Rockne launched his outside offer maneuver, he did not know where it would lead, but as his subsequent uses of the strategy showed, he was often serious about leaving Notre Dame, and it was only after N.D. administrators met his demands and/or his friends talked him out of going that he reembraced the "Gold and Blue."

In early January 1922, Jesse Harper wrote to his protégé about the outside offers and also commiserated, "I was sorry that you had to drop some of your men for professional football. It will be a good lesson for the rest but I know it will hurt your team for next year." Harper referred only to the Green Bay Packers incident, and Father Carey also had that in mind when, in mid-January, he wrote President Burns, "now would be the proper time to secure from the varsity and prospective varsity men . . . the written pledge or promise that they will not play any professional ball of any kind while in school, and that they make the promise with the understanding that if they violate it, they will be ipso facto expelled from school."

This blanket rule did not please Rockne because it included baseball as well as football, and summer leagues in addition to semipro town games. The Notre Dame coach knew how difficult it was to police athletes away from school and how vulnerable his players would be to breaking this regulation. But Carey wanted to put the responsibility directly on the athlete—via a signed pledge—and force the player to accept the consequences.

Rockne might have derailed this internal N.D. reform if, at the end of January, the Associated Press had not broken the Carlinville-Taylorville affair. The *Chicago Tribune* took the story away from its sports department and put the AP dispatch at the top of the front page, headlining "ILLINOIS BARS NINE ATHLETES FOR 'PRO' GAME," and the following day, still using the AP on the front page, "TWO TOWNS BET $100,000 ON 'RINGER' GAME."

The University of Illinois quickly expelled its athletes involved in the game, including a number of stars with years of eligibility remaining. Coach Bob Zuppke was upset but he also loudly condemned the "other teams in the conference who play professional athletes." Zuppke called for a major cleanup, as did the dean of college coaches, Amos Alonzo Stagg of Chicago.

At Notre Dame, some confusion occurred because two athletes were wrongly accused of having played in the game, but on January 30, the eight participants came forward. The *Chicago American* headlined "NO-TRE DAME PLAYERS CONFESS." They included such stars from the 1921 squad as Roger Kiley, Buck Shaw, Chet Wynne, and Eddie Anderson. Then All-American halfback Johnny Mohardt admitted that he had played for the

Racine (Wisconsin) pro team against the Green Bay Packers in the infamous Milwaukee game. The N.D. administrators acted quickly and banned the players from any further participation in varsity sports.

Father Carey went on the offensive, informing the press: "We will stand for no taint or hint of professionalism here, not even if it wrecks our teams forever. My only regret is that we didn't learn of it sooner." His comments, spread by the wire services, angered alums like Joe Byrne, Jr., who wrote Rockne: "All the New York Alumni are with you . . . strange to say, the whole affair is turning to a boost [for N.D.] here now. If you can keep Fr. Carey quiet, we will soothe it over, but his statements in the press are 'cucoos' [*sic*]."

If Rockne believed Byrne, he misjudged the temper of the times. Possibly in the corrupt world of Wall Street and Tammany Hall in which Byrne existed the incident was seen as somehow boosting Notre Dame, but in the Middle West, especially after the full extent of the Black Sox scandal became public during the summer of 1921, the Carlinville-Taylorville affair seriously hurt the schools involved. Amos Alonzo Stagg led the charge for reform of intercollegiate athletics and urged people with information about college athletes engaging in pro sports to come forward, even if they had "evidence against any of our [University of Chicago] athletes." Stagg also condemned all forms of professional football, later arguing that, as the pro game flourished, the "well-known Carlinville and Taylorville incident . . . is likely to be repeated. There is nothing that a bunch of gamblers will not do for their purpose."

Rockne's friends tried to console him with tales of the widespread corruption in college sports and the hypocrisy of Stagg and the other reformers. Former N.D. player Joe Collins wrote, "I don't have to tell you because you already know [about the cheating taking place,] the bigger the school—the smoother they work it—and as a general rule the coach of the institution generally covers up by making a business of lecturing on 'Purity in College Athletics.' "

Rockne himself railed against the hypocrisy of the reformers, particularly those in the Big Ten, and he wrote to the chairman of that group, charging that three conference athletes had played in the Green Bay Packers' Milwaukee game and gone unpunished. In addition, one of the N.D. athletes involved in the Carlinville fiasco said, "If I told the name of every fellow I played baseball against last summer under an assumed name, there would be few stars left to start the football season next year in the Big Ten."

Some members of the "Notre Dame family," particularly former coach and alumni official Frank Hering, wanted their school to circle the wagons and to fire out at the world, exposing the hypocritical Western Conference schools. The men in the Golden Dome shunned this approach, deciding instead on polite public statements and quiet internal reform of their own athletic department.

On February 4, President Burns wrote Byron Kanaley: "When I see you again I shall want very particularly to get your views about these football 'scandals.'" Burns had a plan and needed to persuade the various Notre Dame constituencies, especially Kanaley and the alumni, to accept it. Changes in intercollegiate sports were coming nationally, and Burns, with his academic vision, wanted Notre Dame in step with the reformers.

That was the bottom line in the spring of 1922 for Knute Rockne. His personal feelings about the reform movement were at odds with the changing national and N.D. sentiments—Rockne basically agreed with Joe Collins (because every football program and its athletes cheated in varying degrees, why single out his?), but he realized that he had to live with the new national realities and also accept the altered circumstances at Notre Dame. He disliked Stagg's and Father Carey's crusade but he had to keep quiet about his displeasure. The coach never feared the future and the challenges to come. He had just faced the most serious one of his career and triumphed. His 1921 "Rocket" had crashed but his outside offer strategy, insulating him from the full fallout of the revelations about his players' professionalism, enabled him to escape—and with increased job security and pay.

17

Building a Better Rocket: 1922

NEW 'BIG 3' RULES CURB ATHLETES

TRANSFERRED STUDENT OUT
Propaganda and Special Inducements
to Promising Schoolboys Are Also Prohibited

COACHES ARE REGULATED
Training of Teams Cannot Begin Prior to One Week Before the College
Term Opens.

—Headlines in *The New York Times,* September 24, 1922

The reform of intercollegiate athletics gained momentum in 1922 when the presidents of Harvard, Yale, and Princeton mandated new rules for their schools' sports programs. They wanted to end the abuses of pay-for-play and tramp athletes, hard-to-control coaches, the recruiting of high school athletes, and the general overemphasis on college football to the detriment of higher education. These presidents not only represented the "Big Three" of university sports but also of American academia, and they hoped that their actions would convince other schools to follow.

The NCAA passed a parallel "ten-point code" at its December 1922 meeting and emphasized its opposition to collegians participating in "professional football" and all forms of "betting" on intercollegiate sports. However, member schools were only *urged but not directed to* adopt" the new NCAA code. The Big Ten, with the faculty representatives pushing the presidents, decided to establish an impartial commissioner to enforce its rules—this imitated major league baseball's appointment of Judge Landis as its first "Czar"—and the conference also moved to clean up the corrupt officiating system by giving the commissioner the power to select and assign all game crews.

The big-time football coaches reacted coolly to the reform movement but, pushed by Stagg and Walter Camp, agreed to a few changes of their own. Like the Big Ten, their association's powerful Rules Committee tried to gain control of the officiating situation: instead of coaches hiring their journalist and other friends as officials, the Rules Committee would now send schools a list of approved men and, for each game, the opposing coaches would agree on four. The football conferences were supposed to insure that coaches abided by the Rules Committee's list.

Rockne decided to fight the Rules Committee on a number of fronts; he was already disputing that group's attempt to ban his "Notre Dame shift" but, as important, he probed the weaknesses in the new regulations on game officials. He realized that coaches at nonconference schools, such as Notre Dame, did not have to accept the committee's selections and could negotiate their choice of officials with that group—soon, he had maneuvered the Rules Committee into sending him lists with the names of Walter Eckersall, Harry Costello, Fred Gardner, J. J. Lipski, and most of his other personal favorites. (Glenn "Pop" Warner at independent Pitt used the same tactic.)

The N.D. coach's correspondence indicates that he never lost control of his game-officiating appointments. In July 1922, Harry Costello of the *Detroit News* complained that the Rules Committee had not approved him for that fall's Notre Dame–Army game; however, through Rockne's influence, Costello ended up working the contest. The downside of the N.D. coach's autonomy was that he had to juggle his plum assignments among competing friends (one of the reasons other coaches were glad to accept the lists). J. J. Lipski, a Chicago businessman, grumbled later that summer, "Don't understand why the devil you can't use me on Oct. 28th and Nov. 30th (your good games, not your 'track meets')?" Lipski wanted the high fees that the N.D. coach paid for the premier home contests and not the lower ones for the obscure opponents; Rockne, however, liked to keep the big games for the sportswriters because they would publicize the events and provide excellent coverage. Lipski added a final comment that reveals the occasional tension between the N.D. coach and his referee-pals as well as the sporting world's attitude on

Prohibition—"Glad you didn't come up to the 7% keg party because the rest of us got more."

Rockne not only had to deal with temperamental game officials but also, closer to home, an increasingly assertive Faculty Board of Control of Athletics. Father Burns, in one of his last actions as president, empowered the board to carry out its constitutional mandate and truly oversee all aspects of the school's intercollegiate athletic program. The coach was extremely unhappy with this new situation, and as a concession to his displeasure, Father Matthew Walsh, when he became president during the summer of 1922, removed the reformist Father Carey from the board. However, as Rockne would learn during the following years with President Walsh, this administrator, a superb poker player during World War I days, usually countered the coach's maneuvering with his own.

Thus Walsh, after selecting the young, academically minded Father Thomas Irving as his vice president and chair of the board, permitted his second in command to appoint anti-Rockne faculty members to the 1922–1923 panel. The coach was an "adjunct member" of the board, and the *Scholastic* noted that he "comes in occasionally and looks the place over. He is officially reported to be the root of all the disturbances."

The board shocked Rockne in September when it informed him that "the scholastic record of each of the candidates for the football team was minutely examined and the list submitted by you is approved with the following exceptions," seven in all. The coach lobbied President Walsh to have the ineligibilities rescinded and was successful for all but one of his athletes. But the board had flexed its new muscles and had given the coach a signal that henceforth it would scrutinize player eligibility. The faculty group also became more active in schedule making. In spite of Rockne's distaste for playing Catholic schools, the board seriously considered a game against the University of Detroit and did place a home-and-away series with Saint Louis University on the 1922–1923 lists. However, it allowed the coach to turn down all other entreaties from Catholic institutions.

The board's dealings with Rockne were delicate and involved a large amount of give-and-take. It tended to yield the most in the coach's areas of expertise, especially the East Coast games, and it approved a match against Georgia Tech in Atlanta for 1922. It also urged Rockne to improve relations with Big Ten schools but fought him when he wanted to schedule coast-to-coast excursions. Finally, it reminded him that it had veto power over *all proposed games* and that it would use it on any West Coast contests. The *Scholastic* summed up the group's work and its relations with the coach: "The board has sometimes felt triumphant and sometimes utterly down and out."

The student journalists took their cues from Rockne about how to portray the board, and one even termed it the Ku Klux Klan's "most intimate imitator." The N.D. coach never disguised his contempt for those board members and other faculty who opposed his management of the athletic department and his plans for unlimited expansion. Francis Wallace, his student press assistant at this time, described Rockne's ongoing feud with the professors: " 'If they know so much,' he would say, 'why aren't they out making some money instead of staying here telling boys how to do it for [salaries of] $4,000 a year.' "

> "Football enticed him, and he taught it with a free heart, despite its commercial faults and the bootlegging aspects of recruiting and subsidizing which New Dominion [Notre Dame] practiced, as did all other schools, but in a minor degree.
> Barney Mack [Knute Rockne] didn't have to cheat; he could play the game fairly and win. When [and if] the time came for football to unmask, he would do it cheerfully, lead in that as he had in other points of its development.
> Meanwhile he taught the game hard."
>
> —From Francis Wallace's roman à clef *Huddle*

Rockne's Boswell of this time later wrote about his experiences with his mentor in a number of novels; he termed his "first book, *Huddle,* a fictionalized story of Notre Dame football in which he [Rockne] was the thinly disguised coach," and Wallace used the same character and even fewer veils in a follow-up, *O'Reilly of Notre Dame.* Probably because of their "insider" style—unpopular in an era of "Gee-Whiz" sportswriting and stubbornly innocent fans—these books quickly disappeared, not even cited in subsequent scholarly works on Rockne. Nevertheless, once the key is turned to unlock them, the reader enters the inner sanctum of Rockne's football program.

According to Wallace, the coach "was not too keen about my first book, *Huddle,*" because his double was tough, sometimes ruthless, and often cynical about college sports. The writer attributed Rockne's coolness to his distaste for "having people probe into his personal life" and record his private opinions and motivations, as Wallace did. Indeed, by 1922, Knute Rockne had started to construct a public image contrary to

Shaking Down the Thunder

his private self, and in 1930, when *Huddle* appeared, the coach had firmly established his high-minded and idealistic persona.

In his public speeches, Rockne liked to appear as an apostle of athletics-as-character-builder and quoted such Greek and Roman maxims as "a sound mind in a sound body." But his counterpart in *Huddle* chooses another classical metaphor when he tells a player, "You're a gladiator . . . Just as much as any fellow who ever stepped into a Roman arena. Every man who puts on a suit to entertain the public for money is a gladiator whether he's fighting for money, fame, alma mater or the love of it."

The coach's view of the football-adoring public was no less clear-eyed: "They pay their money and they must be pleased; if you help them escape from themselves, it's thumbs up; if you bore them or disappoint them—thumbs down." Nor did the coach view his work as an exalted calling, imparting high ideals to young men; rather, "I'm a ringmaster. If I give a good show they like me; if I don't, they'll be barking at my heels —alumni, newspapers, students and the great public at large."

"Not you . . . ," a player protests.

"Just let me have two bad seasons in a row and watch them."

Most biographers of Rockne accept the coach's public persona as his actual self and present him as innocent and idealistic; the Hollywood film renders him saintly at times. However, in ignoring his tough-minded and pragmatic view of the world, the biographers fail to recognize that these qualities were crucial to his strength of personality, his great success, and even his best character traits.

In 1922, because of his pragmatism, he did not ban or shun those players who had caused him so much trouble with their escapades in professional football. A puritan like Stagg would have cut them out of his life, but Rockne did not consider their actions sinful and he never turned on them. Quite the opposite: he helped obtain head coaching positions for Eddie Anderson at a Catholic college in Iowa, for Buck Shaw at the University of Nevada, and for Chet Wynne at Creighton; he also hired Roger Kiley to work with him at Notre Dame. In addition, he located a "day job" for Hunk Anderson in South Bend, retaining him as an unpaid assistant with the promise of full-time future employment; then he kept this commitment in spite of the fact that Anderson continued to play pro football on weekends and Stagg and Yost demanded that Rockne fire Anderson because he was "giving college football a black eye."

The N.D. mentor was always loyal to his "boys," and as in Hunk's case, when loyalty combined with the need for an excellent line coach, he would never yield to abstract reform principles. He saw football and life as battles to be won and, a fierce competitor, he focused his intelligence and energies on ways to win. Over the years, his contempt for Stagg grew as the Chicago coach placed his ideals first and produced losing teams.

Rockne was also loyal to his players because he genuinely liked them; furthermore, he demanded so much from them during their Notre Dame careers that he wanted to reward them afterward. His demands on his athletes and himself helped produce winning teams but also immersed Notre Dame in an increasing number of controversies.

> "First I go to the [N.D.] football field and the whole team is shifting— hike, one, two. Then I walk around the campus and the whole student body is shifting—hike, one, two. Then I go see the president of the school and he's shifting—hike, one, two—and do you know, he's the only one doing it legally."
>
> —Bob Zuppke, longtime football coach
> of the University of Illinois

In the early 1920s, Rockne began to perfect the famous "Notre Dame shift"—presnap movements by the backfield so that they were in motion as soon as the ball was in play. In the 1921 Army game, the West Point coaches became so upset with the N.D. shift that they threatened to call the game at halftime; Rockne magnanimously switched to a shotgun formation for the second half and his team continued to pile on the points. (He learned an early form of the shift from Jesse Harper; the scene in *Knute Rockne—All American* of him conceiving it while watching a vaudeville chorus line is pure fantasy.)

Rival coaches considered Rockne's shift illegal and, in 1922, pressured the Rules Committee of the coaches' association to legislate against it. Then the N.D. coach discovered a loophole in the new rules and created an improved version of his offense. The shift controversy continued through the decade, and each time the Rules Committee changed the regulations, Rockne went around or through the new rules—and also accused the committee of discriminating against him and his Catholic institution. For some administrators and faculty at Big Ten and Ivy schools, this ongoing dispute confirmed their view of Notre Dame football as an "outlaw" program.

The Notre Dame shift perfectly fit Knute Rockne's approach to football. Being only five-foot-eight and having learned as a player how to nullify the size and strength of the behemoths, as a coach he preferred quick, smart athletes and he designed his formations to utilize his players' speed and agility. In addition, being a workaholic, he demanded that his teams drill until they had mastered his plays and could execute his offense with absolute precision.

Harry Stuhldreher, who began his varsity quarterbacking career with the 1922 squad, testified to his coach's perfectionism: "Don't forget, when a play goes wrong [in practice], run it over again," Rockne always said; "We leave nothing to chance, everything has to be right." Adam Walsh, a young center on the 1922 team, explained that the coach "spent hours and hours to get precision timing, blocking, and tackling. I worked continuously in passing the ball back, along with blocking and tackling."

Rockne also saw a social and political dimension to his coaching, telling the chair of the Rules Committee: "I have always tried to coach the clever style of football as I appreciate the fact that whenever, in the old days [with battering-ram tactics], Notre Dame outplayed some teams such as Michigan, we were immediately called the 'Dirty Irish' by the 'Lily White' folks" and accused of brutality.

By the early 1920s, Rockne's techniques had gained the attention of fellow coaches and some sportswriters. A coaching colleague described Notre Dame as "one of the few colleges with a real football system, and Coach Rockne is the man who has developed that system to its present state of perfection." And, in 1922, a number of big-city sportswriters began visiting the campus and observing practice, Walter Turnbull of the *New York Herald* noting, "There was no waste motion and no hesitation. Rockne is supreme in his domain and he has no use for slackers. The moment that a man showed any sign of taking things easy the coach was after him like a hornet. He knew what he wanted—and he got it."

"K. K. Rockne is the latest to prove that nothing can long resist full-flung determination. Phoenix-like, he has risen from the ashes of last year's post-season disappointments. . . ."

—*The Scholastic,* "Football Number," 1922

By spring practice of 1922, the N.D. coach, by nature optimistic and full of self-confidence, looked forward to the new season. The *Chicago Tribune* stated his most serious problem: "The disqualifications [of players] together with graduations . . . wreck Notre Dame's chances in football during coming seasons. Coach Knute Rockne will not have a single regular around whom to build the 1922 eleven."

The N.D. coach set about constructing a new team from inexperienced sophomores, and the eventual results, two years later, were the Four Horsemen and Seven Mules. But during spring practice 1922, when he had the departing varsity suit up against the young players for the first Notre Dame "Spring Game" and he watched as the vets mauled the youngsters, he acknowledged that he had many hours of practice ahead. Yet, working with malleable sophomores was easier than trying to deal with war vets and semipros, and he admitted that he was "glad" when the latter group left, adding sarcastically, "They know more football than I do."

Rockne's scheduling technique of opening the season with two easy home games worked perfectly in 1922 as his young team ran over Kalamazoo, 46–0, and then Saint Louis University, 26–0, to gain confidence for the trip to Purdue. Unfortunately for him, local fans were wise to his scheduling trick and many refused to turn out, rendering the total profit from the openers only $811.

The Boilermakers had a new coach, Jimmy Phelan, an N.D. player when Rockne assisted Harper, but the pupil had not learned enough from his masters and N.D. triumphed, 20–0. The Notre Dame student association rented special trains to take a thousand rooters to Lafayette, and in the *Scholastic,* an undergraduate named John J. Cavanaugh wrote about the trip (Cavanaugh began his long N.D. career in this period and was university president from 1946 to 1952).

The following week, Notre Dame rested at home with DePauw, 34–7, in preparation for the crucial trip to Georgia Tech. Not only was the team's first visit to the Deep South financially significant—the total football season profit so far was only $3,547—it was also symbolically important. The Ku Klux Klan, its membership already over four million, was growing rapidly, Atlanta was its national headquarters, and Catholics were one of its primary objects of hate.

By scheduling the game in the South, Rockne had pushed a huge pile of Notre Dame chips onto the public table, and some N.D. faculty and even alumni criticized him for taking too large a risk—they worried that a lopsided defeat would humiliate the school and, by extension, many American Catholics. Rockne needed to redeem his gamble with a convincing win.

Usually he gave one emotional locker room speech a season, and in

1922, he chose the Georgia Tech game as the occasion. However, according to witnesses, instead of beginning by waking up the echoes, he quietly went over the starting lineup and game plans. Then, as he usually did, he read a number of telegrams from important well-wishers. Finally, he retrieved a crumpled telegraph form from his pocket and hesitantly explained that his six-year-old son, Billy, was extremely ill in the hospital and that the wire was his boy's message to the team: "PLEASE WIN THIS GAME FOR MY DADDY. IT'S VERY IMPORTANT TO HIM."

Billy was a team mascot, and the young Notre Dame players reacted to this request by roaring out of the locker room. Ignoring the anti-Catholic taunts of the crowd and the unsettling rebel yells of the Georgia Tech students, the Fighting Irish put away the southerners, 13–3.

When the squad returned to the train station at South Bend, halfback Jim Crowley spotted "Little Billy Rockne rushing up, whooping and hollering . . . You never saw a healthier kid in all your life. He hadn't been in a hospital since the week he was born." But Crowley and his teammates were not angry at their coach for tricking them, attributing the "ploy" to Rockne's desire to motivate his athletes and his obsession with winning.

Notre Dame not only won the Georgia Tech game and the symbolic victory but took home almost $7,000 from the 13,828 white spectators and the 18 "Negroes" who bought tickets. The following week, the Homecoming game, featuring the first visit of the Indiana University Hoosiers to northern Indiana, harvested over $10,000 for N.D. The enlarged Cartier Field held approximately 15,000 and accommodated another 3,000 standees. However, for this game, with special trains arriving from Chicago, Cleveland, and Pittsburgh, as well as railroad cars with IU fans from Bloomington and Indianapolis, the newspapers estimated the overflowing crowd at 22,000. The *Scholastic* headlined its front-page article about the event "THE FATTED CALF—WITH DRESSING."

Rockne hired students to assist him with stadium operations, and Father Hugh "Pepper" O'Donnell was in charge of alumni events. The Homecoming festivities were more elaborate than ever before and they included the launching of the *Notre Dame Alumnus* magazine, with the first volume devoted mainly to the past and present of the school's athletic teams as well as full-page ads for "A Portrait Bust of Knute K. Rockne" and phonograph records of "The Victory March." In addition, alumni and students could now watch motion pictures of the Georgia Tech victory (and later in the season, of other important N.D. games).

Fueling the weekend celebration was the easy win over Indiana, 27–0, as well as large quantities of liquor consumed before and after the game, mainly in South Bend at the Oliver Hotel. Although Prohibition, begun in 1919, was effective in much of the Midwest, it never took hold in areas with large Catholic populations like northern Indiana. Notre Dame's Homecoming was never a dry or dull affair.

After the tumultuous weekends in Atlanta and South Bend, the following week's trip to West Point was somewhat anticlimactic, as was the 0–0 game and the $400 financial loss due to the low Army payout and high travel costs. Some New York sportswriters tried to describe the contest in overheated prose, leaning heavily on its "hard and bitterly fought" aspects; others, like Ed Sullivan (the future TV host), just admired the Notre Dame squad—"the smartest football team we have seen this season."

When the team returned to South Bend late on Sunday night, the entire Notre Dame student body and many faculty and staff members were at the railroad station to hail them. The *Scholastic* noted that "welcoming the football team . . . gains a value far transcending the immediate excitement of being in the crowd . . . The important concern was the tribute" to the coach and players, to the Notre Dame football tradition, and to the "Fighting Irish spirit." The students loved the railroad station hoopla and, as alumni, remembered it fondly. The 1922 student reporter wrote, "Coming through South Bend with crimson torches, yelling one's fool head off, is a worthy deed of praise to the backfield and line which held Army to a tie. It is a tribute to the masculine side of Notre Dame's educational idea." These events were important rituals for the N.D. community and emphasized the uniqueness of the school.

The remainder of the 1922 season produced new highs and lows for the coach, team, and fans. In an easy 31–3 victory over Butler in Indianapolis, the new backfield star, Paul Castner, shattered his hip, ending a career that had promised to eclipse Gipp's. The *Scholastic* devoted the front page of its next issue to an open letter of condolence to him in his hospital bed.

The following week marked the team's first trip to Pittsburgh during the Rockne era and it opened a new vista for Notre Dame football. The coach had scheduled the excursion because of the requests from the area's N.D. alumni, the opportunity to play an easy opponent (Carnegie Tech), and the hope of a big payday in a major league ballpark (Forbes Field). The 19–0 win before thirty thousand spectators, along with the

$9,000 check, fulfilled his expectations, and this game began the long, almost continuous series of Notre Dame visits to the "Steel City"—in the 1920s versus Carnegie Tech and from 1930 on, mainly against Pitt. These trips not only proved financially profitable but also amassed many nonalumni fans in the Catholic communities of western Pennsylvania, eastern Ohio, and West Virginia; the "Coal Field Alums" loved the Fighting Irish victories over the teams of Pittsburgh's Protestant universities.

For the 1922 game, the N.D. fans numbered about five thousand but a year later "some 15,000 rooters in the Notre Dame section sang, yelled and cheered . . . Rock and his Wonder Team from the West." By the 1930s, over half of the large Pittsburgh crowds supported the Gold and Blue. (An added benefit of these visits was that Rockne and subsequent N.D. coaches, right up to the present, have been able to mine this region's rich seam of high school football players—many raised in rabid Notre Dame families—for the Fighting Irish roster.)

Soon after the Pittsburgh triumph, Rockne began to wonder about the wisdom of the road warrior schedule as well as the annual series with Nebraska. The *Dome* noted that "just four days later with only one day of rest between a 1200 mile jump from Pittsburgh to Lincoln," the team lost the season finale, 14–6, to the Cornhuskers and also endured anti-Catholic taunts from the hostile Nebraska fans.

The young team ended the campaign with an 8–1–1 record, although only 4–1–1 against major opponents. The December debacle of the previous year as well as the perfect records of Princeton, Cornell, and Iowa removed the Irish from national championship or bowl game consideration. The perfectionist side of Rockne was dissatisfied but the realist part appreciated the work of the young team as well as the fact that more fans had paid to see Notre Dame football in 1922 than ever before. The final games injected almost $25,000 into the football coffers, bringing the season's net profit to $32,020; this not only covered the annual athletic department deficit but, for the first time, put a five-figure sum of money into the university treasury.

Rockne was pleased with the 1922 season and also with the praise of the N.D. students; their newspaper ended its "Season Review" stating, "We believe that, while they [the national journalists] are picking their All-Americans, they might as well open up a new position on their mythical eleven and choose our own Knute K. Rockne for All-American coach."

18

On the Launch Pad: 1923

"[Rockne] took a truly giant step in the early 1920s when he convinced West Point officials that the Notre Dame–Army game had outgrown the remote facilities on the Hudson.

'Let's play in New York City,' said the astute Rockne, knowing how much razzmatazz the press would make of it. . . .

The game became the biggest annual sporting event in New York."

—Jerry Brondfield, *Rockne*

The biographies of the Notre Dame coach as well as the histories of his school mystify the origins of the N.D.–Army series in New York City. In addition, these breezy accounts assign all of the credit for changing the game site to the N.D. coach; however, archival material at Notre Dame and West Point reveals that Army officials opposed the move to New York for a number of years and that N.D. President Matthew Walsh finally brought it off in 1923.

Immediately after the 1922 contest, many eastern Notre Dame alumni, increasingly unhappy with the difficulty of traveling to and from West Point as well as the lack of accommodations for them there, wrote to Walsh demanding that he try to switch the game to New York City or consider abandoning it. The Notre Dame administrator agreed with their complaints, adding that he did not mind a "break with West Point" because he disliked "playing a team" whose members "according to all recognized college playing standards would be considered ineligible." He also acknowledged: "For some time I have been urging a home and home arrangement with Dartmouth as a substitute. . . . There is so much similarity between [the masculine] spirit of Dartmouth and Notre Dame I believe they would be ideal rivals." Walsh suggested a game with the Ivy school for "next year in either Boston or New York."

The N.D. president's position forced the West Point authorities to agree to move the 1923 contest to the Polo Grounds in New York. Moreover, the opening of negotiations with Dartmouth enabled Walsh to pull off another scheduling coup—he convinced another Ivy school, Princeton, to host the Irish the week after the Army game. Princeton offered only a flat $5,000 guarantee and no opportunity of a gate split at its large stadium, but Notre Dame accepted for the prestige of visiting one of the Big Three schools of American academia and college football.

At a winter football banquet in the Oliver Hotel honoring the previous season's team, Rockne announced the 1923 schedule, ten games in all. Again, few major opponents would visit Notre Dame but he promised that many more would come in the future if the city of South Bend and the school would build a stadium; the mayor agreed to form a committee to explore the matter.

One of the featured speakers at the banquet was sportswriter-referee Harry Costello. He had moved to the *Detroit Free Press* but continued to help N.D. and its coach with promotional articles. Rockne reciprocated by scratching Costello's back in many places, including a nice speaker's fee for the banquet and officiating assignments for the following season. In early 1923, the Detroit journalist informed Rockne that various Big Ten coaches classified him "at the top of your profession. I am taking great pains to see that it is properly published IN THE NEWSPAPERS at the right time." Other sportswriters, particularly the *Chicago Tribune*'s Walter Eckersall, also promoted Rockne's career, and the coach continued to select them as game officials (one player recalled that, after the 1923 Army game in which "Eck" officiated, by chance he "rode back to the hotel in a cab with Eckersall and Rock").

Even with the ten-game schedule announced, Notre Dame continued to receive requests from all over the country for additional appearances. The southern California N.D. alumni pleaded persistently for a December game against USC in the recently built Los Angeles Coliseum. Rockne strongly favored the L.A. contest but the faculty board opposed

it, wanting to blunt the growing criticism of "Rockne's Ramblers." Then
Father McGinn, the school's full-time fund-raiser, sided with the California alums, linking the game to the endowment campaign and predicting
disaster on the West Coast if the university refused to send the team.
President Walsh, however, in one of the first Notre Dame articulations of
the separation of football and institutional fund-raising, vetoed the trip
and pointed out the fallacy in McGinn's argument:

> As far as the probable reaction on the work of the [fund-raising] commit-
> tee is concerned, I question very seriously whether a Coast game would
> be of any assistance. I can easily see you or Father Burns trying to talk
> endowment or building fund with everybody's head filled with football.

For every request to the Golden Dome to emphasize football by
allowing the team to play additional games in faraway locations came a
letter or newspaper report questioning whether Notre Dame ran a "pro
football program" and was serious about academics. A trustee of the
University of Toledo wrote President Walsh in 1923 that a fellow trustee
had charged: "The N.D. football team is barred from the Western Conference because it pays its athletes and other schools do not." As a Catholic, the accusation disturbed her and she wondered, "Is this just K.K.K.
propaganda?"

Walsh replied that the rumors about paying athletes were "a malicious lie," and said: "Notre Dame observes in every detail the rules that
govern institutions that are members of the Western Conference." He
also suggested that the Big Ten would not admit his school into its ranks
because the disputes between the conference members and N.D. "have
resolved themselves into a theological question," that is, their prejudice
against Catholic institutions.

This public stance pushed Walsh to greater vigilance over his athletic
department and an awareness of the two-edged sword of fame and fortune from college sports. Whether his football coach liked it or not, the
N.D. president could not permit much deviation from the Big Ten rules
—as it was, the Irish ten-game schedule was longer than the conference's
limit of eight games per school—and Walsh ordered the faculty board to
enforce the rules, especially such high-profile rules as athletes not playing
more than three varsity years.

Thus, in 1923, when the N.D. authorities discovered from articles in
the New York papers that one of Rockne's starting linemen—listed as a
junior—had played a season at Fordham as well as two at Notre Dame,

they ended his college career. Walsh and the faculty board realized that N.D. football had become too public and too scrutinized to permit questionable athletes on the team.

Even the Notre Dame alumni, the group most rabid about promoting football and giving their beloved "Rock" free rein, were becoming defensive about the public and private accusations against the school. An editorial in a 1923 issue of the *Alumnus* complained: "In the desire to explain how Notre Dame accomplishes the seemingly impossible in football, we have unfortunately been misrepresented [by the press as well as hostile individuals]." The magazine attempted to arm its readers against the charges of misconduct by listing the admission, academic, and athletic requirements for Notre Dame athletes. However, the *Alumnus* did not mention Rockne's special recruiting of athletes or the jobs on and off campus that he made available to them.

> "About 1919, there began to spread . . . a contagion of ready assistance to promising athletes. . . . The result is today that, notwithstanding many statements to the contrary, the colleges and universities of the United States are confronted with acute problems of recruiting and subsidizing [athletes], especially with respect to intercollegiate football. . . .
>
> In the United States, the saying is common that 'every athlete is a needy athlete.'"
>
> —The Carnegie Foundation
> for the Advancement of Teaching, Bulletin 23

Rockne always maintained in private conversation and correspondence that other coaches, particularly in the Big Ten, were cheating in multiple ways, and according to the Carnegie Foundation investigators, he was right. However, he never admitted publicly that during his regime he had an increasingly efficient recruiting and subsidizing system and that he pushed the Notre Dame rules to the limit, sometimes breaking them when he deemed it necessary.

From 1922 on, the faculty board of control attempted to police athletic department recruiting and subsidization. In a 1923 letter to President Walsh, a Chicago alum who had long recruited football players for N.D. complained that the new internal rules were crippling his activities: "I have several times been assured by those in charge of such matters at the University [particularly athletic department personnel], that everything was arranged for a certain boy [whom I recruited], only to have them come back after I had notified the boy, and inform me that nothing could be done" for the recruit. The problem, according to the alum, was that Father McBride, in charge of admissions and student employment, "says that after conferring with Father Irving [the vice president and head of the athletic board], it will be impossible to find a place for the boy."

President Walsh had to balance the faculty board's desire to conform to Western Conference rules with his coach's determination to produce the best possible football team. Walsh tended to side with the academics but he never decisively halted Rockne or his supporters' activities.

The recruiting and retention of the players who became the Four Horsemen and Seven Mules typify Rockne's methods. By 1923, most of them were starters and potential stars but they had arrived at Notre Dame through the usual routes.

Fullback Elmer Layden had played on high school teams in Davenport, Iowa, coached by Walter Halas. After the latter became a Rockne assistant, he recruited Layden, offering him, according to the athlete, "a scholarship to Notre Dame—room, board, and tuition in exchange for a part-time job and . . . for doing what I enjoyed most, playing sports." Big Ten and Notre Dame rules clearly prohibited such subsidization. The conference officially banned all "financial aid for athletic skill" whether granted by school officials, alumni, or boosters—of course, widespread violations of the rules occurred at almost all conference schools.

Halfback Jim Crowley came from Green Bay, Wisconsin, and Curly Lambeau, the Packers' coach, praised his talents to Rockne, adding that "Notre Dame is his choice if he can be taken care of." Crowley received an athletic scholarship similar to Layden's. (In spite of Lambeau's hurting Rockne by playing three N.D. athletes in the infamous Milwaukee game, the Notre Dame coach was far too pragmatic to shun Lambeau's subsequent scouting tips.)

Quarterback Harry Stuhldreher and halfback Don Miller were products of Notre Dame's athletic culture. The former had an older brother at the school who arranged his deal for him. Miller, with three older brothers who had earned N.D. football monograms, never considered any other college. Internal recruiting also produced two of the Seven Mules from interhall football; other linemen came through Rockne's regular external network; for example, Noble Kizer was scouted and helped by former coach Frank Hering, and center and captain Adam Walsh was aided by Los Angeles alum Leo Ward.

By 1923, the recruiting system functioned so well that, according to the *Dome,* Rockne's freshman coach "found it difficult to pick a team from more than one hundred aspirants, many of whom had come to Notre Dame with excellent football reputations." Inevitably, many recruits were disappointed and some left N.D. after a single year. The future NFL star Johnny "Blood" McNally enrolled for 1922–1923, failed to impress the coaches, and dropped out during the spring semester. He later commented: "My one contribution to Notre Dame football was that I used to write Harry Stuhldreher's English poetry papers for him." McNally, a free spirit, also "got in some trouble around Saint Patrick's Day" because of "some pretty good celebrating"; Rockne would try to save his "Monogram Men" from severe disciplinary penalties but not the nonroster athletes.

Stuhldreher, in his book about Rockne—ghostwritten by his wife and a professional journalist—commented on the subsidization system, particularly how the coach obtained summer jobs at the beach resort of Cedar Point, Ohio, for his varsity starters (the same beach where Dorais and Rockne had perfected their version of the forward pass).

Adam Walsh also explained Rockne's South Bend job assistance program, arranged through the coach's contacts with local boosters and his control of season tickets. As a lowly freshman, Walsh worked for the gas company; as a sophomore on the varsity, for a tobacco firm; but, as a junior starter, "Rock gave me and three others the parking concession" for N.D. athletic events, and even though the players farmed out much of the work to student assistants, they still made a handsome profit. "In my senior year Rock gave the four backs [Horsemen] and myself the program concession for home games," worth "$1,500 each" from soliciting program ads, plus an additional amount from program sales. Even in the Roaring Twenties, these lucrative deals for athletes totally violated intercollegiate rules; however, they were the norm for star players in most bigtime football programs.

All of the coach's arranged jobs were beyond the control of Father McBride and his stewardship of on-campus employment for students trying to work off their N.D. bills. Rockne, by tapping his booster friends, could also help his football players pay their Notre Dame tuition and room and board fees; in Francis Wallace's *Huddle,* the coach tells a prospect, "You move out here and I'll see that you get five hundred dollars off regular student rates," that is, someone would pay it for him. Then the coach, in true Rockne fashion, tells the boy that he's right to be cynical about college football: "There are things [in it] I don't approve of either, but it's too big now, and in the meantime we'll just go along with things as we find them."

Later in the book, some athletes explain other benefits of enrolling at New Dominion [Notre Dame]:

In the first place you've got Barney [Rockne], best coach in the business; stick with Barney and you'll get an education touring the country which you'll never get listening to a lot of goofy profs; a guy has as good a chance of making All-American right here as any place in the country.

Wallace was so inside Rockne's world that his description of the recruiting and retention system remains the single best account of how his mentor operated. But, as this writer makes clear, the system pleased the recruits as much as the coach; in the book, after the coach persuades a prize prospect to enlist, the scene ends with the boy elated, walking "down the path with his head somewhere near the golden dome that topped the administration building."

In the 1920s, the men who ran the school from inside that dome did not view Rockne's system as benignly as did Wallace, but they were only able to slow it down, never derail it.

"Barney told him, 'I'm going to start the shock troops [the second string] against them [Army]. . . . When the regulars go in, we'll pass. . . .'

So, equipped with this knowledge, Spike [the N.D. student press assistant] immediately wrote pieces designed for Army eyes; pieces which sang the blues; which told of the battered condition of the Irish regulars and the utter necessity of playing them a full sixty minutes because Barney could not trust his second-stringers.

Football was war, Barney always said, and if the enemy wished to believe what it read in the papers [too bad for them]."

—From Francis Wallace's roman à clef *O'Reilly of Notre Dame*

Early in his head coaching career, Rockne realized the value of a good press—not only for the positive publicity for his program but also to confuse his on- and off-the-field opponents. Jesse Harper had employed students to help publicize some home games but Rockne, taking the practice much further, hired a student press assistant to work full-time for him during the football season. The N.D. coach supplied the material for stories, instructed the assistant on how to shape it, and vetted the copy before release. In addition, Rockne told Midwest newspaper editors to accept articles only from his official press assistant—and to pay the student for the stories—and not to publish anything from on- or off-campus free-lancers. In this way, the N.D. coach tried to control and manipulate the news about his football team.

His first student assistant was Arch Ward, later sports editor of the *Chicago Tribune.* Ward's biographer commented, "Archie's job, quite simply, was to see to it that the football news from Notre Dame was what Knute Rockne wanted it to be—no more, no less." Ward learned the publicist's trade well, and ever after "the journalism that Ward practiced had as its chief objective the glorification of a man [Rockne] and an institution [Notre Dame]."

When Ward left N.D.—he never graduated as he later claimed—the student press job went to Francis Wallace. As a freshman, Wallace had crossed Rockne by reporting on N.D. football for the maverick *South Bend News-Times,* a paper often at odds with the school. However, the N.D. coach recognized Wallace's talent and co-opted him by appointing him Ward's successor. For three seasons, Rockne taught the student his methods and, a few years later, "demanded that I admit that I had learned more journalism from him than I had from the [Notre Dame] Journalism Department, with which he was conducting a feud at the time." The latter quarrel concerned the coach's definition of journalism-as-puffery (Wallace waffled on the answer because, although he revered Rockne, he never lost his independence or his desire to tell the real story).

In spite of the coach's narrow approach to journalism, he was not a provincial, concerned only about the local papers. Wallace related how, because the student assistant spent game days in the press box, Rockne "always wanted to know what the big-shot [urban] writers had to say about his team—and him," and Wallace collected the information. This combined with the coach's sense of how "to put over" his team and himself—he had explained to Ward: "New York is the heart of the matter. That's the big time. When they start noticing us there, everybody else will fall in line."

During a decade of N.D. visits to West Point, from 1913 on, the New York metropolitan press—twelve daily papers as well as the headquarters of the major wire services and press syndicates—noticed the Notre Dame football team and its coach only for the two or three days a year around the Army game. The remainder of the time, the program as well as the Catholic school were far beyond the Hudson River horizon. In 1923, Rockne set out to change Gotham's perception of his team and himself.

"Several features not scheduled as part of the program developed because the [1923 N.D.–Army] game was played in Squire Ebbets' band
box park in Brooklyn. . . .

Before the game began there was a rush on one of the main gates and
the police in charge promptly solved this difficulty with masterly intelligence by deciding to refuse admission to anybody, no matter whether
the would-be spectator carried a ticket or not. . . .

[However, inside,] the Brooklyn police force and all their little pals
were viewing the pastime from the sidelines."

—*New York World,* October 14, 1923

Army and Notre Dame had signed a contract to play the 1923 game
in the Polo Grounds but the park's resident baseball team, the New York
Giants, made it to the World Series and pushed the football game out.
Joe Byrne, Jr., billing himself as "Eastern representative, University of
Notre Dame," helped move the contest to Brooklyn's Ebbets Field, and
he signed the contract for his alma mater; consenting for West Point was
their manager of athletics, Captain Matthew Ridgway (years later, a celebrated army commander).

Byrne, with Rockne's encouragement, also sold and distributed over a
thousand tickets and arranged hotel accommodations for the N.D. team
and traveling party. In addition, Byrne fed the big-city dailies the
pregame articles authored by Wallace.

The 1923 coverage by the metropolitan press indicates, however, that
Notre Dame did not instantly become New York's beloved "Fighting
Irish"—New York journalists still did not use the nickname, and the
"subway alumni" had yet to deposit their tokens. The *New York Daily
News,* the paper with the largest Irish working-class readership, gave
almost no coverage to the 1923 Notre Dame–Army game; it focused its
sports pages on the Giants–Yankees World Series—Casey Stengel was
the hitting star—and horse racing and boxing.

New York newspapers with middle-class readers, such as the *Post* and
Telegram, also gave the N.D. eastern trip minor coverage, and those
dailies with university-educated subscribers, such as the *New York Times*
and the *New York Herald,* never shifted their focus from eastern college
football. Only the downscale *World* and the *Brooklyn Eagle,* because of
the local angle, gave the N.D.–Army contest ample space.

Nevertheless, Joe Byrne, Jr., easily peddled all of his tickets, mainly to
N.D. alums and friends of alums as well as to "inhabitants and patrons of
lower Broadway," and the game sold out the Ebbets Field "bandbox."

Including Byrne's sale, Notre Dame made a profit of $19,400 from the estimated thirty thousand fans.

Most important of all for supporters of the Catholic school, in this first big-city appearance against Army, their team performed exceptionally well, easily winning 13–0. The squad had warmed up for the game with home victories over Kalamazoo and Lombard, and because of Rockne's rigorous training program, the players were in top condition. Showing quickness and speed for all four quarters, they wore the Cadets down. Army had played two previous games, but toward the end of this one, its defense was "dangerously close to a collapse from sheer exhaustion" (*Telegram*). The N.D. men had such an easy time that they began taunting the Army stars, asking whether the rows of stripes on their uniforms signified their many years of college football before enlisting at West Point.

Because the Golden Dome administrators wanted to avoid Notre Dame's being placed in a similar "outlaw" category, they insisted that the players return to campus between the Army and Princeton games, even though it meant spending much of their week on trains. Vice President Irving explained that it was "necessary for us to have the boys miss as few classes as possible . . . we do not want to give others an opportunity to criticize us."

> "Mr. Lawrence Perry, prominent [wire service] sportswriter . . . opens the subject of Notre Dame with the following sentence: 'Notre Dame professors accompanied the football eleven to Princeton and conducted recitations throughout the trip. This is the usual practice. . . .'
>
> Of course it is possible that this was the case. But if there were professors accompanying the team, they must have slept in that rather unprofessorial space between the berths and the Pullman floor. . . . Mr. Perry's opening statement is very interesting as a dream."
>
> —*Notre Dame Daily,* November 1, 1923

Lawrence Perry was one of the first national sportswriters to focus on the Notre Dame football phenomenon, and he became very friendly with Rockne. The N.D. coach fed him the story about professors accompanying the team, and like most journalists of the time, Perry was either too lazy to check the facts and/or chose to use the tale to help promote the source. Rockne liked to put out this kind of counterpropaganda and he was pleased by the wide syndication of Perry's article; however, when he read the *Notre Dame Daily*'s jibe, he felt betrayed by the student journalists and wanted the issue of the paper destroyed to prevent "outside writers" from discovering the facts of the case. (This was the first daily in Notre Dame history, and—in part due to Rockne's displeasure with it—it lasted only one academic year, N.D. reverting to the weekly *Scholastic*, which, with its long lead time, allowed the authorities, including the coach, to censor "objectionable" articles.)

However, most New York sports journalists in 1923 did not visit or inquire deeply about Notre Dame, still regarding it as just another midwestern opponent for their favorite eastern teams. As a hedge against a subpar Princeton performance, one writer pointed out that "Rockne had his men out for practice a few weeks before the agreement of the Big Three [about the start of fall football] would permit [Coach] Bill Roper to call practice at Princeton." Another noted that "for Notre Dame this game is a major affair," a "peak" of its season, whereas for Princeton, the big matches would come later against Harvard and Yale.

In fact, N.D.'s first trip to Princeton was one of the most important games of the Rockne era, not only for the chance to play a founding school of American football but, as significantly, because of the social context. Even more than the trip to Georgia Tech in the Klan-infested South, the Princeton visit represented a crucial challenge for Notre Dame and the Irish Catholic community. The game allowed the Fighting Irish to symbolically battle their most entrenched antagonists, the Protestant Yankees, embodied by snooty Princeton. The resurgent Klan was a fairly new phenomenon, but Protestant contempt for the "Papists" was as old as the first immigration from Ireland, and even in the 1920s, "NINA" signs—"No Irish Need Apply"—still appeared in shop windows and want ads. A large part of Notre Dame's subsequent football fame, and the fervent support of huge numbers of middle-class and poor Catholics for the Fighting Irish, resulted from these clashes with—and triumphs over —opponents claiming superiority in class and wealth.

Like all ancien régimes, the Princeton Tigers were neither prepared for nor even aware of what swept over them on October 20, 1923. They had beaten Georgetown, 17–0, the previous week, and although not expecting a "cakewalk" against the midwestern Catholic school that had defeated Army, they could not begin to handle the speed and execution of the Irish attack. N.D. routed the Ivy power, 25–2, as over thirty thousand fans sat glumly through "the first defeat for the Tiger since the fall of 1921 and her most crushing reverse [in years]" (*World*).

The Notre Dame students followed the contest at the Gridgraphie in the gymnasium and afterward celebrated into the night. A few days later, the school held a huge welcoming ceremony for the team's return from the East. Various dignitaries addressed the crowd, pointing out the importance of the victory and lauding the "Notre Dame spirit" as well as Rockne and the players. An Indiana state senator (and N.D. alum) pronounced, "I think a lot of my friend Rockne but I was most fond of him Saturday night when I learned that he had twisted the Tiger's tail."

Praise continued for months, and President Walsh and Rockne received many spontaneous letters of congratulation. A typical one arrived in January 1924 from a Massachusetts resident, Henry A. Sullivan:

> Permit one of the great unknown to extend his compliments to a great team and a great coach. I was at the Princeton game and also at the Follies that night when you [Rockne] were standing out in back and Will Rogers called you down . . . to be introduced. Those two shows were about as good as I ever hope to see in one day.
>
> Around this town [Salem, Massachusetts] I occupy a sort of commanding position these days because of the fact that I saw Notre Dame play.

The remainder of the 1923 season was dramatically anticlimactic but financially profitable—the Princeton game, with its low guarantee and high travel costs, had netted only $811 for Notre Dame. The following Saturday, the Irish won at home against Georgia Tech, 35–7, before a capacity crowd of twenty thousand, a net profit of almost $13,000 for N.D.

Next, the Homecoming game against a weak Purdue squad resulted in an easy Irish victory, 34–7, another capacity crowd, and a large payday. The Homecoming program was more elaborate than in previous years and, in addition to the usual bonfires and barbecues, included a Saturday morning "Monogram mass" for current and returning lettermen and two Sunday high masses.

The season ran downhill when the trip to Nebraska again resulted in the only N.D. loss of the year, 14–7, and increasingly bad feelings between the schools because of the rabidly anti-Catholic Lincoln fans. The *Notre Dame Daily* published an editorial so critical of Cornhusker "hospitality" that Rockne sent a conciliatory letter to the Nebraska student

newspaper differentiating between the "courteous" university community and the "remarks and actions made by outside hoodlums and small
town sports who happened to attend the game."

Each year the anti-Catholic mob in Lincoln became more antagonis-
tic toward the Notre Dame players and fans. However, Rockne uncharacteristically played the peacemaker and wanted to continue the series,
possibly because of the excellent paydays for his athletic department—
the 1923 net for N.D. was a substantial $16,026; that sum was eight times
larger than the profit from the following week's 34–7 home field win over
Butler. The team immediately returned to the road for an easy 26–0
victory in Pittsburgh over Carnegie Tech and handsome gate receipts.

For Rockne, the final game, against Saint Louis University on
Thanksgiving Day, proved the wisdom of not playing fellow Catholic
schools. Not only did it draw a disappointing crowd of nine thousand in
Saint Louis and provide a mediocre payout but the Irish struggled to a
13–0 win. Before the game, the N.D. coach had received information
that three members of the Saint Louis team had previously "played four
years [of] college ball" and six others were ineligible for such violations as
playing "professional football," but he could not accuse a Catholic institution of such blatant cheating and had to watch the game, teeth clenched.

With the team's 9–1 record, "feelers" came from the Rose Bowl committee, but the faculty board adamantly opposed a West Coast trip. Thus
the N.D. coach and athletic director closed his financial books on the
1923 campaign: almost 200,000 fans paying to see the Fighting Irish, and
a net profit of close to $70,000. For the first time, the Notre Dame
football program not only covered the athletic department salaries and
deficit but also made a substantial contribution, close to $50,000, to the
university treasury. The N.D. coach felt very secure and important when
he went out on the December banquet circuit.

> The Notre Dame Alumni
> To keep their team alive
> Are enrolling all the first-born
> As soon as they arrive;
> At each birth they wire Rockne
> And he tries to put them right
> 'I'm not interested in girl babies,
> And be sure the boys are white.'
>
> —"A Song in Honor of Rock" presented at the Notre Dame
>   Alumni Club of Cleveland reception,
>   December 8, 1923

In 1923, Rockne began to build his reputation—and outside income
—as an excellent banquet speaker. Probably when the coach heard the
song in Cleveland, the lyrics neither embarrassed nor upset him; as a
recent N.D. sports official explains, "Rockne shared the prejudices of the
vast majority of white male Americans of his time." The coach might not
have even noticed the lyrics—in a two-week span, the *Alumnus* noted, he
made "eleven speeches in ten middle western cities before over 2,500
people."

Rockne gave a standard talk in which he "emphasized the value of
good sportsmanship in clean, hard football and the undeniably beneficial
results that accrue to the participants" of the sport. During the remainder of his life, he would repeat these themes in his speeches, rarely
deviating from them. An N.D. historian of this period noted that "[Presi-
dent] Walsh's hand" guided this aspect of the coach's career: "In
Rockne's speeches and writings, which became more numerous and
widely read with the passing years, it was the president's good judgment
that prevailed throughout."

Walsh convinced the coach to try to refute the overemphasis charges
against the Catholic school with the "sound mind in sound body" line.
Rockne, however, insisted upon putting his own spin on this argument,
Arch Ward commenting that not only did the coach "encourage the development of what he called he-men" but also, in his after-dinner talks,
"never failed to belittle the tailor's model, the tea hound, the poser and
the man who can't take it."

One of the coach's favorite after-dinner anecdotes concerned how, in
1923, Notre Dame inexplicably went "cake-eater" by electing as senior
class president a boy of whom Rockne said, "Whenever I met him I
never knew whether to kiss him or slap him." Rockne related how he
became so incensed with this N.D. deviation from his definition of masculinity that he penned a long satire predicting a future football game
with the Irish players "resplendent in green shirt waists, their head gears
resembling a Woodman's toque," and the opposing Nebraska squad "very
striking in a scarlet mauvette tunic and about the waist they had a white
girdle with a Louis XIV buckle." The two teams, featuring such stars as
"M. Bickerdike Pix III," mince their way through a game of tag football
and have tea at halftime. Francis Wallace helped his mentor write and
distribute the piece on-campus in handbills titled "The Society Column
of the South Bend 'Tribune.' "

Rockne so liked his "nightmare" scenario that he lengthened it to a
twenty-minute presentation and narrated it hundreds of times, eventually
substituting Northwestern for Nebraska—the Big Ten team "gaily clad in

purple-mauve tunics . . . and the hosiery specially designed with beige tasseled garters." The coach always concluded the narration by claiming that his satire had the effect on the N.D. campus of restoring "the normal balance in our masculine democracy." Indeed, in addition to its attack on the effeminate, the speech reflected Rockne's fears that Notre Dame would go socially upscale in the 1920s and become very different from the "poor boys" school he had attended as an undergraduate. His proto-typical future N.D. player, "T. Fitzpatrick Pratt," was nicknamed "Two Lump" for his tea drinking preference, and belonged at F. Scott Fitzger-ald's Princeton, not Rockne's Notre Dame.

The football coach did not confine his battle against the supposed decline of American masculinity to the banquet hall; in 1927, he enlisted N.D. students to act out his favorite satire during halftime of the Notre Dame–U.S.C. game at Soldier Field in Chicago in front of 120,000 peo-ple! Rockne's two "effete" teams "took the field clad in assorted ballet tutus, lace gowns and frilly petticoats, and pranced into formation" to play tag football and then to hold a tea party.

Rockne equated reformers of intercollegiate athletics with "tea-hounds" and often worked that point into his after-dinner speeches, warning audiences that "effete easterners are trying to change the game of football from a he-man's sport into a silk stocking contest."

It would be easy to dismiss Rockne as obsessively homophobic, but his speeches and writings must be placed within the context of his era, especially the popular "Christian Manliness" movement and its transla-tion into athletics through the YMCA and other agencies. Arch Ward noted that the N.D. coach's speeches "became almost as famous as his gridiron exploits" and audiences loved his appeal for "he-men" and his denigration of anyone less masculine.

■ ■ ■

"In our telephone conversation this morning I understood you to say that *Rockne said he did not authorize a game or send a telegram saying that a game here on Christmas day would be o.k.* I have before me . . . a letter written by Rockne on October 9th in which he says 'Regarding a game on Christmas day, the faculty here would be in favor of such a game.' . . . [And] On October 10th a telegram signed by Rockne and sent to Leo Ward, which I now have, says: 'Faculty O.K. for Christmas game.'"

—Letter to President Walsh
from Father J. C. McGinn, October 30, 1923

Rockne's increasing fame as a football coach and public personality began to detach him from his Notre Dame moorings and give him the illusion that he could operate under his own rules, not those of the men in the Golden Dome. In his schedule making, he had often talked with a "forked tongue" to the Haskell Indians and other minor opponents, but in 1923, he went far beyond this when, in writing, he promised the Los Angeles alums a Christmas game. He assumed that he could maneuver around or override any faculty board veto, but their intransigence and Father McGinn's detective work left him totally exposed.

McGinn understood the implications of Rockne's actions: the coach had forced the Catholic school either to make good on his commitment or to lose credibility in the midst of the endowment drive. For McGinn, N.D.'s full-time fund-raiser, the only solution was to schedule the game and to rein in the coach. The priest warned President Walsh that it was "absolutely necessary to get matters of this kind straightened out, otherwise we will become the object of ridicule."

When the N.D. president backed the faculty board's veto of the West Coast trip, Rockne was furious, not only at his personal loss of face but also because he felt that, as the author of Notre Dame's athletic success, he should have total control over all aspects of his football program, including scheduling. He then complained loudly to influential alumni about the "lack of co-operation between the Athletic Board and the Coach," and the alums conveyed his displeasure as well as their support for him to the Notre Dame president.

Father McGinn tried to mediate. He reported to Walsh on a New York conference with the alums: A. D. McDonald, the powerful railroad executive, was reluctant "to believe that the Coach has deliberately misrepresented facts" even though Joe Byrne, Jr., confirmed it. Nevertheless, the alums supported Rockne's charges that "a chairman [Vice President Irving] was appointed to the Board who was not at all in sympathy with him" and that the coach "was subjected to the dictation of any member of the Board." Moreover, Rockne wanted a newly constituted athletic board, one where only half the members were priests and the university vice president was not in the chair.

The football coach had gone too far—he had challenged the C.S.C. priests' appointment of Notre Dame officials and their right to run the school as they saw best. Walsh had to oppose Rockne, but the coach would not back down. The resulting impasse continued into early 1924; then relations between Rockne and the administration worsened when the coach learned that Fathers Walsh, Irving, and selected faculty members were writing a new constitution for the Faculty Board of Control of Athletics. The priests wanted to replicate the Big Ten's rules on faculty control of intercollegiate athletics, but unlike the conference schools, they planned to possess the actual—not just the paper—power.

In tight spots during football games, Rockne had a number of favorite plays he liked to use. In February 1924, in this crucial off-the-field situation, he decided to employ the previously successful outside-job-offer tactic.

> "Iowa has been making overtures to the [Notre Dame] varsity football mentor for the past month, and his trip to Iowa City for a conference [with school officials], together with persistent reports from that place and Chicago to the effect that Rockne would probably sign a contract with the Hawkeyes has made the situation take on a serious aspect."
>
> —*Notre Dame Daily,* March 25, 1924

The opening at the University of Iowa occurred because Iowa fans had become enraged at Coach Howard Jones's behavior during the 1923 home loss to Michigan. Despite the fact that Jones's Hawkeyes had won the two previous Big Ten titles, when the referee allowed a Wolverine last-second winning touchdown and Jones, rather than join the crowd in howling protest, supported the ref's decision, the fanatics turned on him. A few months later he could smell the tar and feathers as he departed the state of Iowa.

During the winter of 1923–1924, Hawkeye officials sought Rockne's advice about a good replacement. The Notre Dame coach was noncommittal but, in typically generous fashion, helped Jones obtain another head coaching position. Then, when Rockne reached an impasse with N.D., he told the Iowa people that, with the right offer, he was available.

Ironically, the same university president who previously condemned Rockne's football program now tried to obtain the N.D. coach's services for his school. According to one prominent Iowa alum, the president actually signed Rockne to a three-year contract at $8,000 a year; however, archival documents suggest that throughout the negotiations, the N.D. coach never signed and mainly used the Iowa offer as leverage in his power struggle at Notre Dame.

Irish alum A. D. McDonald assumed the leadership of the campaign to keep Rockne at Notre Dame. After much lobbying, he persuaded the administrators to consider the coach's "reasonable requests," including the hiring of a full-time business manager for the athletic department to relieve Rockne of the mounting paperwork, and a long-term contract for the coach at an increase in pay. McDonald, marshaling other important alumni behind him, informed Walsh on March 21, 1924, that "it is extremely dangerous and uncertain to allow these matters to drag along because, as I told you during my recent visit, Rockne may get himself so tied up with Iowa or some other university that you will be forced to let him go. I shall wait, with some anxiety, word from you in the near future that this whole Rockne matter has been settled and settled right" by placating and retaining the coach.

On March 25, Walsh signed Rockne to a formal contract, committing Notre Dame to employing the coach for "ten academic years of ten months" per annum at an "annual salary of $10,000" (a very high income in the 1920s). That same day, Rockne issued a formal announcement to the press terming the Iowa offer a "rumor" that misled "people to believe that I have in mind going to another school next Fall." He then pledged his lifetime loyalty to his alma mater.

The men in charge of Notre Dame reached an accommodation with Rockne for a number of interconnected reasons: the alumni desperately wanted the coach retained, the students loudly pledged their support for him, and most important of all, when heavyweight members of the inner "Notre Dame family" such as A. D. McDonald spoke to the N.D. administrators about money matters and contracts, the priests tended to listen and to trust their advice. In addition, Father Walsh was a shrewd man— he knew that Rockne's football program now generated more than enough revenue to cover his increased salary as well as that of a full-time business manager, and he believed that he could finesse the coach's demand for "the reorganization of athletic affairs . . . in just the way you [Rockne] think they should be settled."

Ten days after signing the coach to the new pact, President Walsh wrote McDonald that "the suggestions made in your recent conversation with me have been carried out." He added: "The new constitution, governing our Athletic Board, is almost in final shape, and Father Burke, the [new] Chairman of the Board, will send you a copy for comment, before the final adoption."

With Rockne signed, the administrators wrote the N.D. rules for intercollegiate athletics in line with their original intentions, but as a concession to the coach, Walsh ended Vice President Irving's term as chair of the board. The president knew that the board could enforce the constitution at any time, and during Father Burke's eighteen-month term, the group began to use its new powers. Then, in spite of Rockne's protests, Irving's successor as Notre Dame vice president assumed the chairmanship. Apparently President Walsh understood that his struggle with the coach was the equivalent of an all-night poker game and that endurance as well as concentration produced winning hands.

The spring 1924 issue of the *Notre Dame Alumnus* rejoiced at the coach's new contract and at his loyalty oath to his alma mater: "I [Knute Rockne] wish to go on record as saying that if any school in the country feels the need of a coach any time within the next ten years, they will have to leave Notre Dame and myself out of consideration. Notre Dame is a part of my life, and my one ambition is to spend that life at the school that has made me whatever I am."

Within a year Rockne would "contract flirt" with USC, and within two, sign with Columbia University. In 1924, with Iowa, the N.D. coach's outside-offer offense worked well; in 1925, with USC, the strategy gained no yardage; but the following year, like a play used once too often, the Columbia "run" was quickly diagnosed by President Walsh and he threw the coach for a loss.

Father Matthew Walsh and others in charge of Notre Dame were the products of the C.S.C.'s rigorous and unique training. The order tended to produce priests of exceptional toughness of mind as well as intense dedication to their religion and work, regarding the two as inseparable. In the 1920s, no young priest at the school exhibited these qualities more than Father John F. O'Hara, at the time Notre Dame's prefect of religion —the third most important position in the school's hierarchy—and a decade later its dominant vice president and then president.

19

Notre Dame versus Klandiana: 1924

"The University [of Notre Dame] found rich compensations for all the abuse she had received for her athleticism in the fact that her football team, playing the toughest kind of schedule, should give an inspiring example of spiritual life."

—Father Arthur Hope, C.S.C. historian

It was Father John F. O'Hara, the university's prefect of religion from 1921 to 1933, who first made an explicit and public connection between religion and football at Notre Dame. In the Catholic school's sports history, players had frequently gone to mass and received communion before games, but only in 1921, when the team, en route to West Point, used a stopover in Albany to attend church, did the players' religious observance become news. Father O'Hara arranged the excursion from the railroad station to a replica of Lourdes in Albany and for local reporters to cover the event. The wire services picked up the story and Americans learned of the religiosity of the "manly Notre Dame football players." Furthermore, even the non-Catholics on the team attended the mass—the press emphasized this angle—and participated in parts of the ceremony. Subsequently, throughout the Rockne era, the Notre Dame football team's attendance at church during road trips and on game days became important, well-covered rituals.

Another highly publicized event involving Father O'Hara occurred before the 1923 Army annual in Brooklyn. West Point had asked a famous actress to do the ceremonial kickoff; when the N.D. prefect of religion learned of this stunt, he announced, "Elsie Janis will kick off for Army, Joan of Arc will kick off for Notre Dame," and he gave each member of his team a Joan of Arc medal to wear during football combat. He continued to distribute saints' medals before games for the remainder of his N.D. days; press coverage of this practice helped popularize, particularly among Catholic boys, the wearing of medals during sports events.

As the Fighting Irish continued to win during the 1920s, Father O'Hara stressed the religious component in Notre Dame's football success. He preached often on this theme and wrote about it in his weekly "Religious Bulletins." He encouraged team members to receive daily communion, noting: "When timid freshmen see monogram men, their natural heroes . . . approach the Holy Table, they learn what the upperclassmen already know, that devotion to the Blessed Sacrament is a mark of strength and not of weakness." In addition, O'Hara, in his bulletins, drew a correlation between the number of students receiving daily communion and the team's chances for victory—according to his calculations and charts, the higher the number of daily communicants during the week before a game, the greater the likelihood of an N.D. win.

Father O'Hara's missionary zeal was not confined to campus. He sent his sermons and bulletins to alumni and coreligionists around the country and to the Catholic press. One of his colleagues later remarked that O'Hara's efforts, coupled with the fame of Rockne's teams, resulted in such spontaneous exhibitions of faith as the "thousands of rosaries and innumerable prayers [for Notre Dame victory] offered by cloistered nuns on Saturdays of autumn" as well as the prayers of countless other believers for Fighting Irish success. A few Catholic academics, primarily in the Jesuit order, scorned O'Hara's "Football Theology," but the N.D. priest's work sparked a very positive response in most Catholic clergy and in the national lay community.

In part, O'Hara's aggressive Catholicism was a response to the 1920s resurgence of the Ku Klux Klan in America and an attempt to combat the "anti-Papist" forces head-on. Notre Dame's geographic location in Indiana, a pro-Klan state, strongly influenced O'Hara's religious campaign.

"An overzealous lecturer declared to a crowd at North Manchester [Indiana], a college town, that for all they knew the Pope might come there any day. 'He may even be on the north-bound train tomorrow. . . . He may! He may! Be warned! Prepare! America for Americans! Search everywhere for hidden enemies, vipers at the heart's blood of our sacred Republic! Watch the trains!'

Some fifteen hundred persons met the north-bound train the next day. . . ."

—*Atlantic Monthly,* May 1928

Popular histories portray the 1920s in America as "Roaring" and an "Era of Wonderful Nonsense." In fact, the decade began with a major recession plus inflation, and when the economy, shifting to an urban industrial base, finally boomed, it spread prosperity unevenly across the society. Farmers and residents of small towns saw a decline in real income as well as the continuing migration of younger family members to the cities. Increasing numbers of rural Americans became frustrated and angry at these unwanted events and found simplistic explanations more comprehensible and satisfying than complex dissertations about the after-effects of industrialization. Among the threatened and confused populace, demagogues thrived and organizations like the Ku Klux Klan enlisted millions of adherents.

In the South, the Klan pointed to the supposed economic gains of "Niggers" as the cause of social dislocation, and it preached rigid segregation as the solution. In Indiana, the most Klan-infatuated area outside the South, a mainly rural and Protestant population could not find many blacks to blame for its discontent and so it turned against Catholics and Jews. These minorities not only represented strange religions that conducted rituals in the ultraforeign languages of Latin and Hebrew but, because, according to Klan propaganda, they sent their money overseas and were loyal only to the Vatican and Zion, they were clearly "un-American." Exacerbating tensions was rural Protestants' support for Prohibition—part of their desire to impose their moral code on the entire society—and their awareness that many urban Americans, particularly Irish Catholics, mocked the "Drys" of the "Bible Belt." (The Irish-American community considered the Eighteenth Amendment an attack on its social customs and an attempt to obliterate the separation of Church and State.)

By 1924 in Indiana, about a quarter of a million men—30 percent of the white male population—were members of the Ku Klux Klan. A talented rabble-rouser, D. C. Stephenson, organized them and also directed huge Klan rallies and cross burnings across the state. In addition, he helped to elect Klan-approved candidates at all levels of government, including the governorship. Although he was a megalomaniac, for a time Stephenson's plans came true; thus, when he discussed buying Valparaiso

College near South Bend and turning it into a Klan university to eclipse
Notre Dame, the C.S.C. priests took notice.

More directly threatening to the Catholic school during the spring of
1924 was the Klan's intention to hold a week-long "Klavern" in South
Bend and to march upon Notre Dame. The Klan newspaper, *The Fiery
Cross*, promised that more than 200,000 members—the size of the estimated crowd at a Kokomo rally the previous year—would begin arriving
on Saturday, May 17.

The N.D. students, showing Fighting Irish spirit, decided to oppose
the Klan with guerrilla warfare. On Saturday, small groups of students
ambushed arriving Klansmen at the train station and on town sidewalks,
grabbing their robes and hoods and tearing them apart. Skirmishes continued through the weekend, and when some South Bend police intervened on the side of the Klan, a number of students, according to one
vivid report, "were injured seriously and were taken to Hullie & Mike's
Pool Hall where they rested on the tables, red blood staining the green
felt until medical help arrived."

Then on Monday night, a rumor swept the campus that the Klan had
killed a Notre Dame undergraduate. The dormitories emptied and an
army of students marched to the South Bend courthouse, intent on battling the Klan and the local police. President Walsh drove to the courthouse and, standing on the cannon outside the building, informed the
crowd that the rumor about the murdered student was false. He also
advised: "Whatever challenge may have been offered tonight to your
patriotism, whatever insult may have been offered to your religion, you
can show your loyalty to Notre Dame and to South Bend by ignoring all
[Klan] threats." He ordered the students to return to campus, stating that
"a single injury to [another] Notre Dame student would be too great a
price to pay" for fighting the Klansmen.

Rainstorms doused the remainder of the Klan's South Bend activities,
but the organization used the fracas with the N.D. students for propaganda, claiming that the Fighting Irish had destroyed American flags and
beaten innocent women and children, including babies. President Walsh
received inquiries from reporters and concerned citizens about the truth
of the Klan's atrocity stories, and although he tried to refute the "gross
misrepresentations of the conduct of the Notre Dame students," many
Hoosiers believed the Klan's tales.

In the fall of 1924, the Klan threatened another attack against Notre
Dame. Walsh wrote a colleague that "the intended gathering of the Klan

has been instigated by the backers of [Republican gubernatorial candidate] Ed Jackson, who figure that a life sized riot in South Bend would go a long ways towards bolstering up Jackson's candidacy" in the coming election. The fall Klavern never occurred, but over 650,000 Indiana voters elected Jackson, controlled by Grand Dragon Stephenson, as governor. In the new legislature, Jackson backed various anti-Catholic bills, including one proposing the abolition of parochial schools. This increasingly hostile political climate depressed Notre Dame administrators and faculty but also confirmed their resolve to be as independent as possible from the state of Indiana.

However, N.D. could not totally ignore Hoosier politics, and even its football team became involved in the controversy with the Klan. In March 1925, Indiana's powerful United States senator, James E. Watson, wrote N.D. past president Father John W. Cavanaugh requesting his help in scheduling a game between Notre Dame and the Quantico Marines for December in Washington. Watson, a Republican, was socially friendly with Klan leaders and had supported Klan candidates in the 1924 election. Probably the senator wanted to exhibit his political muscle by making the Catholic school give over one of its most valuable prizes—a Notre Dame road game—but he underestimated Notre Dame's independence.

Cavanaugh forwarded the request to Rockne, noting: "I have no use for Senator Watson and don't suppose you will be interested in this proposition for a football game in Washington. . . . Personally I would not shake hands with the Senator nor would I write him any kind of letter for myself. . . . His connection with the K.K.K. in this state has put me on the side lines for life so far as he is concerned."

Rockne offered to write to the senator on behalf of N.D. and he told Cavanaugh, "I will . . . give him the refusal of the Faculty Board" as the excuse for not playing the Marines.

Watson, however, was close to President Calvin Coolidge, and he increased the pressure on the Catholic school by having the White House also request the Quantico game. The N.D. administration agreed with the prior refusal and again Rockne invoked the faculty board's veto. Considering the political climate at this time, particularly in Klandiana, Notre Dame's determination not to please the secular powers illustrates the C.S.C. priests' resolve and courage.

"No Governor can kiss the papal ring and get within gunshot of the White House."

—Methodist Bishop Adna W. Leonard, in a 1924 speech

Beyond Indiana, the political landscape for Catholics was also bleak. In 1924, Al Smith, the Irish-American governor of New York, wanted to run for president, but his campaign sparked anti-Catholic reactions in Klan-dominated regions of the country and also within his own supposedly progressive Democratic party. At the party's convention, Smith squared off against Senator William McAdoo, the son-in-law and political heir of Woodrow Wilson. Before the balloting for the top of the ticket, Smith's supporters tried to pass a platform plank strongly condemning the Ku Klux Klan and its followers. McAdoo's people, according to reports, "proposed a vague and innocuous plank calculated to soothe the sensibilities of the Klansmen" and to parallel the Republicans' appeasement of the Klan. When put to a convention vote, Smith's anti-Klan plank lost. Then, in 102 ballots for the presidential nomination, Smith and McAdoo reached a stalemate and the bid went to the unknown Wall Street lawyer John W. Davis. In the November election, Calvin Coolidge overwhelmed Davis.

But Al Smith had a real constituency: through hard work and savvy, he had moved up in American society from the immigrant Irish-Catholic lower east side of Manhattan to the uptown middle class; in the same way, his strongest supporters had made a similar trek in New York and other urban centers. In 1924, Smith became their political hero, and in that same year, for many of them, Notre Dame became their favorite football team.

20

Blast-off: 1924

"Now a Notre Dame man walks down [New York's] Fifth Avenue, and he sees in the shop windows the old gold and blue alongside the colors of Army, Yale, Harvard and Princeton. He walks up Broadway and he sees neckties advertised in the colors of the same schools—the aristocracy of the gridiron, if you don't happen to know it."

—A "Special Dispatch" to the *Notre Dame Scholastic* from Francis Wallace, Fall 1924

Wallace, trying to make his fortune in the big city, marveled at how upscale Catholic New Yorkers had started to embrace the football team of his alma mater (in this era, few Protestants would wear a Catholic school's colors). He remembered the dress at his Notre Dame as "corduroys and hobnails" and that only one student owned a fur coat; however, recently in a Manhattan "show window," he saw "a great fur coat . . . gaily decorated with a Notre Dame pennant" along with "a sign: 'Going to the game?' " And "the game" involved Notre Dame and Army, not the Ivies.

Alumni of eastern schools had long used football afternoons as opportunities to mix pleasure with business and to solidify their connections to their schools and classmates. Alumni of Catholic colleges, institutions without major football teams, did not have these events—until the Notre Dame football team began to appear annually in New York City.

At the center of Catholic support for Notre Dame football were the

163

school's own alums. Through the previous decade of N.D. eastern trips, their affection for the team had increased, but in 1924, with the scheduled games against Army at the Polo Grounds and the following week at Princeton, their passion exploded into a frenzy of ticket buying and promoting and organizing of social festivities. The letters from Joe Byrne, Jr., to Rockne reveal plans "to assure a 'sell-out' for both contests" and details of the full social weekends, including the involvement of the Marquette Club, the main organization for Catholic university graduates in New York.

Byrne also fed publicity stories to the newspapers, and in 1924 the middle-class and upscale dailies responded more positively to Notre Dame publicity than in previous years. The *New York Telegram, New York Evening Mail,* and *New York Times* were receptive, in part, because of their own high-ranking Catholic executives; in late August, Warren Nolan, the assistant to the publisher of the *Telegram* and the *Mail,* wrote to Hugh O'Donnell, an N.D. grad and the business manager of the *Times,* about obtaining better coverage for Notre Dame football, "whose Catholic affiliations do seem to have hindered 'feature' publicity in sport pages in New York." Nolan suggested that Rockne meet and charm a key writer on his papers; O'Donnell went further and had a *Times* man offer his services "as a press representative" for the N.D.–Army game.

The *Times* reporter emphasized to Rockne that because a journalist-publicist "has an entree into the newspaper offices," he can place his publicity handouts as "daily articles." He acknowledged, "You are probably familiar with this system for handling publicity for football games in New York," adding that his services would cost "from $150 to $300"—the latter figure more than double the average New York sportswriter's monthly pay at this time. Rockne suggested that the *Times* man get in touch with Joe Byrne, Jr., "and anything he may do will be all right with us."

Byrne hired the publicist and also used Francis Wallace's free-lance talents. As a result, the week before the game, in addition to an abundance of features on the two teams, their players, and coaches, "news" articles on the heavy demand for tickets began appearing in the *Telegram* and *Mail* as well as in the *Sun* and *Post.*

The pregame promotion worked, and the contest at the Polo Grounds, enlarged to sixty thousand seats, sold out, "an irresistible magnet for myriads of New York's football fans and society folk" (*Telegram*). Part of the crowd included wealthy Catholics and even some political "notables" (*Times*). The Notre Dame supporters enjoyed the Army's pageantry—the entire Cadet Corps marched into the stadium—but they reserved their cheers for the attack of the Fighting Irish, particularly the quick backfield thrusts and touchdowns by Elmer Layden and Jim Crowley. The N.D. fans became anxious in the final quarter when Army scored a TD; then the Irish line, led by center Adam Walsh, playing with two broken hands, stiffened, Notre Dame hanging on for a 13–7 win. (Walsh later nicknamed his linemates and himself the "Seven Mules.")

Most New York newspapers headlined the victory and provided extensive reports. Grantland Rice led his game account in the *New York Herald-Tribune* with the Four Horsemen metaphor and continued his story for multiple columns; less famous leads but similar coverage occurred in rival journals. However, one New York paper showed minimum interest in Notre Dame's triumph over Army—the *Daily News*. For its writers and Irish working-class readers, college football was still a rich man's sport; the *Daily News* preferred boxing and horse racing, carrying features on current and past champions. Its Sunday edition after the fabled Four Horsemen game ran a long excerpt from the memoirs of John L. Sullivan and a back-page headline: "WHEN HUMPHRIES MET JOHN L." It ignored the suddenly famous N.D. backfield.

During the week following the Army game, the middle-class papers beat the publicity drums for the Notre Dame–Princeton contest and helped turn out forty thousand fans, including many N.D. rooters from New York. For those fans unable to take the train ride to New Jersey, the *New York Sun* featured the game on its outdoor Gridgraphie on Chambers Street. On Sunday, the papers reported in detail on the 12–0 N.D. win, praising Jim Crowley's two touchdowns; but, as W. B. Hanna of the *Herald-Tribune* admitted, it "was not a great game, or very exciting. Rockne's lads fumbled profusely."

Yet for increasing numbers of middle-class Catholics in the eastern United States, the important item was that—for the second year in a row —"their team" beat mighty and obnoxious Princeton. The 1924 victories over Army and Princeton solidified the N.D. football team's hold on its Catholic middle-class constituency; the games also provided the school with the best road paydays to date, $56,500 from the Polo Grounds and almost $20,000 at Princeton—in spite of the latter's unfair contract: "25% of net gate receipts, exclusive of season tickets."

In the weeks after the eastern visit, the New York papers, for the first time, carried details on the remainder of Notre Dame's games. When the team went to the Rose Bowl, the coverage escalated. Not surprisingly, in early 1925, the manager of New York's newest and largest sports facility,

Yankee Stadium, offered a guarantee of $60,000 to Notre Dame and Army to play that year's contest in his showplace. Even less surprisingly, the schools agreed.

> "I grew up hearing stories about how important the success of Rockne's teams was to my family in the 1920s. As German Catholics living in Klan-dominated Indiana, they felt very threatened and insecure. When Notre Dame started to beat the best college teams in the country and attract national attention, all Catholics, not just the Irish, had something to feel proud of. It really built esteem. Like a lot of families, because of what happened back then, we're rabid Notre Dame fans to this day."
>
> —Terri Wenzel, a fourth-generation Hoosier Catholic

In 1924, Rockne's "Rocket" shot over not only the eastern United States but also the Middle West and, at the end of the year, west of the Mississippi as well.

For home games that season, N.D. expanded Cartier Field to twenty-two thousand seats, and although the opening wins over Lombard and Wabash did not sell out the grounds, when the team returned from its eastern triumphs to play Georgia Tech for Homecoming, fans occupied every seat and thousands more stood. In addition to the N.D. alums, increasing numbers of middle-class Catholic supporters from northern Indiana, Illinois, Michigan, and Ohio made the trip by train or car to South Bend. And many local residents, including Protestants and Jews, turned out.

A highlight for the alumni was their presentation at halftime of a Studebaker Big Six Sedan to Rockne. For a testimonial to their beloved coach, Chicago alums Byron Kanaley and George Maypole, a city alderman, solicited money from their fellow graduates to buy the luxury touring car. Not only did the alums want to make the coach happy at N.D. and preempt future outside job offers but they also wished to show their appreciation for "Rock" having "brought fame and glory to their Alma Mater and crowned her with victories beyond fondest hopes." That afternoon, the thorough 34–3 thrashing of the southern school, with the Four Horsemen again starring, added to the Notre Dame victory total and enhanced the alums' affection for "Our Rock."

The following week's easy 38–3 victory at Wisconsin intensified the N.D. grads' passion for the coach and the team. For the game at Madison, many Chicago alums and fans made the short trip north and helped sell out the stadium. With this match, Rockne triumphed on multiple fronts: his quick, alert team, including his reserve units, delighted the Notre Dame rooters and pleased the sportswriters, and his ability to bring off a visit to an important Big Ten school impressed N.D. officials and faculty. This diplomatic breakthrough aided the coach when inquiries from the Rose Bowl committee began, and unlike the previous year, his desire to play in Pasadena did not encounter a hostile administration and faculty board.

To please its expanding numbers of Chicago-area fans, N.D. agreed to allow the *Tribune*'s WGN radio station to broadcast the following week's home game versus Nebraska (marking the first radio broadcast of an N.D. home game). For the contest, the largest crowd in Cartier Field history up to this time, over 22,500, came out. The coach thoroughly enjoyed the match, a 34–6 humiliation of the Cornhuskers, terming the victory "the most pleasing thing that has happened to me in years" because "Nebraska, as usual, was the dirtiest team we played, and after the game, a few of their players even called *me* a few choice epithets."

However, Rockne did not have any time to relax after the Nebraska romp. The following week's opponent was Northwestern, but much more important, the occasion was Notre Dame's first appearance in Chicago's mammoth Soldier Field.

"Chicago was wide open in the twenties and the Notre Dame visits became one of the big annual social events. It really began when they started playing in Soldier Field. It was amazing, you could walk along the sidelines, look in the fancy boxes and see the hierarchy of the Catholic Church, then all the politicians from the governor on down and, of course, all the bigtime gangsters and bootleggers."

—Jack Fishman, a young Chicago lawyer in the 1920s

With the 1920s' prosperity in Chicago, increasing numbers of Irish Catholics in that city reached the middle class and many had connections to Notre Dame, usually through N.D. alumni in their families. For this ethnic subgroup, Northwestern University, a Methodist institution, represented part of the hated Protestant establishment. Thus, in 1924, when Northwestern agreed to host the Fighting Irish, the ticket demand from N.D. fans in Chicago was unprecedented, far exceeding the previous match four years before.

The Big Ten school had originally scheduled the contest for its home grounds in Evanston but then, at Rockne's urging, it agreed to move the game to the expanded municipal stadium in Grant Park, soon to be called

Soldier Field. The week before the game, the N.D. athletic department as well as the Notre Dame Alumni Club of Chicago sold out their huge allotments of tickets. Northwestern also moved all of its tickets—many to N.D. fans—and a crowd of at least forty-five thousand provided a payout of $27,000 to each of the schools.

The spectators watched the Irish win a surprisingly tough match, 13–6, the Four Horsemen stymied for much of the afternoon by Northwestern's line and the N.D. defense struggling to contain Northwestern's All-American, Ralph "Moon" Baker. Nevertheless, N.D. fans were happy with the victory; this first Notre Dame appearance in Soldier Field consolidated and increased the Catholic school's fan base in Chicago, preparing the way for the crowds of 120,000 only a few years later.

The 1924 regular season ended for N.D. in Pittsburgh against a weak Carnegie Tech squad. Winning 40–19 before an estimated thirty-five thousand fans, the Irish gained another $25,000-plus payout. In addition to pleasing their western Pennsylvania supporters, the N.D. athletic department helped a number of Notre Dame East Coast alumni clubs set up special telegraph wires to the game that relayed each play to their gatherings.

After the regular season, because of the team's 9–0 record and the possibility of a unanimous national championship in the final polls, the Notre Dame football phenomenon kept growing, many national as well as regional reporters descending on the N.D. campus to interview Rockne, the players, and the students enraptured by their football heroes. The *Scholastic* printed page after page of praise to the team, and in mid-December, almost the entire N.D. community turned out for a massive rally in the old gymnasium. Among the visiting speakers was Olympic champion Avery Brundage (later, longtime head of the Olympic movement). He proclaimed "Notre Dame . . . the center of the athletic world" and wished the football team well on its final 1924 adventure, a trip to the Rose Bowl to play the powerful Stanford Indians. Ironically, the main reason President Walsh and the faculty board agreed to N.D.'s first postseason trip was to gain the money needed for repairs on and an addition to the dilapidated gymnasium in which Brundage spoke.

> "A flat guarantee of thirty-five thousand dollars—this would have enabled us to make the [renovation and] addition to the gymnasium. . . . however, such a game [as the Rose Bowl] would leave us open to more than our share of criticism as there is a great deal of talk going on

regarding the commercialization of football . . . our [Big Ten] Conference critics were waiting to see what we were going to do."

—President Walsh to Father Matthew Schumacher, October 7, 1924

As soon as the championship potential of Rockne's 1924 team became
evident, N.D.'s West Coast alumni began lobbying for a trip to the Rose
Bowl as a season finale. The Pasadena committee responded quickly and
invited Notre Dame, but as Father Walsh realized, the invitation en-
meshed the Catholic school in the "overemphasis" issue. Complicating
the situation were various disagreements between the Rose Bowl committee and the Pacific Coast Conference, as well as the reluctance of two
of its member schools, Stanford and Berkeley, to play Notre Dame.

When the Rose Bowl decided to ignore the conference and signed
the Haskell Indians as the western representative, Walsh and the faculty
board refused to play this academically questionable opponent and
Rockne balked because of Haskell's athletically minor status. Various
N.D. alums tried to negotiate for a better opponent and prodded USC,
the coast runner-up, to accept the game. The Trojans' coach wired
Rockne that Stanford, the conference champion, "has said . . . that
they would not play Notre Dame on account of [your low] scholastic
standard. U.S.C. would welcome a chance to play Notre Dame New
Year's at Pasadena." Rockne replied, "We would prefer to play Southern
California."

Stanford, however, sat upon a wobbly "high horse"—the team had
swept through the season thanks to its new head coach, Glenn "Pop"
Warner, and his successful but questionable recruiting and subsidization
techniques, as well as his innovative single- and double-wing formations.
With unintended irony, Stanford, trying to evoke the coach's glorious
past at Carlisle and ignoring the shady aspects, had even changed its
football team's nickname to the "Indians."

Not surprisingly, a better financial deal from the Rose Bowl committee enabled Stanford to reconsider its moral position, and in late November, after the Pasadena people increased the proposed payout, Pop
Warner and Stanford agreed to play the Catholic school. However, the
actual contract prompted some criticism: the head of the N.D. Los Angeles alumni, Leo Ward, a lawyer, complained to Rockne that "Notre Dame
pulled an awful 'Brodie' when it signed" for an even split on 60 percent
of the net gate; in other words, if the receipts were $100,000, N.D. would
receive only $30,000. Ward argued that because the Fighting Irish had
become *the major attraction,* the school "could just as easily have had a

60-40 split of the net gate." On New Year's Day, fifty-three thousand fans produced a whopping net gate of $175,000, with the payout to Notre Dame almost $52,000 (although Ward's formula would have greatly increased the N.D. take-home).

In almost 90-degree heat, the Fighting Irish won a tough 27–10 victory over the Indians, led by All-American fullback Ernie Nevers. Stanford actually bested N.D. in all statistical categories, but at crucial moments in the struggle, Rockne's men blunted their opponents' drives by intercepting passes and recovering fumbles. After the game, the two head coaches congratulated one another and promised to meet soon after —they eventually became close friends.

In the 1925 Rose Bowl, three of the Four Horsemen played well but the fourth, Elmer Layden, was spectacular, making key runs, belting long punts, and at a crucial moment late in the contest, intercepting a pass and running it back for a TD for the Notre Dame clincher. However, in his autobiography, the modest Layden downplayed his role and mainly discussed "the round-about trip Notre Dame took to the game," the crowds en route, and the incredible popular response to the Fighting Irish as they crisscrossed the country.

Notre Dame alum A. D. McDonald had put a number of Southern Pacific railroad cars at Rockne's disposal, and the coach scheduled a long football-and-religion pilgrimage to the West Coast and back; appropriately, the only N.D. administrator on the trip was Father John O'Hara.

First, in Chicago, the alumni feted the team and then the squad traveled to New Orleans for a two-day "continuous round of luncheons, banquets, and receptions." The Louisiana city, with its large Catholic population, loved the Fighting Irish, large crowds always gathering for their public appearances. The team next went to Houston, where Father Matthew Schumacher, head of nearby C.S.C. Saint Edward's College, hosted various functions; he also wanted the squad to play a fund-raising exhibition at the University of Texas stadium and guaranteed a crowd of "over thirty thousand," but the N.D. faculty board vetoed the game. Then it was on to Tucson for such events as "a banquet by the Knights of Columbus" as well as four days of football practice at the University of Arizona stadium. Former N.D. player Slip Madigan, coaching at Saint Mary's College in northern California and familiar with Pop Warner's football tactics, joined the team in Tucson. After praising Madigan's "wonderful scouting notes," Rockne used them extensively to plot his strategy for the Rose Bowl game.

Finally, the traveling party went to Los Angeles, where, according to press accounts, "several thousand enthusiasts greeted their arrival" on December 31. The N.D. coach wisely insisted that the many L.A. social events planned for the team take place *after* the New Year's Day game. A majority of West Coast Notre Dame fans were middle-class Catholics, affiliated with such groups as the Ancient Order of Hibernians, but some non-Catholics also became infatuated with the Fighting Irish at this time. A telegram from a San Francisco N.D. alum noted: "H.F. SAYS WE IRISH MUST STAND TOGETHER . . . H.F. IS HERBERT FLEISHACKER, A JEW, BANKER AND MULTIMILLIONAIRE OF SAN FRANCISCO. HE IS A GREAT MAN."

After winning the Rose Bowl and being entertained in Los Angeles, the team visited northern California. The Irish-American mayor of San Francisco hosted them in grand style, and the Catholic archbishop "celebrated mass in the Cathedral in the presence of the squad." For Catholics in the Bay Area, Notre Dame's triumph over Stanford, a bastion of the region's Protestant establishment, was an authentic reason to rejoice.

Then the team traveled to the Pacific Northwest and finally back east through Wyoming and Colorado. At each stop along the way, the local newspapers put the N.D. visit on the front page. Denver even gave the team a huge civic parade—the players were "decorated by the young ladies, 'mugged' by the photographers, and pump-handled by good Notre Dame alumni, good Denver football enthusiasts, sporting editors, Irish cops, Jewish salesmen, and everybody else." From Denver to Chicago, more welcoming receptions occurred.

Finally, in mid-January, the traveling party returned to South Bend. As a result of this Rose Bowl journey of 1924–1925, innumerable Americans in various far-flung locations, chiefly but not exclusively of Irish-Catholic descent, became Notre Dame football fans. As important, many local sportswriters and editors moved Notre Dame to the top of their college football agenda and, in future years, gave the Fighting Irish more coverage than any team outside of their own region.

Notre Dame's athletic culture and Rockne's talent as a coach molded the national championship team, but high-volume press coverage helped shape its enduring fame. In 1924, a number of New York writers with access to the wire services and press syndicates—and a famous photograph—blasted the Four Horsemen and their teammates into the national consciousness, where regional and local newspapers kept their celebrity alive.

Grantland Rice, who first published the nickname for the backfield, always claimed sole authorship of the Four Horsemen phenomenon, and the sports world subsequently believed him. However, the historical record reveals Rice's contribution as being far different than his later self-promotion indicates. Moreover, examining the record not only illuminates the Four Horsemen but also provides crucial information about the role of the press in the amazing popularity of Notre Dame football in the 1920s.

21

The Four Horsemen—
Grantland Rice versus Reality

"The so-called Golden Age of Sports, the twenties and early thirties, was really the Golden Age of Sportswriting. The glories of the Babe, the Manassa Mauler, the Four Horsemen, were tunes composed on portable typewriters by gifted, ambitious, often cynical men who set customs and standards of sports journalism that are being dealt with to this day. . . .

The Golden Age sportswriters hyped the country's post–World War I sports boom, rode the gravy train and then, for the good of the game, maintained the myths and legends as the country slid into a bust."

—Robert Lipsyte, *Sports World*

In the 1920s, increasing numbers of urban Americans acquired disposable income and the leisure time in which to spend it. The rich built country clubs and played polo, tennis, and golf; the expanding middle class attended various sporting events, particularly college football games. As spectator sports grew in popularity, promoters, including some universities, built new and larger stadiums.

Fueling the 1920s sports boom was the press. At the turn of the century, newspaper editors began to realize that stories about sports, along with those on sex and violence, sold many more papers than did "hard news" articles. By the 1910s, circulation managers demanded separate sports sections, and publishers and editors complied. Then, when newspapers increased their profitability by attracting advertisers on the basis of circulation, expanding sports sections began to push many news items and features out of the paper.

In the 1920s, American journalism, in frenetic pursuit of profits, underwent a political lobotomy—a particularly unfortunate operation because, with radio reports and movie newsreels in their infancy and TV unborn, newspapers were the only mass medium for informing the public. The decade's most important stories—the rise of fascism in Europe, military dictatorship in Japan, and the economic instability that led to the Great Depression—rarely appeared in American newspapers in the 1920s, whereas the divorce trials of the rich and famous, the horrible murders of the poor and infamous, and the worshiping of sports heroes and events filled column after column.

Even the *New York Times,* then as now "the newspaper of record," often trivialized serious political and economic issues. In a 1923 editorial about the Ku Klux Klan, the *Times* wrote: "There is in Indiana a militant Catholic organization . . . engaged in secret drills. They make long cross-country raiding expeditions. . . . Worst of all, they lately fought, and decisively defeated, a detachment of the United States Army. Yet we have not heard of the Indiana Klansmen rising up to exterminate the Notre Dame football team."

Newspapers that would not take the fascists or the Klan seriously mainly laughed at the complaints of university professors about the overemphasis of intercollegiate athletics. The press loved and glorified college football with the result that, as the Carnegie Foundation pointed out, "the view of the college" and the purpose of higher education "presented in the newspapers is totally distorted through overstressing of athletics."

When academics criticized the press, journalists usually ignored them; sportswriters paid attention and homage to one person on a college campus—the football coach. The sporting press, including editors, needed the coaches for team schedules, rosters, free rides to and from games, pressbox and locker room passes, game information, quotes, free stadium seats for family and friends, and, when also moonlighting as referees and/or publicity agents, cash handouts. The press did not need the professors for anything other than an occasional quote at which to jibe. The relationship between the sportswriters and the coaches became so symbiotic that one critic complained that "nowadays" schools and their students "appear to have no teams, all teams are commonly referred to by the names of their coaches." (Rockne, with his "Rockets" and other alliterative nicknames, particularly benefited from this practice.)

In the 1920s, most American sportswriters were still poorly paid, but as bylines became common, an aristocracy of sports journalists emerged in New York and the royals began to receive handsome rewards for their utterances. After the 1924 football season, Grantland Rice became the monarch, and his approach to sportswriting replaced the old-time method, which, for all of its dependence on publicity handouts before games, tended to describe the actual events and athletes in fairly direct prose. Rice, however, preferred to turn a ho-hum contest into a mythic struggle or an ordinary athlete into a Greek god or biblical archetype—or a backfield averaging 158 pounds into the Four Horsemen of the Apocalypse.

Grantland Rice, through hard work, self-promotion, and the blind good luck of the Four Horsemen lead, became the first American sports-writer to command a huge salary and, with a multitude of side deals, to achieve a six-figure annual income. Moreover, his hyperbolic "Gee-Whiz" approach came to dominate American sportswriting from the mid-1920s through the 1940s, influencing most of his colleagues as well as a multitude of readers. Paul Gallico was one of Rice's crown princes: "From 1923 to 1936 [on the *New York Daily News*], spinning a daily tale in the most florid and exciting prose that I could muster, part of the great ballyhoo, member of the great gullibles, swallower of my own bait, I belonged to that category of sportswriters known as the 'Gee-Whizzers.'"

Unlike Gallico, Rice never repented, and when he later looked back on the 1920s, he still peered through a golden haze: "Just what odd turn of evolution brought forward so many outstanding [sports] stars in this postwar period? There is no answer to this mystery . . . it must be listed as something that just happened beyond rhyme, reason, or the Milky Way. All that we know is that this Golden Age offered a flame that lit up the sporting skies and covered the world." For Grantland Rice, mystification ruled the universe, to be expressed in romantic language obliterating all serious questions.

Thanks to Rice and his print colleagues, "Gee-Whiz" romanticism

also dominated other sports media for a number of decades. Radio announcers described games and players in a breathless, often fictitious
manner, and Hollywood portrayed sports events and heroes as marvelous
and innocent. *Knute Rockne—All American* is the cinematic equivalent
of Grantland Rice's prose, and even its depiction of the 1920s' press
attention to Notre Dame football—a sudden whirring of newspaper
printing machines and a spewing of front-page headlines—is characteristically mystified. Instead of allowing the audience to view Rockne's
shrewd handling of journalists and the many other factors involved in
Notre Dame's football fame, the filmmakers have the Fighting Irish explode into the national consciousness as "something that just happened
beyond rhyme, reason, or the Milky Way."

Fortunately, the "Gee-Whiz" school spawned its antithesis, the "Aw-
Nuts" men, led by Rice's fellow columnist on the *New York Herald-
Tribune* W. O. McGeehan, and enlisting such sportswriters turned general pundits as Damon Runyon and Heywood Broun. In a column three
days after Rice's famous passage on the Four Horsemen, McGeehan
mocked the "Gee-Whizzers" and the social context in which they operated: "The average reader of the sporting pages is as sentimental as a
seminary girl. You cannot tell the persons hungry for their daily heroes
that a certain champion did not buy his mother a home out of his first
earnings but instead lost the money shooting craps."

Subscribers to the *Herald-Tribune,* the most informative paper of the
period, usually read either McGeehan or Rice, but outside of Manhattan
the "Aw-Nuts" men sank into the Hudson River, whereas the "Gee-
Whizzers" and their imitators thrived in the rest of the country, attracting
millions of readers. Only in a few papers in the hinterlands did any "Aw-
Nuts" sportswriting appear, notably Westbrook Pegler's dispatches to the
Chicago Tribune sports section.

Thus, with little opposition, Grantland Rice and his cohorts helped
promote college football into a huge business and insulated it from public
disapproval. Most sportswriters and editors understood their importance
to the college football boom. In 1925, when Rockne complained to the
sports editor of the *Omaha* (Nebraska) *World-Herald* about the paper's
coverage of various Notre Dame–Nebraska incidents, the journalist
brushed the criticisms aside, reminding the coach, "Tut, tut, Knute. You
know damned well . . . that were it not for newspapers, not five hundred people would be interested in Notre Dame, Nebraska, or the whole
kit and kaboodle of football teams."

"Brazil can cheer about its coffee as Ceylon raves about its tea. Let Florida and California speak with passion of their orange groves as Kentucky points with a finger of pride to the thoroughbred.

But out in Notre Dame, South Bend, Indiana, football grows on trees and bushes. It blossoms upon the vine and leaves the air redolent with the fragrance that comes from the skin of the mole."

—Grantland Rice's lead for his 1923
N.D.–Army game article

Rice lived by the writing proverb that if you throw enough shit against the wall, some of it is bound to stick. Each day he flung out metaphors about athletes and sports events and, indeed, some of his words stuck to the American psyche, notably the Four Horsemen phrase—with a major assist from the famous photograph. The vast majority of his figures of speech quickly disappeared.

For the N.D.–Army game at West Point in 1922, Rice wrote, "Notre Dame's attack is more like a modern war offensive than anything we have seen. The infantry is there to strike through the line, with the air fleet above busy bombing holes in the rival defense." Like many romantics, Rice's infatuation with his words led him far from reality—the Irish attack in 1922 failed to score a single point!

In 1923, after the lame agricultural lead—"Brazil . . . coffee" et cetera—he again tried the war comparison, mixing it with a cinematic one: "Yet even this war-like corps [Army] had nothing to match the swift motion picture known as the Halfbacks of Notre Dame." But then, as sometimes occurs in his prose and doggerel verse, a phrase jumps out at the reader: "Through the tumult and the shouting . . ." On this occasion, Rice knew that the phrase worked and noted it—he eventually used *The Tumult and the Shouting* as the title of his autobiography. Most often, however, he spun out his hyperbolic leads and game stories, sped through his signed columns, met his deadlines, and went drinking with his favorite coaches and athletes.

Even though the 1923–1924 Notre Dame team, chiefly the backfield, became a cornerstone of his fame and fortune, during their actual playing days, Rice was much less interested in them than he subsequently claimed. The Monday after the 1923 victory over Army in Brooklyn, he began his weekend football review by commenting on "Middlebury's great stand against Harvard," a 6–6 tie. And the following Saturday, rather than cover Notre Dame's historic first visit to Princeton, he went to the track and turned his muse upon the feature race.

"Our [1924] team is anything but good as yet, but we hope to keep on improving. Our line, in particular, is not looking well, and our backfield has not got to going yet as a result."

—Rockne to a personal friend, October 8, 1924

The N.D. coach often "talked down" his team to the press before a big game but he was usually honest in his letters to his friends (frequently they bet on the contest). Thus, ten days before the game in which the Four Horsemen and the Seven Mules gained "sports immortality," their coach was pessimistic about their prospects for even winning. Adding to Rockne's concern, quarterback Harry Stuhldreher had injured his throwing arm, admitting, "Every time I raised my hand, the arm went dead and was useless to me" (1920s sportswriters rarely mentioned such key injuries in print, preferring to sell the information to gamblers and/or use it in their own betting). On game day, Rockne convinced his quarterback that he had a special medicine for the arm; after its application and the adrenaline rush of play, Stuhldreher threw adequately (the "cure" was ordinary rubbing liniment).

Grantland Rice watched the first half of the 1924 N.D.–Army game in the pressbox and, with the Irish ahead 6–0 at the break, he began to search for a lead for his game story. During halftime, he chatted with various colleagues and publicists, including George Strickler, the new N.D. student press assistant. Strickler had recently seen the Rudolph Valentino movie *The Four Horsemen of the Apocalypse*, vividly recalling the film effect of "those ethereal figures charging through the clouds—Death, Pestilence, Famine, and War"; thus when a New York writer enthused about the N.D. backfield, the student-publicist offered that they were "just like the Four Horsemen" in the film. Rice heard the remark and subsequently turned it into his lead.

As he watched from the pressbox during the second half, Rice composed what became the single most famous passage in American sports journalism, words that changed the style of sportswriting and catapulted him to the very top of his profession:

Outlined against a blue, gray October sky, the Four Horsemen rode again. In dramatic lore, they are known as Famine, Pestilence, Destruction and Death. These are only aliases. Their real names are Stuhldreher, Miller, Crowley, and Layden. They formed the crest of the South Bend cyclone before which another fighting Army team was swept over the precipice at the Polo Grounds this afternoon as 55,000 spectators peered down upon the bewildering panorama spread out upon the green plain below.

Most sports fans, whether they like Rice's overheated style or not, enjoy this passage. He uses the cadence of biblical verse, alludes to American history—the "blue, gray" and "bewildering panorama" of the Civil War—and even includes a twenties' gangsterism, "These are only aliases."

The night editor of the *Herald-Tribune* recognized the quality of Rice's lead and took the unusual step for that newspaper of putting it on the front page of the Sunday edition. The paper's sports editor, however, gave Red Grange's five touchdowns against Michigan his section's headlines, as did all midwestern journals in their next day's editions.

The Notre Dame victory over Army, 13–7, was hardly apocalyptic, and although other New York sportswriters praised the team, their words were far from Rice's raptures: "Notre Dame's soundly coached team defeated the Army . . ." (the *World*'s lead); "Moving with speed, power, and precision, Knute Rockne's Notre Dame . . ." (the *Times*'s lead). Most reporters described a well-played, interesting game but not the "TITANIC STRUGGLE OF THE AGES." In fact, the *New York Post* writer was critical: "The Notre Dame team of Saturday, taken on its entire game's play, was described by its own supporters as disappointing, West Point astoundingly indifferent . . . [and] on this game Notre Dame is not what it used to be." A *New York Sun* columnist rapped Rockne for having his players wear uniform numbers that did not correspond to "the official program."

George Strickler enjoyed the Sunday *Herald-Tribune*, was pleased about his contribution to Rice's opening, and had the bright idea of telegraphing home to arrange for a photographer to shoot the backfielders on horseback. (Strickler later asked Rice, "What would have happened if all four writers [who heard his Four Horsemen comment] had used the same idea for their lead?" Rice responded, in the understatement of his career, "Well, I don't know. Maybe it wouldn't have been so good if everybody used it.")

When the four Notre Dame players, whose lives were permanently changed by Rice's words, first read them, they "didn't realize the impact it would have" (Crowley) and "felt that people would forget about it" (Miller). Moreover, in that same Sunday edition of the *Herald-Tribune*, in Rice's preview column on the following week's football games, he did not even put the Notre Dame visit to Princeton at the top of the list.

When the team returned to South Bend, George Strickler could only assemble a quartet of work animals—not sleek steeds—for his biblical avengers. None of the players could ride and they nervously sat through the photo session. Nevertheless, when Strickler sent the picture to the wire services, newspapers around the country reproduced it along with Rice's lead. The public "Gee-Whizzed" and the fame of the Four Horsemen started to build.

Grantland Rice, however, had moved on to other players and other teams. Most sports fans would assume that if a reporter has witnessed athletes so phenomenal that they annihilated their opponents like "Famine, Pestilence, Destruction and Death," that journalist would take a short train ride seven days later to see those same football players in action against one of the best teams in the country. Not Grantland Rice —for him, words did not possess real or literal meanings, they were only symbolic formations to play with, enjoy, and make money from, and they were endlessly interchangeable with other expressions, other verbal disconnections from reality.

Thus, on October 25, 1924, with the Four Horsemen of Notre Dame on the field at Princeton, Rice sat at a press table at Baker Bowl in New York watching the Columbia University Lions beat up on tiny Williams College. He began his article the next day: "The Eagle is back in his eyrie. The Lion has returned to his lair. Columbia again is one of the gems of the gridiron."

During the following weeks, as the wire services continued to distribute Strickler's photo along with Rice's lead, the Four Horsemen phenomenon began to explode. In the 1920s, because most newspaper readers could never see their sports heroes in action, they wanted them described as larger than life, and the press inflated the Four Horsemen into the football demigods of the year. Their main competitor was Red Grange, named by Rice before ever seeing him play, "The Galloping Ghost."

The great sportswriter of a later era, Red Smith, a Notre Dame student at this time, noted: "On a campus where a five dollar bill represented wealth, Strickler sold hundreds of 8-by-11 prints at one dollar each" to newspapers, magazines, and individuals around the country. And Smith later wondered—since Rice had been in the upstairs pressbox at the Polo Grounds—"At what angle had he watched the game to see the Notre Dame backfield outlined against the sky?"

Finally, in mid-November, Rice noticed the Four Horsemen fad and started to exploit it. A New York newspaper executive wrote to an acquaintance at N.D., "Rice has gone crazy about the Notre Dame backfield and has personally given you about as much publicity as his paper will permit. Every day he mentions them." In one column, he moved them up to the number-one all-time college football backfield, and in others he offered long doggerel poems to their greatness.

Other journalists imitated his praise. W. F. Fox, an N.D. grad, wrote in the *Indianapolis News:* "From coast to coast they're chanting a toast to the horsemen of Notre Dame" and so on. And through December, the hosannas continued, reaching a peak with the Rose Bowl victory. Many stories about the New Year's game used the Four Horsemen in the headline and/or lead, for example, the *Chicago Tribune* titled Walter Eckersall's account "THE FOUR HORSEMEN RIDE WEST" (thanks to Rockne, "Eck" was also a game official).

In 1925, the Four Horsemen graduated and tried to cash in on their fame. Several played professional football on weekends—when Stuhldreher signed with the Brooklyn pro franchise, it changed its name to the "Horsemen"—and all coached college teams. A few years later, Don Miller was the first to leave football (he became a lawyer), and the others continued more or less successful coaching careers—Elmer Layden with Notre Dame from 1934 to 1940—before becoming businessmen. But for American football fans, they remained the Four Horsemen; Stuhldreher's wife remarked decades later, "Harry has become a football legend. No matter where he speaks or what he says, he is always remembered as the quarterback of the Four Horsemen."

In the history of college football, coaches have assembled many outstanding backfields, but none are better known than the Four Horsemen of Notre Dame. Grantland Rice and his colleagues proved that words are more powerful than the most bruising football "hit" and that words can manufacture apparent realities far different from what actually occurred. No reasonably objective measurement, using football statistics as well as informed opinion, rates the Four Horsemen as the greatest college backfield of all time. In fact, Rockne as well as Rice considered N.D.'s 1930 quartet better. Yet the power of Rice's words, repeated innumerable times, gave the 1924 players a magical aura and, for future generations, rendered them almost literal Horsemen of the Apocalypse.

Thus Rice's passage, detached from its context of 1920s journalism and his other writings of the time, floats through American sports history, assuming a mystified reality. However, Elmer Layden, in his 1969 memoir, offered an excellent antidote to the Four Horsemen myth:

> Even by 1924 standards, we were small. By today's standards, we were almost midgets. We'd probably have trouble getting on most of today's college teams as student managers . . .
>
> I sometimes wonder how I'd have spent those years [since 1924] if George [Strickler]'s idea had fallen flat? . . . One thing for sure, everybody connected with the [1924 N.D.–Army] game collected dividends: our coach, our teammates and Granny Rice.

22

Rockne Threatens to Jump Ship: 1925

"The committee considers that the playing of intercollegiate [football] games in distant cities . . . is wholly bad and is a purely commercial enterprise . . . [and] is one of the great contributing causes to the growing spirit of commercialism in intercollegiate athletics."

—From the Annual Report of the Carnegie Foundation
for the Advancement of Teaching, 1924

Because of the commercial success of college football in the mid-1920s, the reformers increased the volume on their criticisms and began to demand changes. The Carnegie Foundation led the attack and in 1924 issued a brief report listing the most serious problems in college sports—the top three were "commercialism," "excessive expenditure of money," and "too great an insistence on turning out a winning team." Further-more, the main culprit was "the football coach" because he "sets the standard of the whole system of intercollegiate sports and is responsible for many of its most demoralizing features."

The report did not mention Notre Dame or Knute Rockne by name, but by implication, the charges applied to the most successful team of the period and its famous coach. After the 1924 short report, the Carnegie Foundation decided to undertake a massive five-year investigation of col-lege sports and to keep the overemphasis issue at the top of the agenda of American higher education. Their efforts contributed to the climate of opinion within the academy that put Notre Dame and Rockne on the defensive.

During the 1920s, the Catholic school's old antagonist, the Big Ten, also claimed to be in a reform phase. In 1921, the conference prohibited members from playing postseason games, including the Rose Bowl, and the following year it appointed a full-time commissioner to enforce its regulations. During this decade, however, almost every member institution built a larger football stadium—behemoths at Michigan (101,001 seats), Ohio State (81,109), and Illinois (71,227)—and by 1929, all conference stadiums, except three, contained more than 55,000 seats. An official history of the Big Ten noted: "The increased capacity brought in tremendous revenue, and this revenue was plowed right back into the athletic departments." However: "You can't fill a gigantic stadium with a losing team. Consequently the pressure on recruiting began to increase."

Rockne always railed against the Big Ten's hypocrisy, but because he had to compete with their football programs in recruiting, he wanted to match his competitors, particularly in terms of facilities. After the 1924 championship year, he again lobbied for a new stadium at Notre Dame, but as he wrote a friend who sought the stadium construction contract, President Walsh and the faculty board did not "feel that a stadium is the thing to be taken up seriously by them for at least five years."

Rockne's outside-offer adventures did not strengthen his position on this issue, but even more fundamentally, President Walsh reiterated his commitment to build "needed dormitories, class rooms and laboratories" as well as a campus dining hall before considering the construction of a football stadium. Unlike what happened at N.D.'s Big Ten rivals, much of the money from the successful football team moved into the Catholic school's general revenue stream. For the 1924–1925 academic year, N.D. sports generated $332,773, almost 95 percent of it from intercollegiate football, and with total athletic department expenses, including intramurals, at a little over $100,000, the remainder—$231,688, a huge sum for this period—went for various campus projects. The N.D. administrators tightly controlled the money and Rockne had little say in the disbursement of the athletic department profit.

In subsequent years, Notre Dame's successful football program continued to produce significant revenue for the school's building and educational funds, and later helped N.D. weather the Great Depression. It also sparked one of the most pernicious myths in American culture—that college sports generates substantial profits for schools with big-time teams and that these dollars aid academic endeavors. In fact, as the Big

Ten pioneered in the 1920s, at most institutions with major sports programs, athletic departments have always kept and spent all of their revenue and have run deficits—thus, most universities have always lost money on their intercollegiate athletic programs. In 1924, the Carnegie Foundation stated that "the great and constantly growing cost of intercollegiate athletics constitutes one of the gravest abuses" and dangers in American higher education, and that assertion has remained true.

In the 1920s, however, many colleges and universities watched the on-field and box office success of Fighting Irish football and tried to imitate it. Schools launched major athletic programs and justified the enormous cost by arguing that, like Notre Dame, they would achieve national fame and a sizable fortune. In the 1920s, no school duplicated N.D.'s success and many, especially if they built large stadiums, encountered severe financial problems. During the Great Depression, some Notre Dame wannabes, because of their intercollegiate sports costs, almost went bankrupt.

The immutable fact is that in the 1920s and subsequently *no imitator could begin to match Notre Dame's unique formula:* a rich athletic culture, fan identification based on ethnicity and religion, an innovative and charismatic coach, a phenomenal won-lost record, powerful media allies, an immense and increasing number of supporters throughout the country, and most important of all, *the invention of the formula.* The Fighting Irish were there first, and in the beginning, they were also a wonderful novelty. In the harsh world of college sports, imitation mainly produces runners-up and red ink.

■ ■ ■

" 'Virgil N. Evans, a well known football star, released from the Kansas State Reformatory, June 18th, 1924, and paroled to the faculty of Notre Dame, South Bend, Indiana, to play the 1924 season on the college team, has been returned to the Kansas State Penitentiary to complete his sentence.' "

—President Walsh quoting
a newspaper article, December 19, 1924

As the N.D. administration quickly realized, football fame and fortune had an unpleasant downside. Not only did the higher education mandarins distrust Notre Dame's athletic achievements but, in anti-Catholic America, many ordinary citizens wondered how a small parochial school could win a national football championship. Some were willing to believe the wildest rumors about the team. The article about the convict paroled to Notre Dame for the football season first appeared in the *Leavenworth* (Kansas) *Times* but was picked up by the wire services and resulted in many inquiries to President Walsh. He composed a form letter reply stating, in part, that the story "is a succession of lies . . . [and] we all feel greatly incensed over this reflection on Notre Dame."

N.D.'s experience with great football success contradicts one of the other major myths about college sports—that it produces wonderful publicity for the schools involved. At best, the publicity is a two-edged sword, and in Notre Dame's case, although it drew attention to the institution and built up fan support, much of the press coverage was negative and tarred the school with a "football factory" image. In 1925, even the *Notre Dame Alumnus*, the football team's most fervent supporter, admitted that "the unprecedented centering of attention upon Notre Dame" because of the 1924 championship was not a blessing. "Notre Dame is by its nature and function more harmed than helped by publicity, [especially when the stories are] composed of one-tenth rumor and nine-tenths imagination."

In 1924–1925, the N.D. president as well as the coach received many more inquiries than previously concerning the school's athletic program. Typically, the writer was Catholic and inquired whether Notre Dame adhered to Big Ten rules and whether the football players attended regular classes. Usually the writer requested the information "to combat adverse criticism of your football team in this vicinity" or "to settle a dispute." The N.D. authorities patiently explained that the school followed the Big Ten rules in all ways, including academic requirements for athletes.

To insure that the assertion was true, President Walsh strengthened the Faculty Board of Control of Athletics. In 1924, Rockne's nemesis, Vice President Irving, reappeared on two of the board's three committees, and in 1925, when President Walsh changed his administrative team, he appointed his new vice president, Father George Finigan, as chair of the board.

In a letter to Finigan, Walsh outlined his views of the board's duties: "Long experience with the athletic conditions at Notre Dame has convinced me, beyond any doubt, that our standing in the outside world is determined, not so much by the number of victories that we gain as by our strict adherence to what reputable colleges consider the proper standards." Walsh then instructed Finigan to follow "the constitution governing athletics" in all matters, especially eligibility of athletes and finances.

Rockne, who never lost his concern for "the number of victories," attempted an end run around Walsh and the board by enlisting the alumni. He wanted to balance the power of the board with an "Alumni Advisory Committee." The coach assumed that the grads would back him in all disputes with the board and he proposed a group of "eight or ten of our leading alumni" for his committee. Walsh agreed to a three-man group "to act [only] in an advisory capacity to the Board."

"The premature publicity from USC got me in awfully dutch down here [at Notre Dame] . . . I don't know who is to blame for that premature publicity, but it ruined every prospect in the world for me to change [from] here for some time. It made me look very foolish and put me on the defensive as soon as I landed here [after the Rose Bowl trip]."

—Rockne to Amos Santweir,
USC booster, June 4, 1925

The success of the Fighting Irish and Rockne's increasing fame prompted coaching offers from other schools. In December 1924, an important University of Wisconsin alum sounded him out about that school's coaching and A.D. job, but Rockne did not pursue the offer, in part because his close friend and business partner, "Doc" Meanwell, the Wisconsin basketball coach, wanted the Badger athletic directorship. However, in early 1925, during the Rose Bowl visit to Los Angeles, the Notre Dame coach met with USC officials to discuss the head coaching job at that school.

On January 15, 1925, the USC comptroller wired Rockne: "ALL CONDITIONS YOU SUGGESTED IN RECENT CONFERENCE MET. ELMER IS PLEASED WITH ARRANGEMENT AND SINCERELY HOPES YOU CAN ARRANGE AFFAIRS TO COME." (Elmer "Gloomy Gus" Henderson was the incumbent USC coach, and Rockne had requested that Henderson be retained in another athletic department position.) The next day, however, when a Los Angeles reporter published the details of the USC offer and the wire services jumped on the story, negotiations ended. The school telegraphed Rockne: "WE REGRET UNFORTUNATE PUBLICITY WHICH HAS DOUBTLESS MADE YOUR POSITION EMBARRASSING. TRUSTEES UNANIMOUS IN . . . EXTEND[ING] INVITATION TO YOU."

At Notre Dame, President Walsh responded to the news of the Southern California offer by reminding the coach that he had signed a ten-year contract with N.D. and that he could face legal action if he reneged. Rockne wrote USC that he was "on the defensive the minute I landed here" from the West Coast trip "and they had me sweating blood.

I am sorry that the publicity got out the way it did and it has me now in quite bad with a number of the Alumni."

The USC episode marked the first time that Rockne's outside-offer strategy failed. In fact, it soon cost him yardage in his ongoing struggle with the Faculty Athletic Board. Coming off a national championship season and a Rose Bowl victory, he should have been in an excellent position to swat away all attacks from his faculty opponents. But the administrators and professors were restless—ironically, because Notre Dame's football success and the accompanying press attention had produced a whole new set of problems for the board, chiefly in terms of scheduling and relations with other schools.

". . . you must remember that there are thousands of teams wanting to play us now and it is quite a problem as to which games will be to the best interests of Notre Dame."

—Rockne to the sports editor
of the *Cleveland* (Ohio) *News*, February 18, 1925

The Cleveland newspaperman wanted to promote a Fighting Irish game in his city against John Carroll University, a Catholic institution. A few years earlier, with matches hard to obtain, the faculty board might have accepted and overruled Rockne's veto of Catholic opponents because, as the N.D. coach acknowledged, "we have a fine group of alumni in Cleveland [and the city] has many desirable points." But, by 1925, with Notre Dame inundated by requests to play football games in all parts of the country, the N.D. administrators discovered that the football gold had a Midas curse underside—refusing invitations created enemies.

The faculty board instructed Rockne, the point man on football scheduling, to write the rejection letters, and in 1925, he worked out a standard form. He usually began, "You can rest assured that I argued as strongly as I could for this game"—wanting no limits on his program, frequently he did argue for the game, but even when he did not, he never portrayed himself as the "bad guy." However, the coach stated that the faculty board had ruled against the proposed contest because "we are playing five games away from here this [1925] Fall, involving 7,500 miles of travel" and "we are being criticized quite a little bit for the amount of playing we are doing away from home."

The most difficult refusals involved requests for charity games, particularly those made by fellow Catholics and important members of the church hierarchy. By 1925, Rockne articulated what became the standard reply to these entreaties: "We have had hundreds of applications to play for charity and they [the board] are afraid to establish a precedent and to offend all of those who have been turned down."

The faculty board did accept Rockne's position on not playing Catholic schools but, as a result, Notre Dame sometimes strained relations with fellow Catholic institutions. In 1925, Holy Cross in Massachusetts wanted N.D. to play in the inaugural game in its new stadium and worked through many intermediaries, clerical and lay, to obtain the match, but the board and the coach adamantly refused. Rockne later felt vindicated when a C.S.C. priest living in Massachusetts informed him, "The Holy Cross student body and alumni are *not* fond of Notre Dame and are very jealous of our fame in athletics, especially football." The coach replied that he was always "glad to receive [such] letters" because they "help me in my position" against scheduling Catholic schools; however, "I must be as diplomatic as possible, as we cannot afford to have too many enemies."

Yet, in spite of Rockne's diplomacy, the college football world was beginning to divide into those who liked Notre Dame and those who did not, with a diminishing number remaining neutral. Great success sparked envy; moreover, the turndowns of invitations made enemies at Catholic as well as at secular schools. At times, Rockne yearned for the simpler times when he had to scramble to fill a schedule and accepted more rebuffs than he handed out. But by 1925, he and the faculty board realized that there was no turning back and that if Fighting Irish football success continued, it meant increasing numbers of foes as well as friends. (The division of the college football world into Notre Dame lovers and haters has continued—indeed, intensified—to the present day.)

". . . post-season games are not looked on with any degree of favor in college circles. Notre Dame has had its fill of football publicity and we do not believe it would be advisable to give the public the impression that we are seeking more worlds to conquer.

The Faculty Board of Control have adopted a definite policy of discouraging post-season games."

—President Walsh, June 12, 1925

In the early 1920s, the Big Ten prohibited members from participating in postseason games, including the Rose Bowl (and continued this policy for twenty-six years); by mid-decade, such reformers as the Carnegie Foundation called for a ban on all of these contests. President Walsh and the faculty board were alert to these developments and in spite of protests from N.D. alumni and students, especially after the wonderful 1925 Rose Bowl victory, Notre Dame authorities decided to decline all invitations to postseason games (the N.D. ban continued until 1969). One C.S.C. historian pointed out: "This policy, adopted to avoid the accusation of commercialism, was no empty gesture, but actually cost the University the opportunity to earn much money over the years."

Notre Dame fans reluctantly came to accept the bowl game prohibition and offered it as an example of the school's "purity of athletics." Notre Dame's enemies, however, pointed out that, also in 1925, the school scheduled the inaugural game in the USC series and that this biannual trek to the West Coast and the huge payday in the L.A. Coliseum contradicted the anticommercial message of the bowl game ban.

In late 1925, Rockne wrote to a friend: "The Southern California officials came to South Bend and offered the authorities such a fluttering guarantee that they could not turn it down." Walsh and the faculty board justified their acceptance of the offer by arguing that the game was part of a home-and-home series and the trip to California would only occur once every two years; moreover, because of the bowl game ban, Notre Dame would make no other West Coast journeys and could cut down on its travel during the USC away game years. This justification did not totally please N.D. fans or opponents but it reflected the real world in which President Walsh existed—demands from Rockne and alumni for more big-time football as well as the financial rewards from a winning team versus pressure from the educational establishment to deemphasize sports. Walsh could never truly satisfy either side and instead chose a middle course for his school.

■ ■ ■

"This will confirm my understanding of the agreement entered into between you [Knute Rockne] and me [Major John Griffith, Big Ten commissioner] the other day in my office, whereby I am to run two one-half page ads of the Culver Coaching School [owned by Rockne] in the April and May *Athletic Journals* [owned by Griffith] at a cost of $56 per insertion and further you are to write an article on discus throwing for the April *Journal* and another article for the September number on football. . . ."

—Major John Griffith, Big Ten commissioner,
to Rockne, March 3, 1925

The Notre Dame coach also had to deal with the real world, including the fact that the N.D. policy of adhering to Big Ten rules presented new problems in terms of hiring referees. The conference had delegated this power as well as the development of a list of approved officials to its commissioner. The Big Ten head tried to gain pregame agreement on officials from the coaches involved, but he had the final word on all assignments. Moreover, when Big Ten teams played nonconference opponents, they insisted—as a clause in Minnesota's contract for the 1925 game with N.D. stipulated—that "these games shall be played under the rules of the Intercollegiate Conference of Faculty Representatives" (the Big Ten), including regulations on assigning officials.

But Rockne, as usual, perfectly analyzed this new defense and nullified it by using his business and personal relationship with the Big Ten commissioner, Major John Griffith. The latter had started a monthly magazine, the *Athletic Journal,* and needed advertising and articles; in congratulating Rockne on the 1924 season, the Big Ten commissioner noted: "Right now, Knute [Rockne] and Notre Dame are foremost in the minds of football coaches. Why not capitalize on this publicity and in a legitimate way tell these young coaches through the [*Athletic*] *Journal* that you are going to have a coaching school this summer at South Bend." For Griffith, "the legitimate way" was a series of ads for the school and articles by Rockne.

The N.D. coach agreed to the proposal and he continued to place ads and write articles for Griffith's magazine for the remainder of his coaching career. Their business and personal relations became so close that, after Studebaker Motors hired Rockne to promote its products, Griffith's wife asked the N.D. coach, "Aren't you in a position to get us ads from the Studebaker people? You know, the more advertising we get, the more trips we can take with the Rockne-Blackwell tours" (the coach's travel business).

The Big Ten commissioner repaid the N.D. coach for his cooperation in many other ways, including sending Rockne's coaching school material to prospective attendees and, most important of all, by being extremely sympathetic to his requests for game officials. In 1925, the Minnesota and Northwestern games posed a problem for the N.D. coach because powerful Big Ten faculty representatives wanted a voice in the selection of officials. Rockne objected "strenuously" and warned Griffith that if he gave in to the faculty reps, "I will cancel both games and contracts." Griffith took the faculty out of the process and allowed Rockne to veto the commissioner's officiating selections.

Through the 1920s, the Big Ten head was not only amenable to the N.D. coach's requests concerning his games with conference opponents but also agreed to Rockne's use of regular Big Ten officials, especially his journalist friends, for other N.D. contests. In 1925, Rockne wrote, "Dear

John:—Don't forget I want Eckersall for October 17th, Army game, and November 14th, Carnegie Tech game," and added, "I will be up this week [to Chicago] and will have a complete list of the officials that I would like to have and will go over this with you."

> "As you know, I am not much of an official, but I love to travel and so does Mrs. Gardner, and I occasionally have something very close to me that produces much mirth [hip flasks of booze]. And besides, I have never been to California."
>
> —Fred Gardner to Rockne, November 7, 1924

Gardner, one of Griffith's regular Big Ten officials and a Rockne favorite, wanted the Rose Bowl game assignment, but the N.D. coach had to refuse this request, explaining that Pop Warner of Stanford would only "let Eckersall come on from the Middle West." Rockne, who loved to spar with buccaneers like Pop and won this round, added that Warner "was quite provoked because I would not stand for a California official. I wired him that I thought eleven men were enough to play against."

Eckersall thanked the N.D. coach—"It was mighty nice of you to go through with" the Rose Bowl job—but, typically, the Chicago reporter put in for more work, particularly the Notre Dame–Army game in 1925, pleading, "I would hate to lose my identity with this game." (Thanks to his N.D. pal, Eckersall worked this annual contest for the remainder of his career.)

In addition to "Eck," Rockne hired other friends on the Big Ten list for officiating jobs. Because the N.D. coach still controlled all of his home games involving non–Big Ten opponents, he could even extend his list of sportswriter-officials. He signed up Milton Ghee of the *Chicago American* for the Beloit game in 1925, and the journalist wrote him, "I am aggressive and interested enough in working for you that I would like more of your work."

By the mid-1920s, Notre Dame's national success in football provided its coach with great leverage over game officials. In addition to the regular inducements of payment and travel, working a Fighting Irish contest gave a journalist-referee the prestige of being where the action, as well as some of the best stories, in college football were. As Milton Ghee told the N.D. coach, "Please know that I would rather referee for you and Notre Dame than any other team in the country."

Obviously these journalist-referees did not want to incur Rockne's displeasure, nor did opposing coaches who had worked so hard to obtain a Notre Dame game on their schedules protest his choice of officials. From a modern perspective, Rockne's manipulation of the refereeing system seems highly questionable; however, in the world of 1920s college football, the N.D. coach, like his rivals, tried to gain every possible advantage and, characteristically, he succeeded better than most.

> "Rock, wish you would let me know what you think [will be the outcome] of the Nebraska–Notre Dame game this fall and the matter will be kept purely confidential. I have to get enough dough to make the trip to New York and if things are right I can place a lot of dough in Sioux City thru an uninterested party. There will be no sobs or wails if the negative result turns up."
>
> —Bill "Stub" Allison, former N.D. player
> and coach at the University of South Dakota,
> to Rockne, November 6, 1925

In 1924, the Carnegie Foundation warned that students and alumni "regard a bet on their college team as an expression of loyalty to alma mater" and that the wagering on college games, often controlled by professional bookmakers, had become a major problem. Rockne's attitude, however, was pragmatic; in replying to his former player, Bill "Stub" Allison, he did not lecture him on the evils of gambling on college football, he merely advised, "Lay off the betting on the Nebraska game as we have played too terrific a schedule and the boys are getting a little bit all in."

During that same 1925 season, he also answered a West Point officer's complaint about the poor behavior of some Notre Dame fans during the Army's lopsided victory: "There were no doubt a lot of tin-horn sports in our stands who lost money on the game and who may have said anything. These type of men are, of course, detrimental to the game but how can we control them?"

In fact, Rockne contributed to the problem by forecasting the outcome of games in his newspaper columns. Because of his reputation as a "football genius," many bettors, especially in cities like New York, closely followed his tips. By 1925, "plunging" on college football had become so popular that the *New York Daily News*—imitating its horse race betting charts—introduced a weekly "CONSENSUS FOR GRID SCORES," with five experts picking the outcome of Saturday's games. (To feed the growing appetite of working-class New Yorkers for gambling information on college football, the *Daily News* also began to devote much more space to teams like Notre Dame and thus helped spark the eventual formation of the "subway alumni.")

Throughout the 1920s, Knute Rockne and many other coaches publicly predicted the outcomes of college football contests and the betting on the sport increased significantly; a typical Rockne column began, "The way the dope bucket was upset last Saturday . . ."

Part of the N.D. coach's talent was his ability to focus on what he considered his most important tasks—building the best football program in the country and promoting his own career. Peripheral to this work was the reform of intercollegiate athletics, including purging the gamblers, and he regarded the reformers as starry-eyed idealists, not tough pragmatists like himself and his competitors. Thus, in 1925, the Notre Dame coach, in spite of the new constraints placed on him by President Walsh and the faculty board, as well as increased scrutiny by the Big Ten faculty reps, not only found a path through the college football jungle but stayed ahead of his coaching competitors. The corrupt system in which he worked contradicts the later myth that college sports were innocent during the "Rockne era." That the N.D. coach understood such new phenomena as the Big Ten reforms and its commissioner's office and turned them to his advantage is a testimonial to both his high intelligence and his lack of innocence.

"I expect to be in New York early in September and I wish that you would find out which sports writers think that I have been high-hatting them and for what reason. I would like very much to correct this impression as you know it is not so."

—Rockne to Francis Wallace, August 18, 1925

Part of Rockne's job as Notre Dame football coach and athletic director was dealing with the press. He had long known that gate receipts, especially in major cities, were tied to newspaper coverage and so he massaged the egos of the sportswriters of the day. But by 1925, his time was increasingly limited and the demands on it were growing exponentially. Thus, during one typical visit to Manhattan, Rockne only had time for a luncheon arranged by his agent, Christy Walsh, for the two of them and Grantland Rice and Ring Lardner, and he bruised the feelings of some of the uninvited reporters. On other New York trips, especially before the Army–Notre Dame game, he tried to see as many writers as possible. In his correspondence, however, he always targeted the stars for special attention. When Rice praised him in an August column, he responded, "Dear Grant . . . I cannot express in words how keenly I appreciate this fine generosity on your part and I can only hope that some day I may be able to repay in some small way the many favors you have done for me."

A few months later, only a year after the famous Four Horsemen lead, Grantland Rice did not cover the 1925 Army–Notre Dame game in New York, traveling that day to New Haven for the Yale–Penn contest. But Rockne was too savvy to show anger at this slight and he continued his correspondence with Rice, including a long November letter confidentially supplying the sportswriter with the names of players for Rice's *Collier's* magazine All-America team.

Part of Rockne's interest in big-time journalism was personal as well as professional. In 1923, he signed with Christy Walsh's sports syndicate to write articles about college football; the following year, his writing career received a boost when a number of his major competitors—the Big Three Ivy coaches—had to drop their columns because their schools, in a reform move, prohibited them from earning income in this way. As Rockne's fame grew, more newspapers accepted his pieces, paying him increasing sums of money for them.

Christy Walsh, the first sports agent, was notorious for his use of ghostwriters—he titled his memoir *Adios to Ghosts*—and he had as many as four work with his top client, Babe Ruth. In looking back on this "ghostwriting fraud," Paul Gallico marveled at how "much of the hogwash" supposedly written by famous athletes or coaches "was accepted as gospel" by the naive public. Although Walsh did not assign a full-time ghost to Rockne, many of the coach's articles were ghostedited and some were ghostwritten. In addition, Rockne's most famous work, his *Autobiography*, was totally ghostwritten. This, of course, contradicts one of the posthumous myths about "Saint Knute"—that he penned every single word published under his name.

Rockne's agent recognized that his client's "journalism" was important to the growth of the coach's celebrity as well as the fame of Notre Dame football. The signed columns—topped by Rockne's photo—augmented the many newspaper pieces about him and the team, and 1920s sports fans eagerly digested them all. A typical Rockne piece had the coach discoursing on a topic such as "the backfield shift" and, most importantly, featured his Saturday predictions—ghosts usually turned a coach's telegraphed list of winners into prose paragraphs.

Rockne was amenable to his agent's methods, and in a 1924 note to a magazine editor, remarked, "I trust Christy Walsh has turned over our article to you before this. This is the best I could do and you may re-edit it any way you see fit." The samples of prose that are indisputably the coach's, such as drafts of articles in his handwriting, show him to be a laborious author. Writing was far from his natural world of action, and his stilted, prolix style indicates his difficulties. His letters also reveal his problems with syntax and his lack of professional fluency; for example, the next lines of the above-quoted letter to Francis Wallace are: "I will send you some dope on football at the proper time which I hope will help everybody concerned. I shall be very glad to give you any western angles which may be of interest to the east." In 1925, he admitted that even though some people "have taken the point of view that I am clever with English—I am anything but that."

Almost certainly, Rockne's postgame stories for the Sunday papers—a large percentage of his casual journalism—were ghostwritten. The logistics of the situation allowed little alternative: the coach, immediately after the game, mentally drained, surrounded in the locker room by players, reporters, N.D. officials, alumni, and well-wishers, would have had to excuse himself, rush to the pressbox, fend off the journalists there who wanted to interview him, knock out a long article in under an hour, and then dictate it over the phone to a copy editor. The time constraints occurred because most newspapers carrying his postgame column had very early deadlines—the first Sunday edition of his best client, the *New York World,* came out at seven P.M. on Saturday night.

Thus, in 1925, after Army lambasted his team 27–0, did the Notre Dame coach really go to the pressbox and write the well-paced lead— "The best Army football team that I have seen since the World War met the greenest and youngest of all Notre Dame teams"—and follow this with a long, lucid analysis of the game? More likely, in the locker room, Christy Walsh or one of his assistants listened to the coach's rap on the game and efficiently wrote it up in the pressbox. The author of the 1925 piece did an excellent job, with many short, punchy passages: "There was no gloom before the game and there is no gloom now. The boys gave everything they had but they lacked the prime essential for victory . . . experience." This language resembled Rockne's actual speech pattern, but the coach did not believe in writing in this manner—he tried to imitate the complicated, ornate prose popular at the time.

Fortunately for Notre Dame football, Knute Rockne was a much better coach than an author, and after the departure of the Four Horsemen and the Seven Mules, he was able to rebuild while playing a national schedule in 1925.

"The trouble, my dear Rockne, is that defeat is an almost unknown quantity at Notre Dame. If you people out there had a little more of the experience we [at West Point] have had with you, you too might feel as we have felt for so many years . . ."

—Colonel H. J. Koehler to Rockne,
October 26, 1925

Many Fighting Irish fans considered the 1925 football season and the team's 7–2–1 record a failure, but, as the Army officer indicated, Notre Dame and its supporters had been spoiled by the phenomenal success of Rockne's previous years—a 58–4–2 mark—as well as no losses to Army in nine years. Only second-string players returned from the 1924 national championship team, and these, plus a large number of talented but inexperienced athletes, formed the 1925 squad. In his opening games—against Baylor, Lombard, and Beloit—the N.D. coach, in search of a starting lineup, employed "as many as forty and forty-three players in these three practice games, which I use in every sense of the word as practice games."

His team was good enough, however, to win by scores of 41–0, 69–0, and 19–3. Most of the youngsters had played freshman and/or reserve team football against other schools, but they were definitely not ready to meet a strong Army squad in Yankee Stadium on October 17, 1925.

The pregame New York hoopla was greater than for previous Army–Notre Dame contests, and the *New York Times* predicted: "Receipts to run $250,000" and "the game will set a record for New York football attendance and also in receipts." Good seats were at a premium and some New York fans tried all their Notre Dame connections; one of Rockne's former players wrote him that an "individual . . . high up in Tammany [Hall] circles" needed ten tickets, "and of course it would do me good as well as N.D. and yourself to see that ten good ones are forthcoming." The coach replied: "We will take good care of your friend."

On game day in New York, in spite of morning rains, almost seventy thousand people jammed Yankee Stadium. But, except for West Point fans, they left disappointed after watching a lopsided 27–0 Army victory. Rockne was not angry at his young players—he felt that they had given

their best—but he was furious at the Notre Dame fans who heckled the
Army bench and also at some of the N.D. alumni. He later wrote Ed
Barrow, general manager of the Yankees and the stadium: "There were
some rumors which reached me that our alumni, some of them, did some
scalping" of the tickets distributed directly to them by Joe Byrne, Jr., and
the coach vowed to change the distribution system.

Byrne tried to mend fences in a letter to President Walsh, and he also
pointed out that N.D.'s claim on New York football fans was not automatic: "With Notre Dame losing this year, while the papers have been
very fair, you will note that our [post–Army game] publicity has dropped
off considerably due to the fact that we were not champions as we were
in the past."

President Walsh, unlike Byrne, did not regard Notre Dame football
as mainly a business enterprise where winning, because it maximized
publicity and profits, was imperative. The $72,232 settlement check from
Yankee Stadium was more than he had expected and the following Saturday's payday of almost $50,000 from the trip to the University of Minne-
sota was a nice bonus added to the opportunity to play this important Big
Ten school. The N.D. president had to balance academic and financial
pressures, and at this point in the year, when the school began to receive
"feelers" for postseason appearances, he invoked the new policy banning
N.D. trips to these games. Furthermore, President Walsh later accepted
with equanimity the fact that the $190,000 net profit from the 1925
football campaign was $43,000 less than the previous year's solely be-
cause N.D. refused to engage in postseason play.

Rockne enjoyed Notre Dame's first visit to Minnesota—in addition to the
fine payday, his young team executed his offense and contained the Gophers' attack for a convincing 19–7 win. The N.D. coach began to see the
emergence of backfield talent to replace the Four Horsemen: "Red"
Hearden, whom Curly Lambeau had sent from Green Bay, and Christy
Flanagan, loved by the press as an "authentic Irish star," led the rushing
attack.

The following week, the game at Georgia Tech produced another
N.D. victory. Against a good southern team, the Irish earned a hard-
fought 13–0 win. However, Rockne worried that the road schedule was
wearing down his young squad and the next Saturday at Penn State
confirmed his fears—an unimpressive Nittany Lion team held N.D. to a
scoreless tie.

Finally, the Fighting Irish returned for one of the latest Homecoming games in school history, held on November 14 against Carnegie Tech, and an easy 26–0 victory over the weak Tartans. The following Saturday was supposed to be another breather before the Thanksgiving trip to Nebraska, but the visitors, Northwestern, did not accommodate Rockne's scheduling strategy. The Big Ten team was enjoying one of its best seasons, having already beaten tough Carleton College and three conference opponents, including Michigan. The "Purple" almost upset Rockne's squad, losing at the wire, 13–10. (The Northwestern teams of this era fought so hard that journalists began calling them the "Wildcats"—a nickname that remained far beyond its appropriateness.)

More pleasing to Rockne than the close win was the capacity crowd at Cartier Field and the largest home gate receipts to date, almost $60,000, split fifty-fifty with the visitors (another Big Ten rule). Large numbers of Notre Dame and Northwestern fans came by train from Chicago and, because of the sellout, many were unable to obtain seats.

The 1925 season was a turning point in the Notre Dame ticket situation. Only half a decade earlier, Rockne had peddled "ducats" on the streets of South Bend, but after years of great football success capped by the national championship and Rose Bowl victory, the N.D. athletic director had to refuse increasing numbers of seat requests, particularly for the important home games. He explained to one longtime local patron that the demand from Midwest football fans was overwhelming and that even seats for the "Notre Dame family" were scarce. As a result, "the student body is threatening to hang us in effigy while the alumni threaten to fire us." In 1925 and succeeding years, he received many more letters requesting tickets and/or complaining about the lack of them or decent seats than on any other single topic—at least fifty to one.

Rockne tried to distance himself from this problem by turning it over to the athletic department's business manager, Al Ryan, who, in turn, passed it to the ticket manager, Art Haley. But the years of the coach's hands-on approach to ticket selling returned to haunt him when longtime fans as well as sportswriters and friends pleaded directly to him for any available seat. He tried to accommodate them as best he could but often had to turn down their requests, especially last-minute ones.

Similarly, President Walsh became a ticket source of last resort for prominent alumni and important friends of the university. Like the coach, Walsh tried to stay far away from ticket distribution, but he was not immune to all entreaties and sometimes had to come up with box seats at the last minute. On occasion, he bumped C.S.C. priests out of their regular places to accommodate influential alumni. And, as with Rockne's letter files, by 1925 Walsh's correspondence began to fill with ticket requests and/or complaints, and the mail on this topic soon exceeded the letters on any other single issue for the remainder of his presidency as well as the terms of many of his successors.

■ ■ ■

"It afforded much relief to my Irish feelin's to read that athletic relations with Nebraska have been severed.

I witnessed the Thanksgiving Day game at Lincoln. I have been wondering ever since if you men over there [at Notre Dame] would suffer in despicable silence the dirty insult that was offered to the Irish between halves."

—Father H. Ryder, Lowell, Indiana,
    to Father George Finigan, vice president of Notre Dame,
    December 10, 1925

Previous Notre Dame visits to Nebraska had sparked anti-Catholic and anti-Irish insults from the local fans, but because Rockne needed this major game and its big payday for his annual schedule, Notre Dame authorities had ignored such newspaper headlines as "HORRIBLE HIBERNIANS INVADE TODAY" and crowd chants of "Mackerel Snappers Go Home."

By 1925, however, Notre Dame had its pick of big-time opponents as well as opportunities for paydays larger than the Lincoln one. Nebraska supporters seemed unaware of this new power balance, and in October, when the Cornhuskers played at Illinois, members of the Nebraska traveling party regaled the Big Ten people with fables about Notre Dame's academic laxness—specifically, how three N.D. players from the Omaha area were allowed to play for the 1924 Fighting Irish after failing all of their classes, charges that were untrue. Within a few days, accounts of this incident reached Rockne.

The N.D. coach had always tried to smooth out the difficulties with Nebraska but this time he wrote long, vituperative letters to two Nebraska journalists involved in the rumormongering, accusing them of slander. One answered cheekily, "I have never been quite able to forget the case of George Gipp, who was declared ineligible one week and then given the stamp of approval a week later."

The N.D. coach replied: "In these days of the Ku Klux Klan there are bound to be a lot of malicious lies carried around the country," and he challenged "anybody in Nebraska to make a trip here and go through our records and if there is anything wrong in any way, I shall be very glad to pay the expenses of the trip."

With this controversy as background, when the N.D. coach, team, and supporters arrived in Lincoln in late November, they were annoyed to discover storefront windows plastered with a full-page ad from the local paper—the headline "BEAT NOTRE DAME" appeared above a doggerel poem containing such verses as "From South Bend rooter take no 'sass,' / But boldly bellow out, enmasse, / 'These roughneck Irish shall not pass!' " Many windows also displayed large "BEAT THOSE NOTRE DAME ROUGHNECKS" and "BEAT NOTRE DAME" signs, some with the first letter of the first word dropped ("EAT NOTRE DAME").

In 1920s college football, with direct links to its eastern school and amateur gentlemen origins, this kind of partisan rooting was unusual. Administrators tolerated behind-the-scenes athletic department chicanery but demanded public politeness from the university community to "guests" from other institutions; Notre Dame, like the Ivy schools, usually held Friday night welcoming ceremonies for the players and fans of visiting teams. However, in Lincoln in 1925, a C.S.C. priest in the Notre Dame traveling party observed: "The joy of sport seemed to have been completely forgotten in the effort to win. From every corner of the stadium came insulting epithets of 'roughneck Irish, shanty Irish,' and similar expressions" in an attempt to upset the N.D. players and fans. "The crowds in the grandstands, to be sure, were only echoing the spirit voiced by the student body in the insulting song they persisted in singing about the 'roughneck Irish' etc."

During previous anti–Notre Dame incidents in Lincoln, Rockne and the N.D. administrators had always made a distinction between the insulting townspeople and the well-behaved university community. In 1925, this separation disappeared, particularly when, according to the *Nebraska Alumnus,* the "student pep organization," presumably with university approval, put on a halftime "stunt . . . in which four boys, each carrying a brickmason's hod and astride make-believe horses, sought to perpetrate a little fun at the expense of the famous 'Four Horsemen of Notre Dame.' "

This "stunt" outraged Notre Dame supporters. One eyewitness, the publisher of the *South Bend News-Times,* said sharply, "The performance . . . was a ridicule of the Irish, of Rockne and of Notre Dame." Within the context of 1920s America, the halftime show had only negative meanings for Notre Dame—the burlesque implied that the Four Horsemen had not been real college students but hired, ignorant laborers, and furthermore, that Irish Catholics were only fit for menial tasks. Possibly the Nebraska students did not understand the sensitivity of their visitors about this stereotype, but the damage was done.

In previous visits to Lincoln, when Notre Dame had won or played well, the game result and gate receipts compensated for the insults. But in 1925, the Cornhuskers completely outclassed Rockne's young, travel-weary team, beating them 17–0, and the payout was only $34,865, less than four other games that year. Thus, when the N.D. traveling party returned to Indiana, the secretary of the athletic board informed President Walsh that his group was "of the opinion that Nebraska should be dropped from the 1926 football schedule." Rockne did not want to end the series, especially after a shutout defeat, but a few days later Vice President Finigan, chair of the board, canceled the 1926 game as well as negotiations for future contests with the prairie school. He was immediately congratulated by many Notre Dame supporters who had either witnessed the events in Lincoln or heard about them.

Rockne tried to distance himself from the board's decision, even telling the *Lincoln* (Nebraska) *State Journal:* "Personally I do not see anything wrong [in what occurred]." The paper headlined the story "BREAK NOT DOINGS OF KNUTE ROCKNE / NOTRE DAME COACH QUOTED AS SAYING HE DID NOT CANCEL GAME." Rockne's comments angered President Walsh and a week later rebounded back on the coach.

Not every Notre Dame fan congratulated the N.D. administrators on the break with Nebraska. The supervisor of Catholic schools in that state wrote to N.D., "My work has been helped wonderfully by the appearance of Notre Dame [football in this region], it will be hurt to a degree by the absence of Notre Dame."

And many fans who hated the Fighting Irish interpreted the events through their anti–N.D. animus. A South Bend letter writer to the *Chicago Tribune* argued: "Surely the breaking of their contract with Nebraska after Nebraska had beaten them for the third time in four years was enough to convince anybody that their [N.D.'s] system is 'Pick the team that you can beat' . . . Drop the schools that beat you." This letter writer's dislike for Notre Dame probably increased when Rockne wrote him privately: "It is a libelous, slanderous letter . . . but just bear this in mind, brother, a little charity and justice goes a long way further than bigotry and hatred."

Behind the scenes, the N.D. coach tried to reverse the faculty board's decision and continue the Cornhusker series. The Nebraska authorities supported his appeal because the cancellation created a major financial problem for them—the school had built a large, expensive stadium in 1922, and during its first three years, only Fighting Irish visits had filled it.

The men in the Golden Dome were well aware of the Cornhuskers' financial situation but were unmoved by Rockne's and Nebraska's pleas to reinstate the series. For the C.S.C. priests, the era of tolerating anti-Catholic insults was over. Many years passed before the University of Nebraska sold out its stadium again, and even more years, and the passing from the scene of all those involved in the 1925 events, before the Fighting Irish revisited Lincoln.

> "Rock was wrong in ever entering into negotiations with Columbia while under contract with Notre Dame. . . . I know that he is as fine a man as walks but he has been tempted from time to time with flattering offers to coach at other colleges . . . despite the fact that he knew he was under contract to Notre Dame."
>
> —Joe Byrne, Jr., to President Walsh, December 16, 1925

Rockne was incensed at Notre Dame's break with Nebraska; not only had he opposed it but the faculty board had scorned his objections. A few days after the board's decision, he took his anger to New York, where he met with representatives of Columbia University to discuss their head coaching position.

The Ivy school had pursued the N.D. coach, with his encouragement, for a number of years; during the 1923 NCAA meeting in Manhattan, he had discussed the Columbia job with the manager of that school's athletic association, and Rockne later gave this official the impression that he "might be willing to enter into a contract with" Columbia in the future. Rockne's interest in the New York school was more than mere flirtation or an attempt to gain greater leverage at Notre Dame: a number of rich Columbia grads wanted to build "Lion football" to the Harvard, Yale, and Princeton level, and they promised Rockne a well-funded program as well as a huge salary; in addition, as Christy Walsh pointed out to him, working in Manhattan would allow him constant access to the best media deals in America.

When the N.D. coach met the Columbia representatives in early December 1925, they offered him a contract for three years at $25,000 per annum—a salary higher than any other sports coach in the country. Rockne signed the Columbia contract, with the understanding that the deal would remain secret until he had straightened out his affairs at Notre Dame. He would return to New York in late December and, at that time, he and Columbia would announce the agreement.

In what the *New York Daily News* later termed "The Biggest Boner" of 1925, the key Columbia negotiator released the news of Rockne's signing a day after the event. The *News*'s subhead—"Patience Might Have Brought Rockne to City"—and text described what might have occurred if the Columbia man, James Knapp, had kept quiet: "Rockne would have returned to Notre Dame and persuaded the officials there to kindly permit the abrogation of the existing contract, Rockne explaining he had done a great deal for the Hoosiers and that he would like a change in scenery. Beyond a doubt Rockne would have been released."

Francis Wallace confirmed this analysis with his report that President Walsh reacted to Rockne's signing at Columbia with a "bomb"—he informed the coach and his inner circle of alumni friends that "Notre Dame will not stand in Mr. Rockne's way if he wishes to better himself." Walsh was tired of the coach's outside-offer ploys and he decided not to match Columbia's offer—in no way could he pay any football coach $25,000 a year—or to block the coach's exit from N.D. That Rockne had converted to Catholicism a few weeks before and then ignored his commitment to Notre Dame also might have influenced Father Walsh's decision.

But the roadblock to the coach's exit from N.D. turned out to be James Knapp's precipitous announcement. Within hours of his bulletin to the press, newspaper headlines around the country trumpeted "ROCKNE SIGNS WITH COLUMBIA." New York sportswriters were ecstatic, Grantland Rice leading his column: "Knute Rockne's arrival at Columbia is one of the most important coaching moves in the history of the game . . . he will have the Lion of the Hudson roaring before next fall is over." However, unbeknownst to Rice and his colleagues, the deal was unraveling.

When the news broke, Rockne was in Philadelphia with Joe Byrne, Jr., and another N.D. grad. According to Byrne, "when he [Rockne] turned the [Philadelphia] paper over and saw what the contents of the article were, he turned white." Immediately Byrne and other alums began to pressure the N.D. coach to renege on the Columbia contract, and by the next day, they had convinced him to return to New York to tell the Columbia people that the agreement was off.

Rockne was not at his best in this situation. His original plan was rubble and he felt betrayed—he later said, "I took a man's [Knapp's] word like a blamed fool and then he tried to stampede me into the job." Possibly Knapp's strategy in going public was to box Rockne in, allow him no other option than to come to Columbia, but, more probably, the rich alum was so proud of obtaining the famous coach's signature on a contract that he could not keep his mouth shut.

Rockne was also angry at the press for playing up the story, telling a friend, "I am at a loss to understand the tremendous publicity on this Columbia affair but I presume the papers were short of copy. I can assure you [that] I was given a very raw deal."

The negotiations in New York between the coach, accompanied by Byrne and other N.D. alums, versus Knapp and the Columbia people were acrimonious, with neither side willing to agree upon a face-saving formula. Then Knapp slipped away and told the press that Columbia "would not have offered a contract to Mr. Rockne or to any other man, or appointed him as head coach if it had been known that he was under contract to another university and Columbia regrets the entire situation. In view of the foregoing, *the appointment of Mr. Rockne is withdrawn.*"

The coach and his friends were furious at what they considered this final betrayal—Knapp had known all along about Rockne's ten-year contract with N.D.—but they could do nothing about it except, like their opponents, offer a self-serving version of events: Rockne had not been serious when he signed with Columbia and would never have left Notre Dame.

The Golden Dome was silent. President Walsh, using his poker-playing skills, refused to tip his hand. He did not beg Rockne to stay at N.D., nor did he force him out. Instead, he waited for his prodigal coach to return, realizing that a chastened Rockne, with his power to fight the faculty board greatly diminished, would be the perfect head man for a Notre Dame football program under scrutiny by the higher education community.

When Rockne arrived in South Bend, he blamed his troubles on Columbia's treachery and its refusal to accept the fact that, as he told the *Chicago Tribune*, President Walsh would not allow him to break his N.D. contract. Walsh nodded politely in public but privately, he had the coach sign a memorandum stating that he had not asked for a release from Notre Dame. Furthermore, the university could make public the memorandum in the future "in the event that the welfare of the University requires it." Walsh now had Rockne's written admission that the coach had lied.

Unfortunately for Notre Dame, the world saw only the public smiles, and some journalists turned on the N.D. administrators. One New York writer, whom Joe Byrne, Jr., described to Walsh as "a good friend of Notre Dame and a very good friend of Rock's" wrote: "The glistening coat of whitewash applied to Knute Rockne by Notre Dame does not quite cover the football coach . . . It does not seem quite fair to Columbia that Rockne should be absolved of all venality in the affair." And, as Byrne predicted, "others [will] take a little poke at our old friend Rock."

Some sportswriters jabbed publicly, others in private. Typical of the former was Westbrook Pegler's comment that Rockne was "a wizard on his home grounds but something of a hick on Broadway." And, in a letter, one of the coach's Nebraska newspaper antagonists advised, "Better keep away from the big town hereafter. That hard-boiled guy, Knapp, may be trying to sell you the Brooklyn Bridge."

Other observers were more sympathetic to the Notre Dame coach, none more so than the school's students. They devoted a page of *The Dome* to a series of headlines, interspersed with photos of their beloved "Rock": "ROCKNE MAY LEAVE N.D.," "COLUMBIA CLAIMS ROCKNE," "N.D. HEADS ARE SILENT," "ROCKNE DENOUNCES EASTERN SCHOOL," "ROCKNE REMAINS AT NOTRE DAME," "NOTRE DAME WINS AGAIN." For the students, the story proved this line in the "Victory March": "Notre Dame will win over all."

The immediate effect upon Rockne at N.D. was as Walsh had calculated—a diminishing of power in the coach's ongoing struggle with the faculty board and also less power in his administration of the athletic department. In late December, Rockne complained, "My work here is [now] an open book and if they," the faculty board, "pick on me I presume I will have to stand it." At the beginning of January, he wrote a friend whom he wanted to bring to N.D. to coach track, thus relieving himself of that duty, "I find that the Columbia incident has changed matters quite a little and it will not be possible for me to promise you anything for another year as a result." Similarly, Rockne had to put his annual lobbying for a new stadium on hold.

Walsh was too wise to gloat; instead, he ordered Rockne's old antagonist, Father Carey, to research the coach's conflicts over the years with the faculty board as well as his various duplicities and to write a report on them. As a serious poker player, Walsh wanted as many face cards in his hand as possible.

Thus, a year that began with Rockne's fiasco with USC ended with an even greater one involving Columbia. The students believed that the University of Notre Dame had won, and, considering the increased power over Rockne's athletic program gained by the Golden Dome and the faculty board, the students were correct—but not in the way that they imagined.

23

Anti-aircraft Fire
from the Big Ten: 1926

"The authorities here are thinking of applying for admission to the Big
Ten in June. What do you think is the best method of going around and
seeing these faculty men [each school's representative to the conference]
individually before a meeting and who should go? Also, who should make
the formal application when the Big Ten have a meeting in May in Iowa
City. I should appreciate your keeping this confidential and also the
benefit of your advice."

—Rockne to Jesse Harper, March 17, 1926

In early 1926, the Notre Dame administration, with better control of its
athletic department, decided to apply for admission to the Big Ten. The
men in the Golden Dome hoped that membership in a group known for
its reforms and self-proclaimed cleanliness would silence criticism of Notre Dame's football program. To refresh their memories about earlier
bids for admission and to help form their strategy for this one, the N.D.
faculty board questioned such previous vice presidents as Father
Crumley and also asked Rockne to write his predecessor, Jesse Harper
(still a rancher in Kansas).

The time seemed propitious for N.D.'s move because the conference
appeared ready to expand—Michigan Agricultural was a leading candidate for admission—and the Carnegie Foundation had begun its formal

inquiry into college sports. Notre Dame preferred to welcome their investigators as a member of the Big Ten rather than an independent.

Jesse Harper, who led earlier N.D. admission bids to the conference,
suggested that, first, Rockne make a goodwill tour of the member
schools, and then Professor J. E. McCarthy, secretary of the faculty
board, follow up with visits to the faculty representatives. McCarthy, the
young Dean of Commerce and a layman, spoke the same academic language as the Big Ten faculty and possibly he could overcome their prejudices against Catholic higher education. Finally, Harper emphasized that
Notre Dame had to persuade Professor W. E. Moran of Purdue—that
school's longtime faculty rep and the senior member of the conference
representatives—to champion its cause.

In late May 1926, Rockne reported to Harper that his own tour had
gone well except for Michigan, where, "though we had a very polite
interview, it is evident that they are against us." In addition, Chicago and
Illinois were question marks, and "McCarthy and Father Walsh are going
down to Lafayette [on] Saturday to try and induce Prof. Moran to come
up to the meeting if he possibly can."

Walsh's involvement shows Notre Dame's seriousness about this bid,
but Moran could not attend the May meeting; moreover, Chicago and
Michigan had started lobbying against N.D.'s admission. At this point,
instead of a formal application, Notre Dame tried a clever delaying tactic
—it asked the Big Ten members to "appoint a committee to visit" the
Catholic school "and there to conduct an investigation of all conditions,
both academic and athletic." Then, "dependent on the findings of this
committee," it would formally apply for admission at the conference's
late fall meeting.

In Iowa City, the Big Ten schools decided to sidestep the N.D. proposal, voting 6–4 "not to enlarge" the conference, rendering an investigation of Notre Dame moot. However, Rockne, ever the strategist, saw that
the refusal to investigate "still . . . places them in a hole" because they
could no longer accuse the Catholic school of athletic improprieties. He
was particularly pleased because "this silences Michigan and they certainly cannot tell any stories when they very strongly refused to investigate."

The Iowa City rebuff did not end Notre Dame's bid for conference
admission. President Walsh decided to go directly to the presidents of
Michigan and Chicago, the main opposition, and try to persuade them of
N.D.'s acceptability—if they agreed to vote yes, the whole conference
would fall into line. The leaders of these institutions were noncommittal

but suggested that the Catholic school make a formal application at the conference meeting in December. Rockne was not optimistic about this bid, informing Harper that there was "some political intriguing in the Big Ten we don't understand" and possibly could not overcome.

Unknown to Rockne, there was also political intrigue at his own school concerning him. In May 1926, Professor McCarthy visited a number of important alumni and told them that Big Ten hostility to Rockne was the main obstacle to conference admission. McCarthy also condemned Rockne's "business judgment and unethical action with regard to the general interests of Notre Dame." A prominent alum in Columbus, Ohio, upset with McCarthy's visit, wrote to President Walsh that the dean's "general attitude was that there was some consideration of a possible change whereby Rock would be dropped from the staff at Notre Dame," with McCarthy "even mentioning the possible selection of successors." This alum, a former teammate of Rockne's, was unhappy with this prospect but said that he would abide by Father Walsh's decision.

Because the N.D. president wanted to control the coach, not fire him, Walsh vetoed the dean's proposed putsch. Rockne learned of the intrigue a few months later and never forgave McCarthy for it.

During the summer and early fall of 1926, Notre Dame was on its best athletic behavior, trying to bring all of its rules in line with the Big Ten's to strengthen its bid for admission. The faculty board forbade the freshman and varsity reserve squads from playing other schools' teams and instructed Rockne to ask Major Griffith, the Big Ten commissioner, "Do you think the [intramural] Hall teams going away on Saturdays" and playing amateur clubs "would in any way minimize our chances of being received by the Big Ten?" Griffith advised against this and N.D. curtailed the practice in 1926.

In addition, for the 1926 games against Big Ten opponents, Rockne accepted all of Griffith's officiating choices without bargaining. The commissioner did select Eckersall as referee for the Minnesota contest, but he also appointed a Michigan man, Meyer Morton, for the N.D. games against Northwestern and Indiana. Unfortunately for Notre Dame, this move led to a confrontation between Rockne and Morton and contributed to the final unraveling of N.D.'s bid for conference admission.

During the Notre Dame–Northwestern contest, the Michigan official gave out ninety-five yards in penalties to the Fighting Irish and none to their Big Ten opponent. Because, as Griffith wrote Rockne, "a newspaper

man . . . had an exaggerated story of your [postgame] run-in with Morton," the commissioner asked the N.D. coach for a written "statement
. . . regarding what happened and what you said to Morton." He also
informed his friend, regarding "your game with Indiana next Saturday,
[I] told Morton that he has been relieved of this assignment."

The N.D. coach replied that "the only thing" he said to Morton was
" 'It looks to me like a Big Ten suckhole.' " However, for Fielding Yost,
the Michigan A.D. and football coach, the incident confirmed his low
opinion of Rockne and Notre Dame. It also hardened Michigan's opposition to the Catholic school's bid for conference membership.

By November 1926, news of N.D.'s application to the Big Ten and
Michigan's hostility began to appear in the press. One wire service reporter asked Rockne for his version of "the Michigan–Notre Dame
breach of some years ago," and the N.D. coach replied, "We beat Yost [in
1909] . . . 11 to 3 and I don't suppose he has ever forgiven us." Other
inquiries as well as support for N.D. admission came from Midwest football fans; for example, the student paper at the University of Minnesota
strongly endorsed an expansion of the conference to a "Big 12," including
Notre Dame and Nebraska (N.D. and most Big Ten schools favored the
Michigan State Aggies as the other entrant). Rockne thanked the Minnesota student journalist for his support and added, "I cannot say [more] at
this time as the situation is rather ticklish."

The press reports also created countervailing pressure on Notre
Dame from alumni and fans who did not want the school to enter the Big
Ten or any conference. They loved the national schedules and argued
that Fighting Irish football belonged to N.D. rooters from coast to coast.
In their letters to the administration and the coach on this issue, they
urged Notre Dame to remain independent.

As the day of the conference meeting approached, the Big Ten
coaches opposed to N.D. membership began feeding rumors to their
friends in the press. Amos Alonzo Stagg of Chicago reheated tales about
N.D.'s using its "Prep School" as a four-year football training camp for
the varsity (N.D. had phased out the secondary school in the early
1920s). Fielding Yost of Michigan retailed preposterous stories about
Rockne's hiding and training players on the interhall squads for five and
six years before suiting them up for three varsity seasons.

Other Big Ten men claimed that Notre Dame never declared football
players ineligible, no matter how many courses they failed. Rockne angrily answered an inquiry from a Chicago sportswriter about this rumor
with this note: "Regarding envious Big Ten regarding eligibility wish to

say that we had about a half dozen boys this year ineligible but why should we exploit this" by making these facts public "and disgrace the boys?" He added, "just which star in Big Ten football is ineligible this Fall?"

The conference meeting was anticlimactic. McCarthy reported: "The net result of my venture to Chicago with respect to our being admitted to the Western Conference was exactly nothing. I pumped limp hands, talked into unwilling ears, looked into shifting eyes." Michigan had lined up the votes to veto Notre Dame's bid, and McCarthy noted that the Michigan faculty rep "and I were engaged but for a moment in a hand clasp of hatred and a glare of defiance."

Rockne interpreted the rebuff as a triumph for Fielding Yost's religious prejudices—the N.D. coach always termed his rival "a hillbilly from Tennessee and hence very narrow on religion"—as well as confirmation of the Michigan man's professional jealousy of Rockne's accomplishments. Contributing to Yost's animus in 1926 was the fact that Rockne's agent, Christy Walsh, had dropped the Michigan coach from the triumvirate selecting "The Walter Camp All-America Team." After Camp's death, Walsh had secured this prize for his press syndicate and, claiming that no one man could replace Camp, had established the trio of Rockne, Pop Warner, and Yost. In 1926, when Yale allowed "Tad" Jones to join, Walsh bumped Yost, who believed that Rockne was behind this insult and public humiliation.

In the end, the Big Ten's failure to admit Notre Dame was based on misperception, not reality. The conference adamantly refused N.D.'s request "to appoint a committee to visit" the Catholic school and "conduct an investigation of all conditions, both academic and athletic." Instead, the faculty reps chose to believe the rumors about Notre Dame, especially those spread by Yost and Stagg. For "Academic Men" representing universities that considered themselves on the cutting edge of the scholarly research of the day, their acceptance of anti–Notre Dame gossip was reprehensible.

The Big Ten wanted to be the leading reform conference in college sports and it regarded the admission of Notre Dame as an impediment to this goal. However, because most Big Ten members had huge new stadiums to finance and needed winning teams to fill them, they could not even enforce their own regulations, much less provide national leadership. A few years later, the Carnegie Foundation's report on intercollegiate athletics cited the conference schools for a multitude of rules violations and the Big Ten itself temporarily expelled Iowa because of its out-of-control football program.

In fact, if the conference had admitted N.D. in late 1926, the Catholic school could have aided the group's reform efforts. The Notre Dame administrators, with combat experience against a "power coach," could have provided practical advice and help in translating the conference's "paper regulations" into reality. Instead, the Big Ten's prejudices and hypocrisy barred N.D.'s entrance.

Unfortunately for Notre Dame, the rejection also hurt the cause of athletic reform on its campus. Admission to the Big Ten could have provided ongoing reference points and a synergy for the Golden Dome's struggle to control Rockne and his ever-expanding football program. As the N.D. administrators discovered in the next few years, without Big Ten support, they had a more difficult task restraining the famous coach, particularly when he invoked the corrupt recruiting and subsidization practices of his Big Ten athletic rivals as justification for his more modest cutting of corners.

■ ■ ■

"The boys on the campus at Notre Dame tonight think that Knute Rockne has another one of those teams. The Four Horsemen have been gone for two years but this afternoon Rockne sent a new troop of cavalrymen, or cowpunchers, or Cossacks, or something that can ride like hell, and they rode over Hugo Bedzek's Nittany Lions from Penn State by the score of 28–0."

—James Crusinberry, in the *Chicago Tribune,*
October 17, 1926

For all of Rockne's involvement in the bid for Big Ten admission in the fall of 1926, the football coach was still able to accomplish his most important task—produce a winning team. His young 1925 squad had matured and new talent had joined them.

The season opened with the Fighting Irish steamrolling Beloit, 77–0. As usual N.D. played at home and, typically, the school turned down an attractive financial offer to move the contest to a city stadium, in this case "Cubs Park" in Chicago. President Walsh and the faculty board vetoed the move and accepted the low payout from the home opener.

The faculty board had a new chair and Rockne kept his distance: Father Finigan had moved to another position within the C.S.C. order, and Father P. J. Carroll replaced him as Notre Dame vice president and head of the board. Dean McCarthy, still the group's secretary, told President Walsh, "I am looking forward with a great deal of anticipation to our Athletic Committee's meetings with Fr. Carroll at the helm. He usually guarantees action aplenty."

Rockne preferred his action on the gridiron and prepared for the second game, a visit to Minnesota. He wanted a victory and drove himself and his players by emphasizing the toughness of the Gophers, even telling a friend, "I don't believe we can beat Minnesota if reports on them are true. However, we are going to give them a fight."

In Minneapolis, the Irish, with multiple units, ran over their opponents, 20–7, but paid a price—serious injuries to two potential All-Americans, Fred Collins and Joe Boland, and for the latter, the end of his playing career (Boland later became an N.D. assistant coach and, subsequently, the radio voice of Fighting Irish football). Better news for Rockne's program was the $51,165 payout from the huge Minneapolis crowd as well as intensifying press attention.

After the next game of the season—an easy home victory over highly rated Penn State—Notre Dame fans began talking about another national championship. Reporters covering the Penn State game marveled at the depth of the Fighting Irish and how the reserve units displayed almost the same flash and skill as the starters. By 1926, the N.D. coach had so perfected his football system that for fans and "Gee-Whiz" sportswriters, the continuous Notre Dame victories and the Fighting Irish style began to seem preordained and magical.

In fact, according to Francis Wallace, "there was nothing mysterious about his system . . . [Rockne] stressed speed, deception, nifty handling of the ball—all this required detail," and the coach achieved it with long, arduous practices. Other coaches were unable to duplicate his methods, and in 1926, they again attacked his offensive shift plays as illegal, wanting them banned. Rockne countered, "I ascribe most of the popularity of our modern football to the pageantry of shift plays and the thrill of the forward pass"—if these weapons were eliminated, he said, "We will probably have mass on tackle [gang-tackling], wedge plays, assault and battery," and the "mayhem" of boring, old-time football.

The N.D. coach, a natural dramatist, knew that fans loved offensive fireworks and he tried to supply them. His most famous quarterback, Harry Stuhldreher, commented, "In giving the stadium crowds exciting plays, Rockne was paid back in his own coin. Every man in the stands [who rooted for the Fighting Irish] felt that he was fighting with the team [and] this tenseness carried somehow from the field to the stadium and was intensified by the crowds and flowed back again out onto the field."

Rockne's football system provided Notre Dame fans with exciting and winning football teams, and the Rules Committee could never shut his offense down. But, as the stadiums filled to capacity for Fighting Irish games and the team drove toward a national championship, the ticket situation became almost unbearable for the N.D. coach and the school's administrators. In 1926, the game against Northwestern in Chicago as well as the Army annual in New York were officially sold out well before the season began, but many N.D. alumni and self-appointed friends of the university would not accept this reality and pleaded, cajoled, and then screamed for any available seat. Rockne termed some of the Chicago alums "spoiled chaps who feel by pull and special privilege that they are entitled to more consideration than the rank and file." Compounding the problem was the fact that "most of our patronage, of course, comes from non-alumni and we don't want to absolutely not cater to them at all." He received an avalanche of ticket requests for the Northwestern and Army games; at first politely and then with increasing anger, he informed the supplicants of the sellout.

Before the Northwestern contest, scheduled for the Big Ten school's unfinished new stadium in Evanston, scalpers were obtaining $40 (an excellent weekly wage at the time) for a pair of seats. The game did not disappoint the crowd of forty-one thousand; in a tight, well-played match, the Fighting Irish scored early and hung on to a 6–0 lead. Northwestern's All-American halfback, Moon Baker, was the star of the game but could not penetrate the Notre Dame goal line.

The payout for N.D. in Evanston was $52,636, significantly more than the total from the following weeks' home games against Georgia Tech and Indiana. The Fighting Irish easily beat the southerners 12–0, but according to one eyewitness, they were less a "thundering herd" than "domestic cows."

Rockne felt that his players had so mastered his system that he could skip the Indiana game the following week and turn the team over to his assistants, Hunk Anderson and Tommy Mills. The coach went to New York on private business and to scout Army in preparation for the upcoming annual match—he wanted revenge for the past year's 27–0 defeat. His business affairs with his agent, Christy Walsh, were increasingly complicated and lucrative, and on this trip, he accomplished more in Manhattan than at West Point, where he watched Army destroy feeble Franklin and Marshall, 55–0, mainly using reserve units. At Cartier Field against a weak Indiana team, the N.D. offense revived and halfbacks "Bucky"

Dahmen and Christy Flanagan scored two touchdowns each, demolishing the Hoosiers, 26–0. Arch Ward, covering his first N.D. contest of the season for the *Chicago Tribune,* was ecstatic.

■ ■ ■

"I don't know whether John [Balfe, head of the N.Y. alums] assiduously tried to go over my head or he just didn't know any better. I have been coaching football here for fourteen years and this is the first time that I have been sitting around taking orders from an alumnus on how to run our business."

—Rockne to Gerald Craugh, a New York alum, November 2, 1926

Because of problems with ticket scalpers at the 1925 Notre Dame–Army game—some of whom had obtained their supply from N.D. alums—Rockne and the N.D. administration decided to curtail the number of seats sent to the New York Notre Dame Club from ten thousand to two thousand for the 1926 contest. Not only did the president of the club object and demand total control of the tickets, he also wanted to be in charge of the sideline passes. The latter request enraged Rockne, who always personally gave out the passes to his special friends, and he complained loudly to the N.D. administration about the New York alums.

President Walsh sided with the coach and approved a plan whereby the management of Yankee Stadium would send eight thousand tickets directly to Notre Dame and the school's ticket office would handle the requests from most alums. In addition, Rockne decided that the requests from alumni "ordering more than a nominal number" of seats should be "pulled out" and filled last, if then. In this way, N.D. attempted to short-circuit the scalping. Nevertheless, many tickets moved through other channels, the *New York World* reporting that they were "selling for fabulous prices," and according to one of the coach's friends, "if you pass through the Grand Central [Station] tunnels the morning of the game you will be offered by speculators tickets ranging in price from twenty to fifty dollars each."

However, the ticket supply from Indiana so dried up that ten days before the contest, Joe Byrne, Jr.'s assistant wrote Rockne that very few ducats were available for New York sportswriters. Working reporters received pressbox passes and Yankee Stadium gave complimentary seats to the sports editors but, as was the custom, many journalists expected extra tickets for family and friends or to sell on the side. Rockne promptly ordered forty seats from his private reserve sent to a list of eleven important columnists and football journalists, Grantland Rice at their head.

"HAVE ROOM FOR ONE [N.D.] CAPTAIN ONLY ON FRONT COVER ARMY NOTRE DAME
PROGRAMME. WHICH SHALL WE USE?"

—Telegram to Rockne from Harry M. Stevens,
in charge of concessions at Yankee Stadium, October 28, 1926

"USE BOTH OR NONE PLEASE."

—Telegram to Harry M. Stevens from Rockne,
October 28, 1926

Beyond his basic sense of fairness toward his players, the N.D. coach
was too good a sports psychologist to cause divisions on his team by
choosing one of his co-captains over the other. The 1926 Army game was
particularly important to him because of the past year's loss and also
because both squads remained on a short list of undefeated teams, with
the winner gaining the lead in the race for the national championship.

These factors made the pregame ballyhoo more intense than in previous years. Writers like Grantland Rice who usually promoted the contest
contributed their chants, but even journalists not on the N.D. coach's
ticket list joined in. Allison Danzig of the *New York Times* proclaimed,
"Knute Rockne is bringing one of the greatest teams he has ever developed to the Yankee Stadium tomorrow" (in subsequent years, Danzig
always requested special tickets from the N.D. coach); and Paul Gallico
of the *New York Daily News* described the anticipated spectacle in his
florid prose (Gallico would never accept freebies from Rockne or any
other coach and publicly condemned the practice). In addition, the *Daily
News* featured its betting chart, with four of its five experts predicting a
Notre Dame victory by one or two touchdowns.

The New York papers also carried the team's Saturday itinerary: from
its Westchester training camp, it traveled to Grand Central, next a stop at
"St. Agnes Roman Catholic Church on Forty-third Street," then on to
the Vanderbilt Hotel for a pregame meal, and finally, with police escorts,
to the ballpark.

Before the game, Rockne received a note from Walter Eckersall,
scheduled to officiate, "Have you a spare ticket?" Also, "I don't want to
miss the ride to the stadium. Let me know [exactly] where you will be so
that I can bum a ride." "Eck" added, in reference to the Michigan official
who had upset Rockne during the Northwestern game: "Don't pay much
attention to Mr. Morton. We will take care of him before next year."

70,000 FANS WATCH NOTRE DAME
WIN 7 TO 0 OVER ARMY

Christy Flanagan Does Irish Jigstep 63 Yards for the Only Touchdown.

Christy Flanagan, a broth of a boy with the blood of Old Erin in his veins and the fire of Old Erin in his soul, gave New York's record grid-iron gallery—70,000 persons—the thrill of their lives and his team a dearly desired victory yesterday afternoon. . . .

—Front-page headline and lead in *New York World,*
November 14, 1926.

In 1926, Pulitzer's *World,* with increasing numbers of middle-class Catholic readers, stressed the N.D.–Irish connection in its game coverage. When Christy Flanagan scored the winning touchdown, the *World* emphasized his and other players' "Emerald Isle" background—"Another real son of Erin, O'Boyle by name, contributed the point following touchdown"—and the paper repeatedly called the team the "Irish."

The *New York Daily News* also featured the ethnic connection. For the first time, it used the term "Irish" as a nickname for the Notre Dame football team, and the following Monday ran a postgame feature on Flanagan informing its Irish working-class readers: "Despite the fact that his dad and uncles own a [stevedore] company and could have left in his mouth the silver spoon he was born with, they chose to replace that with a hempin line" and made him help out on the docks from an early age.

Grantland Rice, who covered the game, did not pick up on the Irish link and instead flogged his tired horse metaphor, leading, "There was only one Lone Horseman riding against the skyline of fame when Notre Dame met the Army . . ." The next week, he asked Rockne whether Flanagan was a better selection for his *Collier's* magazine All-America team than Northwestern's Moon Baker; the N.D. coach replied, "I would give Baker the shade."

Rockne believed that his system made his players, not the reverse, and unlike his early coaching days when he wanted the Fighting Irish on All-America teams to help promote Notre Dame football, by 1926 he no longer sought the selections—he preferred publicity for his system and his coaching schools. Also, because he helped choose the "Walter Camp" version of the All-America team, he did not want to appear to favor his own "boys." Finally, the N.D. coach had no illusions about the talents of his players, including the press-anointed stars, and Christy Flanagan was a perfect example of how the Rockne system made the hero.

In this period, most New York sportswriters did not really understand the game of football—like Grantland Rice, they were more interested in their prose inventions and writing careers than the realities of the sports they covered. One exception was Joe Vila, an old-timer with the *New York Sun;* in his 1926 Army–N.D. postgame article, he noted that downfield blocking "should be Knute Rockne's middle name . . . He has perfected it [and it has] long been an important factor in attack but neglected unaccountably by many of the present day coaches . . . Christy Flanagan's sixty-three-yard run for Notre Dame's winning touchdown was due almost entirely to Rockne's system . . . Flanagan was protected against [Army] tackling all the way to the goal line."

Frank Leahy, the most successful of Rockne's coaching offspring, always claimed that his mentor was not a football "innovator" but "could take something old and rework it until it looked new and exciting." Rockne's use of downfield blocking in 1926 is a perfect example of how he fitted a neglected but essential part into his shining football machine.

■ ■ ■

"I am going ahead and planning on you to attend and report the Army-Navy game at Chicago, per our conversation. Pop Warner will be there and I am sure Tad [Jones] will be there, making it a great setting for you to select your All-America Team for 1926. It will certainly grab the spotlight for the 'Big Three' [coaches] and get us a lot of timely publicity."

—Christy Walsh to Rockne, March 27, 1926

After the victory over Army, the team returned for a Homecoming game shutout, 21–0, over Drake University of Iowa. Rockne so believed in his system and so sought the fame and fortune promised by his agent that the following week, instead of taking the Fighting Irish to Carnegie Tech, he turned them over to his main assistant, Hunk Anderson. The N.D. head coach went to the Army-Navy game in Chicago to do long-scheduled promotional work for Christy Walsh.

Before the Carnegie Tech encounter, some Midwest newspapers had started to crown Notre Dame the 1926 national champions, and Francis Wallace in the *New York Post* proclaimed: "Rockne and Notre Dame have only to hurdle Carnegie Tech and Southern California to conclude the most remarkable of the many achievements credited to the master coach and the outstanding football school since they began to make national impressions nine years ago."

Christy Walsh made ·all the arrangements for Rockne in Chicago, including a suite at the LaSalle Hotel for the coach and his wife. The agent noted, "I am very anxious to get some publicity pictures before the game of Tad, Pop, and yourself together" (Jones's season at Yale had ended but Warner's Stanford team played and won that Saturday). Walsh also scheduled all three coaches for postgame newspaper columns—probably he had them dictate their comments to ghost editors because, as a letter a week before the game explained, he wanted their copy "as early as possible to catch early editions."

Nevertheless, while planning "this wonderful hit with our papers," Walsh worried, "I certainly would not want to encourage you [Rockne] to do anything that might bring criticism to you." However, the N.D. coach's position was that "the game in Pittsburgh will not be important enough but what I can send it [*sic*] in charge of someone else."

Rockne underestimated Carnegie Tech, in part, because the Fighting Irish had always beaten them easily and also because the Tartans were bit players on the major college football stage. They had a part-time coach—Judge Walter Steffen, who commuted from his full-time judicial job in Chicago—and they did not recruit actively or offer much in the way of athletic scholarships. Yet Steffen was clever and always tried to outwit Rockne on and off the field, for example, never allowing him carte blanche in appointing officials. The N.D. coach complained, "I cannot understand about Steffen as every year he objects to two or three officials. I wonder what he would say if the various defendants [brought before him] all objected to him as a judge every day of the year?" And when Steffen learned that Rockne would be in Chicago, not Pittsburgh, he roused his team in his pregame talk with, "Rockne thinks you're so poor he's gone to Chicago to see some real football players in the Army-Navy game."

Rockne's absence also made his own players overconfident and lethargic. In the first quarter of the game, they quickly fell behind, and for the rest of the long, frustrating afternoon, they could not summon the famous "Notre Dame spirit" and mount an offense. Compounding the team's difficulty was Hunk Anderson's coaching—he carefully followed his boss's pregame instructions and, even when the strategy became inappropriate, would not deviate. The result was a disaster for Notre Dame—a 19–0 pounding by the lightweight Tartans.

Football fans were astonished and most newspapers gave the upset equal billing with the Army-Navy game in Chicago, even though the latter was an exciting tie before a remarkable crowd of 110,000. The *New York Herald-Tribune* balanced Grantland Rice's account of the Army-Navy match with a second-string writer's N.D.–Carnegie game report:

"The choicest surprise-drama of the entire football season was the delectable lot which fell to 35,000 on-lookers at Forbes Field this afternoon." Even from the perspective of sixty years later, sports historians term it "an upset of stupendous proportions . . . considered by many as the greatest in collegiate football annals."

At the time, newspapers discussed Rockne's absence, the *Chicago Tribune* leading its Notre Dame game story: "Without the guiding hand of Knute Rockne . . ." The N.D. coach felt humiliated and for a week was the butt of journalists' jokes. Not only had his team lost to Carnegie Tech but the defeat punctured the 1926 championship dream. Then, adding to his discomfort, some polls awarded the title to Stanford— swashbuckling Pop Warner enjoying a huge laugh at the expense of his friend and rival in South Bend.

Amazingly, Rockne's reasons for missing the Carnegie Tech game later dropped into the black hole of sports history. Not a single biography of the coach or book or article about Notre Dame football mentions his business in Chicago that weekend. Instead, the authors substitute fabricated excuses. Joe Doyle, in *Fighting Irish: A Century of Notre Dame Football*, repeats the most popular one:

> Because Rockne wasn't familiar with the Middies [N.D. had scheduled Navy for the following year], he elected to scout Navy vs. Army at Chicago's Soldier Field instead of going to Pittsburgh for his team's game against Carnegie Tech.
> A powerful Tech team overwhelmed the Irish, 19–0.

This fiction and many others about Rockne arose after the coach's tragic death; the hagiographers, attempting to portray their hero as perfect, tried to pave over all negative biographical facts. Pro-N.D. writers started the "scouting Navy" story in the 1930s and the Hollywood canonization of the coach in 1940 gave it momentum. Later, such loyalists as "Scrapiron" Young fleshed out the fantasy by claiming to have sat with Rockne in the Soldier Field stands while the coach, trying to be inconspicuous, took notes on Navy.

The most amazing aspect of the cover-up is that Rockne's work for his agent that weekend in Chicago was hardly a secret. Christy Walsh told the N.D. coach to be as conspicuous as possible in the pressbox so that the sportswriters would not only comment on "the fact that each" of the three famous coaches "was present" but recognize "that you three are operating as a committee or unit." Walsh's plan succeeded and many reporters noted the presence of the "Big Three" in their stories; in addition, photos of Rockne with Warner and Jones appeared in hundreds of newspapers, and the N.D. coach's column about the Army-Navy struggle was widely syndicated.

That the hagiographers spread the "scouting Navy" fiction in spite of overwhelming evidence to the contrary illustrates their desire to believe in Rockne as a saint. The real Knute Rockne was much more human and interesting than the sanctified version. He proved that the week after the Carnegie Tech game when he took his dispirited team across the country to face an excellent USC squad in the heat and noise of the Los Angeles Coliseum.

> "At every station along the route there were crowds. Paddy [an N.D. player] wondered how they knew, but Spike Parker explained that the railroad company was sending word ahead. They bragged because the Notre Dame team was traveling over its line instead of another . . .
>
> [A typical stop occurred] at Tucumcari, New Mexico, [where] a parish school band led the reception. Little bits of [young] codgers had taken the trouble to learn the Notre Dame Victory March."
>
> —From Francis Wallace's *O'Reilly of Notre Dame*

Southern Cal had pointed all season to this initial game against the Fighting Irish and had compiled an impressive 8–1 record, losing only to Stanford by a point. USC ignored such newspaper headlines after the debacle in Pittsburgh as "N.D. DEFEAT DETRACTS FROM TROJAN GAME" and sold almost eighty thousand tickets for the match.

The Fighting Irish left South Bend on a Monday and spent four days and nights on trains going west. During the frequent stops and layovers, Rockne had the players jog and do exercises in the railroad yards as well as greet the local Notre Dame rooters. The N.D. coach had received scouting reports on the Trojans from West Coast coaches such as Slip Madigan; when his team reached Tucson, he conducted a workout at the University of Arizona stadium and practiced against the Trojan formations.

In his pregame talk, Rockne stressed the importance of winning this game and saving the season. The team responded by scoring the first touchdown but then struggled as USC slowly came back and took the lead. With six minutes left to play, Southern Cal, ahead 12–7, tried to frustrate the Irish with a stacked defense and quick kicks and run out the clock.

Then Rockne, in a master stroke of strategy later termed the "Wooden Horse" trick, removed his starting quarterback, even though the player had performed well, and substituted his fourth-string QB— five-foot-seven, 148-pound Art Parisien—who appeared so infrequently in 1926 that he did not earn a varsity letter. The coach wanted the ambidextrous Parisien to unsettle the Trojan defense with his left-and-right-handed passing. The plan worked perfectly and, with less than two minutes on the clock, Parisien tossed the winning touchdown.

With this victory, Rockne felt that he had restored his reputation as well as the pride of the N.D. team and its supporters. The win over USC ended the 1926 season on an upbeat note and helped sustain the national popularity of the Fighting Irish.

Notre Dame's first visit to the Los Angeles Coliseum also provided the school with its best payday to date—$75,619, four thousand more than it got from the 1926 Army game on the other coast. This brought the total profits from the football season to $251,000—an extraordinary sum for a team in the 1920s, but again, because of the low payouts in Cartier Field and the refusal to play a postseason contest, an amount far below the team's earning potential.

Rockne had to tolerate the Golden Dome's restraints on the revenue-generating power of his football program but he did not have to accept any limits on his personal earnings. His contract contained no stipulations on this question—the school never envisioned an athletic coach with a multitude of outside interests. Throughout the 1920s, as the fame of the Fighting Irish teams and their coach increased, Rockne's opportunities to profit from his celebrity accelerated. In a booming economy, at a time when the president of the United States proclaimed, "The chief business of the American people is business," the N.D. coach willingly obeyed this edict.

Before his coaching career ended, with his commercial ventures— even more than his gridiron achievements—Knute Rockne brought permanent change to his profession. He never claimed to be the premier inventor of football strategy, but off the field he became the first great entrepreneurial college coach, pioneering many new business areas and setting the monetary standard for his successors.

24

Knute K. Rockne Inc.

Dear Knute,
 I just had a letter from Christie [*sic*] Walsh and he seems to be worried that you are going with another syndicate and he has asked me to write you and say any good word I can about him. I just wanted to put in any testimonial I could in Christie's behalf because I know he is a fine fellow and a good hustler. . . .

Sincerely,

Grant Rice

—Grantland Rice to Rockne, March 2, 1925

Rockne's first important private business deal occurred in late 1922 when he agreed to do articles and columns for Christy Walsh's syndicate. This was a standard way for successful coaches to supplement their incomes and, from the beginning of his journalism career, Rockne's friends advised him to play Walsh off other newspaper syndicates and to go with the highest bidder. Probably because such business practices paralleled the N.D. coach's outside-offer experiences with other schools, he willingly listened to all proposals.

 In 1923, with the growing national fame of Notre Dame football and Princeton's refusal to allow its coach, Bill Roper, to continue his columns, the Bell Syndicate urgently wanted the Notre Dame coach and promised him that they "could devote all our energies . . . to selling Rockne."

William Abbott of the *New York World* acted as intermediary and also informed the N.D. coach that "if any long-range assistance is necessary [for your articles] my typewriter is always keen to exercise for football subjects." In the end, Rockne stayed with Christy Walsh and, a year later, after the Rose Bowl victory, again turned down Bell, this time after the intervention of Grantland Rice and others.

In his memoirs, *Adios to Ghosts,* Walsh argued that "a certain amount of illusion is necessary in any form of entertainment and newspaper features are produced to entertain readers. But there is a wide difference between illusion and deceit." Christy, however, did not always notice the difference: "I have never knowingly released copy that was 'fake.' On the other hand there have been emergencies where circumstances forced us to distribute a signed article that had *neither been discussed with, nor approved by the author* but was written by a man who enjoyed the author's confidence and understood his viewpoints on the subject covered."

Not only did these "circumstances" occur when such clients as Babe Ruth were drunk or otherwise indisposed but, because of the primitive state of electronic communication in the 1920s and the deadlines of newspapers, Walsh and his assistants frequently created copy when they could not reach the celebrity. Rockne was more conscientious and literate than most sports "authors," but in all probability, the N.D. coach dictated his postgame pieces and certainly depended upon ghost editors; moreover, in his final years, he allowed ghosts close to carte blanche on his magazine articles and his *Autobiography*.

Walsh placed Rockne's football columns in about fifty papers across the country, mainly Hearst and Pulitzer outlets in major cities and independents in smaller locations. When a newspaper took the N.D. coach's pieces, it also gave more prominence to features about Notre Dame football and carried fuller game stories.

For 1924, Christy paid Rockne almost $4,400 for the football articles, and the following year, close to $6,000 (the average cost of a new house at the time). The coach's other publishing money-maker in this period was his instructional book, *Coaching,* netting him about $7,000. However, he later complained to Pop Warner that the publisher had made almost $20,000 from the deal and had even sold many copies through Rockne's coaching schools; he advised Warner to self-publish a new edition of the latter's coaching book and to keep all the profits.

In 1925, New York newspaperman William Abbott wrote a long profile on Rockne, terming him "a success model for boys," a Horatio Alger figure. According to Abbott, when the Rockne family came from Norway with five-year-old Knute, the "anticipated rainbow [of wealth] in the new land did not quickly materialize. As a young man Rockne toiled hard and unceasingly" and, true to the American dream, ultimately achieved fame and fortune.

Rockne himself subscribed to the Alger formula and proudly pointed to the distance from his hardscrabble childhood on Logan Square in Chicago to his 1920s prosperity. Like many immigrants, he was attracted to the riches of the new world and, with his great talents and appetites, joyfully pursued them. And like those immigrants who invent new ways of amassing wealth, Rockne in his entrepreneurship went far beyond the "signed article" sideline and introduced many other methods for college coaches to increase their outside income.

> Dear Doc:
> I think our [coaching schools'] schedule [for 1928] is o.k.—there is only one suggestion that I would like to make and that is this: to move the Washington and Lee and Notre Dame schools each back a week . . . I ask this as I have a very good offer in Nebraska to run football for just ten days and that . . . will give me a chance to pick up a real nice lump sum of money out in Nebraska which I hate to pass up.
>
> —Letter to W. E. "Doc" Meanwell,
> Rockne's partner in some of his coaching schools,
> September 1, 1927

Rockne began his coaching schools in the early 1920s as informal gatherings at Culver Military Academy in northern Indiana. Other well-known coaches held similar conferences and, in 1922, Rockne also spoke at a number of these. Then, as his fame and drawing power increased, he began to transform his summer coaching schools from a casual pastime to a highly organized and profitable business.

In 1923, he ran one school at Notre Dame and two out-of-state schools; for all three, the host universities paid him a flat fee and kept most of the profits. The following year, he expanded to five coaching schools, and in 1925, after winning the national championship, he set up seven around the country and enrolled well over a thousand student coaches in his programs. He also changed the financial structure—he charged students a fee, thus separating his profits from the host institution's.

In 1925, in addition to a school at Culver, he held one at Notre Dame and convinced his university, as part of its new physical education curriculum, to give two semester hours of credit to his students for his coaching course on campus. He particularly enjoyed the schools at Notre Dame, one year explaining to a friend that this, "of course, will be *the school*, as I will have a gang of my old men [players] back again" as assistants and to liven up the occasion.

At his schools, Rockne often used high school or college athletes to demonstrate his formations and techniques. He soon saw the potential of this untapped source of revenue and had the idea of coaching camps for young athletes long before the concept occurred to his colleagues. He experimented with it at Camp Rockne, his boys' summer camp in Wisconsin and, shortly before he died, planned to develop it on a large scale.

In addition to his own football schools, he also went into partnership with University of Wisconsin basketball coach W. E. "Doc" Meanwell to run coaching schools for football and basketball. These joint operations became so popular that he and Meanwell hired a business manager to help run them. They scheduled four or five a summer at various locations around the country while the N.D. coach also continued with his solo efforts.

In 1927, the fee to attend a two-week session of the Rockne-Meanwell school was $25, and the host university charged an additional $25 for room and board. With an enrollment of at least two thousand students a summer for five schools, the partners took in a minimum of $50,000, and after a fifty-fifty split, as well as expenses and payment to the business manager, Rockne received close to $22,000. In addition, his own schools, depending on how many he scheduled, usually netted him between $10,000 and $15,000, and his guest appearances for brief sessions—where he received a flat fee—always generated handsome profits. In 1928, he charged $2,000 for short spots (that year, Notre Dame paid the business manager of the athletic department an annual salary of $2,500).

In 1928, however, he begged off some of the Rockne-Meanwell schools because, as he wrote his partner, "I have a chance to make $10,000 this summer on this European trip" shepherding a group of rich tourists to the summer Olympics in Amsterdam. He also informed parents of Camp Rockne campers: "Owing to my trip to Europe I am only spending two days in camp myself, [but] ten thousand dollars is being spent on improvements this year and I am confident that the camp will be second to none in the country" (his partner in the boys' camp, a Chicago banker, put up most of the capital—they split the profits fifty-fifty).

From its inception, the camp presented a problem because, as his partner pointed out, "a great many of these boys are expecting you to be there and if you do not spend some little time they may feel that they have been slighted and will not return the following year." The N.D. coach, frantically busy during summers with his coaching schools and other sidelines, never squared his time circle—he could not visit Camp Rockne for long, even when his own sons attended. Fortunately for him, his camp business thrived due to the efforts of former N.D. player and assistant coach Tom Lieb. From its first year of operation in 1925, Lieb did an outstanding job of running the camp and pleasing the campers but, of course, he could never put the Rockne into Camp Rockne.

> Dear Doc:
> I certainly did not know that Texas College was colored. If you want me to, I will write this gentleman over again telling him that it would be out of place for him to attend [our coaching] school in Dallas as, of course, I am entirely responsible, though innocently.
>
> Yours very truly,
>
> K. K. Rockne
>
> —Rockne to R. H. Blackwell, February 24, 1928

On occasion in his coaching school business, Rockne's policy of accepting all cash-paying applicants collided with the bigotry of the era. In January 1928, the dean of Texas College in Tyler wrote the N.D. coach asking whether he could attend one of his coaching schools. Rockne's secretary replied that "Mr. Rockne will be very pleased to see you" in attendance, and she recommended the one at Southern Methodist University. However, when the black educator applied to SMU, an athletic department official there wrote Rockne: "I am sure the negro would not be popular attending [your coaching] school here," and wondered "whether you were aware of the nationality [*sic*] of this college?"

Rockne, always pragmatic, went along with the Southern Methodist prejudice in the same way that he never questioned Notre Dame's long-standing policy not to admit "Negroes." Nevertheless, he claimed that "as far as I am personally concerned, I have no discrimination at all against anyone on account of race, creed or color"—his reply to a black newspaper's inquiry—and, if prevailing opinion and Notre Dame had supported integration, no doubt he would have allowed black coaches at his schools and black athletes on his squads. As an ultrapragmatist, focused on his football teams and ancillary businesses, Knute Rockne had no inclination to become involved in the social and political controversies of his time.

> Director of the Coaching School
> Notre Dame University
> Notre Dame, Ind.
> Dear Sir:
>   We have been asked to recommend a degree man, Protestant, who is strong in Football for a good private school . . . Salary about $1500 [a year], room and board.
>   If you have anyone to suggest for this position, we should appreciate it if you will give us his name and address.
>
> > Thanking you, we remain . . .
> >
> > SOUTHERN TEACHERS' AGENCY
> >
> > —Letter to Rockne, August 13, 1926

The Notre Dame coach, without questioning the implied anti-Catholic prejudice of the prospective employer, replied that he had "given your kind offer" to some of the qualified men attending the coaching school on the Notre Dame campus. Such employment opportunities helped attract coaches to his summer schools and frequently he wrote letters of recommendation for his best students and placed them in jobs. Rockne, however, expended much more time and energy in helping his former players obtain coaching positions. As early as 1920, such colleagues as Zora Clevenger, then A.D. at Kansas State, had asked him to recommend one of his graduating athletes for an open coaching job (Rockne sent Charlie Bachman). As the N.D. coach's professional prestige increased during the decade, in lockstep with the success of his Fighting Irish teams, the requests for Notre Dame "boys" who knew his system grew proportionately. In addition to inquiries from new and old friends—in 1925, Clevenger, now at Indiana, wanted to hire Tom Lieb as a line coach—many unsolicited offers arrived at Notre Dame, especially from Catholic colleges and secondary schools.

The head of Holy Trinity High School in Chicago wrote directly to President Walsh: "We have entered the Catholic High School League [and] most of the teams in that league have Notre Dame men for coaches. It would certainly look bad if we should have a coach, not a Notre Dame man, to lead our team." He sought help in obtaining an N.D. grad. By 1926, the director of the Notre Dame alumni association calculated that "sixty-eight . . . Notre Dame men were head coaches or assistants in universities and colleges about the country," with an even larger number employed by high schools. Some of Rockne's "boys" were on their way to leading positions in the coaching profession—on the West Coast, Buck Shaw and Slip Madigan; in the South, Frank Thomas and Harry Mehre; in the East, "Rip" Miller and Jim Crowley; and in the Midwest, Noble Kizer and Elmer Layden—and many others had embarked on productive careers.

In the coaching placement business, Rockne was far ahead of all competitors. Of course, most employers hoped that his offspring would bring as much fame and fortune to their institutions as the paterfamilias had conferred upon his; however, this never occurred—no other university could duplicate Notre Dame's unique athletic formula. Nevertheless, the employers were usually content with the relative success brought by the N.D. alum.

But some complained. An important booster of the University of North Carolina wrote to Rockne: "In the Fall of 1926 [we] decided to adopt your style and system of football. With that in mind, we procured the services of two of your ex-players, Messrs. Collins and Cserney [Cerney], of your 1924 squad." During their first season, the school "suffered several rather close defeats . . . at the hands of teams we ordinarily should have won from." The N.D. coach, although always pleased to place his "boys" in good posts, worried that many were not ready for head coaching berths and that they would fail. His reply to the North Carolina booster reflected his understanding of this situation and his sense of how college football coaching had evolved from a part-time task to a highly specialized occupation: "You would not expect a lawyer just out of Law School or a doctor just out of Medical School to be as good as men who have been out for some time. This game of football is an integral proposition with a tremendous mass of detail," and he added that boosters and school authorities must be patient with young coaches.

Rockne worked hard to place his former players for practical as well as personal reasons—it spread the fame of his system and coaching schools but also he had real affection for and loyalty to his "boys." They had proven themselves by working extremely hard for him and he wanted to reciprocate; in addition, the successful job placement of the former players spurred on the current ones.

The N.D. coach wrote initial letters of recommendation and as many follow-ups as necessary. Moreover, he was always willing to help a protégé obtain an outside offer to improve his current salary and/or work conditions. He also assisted former players with leaving schools and moving up the college coaching ladder. Thus, in 1927, in one typical example out of hundreds, when he received a letter from the president of the University of Wyoming asking for a candidate to fill the vacant head football job at that school, he pushed "Cy" Kasper from his 1919–1920 squad—at the time in charge of athletics at a small Catholic college in South Dakota. Even though, in a letter to Rockne, the bishop of Sioux Falls praised Kasper's work, character, and indispensability, the N.D. coach felt that his "boy" was both underpaid and ready for a more important position.

Rockne's generosity to his former players had few boundaries and he used every weapon at his disposal to aid them. In 1927, when Chet Wynne, head coach at Creighton University, was negotiating for a pay raise and better job security, his mentor wrote him, "Let me have your dope on who your best players are for my [All-America] selections," because this attention to the Creighton football program would assist Wynne. That same year, when Jimmy Phelan at Purdue wanted to get his team "up" for the Northwestern game and make the Wildcats complacent, he asked the N.D. coach, "In your comments to the press, it will help some to make Northwestern a strong favorite." Rockne replied, "I mentioned in my story [the pregame predictions part of his column] that Northwestern was a favorite." The ploy probably contributed to the Boilermakers' 18–6 upset victory.

From well-placed "boys" like Wynne and Phelan, Rockne extracted a quid pro quo: they sent him detailed reports on Notre Dame opponents. Wynne had always scouted Nebraska for him and Phelan did various Big Ten teams—in the letter with his request about the Northwestern game, he included a report on N.D.'s next opponent, Minnesota. But Rockne was also generous to the former players who could not return favors—he continued to help one 1917 team member obtain coaching jobs even after the man showed unmistakable signs of insanity; in addition, the N.D. coach gave him and his dependents money, paid many of his debts, and eventually approved his confinement in a mental hospital.

Because Rockne saw his former players as surrogate sons, he also shepherded their noncoaching activities. He was particularly pleased to point the Four Horsemen and Seven Mules toward profitable deals. When a banker in Pittsburgh inquired about hiring some members of the famous backfield and line for a proposed professional team, the N.D. coach replied: "Four of them will be assistants in Big Ten schools which," because of Stagg's reform crusade, "makes it impossible for them to play [professionally]." However, Joe Bach and Harry Stuhldreher would be coaching in the East and might be interested. Later, when his former quarterback asked his advice about playing pro football—the reformers in the Coaches' Association wanted to expel *all* members who engaged in the "unsavory" pro game—Rockne replied, "If you just intend to coach for a year or two and then get into business, then I would not pass up any real opportunity to make money as long as it is honest."

In public, the N.D. coach increasingly felt the need to line up with the reformers and disparage professional football; his private correspondence reveals his pragmatic opinions on this and other reform questions.

> Dear Rock,
>
> You no doubt will be surprised at this letter after you have read it.
>
> On account of the poor cattle business and also on account of some trouble with [my partner] Mr. Campbell, I am looking for a [coaching] job so I am writing you to see if you know of any vacancies that I might be able to fill. . . . Anything you can do to help will be greatly appreciated.
>
> I will ask you to say nothing about this to any of my friends in South Bend.
>
> —Letter from Jesse Harper, February 19, 1925

Not only did Rockne assist in the job placement of his "boys" but, in the spring of 1925, he tried to find a head coaching berth for his mentor. Few positions were available and probably at those schools with openings the athletic authorities suspected that the increasingly fast and wide-open game of college football—perfected and propagated by Harper's best student—had passed the old coach by. Rockne did write to Duke and Northwestern on Harper's behalf; to the faculty representative of the Big Ten school he pointed out: "He is a Methodist and would fit in very fine in every respect at your splendid institution. He is the man who took us out of the woods athletically and I cannot recommend him to you too highly."

No one offered Harper a job, and he did not obtain a position in intercollegiate athletics until, with sad irony, he replaced his protégé as athletic director at Notre Dame upon Rockne's death in 1931.

"Westbrook Pegler once described a Rockne speech as 'a battered old oil can giving off champagne.' This phrase was generally supposed to have started one of Rock's most bitter feuds; but I think what really kicked it off was this further quotation from the same column: 'I see Mr. Rockne as a modest man who does not think much of himself, who is constantly amazed to find himself a great national celebrity and who wants to make all the money he can while he can lest the public suddenly get next to him.' "

—Francis Wallace on a 1928 Westbrook Pegler column

The self-confident Rockne probably shrugged off Pegler's comments on his speechmaking and his personality but, most likely, the crack about his money chasing hit a nerve. After the Carnegie Tech fiasco and with the expansion of his entrepreneurial activities, the N.D. coach became more concerned about his image. By the late 1920s, he wanted to be portrayed as a high-minded advocate of amateur sports whose businesses were merely part of this campaign—hence ventures like the guided tour to the *strictly amateur* Olympic Games.

Most journalists, especially Rockne's pals, went along with the new image, and after the coach's death, the hagiographers encased in concrete the unworldly and antimaterialistic "Saint Knute." A few writers, however, approached the truth. Chet Grant, in a private letter, noted that although Rockne "often *publicly* stressed the physical, mental, and moral benefits to be derived by the participants" in big-time football, "he often emphasized in his conversations with me the personally material" and *personally profitable* "side of the public reaction to his spectacles." Francis Wallace wrote of the Rockne character in his novel *Huddle:* "Football coaching being the precarious thing it was, Barney [Rockne] got the money while he could." One other writer appreciated the N.D. coach's business acumen: McCready Huston, a longtime Rockne associate, later wrote about this side of the coach's life in the aptly titled but barely noticed *Salesman from the Sidelines.* Huston argued that "Rockne was his own merchandise" and that he could "have become the outstanding salesman of the United States."

"Rockne does hereby grant unto Wilson the exclusive right and license to manufacture, sell, and advertise footballs, football helmets, football shoulder pads, football kidney pads, football pants, football shoes, football knit goods, and any other items of football equipment identified by the name, facsimile signature, initials and/or portrait of said Rockne and/or any nickname which hereafter may be popularly applied to said Rockne."

—Clause (1) in Rockne's 1927 contract
with the Wilson Athletic Equipment Company

When Rockne entered the coaching profession one of the few ways for successful head men to supplement their salaries was to endorse football equipment. As he began to win games and fame with his Fighting Irish, various sporting goods companies approached him, and in the early 1920s, he signed with Draper-Maynard of Plymouth, New Hampshire. At first, his relationship with them was amicable, but by 1925, his friends, particularly Jay Wyatt, a salesman with Wilson and a frequent referee for N.D. games, advised him that Draper-Maynard was marketing their Rockne products poorly and not paying him nearly enough for the use of his name. That year, the company sold 791 pairs of the Rockne football pants and paid him only $276. By the end of October of the following year, they sold almost 4,400 Rockne pants and sizable numbers of the endorsed helmets and shoulder pads but their check to him was merely $1,624. Thus, when Wilson offered him more money and a much larger line of endorsed products, he agreed to switch to them.

Wilson also promised to market its Rockne goods aggressively. It started with the "Wilson-Rockne football" and telegraphed the N.D. coach: "PACIFIC COAST COLLEGE CONFERENCE ARE GOING TO HAVE A MEETING IN A DAY OR TWO TO ADOPT A FOOTBALL FOR COMING YEAR." Wilson wanted "YOUR PERMISSION TO WIRE EACH COACH UNDER YOUR NAME RECOMMENDING THEM TO VOTE FOR THE WILSON-ROCKNE BALL," and apparently he agreed.

The N.D. coach's deal with Wilson gave him $2,500 up front and a royalty of 3 percent on the sale of the footballs and 5 percent on all other Rockne products. A year later, Wilson introduced a "Rockne-Cadet line" of football equipment for young boys and paid the N.D. coach "fifty cents a dozen on all items." Part of its marketing pitch was Rockne's concern for schoolboy athletics.

Wilson also continued its high-pressure marketing for the high school and collegiate products. In early 1928, "at Mr. Rockne's request," his secretary sent "several sheets of Mr. Rockne's letterhead" to Wilson and the assistant to the president of the company subsequently informed the N.D. coach: "We took a little liberty with your name and compiled a supposed order to be used as an advertising medium for our salesmen. We then had a photostat made of the letter and I am sending you a copy." In the advertising letter, on a facsimile of University of Notre Dame stationery, Rockne extols the complete line of "Wilson-Rockne Varsity and Prep football equipment," sixteen different products in all, and concludes the make-believe communication with: "Very truly yours, K. K. Rockne [signature], Director of Athletics."

Considering the growing mystique of the Fighting Irish and their head man, this dispatch on Notre Dame letterhead must have impressed many school administrators, particularly Catholic school ones, on Wilson's mailing list. The company sold large numbers of Rockne-Wilson products and, by the late 1920s, paid the N.D. coach close to $10,000 a year for the use of his name (at the time, the cost of a four-bedroom "mansion" in South Bend).

Some of Rockne's colleagues also endorsed football equipment, with less lucrative deals, but only the Notre Dame coach was able to break into the 1920s world of celebrity and tie into a wide variety of products, many of them very far from the sports field. Crucial in Rockne's ascent was Christy Walsh, who, in addition to his writing syndicate activities, was in the process of inventing the sports agency business. Walsh was adept at elevating his best clients to star status and at helping them—and himself—cash in on their fame. A typical Walsh move for Rockne occurred in the spring of 1926; he arranged for the N.D. coach to cover the Penn Relays for his syndicate and then to come to New York for an important banquet at the Hotel Astor, where Rockne would meet, among other guests, Governor Al Smith and Mayor Jimmy Walker.

For the Notre Dame coach, all of this led to more endorsements. That same year, Walsh wrote to Rockne, "Babe Ruth has frequently let me use his signature to endorse various things. Now I am anxious to get an endorsement [from you] for him in connection with his Mail Order Health Service which we are just starting off." Rockne replied, "The endorsement you mention for Babe Ruth's Health Service is perfectly O.K." Considering the Bambino's physical excesses and ailments, including gonorrhea, buying the "Babe Ruth Health Service," even upon Knute Rockne's blind recommendation, might have proven an interesting adventure. Safer and less expensive were such Rockne-endorsed products as Barbasol Shaving Cream—"It's the right play at the right moment—that's why I use BARBASOL."

> "I am enclosing herewith a circular on my European trip this summer in which I believe the information is complete. It is my hope to stimulate interest in the Olympic Games and at the same time take over a large party for a trip that will be long remembered."
>
> —Rockne's form letter to prospective buyers
> of his Olympic Tour package, 1928

Rockne had so many agents selling the package that one wrote him, "Soliciting customers for your trip reminds me of the story of the Bootleggers who had to wear badges to keep them from selling [to] each other." The N.D. coach also took along a number of his well-known friends—he wrote Pop Warner that he was "reserving a room for you right next to mine"—and he and they gave informal chats about football, track, and other sports. The tour was a great success and Rockne also did interviews with European papers, thus allowing Christy Walsh to proclaim the N.D. coach "an international luminary."

On the basis of the Olympic Tour success, Rockne organized a boat trip from New Orleans to Havana for the following New Year's vacation. The Football Coaches' Association held its 1928 meeting in the Louisiana city, and at its conclusion, the N.D. coach took a large number of his colleagues to the wide-open Cuban city. Again, his business plan worked well, and although it did not generate the $10,000 he made from the European voyage, it prompted him to expand his travel business.

Mr. Arthur J. Kennedy
Manchester Council No. 92
Knights of Columbus . . .

Your very kind letter inviting Mr. Rockne to come to Manchester [to speak at your group's banquet] is received . . . however, I am sorry to say that this year Mr. Rockne has a contract with a lecture bureau in New York which prevents him from giving any talks except under their auspices. They have, furthermore, booked him rather heavily for the next few months and it will be impossible for him to accept any additional engagements this year . . .

Ruth Faulkner,
Secretary to Mr. Rockne

—Letter from Rockne, December 28, 1927

In the 1920s, when after-dinner speeches were a major form of entertainment and Rockne's celebrity as well as his reputation as an excellent speaker exploded, invitations to the coach from all kinds of groups arrived at Notre Dame. One of the posthumous legends about him is that "Rockne could never say 'No' to a request, especially one that was made in sweet charity's name" (Harry Stuhldreher). In fact, his secretary filled his correspondence files with carbon copies of turndowns similar to the letter to the Manchester (N.H.) Knights of Columbus official. The legend does contain one element of truth but not in the way that the hagiographers intend—Rockne had difficulty saying no when asked face-to-face and subsequently had to beg off by mail. A typical instance occurred in

January 1928 when a priest, having been promised an after-dinner speech to his group by the N.D. coach, wired him, "FOLLOWING CONVERSATION WITH YOU AT CHICAGO HOTEL AFTER THE [USC] GAME, I WROTE TO [YOU AT] NOTRE DAME FOR DATES FOR LECTURE ENGAGEMENT. LATER ON SENT TELEGRAM WITH NO SUCCESS. . . ." Ruth Faulkner replied, "CONTRACT WITH LECTURE BUREAU PREVENTS MR. ROCKNE ACCEPTING KIND INVITATION. . . ."

Contrary to the statement in his standard rejection letter, the contract with the Leigh-Emmerich lecture bureau allowed him to do free-lance speeches, but as he wrote Francis Wallace when the writer informed him of an invitation for both of them to talk to a Rhode Island club, "unless there is a lot of money involved I had better be excused. However, if there is a lot of money involved I might be tempted to throw my hat in the ring."

In his first year with Leigh-Emmerich, he received $125 per twenty-minute talk plus expenses. His standard titles were: "Why We Have College Athletics," "Side Lights of Athletics," and "High Lights of Football as Applied to the Game of Life." The bureau liked to send him on two- and three-week tours, scheduling as many talks as possible.

Rockne's first season with the New York agency was so successful that for the second year they offered, "instead of our paying you a flat price per lecture, we will pay you half the fee for which we book you." The bureau raised its fee for a Rockne speech to $400 but his success also attracted offers from Leigh-Emmerich's competitors. In March 1928, the New York bureau countered one outside offer with a flat fee proposal of "$6,000 . . . for forty lectures, to be given in January and February [1929], approximately twenty a month," plus expenses, or "if you prefer a fifty-fifty proposal, we would guarantee you a minimum of $5,500 for two months—forty appearances, [plus expenses]."

Rockne, however, was not able to cash in on this proposition—his long absences from Notre Dame for his winter lecture tours increasingly angered President Walsh and the latter reminded him in March 1928 that, as Rockne later informed Leigh-Emmerich, "I am employed here at a very high salary for nine months of the year as football coach and athletic director . . . and the President told me that things went all wrong this winter because I was gone." As a result, the N.D. coach could not accept Leigh-Emmerich's or its competitor's offer.

For university administrators in the 1920s, a coach's outside business deals were unmapped territory; moreover, because Knute Rockne pioneered many of these entrepreneurial schemes, the men in the Golden Dome were slow to react to his various conflicts of interest, including his use of the Catholic school's name to advertise himself and his endorsed products. Nevertheless, his lecture tours and long absences from his office were too much for the hardworking Father Walsh. The coach, however, knew that Walsh's presidential term was about to end and he hoped for better luck with his successor, Father Charles O'Donnell.

Mr. Harry J. Allen
Director of Physical Education
Y.M.C.A.
Dayton, Ohio . . .
I have your very kind invitation to speak at your Y.M.C.A. banquet January 31 [1929] and am sorry to say that I have signed up with the Studebaker Corporation this winter to appear at their Salesmen's dinners during the months of January and February . . .

Yours sincerely,

K. K. Rockne

—Letter from Rockne, November 14, 1928

In a clever strategic move, the N.D. coach, rather than try to go back on the lecture tour circuit for a New York agency during the winter of 1928–1929, signed with a large South Bend firm, Studebaker Motors, to do sales talks. Because the car company's headquarters was near Notre Dame, he could claim adherence to President Walsh's mandate. Moreover, the pay ($10,000) was much better than what Leigh-Emmerich or its competitors had offered. In fact, Rockne traveled even more for Studebaker than he had for the lecture bureau—according to his secretary, "from coast to coast all winter . . . away constantly with the exception of a few hours [at N.D.] now and then." But the new Notre Dame president, Father Charles O'Donnell, did not complain, in part, because Albert Erskine, the president of Studebaker, was head of the N.D. lay board of trustees and a great patron of the university as well as of the famous coach.

Rockne continued with other speaking engagements, including some during the football season and at the behest of Erskine. In 1929, the National Association of Finance Companies wanted him to address its annual convention in Chicago, and when he did not respond to its invitation, asked Erskine to "use your good offices" to persuade the N.D. coach to appear. The Studebaker president forwarded the association's letter with the appended note: "Dear Rock. It's worth $300 if you want it." Rockne went to Chicago and gave the talk.

"Before I joined Mr. Hoffman [vice president of Studebaker] on this tour, I was up at [the Mayo Clinic in] Rochester, Minnesota, resting a bit and enjoying myself. Mr. Hoffman called me long distance one day and said he would give me twenty-five dollars a week and my expenses if I would go along with him on a speaking tour of Studebaker meetings. He even said he would pay me a little more than that, but I finally told him that I wasn't interested and hung up. As I said, I was enjoying myself except for a few annoying incidents. Every once in a while a bellboy would come down the hall dribbling one of my checks back to me marked 'no funds.' That wasn't so bad until one of the boys brought one back marked 'no bank.' I immediately called Mr. Hoffman and asked, 'When do we leave?'"

—Rockne's standard opening for his Studebaker sales talks

With self-deprecating humor, the N.D. coach attempted to portray himself as a simple, honest man, interested in making a living but not in amassing wealth. However, his roommate at the Mayo Clinic, the young Frank Leahy, noted that Studebaker's offer to the coach was "a little more than . . . twenty-five dollars a week"—it was $10,000 for the first winter's work with the prospect of a significant increase after that, including a hefty royalty on a Studebaker model to be called "The Rockne." In fact, at the height of his earning power, the N.D. coach's estimated income from Notre Dame and his outside deals was close to $75,000 a year—more than the salary of the president of Studebaker—and an astounding sum for a college athletic coach, not matched by anyone in his profession for another forty years.

In his standard Studebaker speech, usually given to groups of the company's dealers and salesmen, after his opening jokes and some anecdotes about Fighting Irish football, he offered "a few remarks on the psychology that is necessary for success in a football organization [because that] same psychology . . . will make for success in any organization, and particularly in a selling organization."

Rockne loved sports-as-life metaphors, and at a time when most Americans believed that religious leaders explained life's complexities far better than athletic figures, the N.D. coach pioneered with his sports analogies. Athletes and coaches had begun to endorse products but they rarely commented on more weighty matters; Knute Rockne, whose entrepreneurial zest put him on the same wavelength as the era's salesmen, succeeded in his speeches by comparing his techniques in producing winning football teams with a businessman's daily tasks. Rockne worked hard for Studebaker, often giving his standard speech many times in the same day, but according to a company PR man and contrary to the coach's persona, the "professional sales force managing the tours handled Rockne just as other stars are handled."

The promotional work for the automobile company extended past the winter and the coach turned over spring practice in 1929 to his assistants. In addition, he refused less lucrative speaking engagements, even invitations from coaching friends to appear at their football banquets. Again, the reality of his daily correspondence, replete with copies of these turn-down letters, contradicts the legend; an Indiana sportswriter, in his obituary notice on the coach, began one of the most famous posthumous myths: "It was his great desire to help his friends and always turn up for their banquets, regardless of how far he might travel."

Rockne did have trouble resisting some of the money deals put before him. In 1930, an important vaudeville circuit offered him a huge sum—according to one report, $50,000—for an extensive tour à la Will Rogers, but the displeasure of President O'Donnell and personal illness forced him to turn it down.

He was also intrigued by the new medium of radio, and in 1928 he shrewdly accepted an invitation by a Chicago station to help broadcast the Dartmouth at Northwestern game even though they would pay only his expenses. He enjoyed the experience and sent in his bill for $16. By the following year, he referred radio broadcast requests to his agent, Christy Walsh, and his fee increased significantly. As radio became more important, stations and networks offered him more work and, according to one journalist, shortly before he died in 1931, "he had a radio contract . . . worth $30,000." No doubt, with his fame and speaking abilities, if he had lived into the "Golden Age of Radio," he would have earned an enormous amount of money from this medium.

Not all of Rockne's business deals paid off; as a true optimist, he went into the stock and bond business in 1930 *after* the markets had crashed. An item in the *Notre Dame Scholastic* noted: "Coach Rockne will assume a new role in his daily work when he takes possession of a desk in the new brokerage office being opened on the second floor of the Odd Fellows building [in downtown South Bend]." Rockne was a natural salesman with a huge number of contacts in northern Indiana but not even he could stop the Great Depression.

Bonnie's face has become anxious since the moment the messenger appeared. She watches [her husband] Knute's face as he reads the wire and frowns.

BONNIE: What is it, Knute?

ROCKNE [*hands her the telegram*]: I've got to go to California.
BONNIE [*glances at the message, then up*]: But not—not right away?
ROCKNE [*nods without enthusiasm*]: I promised these fellows I'd come whenever they needed me. There ought to be a union for people who can't say no.

—From the film *Knute Rockne—All American*

The Hollywood biopic gives no further explanation for this journey to California in March 1931—the trip during which Rockne died. In reality, the "fellows" in California were film executives at Universal Pictures and they had offered him $50,000 to play the role of the football coach in the movie version of a popular play, *Good News*. He was on his way to close the deal, sign the contract, and receive some money upfront.

According to Elmer Layden, "When the play had been on Broadway, Rock had stepped into the cast one night to give the coach's pep talk . . . one of the highlights of this show," and he was a natural for the film role. After Rockne's death and the national outpouring of grief, Christy Walsh convinced Universal to cash in on the coach's fame and give the film an N.D. slant. It became *The Spirit of Notre Dame*, but after its campus premiere President Charles O'Donnell told the head of Universal that, locally, "it was felt that little of [the real] Notre Dame appeared in the picture."

The hagiographers, including the scriptwriter of *Knute Rockne—All American*, knew the true story of the coach's final journey but chose not to portray him as materialistic. Instead they rendered his motivations as altruistic—he could never say no to an urgent request. However, considering his entrepreneurial zeal and lifelong risk-taking, the actual reasons for his final trip were much more in character with the real Knute Rockne.

25

Anti-aircraft Fire from the College Sports Reformers: 1927

"Not only is he [Rockne] a great field leader but also a strong moral force . . . He has lifted a poverty-stricken school, working among the poorer boys as a duty, to a ranking university. He has elevated the athletic morale of the school to the highest plane, and with it the athletic standards of every Catholic college in the country. . . .

Father [Hugh] O'Donnell, the disciplinarian, told me, 'I would hesitate to accept the responsibility for the behavior and morale of this body of students without the influence of Rockne and athletics.' "

—Hugh Fullerton, *Liberty Magazine*, February 1927

By 1927, the public image of Knute Rockne and Notre Dame began to diverge significantly from the private reality. Not only was the football coach given credit for the Catholic school's academic improvement—in reality, the achievement of Presidents Burns and Walsh as well as such brilliant educators as Fathers George Shuster and Thomas Steiner—but Rockne was increasingly portrayed as a saintlike figure "working among the poorer boys as a duty." In fact, he worked with whomever could play outstanding football, and some of his best players came from very affluent backgrounds, including Marty Brill, an All-American halfback and a millionaire's son, and Fred Miller, captain of the 1928 team and heir to the Miller Beer fortune.

As for Father Hugh "Pepper" O'Donnell's relations with Rockne, during the prefect of discipline's term they had a number of run-ins, including a nasty exchange in 1925 involving a starting quarterback. O'Donnell, although he loved football and had played on the 1914–1915 varsity, wanted Rockne's "boy" expelled from school for violating various rules but the football coach managed to keep him in.

Nevertheless, neither the academic achievements of the Catholic school nor the problems involving athletes reached the public. Rockne had the ear of the press and, through his press assistants, controlled the N.D. football information doled out to journalists; President Matthew Walsh also chose to present a united front to the outside world—to speak as positively as possible about his coach and team, and to handle all internal problems behind closed doors (his predecessors and successors, including Father Hugh O'Donnell when he became president, adhered to this policy).

Reinforcing Walsh's position in the 1920s was the growing importance of the Fighting Irish to American Catholics. The Notre Dame president as well as the head coach received frequent letters from clergy and lay persons conveying their love for Notre Dame football. A dramatic example occurred in 1927 when a priest wrote to Rockne: "As a missionary I seldom get a chance to witness your football games but I do get a lot of chances to hear what the public thinks of them, in almost every state in the Union." The cleric then related how he "went out to reclaim a sinner who had been 25 years away from the sacraments and . . . refused to even talk to me until" the subject of Notre Dame football came up. The lapsed Catholic then said, "I regard Rockne a greater man than Napoleon." The priest "agreed with him of course," and after discussing the Fighting Irish, suggested that he confess his sins. "He knelt down and cleaned up the whole chapter and was in the church with a candle two hours later."

President Walsh and Rockne recognized the naïveté of many of these football fans—increasing numbers of letters came from children and teenagers—but they did not doubt their sincerity. The emotions invested by American Catholics in Notre Dame football placed a unique weight upon the school's administrators, one that began during this era and continues to the present.

The major pressure concerned the purity of Notre Dame athletics: because the Fighting Irish represented a triumph of Catholicism in America, the football team could not win by cheating on or off the field. The Notre Dame president and his coach received many communications, mainly from coreligionists, expressing this article of their faith. In 1927, an N.D. alum, the head of a Washington press syndicate, wrote

Father Walsh: "Detractors of our beloved old institution . . . here-abouts [claim] that Notre Dame is barred from the Western Football Conference [the Big Ten] because the university does not adhere to Conference academic requirements [for athletes]," and the alum re-quested a "denial."

The N.D. president first explained that "whenever a new territory is invaded" by the Fighting Irish—the team had recently played in the Baltimore-Washington area for the first time—"there is the inevitable comeback regarding the very points mentioned in your letter." Walsh then affirmed that the school "has adopted and carefully follows out the application of every rule operative in the [Big Ten] Conference it-self."

The other part of the Notre Dame football burden dropped on Walsh five days later, when the same Washington alum sent him a telegram about the upcoming game against Army in Yankee Stadium: "I DESIRE [TO] EXPRESS BITTER RESENTMENT STEPCHILD TREATMENT ACCORDED US WASHINGTON ALUMNI ON ARMY TICKETS . . . SO WRETCHEDLY LOCATED THAT THEY ARE QUITE EVIDENTLY THE LEAVINGS." In such situations, President Walsh, like many Notre Dame administrators after him, must have wondered how one dismounts from a tiger.

On January 28, 1927, the Big Ten's "Committee of Sixty"—the president, faculty representative, athletic director, football coach, a trustee, and an alumnus of each school—*banned from their universities:*

1. Scholarships, loans, and remissions of tuition awarded on the basis of athletic skill.

2. Financial aid granted for the purpose of subsidizing athletes by individuals or organizations, alumni or oth-erwise.

3. Correspondence or interviews or distribution of litera-ture initiated by athletic directors or coaches for the purpose of recruiting athletes.

4. General or field secretaries used for contacting ath-letes.

5. Employment promised to athletes before registration, or more pay [for campus jobs] than service rendered justified.

Not only did most Big Ten athletic departments have trouble obeying these rules but the new regulations made the Notre Dame coach's work more difficult. Rockne had long believed that the Big Ten reformers, especially Yost and Stagg, were hypocrites but he refused to go public with his opinion. He explained his position to a sports editor: "I know lots of things" about illegal recruiting and subsidization of athletes, "but I keep them to myself as I do not believe intercollegiate football should descend to the level of professional wrestling" with the phoniness exposed and ridiculed by the press and public.

In 1927, as the clamor for reform increased, Rockne felt even less inclined to air his true beliefs. Instead, he used his amanuensis, Francis Wallace; the young journalist placed an article, "The Hypocrisy of College Football Reform," with the important *Scribner's Magazine* and his mentor not only participated in its genesis but saw a draft and later "okayed it [and] gave some added material." The N.D. coach also commented privately to Wallace, "Any time they [rival coaches] all want to come out in the open, I'll take my chances." Until then, it would be business as usual.

In his article, Wallace attacked the Big Ten reforms as naive, wrong-headed, and, above all, hypocritical:

> During the deliberations of the Committee of Sixty . . . somebody suggested that all varsity football candidates be required to reveal, on affidavit, where they received the money with which to pay their expenses the preceding year. This harsh proposal would have given the code teeth, but it might also have been embarrassing to some members of the committee [and thus the committee rejected it] . . . The code remains toothless and there are sufficient holes in it for the bootleggers—and the hi-jackers too—to drive truck-loads of stuff through it.

For a follow-up piece "asking college presidents to reply or comment on" the article, Wallace requested Father Walsh to "endorse my sentiments to any extent." The N.D. administrator, far too canny to become involved in this controversy, particularly on the side of a writer who called the Big Ten presidents "hypocrites," never replied.

> "On the same [banquet] program that evening we are going to have . . . Mr. John T. McGovern, a member of the Investigation Committee of the Carnegie Foundation. Mr. McGovern, I believe, has been appointed by the Carnegie Foundation to investigate [the athletic programs of] practically all colleges of any standing . . . if he has not already been to Notre

Dame, he is intending to go there. This dinner would afford you a good opportunity to become well acquainted with Mr. McGovern."

—Letter to Rockne from Lou Little,
Georgetown A.D. and football coach, April 6, 1927

For many years, Georgetown had tried to get Rockne to attend its annual sports banquet; in 1927, he finally accepted and also waived his usual speaker's fee.

Although the N.D. coach believed that the Committee of Sixty were only pretending to reform intercollegiate athletics, he knew that, unlike the Big Ten, the Carnegie Foundation had nothing to hide and much credibility to lose if it did not thoroughly investigate college sports. Moreover, the foundation had been a major benefactor of his university and the men in the Golden Dome wanted more grant money as well as the academic prestige that accompanied it. Finally, Notre Dame had recently joined the North Central Association of Colleges and Universities and that group's accrediting agency would now scrutinize the Catholic school's academic and athletic programs (the Carnegie Foundation helped initiate and fund these associations and their accrediting procedures).

Thus, at the Georgetown dinner, Rockne was extremely polite to Mr. McGovern and, during the following years, to his superiors, Dr. Howard Savage, in charge of writing the report based on the investigations, and Dr. Henry S. Pritchett, head of the Carnegie Foundation. The N.D. coach treated all reformers warily but he was particularly on guard against these eastern establishment men.

Regardless of the reform climate of the late 1920s, Knute Rockne still wanted to produce winning and dominant football teams. He had met all previous challenges and felt himself up to this one, except the rules seemed to be shifting beneath his feet. In 1928, when one of his Seven Mules enthusiastically recommended a high school prospect in Canton, Ohio, the N.D. coach replied, "I talked to Father Carey [in charge of student admissions] and he says that it is absolutely impossible to accept anyone with [only] fifteen Carnegie units [of high school credit]. As they [N.D.] belong to the Central Association, they must adhere to that absolutely. Personally I regret this very much but I cannot understand how he [the recruit] can be admitted to Ohio State, which has the same ruling."

The hypocrisy of the Big Ten universities galled the N.D. coach, and although he had to endorse their reforms publicly, he had no intention of changing his private methods until he was convinced that the conference coaches had cleaned up their procedures. Rockne began to draw a clear line between public and private behavior and to act in terms of the distinction. Thus, in 1927, when his old friend Charlie Bachman recommended two outstanding "Indian" players, he replied, "Sorry I will not be able to do anything about the two Haskell [Institute] boys as our policy here has done away with that sort of thing. Meaning, by that, that *well known men* would not do us any good here in view of the fact that we really have to lean backwards to satisfy men like Yost, etc."

The University of Michigan athletic director was an ominous bête noir for Notre Dame and its football coach. Rockne attributed his rival's behavior to personal jealousy—he said that Yost couldn't "stand to see anyone else get along"—but the N.D. coach knew that whatever the Michigan man's motivations, Yost carefully watched Notre Dame's football program. As a result, Rockne had to cover his recruiting and subsidization with as much camouflage as possible.

Dear Mr. Trares,

If this young chap you mention in your letter is looking for offers, he is looking at the wrong place as Notre Dame will not give anybody any offer.

So, if he has favorable terms from the other schools you mention I would suggest that he take them.

Yours very truly,

K. K. Rockne

Dear Bodie,

Registration here is supposed to be closed but if you think this boy is awfully good, send him on here and I will take care of him some way or another.

Don't tell anybody about this but just merely send him on and say nothing and leave the rest to me.

Yours sincerely,

Rock

The N.D. coach had always been somewhat suspicious of people beyond his immediate circle, but with the reform movement and the intense scrutiny of his football program, he made a sharp division between trusted friends and the rest of the world. He no longer accepted unsolicited recommendations on players, even from Notre Dame alumni like Trares. However, Frank "Bodie" Andrews had played on the 1916–1917 varsity and had also scouted for him—Rockne respected Andrews's judgment as well as his ability to keep a secret. (The N.D. coach's trust was well placed; none of his inner circle ever revealed his recruiting and subsidization maneuvers—thus aiding the myth that Rockne ran a totally clean program.)

His former players were helpful in scouting, but if they worked as coaches, they had to place their own recruiting interests above their mentor's. Thus, noncoaching grads such as Bodie Andrews, a California real estate promoter; Leo "Red" Ward, a Los Angeles lawyer; Al Feeney, an Indianapolis politician; and Francis Wallace, a sportswriter, became the best "bird dogs" for the coach.

Wallace, originally from the football-rich region of southeastern Ohio, sent such 1920s stalwarts as John "Bull" Poliski and John Niemic to Notre Dame and frequently returned to his home area to search for prospects. By 1927, with growing anxiety about the Carnegie investigators, Wallace sometimes used a comic code to communicate his recruiting to his mentor: "Please let me know when you expect to arrive in New York. . . . I would like to talk to you about some Irish and Polish natives of the great city of Bellaire [Ohio—Wallace's hometown]."

> "The success of the Notre Dame football team [under Rockne] was to a far greater degree the result of the application of perfected routine than of individual brilliance of performers."
>
> —McCready Huston in *Salesman from the Sidelines*

Because of his demanding football offenses and defenses, the N.D. coach wanted as large a pool of recruits as possible from which to select the ideal players for his system. Rockne needed athletes who could meet the physical and mental requirements of his long, tough practices and he knew that high school "hot shots" did not necessarily survive his hard drills and the mud of the Notre Dame training fields. Hence his search for his particular "boys" and his awareness that the more recruits with which he started, the greater his chances of finding the best players to build championship teams.

In a report to Vice President Carroll during the winter of 1926–1927, Rockne's secretary noted that "Catholic boys all over the country," outstanding athletes, "are naturally inclined toward Notre Dame" football. This social fact helped the "bird dogs" enlist prospects and also created a large number of talented walk-ons—the N.D. coach always welcomed them; a few made it to the varsity and others provided cannon fodder for scrimmages with the regulars. The report to Carroll also computed: "An average of thirty boys are developed on our football team each year, making a total of around one hundred and fifty players over a period of five years."

The N.D. coach "red-shirted" before the term was even invented and, as Frank Leahy later indicated, often "Rockne would red-shirt a man for two years. . . . He was most incredible." Leahy, who arrived at N.D. in 1927, also noted: "Rockne had so many players here on [athletic] scholarship that as many as 100 lads would go through Notre Dame and never see [varsity] game action. I loved that man. But I consider that sinful. The idea [of doing it] to keep good players from playing against you—that is squandering humanity."

From the mid-1920s on, Rockne's Fighting Irish elevens were the result of an attrition resembling the Great War's. The N.D. coach began the process each spring: Frank Carideo, eventually an All-American quarterback, recalled a spring practice when the "field swarmed with candidates. The count came to 380," and the following year, there were "370 out for football. Rock believed in groups." By the end of the spring, the coach had his squad down to about 150—mainly returnees from previous seasons and the pick of the past fall's freshmen. After September workouts, he assigned the players to various teams: thirty-five for the varsity's traveling squad; thirty-five for the main reserve unit; and another eighty or so for practices and exhibitions. In addition, every September he held a cattle call for the freshman team —large numbers came out and the coaches selected about seventy-five for the "frosh crew." In 1928, Rockne explained his numbers system to the football coach at Saint Viator College and promised to send him "a sort of sixth or seventh string team" for a game against the Illinois school's varsity the following Saturday (a generation earlier, the N.D. varsity used to play Saint Viator).

For Rockne, the point of this winnowing was to produce the Fighting Irish varsity, the thirty-five members of the traveling squad, and more specifically, the starting eleven—the rules still emphasized one-platoon football (a player removed from the game could not return in the same quarter). However, some N.D. football harvests yielded such excellent second-strings that, in one of his favorite tactics, the coach would start the backups as "Shock Troops" to wear down their opponents and then send in his first eleven to plow the enemy under.

In demographic terms, the 1927 varsity was typical of the N.D. football pool in that eleven members had attended Catholic secondary schools, fifteen others belonged to the faith, and seven were Protestants; in addition, they came from fourteen different states—as far west as California and east as Connecticut although the Midwest predominated with 55 percent of the players.

Moreover, as with most N.D. varsities of this period, the coach's friends had recruited many of the starters and the Big Ten schools had actively sought the midwestern athletes, especially the high school stars. Rockne knew that his "bird dogs" could spot "the kind of men [who] will make good" in his system. In addition, the coach liked to accumulate midwestern recruits because they had excellent football backgrounds, and even though he could start only a small percentage of them, he could frustrate the Big Ten coaches by "stockpiling" the others.

For all of Rockne's maneuvering, when the Carnegie Foundation investigators visited the Midwest in 1927–1928, they found no recruiting violations at Notre Dame and many abuses at Big Ten schools. Because the Carnegie committee had total access to these institutions and every athletic department tried to conceal its sins, the conclusion is that Rockne's recruiting was much less extensive and systematic than that of his Big Ten rivals, and also that he managed to hide the activities of his "bird dogs" from the scrutiny of the Golden Dome—his correspondence with the faculty board and N.D. administrators never touched on his recruiting tactics.

The Carnegie report criticized Michigan, Wisconsin, and Northwestern, as well as Notre Dame's intersectional rival, USC, for "intensely organized, sometimes subtle [proselyting] systems that utilize or coordinate numbers of agents on or off the campus." In addition, at Michigan, Ohio State, Wisconsin, and Purdue, as well as USC, "coaches, managers, athletes, and even university officers combine in broad but intensive and systematic approaches to prominent schoolboy athletes." Most Big Ten schools also used alumni for recruiting—a rich Indiana University grad "hired several special Pullman cars at his own expense to take athletes . . . to the campus of his university"—and Purdue, Wisconsin, Minnesota, Iowa, and Illinois, as well as USC, allowed their campus undergraduate fraternities to help recruit and sub-

sidize football players. The most egregious Big Ten offender was
Michigan, where among other sins, the alumni treasurer got a fellow
grad to "pay . . . [the] expenses in traveling" to Ann Arbor of high
school prospects, then Fielding Yost's athletic department praised the
official for his assistance.

Unlike the recruiting systems of the conference universities, Rockne's
was haphazard and informal. The "bird dogs" did not receive regular or
specific orders from the N.D. football coach or anyone else at the Catholic school. They scouted on their own, only reporting when they found an
excellent prospect; thus, some years Rockne heard from Bodie Andrews
and other years he did not. The whole Rockne "bird dog" network numbered approximately fifteen Notre Dame grads plus about ten men like
Curly Lambeau, whose football opinions the N.D. coach also respected.

The only comment in the 1929 Carnegie report about Notre Dame's
"proselyting" was indirect—the investigators noted the role that "the
loyal alumnus, the devoted priest, the enthusiastic undergraduate, [and]
the professional coach" played in convincing young Catholic athletes to
attend "Catholic colleges." Rockne was pleased with this part of the
report as well as his ability to keep his "bird dog" network under wraps.
Thus, after the Carnegie investigators issued their findings in 1929, partly
as a result of their "clean bill of health" on his recruiting but even more
because of the Big Ten coaches' growing brazenness in this area, he
escalated his "proselyting," setting up an extensive alumni sponsorship
program for prospective N.D. athletes.

> "A subsidy denotes any assistance, favor, gift, award, scholarship, or con-
> cession, direct or indirect, which advantages an athlete because of his
> athletic ability or reputation, and which sets him apart from his fellows in
> the undergraduate body."
>
> —The Carnegie Foundation, Bulletin No. 23

In 1927–1928, the Carnegie sleuths discovered three main forms of
subsidies as well as "miscellaneous assistance": "jobs and work of various
kinds"; loans; and athletic scholarships. Within each category existed "a
scale of subsidizing" from, in the case of jobs, hard and honest work for
little pay to, at the other extreme, sinecures equal in difficulty to the
position of harbormaster in a prairie town.

Notre Dame, because of its long tradition of clergy and students earning their keep, tended to reward most athletes with regular jobs on campus, especially maintenance work. In the 1920s, as student enrollment grew but the number of part-time work positions stayed about the same, the school had fewer job openings for incoming freshmen. Rockne used this situation as an excuse to fend off the self-appointed recruiters—in 1927, he told an alum with a high school "phenom" that "this last year it was very difficult for an athlete who was a Freshman to get a [work] position" and that the coach could promise nothing to recruits. However, that same year and throughout the late 1920s, Rockne frequently wrote to Father Patrick McBride, the longtime N.D. official in charge of campus jobs, about assignments for the "bird dogs'" athletes. In September 1927, he informed McBride: "This will introduce Mr. [Frank] Carideo, who last year attended Dean Academy, Massachusetts. Anything you can do for Mr. Carideo in the way of employment will be very much appreciated. He was a very fine student and athlete at Dean Academy and he is the type of boy I know Notre Dame stands for."

McBride, who loved football and the N.D. coach, understood the subtext of this note, and even though Carideo was an incoming freshman, the future All-American obtained work. In fact, during Rockne's regime, McBride usually assigned over 60 percent of all student jobs to athletes. Thus, in 1927, when one of the coach's scouts wrote him about an excellent prospect in New Orleans who would play for the Fighting Irish "if he could get a [free] ride" through N.D., Rockne replied, "Please have this young man come right on to Notre Dame . . . he will have a *job* here, of course, I am [also] assuming that his entrance requirements are entirely satisfactory." (Paranoia about the reform movement had taken hold —the scout assured the N.D. coach that in a telegram to the prospect, he "did not mention our school—and the wire was safe," that is, not read by nosy telegraph operators.) The Notre Dame chores, especially for underclassmen, were real and sometimes hard.

Rockne, however, did reward his varsity starters with Father McBride's best jobs or various positions around the athletic department. Often, these were the most lucrative and least demanding tasks at Notre Dame. In the summer of 1926, he wrote "Chile" Walsh, Adam's younger brother and an outstanding end: "I shall be able to give you definitely, through Father McBride, the job of sweeping the basketball floor next winter, which will pay $375." And that same week, he promised his best lineman, John Wallace: "You can make yourself some good money parking cars this Fall," an athletic department job controlled by the coach.

He also located off-campus positions for his players. When McBride could not accommodate a "boy" or Rockne wanted to reward the athlete with more pay, he would use his "downtown" South Bend friends. In addition, he had a large network of contacts throughout Indiana and other states to secure summer employment for players. He always tried to place a few varsity starters in the Cedar Point resort area of Ohio where, as undergraduates, he and Gus Dorais had been lifeguards. In the late 1920s, when an important N.D. alum became a powerful alderman in Chicago, controlling many city positions, Rockne usually asked him for summer work for some of the "boys." In addition, he used his pull with the alderman for positions for incoming as well as graduating players: "This is John Bachman, brother of Charlie, our old star. He will be entering school next February and he needs a job between now and then"; "This will introduce to you 'Chunky' Murrin, one of our guards who graduates February 1. He is desperately in need of some work to clear up some debts."

When all else failed, the N.D. coach was willing to fall back on a "phoney" job financed by an alum. Frank Hayes, Rockne's partner in Camp Rockne, wrote him in 1927 that Father McBride had refused employment to a recruit whom Hayes had sent to N.D. The player "had an opportunity to go to the University of Wisconsin with all expenses provided for" and Hayes suggested, "If you cannot get him a position for $100 in the gymnasium to pay off expenses for the balance of the semester, kindly get him a 'phoney' job and I will send [you the money]." Rockne agreed to the arrangement and promised a real position for "the year following."

Rockne's players truly appreciated his help, but their off-campus employers usually demanded a quid pro quo—more and better Notre Dame football seats. The N.D. coach often placed athletes through a wealthy Cleveland alum, John P. Murphy; in return, Rockne received such requests as, "I have invited some very prominent people to go to the [N.D.–Navy] game, and I would appreciate very much exchanging these tickets for better seats." The coach promptly replied, "I am enclosing herewith the [prime] tickets which you must keep strictly confidential as the [ticket] situation here is almost hopeless."

The Carnegie investigators did cite Notre Dame "for jobs that provide tuition, board, and room in return for very nominal services," but they found much worse situations at Big Ten schools—make-work or phantom positions for athletes as well as highly elaborate systems of off-campus and summer employment. They listed Wisconsin, Northwestern, Ohio State, Minnesota, and Chicago as offenders, but again they charged

Michigan with the greatest number of violations. A few years later, a study of the Big Ten detailed these "easy 'no work' jobs," including regular payment from alums "betting the athlete $50 that he cannot jump over a traveling bag."

> "This will introduce you to Austin Downes, one of our [N.D.] athletes who will have to drop out of school unless he is able to get some [financial] help from some source or another.
> Father Hugh [O'Donnell] expects to discuss an Alumni Loan Fund at your banquet on the fourteenth. Do you think that it would be easy to get the alumni interested in, say, $5.00 a man so as to create a loan fund to help keep a boy like this in school?"
>
> —Letter from Rockne to Chicago Alderman George Maypole,
>   February 8, 1927

For this fund, the N.D. coach expected $5 from each of the approximately three thousand active Notre Dame alumni. However, before he and Father Hugh O'Donnell could launch the idea—and the semipublic campaign necessary for success—the Notre Dame administration vetoed it. Not only would the fund violate the Big Ten's rules but the N.D. authorities wanted the alumni to contribute directly to the university, not to separate athletic department projects.

Rockne knew that loan funds for athletes existed at many schools and he wanted one for his athletic program. The Carnegie investigators confirmed the widespread existence of "loans as subsidies," particularly at Georgia Tech and USC, as well as at some Big Ten schools. The alumni frequently left the due dates blank and subsequently "forgave" the loans.

The loan scam often connected to direct athletic scholarships—not officially allowed in this era or until many years later. Higher education authorities as well as the general public believed that universities should give grants to students on the basis of academic ability only and greatly disapproved of awarding money for athletic prowess. Nevertheless, many coaches arranged full-year subsidies covering the cost of athletes' tuition, room and board, and other expenses. Some schools accepted the money directly from an alumni club or booster group, applying it to the recipient's bill, and because the athlete never handled the money, the institution claimed that he was a pure amateur. In fact, as critics pointed out, the player was a professional because his athletic scholarship was barter payment for services rendered—that is, playing sports for the university's team.

In 1927, Penn State abolished all of its athletic scholarships, and when its athletic department manager informed Rockne, he replied, "I believe your Board has been rather drastic in taking the action they have." He argued that Notre Dame's version of the athletic scholarship system worked well, "about ten or twelve of our Alumni Clubs . . . give a scholarship which includes tuition only . . . and these are supposed to be based on competitive examination. According to my check-off last spring about half of these chaps [the grant holders] were athletes."

These were the official N.D. scholarship holders but their number is far from Frank Leahy's estimate. Possibly Rockne understated his numbers or Leahy exaggerated his but more likely Leahy conflated all of the loan recipients and the job holders—he worked on- and off-campus during his playing career in the late 1920s—with the scholarship winners. In any event, Rockne took care of large numbers of his "boys" in a great variety of ways, few of them in accordance with the Committee of Sixty's strict rules but most covert or benign enough to avoid the attention of the Notre Dame administration.

In their investigations around the country, the Carnegie Foundation also discovered academic fraud concerning athletes: questionable admissions, passing grades for easy courses, and so on. Because academic laxness for Fighting Irish football players was one of the ongoing allegations against the Catholic school, N.D. administrators monitored the coach closely in this area. He was allowed to move some players out of afternoon classes to morning sections of a course so that they could attend football practice, but his athletes had to pass regular Notre Dame courses to remain eligible to play. The "boys" got some breathing room if they were Physical Education majors—and many were—and took the practicum classes in football, basketball, and other sports. Nevertheless, like all Notre Dame undergraduates, they had to pass a large number of required courses, and as a Catholic school, N.D. had a full complement of these.

Dear Rock—

Reports here that Cavosie [an outstanding Big Ten player is] going to Notre Dame.

As your friend, I advise you not to let him enter if you can keep him out. [He] Is a great football man but notoriously dumb in the head. If by chance he ever got eligible for you, your good friends (?) would knock you and your school more than enough. You can not stand the criticism of being an 'easy' school. Too many would like to account for your success by giving that as a reason . . .

"Doc"

—Letter to Rockne from Wisconsin basketball coach
W. E. "Doc" Meanwell, September 15, 1927

Dear Doc:
   All I can say, Doc, regarding the note on Cavosie is that he couldn't get in here for love nor money. . . . [This] School flunked out a half dozen [football] boys this year, one of whom was Danculovic of Aurora, Minnesota—and what a sweet athlete he was!

Kindest regards,

Rock

—Rockne's reply to Meanwell, September 17, 1927

The case of Paul Danculovic illustrates the limits of Rockne's power at Notre Dame. The coach's "bird dogs" claimed that the player was the athletic equal of his Minnesota contemporary, the great Bronko Nagurski, but from the beginning of his Fighting Irish career, Danculovic had difficulty—Rockne advised him after his freshman year, "Your weakest point in football [is your] inability to catch on to signals."
   Nevertheless, like every college football coach in the history of the sport, Rockne would go many extra miles to try to utilize such a talented player on his team, including appealing to the N.D. administration to overlook the athlete's problems. In February 1927, he wrote the academic dean: "A couple of alumni and myself have taken an interest in him and unless he can get back into school, it may be that his career will be entirely frustrated."
   The dean gave Danculovic another chance but the athlete did not help himself; the following August, Father Hugh O'Donnell informed him that his academic and personal "conduct during the summer session . . . convinced the Board that you were not seriously interested in your work here," and the board asked him to leave Notre Dame.
   Rockne could not reverse this decision but he did not abandon the athlete. He sent telegrams to some of his "boys" who headed football programs—for example, to Harry Mehre at the University of Georgia: "CAN YOU USE CRACKERJACK HALFBACK AND END, DANCULOVIC BY NAME?"—and

eventually placed the player as well as his brother with Hunk Anderson, at the time head coach at the University of Saint Louis.

Rockne's actions underline his generosity toward all of his "boys"— past and present—as well as the differences between Notre Dame's self-imposed standards and the looser regulations of many other schools. Danculovic was grateful and later wrote his old coach, "We are mighty glad you advised us to come here because Anderson and his assistants, former Notre Damers ["Chile"] Walsh, and ["Bucky"] Dahmen have taken real good care of us."

The proliferation of Notre Dame men in the college coaching profession was a source of pride to the coach and the school but, in the late 1920s, it also created new problems, particularly in terms of Fighting Irish schedules.

> "The more I see of games between Notre Dame men, the more I think that they had better not play [each other]. There has been more bad blood between Notre Dame coaches than is good for the game and personally there is no one more sorry than I am that these things happen."
>
> —Rockne to Gus Dorais, his N.D. undergraduate roommate, and teammate, and at the time of the letter, head football coach at the University of Detroit

Rockne wrote his close friend concerning a number of vicious incidents that occurred when the latter's Detroit team encountered the University of Saint Louis varsity, coached by another friend, Hunk Anderson. According to Dorais, the Saint Louis starters were "eleven popeyed maniacs" and played incredibly dirty football. Then "between halves Hunk added fuel to the fire by publicly calling me a dirty little son of a bitch and other choice descriptions of a like nature." Dorais, sensitive about his height (he was five-foot-seven), admitted to Rockne: "If I could have made the score 100–0, I would have gladly done it." Instead he had to settle for a 38–0 thrashing of Saint Louis. (Hunk's failure to control his players was a portent of one of his major problems during his years as Rockne's coaching successor at N.D.)

This "bad blood between Notre Dame coaches" added another argument to Rockne's list of reasons for not playing Catholic schools—an increasing number of them had N.D. men as coaches. Nevertheless, in 1927, the Notre Dame administration and the athletic board, after many years of pressure from Detroit-area alumni, agreed to schedule Dorais's University of Detroit squad for that fall. With this move, N.D. officials hoped to counter the growing criticism in the American Catholic community that N.D. would not aid its colleagues by scheduling a big football payday with them, and that Notre Dame wanted all the football glory plus all the Catholic fans for itself.

Even before the game with Detroit took place, N.D. made it clear that no return contest would occur. The faculty board did, however, schedule the 1928 home opener against Loyola of New Orleans, in part to counter the gossip that Notre Dame would never play a second Jesuit school. As a result, many Catholic institutions, particularly those in New York, Boston, and Washington, bombarded Notre Dame with requests for games, but N.D. officials decided to refuse all entreaties. This decision was based mainly on the rumors (and facts) that other Catholic schools did not observe regular intercollegiate athletic rules; certainly N.D.'s experience with the University of Saint Louis confirmed this belief. Because of this problem, Notre Dame subsequently passed on the great Fordham and Boston College teams of the era. After 1928, the Fighting Irish did not play a Catholic institution until 1951—Detroit again—and then waited almost a quarter of a century before scheduling another—Boston College in 1975.

The N.D. administration also responded to all appeals for "charity [exhibitions] and games of this sort" by having the athletic director explain that "the authorities here have already turned down Cardinal Mundelein and various Catholic schools which have been destroyed by fire or razed by cyclone" because "to play one football game for charity would merely get them into an impossible situation. We would not only have the enmity of the ones we turned down but we would have to accept the many others for years following."

In addition, the administration remained opposed to postseason contests, and in 1927, the school refused many attractive offers, including a $100,000 guarantee from Southern Methodist for a Christmas game in Texas. Rockne exclaimed to an SMU official: "The size of the guarantee is the biggest I ever heard of [but] our Faculty cannot see how it is possible for us to play any other game away from home this Fall without incurring criticism that would be unanswerable."

During the late 1920s, Notre Dame could dictate scheduling terms with Catholic schools and most intersectional opponents, but the Big Ten, notably such conference heavyweights as Michigan, Illinois, and Ohio

State, shunned the Fighting Irish. In 1927, when Rockne wrote the Minnesota football coach proposing "another three-year contract with you" for games beginning the following season, that university declined. Minnesota ended the series, in part, because of pressure from conference "reformers" such as Stagg and Yost.

The same year, a number of schools, led by Missouri and Kansas, explored the possibility of forming a "Missouri Valley Conference" and asked Notre Dame to consider membership in it. The faculty athletic board canvassed the various Notre Dame constituencies about the proposal and discovered unanimous opposition: one heavyweight alum wrote that joining "such a Conference . . . would tend to take Notre Dame out of national prominence," and another strongly argued in "favor [of] remaining the 'free-lance' that we are at the present time . . . ours is the only *national* team in football."

Becoming a charter member of the Missouri Valley Conference was soundly rejected and, by 1927, even the desire for membership in the Big Ten was fading. In November of that year, President Walsh remarked: "If a vote were taken among our Alumni and friends at the present time, I seriously question whether approval would be given to our joining the [Big Ten] Conference, as it is universally felt that we are much better off in our present situation." Thus, by 1927, Notre Dame began to see its independent position in college football as a distinct plus and this attitude shaped its future determination to go it alone.

■ ■ ■

"I must admit that I don't know how refs were hired and assigned in Rockne's time. I suppose that some officials were hostile to us but probably Rock didn't even care . . . I don't know to this day how he got his refs. No one ever talked about it back then and it all got buried afterwards."

—Edward "Moose" Krause, N.D. athlete in the early 1930s, later the school's longtime athletic director, in a 1992 interview with the author

In addition to parrying the suggestions for various contests and conferences involving the Fighting Irish, Rockne also had to deal with requests from referees to work his scheduled games. Jay Wyatt, the Wilson sporting goods salesman and regular N.D. game official, and Frank Birch, another Rockne favorite ref, heard that "Southern California will ask for new officials [rather than us] for your [1927] game"; Birch questioned the N.D. coach, "Is this possible? I know [that] I was criticized for 'handing you the [1926] game on a silver platter,' " but according to the official, the charge was unjust.

The N.D. coach replied that USC had indeed vetoed Wyatt and Birch but he promised, "In another year I shall try to work you in either [our] Army or Navy game." However, late in 1927, Birch requested the following year's USC game and Rockne agreed to recommend him, noting that there would always be public disputes over referees' decisions; for example, "the trouble" a few weeks previous when a controversial call resulted in a Trojan defeat, "was almost entirely caused by the newspapermen in Los Angeles who, I understand, lost heavily on betting."

Rockne tried to insulate his games from the vagaries of officiating by working as closely as possible with Major John Griffith, commissioner of the Big Ten. The N.D. coach's 1927 files contain many letters between them, some concerning referee assignments but also some about Griffith's magazine, the *Athletic Journal*. The Big Ten commissioner would remind Rockne that "we are now ready for your [advertising] copy" for the coach's various businesses and, in 1927, he also asked for "a short endorsement of the *Athletic Journal*, which I can use in an effort to increase the *Journal* circulation." The Big Ten commissioner tried to wrap his request in high-sounding phrases about his magazine's "mission . . . [for] doing some good for the cause of amateur athletics," and the famous coach obviously liked this line—it fit his new image as a champion of the same cause—because, in his endorsement, he wrote: "You are filling an absolute need in the cause of amateur athletics."

Nevertheless, beneath the inflated language was the nuts-and-bolts business of obtaining officials for N.D. games, and in 1927, Rockne admitted to a man at Michigan Agricultural that he "asked Mr. Griffith personally, not the Big Ten Board but Mr. Griffith, to pick our officials." Of course, Griffith knew that Walter Eckersall of the *Chicago Tribune* was Rockne's first choice and the Big Ten commissioner assigned the reporter to as many N.D. games as possible. In addition, as the coach notified Griffith in late September 1927, "I am having Eckie and Lipp [J. J. Lipski] come down and work my freshman scrimmage [against the varsity] next Saturday."

After Eckersall's September visit, the N.D. coach wrote him that Art Haley, the ticket manager, was "taking personal care of your tickets [for N.D. games for your family and friends] and you may rest assured that they will be good ones. It was very nice of you to write that nice story [about us] this morning and I assure you I appreciate it very much." Indeed, a major part of Rockne's friendship with "Eck" was the quid pro quo of exclusive information from the coach and good press from the reporter—"Eck" added in one 1927 note, "See you Saturday and if you have any fresh dope, shoot it along." Nevertheless, the main ingredient of their relationship was the coach's hiring of Eckersall to referee N.D. games and other tasks:

> Dear Eckie,
>   You have been selected to work as head linesman in our Southern California game in Chicago on November 26 [1927] . . .
>
> K. K. Rockne
> Director of Athletics
>
> —Rockne to Eckersall, September 20, 1927

> Dear Eckie,
>   Confidentially, we have decided to give you $250 [the price of a new Dodge coupe] to handle the publicity in Chicago for our California game November 26 . . .
>
> K. K. Rockne
> Director of Athletics
>
> —Rockne to Eckersall, November 17, 1927

The Carnegie Foundation investigators noted: "During the early days of this enquiry the statement was frequently made to members of the staff that the newspaper publicity accorded to many coaches was bought and paid for in cash or in kind. In view of the seriousness of the charge, special steps were taken to study it. . . . No such accusation was clearly substantiated." Thus Rockne's payment to Eckersall in 1927 was unusual and the N.D. coach must have considered it so because he began his letter "Confidentially . . ." Moreover, why, ten days before the game, did the N.D. coach believe that extra publicity for the Chicago contest was even necessary? Although the game was scheduled for cavernous Soldier Field, the Notre Dame athletic department could not begin to meet the demand for seats—the N.D. ticket manager exclaimed to one alumni official, "We could have easily sold 100,000 more tickets for the Chicago game."

By 1927, with reformers peering into all corners of college football, for a journalist to accept "flak" money for a particular game and then to work that contest as an on-field official was well beyond the usual corrupt practices of the day. If the Carnegie investigators or the Big Ten's Committee of Sixty had discovered Eckersall's arrangements with Rockne, they would have censured them and, in the Big Ten's case, probably banned both men from future contact with conference schools. Ironically, the man in charge of policing the Big Ten and enforcing its rules, Commissioner John Griffith, probably did know about the Eckersall-Rockne deals, but he was so compromised by his business and personal relations with the N.D. coach that he never said a word.

No evidence exists, however, that Eckersall ever "threw" a game for Notre Dame. The years of his relationship with and payments from Rockne made him extremely sympathetic to the "Notre Dame shift" and its controversial timing—some refs whistled it down as illegal—and his preseason work for the N.D. coach familiarized the Fighting Irish players with his officiating and he with them. "Eckie" was definitely on Rockne's football wavelength but he did not always rule in favor of the Fighting Irish or, as important to the N.D. coach, consistently make decisions against them. Finally, as in Rockne's dealings with all game officials, with "Eckie" he wanted every possible advantage and if paying him for public- ity work helped, he did it.

■   ■   ■

"My earliest memory of a Notre Dame game was as a young boy going on an excursion train from Chicago to Detroit to see the Fighting Irish play there. There were special cars for N.D. rooters and I remember bootleggers coming down the aisles selling booze in these little brown medicine bottles. Everyone wore Notre Dame colors and had a great time. I assume we won."

—A longtime Notre Dame fan and alumnus of the school

By the late 1920s, Fighting Irish fans not only followed the team to road venues but turned out in great numbers for home games, with one proviso—the visitor had to be nationally ranked. Thus, the home opener against tiny Coe College of Iowa drew only about ten thousand, and the N.D. alumni magazine noted: "If it hadn't been for season tickets it is possible that Coe would have drawn [many fewer spectators]." The game itself was a 28–7 yawner, with Christy Flanagan and Elmer Wynne (Chet's brother) scoring touchdowns.

Rockne, however, worried about the following Saturday's trip to De- troit, telling Joe Byrne, Jr., that he expected Gus Dorais's Titans "to give us all kinds of trouble." Detroit had lost to Army by only 6–0 the previous week, but in front of a sellout crowd of almost thirty thousand in its new stadium, Dorais's team could not contain the speed of the Fighting Irish attack, and N.D. won, 20–0.

The third game—against Navy in Baltimore—filled that city's new

Municipal Stadium with an estimated fifty thousand spectators, many of them cheering for Notre Dame in spite of Baltimore's proximity to the Naval Academy's campus. One fan had boasted to President Walsh, "This Baltimore is probably the largest and most enthusiastic Catholic city in the United States." For the Fighting Irish, John Niemic, one of Francis Wallace's discoveries, led the attack and the team easily beat the Middies, 19–6.

Westbrook Pegler covered the event for the *Chicago Tribune* syndicate and his slant on Rockne's "All-Nations" team pointed to an important aspect of the growing Notre Dame mystique: "Traditionally known as the Irish or Romans," in fact, according to this writer, Notre Dame's teams had long been an ethnic mixture, "with such names as Mohardt, Anderson, Stuhldreher, Voedisch, Leppig, and Niemic . . . that cannot be found on tombstones in the graveyards of Galway or Connemara . . . [but] on the gravestones of Württemberg, Kovno, Warsaw, or Helsingfords." As the Fighting Irish nickname took hold—in 1927, President Walsh gave official university approval to it—friends and enemies liked to recite the many non-Irish names on the N.D. roster. Pegler publicized what the Norwegian-born Knute Rockne had said years before—the Fighting Irish represented every European group trying to make it in America.

For its fourth game, N.D. visited Indiana University and filled that school's new stadium in Bloomington. Unfortunately for the visitors, it was the smallest structure in the Big Ten and the twenty-four thousand spectators provided a small payout. The crowd, except for the N.D. rooters, quietly watched Notre Dame win 19–6.

Fighting Irish fans had become somewhat spoiled and the next Saturday only seventeen thousand showed up at Cartier Field to see their team crush Georgia Tech, 26–7. However, for the following week's contest against powerhouse Minnesota, at least twenty-eight thousand packed into Cartier in a snowstorm and many more were turned away. The fans wanted the Fighting Irish to beat one of the strongest Big Ten teams but, after sixty minutes, left relieved with the 7–7 tie.

Notre Dame had won every home game for twenty-two years and seemed ready to continue the streak when the team turned an early fumble by Minnesota quarterback Fred Hovde into a touchdown. But N.D. had not reckoned on sophomore Gopher tackle Bronko Nagurski—subsequently an All-American at line *and* backfield positions, the only player ever to win such honors. The young Nagurski totally dominated the line play and shut down the N.D. offense; then, late in the contest, he forced a fumble that set up the tying touchdown. He later said, "Nothing I did afterwards in college [even scoring winning touchdowns] could compare with causing and recovering that fumble [and ending the Notre Dame home winning streak]."

When, the following Monday, Grantland Rice wired Rockne for assistance with the sportswriter's All-America team, the N.D. coach mainly named Minnesota players, including Nagurski. Rockne also invited Rice to drop by his hotel before the next week's game against Army in New York.

> "The Army–Notre Dame game is not merely a football game. It is an institution. Everywhere all over the country, when these two teams meet —the city people, town's people, and country people, North, South, East and West—watch with keenest interest the outcome. It is everywhere admitted there is no game which has so captivated the imagination of the American public."
>
> —Notre Dame Vice President P. J. Carroll, March 15, 1927

By the late 1920s, the N.D. administrators understood and cherished the importance of the annual against Army in New York. However, they did not enjoy the resulting ticket problems. In August 1927, President Walsh notified a friend that henceforth Arthur Haley would handle all tickets and "even in the case of my close friends . . . all requests" would go through this channel. Walsh kept his word, deflecting many important people to the ticket manager; he even answered the request of a New York newspaper columnist with, "I need not tell you how grateful I am for your kindly interest in Notre Dame, and whether or not you are able to obtain tickets [to the Army game from Haley] may your column prosper."

With Walsh adamant, many N.D. fans turned to Rockne. A Justice of the New York State Supreme Court explained that he had requested his usual three hundred tickets to the Army game "for the accommodation of various friends of mine among the clergy, leading public men and other prominent men, and personal friends, all of whom of course are friends of Notre Dame"; however, "Manager Haley says I will receive only 25." The N.D. coach replied: "I have just stepped out of the [ticket] picture entirely," and suggested that the judge complain to President Walsh and the faculty athletic board.

To his friends, Rockne was candid: "It looks like an impossible situation as long as the New York Alumni insist that the game in New York is played for their private benefit. . . . [Some] feel that they ought to be able to give five tickets for every [insurance] policy they sell so that the old school will appreciate what great alumni they have." But for his cronies, he produced tickets, writing Rupe Mills and Joe Byrne: "Now for the 'under the hat stuff' . . . Nothing must be said to anyone about these 2,000 tickets or our name is mud."

Similar ticket problems and solutions occurred with the press. As Rockne's fame grew—the week of the Army game, *Time Magazine* put him on its cover—more reporters and editors asked him for extra seats. He refused most ticket requests from minor and regional newspapermen but he continued to distribute the usual number to key New York sportswriters and columnists. He also accommodated the important editors of the day—to Herbert Bayard Swope of the *New York World* he wrote, "We were entirely sold out when we received your wire but of course we pulled some strings and fixed you up."

The demand for seats at the 1927 game was so great that Yankee Stadium did not put any on public sale, dispensing all of its allotment to favorite customers. The *New York Sun* estimated that the ballpark refused at least 100,000 requests, and the *New York Daily News* featured a poem with the lines "The scalpers are coming, hooray, hooray . . . To charge fifty bucks for the Mule-Irish fray" (few of their readers earned a weekly salary of $50). A ticket to the game was so prized that the *Daily News* made a "pair of ducats" the award to the winner of its "Pick 'Em" college football score contest. For two Notre Dame–Army seats, it reported, "10,757 Amateur Selectors Got into Game."

Through these contests and its increasing coverage of the Fighting Irish, the *Daily News* helped popularize the team among its working-class readers. However, most of these fans, lacking the connections necessary to obtain seats, could only dream of seeing their new favorites in action. This social reality contradicts the myth that, as soon as the Notre Dame–Army series moved to New York, large numbers of poor Irish took the subways to the games—hence the term "Subway Alumni." In fact, in the 1920s, these fans were first nicknamed "Curbstone Alumni," probably because many of them stood on the sidewalks and curbstones in front of the Gridgraphies provided by various New York newspapers and from these "choice locations" cheered on the Fighting Irish.

"I am sure that the faithful will be interested to know why I pick Army to defeat Notre Dame [today]. . . . It isn't as if Notre Dame were playing

De Witt Clinton High School. Nossir, that Army team has some of the best football players in the country—in fact, most of them, and any time they shake together and play as a unit they will be every bit as formidable as Rockne's team, which is not unbeatable."

—Paul Gallico in the *New York Daily News*,
November 12, 1927

The reputation of the Fighting Irish was so great that of the ten selectors in the *Daily News*'s betting chart on the Notre Dame–Army contest, only Gallico and one other writer predicted an Army victory. Rockne, however, knew the reality of the situation and a month earlier had told Joe Byrne, Jr., "Am going to try to beat the Navy but I know that I have no chance against the Army."

The N.D. coach's pessimism came from experience. In 1926, when his team edged West Point, they faced a starting eleven featuring nine players with previous college playing experience, and for the 1927 season, Army had acquired other former All-Americans. Moreover, their offensive stars, "Light Horse" Wilson and "Red" Cagle, were in their seventh and sixth years, respectively, of major college football and superior to most NFL running backs. (In late 1927, the Naval Academy, tired of West Point's flaunting of the three-year eligibility rule, pulled out of the series with its service rival.)

Notre Dame's best hope in this year's Army annual, as explained by a New York journalist, was that the Army men "have played so much football" during their careers "that they find it difficult to get the old college excitement. If things go badly, they cannot rouse themselves."

With headlines in the New York press proclaiming "KAYDET VETERANS SEEK REVENGE FOR 1926," West Point prepared intensively for the Yankee Stadium contest. Rockne intended to give Army the best game possible, and sportswriters termed the final workout at Cartier "punishing." In addition, the N.D. coach prepared a number of surprises: to help his passers see their targets better and his ball carriers locate their blockers more easily in the Yankee Stadium twilight and against the dark Army uniforms, he substituted bright green outfits for the regular dark blue Notre Dame suits; he also changed the players' numbers from those he had sent to Harry Stevens for the game program, thus confusing the fans, the press corps, and, he hoped, the Army coaches.

The green uniforms had no apparent effect on the outcome of the contest but they helped the Fighting Irish nickname gain momentum. The *New York World* and the *New York Daily News* used the term in their coverage and the *New York Times* allowed "Irish" to creep into its columns for the first time. The *New York Herald-Tribune* reported that when the team ran onto the field, the "Celtic representation" in the crowd "took to this display of green immediately and cheers from all [their] sections" arose.

As for the game, all of the shouts of the Fighting Irish supporters and all of Rockne's tricks were of no avail—the eighty thousand fans, among them Babe Ruth and Lou Gehrig as well as various politicians and church dignitaries, saw great runs by "Light Horse" Wilson and "Red" Cagle and an easy Army victory. "18–0! IT'S THE MULE'S HOOF," blared the *Daily News*, and it subheaded, "It Was an Unlucky Day for Those Irish!"

Many reporters complained about Rockne's trick of switching uniform numbers, but one pressbox wit observed, "The Notre Dame backs could have been wearing Klansmen outfits for all it mattered. They did nothing that made it worthwhile breaking their incognito." Walter Eckersall, after working the game as umpire, was more generous to his friend's players, and in his *Chicago Tribune* game story, he noted that the Fighting Irish showed "the effects of the hard schedule." Two days later, in a letter to the N.D. coach in which "Eck" tried to nail down officiating assignments for the following year's Army and Navy games, he was more direct: "If a little better judgment had been used in the selection of plays in the second quarter, the result would have been different."

Fortunately for Rockne and his team, they did not have to end the season on this down note. The big game against USC at Soldier Field was two weeks away and they could prepare by working out against Drake University in Des Moines, Iowa.

"The [Chicago] city council, absorbed as it is in the matters of widening streets, paving alleys, and getting good fight tickets, found time the other day to draft a set of resolutions extending the freedom of the loop, etc., to the Notre Dame and Southern Californian football teams when they come here on November 26 for a game in the Grant Park stadium."

—*Notre Dame Alumnus*, 1927

The New York papers and national wire services continued to follow the Fighting Irish closely, even after the thumping by Army. Some sent reporters to cover the road game against Drake and to travel to Chicago for the USC match. The *Daily News* put the N.D.–Drake game on its predictions scoreboard and again Paul Gallico was closest, forecasting a 27–0 victory. Rockne's team won 32–0 before only 8,400 in Des Moines, reporters terming it "a practice gallop" and "a breather in preparation for" USC.

The Southern California contest marked the first visit by a major West Coast team to Soldier Field, and the pregame sale exceeded even the 1926 Army-Navy contest in that city. In addition, midwestern politicians and other notables clamored for seats and the Notre Dame ticket office was deluged with requests. Rockne tried to distance himself from the ticket demand but had to respond to certain people. Ten days before the game, he answered the plea of Harvey Woodruff of the *Chicago Tribune:* "I will get you twenty [additional] tickets for the Chicago game but it must be kept under your hat. We are in a terrible dilemma and we are trying to pull out as best we can. We are always glad to take care of our friends, however." And four days before the event, the N.D. coach obtained a box for Colonel McCormick, the *Chicago Tribune* owner and publisher, but returned his check; the seats were compliments of the Catholic school.

Southern Cal took the field with a 7–0–1 record, the only blemish a tie with powerful Stanford. None of the names on their fifty-man roster resonates for the modern football fan—however, reserve lineman Marion Morrison, although possessing limited football talent, became famous as actor John Wayne. The Trojans, directed by former Iowa coach Howard Jones, played conservatively, and one New York sportswriter observed: "A much more animated spectacle than the game was the crowd. The game was an early ten-minute affair [with both teams scoring touchdowns] and after that a game of kicking, imperfect forward passing, and mauling by this side then by that and altogether unproductive." Notre Dame made its PAT and eventually won 7–6.

The *Chicago Tribune* headlined "RECORD CROWD OF 117,000" and featured pages of photos of the amazing scene. In addition, their reporters listed the many celebrities present and mentioned: "Not all of the boxes were occupied by notables and society folk, for the gangsters and detectives called off their shootings until after the game and [they] were out in almost full force except a few, who didn't have tickets and were left in jail, but all the 'big shot hoodlums' were there, behaving just like gentlemen."

The only controversy of the afternoon involved an umpire's call against USC. Late in the game, a Notre Dame defender, after intercepting a pass near his goal line, was tackled so hard that the ball flew loose and rolled out of the end zone. USC demanded a safety and an 8–7 lead, but—though subsequent films of the game showed the N.D. defender running with the ball—the official ruled that the N.D. player "never had possession of the intercepted pass." All four officials were from the Big Ten list, including Commissioner Griffith working as the field judge, but USC coach Howard Jones had a nasty case of déjà vu—the official who ruled that the N.D. player "never had possession of the intercepted pass" was the same umpire who, with an ultracontroversial call, had cost Jones his job at Iowa years before.

Rockne stayed out of the dispute, taking the line that "Notre Dame was not in any way involved in the misunderstanding except as one of the competing teams." He did enjoy the fact that the "four officials were chosen by Southern California." USC, assuming that the Big Ten commissioner was their best insurance against pro–Notre Dame men, had applied to Griffith directly and, not surprisingly, Rockne had gone along with their plan.

"Notre Dame's and Southern California's athletic departments are each at least $150,000 richer as the result of the game played in Soldiers Field yesterday. Even at low estimates, gate receipts exceeded $350,000. Excluding all complimentary tickets and gate crashers, at least 110,000 persons paid from $3 to $7 for their seats. Rental of Soldiers Field was $40,000, and allowing $10,000 for other expenses, the fifty-fifty split of the remaining receipts will net each school $150,000."

—The *Chicago Tribune*, November 27, 1927

The final numbers for the 1927 Notre Dame football season reveal a profit of $331,454, and some of the big autumn paydays were outstanding—the Soldier Field game earned $123,909 (the *Tribune* guessed high), and the Yankee Stadium annual, $103,389. The approximately $65,000 from the Navy game and the total of $47,535 for the visits to Detroit, Indiana University, and Drake were respectable. The only financial problem was the revenue from the home contests at Cartier Field. Rockne wrote a member of the N.D. lay board of trustees: "Our income this year at home, net, was $48,000—a year ago it was $33,000. It will never be any bigger and our home schedule will absolutely die unless we get a Stadium."

The editor of the N.D. alumni magazine also complained in print: "The Minnesota game this year was evidence of the inadequacy of Cartier Field to handle a big crowd. Rockne stated that both teams lost $75,000 by playing at South Bend instead of Chicago."

By the end of the 1927 season, when even officially vetted publications like the *Notre Dame Alumnus* called for a new Notre Dame stadium, the drumbeats for its construction began to drown out all other discourse in the Golden Dome. Immediately after the triumph at Soldier Field, Rockne decided to force the issue.

Dear Father [Walsh]:

You will pardon the appearing formality of this note but I wish to hereby tender my resignation to you as Head Coach and would appreciate your accepting at your convenience.

Yours very sincerely,

K. K. Rockne
Director of Athletics

—Letter from Rockne to President Walsh, November 28, 1927

For five years, the Notre Dame football coach had lobbied to replace wooden Cartier Field with a new stadium, complaining that he was "presenting a first-rate production in a third-rate setting." President Walsh resisted, preferring to construct dormitories, academic buildings, and even other sports facilities before investing in a huge football structure. In addition, the N.D. president knew that the higher education authorities regarded mammoth football stadiums as symbols of the overemphasis of intercollegiate athletics. Many members of the C.S.C. order agreed with Walsh's priorities and also felt that "the homey confines of Cartier Field better typified the family spirit of a small institution like Notre Dame." (Later debates on enlarging or reconstructing Notre Dame Stadium reprise many of these arguments.)

Rockne, truer to the spirit of the Roaring Twenties than his adversaries, dismissed their objections by listing the benefits to his football program: more and better teams willing to visit N.D., much more revenue, and more fame for the Fighting Irish. At times, the Notre Dame coach became so frustrated with President Walsh's opposition to the stadium that he informed alumni friends of his willingness to accept the next outside offer. The great strategist miscalculated with this ploy; an N.D. official told Francis Wallace, "Actually the rumors and reports of his leaving for other schools only got in the way of the stadium he wanted. Notre Dame knew that without Rockne to fill it, a big stadium might become the same debt-ridden white elephant as at other colleges."

Rockne's campaign finally attained critical mass at the end of the 1927 season. He had again proven that his Fighting Irish teams could attract huge numbers of paying spectators and that Cartier Field was inadequate for such major visitors as Minnesota—even though the crowds had not come out for Georgia Tech or Indiana. Moreover, shifting home games to Chicago's Soldier Field was not a solution—it created as many problems as it solved. As Rockne later explained to a Naval Academy officer, because only forty-five thousand seats at the lakefront facility were between the goal lines, "the washback from bad seats in Chicago is terrific. Seventy thousand people do nothing but abuse us after every game there."

Thus, at the November 1927 meeting of the N.D. lay board of trustees, President Walsh agreed to establish three committees to investigate the feasibility of constructing a new stadium. Walsh did not want this information announced publicly but newspapers soon had the story— probably from Rockne—and in the form of a done deal. The *New York Herald-Tribune* headlined "NOTRE DAME TO BUILD $800,000 STADIUM," and carried the AP text, "A stadium seating 50,000 persons is to be built." Then, two days after the 1927 season ended, Rockne submitted his resignation to Father Walsh. The precipitating factors were probably the president's insistence that the stadium was not a fait accompli and the coach's frustration at the slow N.D. administrative process. Walsh did not accept Rockne's resignation but, through an alumni official, he issued an addendum to his instructions to the committees: "It is understood that the University is not committed to the building of a stadium if an undue financial burden is placed upon the University, or if any other adverse contingency, not at present foreseen, should arise." The final clause was broad enough to include Rockne's departure to another school.

The key committee was Finance—Rockne was not a member, instead being appointed to the Site and Construction group—and money men such as Albert Erskine, head of Studebaker, tried to figure out the best way to pay for the project. A South Bend civic leader suggested that the city build the structure and rent it to N.D., but few political groups in the region would support this plan. More feasible was the issuing of bonds by Notre Dame—many schools had done this—but President Walsh objected, pointing out that "there would be criticism of the University if its credit were used for a stadium instead of for urgent academic needs." Another strategy, the one eventually employed, was self-financing—the ten-year leasing of all boxes and prime seats for cash up front. No other university had financed its stadium in this way—but no other school had such devoted football fans.

The mandate for the third committee was "to consider the need for a stadium." Rockne railed against the group's very existence but because Frank Hering, an early N.D. football coach and a great Fighting Irish supporter, chaired it and coordinated all the other committees, the N.D. coach need not have worried about its final decision. A crucial member of this committee and a key player in the stadium construction process was Father Charles O'Donnell, soon to become president of Notre Dame when Father Walsh's six-year term ended in 1928.

O'Donnell, a poet and an English teacher, greatly disliked the pejorative nicknames given the team, specifically the "Ramblers," the "Nomads," "Irish Roamers," and "Irish Wanderers." He wanted to erase them and he accepted Rockne's argument that only a large home stadium would accomplish this. He told the *New York Times* that "it is not sound academically to have a roving set of collegians," and, as president, he indicated to the Provincial Council of the C.S.C. that the excessive road schedules are "unfortunate from an academic point of view, and it leaves the school open to the charge of commercializing athletics." Critics countered that building a huge university stadium, used only for big-time football and for five or six afternoons a year, was even more commercial, but O'Donnell, with the din of the negative nicknames in his ears, disregarded this point.

During the following year, in spite of Walsh's "second thoughts" about the project and Rockne's distracting tantrums at the committees' long deliberations, all three groups eventually voted to go forward. O'Donnell, as N.D. president, presented their reports to the C.S.C. Provincial Council. Rockne explained the slow N.D. procedure to an engineering firm: "This all seems very nonsensical and silly but you have to understand the intricate workings of an organization of this sort to have the proper patience"—he had acquired it once the outcome was no longer in doubt. The C.S.C. order approved the stadium plan and awarded the contract to the Osborn Engineering Company of Cleveland, Ohio.

Ironically, Osborn's winning bid was to construct at Notre Dame a half-size replica of the stadium it had built for the University of Michigan at Ann Arbor in 1927. As Rockne told a business friend, "Hadden [Engineering] built the Northwestern stadium [for] $40 a seat and Osborn built the Michigan stadium [for] $10.50 a seat. Osborn is building ours to cost $10.50 a seat." In addition, the various levels of government in the South Bend region cooperated by constructing highways to the stadium and improving access from such cities as Indianapolis, Chicago, Cleveland, and Detroit. The railroads also upgraded their facilities to and at Notre Dame, and in the first decade of the stadium's existence, they transported the majority of visiting fans to Fighting Irish home games.

During the Great Depression of the 1930s, many football stadiums became bleached white elephants for their universities but Notre Dame's structure, usually less than half full, drained no money from the Catholic school. The key was the original self-financing, and although Rockne had not conceived the method, he was crucial to its success. As a business writer later commented, "Notre Dame's stadium speculation was mini-mized more than that of other universities because Rockne had so worked up his national schedule that the income could be counted in advance."

For 1928, the schedule included trips to Atlanta and Los Angeles as well as the annual encounter with Army in New York. That particular con-test—the "Win One for the Gipper" game—became the single most famous event in Notre Dame football history.

26

Al Smith and
"Win One for the Gipper": 1928

Dear Rock,
   I have a notion that the athletic prosperity which we have enjoyed in the last seven or eight years has had some connection with our business prosperity and I further am afraid that if we change administrations in Washington [from the Republicans to the Democrats and Al Smith] that we may suffer a business reaction and with it our building program in athletics, etc. will be affected. . . . [If you] would be willing to issue a brief statement showing why you are for Hoover, the [Republican] committee could make good use of this by sending it around to the schools and the colleges.

—Major John Griffith to Rockne, September 20, 1928

The historical ironies within the Big Ten commissioner's request to the Notre Dame coach are multiple—not only did the Hoover administration subsequently preside over the onset of the country's worst economic depression but, in 1928, the Republicans conducted the most anti-Catholic political campaign in American history. According to one expert, "its virulence [surpassed] the height of the [anti-Catholic] Know-Nothing agitation of the mid-nineteenth century."

Governor Al Smith of New York, after losing the Democratic presidential nomination in 1924, continued to run his home state efficiently and won the top spot on his party's ticket in 1928. Smith, proud of his Irish-Catholic working-class origins, believed in the popular image of

America as a "melting pot" and a "land of opportunity." He was genuinely surprised and bewildered when, venturing into the heartland to campaign, he encountered vicious attacks on his religion as well as disbelief concerning his adherence to the separation of Church and State.

Not only did Protestant Baptists and fundamentalists, with their Ku Klux Klan sympathies, consider him the "Devil's Disciple" and the "Pope's Son," but most other Protestant denominations also opposed him —Lutherans because of their founder's break with Rome, Methodists for his anti-Temperance position, Episcopalians out of snobbery, and even Unitarians because the Catholic church supposedly persecuted their brethren in Latin countries.

H. L. Mencken, the great journalist, commented, "I daresay the extent of bigotry prevailing in America, as it has been revealed by this campaign, has astounded a great many Americans." But not the cynic from Baltimore, who satirized the American "Booboisie" and, traveling with the Smith campaign, marveled at rumors that "the Catholic candidate would annul Protestant marriages, that Protestant children would be declared illegitimate, and that the Pope had his bags packed, ready to move to Washington once Smith was elected."

The Republicans encouraged the belief that a Smith victory would bring "Rum, Romanism, and Ruin," and played upon rural and small-town fears concerning Smith's religion, urban background, and anti-Prohibition stance. The New York governor believed that "the noble experiment" had mainly caused lawlessness and the weakening of government; his public and private honesty on this issue—most politicians publicly endorsed the Volstead Act and privately imbibed—drew the wrath of Prohibitionists. Smith's "wet" position also sparked anti-Irish slanders and, according to a political commentator of the time, revived cartoons of " 'Paddy' . . . a gorillalike personage with a stovepipe hat (a shamrock stuck in the hatband), a shillelagh in one hand and a beer mug in the other."

Even educated Protestants reviled Smith's and his wife's Irish origins and mocked "the figures they would cut as President and First Lady, how it would be like putting the comic strip characters Maggie and Jiggs in the White House which would soon reek of corned beef, cabbage, and home brew."

Dear John:
Your letter regarding the Hoover [endorsement] proposition is just received.
Confidentially the Smith people wrote to me several weeks ago about

making some speeches for Smith and I have talked it over with the
school authorities. . . . They feel that they must absolutely keep out of
politics because they are asking favors from both sides . . . while their
attitude may seem rather weak, still they feel that they must keep out of
it. I think you can see their position.

They feel that my name is so closely connected with the school that I
had better stay out, also.

—Rockne to Griffith, September 22, 1928

In the late 1920s, the coach of the Fighting Irish was well aware of
anti-Catholic prejudice but, as a pragmatist, either ignored it or used it
for his own ends; for example, after a Chicago magazine printed an article criticizing N.D.'s disbursement of seats for the 1927 USC game,
Rockne wrote the publisher, "I was very much hurt personally when I
read that Ku Klux article in your club magazine—I thought at first it was
written by Senator Heflin [of Alabama, a notorious anti-Catholic]." On
the religious issue, as in all other aspects of his career, Rockne preferred
to initiate action, not have it thrust upon him.

Thus, when the Democratic national committee invited the Notre
Dame coach—a famous American and a convert to Catholicism—to head
a campaign subcommittee and to speak on behalf of Al Smith, he declined, claiming that "school authorities stand firmly on [the] decision
that regardless of our personal feelings they will have to keep [N.D. and
me] out of politics." Publicly, the coach pushed the blame toward the
Notre Dame administration; however, in the internal letter that officially
stated the school's policy, the new president, Father Charles O'Donnell,
wrote Rockne, *"Confirming your own judgment in the matter,* we have
reached the conclusion that it would not be well for you to identify
yourself and us . . . with either presidential candidate."

By September 1928—like most Americans—the Notre Dame coach
and the school's administrators knew that Al Smith's campaign was
doomed. Rockne embraced neutrality to maintain his public image as a
national figure above politics and to further his business interests—his
desire to sell himself and his endorsed products to maximum numbers of
consumers, many of whom opposed the Catholic presidential candidate.
The university chose neutrality out of political expediency—with Smith's
expected loss, they would have to live with Republican administrations in
Washington and Indianapolis. Through the fall, the Republicans engaged
in campaign overkill and, in early November, won in a huge landslide.
Even parts of the "Old Confederacy" voted for the GOP—the party of

Lincoln—for the first time since the Civil War, and Smith lost a total of forty states, including New York.

Considering the importance of Rockne and Notre Dame to American Catholics, and the virulence of the attacks upon the faith, neutrality was pragmatic but not laudable. However, the following spring, in an act of contrition that undercut much of N.D.'s political gain from its election position, the school awarded its highest honor, the Laetere Medal, to Al Smith. The alumni magazine summed up the reasons for the change of heart: "Few public men have been identified so insistently" and, considering the attacks upon him, "with such varied motives, as Catholic. The faith of but few Catholic laymen has been exposed to the public as was his. The staunchness of that faith . . . made of his recent campaign a Mission of inestimable value to the Catholic Church in America."

Rockne also tried to make amends for his neutrality and, in November 1928, the magnitude of Smith's defeat and the humiliation felt by American Catholics contributed to his decision—four days after the election and in the locker room at Yankee Stadium—to pull out the oratorical stops in his speech to the team during the Army game.

My dear Rock:

I am convinced that the public is with you in the present situation at Notre Dame [after losing two of your first four games]. While, of course, you [at N.D.] are meeting a lot of rejoicing in other camps over [other squads] being able to defeat your team after [you have had] so many successful years, I am sure you will find that it [the losses] will prove beneficial to Notre Dame in the long run. You will get a wonderful response in the future.

—Letter from Glenn Thistlethwaite,
University of Wisconsin head football coach,
to Rockne, October 25, 1928

Thistlethwaite's prediction that Rockne would turn a bad situation to his advantage was amazingly prescient. For 1928 was the N.D. coach's single worst year—the Fighting Irish ended 5–4—and yet the season is now remembered for only one event, the "Win One for the Gipper" game, a victory made memorable because the coach's plea enabled a young, struggling team to beat a powerful one. Notre Dame was rarely the underdog during the Rockne era but this upset, later mythologized by the Hollywood film, helped perpetuate its "small Catholic school versus the Titans" image.

Before the 1928 season began, Rockne wrote to George Strickler, the originator of the Four Horsemen idea, that "our team looks terrible . . . whether we go any[where] or not is doubtful." Not only was the squad "light" but it was inexperienced; nine of eleven starters from the previous season had graduated and of the remaining varsity players, only seven were seniors. The Notre Dame football pipeline was not empty—the 1929 and 1930 teams were superb—but, as occurs in all sports organizations, this was a dry year.

Even the home opener, usually a laugher, was tough. The *Chicago Tribune* headlined "N. DAME GETS A SCARE BUT NIPS LOYOLA [OF NEW ORLEANS, 12–6]." Rockne knew that the following week's visit to Wisconsin would be difficult but he did not expect a 22–6 ambush by the Badgers. This marked N.D.'s first loss to a Big Ten team in eight years and the Fighting Irish had aided the enemy: "Fumbles, fumbles, and yet more fumbles coupled with a pass defense that cracked badly at times," admitted the *Notre Dame Scholastic.* Masterminding the Badgers' aggressive play was their assistant coach, Tom Lieb, former Rockne player, assistant, and the director of his summer camp in Wisconsin.

The N.D. coach did not mind Lieb using his knowledge of the Fighting Irish to help his present employer, and he continued to share scouting reports with him. However, Rockne needed ticket office help more than scouting tips for his next game—a Soldier Field contest against Navy. The Middies were weak but their first match against Notre Dame in Chicago had sparked an enormous demand for seats. N.D. sold its allotment months in advance and its A.D. then had to locate seats and sideline passes for various luminaries, even Mayor Jimmy Walker of New York.

Rockne also set aside large blocks of extra seats for the Chicago press corps, knowing full well that the sportswriters would scalp many of these ducats: for Tom Barry of the *Herald-Examiner,* "twenty-two tickets on the thirty yard line which I got by chiseling and fighting around as best I could"; to the sports editors of the *Tribune* and *American,* fourteen each, as well as many more to individual writers on their papers; and to the sports editors of the *Daily News, Evening Post,* and *Journal,* ten, ten, and nine respectively; and the wire services, six each. In addition, Rockne sent Walter Eckersall his freebies as well as money for "publicity"; "Eckie" also worked the Soldier Field game as an official and when he did not receive his "flak" payment after the contest, he whined, "I know you are busy but don't forget our little agreement concerning the Navy game."

Again, Rockne did not need Eckersall's help to promote the game. One Sunday paper headlined "BIGGEST CROWD IN FOOTBALL HISTORY SEES

NOTRE DAME DEFEAT NAVY." At least 120,000 in Soldier Field watched John Niemic throw a perfect touchdown pass in the fourth quarter to enable the Fighting Irish to squeak by, 7–0. The N.D. coach was pleased by the wonderful payday but not by the unconvincing victory. A few days later, when a University of Pennsylvania official proposed a future Penn–N.D. match, Rockne replied, "With the terrible team I have I will be in no mood to discuss any games until I come down east [in a few weeks]."

Rockne's immediate task was to take the squad to Atlanta to play an excellent Georgia Tech contingent—so powerful that they became national co-champions and won the Rose Bowl. For the Fighting Irish, mid-October 1928 was not a good time to visit Atlanta—the Ku Klux Klan and fundamentalist preachers were trying to convince southerners to place their fear and hatred of Catholics ahead of their aversion to the Republican party of Abraham Lincoln and to vote against Al Smith.

In the locker room before the game, however, Rockne did not attempt to rouse his troops as he had in a famous pep talk during Notre Dame's first visit to Atlanta in 1922, when he employed the fictitious hospital bed request of his son, Billy. He knew that his team was tired after the Navy game and also that because N.D. had easily defeated the Yellow Jackets every year since the inaugural, a fiery pep talk probably would not work. As a result, according to a newspaper account, "a great Tech machine pounced on Rockne's youngsters," scoring an early touchdown, "and came through for a [13–0] victory as Atlanta went wild."

Rockne was most upset with his team's lack of killer instinct. He told a friend, "We fumbled the Wisconsin game away but in the [Georgia Tech] game we got on the goal line four times but failed to score. We are simply not playing good enough." He was also angry at an attack on his coaching by the *Atlanta Journal's* "Fuzzy" Woodruff, the South's most famous sportswriter, and he wrote the editor, "I am surprised that a paper of such fine, high standing [as yours] would allow a zipper to write in his particular vein . . . the article by Fuzzy Woodruff was not called for."

Fortunately for the N.D. team, it could take a week off from its road schedule and the following Saturday, at Cartier Field, host Drake. The easy victory, 32–6, over the Iowa school—Drake's only loss of the season—showed the coach that his team still had potential, but he had to find a way to energize it. He wrote a friend: "If I had a second string to take up part of the burden I might sneak up on someone [good] . . . I have hopes that [the starters] will keep improving and that the morale will stay just as it is."

For the next game, against a weak Penn State squad in Philadelphia, the young team remained on its plateau. Francis Wallace, traveling to Philadelphia for the *New York Daily News*, remarked in a pregame article that many fans would "not be satisfied unless Rockne, the magician, pulls some rabbits out of the hat. They can forget that idea right now because if the Hard Rock from Over Yonder has any rabbits up his sleeve he will save them for Army next week." On a foggy, rainy afternoon in Philly, Notre Dame won 9–0 in, as one reporter commented, "not a very impressive display . . . by the victors."

During the following seven days, the Fighting Irish football team traveled back to South Bend and then returned east for the game against Army. In midweek, Al Smith lost the election. No one, not even Knute Rockne, knew that from this dark, depressing time the most famous victory in Notre Dame football history would emerge.

AFTER ELECTION . . . ROCKNE'S REVENGE

If there is any such thing as firing all your barrels in one game this will be the Notre Dame idea on Saturday.

In the first place, Rockne is still nursing the hope of revenge for what the Army slipped his team a year ago. In the second place, both Rockne and Notre Dame understand that here is one game that can wipe out every adverse mark made [against N.D. and against Catholics] this year.

—Headline and Grantland Rice's
comments in the *New York Herald-Tribune*, November 7, 1928

Even the worst team of Rockne's coaching career could not diminish the demand for seats to the 1928 Notre Dame–Army game. Arthur Haley, the N.D. ticket manager, told one alum that "we are returning over 1,000 dollars a day for Army tickets" and the refunds increased as game day approached. Typical of Haley's problems was the fact that there were "over a hundred priests who ordered tickets for this game" as well as a large number who received comps. Part of the ticket demand was a result of the growing popularity of radio; in 1928, as a goodwill gesture to its alumni and to augment the number of Fighting Irish supporters, Notre Dame allowed the new networks of NBC and CBS to broadcast its games for free.

In its pregame coverage, the New York press took its cue from Grantland Rice and played up the angle that the Fighting Irish could "retrieve a somewhat lumpy season by bagging this one contest." Army was unbeaten, including victories over powerful Yale and Harvard, but Rice noted: "Psychology can play a tremendous part in any one football game, and psychology could be one of Rockne's leading stars [against West Point]."

The N.D. coach always read and enjoyed Rice's work—he told him the previous fall that, "as a lover of football, I wish there were more writers like you, though just now there is just one Grantland Rice." Rockne particularly appreciated the journalist's "Gee-Whiz" style and his embellishments for the sake of drama. No doubt, before the 1928 Army game, he read Rice's *New York Herald-Tribune* pieces and took his advice as well as his style to heart.

> Dear Coach Rockne:
> I have been interested for some years in many of the problems of psychology and athletics. . . . I have heard it said that you do not key your men up to their games.
>
> —Psychology Professor Coleman Griffith
> to Rockne, December 9, 1924

> Dear Mr. Griffith:
> I do not make any effort to key them [my players] up, *except on rare, exceptional occasions.*
>
> —Rockne's reply, December 13, 1924

Although the Notre Dame coach became famous for his locker room talks, legend outstripped reality. Paul Castner, a former Rockne player and a longtime associate, stated that the coach "himself said that one talk a year was enough and I don't believe that he gave many of the emotion-packed talks that the myth has him giving every game." For 1928, however, Rockne decided to wheel out the oratorical artillery to attack Army.

Much of Rockne's speaking success came from his acting ability. Even the Notre Dame clerics, including former President John W. Cavanaugh, acknowledged that "there never was a greater showman than Knute Rockne. All his life long he was a play actor." And a C.S.C. historian who long observed him wrote, "Rockne had a great sense of the dramatic . . . in company, Rockne was always the actor, a very clever and telling actor, with a superb stage presence."

Jim Crowley, the "Horseman" who related the story of his coach's plea to win the 1922 Georgia Tech game for little Billy Rockne, once listed other locker room talks where his mentor fabricated stories. Crowley concluded, without hostility to Rockne because he loved his dramatic side, "They were all lies, blatant lies. The Jesuits call it mental reservation, but he had it in abundance." In addition, the N.D. coach's private correspondence reveals many instances where he attempted to extricate himself from tight spots with half-truths or even total fictions. When he wanted something badly enough, he would stretch facts to their breaking point and beyond.

Rockne's success as a speaker also depended upon his rapport with and control of his audience—in the case of the locker room talks, his team. Paul Gallico, sports editor of the *New York Daily News,* visited the Notre Dame training camp before the 1928 Army game and observed: "To the boys it is a romantic thing that they are doing, and they are in love with it and all its rituals and Rockne is the high priest . . . He stalks among them, author and chief actor in the show and the boys simply hang upon his words." The younger the team, the more naive the players, and the 1928 Notre Dame varsity was the youngest since 1922.

> Dear Cy:
> I have your letter with enclosure [from the *New York Daily News*] and I am certainly surprised at the article by [Francis] Wallace.
> *Of course I have had no contact with Wallace in six years* but I am asking him as a personal favor to me to lay off [the negative remarks about the University of Nebraska football program].
>
> —Letter from Rockne to Nebraska
> journalist Cy Sherman, March 5, 1928

The magnitude of Rockne's lie about "no contact" with his protégé, Francis Wallace, during the previous six years is breathtaking. Probably he was peeved with Wallace's article—in 1928, the N.D. coach sought a resumption of football relations with Nebraska and he also wanted his coaching school in that state to succeed—but to lie so boldly transcended his normal impulses.

Thus, later in the year, in a much more important situation, for the N.D. coach to concoct a story about the last wish of a long-departed player—who, unlike Wallace, could not contradict the tale—was a small fib compared to his documented whoppers. In addition, Gipp's "final words" belonged to a subgenre of American sentimental fiction—the deathbed and hospital request—that was extremely popular in this era, for example, the pleas, mainly fabricated by "Gee-Whiz" sportswriters, from young invalids to Babe Ruth and Lou Gehrig resulting in magical home runs. The Notre Dame coach liked these famous "last prayers" and used a number of them in locker room talks during his coaching career.

But why George Gipp? He had died eight years before—during all of that time Rockne had never mentioned his supposed dying request—and his memory was a bit of an embarrassment to the Notre Dame coach and the Catholic school. Not only had Fielding Yost conducted a public squabble about Notre Dame's allegedly "welching" on Gipp's funeral expenses but anti–N.D. reporters, including Nebraska's Cy Sherman, had mocked the school's "overlooking" Gipp's academic failures. Moreover, although the press had mentioned Gipp's athletic accomplishments in the years after his death, by 1928 his memory had slipped under the hooves of the Four Horsemen as well as such great running backs as Red Grange.

But Gipp remained vivid for at least one journalist. Francis Wallace had seen him play for Notre Dame and, two days before the 1928 Army game, he wrote a *New York Daily News* article emphasizing Gipp's role in the 1919 and 1920 N.D. victories at West Point and how the latter contest "earned [him] a rating as the outstanding player of the year."

Not only did Rockne and the team—training in Westchester County —see this article but apparently so did W. O. McGeehan of the *New York Herald-Tribune*. On Friday morning, the leading exponent of "Aw-Nuts" sportswriting provided his readers with a full-page laudatory column on "Gipp of Notre Dame." McGeehan termed him "the greatest individual football player I ever saw" and described at length his outstanding game on the plains of the Hudson in 1920.

McGeehan's praise and particularly his conclusion must have astonished Rockne: after discussing Gipp's death, the writer added, "What manner of youngster he was personally I never knew, but I imagine that he was of the type of Hobey Baker of Princeton. I suppose that the men of Notre Dame remember him with the same emotion with which the men of Princeton remember Hobey Baker. They should especially when the Army–Notre Dame games roll around."

Hobey Baker, the model for generations of eastern establishment youth, had been a superb athlete and sportsman, so clean-cut and high-minded that even his cynical classmates admired him and were devastated when he died at the end of World War I. Off the field, he was the antithesis of the gambling and hard-drinking Gipp. That W. O. McGeehan, the most skeptical sportswriter in New York, whitewashed

Gipp's reputation gave Rockne the sanction to use the memory of his former player in any way that he saw fit.

No doubt, the N.D. coach read the Friday *Herald-Tribune* at the training camp in Westchester County. Rockne had long believed, and had written in his book, *Coaching,* that "the history or traditions of the school are a great thing to recite to your team, and to keep before them. Exaggerate these as much as you can." And he told Walter Eckersall, scheduled to referee on Saturday, that although this team was young, because Notre Dame "has a lot of tradition, these kids will fight it out until the [final] whistle blows."

Whether Rockne conceived his plan to use the Gipp deathbed story the day before the game or on the spur of the moment in the locker room is unknown. Grantland Rice, the other featured columnist in the *Herald-Tribune,* claimed in his memoirs that the N.D. coach telephoned him on "Friday night before the game," suggesting, "Grant, the boys are tucked in for the night. How about coming down and sitting around with Hunk [Anderson] and me here at the hotel?" Instead, Rice persuaded Rockne to come to his apartment—Hunk presumably remaining with the "boys" —and during their long chat the N.D. coach revealed, for the first time, Gipp's dying words. Rockne then added, "Grant, I've never asked the boys to pull one out for Gipp. Tomorrow I might have to."

This conversation is cited by sports historians as the best proof of the authenticity of George Gipp's request—no one heard him speak the words to Rockne but, eight years later, the coach did not invent them in the locker room because, the night before, he related them to Grantland Rice. Moreover, Rockne would not have lied to the most important sports journalist in America. Unfortunately for this argument, the originator of "Gee-Whiz" sportswriting was as great a fantasist as the N.D. coach.

Grantland Rice was not in New York that Friday night! The following Sunday's *Herald-Tribune* featured his eyewitness account of the Saturday game between high-flying Georgia Tech and Vanderbilt in Atlanta, and newspapers in that city noted his presence in the pressbox. For the writer to cover that event, he had to be in Georgia on Friday night or on a train moving through the South. But a few thousand miles of railroad track never kept Grantland Rice from inventing an imaginary meeting, particularly one that gave him an exclusive preview of the most famous locker room speech in sports history. He compounded his lie by placing Hunk

Anderson in New York on that Friday night; in fact, the head coach of the University of Saint Louis football team was in the Missouri city, awaiting his Billikens' Saturday afternoon home game against Loyola of Chicago.

In the end, only Rockne knew the truth about the authenticity of Gipp's dying wish. However, all the circumstances in 1928—the pressure to alleviate Al Smith's election loss and the humiliation of American Catholics, the necessity of beating Army to salvage the terrible season, the whitewash of Gipp by W. O. McGeehan, and, finally, Rockne's extraordinary talent and long history as a storyteller—indicate that *George Gipp's legendary request was first made on Saturday, November 10, 1928.*

Many controversies surround Rockne's speech to the Fighting Irish at Yankee Stadium on that day in 1928, not the least of which concerns his actual words. The most famous version is:

"He [Gipp] turned to me [on his deathbed].

'I've got to go, Rock,' he said. 'It's all right. I'm not afraid.' His eyes brightened in a frame of pallor. 'Some time, Rock,' he said, 'when the team's up against it; when things are wrong and the breaks are beating the boys—tell them to go in there with all they've got and win just one for the Gipper. I don't know where I'll be then, Rock. But I'll know about it, and I'll be happy.' "

—Rockne in *Collier's*,
November 22, 1930; reprinted in
his posthumous *Autobiography*, 1931

This was the N.D. coach's only printed rendition of the speech and many later accounts of the event, including the Hollywood biopic, follow this autobiographical passage. It is doubtful, however, that Rockne actually said these words. Not only did they first appear two years after the event but, in all probability, Rockne's ghostwriter at *Collier's*, John B. Kennedy, wrote them. Rockne's correspondence reveals his use of Kennedy's services, and the *Collier's* narrative of this event both fits the professional writer's style—"brightened in a frame of pallor," and so on —and contains howling errors that the coach-as-author would not have made. In describing the immediate consequences of the speech, the writer says, "the boys came out for the second half exalted, inspired, overpowering. They won. As Chevigny slashed through for the winning touchdown he said: 'That's one for the Gipper!' " End of story.

In fact, after the halftime interval, Army broke the 0–0 count with a TD, and later, Jack Chevigny scored the tying touchdown. Then, in the fourth quarter, the Notre Dame coach made a brilliant strategic move to win the game. He substituted an obscure end for one play—the winning touchdown pass—and the player gained Notre Dame fame as Johnny "One Play" O'Brien. Surely if Rockne had written these passages about the 1928 Army game, he would have remembered the scoring sequence and his masterstroke.

"They were underdogs and that helped. They had Rockne and he helped. Football people knew that Rockne would fire the boys up in his speech before the game. This is what he told them—and then perhaps you can understand the cold forgetfulness of self of those Irish kids.

'On his deathbed George Gipp told me that some day, when the time came, he wanted me to ask a Notre Dame team to beat the Army for him.'"

—Francis Wallace in the *New York Daily News*, November 12, 1928

Wallace broke the story of Rockne's speech two days after the game. He had not been in the locker room but Joe Byrne, Jr., an eyewitness, told him about the talk and, on Monday, he published the story in his paper under the headline "GIPP'S GHOST BEAT ARMY," with the subhead "Irish Hero's Deathbed Request Inspired Notre Dame."

When the *Daily News*'s Monday article appeared, the N.D. coach was angry at his protégé for going public with the story. Wallace attributed Rockne's displeasure to the writer having "violated a [locker room] confidence," but possibly the coach did not want the tale known because he worried that it would not withstand press and public scrutiny. Certainly Gipp's request was at odds with his character in life—one wit later noted that "it would have been much more like him to ask Rock to put down a bet for him some day when the Irish were a sure thing." In addition, according to Gipp's teammates, he "never referred to himself as 'the Gipper,'" and that nickname only caught on *after* the 1928 incident.

No wire service or New York newspaper picked up Wallace's "death-bed request" story—probably because of their low opinion of the *New York Daily News*—and it remained in semi-obscurity until the *Collier's* piece two years later and the subsequent reprinting in the posthumous *Autobiography*. Only when Hollywood featured it in *Knute Rockne—All American* did it enter the mainstream of American culture.

Other controversies surround the famous speech. Did it occur before the game, as Wallace implied, or at halftime, as most of the players later claimed? Ted Twomey, the starting right tackle, recalled that before the game, Rockne brought Jack Dempsey into the locker room and the great fighter spoke at length to the team, ending with "Go out there and beat Army!" In all probability, the N.D. coach would not have attempted to top Dempsey's appeal and would have saved his Gipp speech for half-time. Twomey also described the emotional sea in which the team swam: "As we approached Yankee Stadium there were Irish cops on every corner hollering, 'Beat Army! Beat Army!' It was terrific, and really got us keyed up for the game."

The game itself was very different from the later depictions of it, particularly the movie version. The first half was tough, mean football, and although Notre Dame had the best scoring drive, the Fighting Irish stalled when their fullback fumbled on the Army two-yard line and the Kaydets recovered in the end zone for a touchback. The half ended 0–0. In the locker room, according to Joe Byrne, Jr., the N.D. coach launched his Gipp talk with a description of the player's career, his illness, and his hospital room; finally, Rockne announced the dying wish.

One of the N.D. assistant coaches, Ed Healy, later said, "There was no one in the room that wasn't crying, including Rockne and me. There was a moment of silence, and then all of a sudden those players ran out of the dressing room and almost tore the hinges off the door. They were all ready to kill someone." Unfortunately for N.D., it was not yet Army—the Kaydets took the second half kickoff and slowly moved down the field, with "Red" Cagle leading the attack, and scored a touchdown.

But Notre Dame hung in the game and, near the end of the third quarter, Jack Chevigny plunged over from the two. Even the cynical Westbrook Pegler in the pressbox noticed that the Fighting Irish were playing with special intensity; he wrote the next day—before the Gipp story was known—that the N.D. comeback "must have been one of those strange mind-over-matter affairs that the coaches . . . talk about with such simple faith."

At 6–6, the teams battled through the fourth quarter until Rockne sent in Johnny O'Brien with a pass play. He ran his pattern to the goal line and Niemic, on the forty-three-yard line, hit him perfectly for the touchdown. Notre Dame missed the PAT but was ahead, 12–6. Army did not give up; Cagle returned the kickoff to the N.D. thirty-one-yard line, then battered his way to the ten, where, according to a journalist, he "has to be dragged out of the game because he is groggy from the sustained pummeling he has undergone since the opening scrimmage."

On a pass-and-run, Army then moved the ball to the one-foot line, but before the Kaydets could attempt another play, the referee blew the final whistle—starting a huge controversy about whether he had ended the game too soon and robbed Army. A telegram from the *New York World* demanded that Rockne state "WHAT THE SITUATION WAS WHEN WHISTLE ENDED ARMY GAME . . . WHOSE BALL WAS IT?" According to the rules, if the Kaydets had made a first down, they were entitled to another play. However, in a telegram to Francis Wallace, the N.D. coach replied: "PERSONALLY THINK THE MATTER OF NO IMPORTANCE." He elaborated: "THEY [OUR PLAYERS] CLAIM ARMY DID NOT MAKE FIRST DOWN BY OVER A YARD BUT BEFORE ANYTHING COULD BE DONE WHISTLE SOUNDED AND GAME WAS OVER. . . . MATTER IN MY OPINION IS OF NO IMPORTANCE."

The referee who blew the whistle was Walter Eckersall. The *Chicago Tribune* writer later felt badly about his call, and Wallace wired Rockne: "ECKERSALL AND [WEST POINT COACH] BIFF JONES CLAIM ARMY BALL WHEN GAME ENDED. I AM HOLDING THE BAG [IN DEFENDING NOTRE DAME]." But a day later, Eckersall blurred his story, telling Wallace and the *Daily News,* "As time was up when an Army man made a plunge, I did not pay any attention to the ball reverting back to Notre Dame or remaining in possession of the Army." Rockne shunned the controversy and he wired Wallace, "IT WAS A GREAT GAME AND THE SCORE IS TWELVE TO SIX."

The subsequent accounts of the 1928 game always portray the Notre Dame win as inevitable—once the Fighting Irish heard the "Win One for the Gipper" speech nothing could stand between them and victory. In reality, if Kaydet star "Red" Cagle had been able to remain and function or if Eckersall had not blown the final whistle when he did, Army might well have scored the tying touchdown. One New York columnist believed that if the game had continued "ten seconds more . . . the Army almost certainly would have scored, as its desperate attack had Rockne's team backing up in bewilderment." With the TD and conversion, the 1928 result would have been Army 13—Notre Dame 12; without the PAT, a 12–12 tie. With either score, Knute Rockne's invocation to the memory of George Gipp would have gone to the same unmarked grave as all the other locker room speeches that failed to bring victory.

One can also speculate on what the absence from history of the "Gipper" speech would have meant for the Hollywood film on Rockne and especially the political career of the actor who portrayed George Gipp.

Would Ronald Reagan have been as successful, particularly in appealing to the crucial voting bloc of "Reagan Democrats"—many of them Catholic—without his appealing campaign slogan, "Win One for the Gipper"? But football games and elections cannot be replayed; Notre Dame won the famous game and Ronald Reagan triumphed.

■   ■   ■

TARTANS UPSET TRADITIONS IN 27–7 WIN

Notre Dame Drops First Contest on Cartier Field in 23 Years.

Carnegie Tech's Tartans shattered a quarter century old tradition to defeat Notre Dame, 27–7, last Saturday on Cartier Field.

—Headline and lead in the *Notre Dame Scholastic*, November 30, 1928

A week after the emotional victory over Army in New York, Rockne was disappointed but not surprised by his team's loss at home to Carnegie Tech. He had long believed that in "keying up" a team for a game, a coach risked a subsequent letdown. Francis Wallace, who traveled to South Bend to cover the Carnegie Tech game, echoed his mentor's fears in an article headlined, "SKIBOS HAVE PSYCHOLOGICAL EDGE," explaining that "Notre Dame is liable to be strutting around this week . . . thinking, 'We beat the Army, who is Carnegie Tech?' "

The clever Chicago judge Walter Steffen coached the Tartans, a.k.a. Skibos (the name of Andrew Carnegie's Scottish castle), and the team remembered knocking N.D. out of national championship contention with an upset two years before. In 1928, with a heavier line and faster backfield than the 1926 contingent, Steffen "keyed" his squad for the visit to Cartier Field.

The accounts of the game differ. The *Chicago Tribune*'s Arch Ward, increasingly assuming the position of "Notre Dame Cheerleader No. 1," led his game story: "Never before did a football team fight harder than Notre Dame in the mud and water of Cartier Field today. But all the fight and all the courage the Irish could develop was inadequate and they went down in defeat before a big, powerful team from Carnegie, 27–7."

Rockne saw the game differently, writing a friend that his team "gave out physically, mentally and nervously . . . they tried but it wasn't nearly enough." He also told Grantland Rice that the Carnegie Tech quarterback "made some terrible mistakes Saturday," including one that "gave us a touchdown," N.D.'s only score.

The home field defeat—the first since 1905—shocked Notre Dame rooters. However, rival fans as well as N.D. haters and others rejoiced; Francis Wallace described the phenomenon in *O'Reilly of Notre Dame*—his hero had to spend the following "winter . . . listening to Tech [fans bragging], and not only Tech [supporters], because it seemed that a lot of people who were with Notre Dame when it won, turned against it when it lost."

"SON FIGHTS FOR LIFE AS ROCKNE DIRECTS N. DAME.

While Knute Rockne, coach of the Notre Dame football team, watched his team battle Southern California in Los Angeles today, his 2 year old son, Jack, was in St. Joseph's hospital here [in South Bend] waging a fight for life."

—United Press dispatch, December 1, 1928

The final game of 1928 provided the Fighting Irish with a last chance to avoid their worst season since the 5–4 record of 1905. Rockne not only worried about his football predicament but also about the critical condition of his youngest son, unable to breathe properly because of a peanut lodged in his lung. The N.D. coach did not mention his son's plight to the team, but even if he had used it in his pep talk the 1928 Trojans probably still would have beaten that year's Fighting Irish. (His son subsequently recovered.)

USC coach Howard Jones had assembled a powerhouse and it breezed through most of its season, including a convincing 10–0 victory over its nemesis, Pop Warner's Stanford. West Coast fans wanted to see the Trojans beat the Fighting Irish and, weeks before the game, they bought all available seats in the Los Angeles Coliseum. This put extra pressure on the Notre Dame ticket office and Rockne received many special requests, including one from N.D. alum Joe Gargan for "a good box and two sideline passes" for his brother-in-law, financier Joseph P. Kennedy. Rockne was aware of Kennedy's importance and put aside the box and passes but, as game day approached, he returned them to the ticket office. He explained in a telegram to Joe Byrne, Jr.: "GARGAN PROMISED TO SEND MONEY FOR THESE BOXES WHICH [MONEY] HAS NEVER BEEN RECEIVED. HE MUST QUIT BEING A SPONGER AND PAY HIS WAY THROUGH THE WORLD. I HELD THESE BOXES JUST SO LONG AND DID NOT RECEIVE ANY MONEY SO LET THEM GO." Rockne, a self-made man, had no sympathy for the "spongers" of the world.

In the USC game, Notre Dame fought gamely and even managed two

touchdowns but the Trojans easily scored four and won, 27–14. The defeat
ended the worst season of Knute Rockne's coaching career. However, the
repercussions from the 5–4 record were just beginning, the grumbling of
Notre Dame boosters soon intensifying to a roar of outrage about the
"Failing Irish." This was the year for Rockne to try the 1920s coaches'
tactic and declare: "You're a great coach when your team wins every
game. But when you drop four or five, *you make 'em believe the main idea
is to build character.*" (The exact origin of this truism is unknown although, very possibly, the N.D. coach was the source—a number of his
newspaper pals, including Francis Wallace, publicized it widely.)

> "In 1928 . . . I met the late W. O. McGeehan on a train en route to
> South Bend, he smiled and said:
>   'Just before I left the office I wrote a column which said I was going
> out to Notre Dame to investigate the rumor there was a university lo-
> cated there.' "
>
>   —The opening of Francis Wallace's *Notre Dame:
>   Its People and Legends,* 1969

For many years, the skeptical McGeehan had mocked "Mr. Knute
Rockne's Wandering Irishmen" and wondered in print "if Notre Dame
has a campus?" Even after the 1928 laud to Gipp, he wrote: "The Notre
Dame boys live in Pullmans for the entire football season . . . The Pullman company will be advertising their cars" as perfect preparation for
such difficult tasks as taking on the Army.

Because the 1928 upset of the Kaydets piqued his interest, the New
York writer decided to visit Notre Dame and cover the Carnegie Tech
game. He telegraphed his plans to "Knute Rockne or Manager Notre
Dame football team," and asked: CAN SOMEBODY ARRANGE PLACE [FOR ME]
TO STOP OVER NIGHT [AND] ALSO ARRANGE FOR PRESS RESERVATION AT GAME?"

The N.D. coach wired back: "HOTELS ALL FILLED AND AM INVITING YOU
VERY CORDIALLY TO BE MY HOUSE GUEST, DELIGHTED TO HAVE YOU." No doubt
McGeehan's praise of Gipp had put Rockne in a positive mood toward
Grantland Rice's main rival. In addition, the N.D. coach probably saw
the visit as a chance to convert a hostile and important writer to his point
of view.

The strategy worked—at least to the extent of informing McGeehan
about the reality of life at Notre Dame. The journalist inspected the
school, including the financial records, and concluded that the profits
from football "go to the improvement of the university. . . . They are

building new dormitories" and classrooms with the money. Then, after describing campus life in detail, he stated, "Notre Dame is no place of mystery and no football recruiting camp [a standard anti-N.D. charge], but just an American university with some fine traditions and some very human American undergraduates."

The following Monday, back in New York, McGeehan began his column: "So much misinformation has been circulated concerning Notre Dame that your correspondent feels inclined to devote one more column in an attempt to show that this institution primarily is a university and not a football recruiting station." Later in the week, in response to irate letters accusing him of "wearing a blindfold" while at N.D., McGeehan repeated his findings.

The columnist's work came at a crucial time for the Catholic school. McGeehan's discussion of the academic side of the university provided a counterweight to the howling discontent of many Notre Dame football fans, especially the boosters, over the 5–4 season. McGeehan termed the latter group "assistant alumni," and defined a typical member of the N.D. species as "one who, while he has never attended Notre Dame and never even passed through South Bend, is thoroughly" obsessed with Fighting Irish football. After the 1928 season, in spite of the victory over Army, many "assistant alumni" as well as some regular alums demanded a return to championship-caliber teams, no matter what the cost to the university's academic reputation. Their cry, from the title of Paul Gallico's column about the 1928 N.D.-Army game, was "LET US OVEREMPHASIZE." Rockne sympathized with and covertly encouraged them.

The *South Bend Tribune* opposed this sentiment; it reprinted McGeehan's work and also editorialized: "In the final analysis it may be well that Notre Dame does not retain national football supremacy year after year. When the low spots are reached, the academic merits of the institution behind the football team are more obtrusive. Entirely too many Americans, thrilled by the exploits of Notre Dame football teams, have gained the impression that our university is one of those in which sports is overemphasized."

The N.D. authorities embraced this position and had the *Notre Dame Alumnus* reprint the entire text of the *South Bend Tribune*'s editorial as well as many of McGeehan's comments. The alumni magazine also underlined a passage in the editorial that later became the Catholic school's credo during future bad as well as good times on the gridiron: "*Notre Dame is not a football team; it is a great university. Football teams come and go; some are triumphant, others know defeat. On the football fields,*

Notre Dame is up today and down tomorrow. However, the academic Notre Dame, the true Notre Dame, suffers no recessions."

■   ■   ■

"I noticed in press reports in the Chicago and South Bend papers that you [Rockne] have completed arrangements with Nebraska by which Notre Dame and the University of Nebraska will resume athletic relations in football beginning 1930. I am not assuming that this is true. I merely call your attention to it."

—N.D. vice president and head of the athletic board,
Father P. J. Carroll, to Rockne, July 16, 1928

Throughout 1928, Notre Dame officials, alert to the ongoing Carnegie Foundation investigation and the debate about overemphasis, tried to control the school's most famous employee. Tension between the administration and Rockne increased in midsummer when a number of newspapers reported that the Fighting Irish would resume athletic relations with Nebraska. The N.D. coach was the source of the reports, and although the athletic board, at Rockne's urging, had set up a subcommittee to listen to Nebraska's proposals, the Golden Dome—particularly during Al Smith's election campaign—was not about to agree to football games against a university with rabid anti-Catholic fans.

Much of Rockne's unhappiness with the N.D. administration focused on the issue of schedule making. At the beginning of his coaching career, he had arranged games with whomever he wanted, but by 1928, the athletic board had gained full control of scheduling—this reality, compounded by the fact that many of his rival coaches still made up their own lists, constantly annoyed him. Then, in September, when Father Carroll was replaced by an even tougher-minded vice president and athletic board chair, Father Michael Mulcaire, Rockne's input on scheduling decreased further. He sarcastically referred to the athletic board as "this august body" and, in October, told a coaching colleague that the group "voted to cut down our schedules and terrificness"—difficulty of opponents and travel—"starting immediately. I was pretty severely censored for putting on such hard schedules . . . the authorities are going to cut me down to four hard games and four easier games a year." However, "from the looks of things," contracts already signed, these changes "will not be [in effect] until 1931."

The athletic board acted in response to faculty discontent about the coach's "overemphasis" as well as outside criticism of his "Nomads." Yet, the N.D. administrators could not ignore the fact that, in spite of the worst season by a Rockne team on the field, the 1928 Fighting Irish were packing all their road venues, including huge urban stadiums, and producing a substantial amount of money for the school. In November, the coach told a friend: "We are having some beautiful gates and it looks like we are going to gross over $600,000 [for the year] for our share." Rockne felt that he was responsible for this financial success and he could not understand why some N.D. faculty members and administrators neither appreciated nor even approved of his accomplishments.

In the end, the year's total receipts were $723,692, but the expenses were $237,940. Not only did travel costs of close to $40,000 eat up a chunk of the income but the expense of running a big-time football program was escalating; for example, "wearing apparel" (uniforms, capes, etc.) cost $12,506. The Carnegie Report later criticized Notre Dame for this "lavish" expenditure and Rockne's faculty critics complained about all of his extravagant purchases, contrasting them with the school's "parsimoniousness" on such essential items as periodical subscriptions for the library.

The N.D. coach always justified his spending with the argument that his main adversaries, notably the Big Ten coaches, spent "ten dollars for every one" of his and that for his program to remain competitive he had to purchase the latest equipment. His justification subsequently became a Holy Commandment in the coaching profession and helped start and perpetuate the "Athletics Arms Race."

For 1928, net profits for Rockne's football program approached $500,000, and if Notre Dame did not applaud his efforts, other schools might. His Los Angeles "bird dog," Leo Ward, wrote him in late November 1928: "I have inquiries from Jesuit College here . . . which is now expanding and building about eighteen miles west and near the Ocean whether or not you would be interested, in the future, becoming athletic director after the school is erected." Ward suggested a meeting with the Jesuits when the coach was in L.A. for the Southern Cal game; Rockne replied, "I would be glad to meet the people any time you say." Rockne never took the job but if he had, the athletic history of Loyola Marymount would have been very different.

"There was only one time when I [as A.D. at Ohio State] felt justified in hiring a man [as head football coach] without talking to anybody else. That was after the 1928 season when we were looking for a successor to Dr. Jack Wilce. . . . I was sitting in my office when a call came from Major John Griffith, Athletic Commissioner of the conference. He said

he had a 'young fellow' in his office who was interested in our coaching
position. He was Knute Rockne. So he put Rockne on the phone and
sure enough he was interested in leaving Notre Dame and in getting into
the Big Ten."

> —Lynn St. John, longtime Ohio State athletic director,
> to Francis Wallace

According to Wallace and other friends, Rockne considered the Ohio
State job mainly because he believed that the Notre Dame administration was going to renege on its promise to build a new stadium, using the
"football profits" to construct "other buildings instead." He was also unhappy with the restrictions on his lucrative lecture tours—he had not yet
signed with Studebaker; in addition, he relished the challenge of playing
Big Ten schools like Michigan and Illinois—if he coached Ohio State,
Fielding Yost and Bob Zuppke could not avoid scheduling games against
his team.

By the late 1920s, Ohio State had already developed a large number
of demanding, win-at-all-costs football fans. After a 4–4 season in 1927, a
Toledo sportswriter wrote Rockne: "Everyone around here is busy firing
Jack Wilce at Ohio State, and the Toledo alumni will recommend [former
N.D. player] 'Slip' Madigan . . . for the post." In 1928, with a 5–2–1
campaign, including a win over Michigan, the demands for Dr. Wilce's
"scalp" increased and the coach resigned to return to medical practice.
Newspapers soon carried reports that OSU was pursuing Rockne along
with repeated "No comment" statements from Ohio State officials—they
remembered Columbia University's blunder during its courtship of the
N.D. coach and did not want to ruin the potential deal by going public
too soon.

Whether Rockne was seriously considering the OSU job or testing
the new N.D. president, Father Charles O'Donnell, is unknown. Most
likely, he was engaged in both activities—if O'Donnell did not accede to
his demands, he would have continued to negotiate and possibly sign
with Ohio State. However, O'Donnell supported the stadium proposal
and assured the coach that he would move the committees along and
"petition . . . the Provincial Council [of the C.S.C. order] for permission [to build]."

Moreover, according to an Ohio State trustee, "It was shortly after
this that Rock made a deal with Studebaker to lecture" for them and this
helped "keep Rockne in South Bend." Albert Erskine, the head of the
automobile company and of the N.D. lay board of trustees, was a key
player in this arrangement and persuaded President O'Donnell to agree

to it. Thus, in early January, the N.D. coach told a journalist, "My situation here is that I will be here four more years regardless"—the remaining years on his ten-year contract—"so there can be no change from this as the land lays now."

The N.D. coach was temporarily happy with the way the land at Notre Dame lay, especially the area that would become the site for the new stadium. He had finally nailed down the approval to build the structure and he had also increased his lecturing income. Although it took some questionable maneuvering on his part to achieve these goals, the worst on-field year of Rockne's coaching career ended on a positive off-the-field note for him.

27

Rockne Attacks
the College Sports Reformers: 1929

"He did things recruiting that would appall a modern coach. In fact, it is said that they [N.D. administrators] were getting ready to move on him when he died."

—Frank Leahy on Rockne's recruiting during a period when Leahy played for him and then was a student assistant

In early 1929, after winning his most recent power struggle with the Golden Dome and deciding to stay at Notre Dame, Rockne confronted two major and connected problems—how to avoid another debacle like the 1928 season and how to produce championship teams in an increasingly cutthroat recruiting environment. The Carnegie investigators had completed their visits to Notre Dame and although they had not yet issued their report, privately they gave the Catholic school relatively high marks. The N.D. coach no longer had to worry about them but he was at a crossroads on recruiting. He wrote his mentor, Jesse Harper: "The way these other schools are proselyting has me worried as I don't know where it's going to end."

But the N.D. coach did not intend to wait passively to find out. He knew that in the never-ending war of big-time college football he had to march or die and soon he saw a route. He began by enlisting the help of the Notre Dame alumni president, Donald Hamilton (he had been a QB in the pre-Harper era but had lost his eligibility by playing summer pro baseball). In January 1929, Rockne wrote the alum president: "My plans have crystalized and are quite ripe and I believe, with an organization, we can put things over in great shape." The N.D. coach suggested a meeting with such key alums and football supporters as Alderman George Maypole of Chicago, Al Feeney of Indianapolis, and Joe Byrne, Jr., of New York—"This will give us a quiet, select crowd who can keep their mouths closed and who are interested in the old school and results." Rockne's plan was to establish a national "proselyting" organization with alumni recruiting prime athletes in their areas and sponsoring them at Notre Dame.

Hamilton, an Ohio attorney, worked on the agenda of the meeting and also wondered about such issues as letters from recruiters to prospects because "such letters not carefully worded, might do us some harm if they should fall into the wrong hands." The N.D. coach immediately replied, "I am against letter writing [to recruits] very much—put nothing in writing."

In late January, Hamilton, either because he was nervous about the plan and/or wanted the N.D. administration's approval, requested a private meeting with President O'Donnell. The latter replied that he was about to leave on an extended working vacation and suggested a conference with Vice President Mulcaire. Apparently this meeting did not occur nor is there any further correspondence between the alumni president and O'Donnell on this matter; probably Rockne convinced Hamilton and the other special recruiters to proceed quietly and without informing the Golden Dome. Certainly Frank Leahy's comment—"They were getting ready to move on him when he died"—suggests that the administrators only learned of the recruiting scheme a year later.

For Rockne, the irony of the new "proselyting" was its similarity to recruiting during his years as a player and a young coach, the waning of the "tramp athlete era." In the spring of 1929, grumbling that recruiting now required "a lot of the old-time chiseling," he organized his national network. By September, he began to see the results when the athletes— with alumni from Los Angeles to New York "taking care of a man each" —arrived on campus.

The new recruiting organization built on the old "bird dog" system as well as the coach's regular jobs on- and off-campus for players. However, it pumped much more cash into the pipeline and also produced more athletes expecting "free rides." Some Los Angeles alums sent on Larry

Vejar, a fine young quarterback, but once on campus, the player protested when he had to pay personally for his incidental expenses, for
example, his subscription to the *"Scholastic—$3."* His main L.A. sponsor
wrote to Rockne about this and the N.D. coach replied, "This boy Vejar
evidently has got the point of view of a young man . . . on that Chamber of Commerce team in Los Angeles known as the University of Southern California."

Because his opponents were outspending him in this aspect of the
"Athletics Arms Race," Rockne responded by recruiting in different and
more expensive ways. Frank Wallace, still "bird-dogging" in the
southeastern Ohio region, suggested that one prospect, "as good as
Niemic," needed a year of prep school and wondered if Alderman Maypole could pay for it. Rockne replied, "I know George will be able to
handle him."

The Notre Dame coach not only had to compete with big-time opponents like USC for players but sometimes against his own "boys." Harry
Stuhldreher at Villanova particularly enjoyed this game, and Wallace reported: "Since Stulie gets such a kick out of getting a boy away from old
alma mater you might be interested in knowing that he's after this chap
[Wallace's prospect]." Rockne became so angry with the quarterback of
the Four Horsemen that he wrote a Philadelphia friend, "Regarding
Stuhldreher, I hear an awful lot of little lies he has been telling about me
personally . . . tell Harry for goodness sake to quit telling them as they
are somewhat annoying . . . I am through giving these fellows [N.D.
players now coaching] my latest stuff in football and having them say that
they gave it to me."

The world of high-pressure recruiting produced other difficulties for
Rockne. A prominent Detroit alum wanted one of the new athletic scholarships to go to his nephew; Rockne had to inform the alum that the boy
was "too small to ever play football at Notre Dame."

In addition, the coach had to adhere to his school's policy of refusing
football transfers—he informed N.D. supporters beyond his special circle
that this was "a very good rule"—but privately he tried to circumvent it.
Former Notre Damer Harry Mehre, coaching at Georgia, told him about
"a Jew boy by the name of Gellis here for most of last season. He had
played one game with Wake Forest College freshmen the year before.
That makes him ineligible in the Southern Conference [where Georgia
played] . . . Gellis is the best looking backfield prospect I have had
since I have been down here" and could Rockne use him? The N.D.
coach replied that he was "very interested," and he wrote Joe Byrne, Jr.,

The 1909 team with coach Shorty Longman in his bowler hat.

Head coach Jesse Harper and assistant Knute Rockne, circa 1916.

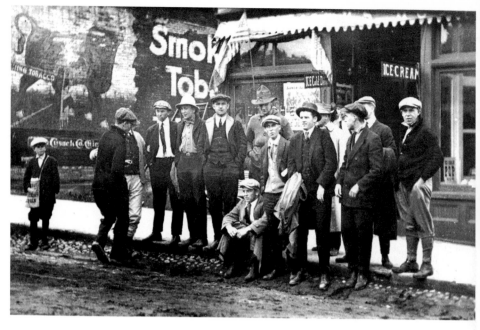

Notre Dame students hanging out at Hullie & Mike's, circa 1916.

The Notre Dame football field in the 1910s.

George Gipp at football practice, 1920.

Hunk Anderson, Rockne, and Tommy Mills in coaching attire, circa 1926.

Rockne promoting a car
outside the new Notre
Dame Stadium, 1930.

Poet-President Charles
O'Donnell during the N.D.
visit of the greatest poet of
the century, William Butler
Yeats, 1933.

Vice President John O'Hara greeting his new coach, Elmer Layden, 1934.

Elmer Layden with some of his assistants: from right to left, Joe Boland, Chet Grant, and Joe Benda. Rockne looks down.

Arthur Haley arrives in Hollywood with (from right to left)
his wife, Bonnie Rockne, and Gale Page, who played Bonnie
in the Rockne biopic, 1940.

President Hugh O'Donnell watches Frank Leahy sign his official coaching contract
at N.D., 1941.

in New York, Gellis's hometown, that "there is a certain lad I want you to see regarding coming to Notre Dame." Typically, Rockne was coy about the player's background: "He was with Harry Mehre a short time at Georgia but cannot go back for some reason or other."

In the fall of 1929, Gellis entered Notre Dame and, in addition to what he received from Joe Byrne, Jr., Rockne gave him one of the plum jobs in the athletic department, "acting as a caretaker in the gym." The N.D. coach had other transfers on his 1929 and 1930 teams, including star halfback Marty Brill from Penn. (Brill was also Jewish, as was his backup, Clarence Kaplan, and two varsity linemen, Abie Zoss and Norm Herwit; running back Marchy Schwartz was half Jewish; in addition, Bernard Hennes, a Jewish alum of N.D., sponsored a number of Jewish players, including Sam Goldstein, an outstanding freshman tackle. Rockne, a philo-Semite, was pleased to include them all in the Fighting Irish.)

As the recruiting system moved into a higher gear, the N.D. coach contacted many more athletes and inevitably some got away. One of Byrne's assistants told Rockne about a wonderful New Jersey high school football and baseball player named Joe Medwick, such an "exceptional hitter" that professional baseball teams tried to sign him but "he wants to continue his education and Notre Dame to him means the ultimate in colleges." The N.D. coach replied that "confidentially . . . you can consider the matter all set [for Medwick to come here] if the boy just goes through with everything [and applies for admission]." However, Joe "Ducky" Medwick decided to bypass college and enter pro baseball, eventually named to the Hall of Fame.

For Rockne, a more serious downside to the intensive recruiting system was involvement with high school "hotshots" shopping around for the best "free rides." Although for the majority of Notre Dame recruits coming to the Catholic school and playing for the famous coach was still very special, some star athletes treated the recruiting process cynically and merely sought the best financial deal. Al Feeney, the coach's man in Indianapolis, arranged for two excellent Indiana high school players to enroll at Notre Dame, and Rockne told his old friend, "These two boys will be taken care of for four years as you and I understand" it. However, when they arrived at N.D. in the fall of 1929, they complained about their dormitory accommodations and their freshmen jobs, then left campus. Rockne commented, "Evidently these boys have been spoiled by "the deals offered by" some of the other schools and they probably expected a private suite in one of the larger halls with a job that required no work . . . [they] have been spoiled and pampered . . . why they should expect a private suite down here is more than I can see."

The answer was simple—in the world of big-time recruiting, such expectations were not out of line and although Rockne wanted to intensify his efforts, he could not "promise the moon." What he could provide were enhanced and guaranteed versions of the old Notre Dame packages as well as summer jobs for his varsity—the 1929 correspondence contains letters to such N.D. stalwarts as Alderman George Maypole: "This will introduce to you Mr. [Manny] Vezie, our right end . . . he must have a job to carry him over." In addition, Rockne could help athletes prepare academically for Notre Dame, for example, he wrote a Toledo alum: "Everything is O.K. regarding [your recruit] Keefe except that he must have his mathematics [to get in here]. Can you not arrange for a private tutor" to help him this summer?

Though Rockne could hide his recruiting organization from the N.D. administration he could not conceal the academic problems of his athletes. Most did well enough to stay eligible—a few were excellent students—but some had classroom difficulties. One of his varsity halfbacks did so poorly academically in 1928–1929 that he flunked out. Rockne protested vigorously and the case went all the way to the president. O'Donnell reviewed it and ruled that "this is a clear case of scholastic deficiency which has been handled with all possible consideration." Appeal denied.

Rockne realized that although O'Donnell was more tractable than Father Walsh had been, the new president endorsed certain rules that even the famous football coach could not circumvent. Foremost among these was O'Donnell's adherence to N.D.'s scholastic requirements. O'Donnell, a protégé of former president James Burns, had a strong sense of Notre Dame as an academic institution and he wanted to move it—and its national reputation—in that direction.

Miss Harriet Monroe
Poetry: A Magazine of Verse
Erie Street
Chicago, Illinois

Dear Miss Monroe:
    The fact that I was not mentioned in your review of the season's poetry, in this morning's *Tribune,* can of course mean only one thing— you have not received my new book of verse! For all the brave front, this assurance is only assumed. . . .

I enclose a sonnet. Before your temperature goes up, let me hasten to add this is the first sonnet I have ever sent to you [for publication in your magazine].

Rev. Charles O'Donnell

—Letter from President O'Donnell, December 15, 1928

Father Charles O'Donnell was unique among Notre Dame presidents —his predecessors and successors—in his love of literature and his skill at writing. His work transcended the traditional Catholic liturgical verse of his day and qualified for a place in such avant-garde magazines as Harriet Monroe's *Poetry*—she accepted his sonnet and many other poems. But O'Donnell was not an aesthete snob, he appreciated a great variety of authors—he boasted that he "was one of the first to recognize that Ring Lardner wrote sense, and wrote with art"—and he particularly liked the newspaper columns of Rockne's nemesis, Westbrook Pegler, telling the sportswriter, "I should welcome you to Notre Dame any time you find it possible to come here."

O'Donnell had come of age in the C.S.C. community at Notre Dame and enjoyed its athletic traditions and success but, as president, he was often annoyed at having to ride the football tiger. He wrote a C.S.C. friend at another school: ". . . last night Notre Dame and Purdue conducted a radio debate which was broadcast from Chicago. Not a line about this goes into the papers—but imagine a football game between Notre Dame and Purdue. Also, last night the University Theatre presented *The Taming of the Shrew*. . . . But who would believe that Notre Dame has any interest in Shakespeare, certainly not" Rockne's friend, "Will Rogers?"

O'Donnell tried to correct this imbalance in public perception by bringing such famous Catholic writers as G. K. Chesterton to campus and also by encouraging the coach to mention the school's academic achievements in his lectures. Then, in a February 1929 speech in New York, the new president bluntly stated, "We deplore the excessive and almost exclusive eminence of Notre Dame as a place where a football team is turned out."

Although life for Rockne under the new regime began amicably with the resolution of his grievances about the stadium construction and his lecture tours, during the spring of 1929 the coach became unhappy again. In part, he disapproved of O'Donnell's attack on N.D.'s football fame, but more specifically, his faculty opponents had not quieted— indeed, they had coalesced around the new vice president, Father Michael Mulcaire, a resolute Rockne foe, and had enlisted Father Vincent Mooney, head of the Physical Education Department, in their ranks. The coach complained privately to a journalist: "Under certain conditions this could be the best place imaginable but [right now it is] anything else with the present personnel . . . there is sand in the ointment."

In late June, the coach's discontent erupted when he received word about the president's refusal to readmit the flunked-out halfback. He fired off a telegram—he was in Virginia at one of his coaching schools— to O'Donnell: "PLEASE ACCEPT MY RESIGNATION TO TAKE EFFECT IMMEDIATELY. PROSPECT OF CONTINUING WITH MOONEY AND KEOGAN TOO MUCH FOR ME. PLEASE ANNOUNCE TO PRESS SO I CAN GET ANOTHER JOB."

In a follow-up letter, the N.D. coach explained that he was "convinced that" the flunked-out player "was railroaded unfairly" and "that athletes have been persecuted in recent years." More important, however, was the "fact that [basketball coach George] Keogan was hired [originally] over my objections; that he was rehired [in 1929] for three years without consulting me; the fact that Father Mooney was made head of the Physical Education Department . . . that his name appears above mine in the catalogue," and many other embarrassments and slights resulting from these "facts."

The N.D. coach then charged that there was "an organized political group [at Notre Dame] who are against me personally." There were "a few of the younger [faculty] men who have had nothing to do with the success of the school . . . and who, by lack of judgment and experience, have a pathological point of view, at least as far as I am concerned, which makes me believe that the situation can best be solved by the method I mentioned" (immediate resignation and departure). Rockne added: "The attempt by a small group to put Father Mooney in as Director of Athletics is a very foolish move, as you would be only doing what other Catholic schools are doing and are sadly having no success." Finally: "As far as I am concerned, I want to be somewhere where I can be contented [and] I shall appreciate a wire from you [accepting this resignation]."

President O'Donnell, like Father Walsh before him, despaired at ever satisfying his famous football coach. The priest, as a member of a religious order, had little sympathy for the ego and demands of a prima donna employee. But, as a sharp observer of his world, he understood the importance of Knute Rockne to Notre Dame's success as well as the coach's celebrity status in America. Moreover, the new president knew that with stadium construction and financing about to begin, he needed Rockne at Notre Dame. O'Donnell's compromise was to convince Rockne to continue as athletic director, to have Father Mooney take a leave of absence from Notre Dame to pursue his Ph.D. degree, and to keep Father Mulcaire as vice president and head of the athletic board.

As with all compromises, the adversaries were not truly placated, but O'Donnell managed to calm the coach and gain his cooperation. Later in the summer, when Francis Wallace wanted his mentor to collaborate on a *Saturday Evening Post* article attacking the reform movement in college sports, Rockne informed him, "I have just had a long session with our president regarding the article and it is his opinion that I had better not have anything to do with it in any manner as it might jeopardize our relations with some schools." Rockne privately sent Wallace a large amount of information for the piece, chiefly on the hypocrisy of Fielding Yost and Bob Zuppke, but he warned the young writer not to "use Notre Dame too much in the article . . . [President O'Donnell] is, of course, very touchy on Notre Dame's situation."

"We had quite a job in New York as it was strictly a political situation but the coaches for the first time in their history were organized with a solid front with the exception of Fielding Yost and a few others, who evidently want to play ball with the 'powers that be' [college administrators and reformers] for some selfish motive or other."

—Rockne to Jesse Harper
after the coaches' annual convention,
January 1928

The N.D. coach had long opposed the reform movement but had kept his opinions private—he believed that the reformers like Yost were hypocrites and that their proposals would never work, but he saw no point in creating public controversy as well as difficulties with the Notre Dame administration by joining the opposition. However, as the reform movement gained momentum in the late 1920s, his private dissatisfaction grew, particularly on the issue of university control of football coaches.

When former Notre Damer Pete Vaughan, coaching at Wabash College, wrote him, "We got a new President last fall and he and I sure do disagree on athletic matters," Rockne replied, "My point of view is that a man either runs his [athletic] department," as he sees fit, "or he gets run out," and he offered to help Vaughan obtain another job. Rockne continued to watch the Wabash situation, later grumbling that the school "has ceased to be an athletic institution and has become quite literary and highbrow. This is too bad because Wabash, in my mind, used to be the greatest school in the State [of Indiana]. It is pretty tough on Pete Vaughan, too, as Pete can do pretty well coaching football players but he is a little out of his element handling the Phi Beta Kappas." (Vaughan was one of the "hard men" from the pre-Harper era at N.D.)

Rockne also privately discussed "the question as to whether the game of football was being taken away from the coaches" with Major John Griffith. The Big Ten commissioner, like his coaching friend, condemned the involvement in college football of university officials—trustees and presidents, as well as faculty—"many of them are like the parasites who try to get publicity and notoriety from this or that contact with Dempsey, Tunney, or any other athletic great." Considering that the commissioner headed the Intercollegiate Conference of Faculty Representatives, his condemnation of "jock-sniffing" faculty is noteworthy; however, Griffith disputed Rockne's coach-centered point of view, telling him that "football is primarily for the players and the public . . . [coaches] have a part in the game but after all the game is bigger than the individuals [coaching and administering it]."

Throughout their correspondence, the Big Ten commissioner cautioned his friend about becoming too active in the coaches' opposition to the reform movement. Griffith particularly warned against condemning the NCAA because that group was trying to broker a compromise between the educational reformers and the intercollegiate athletic establishment. If the coaches tried to "take the administration of football in all of its aspects into [their] own hands," Griffith argued, they would mainly aid their enemies. At the present time, he thought, college sports people were "apprehensive lest when the Carnegie report is published, there will be another upheaval comparable to that which occurred in 1906" (when President Theodore Roosevelt forced major changes in the rules and the structure of the sport).

Rockne disagreed: "If this be treason, make the most of it. If we coaches are just going to be the goats while the administrators and directors of athletics and other parasites hold their positions indefinitely I am going to get out of it just as fast as I can." (Significantly, although an A.D., he identified only with the coaches; however, back at Notre Dame, he demanded the power and perks of the A.D.'s position.)

At the 1927–1928 coaches' convention in New York, Rockne helped lead the opposition to reform and enjoyed the rout of Fielding Yost, boasting, "In the test vote . . . he was beaten fifty-eight to sixteen and after that he ran for cover." Not only did the N.D. coach abhor Yost's hypocrisy but—as his traveling companion, McCready Huston, explained—he considered "the whole crusade for deflating intercollegiate football as a menace, because it was . . . a threat to an established profession [coaching] and partly because he looked on it as an effeminizing trend."

In 1929, Rockne also began to incorporate his opposition to reform into his after-dinner speeches, especially to Notre Dame alumni. The *Washington Evening Star* described his talk to N.D. alums in that city: "In a quaint aside, Mr. Rockne observed that the Notre Dame faculty seems determined 'to pay some attention' to academic standards in the acceptance of students. He indicated that other universities, too, nowadays scrutinize the 'credits' with which a would-be matriculant turns up. Mr. Rockne concedes the indispensability of mental equipment for college men, but boldly declares that educational authorities overstress its importance and underestimate personality." Furthermore, "the registrar of admissions accords the accolade of preference to the fellow with greater Phi Beta Kappa prospects. The Notre Dame coach thinks this is all wrong. He believes college [admissions] directors in particular take a myopic view of the significance of football [and discriminate against] the brawny boy because he is not so strong on math" and other academic subjects. However, "four years of football are calculated to breed in the average man more of the ingredients of success in life than almost any academic course he takes."

Thus Knute Rockne, ahead of his coaching colleagues in so many areas, attacked academic admission standards for athletes long before that position became a major tenet of the coaches' credo. The Washington paper termed his stance on this issue "revolutionary"; however, it subsequently became the orthodoxy of "special admits for athletes."

Rockne's comments about the Notre Dame faculty also indicate the light-years between his coach-centric universe and the academic galaxy of the N.D. professors, especially the younger and more intellectual priests and laymen.

■ ■ ■

"The predominance of sports in schools, in the national life, in the press, not only crowds out what is, or should be, more important, but it creates an atmosphere in which those important things are made to appear superfluous."

—Abbé Dimant, *The Art of Thinking*

In a preface to the Carnegie report, the head of the foundation, Henry S. Pritchett, quoted the Catholic philosopher to bolster his attack on the "commercialism in college athletics." For Pritchett, the years of investigation had produced overwhelming proof that college sports, particularly football, were corrupt and a cancer within American higher education: "The question is not so much whether athletics in their present form should be fostered by the university, but how fully can a university that fosters professional athletics discharge its primary [educational] function?"

Pritchett saw "the paid coach, the gate receipts . . . the recruiting [system]" and the alumni and boosters as the engine of the commercial sports machine. He argued that because "the defense of the intellectual integrity of the college and university lies with the president and faculty," these authorities must "correct this situation."

The body of the Carnegie study, "Bulletin No. 23," written mainly by Howard Savage, presented the results of the investigation—a massive amount of data revealing, among other facts, that at least "one in seven" of all college athletes was "subsidized" and that among starting football players, almost half received special, usually financial, aid.

The report not only demolished the claims by university officials that recruiting and subsidization did not exist but it attacked the cherished rationales for college sports: "The supposed advertising values of success at football and a few other branches [of sports] has led some institutions to . . . a naive and undue regard to the notice which a victorious team or an athletic event attracts." Mentioned among these culprits were USC and Notre Dame.

The Carnegie Foundation noted, however, that the Catholic school was among "fifty-two institutions that cooperated fully, even to an analysis of 'hard' and 'easy' courses," and that it was one of the institutions that kept "excellent account of all student athletic activities." But the Carnegie people were not sympathetic to the football "commercialism [that] has made possible the erection of fine academic buildings and the increase of equipment from the profits of college athletics . . . those profits have been gained because colleges have permitted the youths entrusted to their care to be openly exploited. At such colleges and universities the primary emphasis has been transferred from the things of the spirit or the mind to the material."

The report did not tag any specific school with these sins, but even a casual observer of college football in the 1920s could move from this general criticism to the specific—Notre Dame and its successful teams. Similarly, the report never attacked Rockne by name, but anyone familiar with his situation knew that of the "242 coaches" in the report's sample, the N.D. head was among the "seven coaches of the study [who] received $10,000 or more as annual salary."

The Carnegie people deplored these high salaries, particularly at a time when faculty were so poorly paid, and they called for a return to "amateur" athletic mentors. However, the reformers acknowledged that the professional "drill-masters" were in the ascendancy and, in a discussion that applied to the most famous coach in college football, they admitted that the "preference for the 'driving' coach is not by any means confined to the alumni. . . . At a number of institutions . . . athletes have expressed preference for the 'driver,' whose teams win, over the gentler man whose efforts end in defeat or mediocrity."

Another important section of the Carnegie study concerned the press and college athletics. The authors detailed how sportswriters worked closely with football coaches to promote mutual self-interests, and how the press inflated the coach to a more prominent position than his team and his university. The report also condemned the "sensationalism" resulting from the ever-increasing press coverage of college sports, but it blamed the universities as much as the newspapers for this situation. Then, in a conclusion that indicted all schools involved in big-time intercollegiate athletics, the reformers insisted that the extraordinary publicity generated by college sports undermined the academic seriousness of the university and the reasons for its existence.

Not surprisingly, considering the media's vested interest in promoting college sports, most newspapers gave the Carnegie report short shrift. Many ignored it, others carried cursory wire service summaries, and some mainly ran the denials from schools accused of illegalities by the Carnegie investigators. Even the *New York Herald-Tribune,* probably because of the importance of its sports pages to its advertising and circulation, refused to cover the report as news and, of their columnists, only W. O. McGeehan commented on it. The one journalistic exception was the *New York Times*—it provided multicolumn coverage, offering a detailed summary as well as many follow-up stories.

The *Chicago Tribune* had a schizophrenic response. Because the Carnegie report had not overly censured the universities of Chicago and Illinois, the paper ran photos of their athletic directors with the inaccurate caption "THEIR WORK PRAISED." But because the report indicated infractions at other Big Ten schools, the *Tribune* ran such articles as "GRIFFITH CALLS CARNEGIE REPORT UNFAIR TO BIG TEN" and "N.U., MICHIGAN DENY 'UNETHICAL SPORTS' CHARGES." Its oddest story was "IOWA JUBILANT"— the previous spring, the Big Ten faculty reps had expelled the Hawkeyes from the conference for flagrant violations of recruiting and subsidization rules but the Carnegie report had bypassed the sins of this school and focused on those of other conference members.

Public reaction to the Carnegie study varied. William Howard Taft, Chief Justice of the Supreme Court and a former U.S. president, agreed with its findings and called for a cleanup of intercollegiate athletics. However, most politicians, particularly those from states with big-time college football teams, were noncommittal, and the man in the street could not decide. The *Chicago Tribune*'s "Inquiring Reporter" found one who believed "it probably will clean up athletics," but another who said, "I'm laughing yet. I am a college man and I think the Carnegie Foundation report is a lot of nonsense."

Westbrook Pegler articulated the skeptic's position: "The Carnegie report, substantiating conditions which have been commonly known to exist," would change nothing because, in the history of college sports, "as the rules and agreements took on greater solemnity, the cheating has grown correspondingly shrewd and serious." For Pegler, it was "only the pretense and concealment, couched in resolutions and agreements of the most elaborate amateur piety, that is immoral, but this is familiar in so many phases of American life that it has lost its power to shock."

W. O. McGeehan was equally skeptical and considered the report "quite as unimpressive as was Mr. Ford's peace ship when the World War was getting under way"—the automaker had chartered a boat and traveled to Europe in a quixotic attempt to halt hostilities. The leading exponent of "Aw-Nuts" sportswriting also pointed out the basic absurdity of football overemphasis: "None of the colleges would cheat in any academic matter. They would not, for instance, intimate to a particularly brilliant student in some other university that if he transferred to Whatsis, he would be sure of his Phi Beta Kappa key," but "this sort of thing is done in regard to intercollegiate football."

McGeehan also scoffed at the charges by Commissioner Griffith and others that the Carnegie investigators had found illegalities where none existed: "I happen to know that this report could have been much more sensational than it was." He wryly added, "Old grads from colleges mentioned as almost strictly ethical in a football way are saying nothing whatever. Probably some of these are refraining from taking a bow because they are wondering how they got by."

As this columnist undoubtedly expected, many readers wrote to him about the Carnegie report. Some confessed their own "proselyting" sins, but one condemned him for overlooking the crimes of specific schools, including Notre Dame, adding, "you have omitted to mention that 'Rock' is no less than president, registrar, treasurer and coach of the South Bend campus." The *New York Herald-Tribune* writer replied angrily:

> In fact, the point of view on athletics at Notre Dame is less distorted than the point of view of a majority of universities of the country. The Fathers of the Holy Cross, who have charge of the University of Notre Dame du Lac, can be depended upon to see that football is kept in its place.
>
> I am so vain that I believe that I can detect bunk as quickly as the next man. I found no bunk at Notre Dame, and . . . I am convinced that the standards and the ethics at South Bend are quite as high as any member of the "older institutions," including the "Big Three" [Harvard, Yale, and Princeton].

Not everyone accepted McGeehan's assurances; N.D. haters and their allies pounced on the report's few negative remarks about the Catholic school. Rockne believed that there was "a decided effort on the part of [hostile] newspapermen to discredit Notre Dame, which has a common source"—Fielding Yost. In addition, some reporters revived false rumors that the N.D. coach received a large percentage of the gate receipts from Fighting Irish games and that his salary was much higher than the report implied. He told a friend, "I couldn't help but deny the story on the fancy salary as we would not only have had trouble with the Carnegie Foundation but with the Income Tax people in Washington." In fact, his salary was only a minor part of his annual income; the Carnegie investigators and the press never added up the money from his outside deals and he was not about to divulge that total to them.

As a result of the Carnegie criticism of Michigan's athletic program and its relatively clean bill of health for N.D., Fielding Yost's animosity toward Rockne and the Catholic school increased. When some Michigan alumni, prompted by the "new level playing field," suggested a game between their school and the Fighting Irish, "Yost called a meeting of the [Michigan] varsity coaches to learn their attitude toward such a game" and, of course, they voted "thumbs down" on it (AP report). Michigan's actions infuriated Rockne and he replied to a fan's inquiry about Yost's hostility to N.D.: Yost "is the Senator Heflin [a rabid anti-Catholic] of Middlewestern athletics . . . [and] would do the game a lot of good if he should resign . . . He has lost all influence among all athletic men and, as far as this letter is concerned, I don't care to whom you show it."

Considering the N.D. coach's illegal recruiting and subsidization during the nine months *before* the report's publication, he was fortunate not to get knocked off his high horse.

The Carnegie findings did shake up the Big Ten conference, but mainly in favor of reinstating Iowa. In a story concerning this move, the *Chicago Tribune* reported: "One thing was certain, however, and that was Notre Dame will not seek membership in the Big Ten . . . the Ramblers have no contemplation whatsoever of joining the conference if Iowa does or does not gain reinstatement." In the event, Iowa came back and N.D. happily stayed out.

COACH ROCKNE FINDS FOOTBALL
NOT COMMERCIALIZED ENOUGH

Knute Rockne, here [Buffalo, New York] to speak at the annual Canisius College football dinner, said in an interview today that he did not believe college football was over-commercialized. He went even so far as to say that "it is not commercialized enough."

—AP report, December 17, 1930

In the aftermath of the Carnegie Report, the N.D. coach became more aggressive and outspoken in his defense of big-time college football. He argued that "football isn't commercialized enough because *there are only about twenty-five out of a thousand colleges making any real money out of it.*" He also rejected the reformers' solution to this financial problem—drop big-time football with its huge expenses and play the sport at the club level—because deemphasis would eliminate the highly paid coach and, at those few schools making money from the sport, it would obliterate many athletic department activities supported by the successful football program. Hence he believed that a more "commercialized" form of the game was the only way for more schools to make money through college sports. His position subsequently became the standard athletic department line but, sixty-plus years later, the pot 'o gold eludes as many schools as it did in his era.

The N.D. coach continued his public opposition to reform until his death in 1931, and a famous echo of his campaign appeared in the film *Knute Rockne—All American.* In an incident that never occurred—his appearance before a congressional-like committee investigating college sports—his film character passionately justifies big-time college football. His culminating argument is that it channels "every red-blooded young man's

. . . natural spirit of combat" into a healthy substitute for war, otherwise America will always be at war.

This speech, however, belongs more to its time, 1939–1940, than to Rockne's attack on the reformers ten years earlier. The scriptwriter, Robert Buckner, focused on the substitute-for-war theme because he wrote during a period when many Americans, including himself, wanted to excuse their country's isolation from World War II. In any event, the real Rockne would have enjoyed the conclusion of this scene when his character totally converts the skeptics and routs the reformers.

Unlike the make-believe world of the film *Knute Rockne—All American*, the real Notre Dame struggled with "Bulletin No. 23" from the Carnegie Foundation. The alumni magazine editorialized that "Notre Dame was damned, after a fashion, with faint praise"—the investigators found few outright abuses at the school but because of "the particular bête noir of large gate receipts," the report implied that "Notre Dame must essentially have dipped its academic garments in the mud of the gridiron."

The Carnegie Foundation's equation between financial success from big-time football and intellectual and spiritual impoverishment particularly bothered President Charles O'Donnell. In a number of public speeches and interviews after the report's release, he downplayed the amount of money that his school actually earned from football and also pointed out that, at a time when the total endowment of the Big Three schools (Harvard, Yale, and Princeton) approached $160 million, and the total for Columbia, Chicago, and Stanford was at $142 million, Notre Dame's barely reached $1 million. He understood the Carnegie report's arguments but he felt that the eastern establishment men exhibited a large amount of misguided snobbery—because their alma maters could build innumerable "ivory towers," they had no right to criticize a poor Catholic school for using its profits from football to improve its physical plant and academic facilities.

Although Notre Dame, through the efforts of Presidents Burns, Walsh, and O'Donnell, had entered the mainstream of American higher education, it was still far from the secure islands of the well-endowed private and public schools. It had its own religious and cultural traditions —including its athleticism—and even though the Carnegie people criticized its values, O'Donnell and his fellow C.S.C. priests were determined to guide their university by them.

Notre Dame needed this collective self-confidence for the 1929 football season because, with the ongoing construction of the new stadium, the Fighting Irish became true "nomads," playing all their games on the road and in a number of the largest venues in America.

> "We will either have a pretty good year [in 1929] or an awfully bad one but our spirit of optimism has already brought into the coffers a complete sell-out for the Southern California and Army games, as well as Indiana, and it looks like we may stand a chance of netting around $400,000 . . . in which case the spirit of optimism will have done its job of bringing in the shekels at the gate. Next year I will sing the blues in the well known manner of Gil Dobie."
>
> —Rockne to Oregon State coach
> Paul Schissler, October 1, 1929

Uncharacteristically, before the 1929 season, the N.D. coach predicted great success for his squad. Usually he preferred the pessimistic style of Cornell coach "Gloomy" Gil Dobie, but to insure large gates on the road, he employed the upbeat approach. In addition to a good crowd at Indiana, Rockne hoped that the opening game would provide "the acid test" on whether this will "be a good team or a bum one." But, during a long afternoon, the Fighting Irish struggled to a 14–0 victory over a weak Hoosier contingent, one observer jibing, "Those who say the current Notre Dame football club is the greatest since the famed Four Horsemen era will have to wait another day to prove it."

But the N.D. coach knew that the 1929 squad was much better than the previous year's team—the best players had returned and many outstanding freshmen had joined them—and he carefully prepared three full units to take on the ultimate road schedule. In addition, with no home games to offer referees, he had to work hard to obtain the game officials he wanted. However, Major Griffith was particularly accommodating this year: he placed George Strickler, Rockne's former press assistant and, in 1929, with the *Chicago Herald Examiner,* on the Big Ten's officiating list and assigned him to the N.D.–Wisconsin game; Griffith also took in another Rockne-approved journalist, Frank Haggerty of the *Chicago Daily News.* Furthermore, after the season, Donald Hamilton, N.D. alumni president, wrote Rockne that "Griffith will O.K. me with you" on the Big Ten officials' list for future years.

But bad luck intervened for the N.D. coach in 1929 when, after setting up Walter Eckersall for Notre Dame's key games, the sportswriter became ill and could not fulfill most of his assignments. Before the Indiana game, Griffith scrambled to replace him with another official and did so throughout the season—"Eck" could work only the N.D.–Northwestern game. Eckersall's personal life intruded upon his frenetic professional activities; he was a bachelor and, according to an authoritative account, exceptionally "loyal to his widowed mother. Her death in 1929 profoundly affected him and caused his health to fail. Within a year, he died."

Rockne's health also declined in 1929. Before the second game of the season—against Navy in Baltimore—he suffered an attack of phlebitis and a blood clot in his right leg threatened to move to his heart. His doctors convinced him not to go east with the team, and the United Press reported that this "was a blow to Irish fandom which believes that the bald-headed figure down on one knee at the sideline watching the ebb and flow of battle is an assurance of victory."

In fact, by 1929, the N.D. coach had so perfected his football system that with a sufficiently talented and deep team, as well as excellent assistant coaches, he did not have to be on the sidelines for every game. The key in 1929 was the quality and quantity of the team and the return of assistant coach Tom Lieb from Wisconsin. In addition, Rockne was even better organized than in previous years. Among other innovations, he used what he called his "chart of play": these charts—now standard procedure but in the late 1920s very innovative—diagrammed and analyzed the game performance of each player, breaking down his work on every single play. Thus, during practices, the N.D. coaches put the players through the regular, arduous drills and then focused on correcting specific weaknesses.

On the eve of the Navy game, Rockne sent a long "Night Letter" to Tom Lieb with careful game instructions. It began: "To shake Elder loose you have [play number] thirty-five and thirty-seven dash one to the left. Another man to shake loose . . . is Kaplan on fifty-four dash two from punt formation," and so on. The morning of the game, the N.D. head coach telephoned the players at their hotel and talked to each member of the first two units. Westbrook Pegler observed the scene and wrote, "Rockne achieved something unique when by the power and ardor of his pleas, he sent the boys turning from the telephone, one by one, blinking tears out of their eyes." In 1929, in quest of a national championship, Rockne gave more pep talks than usual, but instead of deathbed or hospital requests from children or departed players, he used his own illness as a prod.

Pegler covered the game for a press syndicate and he lead his story, "A typical Knute Rockne football team, trim, smart, well-schooled in both hard and allusive football and backed by a full complement of substitutes who were almost interchangeable with the regulars, beat the Navy again . . . 14–7."

Most readers loved the story of Rockne's telephone pep talks, but a few days later, an obscure writer on the *Chicago Evening Post* satirized them by having an N.D. player exhort his teammates: " 'De coach is back home fightin' a losin' fight wid a blood clot . . . he says he ain't gonna live troo dis game anyway, but if we don't muss up dese [Navy] palookas plenty, he'll cry his eyes out in hell for a hundred years. Now, how about it, youse babies."

This burlesque, particularly the portrayal of the Fighting Irish "as an untutored delegation of bully-beef thugs," infuriated Notre Dame fans and a group of alumni called upon the managing editor of the newspaper. To mollify them, he offered to fire the writer immediately, but the N.D. visitors were satisfied with a lesser punishment—the offender would "remain with the paper on probation, as a copy reader only."

Before the third game of the 1929 season, the Catholic school encountered enmity from a more traditional source, the Big Ten faculty representatives. This group wanted to prevent Wisconsin from playing N.D. at Soldier Field, claiming that the encounter smacked too much of "commercialism"—as opposed to the "campus entertainment" provided to 101,000 paying customers at Michigan, 81,000 at Ohio State, and so forth. But Rockne complained to the Wisconsin authorities that "the Big Ten Faculty Committee [wants to] make a show of us in public by denying us permission," and Wisconsin agreed to go through with the Chicago game. A more expected problem for Notre Dame contests in that city was ticket requests. In 1929, even with three games at Soldier Field—Wisconsin, Drake, and USC—and a visit to Northwestern in Evanston, the demand was phenomenal. Before the season began, a Chicago alum wrote Rockne: "The Notre Dame Club of Chicago is getting ready to take the roof off the town for your four appearances this Fall," and requested a huge number of seats. In addition, the press required its full allotment for the games—this was the all-time bumper year for Chicago sportswriters to scalp N.D. tickets.

For the Wisconsin game, Rockne's doctors kept him from traveling to Chicago and assistant coach Tom Lieb came into his own. A Madison reporter noted in a pregame article that Lieb "knows every formation and play in the Badger repertoire and more than that, Lieb knows the strength and weakness of individual Wisconsin players whom he coached last year and the year before." Before ninety thousand fans, the Fighting Irish rolled to an easy 19–0 win, with Joe Savoldi, a junior fullback, leading the attack.

The following game was at Carnegie Tech. The situation reminded Rockne of N.D.'s last visit to Pittsburgh—he had turned over the team to Hunk Anderson and the Tartans had stopped the 1926 national championship drive. He also feared a replay of the 1928 upset that ended the N.D. home field streak. Tom Lieb was a more competent substitute head coach than Hunk, but Rockne insisted on making the trip.

Adding to his incentive to travel was Grantland Rice's proclamation after the Wisconsin win: "The South Bend Cyclone . . . [has] swept out ahead of the national football procession." The N.D. coach wanted to retain the number-one rating; privately, he thanked Rice "for the very fine things you have been writing about our boys . . . it has helped them because it has been right along the same thing I have been trying to do—build up confidence."

The coach, in a special wheelchair, accompanied the team. In the locker room before the game, he spoke briefly but sharply: "A lot of water has gone under the bridge since I first came to Notre Dame—but I don't know when I've ever wanted to win a game as badly as this one." Then his voice rose and he chanted, "Go out there and crack 'em. *Crack 'em.* Fight to live. Fight to win. *Fight to win—win—win—WIN!*" His body shook and his doctor worried that he would expire on the spot. Francis Wallace, observing the scene, noted, "Rock wanted to win more than he wanted to live."

The Notre Dame coach also directed the team from the sidelines, basing much of his attack on running quarterback Frank Carideo. But Carnegie Tech coach Walter "Wally" Steffen almost outfoxed his N.D. colleague; as Steffen explained on the train back to Chicago, where he worked as a judge, his strategy was "to prepare for Carideo getting away from the first men to reach him but to send enough other fellows . . . to put a blanket on him before he got too far." Steffen's defense worked and the game was scoreless until the third quarter when Joe Savoldi broke loose for a touchdown and the 7–0 winning score.

Rockne returned home exhausted. He received hundreds of get-well phone calls and telegrams, the most unusual coming from Westbrook Pegler, who, for all of their professional differences, wished him well personally: "WHY DON'T YOU GO TO BED AND STAY THERE UNTIL YOU GET BETTER. A GUY OF YOUR AGE AND EXPERIENCE SHOULD KNOW ENOUGH TO TAKE A COUNT OF NINE. . . . WHAT DIFFERENCE DOES IT MAKE IF THIS TEAM DROPS A GAME OR TWO? IF YOU HAVE TO WIN TO KEEP YOUR FRIENDS THEN YOUR FRIENDS AREN'T

WORTH WINNING FOR. YOU WILL MEAN PLENTY TO POSTERITY BUT WHY THE MAD
RUSH [TO GET THERE]? FOR GOD'S SAKE WHY DON'T YOU STOP?"

The sportswriter did not understand the N.D. coach's perfectionism.
It made an enormous difference to him if the Fighting Irish dropped "a
game or two." The same personality trait that drove Knute Rockne to
produce the best possible team made it impossible for him to ease up. By
the end of the 1920s, he had become the new prototype for the coaching
profession. The casual head men like Judge Wally Steffen were increasingly obsolete, and the Rockne model of insatiable perfectionism would
soon predominate, emulated by but burdening many future coaches, including at Notre Dame, Frank Leahy and Ara Parseghian.

After the Carnegie Tech win, Rockne continued to train the team from
his wheelchair, often hoisted onto the top of a car to move him around
the practice field. However, when a medical specialist warned that he
might not return from his proposed trip south for the following week's
game at Georgia Tech, he reluctantly turned the team over to Tom Lieb.
The Yellow Jackets, 2–2 coming into the contest, were far weaker than
their previous year's championship form. Although Georgia Tech scored
first, Frank Carideo and Jack Elder brought the Fighting Irish back for a
26–6 romp.

For the next game—against Drake at Soldier Field—Rockne promised to stay home in order to be with the team the following Saturday,
also in Soldier Field but against high-flying USC. The easy victory over
Drake, 19–7, served mainly as buildup for the N.D.–Southern Cal contest.

Rockne told Grantland Rice that "Pop Warner wrote me that they
[USC] have three wonderful teams, one as good as the other, and I don't
see how they can be beaten," but he was determined to find a way. He
also invited the sportswriter to have dinner with him on Saturday night in
Chicago; Rice used the N.D. coach's comments in his pregame stories
and accepted the invitation.

On Wednesday before the game, the *Chicago Tribune* banner-headlined "ROCKNE DIRECTS N. DAME DRILL FOR TROJANS," and subheaded "Wants
No Opponent Left on His Feet." Most Chicago newspapers pumped the
event with similar attention, and their sports editors and writers clamored
for more tickets to scalp. Rockne wrote one editor, "I note where you tell
me you want thirty [prime] seats for the Southern California game.
You're [almost] worse than Eddie Geiger of the *Chicago American*—he
only wants the East Stand."

As usual, Chicago alumni and fans sought seats, cajoling, begging, and promising favors in return. Back in South Bend, the local partisans, many of whom could not obtain tickets, were equally fanatic. On the eve of the USC game, six thousand, including the entire student body, turned out for a huge bonfire and pep rally on the Notre Dame campus. In a steady drizzle, they fed the fire until the flames soared a hundred feet high and for hours they sang the N.D. fight songs. Then, as Arch Ward reported: "Following the bonfire more than 3,000 students snake danced to the main business section of South Bend."

Southern Cal won ten games in 1929, including a 76–0 thrashing of UCLA and a victory over Stanford. But Notre Dame was the "Big Game" for them and at least 120,000 fans, including many from the West Coast, arrived at Soldier Field to see if the Trojans could repeat their previous year's triumph. Like Rockne, USC coach Howard Jones trained his team with long, hard drills, and the 1928 game reflected the coaches' methods. Old-time Chicago sportswriter Harvey Woodruff led his game story: "Notre Dame and Southern California gave the greatest exhibition of football fundamentals ever seen in a college game by a Chicago crowd."

The teams fought to a 6–6 halftime tie, and in the N.D. locker room, former player Paul Castner spoke about the meaning of "Rock" to the Fighting Irish and the risk he took by coming to this game. One observer wrote, "Beefy linemen swallowed their Adam's apples. Chunky Savoldi was watching Rock and trying hard to keep from crying." Then the N.D. coach "raised himself in his chair. 'Go on out there, go on out there, and play 'em off their feet in the first five minutes.' He was shouting, 'They don't like it. Play 'em. Play 'em. They don't like it. Come on boys, Rock's watching.' "

Six minutes into the second half, Savoldi scored a TD and Carideo converted. Then the Trojans notched a second touchdown on a ninety-five-yard run but they missed the PAT, eventually losing 13–12. Notre Dame fans rejoiced and many snake-danced through "The Loop." Again the newspapers featured the story of the locker room talk, the fans loving it but a few skeptics scoffing. A nonsports columnist in the *Chicago Daily News* offered, "Coach Knute Rockne, in a wheel chair (sniff, sniff), was trundled lovingly into the dressing room between halves Saturday (boo, hoo) and raising himself painfully (we c-c-can't s-s-stand much m-m-more of this) spoke." Then, after repeating the text of the speech, the journalist concluded, "Football a rough sport? Don't laugh. Cry."

The gulf between the infidels and the Fighting Irish fans was larger than Lake Michigan. The jokes about Rockne's locker room talks infuriated Notre Dame people, even provoking accusations of anti-Catholic prejudice. N.D. supporters sent Rockne copies of their letters to the *Chicago Daily News,* with passages such as, "The article in question is smeared all over with the taint of Klanism which unfortunately is, and has been, rampant in our state."

Yet, for Notre Dame fans, satires by their rooters on Fighting Irish players were another matter. The emerging hero of the 1929 season was Joe Savoldi, not only because he scored the key touchdown in the USC game but also because the following week he went over twice against Northwestern, leading N.D. to a 26–6 victory. The *Notre Dame Alumnus* printed a poem "written for Mr. Rockne" by a member of the class of 1921 entitled "Savoldi's Keed":

> *I nota' know he's olda' man,*
> *But papers say he's Italian,*
> *I bat he's glad, I ama' too,*
> *Maybe he send some fruits ta you.*
>
> *Deesa Swartz is good, dees' Elder too,*
> *So's all de' resta 'Micka' crew,*
> *So—I t'ink you should, for deesa' fall,*
> *Just geev' Savoldi's keed de ball.*

At first, sportswriters termed Savoldi the "Wandering Italian," and in postgame stories gently alluded to the fact that he was not the brightest player to ever pull on the pads at N.D., for example, "he found Rockne's system hard to master." After the Northwestern game, the journalists called him "Jumping Joe" and that nickname stuck—he used it later when, after leaving school early, he became a professional wrestler.

Rockne was too exhausted after the USC victory to return to Chicago for the Northwestern contest. He knew that his system worked and he hoped to save his strength for the season finale against Army in New York. At Evanston, his Fighting Irish won easily, and in New York W. O. McGeehan wrote in his column:

> I always have maintained that Knute Rockne is the greatest football coach in the country. I submit the achievement of his Notre Dame team against Northwestern as evidence. . . . In this game it was demonstrated that a great coach could train a team so thoroughly that it could go forth and take care of itself in battles afar. Theoretically, that is what every coach is supposed to do.

In New York, in late October 1929, the stock market crashed and newspaper editorials predicted difficult economic times ahead. However, football fans, in their frenzy to obtain tickets for the November 30 N.D.– Army match, ignored the financial news and bid up the scalpers' price to $300 for a box (a year's rent on a West Side apartment) and $100 for a pair of grandstand seats. Moreover, because Navy again canceled its meeting with its service rival, West Point fans regarded the Fighting Irish visit as the "Big Game" and frantically joined the ticket hunt.

Ticket seekers besieged President O'Donnell's office and, in addition to turning down requests from such notables as the president of Villa-nova, he had to deny the appeals of long-lost friends and relatives. To one, he began: "Your letter" after so many years of silence, "does not surprise me as much as you might imagine. All sorts of persons . . . are now writing me for football tickets [to the Army game]."

Complicating the president's problem were the machinations of the Notre Dame Club of New York. The N.D. alums tried to bully O'Donnell into restoring the old ticket system whereby they distributed thousands of seats to whomever they wished and at whatever prices they wanted. The president reacted by trying to end their small allotment. The C.S.C. Provincial's office had to intervene and it allowed the allotment in 1929, but O'Donnell told his friend Father Michael Shea that "this is the last time any group of alumni will enjoy special privileges of this sort." Fur-thermore, because of his "disappointment that Notre Dame men should behave in a manner so juvenile . . . I have decided not to attend the game." He asked Shea, the composer of the "Victory March," to use the N.D. president's enclosed box at Yankee Stadium and to act "as host in my stead" to the various dignitaries in attendance.

Rockne was also under siege. Ticket seekers, after perfunctory inqui-ries about his health, begged, bluffed, and/or demanded seats. Everyone from former Army All-American Elmer Oliphant to lifelong Notre Dame fan Ring Lardner thought Rockne could help them, but the N.D. coach deflected most requests—he did send Lardner two seats and also ob-tained three hundred for his friend Joe Byrne, Jr.

The N.D. coach was still generous with the working press and he enjoyed the spectacle of the austere John Kiernan and Alison Danzig of the *New York Times* in line for handouts like their grubbier colleagues on the tabloids. He was extra polite with the *Times* men but with the tabloid writers he was direct; after the Carnegie Tech game, he wrote Paul Gal-lico, sports editor of the *Daily News*, "Don't ever let this fellow [Jimmy] Powers, whoever he is, write up any more of our games." Rockne was angry at Powers's comments about his coaching strategy during the game, but Gallico—who would not accept freebies—kept the young reporter, at the beginning of his long sportswriting career, on the Notre Dame beat.

By the week of the N.D.–Army game, the *New York Herald-Tribune* banner-headlined "300,000 SEEK TICKETS TO NOTRE DAME GAME" and noted that "New York has never seen anything like the demand for admissions to the big game." In 1929, many fans—as if not wanting to face the reality of the stock market's collapse and their loss of millions of dollars in "paper profits"—turned to this sporting event for even more escape than usual. For the multitude who could not afford a scalped ticket, the *Daily News* ran its annual contest—"First prize is a football bender as will knock your eyes out—two tickets to the Notre Dame–Army game, dinner afterwards."

One sportswriter explained the party atmosphere for the game: even with Prohibition, "this city will be cut down to the pattern of a campus for the occasion; its speakeasies will resemble college fraternity houses, the cafes will be alive with raccoon-skins and it will be hard to find space [for drunks] to lie down on the sidewalk." At the game, played on a bitterly cold day, even the drinking in the stands was wide open: "The New York policemen, apparently from humanitarian motives, considered the contents of flasks as medicinal" (*Herald-Tribune*).

Before the contest, Rockne told Grantland Rice that he did not know if he could make the trip "as the doctors think I have gambled too much already with this leg" and, in the end, because of the winter weather, he stayed home. Again he telephoned the team—this time at Yankee Stadium an hour before kickoff—and afterward, like millions of Americans, he listened to the play-by-play on the radio.

Army had already lost to Yale and tied Harvard, but the N.D. coach warned: "Anyone who picks Army for a pushover doesn't know what he is talking about." Not only was this the big game for West Point but coach "Biff" Jones had announced his departure and his players wanted him to go out a winner.

On an icy field, with the wind-chilled temperature well below zero, the teams slugged to a scoreless tie until late in the second quarter. Then "Red" Cagle, in a sad conclusion to his great multiyear college career, threw deep into N.D. territory, directly into the zone covered by Jack Elder, an exceptional athlete and an Olympic-caliber sprinter. The N.D. player intercepted and Cagle compounded his error by not covering the sideline. Elder sped up the lane for ninety-six yards and the touchdown. Notre Dame then sat on the 7–0 lead and won by that score.

Fighting Irish fans around the country celebrated the perfect 9–0 season. When the team arrived back in South Bend, thousands of supporters, including the entire student body, "stood in a driving snowstorm and biting wind to give [the players] a rousing welcome" (AP report). Some sportswriters declared N.D. the national champions but many others wanted the Fighting Irish to put their undefeated season on the line in the Rose Bowl game to gain the award.

Controversy also occurred over whether N.D. had played too conservatively in the second half of the Army match. Columnist George Trevor of the *New York Sun* discussed the team's "safe and sane football" strategy, with which he agreed, but because of these comments, as he wrote Rockne, "I was deluged with abusive letters from self-constituted boosters who never have seen Notre Dame, Ind., charging me with 'religious prejudice,' 'being a Ku Kluxer,' etc." For these fanatics, any suggestion that the Fighting Irish played less than all-out offensive football was heresy and they reacted with vituperation (some Notre Dame fans have maintained this attitude up to the present).

Rockne, who approved of the Army game strategy, answered Trevor: "Our school has been very unfortunate in some of the synthetic rabid nuts who have attached themselves to us and I sincerely hope that you pay no attention to the crazy stuff that they may send you." The N.D. coach also ignored fan appeals for a Rose Bowl game appearance, even though undefeated Saint Mary's of California, coached by his "old boy" Slip Madigan, and undefeated Purdue, headed by former Notre Damer Jimmy Phelan, were listed as possible opponents. Rockne knew that he could not travel to the coast and he discouraged all Rose Bowl talk.

President O'Donnell and Vice President Mulcaire simply followed the long-standing policy of no Notre Dame appearances in exhibition and postseason games. One bowl official suggested that the school circumvent this rule by giving the Rose Bowl payout to charity. However, to avoid the quagmire of benefit games, the ban included appearances for charity, even Catholic ones. President O'Donnell said of the never-ceasing requests for the Fighting Irish to raise money for various causes, "You would hardly believe how many persons there are who are anxious to give us opportunities of doing good."

In addition, with the Carnegie report recently issued, O'Donnell was sensitive to the charges of "commercialism" as well as the press speculations on the amount of money the school had earned from its 1929 season. The N.D. administrator knew that a Fighting Irish appearance in the Rose Bowl, even though it would add at least $150,000 to the football profits, would comfort the Catholic school's enemies. Moreover, the Big Ten, adhering to its no-bowl-games policy, had barred conference champion Purdue from making the trip to Pasadena.

The internal N.D. financial statement put the net profits from the 1929 football season at a healthy $541,840. Nevertheless, on the eve of a financial depression, another major payday would certainly have helped the Catholic school. The self-financing on the stadium was proceeding well—the athletic department had received almost $208,000 in payments for box seats—but President O'Donnell worried about whether, in a floundering national economy, fan purchases would match the total price tag, $750,000.

Rockne remained optimistic. At the end of the season, he pronounced, "It will be great next year playing in our own stadium." He also sent a special "Holiday Greeting" to his friend and supporter Grantland Rice: "Merry Christmas to you and yours."

Thus the 1920s concluded for two of its most famous personalities. Neither realized that the end of the decade marked the finish of an amazingly prosperous period in American sports, later called "The Golden Age," and in the country's history. Rockne never coached again in New York—the "Gipper" contest had been his final game there—and the Notre Dame–Army circus of 1929 was the last great New York sports party of the Roaring Twenties. When the teams next met in that city two years later—they played the 1930 game in Chicago—they encountered a New York and an America well into the Great Depression.

28

Rockne's Last and
Greatest Rocket: 1930

Reverend and Dear Father [O'Donnell] . . .

[My novel, *Huddle*] is not yet sold [to a film company] but I believe it
now has a very good chance, depending perhaps on my securing your
consent to use the University. . . . [it is] a story of Notre Dame with
the physical background and traditions of the university woven into
it. . . . whether we like it or not, Notre Dame *is* identified with football; we know there is nothing to apologize for; the opportunity is here to
show the general public that there is a University there.

I have not been able to get in touch with Mr. Rockne but if he cares
to, he can pick up a year's salary, possibly, for doing little more than
lending his presence [to the film] for two weeks. . . .

Sincerely and with many thanks for your consideration [in this mat-
ter], I remain,

Frank Wallace

—Letter to President O'Donnell, July 15, 1930

In 1930, a number of Hollywood companies wanted to make movies
featuring Notre Dame football. One proposed a sentimental sports-and-
love-story, *Toplitzky of Notre Dame,* and after the newspapers reported
President O'Donnell's displeasure with the idea, the Carnegie Foundation congratulated him for his public stance that "Notre Dame desires to
be known primarily for scholarship and research," not football.

When O'Donnell received Wallace's proposal for a Hollywood version

323

of *Huddle,* the president wrote to Howard Savage of the Carnegie Foundation asking his advice on the matter. The reformer acknowledged that Wallace's project has the virtue of giving "you, as it should, the powers of a censor, and shows due respect for your functions as the guardian of the University's good name," but he advised that even if the movie were shot on campus "the University's name does not appear in the film."

O'Donnell replied, "I quite agree with your judgment," and informed Wallace of N.D.'s position, adding: "Mr. Rockne is convinced he should not personally appear in the film. His convictions are based on principle and not to be shaken." O'Donnell did not define the N.D. coach's "principle" but, considering Rockne's dislike of Wallace's portrayal of him in the book, undoubtedly he did not want to see that portrait on the screen. Although his protégé knew how to tempt him, in 1930 his outside income was excellent and his desire for a wholesome public image—as opposed to the cynical coach in *Huddle*—was strong. As O'Donnell wrote Wallace, "If, then, this picture is to be made at Notre Dame, Mr. Rockne must be counted out of it altogether." Without the famous coach's participation, and with the Golden Dome's restrictions, the film project died.

Throughout 1930, Rockne's dealings with President O'Donnell were fairly amicable. Construction on the stadium proceeded well and the administrator approved the coach's usual projects, such as his summer coaching schools on campus, even agreeing that "the University will receive 25% of [N.D.] tuition fees" from these courses, with Rockne keeping 75 percent.

They also agreed on a temporary change of venue for the Army annual. Both were exasperated with the antics of the New York alums and felt that removing the contest from that city for a year would show the New Yorkers, in a most emphatic way, who controlled Fighting Irish football and who was in charge of tickets. A few weeks after the 1929 game, Rockne wrote a friend in Philadelphia: "We are interested in getting some other place to play besides New York City and your dope on the Municipal Stadium [in Philadelphia] is received with much interest."

West Point owed N.D. a favor for continuing the series when other schools, particularly the Naval Academy, had dropped Army from their schedules, thus the Kaydets agreed to a one-year move. Philadelphia proved impractical because the Fighting Irish had already scheduled a game against Penn there for 1930, but Notre Dame had no games planned for Chicago's Soldier Field and the schools agreed on that site.

Even with the move, the New York alums proved indefatigable and incorrigible; they turned their attention to the Penn contest at Franklin Field in Philadelphia. One of their officials wrote N.D. ticket manager Art Haley that because this was "the only game that we have in the East this year . . . we are of the opinion here in New York that we could possibly dispose of 10,000 tickets." Thus, "we contemplate notifying our alumni here that we have the tickets and *they could purchase them through us.* . . . This would relieve you and your office of a great deal of work."

Beneath this apparently kind offer lay the New York alums' attempt to acquire a huge block of Notre Dame football seats and to dispose of them as they wished, at whatever price they wanted to charge—often well above face value. The New Yorkers must have thought that the men in Indiana were "rubes," but the N.D. administrators did not fall for the scheme. Haley informed the New York Notre Dame Club: "The football committee here permits only the purchase of tickets *through this office by regular application blank,* and we will be pleased to send you a number of application blanks if you so desire."

Vice President Michael Mulcaire, a smart young economist, chaired the football committee, and he not only wanted to control the tickets but also Rockne's athletic department spending. Unlike his polite predecessors in the vice president's office, Mulcaire was blunt and hot-tempered. Inevitably, he clashed with the coach over financial matters. One member of the 1930 faculty athletic board related how Rockne wished to buy a $10,000 tarpaulin for his new football field. Mulcaire vetoed the idea, stating, "Our projected football budget is far over the top now. We simply don't have the money."

Rockne, however, decided on an end run and purchased the tarpaulin, paying for it out of athletic department miscellaneous funds. In a similar way, according to Scrapiron Young, the N.D. coach brought him back to Notre Dame as a full-time trainer over Mulcaire's objections and "for two years, I was the high-salaried guy who was paid from the petty cash fund."

Rockne told Clarence Manion, longtime Dean of the Law School and a fervent supporter of Fighting Irish football, that "the criticism by board members was nothing more than calloused ingratitude on the part of the stuffed shirts for what he was sincerely trying to accomplish for the university." Within the value system of big-time college sports, the N.D. coach was correct. He knew that for the Catholic school to continue to win in college football, it needed the latest weapons in the "Athletics

Arms Race" and he never stopped trying to acquire them. The faculty men, however, did not share the N.D. coach's values and they again attempted to bring athletic department spending more in line with academic expenditures—for example, they pointed out that, in 1929, Rockne had paid $15,400 for football uniforms, a sum equal to the N.D. library's budget for book acquisitions.

Because of the huge amount of football receipts, Rockne could quietly move large sums of money around, and in this way he also obtained what he wanted for Notre Dame Stadium. When Scrapiron Young saw his new quarters, he raved about "a training room of such elegance as to dazzle the eyes. Embracing the last word in modern training equipment, it was a far cry from the insignificant thing of six years previous" when he first arrived at Notre Dame as a student. With the new stadium, Rockne had committed N.D. to big-time college football and the school could not easily return to the more casual days at Cartier Field.

■　■　■

> "St. Louis [University], however, was like all Jesuit schools. You have a president who wants to build a good sports program, and then they switch every so often and get a new one who doesn't like football, everything that was built could be torn down in a hurry. You never know where you stand with Jesuits."
>
> —Hunk Anderson in his memoirs

In 1930, Rockne's former assistant confronted a new president at Saint Louis University who "indicated that he would scuttle the sports program which I had just begun to build." Anderson wanted out and was willing to return to his assistant's job at N.D. Thus, when Loyola of Los Angeles, a Jesuit school building up intercollegiate athletics, hired Tom Lieb as its new head coach, Rockne brought Hunk back. These personnel moves became crucial for Notre Dame a year later upon Rockne's death: Lieb, his best assistant and potentially best successor, had departed—and President O'Donnell would not ask him to break his three-year contract with a fellow Catholic school to return—and the N.D. coaching job went to Hunk, an excellent line coach but a poor head man. As one N.D. grad of this era remarked, "The Jesuits giveth and the Jebbies taketh away. It's the *giveth* that you have to worry about."

In 1930, because of concerns about Rockne's health and a recurrence of his crippling phlebitis, the N.D. administration reluctantly agreed to hire other full-time assistant coaches: Jack Chevigny, one of the heroes of the "Gipper" game, for the backfield; "Ike" Voedisch for the ends; and

"Manny" Vezie and Bill Jones for the freshman team. Rockne finally achieved the full complement of assistants that his Big Ten rivals possessed and, like his fellow program heads, he maintained a personal distance from his assistants. "Manny" Vezie later remarked, "I do not pretend to know Rock outside of the football field for, as you know, my only association [with him] was on the field itself."

The assistants worked hard for their money—Hunk earned $8,500, double the salary of the highest paid N.D. professor at the time—and had to supervise over three hundred players in varsity, reserve team, and freshman practices. Rockne's massive recruiting system continued, although Art Haley was increasingly in charge of job allocation. Even old Rockne pals dealt with Haley; one Washington State "bird dog" sent future All-American Tommy Yarr to N.D., and when his recruit became a starter in 1930, wrote Haley, "I feel like a very proud father already."

Other prominent alums also helped out. Frank Hering put up $280 in cash to be "awarded for proficiency in spring football," and Rockne maintained his on- and off-campus jobs program, with N.D. officials doing much of the paperwork. In early 1930, concerning spring semester jobs, one of them wrote the coach, "I have taken care of most of the boys you mentioned in your letters," and during the summer of 1930, he informed players about their fall work positions.

Summer job placement also continued. Frank Leahy, a senior in 1930, related how he "worked for Hugh Mulligan, head of the Chicago Asbestos Workers' Union, for $70 a week, an enormous sum for the time and . . . only the ten Notre Dame players on the job were paid so handsomely. The athletes were [also] encouraged to open bank accounts with the understanding that a prize will go to the man who has the largest balance at the end of summer." Leahy won "the extra $150." Then, in the fall of 1930, he solicited ads for the N.D. game programs.

Frank Leahy needed the cash. From extremely poor circumstances in North Dakota, he had arrived at N.D. in 1927 as a result of the old "bird dog" system but with almost no money. He was afraid to approach Rockne to "help him out," but a family friend and former Rockne player, Earl Walsh, explained the young man's "financial condition" to the coach. Rockne thanked Walsh for writing, "otherwise I should not have known his [Leahy's] situation so thoroughly—you may rest assured that I will help the boy all I can." And he did, providing Leahy with better and more lucrative jobs as the player worked his way up the Fighting Irish depth chart and also proved himself to be a dedicated football man.

Unfortunately for his on-field career, Leahy suffered frequent injuries—and insisted on playing even with broken bones—but he gained much more from his student years at N.D. than glory on the gridiron. As his biographer explained, Frank Leahy "was part of a growing number of young men who had come to a university with the idea of majoring in a sport," and the future head man admitted, "there was only one thought in my mind, I wanted to learn all I could from the great master, Knute Rockne, so that someday I could coach."

Because of the severity of one of Leahy's injuries, Rockne took him to the Mayo Clinic, and he also made him a student assistant coach in his senior year. For Frank Leahy, Rockne "became my patron saint." While the younger man had the opportunity of actually knowing the great coach, for many Americans who never met him, Knute Rockne also became a kind of patron saint. A key document in this secular canonization appeared in 1930—the *Collier's* edition of the coach's autobiography and the basis of the film *Knute Rockne—All American.*

Dear Knute:
   The Mentor, one of the Crowell monthly magazines, wants an article to be signed by you on football; not the technical side but the human side of the game.
   With your consent I can prepare this from material of yours with which I'm acquainted, including one of your books.
   The Mentor is willing to pay you an honorarium of $200, and, of course, the matter, being yours, will be submitted for O.K. by you.
   Can you kindly give your consent?

Cordially,

John B. Kennedy

—Letter to Rockne, July 3, 1929

Kennedy was a professional writer of fiction as well as nonfiction and an associate editor of Crowell's flagship magazine, *Collier's: The National Weekly.* He had met the N.D. coach in New York on a number of occasions but, in using the "Dear Knute" salutation, showed that he did not know Rockne or his work well—only the coach's family and a few older C.S.C. priests addressed him in that manner; all of his friends and colleagues called him "Rock."

The coach replied, "Regarding the article on football . . . it is entirely o.k. with me so go ahead and do your darndest." A few weeks later, the ghostwriter sent the manuscript and noted, "we believe you can accept [it] with very few changes. It covers many things I have heard you say, and some you have written, and for the rest it is simply an historical sketch."

Rockne subsequently approved "the article which you wrote and which I think is a dandy." Kennedy's essay was approximately five thousand words—the vast majority of it the ghostwriter's "historical" sketch. The coach suggested one minor factual insertion; Kennedy made the change and forwarded a check in payment for the magazine's use of the coach's byline.

The article, "Football—A Man's Game," appeared in *The Mentor* of November 12, 1929, signed by Knute K. Rockne and without a hint as to its real authorship. In polished prose, with much inaccurate information about football's ancient origins, the ghostwriter concocted a noble lineage for big-time college football and its coaches.

In 1929, Kennedy continued to correspond with Rockne and the next year played a crucial part in the series of magazine pieces for *Collier's* that became the *Autobiography of Knute K. Rockne*. Unfortunately, their 1930 letters are lost, but contemporary witnesses supply accounts of Kennedy's work for the N.D. coach and internal analysis of the *Collier's* pieces provides further insight. Then, after Bobbs-Merrill brought out the *Autobiography* in book form in 1931, the ghost reappeared:

> "Mr. Kennedy of *Collier's* has written in about the complete absence of credit to him for his help on the autobiographical material . . . we [Bobbs-Merrill] have never understood that Kennedy's contribution was more than a rather technical advice of the preparation of the material. It would seem from his letter that he feels he had a real part in the writing of the material. I have already written Mrs. Rockne about this."
>
> —A. H. Hepburn, senior editor, Bobbs-Merrill,
> to Father John W. Cavanaugh, October 19, 1931

The former president of Notre Dame contributed an introduction and postscript for the 1931 *Autobiography* and had helped the widow, Bonnie Rockne, prepare her short introduction to the book. All of Bobbs-Merrill's correspondence and contracts with her were based on the premise that her husband was the sole author of the *Collier's* articles. With the book in the stores and the publisher in a legally vulnerable position, the company tried to ascertain the truth, but the widow was not forthcoming. Hepburn, the senior editor, noted a few weeks later, "Mrs. Rockne seems to be a very elusive lady. She replies to none of our letters."

John B. Kennedy, however, pressed his case with Bobbs-Merrill,

Hepburn informing Cavanaugh, "We have since had another letter from Mr. Kennedy in which he assures us that he really did write the Rockne [memoir]." Bonnie refused to comment and, finally, the editor alerted the former N.D. president, "It now seems clear that on future editions of THE AUTOBIOGRAPHY we will have to, in some manner, give credit to Mr. Kennedy for his share of the work . . . in the next week or so, send me text for a notice that can be placed on the title page. You may wish to confer with Mrs. Rockne about the matter."

Cavanaugh, known in his time as a hard-nosed administrator, disliked Bobbs-Merrill's solution, writing Hepburn, "*Collier's* sold the public this copy [of the autobiography] as Knute K. Rockne's own writing. The public bought it believing it was Rockne's own stuff . . . even though all the contention of Mr. Kennedy be correct, the *Collier's* people have made it impossible for anyone to make the acknowledgment suggested in the forthcoming edition. . . . If the announcement goes as suggested it will be a loud shout to the public that *Collier's* does funny things." Moreover, "most publishers under these circumstances, and assuming that everything that Kennedy says is true, would remain clamorously silent."

For Father John W. Cavanaugh and Bonnie Rockne, acknowledgment of a ghostwriter was totally contrary to the "Saint Knute" version of the coach's life that they wanted to erect, particularly the widow's insistence on portraying her husband as a "scholar" as well as a football coach. In the end, Bobbs-Merrill rendered the issue moot by declining to bring out a second edition. As for John B. Kennedy, a young writer making his way in a very competitive field at the beginning of the Great Depression, he decided not to "make waves" and quietly moved on to other projects.

> "In his autobiography Rock has himself exclaiming [circa 1910]: 'Who ever heard of Notre Dame? They never won a football game in their lives.' Actually Notre Dame had gone undefeated the previous year (1909) and one of its victories, over Fielding Yost and mighty Michigan, had shocked the Midwest [and Knute Rockne] and begun an athletic quarrel . . . which Rockne himself was to keep at a stir [by mocking Yost's 1909 loss for the rest of his life]."
>
> —Francis Wallace on
> the *Autobiography of Knute K. Rockne*

This obvious mistake and others in the text occurred as a result of the N.D. coach's circumstances in 1930 when his autobiography was written. Throughout the year he was exceptionally busy, juggling at least five full-time jobs—supervisor of stadium construction, N.D. athletic director,

N.D. football coach, Studebaker sales lecturer, and business entrepreneur. Moreover, as America's most famous sports coach, he dealt constantly with many people seeking a piece of his glory. But he had not totally recovered from his phlebitis and often felt ill.

In the early years of his coaching career, Rockne vetted all articles on football emanating from Notre Dame; a decade and enormous national acclaim later, he could no longer perform this chore. In 1930, when the *Official [Notre Dame] Football Review*, written by N.D. students, jeered at and upset some Chicago sportswriters, Arthur Haley reminded the coach that because of time constraints as well as "your illness the past season you did not get to censor the book before publication."

Nevertheless, according to sportswriter Edward Burns, when *Collier's* offered Rockne "twelve grand for eight magazine articles," he could not resist. Part of the inducement was the assignment of John B. Kennedy to the project to perform the same function as he had with *The Mentor* article. Neither *Collier's*, the ghostwriter, nor the N.D. coach saw the deal as anything more than a series of quick articles for cash; certainly no one anticipated that Rockne would die the following year and that the casual pieces would come to be regarded as a sacred last testament, with the 1931 *Autobiography* replicating the *Collier's* text—and mistakes—almost word for word and the Hollywood film reproducing the errors for future generations of Americans.

Internal evidence, as well as Kennedy's assertions, indicates that the ghostwriter composed most of the text and thus made many of the factual errors. In preparation for writing, Kennedy researched the coach's printed writings as well as articles about him. He also visited Notre Dame and, according to former president Cavanaugh, the writer and the coach spent time "talking over incidents and episodes" in Rockne's life.

Back in New York, Kennedy shaped the material for dramatic emphasis, adding fictional elements of his own creation, and wrote a draft. Then, as with the *Mentor* piece, he sent sections of the completed manuscript—it appeared in *Collier's* over a two-month period—to the coach for his approval.

The ghostwriter worked fast and on deadline and did not spend much time fact-checking previous sections or even current ones—it was up to Rockne to catch the errors. Moreover, because the proofreading schedule for these articles paralleled the one for the *Mentor* piece, Kennedy started sending manuscript sections to Rockne at the beginning of fall football practice and continued for the next month or so—the busiest time of year for the N.D. coach.

This piecemeal approach resulted in many factual mistakes; for example, the description of the "Win One for the Gipper" speech and the blunder on Jack Chevigny scoring the winning touchdown appeared in the article "Gipp the Great," November 22, 1930. However, in an earlier essay in the series, "Tuning Up the Team," November 8, 1930, the narrator described Johnny "One Play" O'Brien's work in the famous game and the actual winning TD in detail as "a shining example of unselfish effort for the team." Obviously Rockne proofread some parts of the manuscript more carefully than others and suggested a number of editorial changes; ironically, he did a particularly sloppy job on what became the single most famous page of the autobiography—the "Win One for the Gipper" passages.

Thus, as discussed previously, because the evidence clearly indicates that George Gipp did not make this speech on his deathbed in 1920 and that Rockne uttered a very different version in the locker room during the 1928 Army game, *the authorship of the most quoted request in American sports history belongs to John B. Kennedy.*

Considering how the ghostwriter and the coach worked, the inaccuracies and contradictions in the text become understandable, even inevitable. Less explicable are the passages that falsify Rockne's beliefs; for example, "From the beginning of my coaching career, with whatever faults I brought to my profession, I at least had intelligence enough to recognize that the faculty must run the institution. The school is their school, and the coach must bear in mind that his is an extra-curricular activity like glee clubs, debating societies, campus politics, publications and so forth." Possibly Kennedy wanted to present the N.D. coach on the reformist side of the "overemphasis" debate and Rockne overlooked these lines and similar ones or went along with them to soften his anti-reform image. But, as hundreds of personal letters and public utterances during his career reveal, he certainly did not endorse faculty sovereignty over his athletic program nor consider intercollegiate football just another extracurricular activity!

The above quote segued into one of the most famous passages in the *Autobiography*, repeated in the coach's speech at the end of the Hollywood biopic: "If a player flunks in class, he's no good to the coach or the school, and the coach who goes around trying to fix it for athletes to be scholastically eligible when mentally they're not, is a plain, every day fool." In fact, Rockne fought to keep many of his starters scholastically eligible, and only the vigilance of the C.S.C. priests and lay faculty and

their obstinate desire to make Notre Dame a serious academic institution
kept him in check.

The final irony concerning these and many other passages in the
Autobiography is that they became a cornerstone of the Rockne legend
at Notre Dame and elsewhere. Held up as scripture to subsequent Fighting Irish coaches, his successors could not violate the master's creed—
even though the great man had neither written the words nor lived by
them. Notre Dame coaches up through Leahy, who knew the reality of
Rockne's career, chafed under the restrictions, but later generations of
N.D. coaches as well as the men in the Golden Dome accepted the
passages in the *Autobiography* as literal truths and tried to fulfill them.
Notre Dame has erected many memorials to Knute Rockne; possibly it
should build a small one to John B. Kennedy.

THE KING HAS A PALACE

With the completion of the magnificent Notre Dame Stadium, Knute
Rockne's teams, the royalty of football, now are housed in a manner to
which public opinion has forced them to become accustomed.

—Headline and article opening
in the *Notre Dame Alumnus*, September 1930

The most appropriate memorial to Knute Rockne was never named
after him. During the stadium construction, many N.D. students and
alumni as well as fans and sportswriters lobbied for the coach's name to
go over the front entrance. However, as longtime alumni director James
Armstrong explained, "Rockne requested that the new stadium be called
the Notre Dame Stadium, shutting off the natural efforts of admirers to
designate it in his honor." Whether through modesty or because he knew
that the N.D. administration opposed putting his name on the structure
—it suggested football overemphasis and glorification of coaches—he
squelched the "Rockne Stadium" campaign. After his death, to avoid
changing the title, Notre Dame officials invoked his injunction and decided to build another kind of memorial to him, one consistent with his
love of his school's athletic culture—a large intramural facility bearing his
name.

Even in difficult economic times, Notre Dame financed the structure by
selling all of the ten-year leases on the stadium boxes and prime seats.
The school put the sale over the top by promising the lessees the oppor-

tunity to buy the best seats for *all N.D. road games* for the next ten years. Nevertheless, the Depression began to affect the football gate receipts. The first game at Notre Dame Stadium took place on October 4, 1930, with the national champions hosting Southern Methodist, and only 14,751 fans came.

N.D. pulled out a 20–14 win in the final minutes and invited supporters to return for the "Stadium Dedication Game" against Navy the following Saturday. During the week, the N.D. ticket office received a different kind of complaint; one irate fan wrote, "Two people went in the auto with us to Notre Dame last Saturday who had no tickets for the game in advance, and they got seats on the 50 yard line," whereas the letter writer's seats in the N.D. rooting section, ordered by mail long in advance, were much worse.

Promoters, including some Notre Dame grads, advertised "Special Football Excursion Trains" from Chicago and for the Navy game helped boost the crowd to 40,593. This was far below the expected turnout, and the photographer hired by the athletic department to supply publicity photos of the event wrote Art Haley, "As per our agreement, we are fixing up the foreground so that it will appear like a full crowd in the stadium."

The ceremonies at the dedication were also an exercise in image building. Notre Dame publications extolled the school's glorious football past and elevated various gridiron heroes to "immortal" status, none more so than George Gipp—the N.D. community knew about Rockne's locker room talk at the 1928 Army game. One author in the *Notre Dame Alumnus* proclaimed Gipp, "the world's most perfect gridiron gentleman," and even President O'Donnell, in his dedicatory address, read a eulogy to the player by an anonymous student poet. With references to Gipp's deathbed conversion and the school's "spiritual guardian, Our Lady," the poet intoned, "You wore Her armor, battling in Her name, / What though you scarcely knew its august power," and concluded, "O Lady, you have taken our best . . . Be good to him."

Father O'Donnell, at Notre Dame during the Gipp years, knew the facts of the player's life, but he also believed that death could transform sordid reality into an uplifting spiritual tale. Thus he eulogized Gipp and, six months later, upon the death of Rockne, ignored the coach's less than perfect character and praised him as a secular saint.

■　■　■

"I have a creepy feeling about the Savoldi case. To me, and to other priests with whom I have discussed the case, it is as if Almighty God had laid his cards on the table to test our willingness to place [religious] principle above everything."

—Rev. John O'Hara, N.D. prefect of religion,
to President O'Donnell, November 11, 1930

Of all Notre Dame officials, Father O'Hara equated religious faith with winning football. A few weeks after the dedication of the new stadium, the hero of the 1930 season, Joe Savoldi, severely tested O'Hara's formulation. Outstanding the previous year, the big fullback led the N.D. attack in the opening victories of 1930 and was on his way to All-America honors. Then he filed for divorce—no one at N.D. even knew that he was married—in a South Bend court.

In this period at Notre Dame, and for many years after, the school did not allow married men in the undergraduate student body and, as a Catholic institution, has never condoned divorce. Savoldi had thus committed two offenses, and Francis Wallace pointed out a third: "Joe hadn't learned not to sue for divorce in the middle of the football season." The dilemma for Notre Dame was whether to ignore the star athlete's transgressions or enforce the school's disciplinary code and expel him.

The South Bend press so supported Fighting Irish football and so feared Rockne's displeasure that the reporters who discovered Savoldi's legal action tried to talk his lawyer into withdrawing it and their newspapers sat on the story. Finally, the N.D. authorities learned of the divorce petition and O'Hara outlined the school's options in his letter to O'Donnell: "If Savoldi is dismissed we will incur the enmity of our most embarrassing friends, the synthetic alumni (and God be praised if we can get rid of some of them!). If he is retained, we will disappoint a legion of Catholics, from the highest Cardinal to the lowest grave digger, who regard Notre Dame as a strong citadel of God's Kingdom on earth." Although O'Hara was one of Rockne's staunchest supporters and an advocate of big-time football, for him the solution was simple: dismiss Savoldi. "It looks to me as though the stage is set for a stand and a pronouncement on the sacredness of Catholic marriage, the sort of stage St. Paul would have longed for."

Rockne knew better than to argue with the C.S.C. priests on this issue. He instructed the press to publish the facts as well as the names of other married college players, including Southern Cal's star, Ernie Pinckert. He then called Savoldi to his office and suggested that he leave school before being expelled; in addition, according to a witness, the N.D. coach offered to help the athlete in any way that he could and wrote out a $1,500 personal check to start him in his postcollege life. (Savoldi soon signed a pro football contract, and within a year, in the NFL and particularly as a professional wrestler, began earning big money.)

The player's departure prompted newspaper headlines in many cities and a barrage of editorial comment. The national Catholic paper, *The Tablet,* praised the school's actions, declaring, "There are things greater than victory or success. Here is a fitting reply to those who speak of the over-emphasis of football." However, a laudatory editorial about N.D.'s actions in the *Pittsburgh Catholic* prompted a letter from a woman who inquired, "Perhaps Our Blessed Lady has more interest in the brave men and women who are facing [the] Depression with faith . . . and keeping their children in our parochial schools than in any football team."

Most sportswriters felt that Notre Dame had acted foolishly and had jeopardized the 1930 Fighting Irish national championship drive. Arch Ward in the *Chicago Tribune* also saw the incident as part of the ongoing struggle between Rockne and the faculty: "We can't help wondering if the faculty would have ruled similarly if the student involved had been less publicized?" Ward underestimated both N.D.'s adherence to principle—the authorities dismissed many unknown students for lesser religious offenses than Savoldi's—and the Catholic school's desire to have the Fighting Irish achieve football glory as an illustration of faith, not as an example of cynical pragmatism.

President O'Donnell, in a letter to a C.S.C. friend at another school, summed up the Notre Dame position in the Savoldi case: the course of action "was clear; there simply wasn't anything else to do [but dismiss] the poor boy." He added, "There has been no squawk from the coaches or the [other] boys themselves, nor from anybody except a few illiterates who write anonymous letters in lead pencil."

O'Donnell's final comment and O'Hara's views on the "synthetic alumni" reveal the administrators' contempt for rabid Notre Dame fans demanding that the team win at any cost. In this period, N.D. authorities began to make a clear distinction between "Fighting Irish football fanatics" and the "Notre Dame family," that is, the campus community and those alums and friends of the Catholic school concerned about its academic and religious development as well as its football team.

To know the Rockne of today and the Rockne of several years ago makes it easy to understand that he might be serious about abandoning the work that has had him in the headlines.

—Headline and comments in
the *Chicago Tribune,* October 17, 1930

Rockne had always coached by giving physical demonstrations of his offensive and defensive techniques and, in 1930, his chief frustration was his inability to teach football in this way. He had endured the restraints of 1929, but the following year, even with his phlebitis in abeyance, he could not move well: "Under such conditions, he doesn't think that he can do a team justice. That's why he thinks that he might have to give up [coaching]."

Nevertheless, the N.D. head still did most coaching tasks superbly. For the 1930 season, he assembled and supervised the training of three formidable units as well as multiple reserves and, as usual, he also lined up sympathetic referees. With Walter Eckersall deceased, Major Griffith assigned longtime Rockne favorites Frank Birch, Jay Wyatt, J. J. Lipp, and Fred Gardner to three or four N.D. games each, and he gave John Schommer—a Rockne request ever since his controversial game-deciding call in the 1927 USC contest—four plum assignments, including the Army annual. However, as the season unfolded, all the N.D. coach needed from the officials was for them to show up—his Fighting Irish breezed through the schedule.

For the N.D. stadium dedication game, they walloped a strong Navy team, 26–2, with Savoldi scoring three TDs (his divorce controversy broke a month later). The following week, in preparation for Carnegie Tech, the newspapers headlined "ROCKNE VIEWS GAME WITH USUAL ALARM," but even the visit of Judge Steffen's squad could not produce authentic worry. Rockne cited various injuries but a newspaper pointed out, "2 INJURIES CUT IRISH VARSITY TO A MERE 120 MEN." Before almost thirty thousand fans at home, the team rolled to a 21–6 victory, one writer noting that the starting backfield—"without a Son of Erin in it"— was "splendid."

For the next game, the Fighting Irish traveled to the University of Pittsburgh to inaugurate that school's new stadium. The structure cost $2 million—compared to N.D.'s $750,000—and, according to Francis Wallace, was a sad example of many college stadiums of the period, financed with "interest-hungry bonds which became concrete chaplets around the necks of the schools."

The fans in Pittsburgh watched N.D. score five touchdowns in twenty-five minutes and win 35–19. One reporter invoked the Notre Dame "echoes": "Eighteen years ago Notre Dame defeated Pittsburgh, 3 to 0. . . . This afternoon, for the first time since 1912, Notre Dame again met Pitt. . . ." By 1930, the Fighting Irish had accumulated enough history that invocations to the school's football past became increasingly common and, in subsequent years, gained great momentum.

The team returned home to play Indiana but the visit of the Big Ten squad produced only 11,113 spectators. Savoldi starred with two TDs and the Irish rolled up the Hoosiers, 27–0. A few days later, the low attendance at this contest and others in 1930 prompted the president of Purdue University, "after a careful study of this year's football activities in all parts of the country . . . [to] come to the pessimistic conclusion that public interest in our intercollegiate athletic contests has reached its peak and is receding . . . The time may be near when we may have to restrict intercollegiate athletic activities."

Nevertheless, a Fighting Irish road game in a large city was still a major attraction. The same newspaper page with the Purdue president's statement carried the headline "78,000 TO WATCH NOTRE DAME AND PENN PLAY TODAY" and the story of how the first contest between Notre Dame and the Ivy school would fill Philadelphia's huge Franklin Field. Not only were local fans interested but N.D.'s only appearance in the East that season drew large numbers of people from New York, including Mayor Jimmy Walker.

The Fighting Irish routed Penn 60–20, one of the highest totals recorded in a game between big-time college football teams in this period. All the members of the N.D. backfield scored, but the star of the day was Marty Brill with three TDs. The Jewish halfback, a native Philadelphian, particularly enjoyed the victory because he had started his college football career at Penn and, failing to gain a starting berth there, transferred to Notre Dame.

Grantland Rice later acknowledged, "The Notre Dame backfield which struck Pennsylvania . . . was the best all-around combination I ever saw." Frank Carideo was a superb triple-threat quarterback and Joe Savoldi was an agile and powerful fullback (both were popular with Italian-Americans and helped forge that ethnic group's link to N.D. football). Marty Brill was an excellent blocker and, as the Penn game proved, dangerous in the open field, scoring all of his TDs on long runs; Marchmont "Marchy" Schwartz was a quick and hard-to-tackle runner—Rockne described him as exceptionally "smart from the Jewish blood in him."

One Notre Dame alum of the period remarked, "This backfield should be more famous than the Four Horsemen—even Rock said they were a lot better—but the press would only go so far with a Fighting Irish backfield consisting of two Wops and two Hebes. Also the Italian and Jewish gangsters in Chicago and New York loved them and this embarrassed the priests. Of course, Savoldi also got himself expelled." That the unit did not stay intact for the whole season probably contributed most to their lack of fame, but the fact remains that, in an age of nicknames, neither Grantland Rice nor any other reporter gave one to this backfield and many writers seemed relieved by the Irishness of Savoldi's replacements, Larry "Moon" Mullins, Dan Hanley, and Paul "Bucky" O'Connor.

Savoldi's last appearance was against Penn, and Rockne considered Mullins an adequate sub for the next game, an easy 28–7 home win over Drake. The team was now 7–0 and, in spite of the worsening Depression, their fans and the public clamored for seats for the final road games against Northwestern, Army, and USC.

Because of the ticket demand for the match in Evanston, the president of Northwestern University suggested that the NU–Notre Dame game be transferred from Dyche Stadium to Soldier Field and that the extra gate receipts—at least $100,000—go to "poor relief." After much soul-searching at N.D., President O'Donnell and the faculty athletic board decided to make an exception to the school's policy of not involving the Fighting Irish in benefit games and agreed to the proposal. However, in one of the Big Ten's most vicious and counterproductive actions against the Catholic school, the conference faculty representatives invoked a little-known rule forbidding "transfer of a game from a home gridiron to a field within a radius of 100 miles of another Big Ten university"—in this case the University of Chicago—and refused to allow Northwestern to play the Fighting Irish at Soldier Field. The rule was intended to prevent a member school from hurting the home gate of another—however, Chicago was scheduled *at* Michigan on the day in question.

Midwestern newspapers condemned the Big Ten and, on game day, the *Chicago Tribune* pointed out that "only 48,000 persons have seats" in Evanston but "three times that number could have been sold [and Soldier Field filled]. Prices as high as $50 have been paid for good locations against a face value of $3 for the coveted pasteboard." Westbrook Pegler underlined the absurdity of the Big Ten's action: "Consequently, the ticket scalpers got the excess revenue and the destitute, who might have received some relief in their present jobless desperation, got nothing more satisfying than a fine example in the strict observance of the rules." In practical terms, according to one newspaper, "$100,000 could have fed 1,000 indigent families for half a year."

Part of the demand for tickets to the NU–Notre Dame game resulted from the quality of the teams. Northwestern entered the contest at 7–0 and had already clinched a share of the Big Ten title. But Rockne's very best edition of the Fighting Irish beat the Wildcats 14–0; Marchy Schwartz led the ground attack, and Frank Carideo, passing and kicking superbly, later proclaimed this "my greatest football game." In the Northwestern locker room afterward, coach Dick Hanley, a personal friend and rival of Rockne's, wept in frustration at the loss.

> There is certainly something wrong somewhere as the tickets [for the N.D.–Army game in Chicago] which you have sent me are nothing more than general admission and are certainly not worth $4.00 each. I consider it a rotten shame when every Chicago politician, bootlegger, gangster, and bartender can show you tickets on the forty or fifty yard line [at Soldier Field].
>
> This is not hearsay as this has occurred year after year [for games in Soldier Field]. I have come to the conclusion [that] being a Notre Dame alumnus means nothing at all when it comes to buying football tickets, otherwise it is a wonderful thing.
>
> Yours very truly,
>
> F. J. Oelerich
>
> —Letter to the "University of Notre Dame," November 19, 1930

The ticket demand for the first Army–Notre Dame game in the Midwest exceeded all expectations. In part, as an escape from the worsening Depression and an attempt to recapture the giddiness of the Roaring Twenties, the alumni of the schools, their friends, and the general public frantically sought good tickets; in addition, politicians and other notables insisted on large blocks of "well-located" seats. Rockne, according to one witness, "was denied deserved rest by the innumerable telegrams and telephone calls from an army of ticket seekers."

Art Haley, at N.D., received the brunt of the complaints from alums, especially the gripe, "Is this fair to send an alumnus such ducats . . . when I know non-alumni and politicians around Chicago [who] have tickets on the 30 to 40 yard line." Many politicos, notables, and scalpers obtained their "ducats" from the city officials in charge of Soldier Field—for important games, the South Park commissioners purchased at least fifteen thousand good seats at face value for private resale and distribution; Rockne never publicly disclosed this practice, probably because he did not want to upset his working relationship with the Chicago authorities, and Notre Dame silently endured the alums' abuse.

The day before the 1930 Army–N.D. contest, Haley predicted an all-time record crowd for a college football game of 125,000. Visiting sportswriter Paul Gallico, from the *New York Daily News*, remarked: "The pre-contest festivities [aided by liquor] bottles at five dollars a pint," were particularly uproarious, and "some of the furniture came out of the window of the Auditorium [Hotel, N.D. fan headquarters] about five a.m. this morning."

On game day, the air whooshed from the hoopla balloon. Not only did the 1930 Army–Notre Dame contest not break the attendance record, it reflected the gloom of the new era. Gallico began his coverage from the pressbox with, "It is cold, it is dark. It is alternating between a smoky drizzle and a pouring rain. Snow, muck, and straw lie banked around the field." The weather was so bad that the scalpers outside the stadium had to unload their tickets, by game time offering half of face value. Westbrook Pegler, in a description that caught the atmosphere of the Great Depression as well as Soldier Field that day, wrote, "The damp heavy air was foul with the breath of the railroad locomotives down in the cut and with the outpourings of the city chimneys. You didn't breathe it but bit off hunks of the atmosphere on this lake front and Fletcherized [vacuumed] it in."

The headline writer on Pegler's article was less literary: "RAIN AND SLUSH MAKE PLAYERS ALL LOOK ALIKE." Yet, over 100,000 spectators sat through the slow, often brutal game, watching the teams slog to a scoreless draw for over fifty minutes of play. Then suddenly Marchy Schwartz broke loose and, following his downfield blockers perfectly, scored on a fifty-four-yard run. Carideo made the PAT but, in the dying minutes, Army blocked a punt and recovered the ball in the N.D. end zone for a touchdown. The Army coaches debated whether to kick the tying PAT or to try a pass play—the choice of a hot-tempered young assistant. The head coach sent in the kicker, he missed, and Notre Dame won, 7–6. (The Army assistant, "Red" Blaik, later became the greatest football coach in West Point history and the bitter rival of N.D.'s Frank Leahy.)

The newspaper accounts of the game portray the event in dour terms. Paul Gallico complained, "never have I been quite so remote from a sporting event that I was supposed to be covering . . . all I saw were twenty-two figures, unrecognizable as human beings and certainly not to be identified with any particular institution, squirming about in the muck." In addition, as the *New York Times* reported: "MANY HURT IN CRUSH AFTER ARMY GAME"—after sitting in the terrible weather for three hours but staying until the final whistle, the crowd "pushed and jammed its way out of Soldier Field," causing many injuries, some people requiring hospitalization.

What began for Paul Gallico and others as a great party weekend in Chicago ended, as the title of his final article from that city recorded, in "THE RETREAT FROM MOSCOW." Even the Chicago river of booze ran dry— "what wasn't drunk up on Friday night was consumed during the game" —and the postgame parties were jittery and unpleasant.

The previous year's Army–Notre Dame game in New York had sparked that city's last bash of the 1920s; the 1930 events in Chicago started as an attempt to reignite the Twenties' spirit but ended as a reflection of the increasingly "Dirty Thirties."

No one suspected that this N.D.–Army game was Rockne's last. From the first encounter between the schools in 1913 on the plains above the Hudson, he had played a crucial part in molding the series into one of the great annual sporting events in America. At the conclusion of the Soldier Field game, he went to the Army locker room and chatted with the Kaydet coaches and players; he genuinely liked the military academy men and they, him. The following March, when West Pointers learned of his death in a plane crash, the Army head coach, Ralph Sasse, told his PAT kicker, "I can honestly say that I am glad you missed that kick. If you'd made it, Rock wouldn't have won his last Army game."

■ ■ ■

NOTRE DAME 11 FACES 19TH LABOR—WEARILY!
Compared with these 'Irish by Environment' kids, Hercules was just a bush leaguer. He had seven labors to perform. These lads have already completed eighteen [straight victories over two years] and, considerably battered, are making a cross-country journey in search of the most difficult of all.

—Headline and lead in Francis Wallace's article,
New York Daily News, December 2, 1930

To complete the 1930 schedule, the Fighting Irish traveled to Los Angeles to meet a powerful USC squad. The Notre Dame team and entourage, including some alumni who had rented railroad cars and sold packaged tours, headed for the West Coast in early December. Wallace noted, "The train is a complete, moving city. We have a bishop who says mass," a doctor, sportswriters, and even some wives and children.

For the N.D. coach, the only cloud in the western sky was the season-ending injury to fullback Larry "Moon" Mullins—Savoldi's main replacement—in the Army game. Behind Mullins on the depth chart was an inexperienced sophomore, Dan Hanley; instead of using him, Rockne decided to try an excellent second unit halfback, "Bucky" O'Connor, in the starting fullback slot. But the coach did not want to reveal his team's vulnerability at this position to the press and USC.

When the train stopped at Tucson and the Fighting Irish held a full practice at a local stadium in front of a large crowd as well as some Los Angeles sportswriters, Rockne pulled his last major deception. He had O'Connor pretend to be Hanley, wear his number, and work with the first unit; the coach praised "Hanley" to the press while the halfback tried to master his new role in the Fighting Irish offense. According to Chicago sportswriter Warren Brown, with the N.D. traveling party, Rockne's "gamble consisted in taking a chance that one of the company [present] might recognize O'Connor by sight rather than by number. None did."

When the team arrived in Los Angeles, "five thousand cheering alumni and team followers greeted the squad at the station" (AP). Notre Dame had sold its allotment of tickets over a month before and USC expected a full Coliseum. The California prosperity of the 1920s had ended but the region had not slipped into the same Depression as the rest of the country. That year in Los Angeles, the big football game was the Notre Dame–USC match.

The Trojans were strong and deep, accumulating 376 points in their first eight victories to their opponents' 32, running up scores against California, 74–0; UCLA, 52–0; and Stanford, 41–12. However, part of the Trojans' success resulted from the fact that their opponents, especially Cal-Berkeley, deemphasized football in the wake of the Carnegie report. During the season, the student newspaper at Berkeley accused USC of running a professional football franchise, and even though this embarrassed Southern Cal, it did not prompt school officials to change the Trojans' football recruiting and subsidization system.

More embarrassing to USC was Notre Dame's easy 27–0 victory over their team. Scoring the second touchdown on an eighty-yard run, while wearing his own number, was "Bucky" O'Connor. Eventually, Dan Hanley substituted for him and also racked up impressive yardage.

As in the past, a Rockne deception proved to be overkill, and some sportswriters resented it. Bill Henry of the *Los Angeles Times,* who had interviewed O'Connor in Tucson while the latter pretended to be Hanley, jibed, "It's a shame, a dirty shame, when a coach loses all his really good players and has to fall back on 'bums' like this fellow, Bucky O'Connor. Poor old Rockne . . . I presume that if Savoldi had been in there, instead of running 80 yards for a touchdown, he would not have stopped [until] this side of Santa Monica."

Notre Dame fans rejoiced at the victory, and a C.S.C. friend of President O'Donnell's, who had attended the game, wrote him, "After Notre Dame had made its third touchdown, an enthusiastic Irishman, a little the worse for a high-ball or two, rose in his place, took off his hat and thus saluted the gathering, 'Hey, you—Methodists! You may beat Al Smith, but you can't beat Notre Dame.' "

O'Donnell probably enjoyed this story but even more pleasing were the words of the popular West Coast "Radio Minister," the Reverend Robert Shuler. In a sermon on the Sunday after the game, Shuler condemned USC as "a great Methodist university that seems to have its mind bent [toward sin]. Their college humor magazine devotes half its space to jokes about gin and women." On the other hand, "Notre Dame has for years been known as the team that prays." Shuler implored Protestant institutions to take religion "as seriously as our Catholic schools take the teaching of Roman Catholicism" and, in this way, achieve N.D.'s success on the gridiron. Other Americans also made an equation between religion and winning football. When the Fighting Irish traveled home from the West Coast, in towns and cities along the route the local Catholic clergy, lay officials, and parochial school students turned out en masse at the railroad stations to hail the players and coaches. The Notre Dame alumni magazine began its feature on the 1930 team—proclaimed national champions after the USC win—with the quote "Gangway for God."

But the Fighting Irish also attracted increasing numbers of non-Catholic supporters. Like the most successful baseball team of the period, the New York Yankees, many sports fans loved Notre Dame's winning record and style, reporters later noting, "There's little doubt that [these were] this era's two most popular teams . . . And each team was led by the country's most dynamic personalities of the time—Babe Ruth and Knute Rockne."

The apotheosis for Rockne's Fighting Irish came when they arrived back in Chicago on December 10, 1930. The city gave them a huge ticker tape parade, decorating the route with blue-and-gold Notre Dame banners. One newspaper compared it to the "attention usually reserved for heroes back from the wars, [and] transatlantic flyers" like Charles Lindbergh. This amazing public reception—repeated later in the week in New York for Rockne—never occurred again in Notre Dame football history, even for the greatest triumphs and multiple national championships of the Leahy era.

After the tumultuous Chicago welcome, the team traveled to South Bend, where a crowd of at least twenty-five thousand greeted them. The entire university as well as a large percentage of the local population turned out, and businesses in South Bend closed for the afternoon. Various speakers praised the squad and also quoted the words of such national figures as Pop Warner—"The greatest team I have ever seen"— and "Chick" Meehan (NYU coach)—"The team is the greatest in football history."

After the train station festivities, Notre Dame students stayed in town and celebrated into the night. They roamed the streets and, among other activities, "cuffed about . . . a local bookmaker, who was reputed to have laid odds on [a] Southern California [victory]" (AP). They felt that this national championship—the only totally unanimous one of Rockne's career, seven different agencies proclaiming his Fighting Irish the "Number One" team—was the high-water mark in Notre Dame football history.

For all the celebration after the 1930 season, the final revenue caused a bit of concern in the Golden Dome. Income from football was $897,173 but athletic department costs had soared to approximately $347,000, including almost $42,700 for travel and $14,550 for uniforms. In addition, stadium and practice field expenses were close to $27,200. Nevertheless, Notre Dame made almost $540,000 from its football team in the first full year of the Great Depression—an amount far exceeding every other school's college sports profit.

Yet President O'Donnell worried. Even before the new stadium opened he had told a group of alumni, "Economically, a stadium means a tremendously increased overhead [for maintenance and upkeep], and it means an investment of $750,000 lying idle for all but four or five afternoons of the year. . . . It remains to be seen just how often in the course of a season a crowd of 57,700 will fill the stadium at Notre Dame. There is no question but that, from the mere financial point of view, building and operating a stadium is not the money-making scheme it is represented to be."

The 1930 home attendance was only 42 percent of capacity—146,849 seats went unsold. The financial profit came from the road games in major cities, but some economists predicted that as the Depression worsened and Americans had less money to buy essentials and *much less* disposable income, they would not purchase tickets to sporting events. After the 1930 season, the Carnegie Foundation reported significant decreases "in the gate receipts at football contests at twenty-five well-known universities, including Yale, Harvard, Princeton, the United States Military and Naval Academies."

Knute Rockne, however, remained optimistic. In an elaborate ceremony on the steps of New York's City Hall, he accepted the Erskine Award for the best team in college football and he predicted great days ahead for his sport. Named after and endowed by Albert Erskine, the head of Studebaker and the N.D. lay board of trustees, the award attempted to transcend all the other championship polls and establish the most comprehensive one in the country. Two hundred and sixty-one sportswriters received Erskine Award ballots and they overwhelmingly selected the Fighting Irish "Number One."

The award included a free Studebaker for the coach of the championship team. Rockne already owned a number of Studebakers but he was pleased to accept another. However, unbeknownst to the coach and the award donor, the 1930 ceremony marked "the most important Notre Dame moment" for this prize. The following spring Rockne died, and a few years later, Albert Erskine, after severe financial reverses, committed suicide and the award ended.

Rockne had already seen the shadow of death. During the summer of the previous year, one of his closest friends, Rupe Mills, had died in a tragic accident. Mills and Rockne were teammates and classmates at Notre Dame and close after graduation; "Rupe," along with Joe Byrne, Jr., and a few others, formed what the N.D. coach called "The Old Gang." The coach later wrote, "I have not been able to shake off the effect of poor Rupe's death. It has brought home more than anything that has ever happened the fact that we can't tell when the same thing is going to come to any of us."

29

The Death of Reform
and Rockne: 1931

Dear Father Charles [O'Donnell] . . .
I have some inside dope that the committee [of the North Central Accreditation Association] involved in the investigation [of midwestern college sports] is made up of some fanatics of the Ku Klux type or anti-athletics [fanatics] and will move heaven and earth to see athletics abolished in American colleges.

The men doing the investigating include Dr. [Howard] Savage of Oberlin, who is a rabid anti-athletic man; T. N. Metcalf of Iowa State, who is against athletics; and C. H. Whitten, the head of the Illinois State High School Association, who published some very anti–Notre Dame notes in his personal comments in his [Association's] own magazine last December. . . .

—Rockne's last posted letter
to President O'Donnell, March 10, 1931

In 1931, the Carnegie Foundation scheduled publication of an update on its work on intercollegiate athletics, and other educational groups, like the North Central Accreditation Association, wanted to institutionalize the reform process by establishing ongoing investigative committees. Heading the North Central effort was Dr. Howard Savage (the main author of the 1929 Carnegie report), and an intramural-minded athletic director, T. N. Metcalf (later, the A.D. at the University of Chicago when that school pulled out of Big Ten football). Rockne and other big-time

347

coaches continued to fight the reformers, and in his letter to President
O'Donnell, he invoked the usual bogeyman—"fanatics of the Ku Klux
type"—as well as C. H. Whitten, an Illinois official involved in an anti–
Notre Dame incident.

When, the previous December, the president of Loyola of Chicago
abolished his school's college football program because of its "lack of
educational value," Whitten publicly cheered, "Whenever Loyola is mentioned, it is likely to be thought of as an educational institution. This
certainly is not the case with Notre Dame."

Rockne was incensed, professionally and personally—one of his favorite "old boys," Roger Kiley, had coached Loyola throughout the
1920s. President O'Donnell also did not appreciate the gratuitous insult
to his school, writing a prominent N.D. alum, "I despair of getting the
average outsider to understand that the newspapers' picture of Notre
Dame football is not the campus reality. Football grows naturally out of
our mode of life, but the life is so much more important than the game."

Notre Dame officials worried that the 1931 Carnegie Foundation update
would again castigate the university. However, the new report—"Bulletin
26"—focused as much on the impact of the Depression on college sports
as on the need for reform. The *New York Times* headlined "[CARNEGIE
FOUNDATION] FINDS SPORT IN 'LEAN DAYS,' " "LACK OF INTEREST [IN BIG-TIME
FOOTBALL] BY PUBLIC AND STUDENTS NOTED," "FOUR OUT OF FIVE SCHOOLS FORCED
TO RETRENCH ON ATHLETICS—PARTICIPATION [IN INTRAMURALS] MORE GENERAL."

The Carnegie update presented financial information on the decline
in football gate receipts and the resulting cuts in many schools' intercollegiate athletic programs; for example, Purdue "abandoned" teams in ten
sports. In addition, the update noted: "Almost every current indication is
to the effect that the undergraduate is tiring of 'bigtime' athletics" and, if
interested in sports, preferred intramurals. However, Notre Dame was
an exception to this trend. The students loved their Fighting Irish and
big-time football and, unlike other schools discovering intramurals, N.D.
already had the largest program in the country in terms of percentage of
participants.

Most pleasing to the Catholic school, the 1931 Carnegie update actually praised it for a number of achievements: "The completion of the
Notre Dame stadium has already begun to diminish the number of football games played by its teams on alien fields," moreover, N.D. has resisted "post-season . . . irregular or extra" games and managed to

"increase intramural facilities"; in addition, "At Notre Dame, academic aspects of [athletic] eligibility have been rescrutinized . . . amounting practically to an increase in academic requirements" for athletes; also N.D. "has further restricted its basis for the award and compensation of jobs and work" to athletes.

Rockne had protested the latter restriction but because of the Depression the school had to spread its work positions among many more students, needy nonathletes as well as jocks. Nevertheless, the N.D. coach still had his unofficial job network on- and off-campus, and the administrators only gained full control of the work-for-athletes situation during the regimes of his successors.

The Carnegie Foundation update, however, did criticize Rockne, not by name but by profession. It reiterated the argument that major problems "will continue as long as the illusion continues that college sport belongs to coaches, writers, business groups, alumni, and the general public rather than to colleges." The reformers found the alliance between the press and the coaches "insidious" because the newspapers' self-proclaimed "vested right in intercollegiate football arises from the number of coaches who syndicate their views" in articles and columns. The press made money from the pieces by and about coaches as well as the "splashy" coverage of their teams—thus it shunned serious discussion of the problems in intercollegiate athletics. Then, sealing "the vicious circle," the papers provided the leading coaches—Rockne, Warner, et al —with an unobstructed platform to "praise the sport of football, reply to its detractors, real or imaginary, and strive to assure the public that 'all's well with the game' *upon which their livelihood depends.*"

As in its earlier studies, the Carnegie Foundation's main complaint concerned the commercialism of intercollegiate athletics and the contradiction of huge sports businesses operating within serious academic environments. But the update contained a surprisingly optimistic conclusion —the Depression would end the commercialism: "The deflation of American football has begun . . . the poverty that results from a decline in football gate receipts will lighten parts of the task of those who administer college athletics [that is, faculty and presidents]. The return to a more sincere appreciation of the values of sport and sportsmanship [as opposed to mass spectatorship] is under way."

This ended the Carnegie Foundation's attempt to reform college sports; it fired a few brief volleys later in the 1930s, one aimed at N.D., but "Bulletin 26" was its last substantial effort. Rather than continue the investigations, reports, and proposals, as well as the pressure on specific schools and conferences to reform, the educational mandarins retired from the field, hoping that the Great Depression would do their work for them.

In the history of American intercollegiate athletics, reformers have launched many cleanup campaigns, and in all cases, the college sports establishment has fought back, never willing to yield a millimeter and always adept at "damage control." Of all the reform movements, the one begun by the Carnegie Foundation in the 1920s came closest to attaining critical mass and, combined with the Great Depression, might have permanently changed the nature of American intercollegiate athletics. However, in an amazing display of lassitude and laissez-faire, in 1931, at a crucial moment in its campaign, rather than press on, the Carnegie reformers exited and most of their followers, like the North Central Association, became discouraged and also withdrew. (Later reform efforts, particularly those led by the American Council on Education in the 1950s and the NCAA Presidents' Commission and the Knight Commission in the late 1980s, again forced the college athletic establishment into a "damage control" mode but, like the Carnegie Foundation attempt, failed to bring fundamental changes to college sports.)

Without an organized opposition, big-time college sports, albeit in slimmed-down form, survived the Depression and World War II; subsequently, it grew more immense and powerful than even its most optimistic proponents, like Knute Rockne, had dreamed.

■ ■ ■

"Back in 1930, Christy Walsh [Rockne's agent] had obtained Knute Rockne's consent to make a moving picture in which he was to play an actual role on the screen. The various elements which were to go into this feature [film] had been incorporated into a contract. This contract was to be signed on a certain day. In order to keep that engagement, Knute Rockne took off on the airplane trip which proved fatal."

—*Notre Dame Alumnus,* October 1931

The N.D. coach's last days were typical of his life—frenetic activity, entrepreneurial pursuits, and disputes with officials at Notre Dame. He argued with the faculty athletic board and its chair, Father Mulcaire, about whether to renew the contract for the USC series; the vice president objected because the game involved "too much train travel," and Rockne countered, "I see the day coming when most college teams will be going by air exclusively. As a matter of fact, I'm flying to Los Angeles next week."

First, he went to Florida to visit his wife and youngest son, vacationing there, then he returned to Notre Dame for a day. In previous years, the N.D. administration had tolerated his long winter absences to travel to the Mayo Clinic for treatment, to Florida for recuperation, and to lecture for Studebaker, but by 1931, with his health improved, his inattentiveness to his duties was much less acceptable. Thus, in his last day at Notre Dame, Rockne tried to see Father O'Donnell to justify his impending trip to Hollywood. The N.D. president was unavailable and the coach left a copy of the Universal Pictures' contract and a note on O'Donnell's desk: "They have offered me fifty thousand ($50,000) dollars for this proposition, *which, however, doesn't interest me at all*. . . . Please wire me collect at the Hotel Biltmore, Los Angeles, where I will be Wednesday."

Rockne's comments prompt a question—why travel so far to inform the movie executives of a complete lack of interest in their project? However, the N.D. coach, a master strategist, added in his note to O'Donnell—"The only thing is I thought perhaps there might be a chance to put out a picture that might be instructive and educational as regards Notre Dame in every sense of the word." Rockne knew that the N.D. president would approve of this explanation and feel much more positive about the trip than if the coach appeared to be leaving on another of his private money-making ventures. In any event, O'Donnell was not available to respond and the coach left campus.

> "[Rockne often said] 'I like to travel by air. With a good plane and a good pilot, it's as safe as any other method. . . .'
>
> An additional impelling factor [in his decision to fly] was that he got a thrill out of the speed at which he cut over the country in the air. He was forever buttonholing his friends to tell them how fast he had made a run to Miami to visit his wife and daughter, to Atlanta on business, and elsewhere."
>
> —Delos Lovelace in *Rockne of Notre Dame*

After leaving Notre Dame, Rockne had dinner in Chicago and then went by train to Kansas City to see his two eldest sons, attending a prep school there. After visiting them, he boarded a small plane scheduled to hop-skip across the western states and end its run in Los Angeles. Commercial air travel was in its infancy but the N.D. coach, who loved speed on the gridiron and in other aspects of life, wanted to reach California as soon as possible.

In western Kansas, with ice collecting on the wings, the pilot lost control and the aircraft went down. A number of farmers and ranchers heard the crash and rushed to the wreckage, where they discovered the corpses of all eight passengers and crew, most of the bodies mangled beyond recognition.

Within an hour, the airline company released the news that the famous coach was on the downed plane. Radio reports prompted scavengers to hurry to the scene, and the AP later headlined "MOST OF SHIP CARRIED AWAY FOR SOUVENIRS." Also arriving from his ranch in Sitka, Kansas, was Jesse Harper, shaken by the death of his forty-three-year-old protégé. William Allen White, the famous editor of the *Emporia* (Kansas) *Gazette,* described the crash site: "An endless stream of curiosity seekers trudging from their motor cars along the road. Miraculously there had been no fire. So died the great Viking of football, on a hill overlooking a prairie, at the crossroads of the old forgotten stage road and the new highway of the air."

> "Anybody who was old enough in 1931 to remember, can probably tell you just where and how he received the shock of Rockne's death."
>
> —John McCallum in *We Remember Rockne*

For many Americans, Knute Rockne's death was a riveting moment in their lives, analogous to the responses by later generations to the sudden deaths of John F. Kennedy, Martin Luther King, and Robert Kennedy. Beyond the "Gee-Whiz" curiosity and sympathy sparked by Rockne's being one of the first famous Americans to die in a commercial air crash, his passing seemed to mark an important historical boundary.

As the first of the great 1920s heroes to depart, his end dramatized for many people, in ways that economic statistics never could, the unalterable fact that the "good times" had expired. As a man who appeared to control his destiny and was the winningest coach in football history, his premature death signified defeat. Moreover, the demise of this apostle of optimism seemed to mock the national hopes for a brighter future and confirm the predictions of a dark and gloomy time.

Rockne had also touched numerous Americans, particularly those belonging to religious and ethnic minorities, in ways inaccessible to other 1920s heroes, and many persons treated his passing like the death of a family member. Thus the reaction to the news of the fatal accident was unprecedented.

In a pretelevision age, people flooded the switchboards of local newspapers with phone calls seeking information about the plane crash. After the first wave of inquiries, the telephone operators at the *Chicago Tribune* began answering every call, not with the name of the paper but "Yes, it's true about Rockne."

When national radio broadcasts and the afternoon papers confirmed his death, many people cried openly. The reaction at Notre Dame was shock and disbelief; former President John J. Cavanaugh noted that "the world went pale, trembled, almost wept. On the campus at Notre Dame, men with frozen faces looked hard into one another's eyes and passed by unspeaking."

The coach's old friend and an N.D. alum, Dr. Michael Nigro of Kansas City, had the unhappy task of assembling his remains and putting them in a casket. A later legend states that "when his body was recovered, his rosary was clasped tightly in his hand," however, neither eyewitnesses nor Dr. Nigro ever mentioned this. The Kansas City physician also brought the two eldest Rockne sons with him to the crash site and then shepherded them and the casket on the journey back to South Bend.

In Chicago, the funeral party had to go from the Dearborn Street terminus to the La Salle Street station and the train to South Bend. Almost ten thousand people crowded into the railroad terminals and many more stood in the streets en route; some hoped to catch a glimpse of the casket of the famous man, others wanted to pay homage to him. N.D. trustee Byron Kanaley wrote President O'Donnell, "I was at the station last night when the casket came in. It is a very sad affair, but I imagine that is the way he would like to have gone had he had a choice."

Kanaley's comment, stating his personal feelings as well as his interpretation of events, was a typical reaction to Rockne's death. Other responses ranged from private, specific memories to public, abstract pronouncements, from sincere condolences to hypocritical untruths, as well as a quotient of the semi-articulate and the bizarre.

Among the strictly personal reactions, Etta Eckersall, sister of the late journalist Walter Eckersall, wired the widow, Bonnie: "WITH HEARTFELT SYMPATHY. KNUTE AND MY BROTHER WALTER WERE WONDERFUL FRIENDS AND ARE NOW JOINED IN HEAVEN." Most of "Rock's Old Boys" also sent notes, including Joe Savoldi: "My deepest sympathy for the loss of one of my dearest friends." However, many persons who knew the coach well transmuted their private sentiments into an ideal Rockne for public consumption. Major John Griffith, Rockne's pal at the Big Ten commissioner's office, first telegraphed the widow, "I AM HOPING AND PRAYING THAT IT ISN'T TRUE," but subsequently announced, "Knute Rockne's death is a greater loss to society than to football. . . . His true worth to society will be recognized more and more as time goes on." Even Grantland Rice abandoned hyperbole in his initial wire and offered real sympathy: "I JUST WANTED YOU TO KNOW HOW DEEPLY I FEEL FOR YOU AND THE CHILDREN. I STILL CANNOT BELIEVE IT IS TRUE." But he later penned inflated doggerel to honor his friend: "O, spirit brighter than the flaming ship / That drove you downward on life's final trip," and so on.

Other responses, particularly from public figures who had never met the N.D. coach, were the authors' abstract projections of the meaning of his life. Herbert Hoover, president of the United States, proclaimed, "I know that every American grieves with you [the family]. Mr. Rockne so contributed to a cleanness and high purpose and sportsmanship in athletics that his passing is a national loss." In this era, United States presidents rarely encountered or commented on sports figures, especially those from Catholic schools, thus Hoover's remarks indicate the national impact of the coach's death.

The king of Norway extended his country's condolences, and various governors, senators, and lower ranking politicians added theirs. Famous athletes of the 1920s, who had shared the spotlight during the "Golden Age of Sports" with the N.D. coach, also telegraphed the widow: Babe Ruth, "IN YOUR GREAT SORROW YOU HAVE MY DEEPEST SYMPATHY"; Lou Gehrig, "MY HEARTFELT SYMPATHY IN YOUR GREAT SORROW"; and Jack Dempsey, "MY HEARTFELT SYMPATHY IN THIS YOUR HOUR OF GREAT SORROW."

More personal were the messages from fellow coaches, especially his friends in the profession. Lou Little, who had moved from Georgetown to Columbia with Rockne's blessing, wired: "I WISH THAT THERE WAS SOMETHING THAT WE COULD DO TO HELP YOU [BONNIE] IN YOUR HOUR OF SADNESS. THEY HAVE TAKEN OUR LEADER AWAY." And even players from opposing teams praised him: "HAVE PLAYED AGAINST YOUR HUSBAND'S TEAM AT GEORGIA TECH. THE WHITEST MAN THAT EVER LIVED. WE LOVED HIM DOWN HERE AT TECH. RAYMOND C. EUBANKS, ROME, GEORGIA."

After the immediate telegrams came the written tributes in the press. John Kieran in the *New York Times,* referring to the killing ground of

World War I, began his moving eulogy "In Artois and Picardy one soft phrase stood out in a hard war. 'Bill, he went West.' And yesterday Knute Rockne went West." Will Rogers, in his widely syndicated column, offered, "We thought it would take a President or a great public man's death to make a whole nation, regardless of age, race or creed shake their heads in real sorrow and say, 'Ain't it a shame he's gone?' Well, that's what this country did, Knute, for you. You died one of our national heroes."

Like Rogers, other writers described the national mourning caused by Rockne's death. A reporter in Youngstown, Ohio, noted that on the same day as the plane crash in Kansas, a massive earthquake hit Nicaragua, killing hundreds of people. However, the citizens of Youngstown were mainly concerned about the coach: "Newspapermen have an old maxim to the effect that the death of one local man means more to their readers than the death of a thousand Chinamen. . . . Rockne was not a Youngstown man, nevertheless he was such a national figure that the fatal accident brought genuine grief to hundreds of Youngstown homes."

This identification with the N.D. coach by ordinary Americans was the most striking aspect of the mourning prompted by his death. Many people identified with his immigrant roots, his humble childhood, and the individuality and uniqueness of his achievements. Unlike famous political, business, and professional leaders who had taken well-worn routes to prominence, Rockne had helped pioneer a new field—big-time college football—and was crucial in the invention of something unique—a national team, the Fighting Irish, with a national following. For many contemporaries, he embodied the American dream better than any other figure of his era: movie stars were remote and unreal, industrial giants like Henry Ford and Thomas Edison were cranky and idiosyncratic, and great athletes like Babe Ruth and Jack Dempsey were bound by their waning athletic skills. Knute Rockne, with his ordinary looks and manner, was both completely human and also at the top of his exceptional powers after two consecutive national championships.

Thus the most touching messages received by the widow and Notre Dame were from ordinary citizens and groups: the Norden Lodge, Sons of Norway, in Tacoma, Washington, "wept over the untimely death of a beloved" countryman; the B'Nai B'Rith of South Bend grieved for "our beloved friend 'Rock.'" Thousands of people sent such messages, others mailed scrapbooks dedicated to the coach and his Fighting Irish, and many persons sent poems of bereavement. The N.D. alumni magazine printed a selection, the editor commenting: "Geniuses, schoolboys, women, priests, and paupers appear in this corner of Rockne [tribute] verse. It is only indicative [of the] flood of verse." Predictably, most of the poems were extremely maudlin, but an occasional couplet glimpsed the coach's character: "Into the game [of life] he stormed his way, / And he molded the game to his need."

Similarly, most of the newspaper editorials about Rockne's life were treacle and could fill the obituary of any "Great Man," but a few editorialists transcended the elegiac genre. The *New York Herald-Tribune* had observed him throughout the 1920s and termed him: "A football genius, a coach who influenced the game more than Walter Camp, Glenn Warner, or any of those great strategists [because] Rockne was as great a promoter as he was a coach. He might have been a P. T. Barnum or a 'Tex' Rickard. . . . Lovers of the game are worried by its hippodroming features, its offensive ballyhoo, its commercialism, [but the N.D. coach] was everything to big-time football."

The editorialist at the *South Bend News-Times*, who knew him personally, supplied real insight: "Mr. Rockne's death was in keeping with his life. He was not bound by the confines of his job or geography. The whole earth was his apple and from it he took zestful bites . . . He died in flight before he had reached his zenith. Age and the pressing forward of competitors would have held him to the ground eventually. Rockne, a sad and broken man, was an impossible thought. He meant action and the continual clash."

The funeral occurred during Easter week and CBS Radio broadcast it to the nation. Many businesses around the country and almost all in the Saint Joseph Valley, the home area of Notre Dame, closed for the afternoon. Thousands of people lined the streets as the funeral cortege went to and from the Notre Dame church. Members of his current N.D. championship team served as pallbearers and some of his graduating class of 1914—Joe Byrne, Jr., Al Feeney, and Gus Dorais among them—formed the honor guard.

President O'Donnell conducted the service and behind him on the altar stood three former presidents of the university—Fathers Cavanaugh, Burns, and Walsh. Of all the words that Father Charles O'Donnell, the poet-president, ever wrote or spoke, his funeral sermon on this day became his best known and most repeated: "In this holy week of Christ's passion and death there has occurred a tragic event which accounts for our presence here today. Knute Rockne is dead. And who was he? Ask the President of the United States, who dispatched a personal message of tribute to his memory and comfort to his bereaved family. Ask the King of Norway, who sends a special delegation as his personal representatives to this solemn service." Then, after hailing the political, religious, academic, and journalistic delegations also in attendance, O'Donnell discussed the many ordinary Americans enthralled by Rockne, "whose death has struck with dismay." For all these people, high and low, the Notre Dame coach was special and unique.

Nowhere in O'Donnell's sermon is there a whisper of the many disagreements over the years between the coach and the Golden Dome. Not only would O'Donnell and the past presidents flanking him have felt that the mention of their difficulties with the deceased was inappropriate at this time but, most likely, grieving for a man with whom they had maintained long and ambiguous relationships, they preferred not to remember contentious past events at all. Similarly, O'Donnell did not touch on the aspects of Rockne's character that were less than sterling; instead he pictured the coach as a secular saint, "the true American character . . . an inspirer of young men in the direction of high ideals that were conspicuously exemplified in his own life."

This sermon articulated the Notre Dame position on the departed coach. James Armstrong, in the alumni magazine, offered his version: "Praise of Rockne forms a litany that brings a responsive *Requiescat* from the hearts of the world. Inspirer of youth, maker of men, apostle of sportsmanship—death has removed a character whose influence stretched far beyond his official sphere."

Others in the "Notre Dame family" put the coach's death within the context of the university's history. The bishop of Oklahoma, "an alumnus, albeit an honorary one," compared the deceased to Notre Dame's founder: "Rockne was Sorin without a cassock and breviary. Perhaps he did not pray as much as Sorin, but he knew he could rely on others making up the deficit." This comparison seems apt—both men possessed builder's visions as well as the obsessive determination and ability to turn their dreams to reality. Moreover, their visions built the University of Notre Dame and its most famous product, Fighting Irish football.

> "I read that youth has no idols nowadays. But they had one [Rockne] at Notre Dame."
>
> —Westbrook Pegler

"Football has lost its most colorful figure and outstanding coach."

—Fielding Yost

"I was impressed with his human qualities, his warm, generous, unselfish personality."

—Amos Alonzo Stagg

No doubt unwilling to swim against the high and rushing tide of public opinion, and also not wanting to speak badly about the dead, Rockne's former enemies—even Pegler, Yost, and Stagg—offered kind words to their fallen adversary. The University of Chicago coach did append his with the sly and accurate comment, "Rockne was always ready for the give-and-take of life—and willing to give more than he took." Yost's main complaints about the N.D. coach had always concerned recruiting and subsidization. From the Michigan man's point of view, with Rockne gone, possibly Notre Dame would change its procedures in these areas; at the minimum, Rockne's successors would never be as wily as the master nor would they have the professional clout and nerve to deride Yost's own cheating. Thus the Wolverine A.D. was generous in his bereavement statement—but he still refused to schedule a football game between his team and the Fighting Irish.

Westbrook Pegler had admired some of Rockne's qualities during his life, therefore this writer's omission of negatives was not difficult. However, for a number of other journalists, the embrace of the N.D. coach in death was a complete reversal. John Tunis, a leading critic of big-time college sports, had written scathingly about Rockne and the Fighting Irish for many years, referring to Notre Dame games as "great gladiatorial contests." In one particularly controversial column in the *New York Post,* he "wished that professional football would develop more rapidly in technique and popular appeal" so that the college game "could return to moderation" and "amateur status," unlike the version exemplified by Rockne's "Ramblers." Nevertheless, after the coach's death, Tunis wrote lovingly about him. This writer had once predicted that an adoring public would elevate the Notre Dame coach to "Saint Knute Rockne" status and, after the tragic accident, Tunis helped fulfill the prediction by incorporating a sanctified version of the coach into a number of his football novels for boys.

Bill Cunningham, the main sports columnist of the *Boston Post,* had also criticized Rockne and Notre Dame, once even suggesting—and receiving a flood of angry letters from N.D. fans as a result—that college football would greatly benefit if the Fighting Irish lost more often. He had also retailed such anti–N.D. slanders as "If he [Rockne] wants to ordain football practice at 10 a.m. he can, with all classes dismissed at his order." Upon the coach's death, Cunningham wrote: "The spontaneous and sincere expressions of sorrow from men in every walk of life should forever silence the criticism that [college] football is overemphasized . . . One man like Rockne means more to our country than a million reformers."

With the coach's critics either silent or joining his supporters, the result was hagiography. In 1931, a number of instant lives of "Saint Knute" appeared—most lifting anecdotes and "facts" from the coach's 1930 series in *Collier's*. These books tried to cash in on the national bereavement; the most adoring and commercially successful was Warren Brown's *Rockne*.

A veteran sportswriter and a graduate of San Francisco Catholic schools, Brown had covered the Fighting Irish for a number of years for the *Chicago Herald-Examiner*. His private letters to Rockne show that he knew the inside workings of the N.D. coach's operation, but his biography never revealed this knowledge. Instead, Brown stayed within the hagiographical genre and obtained a foreword from Father Charles O'Donnell.

The President of Notre Dame found Brown's work "a truthful portrait of the Rockne we knew, against a background accurately and sympathetically portrayed." O'Donnell would not deviate from the official line on the coach's life. His position was pragmatic; in his grief, he came to believe that Rockne had been a great man and of inestimable value to Notre Dame, thus, from his point of view, to speak ill of the coach—or even to portray him as he had been in life—served no purpose.

Later in the decade, during preliminary work on the film *Knute Rockne —All American,* the screenwriter mainly used four works to research the coach's life: the *Autobiography* from the *Collier's* series; the hagiographies by Warren Brown and Harry Stuhldreher; and the special issue of the *Notre Dame Alumnus* devoted to the death, funeral, and the public reaction. (The screenwriter relied most on the *Autobiography* and the *Alumnus*.)

The memorial issue of the alumni magazine not only contained O'Donnell's funeral oration but many other items that helped shape the official portrait of the N.D. coach. Christy Walsh contributed a piece entitled "Happy Landings." Rockne's agent, a master mythmaker, discussed the coach's last plane flight and let loose various legends, including: "You died . . . thinking of others, waiting for you in California." Walsh did not mention the film deal or that the "others" were executives at Universal Pictures—even though the agent immediately picked up the ball on the project and soon scored with it as *The Spirit of Notre Dame*, a sports potboiler exploiting the school's name.

In the same issue of the alumni magazine, James Armstrong, the editor, in detailing the chronology of the coach's last days, related: "The trip by air during which he was killed was to fill a speaking engagement 'because he did not want to let a friend down,'" with the quote unattributed. Again, not a hint of the proposition from Universal Pictures. These versions portrayed the coach's last actions as altruistic; no doubt the authors realized that the revelation of the $50,000 deal would render Rockne materialistic.

Nevertheless, the secular canonization of the coach was not instantaneous and the hagiographers struggled before they all read from the same page. In the October 1931 *Notre Dame Alumnus*, a non-bylined promotional article for the movie *The Spirit of Notre Dame* noted that Rockne had been on his way to Hollywood to sign the film contract when he died—though there was no mention of the $50,000. Probably this author assumed that the reference to the great coach's involvement in the project would help sell tickets to the movie. Eventually, the film *Knute Rockne—All American* sanctified the Walsh-Armstrong versions, setting in stone the coach's parting line, "I promised these fellows I'd come whenever they needed me."

The transformation of the reasons for the final trip is one small example of the massive rewriting of Knute Rockne's life that began shortly after his death. The motivations behind the campaign were complex: some revisionists acted out of grief, loss, even guilt; others embraced the sentimental tradition, the glorification of the dead, and the cultural impulse toward myth rather than reality; and many felt a need for a hero and/or a secular saint during a dark Depression.

Propelling and aiding the revisionists was the fact that the object of their attention could never contradict them. Rockne was gone, and although in his final years, he frequently polished his image, he never considered himself a candidate for sainthood and undoubtedly would have objected to secular canonization.

James Armstrong, in an editorial in the special memorial edition of the *Notre Dame Alumnus,* summed up the situation well:

> Knute Rockne, alive was mortal, subject to death, subject to error, as are we all.
>
> Dead, time is no longer an element. . . .
>
> He is unlimited by time and space, bonds that troubled his restless life. . . .
>
> With the fatal plane crash, crashed too those barriers which success inevitably builds about itself.

This last comment is a bit obscure. Did Armstrong mean that Rockne's success—and the demands on his time and energy resulting from it—had erected "barriers" between the coach and the "Notre Dame family," including the alumni, whom Armstrong represented? But death "crashed . . . those barriers" and detached Rockne from the "bonds" of his worldly concerns. Armstrong went on to proclaim that the coach now belonged to "each of us" because *"Knute Rockne can now be molded into that particular form which each of us may prefer."*

As if on cue, a horde of other writers created their own versions of Rockne but, unlike Armstrong, without any awareness that their "particular form" of the Notre Dame coach was exactly that—*their form, not his reality.* Moreover, using this special issue of the alumni magazine, many of these authors claimed the editor's favorite "forms" of the mythic Rockne as their own:

> *A man who believed in God.*
> *A humble man.*
> *A husband and a father.*
> *A scholar.*
> *A teacher.*
> *An advisor.*
> *Lover of boys.*
> *Idol of boys.*
> *Believer in clean living.*
> *Advocate of right thinking* . . .
>
> *To everyone—a friend.*

Thus, the flesh-and-blood Knute Rockne disappeared from public view. Fortunately, he was kept alive in the works of Francis Wallace as well as the occasional comments of a few others who knew him. And, through chance and an obligation to history, the University of Notre Dame preserved the bulk of his daily correspondence; his actual words can return to demolish the "barriers" that the mythmakers erected around him.

III

"Rally Sons
of Notre Dame"
1932–1941

30

In the Depression: 1931–1941

"In the past few days, disquieting rumors have reached us [at Notre Dame] regarding the stability of the major banks in Chicago . . . [specifically] that one of the big banks was on the point of collapse and that, fearful of possible riots, the city or State officials had already given orders to move the national guard in Chicago at a moment's notice. I give you this for what it is worth but I should like to know what, in your estimation, it is worth?"

—President Charles O'Donnell
to Chicago banker Byron Kanaley,
January 2, 1932

The head of Notre Dame sought Kanaley's opinion because, like most Americans in the early 1930s, Father O'Donnell feared putting money in a bank and suddenly discovering that the institution had collapsed, wiping out all deposits. He pointed out to Kanaley that Notre Dame placed most of its money in Chicago because, up to now, "we have felt comparatively safe" with the Illinois banks as opposed to the ones in South Bend. He was relieved to learn a few days later that the main Chicago banks were solid; however, the N.D. administrators carefully monitored this situation throughout the Depression.

Between 1930 and 1934 approximately twenty-one thousand American financial institutions failed, including almost ten thousand banks, and during that same period, the Gross National Product declined 30 percent while unemployment reached 25 percent. Moreover, the employed worked shorter hours for less money than during the previous decade. A general deflation occurred and although prices declined, average earnings sank lower. All sectors of the economy suffered and higher education was particularly hard hit: public universities underwent drastic cutbacks in government funding; private schools could no longer depend on alumni or church donations; and commercial ventures like college sports became financial liabilities. One study of the Big Ten conference noted, "admission prices [to athletic events] were cut, attendance still fell off. One of the [athletic] directors stated that revenues were cut in half." In addition, the wild expansion of the 1920s left a massive debt-servicing hangover for the next decade and many universities had difficulty paying the interest on their 1920s building projects, especially huge new stadiums.

A historian of the period commented, "What caused the Depression after the [stock market] crash of 1929 was not so much the crash itself but a loss of confidence. It shattered the mood that the economy would go on upward forever." New Yorkers experienced the psychological "Depression" first and most keenly. In 1931, Notre Dame alum Ambrose O'Connell, a Manhattan banker, explained to a friend on campus at N.D., "New York has felt the effects of the Depression very much due to the fact that everybody in town from a hired girl to a bank president was 'playing the Market.' New York was probably harder hit than any other place in the country due to individual speculation." As the media center of the country, New York pessimism spread outward.

In the early 1930s, public confidence in many political institutions and most office holders, especially President Herbert Hoover, also dropped precipitously. This situation produced an odd irony for American Catholics: if Al Smith had won in 1928 and the Depression had started during his presidency, it might have sparked anti-Catholic riots in the country; however, Smith's humiliating defeat seemed to relegate his coreligionists to second-class citizenship. A 1931 editorial in the *Notre Dame Scholastic* observed that it was "discouraging for a Catholic student interested in a political future to know that he has two strikes on him before he even begins; and it is particularly paradoxical that in these days when some different sort of leadership is most in need, a talented Catholic must sit far back in the back seat—with his religion."

In 1932, Franklin Delano Roosevelt won the presidency and, more out of desperation than conviction, tried various innovative economic solutions.

Among his close advisers were Notre Dame alum Frank Walker and
James Farley, an honorary N.D. grad. Although Roosevelt did not end
the Depression during his first or even his second term, he slowly restored public confidence and prepared the country for the economic
boom of World War II. Furthermore, by appointing members of religious
minorities, chiefly Catholics and Jews, to important positions in his administration, he gained the approval and support of these groups.

> "In 1920, the network of Catholic colleges and universities consisted of
> 130 schools enrolling 34,000 students, mainly in undergraduate and pro-
> fessional programs. Twenty years later, Catholic higher education had
> grown to 193 colleges and universities, and attendance had risen to
> 162,000."
>
> —Father William P. Leahy, S.J.,
> *Adapting to America*

Hard economic times did not stop the movement of American Catholics into the middle class and their entrance into higher education, both
at parochial and public institutions. Nevertheless, disparities occurred
among different Catholic ethnic groups and in different regions of the
country. One sociologist reported that during the Depression, "22 percent of [university-age] Eastern Irish Catholics . . . went to college as
compared to 43 percent of those" west of the Alleghenies. The relative
affluence of midwestern Irish Catholics benefited Notre Dame—in 1931,
close to 60 percent of its student body came from the Midwest—as did
the school's improving academic reputation.

In the 1930s, when American Jesuit colleges became more conservative in curriculum, their chief rivals—Catholic University in Washington,
D.C., and Notre Dame—edged further into the educational mainstream,
establishing more professional and graduate schools. In 1934, a national
evaluation of American graduate education gave "approval ratings" to
only six programs at Catholic institutions, all of them at Catholic U.
and N.D.

But Notre Dame's main academic mission remained undergraduate
education. In 1931, enrollment reached a new high of 3,227, slowly declining from this peak during the remainder of the decade. Unlike many
other colleges and universities in the Depression, N.D. did not curtail
services for students, fire faculty, or cut salaries—very common practices.
The school's fiscal conservatism in the 1920s, especially its policy of constructing new buildings, including the stadium, with cash up front,
helped balance its books during the 1930s. In addition, wise investments

by its lay board of trustees kept its endowment intact, and its contacts in the Roosevelt administration insured a steady flow of National Youth Administration money to subsidize students.

The majority of Notre Dame undergraduates studied business, engineering, law, and education, and only a minority focused on pure science or liberal arts. Most tended toward political apathy or conservatism; a typical student leader of the mid-1930s, William E. Miller, later served as Barry Goldwater's vice presidential running mate. On campus, as Ed "Moose" Krause, an undergrad in the early 1930s, observed, "this was a man's school then. We felt we were a very select school from the point of view that it was a man's school and we looked down on the big state schools with their social fraternities, coeds, and political agitators."

Much of the masculine N.D. culture centered on athletics. Father John O'Hara surveyed the alumni every year from 1921 to 1936, and to the question about their "most common form of diversion at school and at home," the majority consistently answered, "Athletics was first in both places." Typically, Notre Damers loved playing and watching sports and, as students, made fewer distinctions between intramural and intercollegiate athletics than at most schools with big-time college sports programs.

Thomas Strich, a retired N.D. professor, recently remarked that in the early 1930s, "as a student I liked living with the players. I am uneasy when I encounter places where the athletes are virtually segregated. Even the bums, and we had our share, were bums in reality, not [campus] legend. I don't want to project the holier-than-thou image we've brought on ourselves lately."

■   ■   ■

Dear Father O'Hara,

George Keogan [N.D. basketball coach] has undoubtedly called to your attention the fact that we are using a colored boy on our basketball team [at the University of Detroit].

Inasmuch as I knew nothing of this 'gentlemen's agreement' among coaches—not to use colored boys—which George says actually exists . . . I do not see the justice of it. Last fall, we played against quite a few negroes in football. Michigan State had at least four on their squad. Track teams are full of colored boys. This is the only one [at Detroit] we ever had in any sport and I am mighty sorry to get in a mess [with N.D.] over him.

—Letter from Gus Dorais, A.D. at the University of Detroit,
to Father John O'Hara, acting president of Notre Dame,
February 3, 1934

Notre Dame had always been socially progressive in mixing rich and poor boys and in welcoming Protestants and Jews into its Catholic "family." Furthermore, starting in the early 1920s, the school had enrolled a sizable number of Latin American students and even a few Asians had entered over the years. Nevertheless, it adamantly refused to admit "Negroes." The school administrators argued that because few "coloreds" were Catholic, fewer still sought admission to Notre Dame. But when any tried, even when sponsored by priests, the N.D. administration always took the position: "We have at Notre Dame a large number of boys drawn from the extreme South and . . . question the advisability of exposing a well deserving colored boy to the prejudice that unfortunately the Southerner carries with him," as President Walsh wrote in 1922.

Father O'Hara repeated this line in the 1930s, informing an African-American applicant, "There are so many Southern students at Notre Dame that I feel certain a colored student would find himself in an embarrassing situation if he were to enter here." However, the demographics of the N.D. student body contradicted him: in 1931, only 40 men, a bit over 1 percent—out of 3,227 students—came from the "extreme South," with another 2 percent from "border states," and those percentages remained constant for many years. Moreover, in response to Gus Dorais's letter about the black basketball player, Father Leonard Carrico, another N.D. official, noted, "I am a Southerner by birth [and upbringing] but still I cannot see why there should have arisen any difficulty about that matter [of his playing against us] here in the North. I know that in football we play teams now and then which have colored members, and I do not understand why there should be any agreement to the contrary in regard to basketball."

But O'Hara backed his basketball coach's protest, informing Dorais, "At first, I could see no objection to your using a negro on your team, but George [Keogan] pointed out to me that there is a difference in a game where there is such close physical contact between players scantily clad and perspiring at every pore."

As Dorais and Carrico indicated, African-Americans had entered intercollegiate athletics and, for a northern school, Notre Dame was slipping into the segregated minority. By the early 1930s, most Big Ten institutions annually admitted a small number of qualified black students and their athletic departments began seeking black athletes. The first college sport to approach total integration was track-and-field, and the achievements of Big Ten schools in this area were significant: Iowa sent conference broad jump champ Edward Gordon to the 1932 Olympics, where he won a gold medal in his event; Michigan's Eddie Tolan also found gold in 1932 in the 100- and 200-meter sprints; and the most famous product of Big Ten integration was Ohio State's Jesse Owens, triumphant in the 1936 Olympics in Berlin. In addition, by the early 1930s, African-Americans began appearing regularly on Big Ten football rosters and, in 1931 and 1933, the Fighting Irish played against a number of black athletes on Indiana University's squad.

A final irony in Notre Dame's refusal to integrate occurred in 1933, when O'Hara brought one of the Four Horseman, Elmer Layden, from Duquesne University to head the N.D. football program. At the Pittsburgh school, run by the integrationist Holy Ghost Fathers, Layden had coached and worked with African-Americans, including an outstanding black quarterback. Once back at Notre Dame, he abided by his alma mater's segregationist policy.

Throughout the 1930s, Notre Dame remained not only white but, with O'Hara's prodding, it became more homogenous, the percentage of middle-class Irish Catholics increasing every year. Some members of the C.S.C. community deplored the school's direction, especially its failure to integrate, and the religious order assigned a priest to full-time work in an African-American parish in South Bend. Eventually, after World War II, Notre Dame enrolled its first black students and then, in the 1960s under Father Theodore Hesburgh's leadership, moved to the forefront of the Civil Rights movement.

Unlike many schools with big-time athletic programs, N.D. did not begin integration with highly visible black athletes and subsequently increase the number of African-Americans in the student body. With its top-down authoritarian structure, the Notre Dame president made the key decision on this and all other major questions; if a conservative like O'Hara, he continued segregation; if a liberal like Hesburgh—the most important N.D. president since Sorin—he ordered total integration in all facets of the university's operation.

31

After Rockne in 1931

"The sudden blotting out of such a real celebrity [as Rockne] leaves you at first bewildered and deeply shocked. A thousand questions surge through your mind. What's going to happen? What will Notre Dame do? How could it have happened? Who can take his place? What will become of his system? How can they get along without him? What will we do for stories this fall? How can things in football go on?"

—Paul Gallico, *New York Daily News* sports editor, April 1, 1931

For the "Notre Dame family" as well as the legions of sports fans and journalists, the death of Rockne prompted immediate grief—but then questions about the fate of his great product, Fighting Irish football. Francis Wallace admitted that "latent in the spontaneous national tribute to the coach was the haunting question: What now? What happens to the monument [he built and] so many people thought so important? Can Notre Dame find another man to fill the popular image Rockne created?"

The men in the Golden Dome set about to answer the final question first. They decided not to seek one man but two—to separate the jobs of athletic director and football coach—even though this move, in the Depression, would cost them an extra $10,000 a year.

First, they sought a new athletic director. They had noticed and chatted with Jesse Harper, Rockne's predecessor, at the functions surrounding the funeral but, contrary to the various histories of Notre Dame football, he was not their original choice to replace Rockne as A.D. Instead, President O'Donnell contacted Major John Griffith, commissioner of the Big Ten, and invited him to become the Notre Dame athletic director.

O'Donnell then went to Chicago to meet with Griffith—the latter's acceptance of the position would have been a coup for the Catholic school and added significant weight to its side of the ongoing arguments with Yost of Michigan, Stagg of Chicago, and their conference allies. But Griffith, who wanted to build the NCAA as well as retain his commissionership, declined the offer. O'Donnell wrote him in late April that his refusal was "a real disappointment to us [but we are] proud of your friendship for Notre Dame."

The N.D. administrators next turned to Harper, who, because of the depression in the cattle and farm business, was pleased to return to intercollegiate athletics. However, he knew that Rockne would be difficult to follow. A few years before, Harper had told his protégé, "You are at the head of them all at present and hard work will keep you there for many years. Next to your wife and mother, your great success means more to me than to anyone else." The mentor realized that Rockne's fame came from coaching—"Your teams each year show to me your extraordinary ability as a coach and a handler of men. I know I appreciate your ability more than anyone"—and Harper, upon his return to N.D., to avoid any comparison with his great pupil, stayed far away from the coaching aspects of the football program, rarely even commenting upon the work of Rockne's gridiron successors.

Jesse Harper took up his A.D. duties in early May 1931. Arthur Haley, the athletic department business manager, wrote the president of the N.D. alumni association that "Mr. Harper arrived last Friday, and is gradually becoming acquainted. In fact, just now Nobe Kizer and Piggy Lambert from Purdue, also Frank Hering, are in his office."

Because Haley provided athletic department continuity, increasing numbers of alumni and other members of the N.D. family developed personal relations with him and wrote him about athletic department matters—also, friendship with Haley did not hurt their chances for more and better football tickets. John Neeson, president of the alumni association, began a letter in April 1931: "It doesn't seem possible to come down to earth and realize what has happened. Things go all right for awhile until I am suddenly startled into a realization that Rock has gone." But later in the letter, he remarked, "you also told me not to throw down the tools regarding certain [football] prospects . . . Under the changed conditions I don't, of course, know what to do." Haley replied, "Just keep after them about attending here."

When Harper returned to his ranch in June, as well as during other absences to attend to his cattle business, Haley ran the athletic department. In one letter to his new boss, he noted, "Miss Faulkner left Saturday in a calm mood, bringing in the keys for her desk and the files. There have been several applicants [for her job] but I am going to take a little time [in selecting one]." Why Ruth Faulkner, Rockne's wonderfully efficient secretary, departed is unclear. In a note to President O'Donnell asking for "permission to use your name as a University reference," she mentioned that she "was forced to leave Notre Dame . . . for obvious reasons" but she did not explain them. Possibly she and Harper clashed or the new A.D. regarded her loyalty to the old regime and Rockne's modus operandi as a negative. Nevertheless, there is a poignancy about her exit into the cruel Depression job market.

The Notre Dame administration, particularly Vice President Mulcaire, instructed Harper to monitor the athletic department books carefully and the A.D. worked hard to fulfill this mandate. In Harper's notes to Haley, he commented on such minutiae as the football managers' stationery—"Do not allow them to have as much printed as [in 1930–1931]; we can order more for them at any time." One of the managers later recalled "sitting up half the night in the [dormitory] bathrooms— the priests switched off all the other lights at eleven—just trying to get our ledgers to come out right. Harper went over those things with a magnifying glass. You would've had to get a receipt from a pay toilet [to please him]."

The new A.D.'s methods, of course, were the opposite of Rockne's, where large sums of money moved about unaccounted for, only to appear in the form of $10,000 tarpaulins and other accessories for the football program. But the N.D. administration wanted total control of all financial matters in the athletic department and the new A.D. cooperated fully with this policy. In fact, this fiscal accountability became the most important legacy of Jesse Harper's final tour at Notre Dame.

Starting with Harper, all N.D. athletic directors have had to seek permission from the vice president for major expenditures and, in regular audits of their financial books, justify all minor costs. Never again was a Notre Dame A.D. or coach, even the powerful Frank Leahy, allowed to operate with the near autonomy of Rockne. Moreover, a large part of Notre Dame's subsequent strength in college sports came directly from this tight institutional control of its athletic department finances. (In contrast, big-time athletic departments that operate as autonomous or semi-independent units often produce financial scandals as well as huge annual program deficits for their host schools.)

> "It was all news to us at Notre Dame when the matter [of a supposedly scheduled game with Oregon State] was taken up with Mr. Harper after his appointment as Athletic Director. We had no record of Mr. Rockne's negotiations with Mr. Schissler [of Oregon State], and the matter had never been presented to the Athletic Board."
>
> —Vice President Mulcaire
> to the chairman of the board of athletics,
> Oregon State University, October 2, 1931

In addition to his idiosyncratic bookkeeping, Rockne's casualness about other aspects of his athletic directorship returned to trouble his successor. In June 1931, Paul Schissler, A.D. and coach at Oregon State, informed Harper that Rockne had promised, in writing, a Fighting Irish visit to his school in 1933 and that Oregon State had already announced the game to an ecstatic local press and public; thus the West Coast school could not understand why the N.D. faculty athletic board had not yet approved the contest.

It soon emerged that Rockne had made the promise without consulting the board, probably hoping that he could bluster the faculty men into accepting the game or making them the fall guys in an N.D. refusal. Harper played it by the book—he indicated to Oregon State that, as Notre Dame A.D., he lacked final authority in this matter—but he did write Vice President Mulcaire: "I have been afraid all the time that we might be in a jam" because of Rockne's promises "and I have kept the 1933 schedule open so that we could take care of" problems like Oregon State. In the end, the board refused to sanction the West Coast trip and the Fighting Irish never played Oregon State.

> "When Harper came in, he went on an economy kick and cut the athletic scholarships practically in half.
>
> 'The coaching part was easy,' Anderson says. 'That part of it never bothered me because I had learned a lot from the Great Guy [Rockne]. But when you go from 36 scholarships down to 20, and you lose at least five more of these in the general process of things, then you have practically nobody left [who can play football].' "
>
> —Hunk Anderson,
> quoted in *Wake Up the Echoes* by Ken Rappoport

Following Knute Rockne as head coach of the Fighting Irish was a near-impossible task, but many candidates applied for the job. Typically, Rockne had complicated the process; Francis Wallace explained that "he had a habit of saying to the hometown friends" of one of his "old boys" in coaching, that " 'If I should ever leave Notre Dame, I'd like Joe here to succeed me.' " Therefore many would-be heirs appeared, but Hunk Anderson, his main assistant on campus, was not among them, expecting the position to go to one of the "former Notre Dame stars [already] coaching a major university."

The N.D. administration wanted to hire an athletic director first, and by mid-April 1931, after spring football practice should have started, they had not settled upon one. Then, when Harper signed, President O'Donnell decided to finesse the head coaching issue—press and alumni campaigns for various candidates were heating up—by announcing: "Anderson will be in charge, but he will be the senior coach, and Jack Chevigny the junior coach. Rockne cannot be displaced as head coach." O'Donnell also told the team before it began spring practice, "The eyes of the football world are on Notre Dame. It wants to know what Notre Dame will do without Rockne. You will answer."

Hunk Anderson always claimed that he was handicapped from the very beginning of his "senior" and then "head" coaching career at Notre Dame. In his first conversation with Harper in late April 1931, the A.D. reportedly said, "There will be no proselyting . . . I am under orders to 'tighten the drum' [financially]"; athletic scholarships were "cut to twenty."

Hunk responded, "How do you expect to have a football team?" Harper told him to complain to the vice president. Father Mulcaire informed him, "Rockne ran things pretty much the way he wanted. Now the priests are going to run things around here. The only time you are going to be 'boss' is when you get behind that green fence [on the practice field, and during games]." Therefore, according to Anderson, he coached in a straitjacket, and as Rockne's recruits played out their eligibility, the Fighting Irish declined, ending with a horrible 3–5–1 record in 1933 and his firing.

Every history of Notre Dame football accepts Hunk's explanation at face value and bemoans his colossal handicap in trying to continue the master's success. However, Anderson learned many things from his mentor, including self-serving exaggeration.

Notre Dame internal memos reveal a very different situation from Hunk's version of events. In January 1931, Rockne sent the N.D. administration his "scholarship list" of thirty-nine football players "for the second semester." He controlled the awarding of these grants-for-work and also, usually upon his recommendation, at least one hundred other players received various deals from the N.D. official in charge of campus jobs. This system continued through Hunk Anderson's years. In January 1932, the athletic department accounted for $28,588 of B.R.T. (Bed, Room, and Tuition) aid-for-work, the bulk of it for football players; because B.R.T. at Notre Dame at this time was about $375 a semester per student, this amounted to either *seventy-six full B.R.T. grants or, more likely, a much higher number of players on aid,* many receiving partial grants. For 1933, Notre Dame continued to help its intercollegiate athletes, the university comptroller noting that *142 men, the vast majority in football,* "account for 34% of the total number [of students] employed and just over 50% of the service credit dollars [for the university]."

Then, in early 1934, the N.D. comptroller listed *"102 . . . football players"* on grants-for-work; of this group, "67 boys . . . are receiving the maximum allowance" of "B.R.T." and thirty-five, various smaller amounts. Because fifty-three freshmen were on the list, obviously Hunk and his assistants had been able to use the grants as inducements in recruiting. Furthermore, because the list included fifty-three sophomores and juniors, Hunk must have also recruited the majority of them.

Like many of Rockne's special pleadings, Anderson's contained both a grain of truth and an absence of context. Mulcaire and Harper did seize control of the athletic department's finances and they did trim the number of so-called football scholarships. But Rockne's thirty-nine and Anderson's twenty-down-to-fifteen referred only to the grants over which the football coach had *unilateral control;* Hunk always implied that these were the *total number for his entire team* and the historians of Notre Dame football turned his implication into "fact." In reality, although Hunk's unilateral numbers were lower than Rockne's, Anderson still had plenty of players—always over one hundred receiving N.D. aid—from which to select his varsity units.

The real difference between Rockne's subsidization of football players and his successor's was that under Anderson the off-campus and summer jobs dried up—more a result of Hunk's personality than Mulcaire's and Harper's assertion of control. Unlike the affable Rockne, Anderson was, according to Francis Wallace, "toughness personified, with a voice like the sound of a blacksmith striking an anvil." In his roman à clef *Autumn*

Madness, Wallace assigned Hunk the role of "Bull" Cardon, "the high priest of the tough guys. He never left the campus unless it was absolutely necessary."

As an N.D. assistant coach and as head man at Saint Louis, Anderson had never liked dealing with the public; as Fighting Irish senior and then head coach, he neglected this important aspect of his Notre Dame assignment. Arthur Haley, the athletic department business manager, maintained a remnant of the off-campus job network, but because he lacked Rockne's contacts and clout, his version was far from the master's. Because of the Depression, if Rockne had lived he would have had to work extremely hard on the off-campus job program; because Hunk tended to ignore the locals and the alumni, at a time of massive unemployment, the network dried up. These part-time and summer positions were the gravy in Rockne's subsidization system, they rewarded the varsity players and helped keep team morale and loyalty to the coach high. Their absence contributed to Hunk's downfall.

Francis Wallace always considered Anderson an outstanding assistant, frequently terming him the "Top Sergeant to General [Rockne]." Anderson's role in his mentor's football program was essential but one-dimensional; in *Autumn Madness,* Wallace explained Hunk/Bull's strength: "football was a tough game played by hard people and it had to be taught that way. [As assistant coach], 'Bull' did the kind of teaching that paid dividends. He kept the temper of the squad hard. There was no percentage in scouring the coal and iron countries for young men and then permitting them to be softened up."

Hunk was unable to move from the one-dimensionality of his top sergeant role to the multifacets of a general's job. Hunk's failure resulted from his own inadequacies compounded by the extraordinary pressure placed upon him by Fighting Irish fans, not the supposed cutback in "football scholarships" ordered by Mulcaire and Harper. A Notre Dame squad of at least one hundred receiving aid, supplemented by outstanding reserves on the hall teams, was deeper and better than almost any other big-time college football program in America. In the early part of the 1931 season, the flaws in Anderson's coaching appeared. By the final games of the year, they were glaringly obvious.

"Notre Dame's [football] cause goes even deeper on the emotional side. It is the memory of the late Knute Rockne, who placed Notre Dame on the highest national gridiron pedestal [that motivates the team]. 'Rock

Wants This Game,' placarded on the South Bend dressing room, will be
augmented by a player spirit of 'Let's Do It for Rock.' "

—Front-page *Chicago Tribune* article,
  October 10, 1931, before N.D.'s first game of the season

As soon as President O'Donnell promoted Anderson, questions arose
concerning Hunk's ability to do the job. Spring practice went unevenly
and then, for the first time in his life, Hunk became seriously ill, having
to go to the Mayo Clinic in June because of an acute sinus condition, and
a month later almost dying from a neglected appendicitis. Father Mulcaire reported, "he was pretty close to the border for a while."

Anderson recovered and opened fall practice in September. He had
five assistants, and immediately Jack Chevigny, in the ambiguous role of
junior coach, caused problems. The former halfback was in charge of the
backfield but he also wanted total control of the offense. Hunk later
admitted that "Chevigny, my assistant, became impossible to handle,"
even "countermanding my orders [during games]." The ongoing conflict
between the two slowly eroded team morale.

The Fighting Irish opened the 1931 season in Bloomington, Indiana,
with fans and journalists asking: "What will Notre Dame do without
Knute Rockne? That thought dominates pre-game discussion. And the
corollary. What will Notre Dame do under the coaching of Hunk Anderson?" Coaching under a microscope is never easy but, in Hunk's first
game, the Fighting Irish, led by Marchy Schwartz's triple-threat talents,
and halfback Joe Sheeketski, one of Francis Wallace's Ohio boys, demolished the weak Hoosiers, 25–0. As significant was the half-filled stadium
and the low payout for N.D., $10,000 and change.

With the Depression biting deeply, fewer fans were attending football
games and, the following week, for the Notre Dame–Northwestern game
at Soldier Field in Chicago, the unprecedented occurred. There were no
ticket problems—the crowd filled only half the stadium's capacity. Ironically, this year the Big Ten had allowed the contest to be moved to
Soldier Field and staged as a partial charity benefit; President O'Donnell
explained that all receipts "in excess of" the regular payout if the game
were played as scheduled at Notre Dame "are to be turned over to the
[Illinois] Governor's Commission for the relief of unemployment."

On game day, "Tug" Wilson, Northwestern A.D., urged Chicagoans
to buy the "nearly 36,000 unsold [good] seats" because they would pro-

vide $70,000 for charity, and if fans totally filled Soldier Field, much more money would go to the unemployed. Unfortunately, the payout for the event, after expenses, was slightly below what the schools would have earned in Indiana, thus the charity attempt failed. Those fans who came sat through a cold rain, witnessing a dispirited 0–0 tie. The field was extremely wet and the players "floundered and skidded around the slippery turf" *(Chicago Daily News)*. Marchy Schwartz could not break open the contest as he had done in 1930 at icy Soldier Field against Army. The tie also ended the Irish's twenty-game win streak and marked the first time that N.D. had failed to beat Northwestern since 1903.

The following Saturday in the home opener, "the pent-up fury of Notre Dame's big football army fell on the valiant but out-classed Bull Dogs from Drake [University]" (AP report). N.D. won 63–0, but the small crowd produced only $8,000 for Harper's athletic department books.

Pittsburgh visited next, followed by Penn. The Fighting Irish, led by Schwartz, had no trouble with either eastern team, winning 25–12 and 49–0. But, as Arthur Haley reported to Harper, the Pitt and Penn visits produced only $27,000 and $20,000 for N.D., whereas "our check from [road games at] Pittsburgh last year was $80,000 and $112,000 from Penn." So far, no visitor had come close to filling Notre Dame Stadium, and the home part of the series with big-city schools was causing financial problems. In addition, the 1931 trip to Carnegie Tech provided a lower payday than past games in Forbes Field.

The Tartans were slipping out of big-time college football—Judge Wally Steffen resigned two weeks later—and the Fighting Irish easily beat them, 19–0. However, some observers felt that N.D.'s 104 yards in penalties, high for this era, marred the winning effort. In his coaching, Anderson emphasized "hard play" and his teams tended to collect penalties. Moreover, he never attempted Rockne's manipulation of the referee assignment system and his squads often confronted four unsympathetic officials from their opponents' areas of the country.

This occurred on the next road trip when N.D. visited Baltimore to play Navy. In beating a weak Middie squad, 20–0, the team again accumulated unnecessary penalties; they also failed to impress eastern sportswriters who saw Hunk's version of the Fighting Irish for the first time. Westbrook Pegler wrote, "It is a very good thing for the Notre Dame football players that they are not beholden to some prize fight commission for their licenses, their gate money, and their training expenses . . . A stern and fearless fight commission with the honor of the grand old game at heart might suspend them for not trying, withhold their remuneration and make them walk home to South Bend."

It was unfair to expect a team headed by a line specialist like Hunk Anderson to play with the offensive panache of Rockne's championship squads, but the eastern fans were merciless, and a few days after the Navy victory, Walter Winchell, the famous gossip columnist, ran a "blind item" about Hunk and Notre Dame: "What successor to a late mid-Western football coach may lose his job because his religion differs from that of the university?" Anderson, 6–0–1 after the Navy victory, could not be attacked for his record, but he was a Protestant and the New York N.D. alums were restless, one of them apparently feeding this story to Winchell.

When sent the clipping, President O'Donnell replied, "The University's policy is to ignore ill-humored and ill-considered comments of this sort in the belief that they do not injure the University in the estimation of fair-minded people." However, the sender made the point that it would be "a very sorrowful thing for your institution and its followers, among whom you have millions throughout the nation, to have the general public feel that Coach Anderson was going to be dismissed on account of his religion."

For Father O'Donnell, this argument as well as the fact that he had appointed Hunk in the first place, convinced him to stay with Anderson long after the latter's weaknesses became evident. The disastrous final two games of the 1931 season did not shake the president's resolve.

"With 52,000 spectators looking on thunderstruck in the beautiful new red brick stadium that stands as a monument to Knute Rockne, Southern California . . . performed the almost incredible feat of spotting its opponents a 14–0 lead going into the final period and then proceeding to pile up 16 unanswered points in the space of fifteen minutes to win, 16–14."

—Allison Danzig,
The New York Times, November 21, 1931

The press ballyhooed USC's first visit to Notre Dame Stadium, billing it as "The Clash of the Colossi" for the national championship. More than 150 sportswriters requested press credentials from N.D. and close to a hundred radio stations carried the contest. The pregame buildup produced the first sellout in Notre Dame Stadium history.

In reality, these were not the two strongest USC and Notre Dame teams of the era. Previous games had revealed the N.D. weaknesses and the Trojans had lost their opener to Saint Mary's—coached by Rockne's "old boy" Slip Madigan—and had beaten a number of mediocre opponents by various scores, including 6–0 over a deemphasized Cal-Berkeley. Yet, Southern Cal was up for this contest—it had been humiliated, 27–0, in Rockne's final game the previous year and it had not beaten N.D. since 1928. That contest, twenty-six games ago for the Fighting Irish, also marked the last time Notre Dame had lost.

The first three quarters pleased but did not surprise the home crowd. Marchy Schwartz ran the offense and notched the only TD of the first half. Then the Irish scored another touchdown on their first possession of the second half and ended the third quarter with a 14–0 lead. However, throughout the day, the officials had frequently penalized the undisciplined N.D. players, and when USC's offense finally started to move in the fourth quarter, the Notre Dame defense cracked. A pass interference call set up the first Trojan TD, the kicker missing the PAT.

With USC coming back, Hunk Anderson made a series of disastrous substitutions, pulling off many of his first unit players and then not being able to reinsert them because of the era's one-platoon rule—a player removed in one quarter could not return until the next. Hunk later explained that he was engaging in good "sportsmanship," trying not to run up the score, but eyewitnesses felt that either he miscalculated the USC momentum or simply lost control of the situation.

The Trojans marched to another TD and, with the PAT, were now within a point, 13–14. Hunk ordered his team to stick to its regular offense, grind out first downs, and run out the clock—but lacking most of the regular backfield, the Irish could not move or hold the ball. With four minutes left, Southern Cal drove again. A long pass to a lineman sent them deep into N.D. territory—Francis Wallace described the pass as a "sucker play, the *tackle eligible*, which should never happen against an alert team." Then the Fighting Irish defense stiffened and seemed to stop USC—until an N.D. penalty gave the Trojans another chance. Southern Cal opted for a field goal, and the successful three-pointer made the score 16–14, capping one of the great comebacks in college football history.

For a long time after the game, many Notre Dame fans remained in their seats, stunned. Mayor Jimmy Walker of New York, in attendance, wept, as did others in the crowd. Not only had the twenty-six-game undefeated streak ended, but for the Fighting Irish to snatch defeat from the jaws of victory seemed impossible to comprehend. It was one thing to win without style—Hunk's team had done that all season—but to lose like this was too much, and many N.D. fans left the stadium calling for Anderson's scalp.

In the creation of Notre Dame football, many victories stand out—the 1922 triumph in Atlanta over Georgia Tech, the 1925 Rose Bowl win over Stanford, the 1928 victory in the Army game—but some of the defeats are almost as important. At the head of the list is the 1931 loss to USC *For Fighting Irish fans, it illustrated the way that a Notre Dame team must never lose.*

On occasion, Rockne's good teams had failed in close, hard-fought games, and some of his thin squads had been overwhelmed by superior opponents, but never had the great coach blown a two-touchdown lead in the fourth quarter through a combination of bad preparation—the referees and the Fighting Irish not understanding the penalty rule parameters, the players not alert for "sucker" moves—and bad sideline tactics—the fatal substitutions, the inflexibility in the face of changed circumstances.

Rockne's victories had spoiled Notre Dame fans, but as important, his brilliant coaching had also set a standard against which all his successors have been measured. After Rockne, Notre Dame coaches not only had to win with style but could never lose through incompetence. In the USC game in 1931, Hunk Anderson failed this test; the following week, at Yankee Stadium, he added to his woes.

"Out of their pockets, the citizens of this place [New York] and a few other places . . . will contribute about $320,000 tomorrow afternoon to watch Notre Dame and the Army proceed with a football controversy which has come to be valued as New York's one big game."

—Westbrook Pegler,
Tribune syndicate, November 27, 1931

Following the 1930 Army game in Chicago, President O'Donnell decided that the New York alums had finally accepted the Golden Dome's control of the annual contest and he approved the move back to Yankee Stadium for 1931. Arthur Haley handled all ticket requests out of the N.D. athletic department office and throughout the fall did a brisk business. However, because of the Depression, many ticket seekers assumed that they would be able to obtain large numbers of good seats, Haley sarcastically informing one alum, "I received your very modest request for Army tickets. As the fellow says, 'If these aren't on the 50 yard line, I hope they are in the center of the field.'"

Notre Dame sold its allotment well before game day, and Haley kept a few in reserve for special friends of the school, including Mayor Jimmy Walker, almost a Notre Dame mascot by this point, and Rockne's former agent, Christy Walsh. Army also moved all of its tickets, one sportswriter noting, "The cash response of the West Point and Notre Dame graduates and the general public to this attraction was a happy surprise" to the Army's athletics manager, "who has put on his show in the presence of empty seats this fall," including at Yale and Pittsburgh. By game day, scalpers were asking $50 a ticket and a sold-out Yankee Stadium produced, after rental cost and other expenses, almost $137,000 for N.D. and an equal amount for West Point. The response proved that, even during the Depression, the Notre Dame–Army annual was special and had "become such a gala occasion that it attracts nearly as much national attention as the World Series or the Kentucky Derby" (United Press).

The 1931 Kaydets lacked the running power of previous editions and had wandered through a lackluster campaign, losing to Harvard and tying Yale (both schools were deemphasizing), and being stomped by Pitt 26–0 —N.D. had beaten the Panthers, 25–12. One sportswriter pointed out that Army was "rated only as a very nice, earnest lot of football players and any thought on their part of winning the [Notre Dame] game would be regarded as something close to impudence." Moreover, the *New York Times* indicated that football fans had "the expectation of seeing the Ramblers from South Bend make Army pay dearly for the [USC] breaking of their three-year winning streak a week ago."

In the event, the Kaydets outplayed the not-so-Fighting Irish, and the West Point coaching staff outsmarted Hunk Anderson and his assistants. Army scored the only TD of the first half—the key play a basketball-style pass to its main scoring threat, Ray Steckler. Meanwhile, the N.D. offense sputtered and, according to one writer, "Notre Dame suspected that the Cadets knew their signals." In fact, Anderson had not changed the "number-series" used by his predecessor and his offense employed Rockne's sequences in a much more predictable manner than had the master. Thus the Kaydets were ready for N.D.'s attack, particularly the aerial game—during the long afternoon, the Irish completed only three of eighteen passes, with four intercepted.

Army scored another touchdown in the fourth quarter and coasted to a 12–0 win. New York N.D. alumni and fans, after the Southern Cal debacle, sat stunned during the second half, always expecting a Fighting Irish comeback, appalled by the ineptness of the offense and the lack of spirit displayed by Hunk's team. After the contest, Army fans, coaches, and players were jubilant; "the Notre Dame quarters, on the other hand, were far from merry. . . . Most crestfallen of all was Hunk Anderson" (*New York Herald-Tribune*).

The New York alumni, the Fighting Irish boosters, and the press were not sympathetic to the coach's plight and began calling for his head. However, the response at Notre Dame was to raise the drawbridges and rally round Hunk. After all, he was a "Notre Dame man," the close friend and teammate of the legendary George Gipp as well as the longtime assistant of Knute Rockne. The *Notre Dame Scholastic* editorialized: "Malicious rumors that have circulated on the outside by the customary football 'nuts,' veiled newspaper insinuations, and pussy-footing columnists have indicated that Anderson is not the man for the job because of these two heart-breaking defeats . . . [But] Anderson is senior coach at Notre Dame because the entire University has confidence in his ability. And that is why the undergraduates hope he will continue in his present capacity."

The N.D. administrators had no intention of being forced by outside partisans to fire Hunk and they responded to the calls for his ouster— when junior coach Jack Chevigny resigned to go to Texas—by conferring the title of head coach upon him. They hoped that the final two games of the 1931 season were aberrations and that Hunk would resume Rockne's winning ways. But their fears, as well as informed alumni such as Francis Wallace, told them otherwise.

In late 1931, the men in the Golden Dome confronted a unique situation in Notre Dame history—no head football coach had been hired since 1917 or fired within memory; indeed, so little resemblance existed between the pre-Rockne and the post-Rockne eras that precedents were useless. Thus President O'Donnell, overreacting to the howls of the "synthetic alumni," gave Hunk an open-ended contract and did not set up a timetable to review his job performance. O'Donnell wanted Hunk's teams to win as Rockne's had, rendering all questions about Anderson's coaching moot. The N.D. president did not realize that Notre Dame football, now a national institution, needed clearly marked procedures for hiring and firing coaches, and his decisions in 1931 cost the school dearly two years later when Hunk's last team produced a 3–5–1 record. (A generation later, President Hesburgh instituted regular procedures, including five-year contracts for N.D. coaches, with an automatic review in the fifth year.)

At the end of the 1931 season, the Notre Dame administration not only worried about Anderson's coaching abilities but also about their great money machine, Fighting Irish football. Was it as Depression-proof as they thought? The team had finally filled its new home stadium, but road receipts, except in New York, were down, and clearly Notre Dame needed to win to keep its large share of the decreasing college football market. The final profit for the season was a bit over $400,000—down 26 percent from the 1929 high-water mark—but costs, even under Harper's tight fiscal reign, had reached $258,000; if football revenue dropped precipitously as it had at other schools, expenses could not shrink nearly as quickly. Moreover, problems in raising funds for the Rockne Memorial were a frightening portent of possible bad times ahead.

> "We have decided to enter upon a nationwide campaign to raise a fund of a million dollars, $650,000 of which will go to the erection of the Rockne Memorial Field House, and $350,000 of which will go to its endowment [for maintenance and upkeep]."
>
> —President O'Donnell's announcement
> of the Rockne Memorial, June 6, 1931

After consulting the various constituencies of the Notre Dame community, O'Donnell decided that the most fitting memorial to the great coach would be the erection of an intramural facility bearing his name. A few months after Rockne's death, O'Donnell invited Albert Erskine to head the campaign, and several high-profile Americans, including Al Smith, Admiral Richard E. Byrd, and Will Rogers, to serve on its board of directors. The N.D. president expected all the money to be obtained by the end of the year.

He soon realized that in the midst of the Depression, fund-raising— even for a memorial to a beloved public figure like Rockne—would be difficult. Nevertheless, when the president of Northwestern University suggested making the October game between the schools at Soldier Field "in some way a memorial to Coach Rockne," with some of the gate receipts going to the fund, O'Donnell refused, stating that "no part of the surplus proceeds of this game should be set aside for any purpose other than that originally agreed upon," relief for the unemployed. Similarly, when Notre Dame received other suggestions for gaining money for the Rockne Memorial—for example, a New York group wanted a Fighting Irish alumni team to play an exhibition against the professional New York Giants—the school rejected the schemes, O'Donnell explaining, "In the public mind, the University would be in the position of playing a benefit game for one of its own projects after declining several invitations to play for [other worthy causes]."

As a result, Notre Dame had to rely on more traditional fund-raising methods, among them solicitations of the rich as well as the not-so-wealthy. In November 1931, O'Donnell mentioned to a concerned alum that the superior-general of the C.S.C. order, "now in Montreal [Canada] has agreed to call upon [mining baron] Mr. Timmins in behalf of the Rockne Memorial." In addition, the memorial board established a plan to pass contribution buckets at college football games throughout the nation.

Unfortunately for N.D., neither the wealthy nor anyone else gave enough to allow the Rockne Memorial to proceed—Timmins and other millionaires were unreceptive and the contribution buckets produced very small amounts. Even the Notre Dame alumni and students could not provide much—only about 10 percent of the 4,670 alumni contributed and the men on campus came up with less than $500. At the end of 1931—"the scheduled termination date"—$126,000 in cash was in the Rockne Memorial fund, with another $34,000 pledged. This total was so far from the $1 million necessary to build and operate the proposed facility that O'Donnell suspended the drive. (President O'Hara renewed it in 1937 and raised another $200,000; the university bridged the difference and completed the structure in late 1938, assuming the maintenance and upkeep in perpetuity.)

The failure of the 1931 Rockne Memorial drive made the N.D. administrators even more financially wary than usual. They believed that Americans wanted to contribute to a monument to the revered coach—the national outpouring of grief prompted by his death indicated as much—but the Depression was proving so deep and intractable that most people did not have money for charity or much else. For Father O'Donnell and his associates, the lesson of the failed drive was that they had to run a very tight financial ship, spend as little as possible, and insure that Fighting Irish football continued to prosper. The annual profit from football provided the revenue to fund the school's entire intercollegiate and intramural programs as well as many other student activities and special projects. Without the football money, the quality of life at Notre Dame would decline dramatically.

Football profits had already turned to deficits at dozens of other schools involved in big-time college sports. Even more than the death of Rockne, the Great Depression would test the strength and uniqueness of Fighting Irish football.

32

The Demand for Perfection: 1932

"As in past years talk of a national championship is already heard around the campus. People who know anything about the vicissitudes of the sport [of football] are keeping their mouths closed and are sitting tight. The spirit of buoyancy is contagious, nevertheless. Notre Dame students, like everybody else, are prone to believe those things which they want to believe."

—Editorial in the *Notre Dame Scholastic*, October 7, 1932

With the departure of Jack Chevigny to Texas, Hunk Anderson shook up his coaching staff, replacing most of Rockne's last assistants with recent N.D. grads Nordy Hoffmann, Tommy Yarr, and Marchy Schwartz, only carrying over Ike Voedisch. The head of the Notre Dame alumni association was so concerned about Hunk's moves that he wrote directly to President O'Donnell about them. The latter responded: "We admit [that our coaching staff] is experimental but are expecting it will be a successful experiment. The three young fellows are keen as can be on their assignment[s]."

For the coming season, because business conditions continued to deteriorate, A.D. Jesse Harper decided, with Vice President Mulcaire's permission, to reduce ticket prices. But during the summer, Arthur Haley informed Harper that the "ticket sale is moving slowly. Up to date we have sold 281 season tickets"—separate from the long-term leased boxes and seats. The A.D. replied that he was "not surprised the season ticket sale is going slowly even at the very low price. I do not anticipate we will have a very large crowd at either the Haskell or Drake game. I doubt very much if the Haskell game will pay out," that is, make a profit.

Because of the Depression, Harper wanted only four home games, moving the return match against Navy from N.D. to Municipal Stadium in Cleveland, Ohio. For the opener, the Fighting Irish hosted the Haskell Indians thanks to a deal that Rockne had made years before with an acquaintance, Lone Star Dietz, and the second game of the season was a result of the former coach's friendship with his fellow Norwegian, Ossie Solem, at Drake. The faculty board reluctantly agreed to the Haskell game but always approved of the visits by Drake, an upscale private school.

Harper's pessimism about the gate receipts proved accurate; only 8,369 paid to see Haskell, and the crowd of 6,663 for Drake marked an all-time low at Notre Dame Stadium—a record no doubt never to be broken. The gross receipts to N.D. from these games was $7,207, and the third contest of the year, at home against Carnegie Tech, only brought in 16,015 fans, paying the home team a little less than $9,600. Rockne's promise of filling the stadium by entertaining the best opponents in the country went awry because he had continued his longtime scheduling technique of hosting early-season patsies. Jesse Harper and then Elmer Layden, with faculty board approval, eliminated these "track meets."

At first Hunk Anderson was grateful for his mentor's scheduling ploy, his team rolling up scores of 73–0, 62–0, and 42–0 in the opening three games. Unfortunately for him, these results created even higher than usual expectations among Fighting Irish fans and the press, some sportswriters hailing the team as "Point-a-Minute Champions." Reality intruded the following week during the visit to Pitt.

The University of Pittsburgh administration, because of the need to fill its heavily indebted stadium, had given a smart and ruthless coach, Jock Sutherland, carte blanche in recruiting and subsidization, and he responded by building powerful teams of semiprofessional athletes. The previous year, his Panthers had lost only to Notre Dame and he wanted to avenge that defeat in 1932 and charge through the entire schedule. Before more than fifty-five thousand screaming fans in Pittsburgh, Notre Dame dominated play through most of four quarters but could not score. Then, with key interceptions of N.D. passes, Pitt struck for two TDs within a single minute to pull ahead 12–0. One sportswriter, under the

subhead "Irish Become Panicky," commented, "Notre Dame's van-
quished heroes were too bewildered to realize what was happening. It is
seldom that Notre Dame teams are seen in such a mental state."

In the final minutes, trying desperately to come back, the Fighting
Irish came totally apart, the Associated Press describing "the strangest
picture of all . . . the sight of a Notre Dame team, its assurance and
cohesion absolutely destroyed, passing wildly like a bunch of high school
kids in a demoralized effort [to save themselves]." The game ended 12–0.

Other writers and many N.D. rooters pointed to the yielding of two
touchdowns within a single minute as a new and dubious record in Notre
Dame football history and they compared the debacle to the previous
year's loss to USC. More disturbing to the men in charge of the Catholic
school were the irate letters from alumni and even fellow clerics. A priest
in Pittsburgh, after witnessing the game, handwrote a letter to President
O'Donnell, who had a copy typed and circulated:

> [Anderson] is ruining your great school. . . . Hunk is not for Notre
> Dame. Notre Dame should wake up and fire Hunk. . . . Perhaps you
> don't want to be so great. Well, in this case you have to be great for God
> and Church. I go here, there, and everywhere on missions, and all I hear
> is Notre Dame, Notre Dame. People will be heart-broken now. Priests
> are sick now. Saturday night I could hardly preach. I would be tempted
> to hang Anderson and all who are for him."

Father O'Donnell, always cool when responding to emotional out-
bursts, replied: "I know that your letter . . . was written with the greatest good will in the world and inspired by your love of Notre Dame."
After other soothing words, he noted, "we do not feel about this quite as
you do, and of course you will be big enough and broad enough to realize
that there are two sides to every question." Yet, the letters and the defeat
at Pitt began to shake his confidence in Hunk.

Similarly, the *Notre Dame Scholastic* ran a cartoon showing a group
of students pointing fingers labeled "CENSURE," "CRITICISM," "BLAME,"
"FAULT," and "CONDEMNATION" at Hunk and the players. However, an editorial in the same edition called for calm and argued that it was "as
illogical to lay the blame at the feet of one individual [Hunk Anderson] as
it is to hold Mr. Hoover responsible for the Depression." The problem
for Notre Dame rooters, according to the student paper, was that the
"unexpected defeat apparently blasted away the possibility of an Irish
national championship" and this was "too large a pill to swallow." Even
Jesse Harper stepped in, telling the press, "Rumors can fly where they

will but Anderson will be back at Notre Dame [next year] as head football coach. The fact that he lost a game is no reason to fire him. We at Notre Dame feel he has done a fine job."

Not all the letters sent to President O'Donnell condemned Hunk. One angry alum supported him, pleading that he was "trying to do a coaching job for your institution under the most trying and unfair conditions," working under Jesse Harper, an incompetent. The alum was well informed, mentioning that "you tried to secure John Griffith [as A.D.]. He would have been a very able man." But he believed that hiring Harper "was indeed a mistake; to bring any man back who had been out of the business for seventeen years" was folly.

If President O'Donnell had doubts about Harper, probably the following game's result alleviated them. The one series for 1932–1933 that the new A.D. had added to the schedule was a home-and-home with the University of Kansas, where he had many friends. After losing to Pitt, the Fighting Irish traveled west and walloped the Jayhawks, 24–6.

The Notre Dame football situation intrigued the regional and national press, and Arch Ward, now sports editor of the *Chicago Tribune*, wrote to President O'Donnell, asking him to grant a special interview to the reporter assigned to cover N.D.'s coming home game against Northwestern. O'Donnell replied affirmatively and also invited Ward to visit at any time. (Ward did, frequently staying at Arthur Haley's house.)

Against Northwestern, before the best home crowd of the season, 31,835, Hunk's team won easily but did not convince the skeptics. The Wildcats were 2–3–1 entering the game and rolled over, having their tummies rubbed for a 21–0 count. In the *New York Daily News*, Francis Wallace termed Hunk's team "a curiously ineffective Notre Dame squad which failed to satisfy its adherents. Blocking, always a decisive factor in the Irish running attack, was ineffective today and the flashy backs were stopped cold."

Nonetheless, the home crowd put close to $46,000 in Harper's till, and the following Saturday, over sixty-one thousand fans in Cleveland provided almost $70,000 in receipts for N.D. Like the Northwestern visit, this game proved more of a financial than artistic success. Navy came west with an unimpressive 2–4–1 record, and although led by a spectacular Chinese-Hawaiian back, Chung-Hoon, the Middies were no match for the Fighting Irish. Moreover, the 12–0 victory failed to convince the Cleveland crowd that this was "big-time football." According to one sportswriter, "They saw a victory which was almost as disastrous to Notre

Dame's reputation as the defeat at Pittsburgh last month." The Fighting Irish should have scored at will but "this impotence, portent of what now may be expected against the Army and Southern California, was a complete surprise. To Notre Dame players and coaches it was a catastrophe."

Hunk and the team did not see it that way—they were happy to win, albeit frustratingly, on a cold day on Cleveland's windswept lakefront. *The real catastrophe was their inability to please the boosters, to dominate opponents as Rockne's best teams had done, to achieve a perfection that, increasingly, existed in the minds of the fanatics, not the record book. For all of Hunk's faults and failures, no coach could field a team equal to a myth.*

> "This is by no means the biggest football game of the day. Notre Dame has lost a game, Army has lost one. And yet it has the Big Town in something approaching a mild hysteria. It's bigger than the heavyweight fights, bigger than the World Series. And it so happens, it always is . . .
>
> The Big Town loves a show and the gray-coated Cadets, with their precise, breathless maneuvers, never fail to produce. But perhaps more important is that the Big Town has adopted Notre Dame."
>
> —Joe Williams,
> *New York World-Telegram,* November 25, 1932

In the Depression, some Notre Dame football traditions ended—after 1931, the Fighting Irish stopped making regular visits to Soldier Field—and other expected customs did not begin—after the 1931 USC game, N.D. failed to sell out its stadium for many years. But the annual against the Army in New York had a life of its own, becoming an always dependable payday—never less than $130,000 for each school throughout the 1930s—and a wonderful ritual for the Notre Dame team and their national following.

In 1932, with the resumption of the Army-Navy annual and its semi-permanent move to Philadelphia, the N.D.–Army match took on added significance for New Yorkers, becoming the city's biggest "Big Game." As the event approached, the ticket requests to Notre Dame escalated in volume and intensity, including one from the private secretary of Franklin Delano Roosevelt: "The Governor, who is the next President of the United States . . . wants [seats for a party of ten] as near the forty yard line as possible." Other politicos, such as the governor-elect of New York, Herbert Lehman, also obtained tickets from N.D., and lesser luminaries such as Congressman Emanuel Cellar sent frantic telegrams pleading for seats—Haley replied to Cellar: "CAN FURNISH YOU A NUMBER BEHIND GOAL

POSTS." In addition, many requests came from church dignitaries, from the Cardinal of New York to a host of lower prelates.

On game day, one writer noticed that "on the way to Yankee Stadium, you passed apple vendors on street corners and bread lines were strung out all over town." Yet the match was a sellout and scalpers got $50 for a pair of "ducats," illustrating the extremes of wealth and poverty existing in New York in flush times and Depression. Westbrook Pegler observed that the 1932 "crowd was one of those New York football opera gatherings which . . . adorn the Notre Dame–Army games with big names, the trappings of wealth and moral and financial appreciation. There were automobiles in the lots and streets around as far as the eye could glare, most of them in the upper brackets in price, and there was enough mink and sable in the park this afternoon to patch a hole a mile square."

The rest of the country also loved the N.D.–Army spectacle, both the CBS and NBC radio networks broadcast the game nationally, frantic Graham McNamee announcing. The schools did not charge the networks any rights' fees, believing that the broadcasts were in the public interest and also built fan support and future gate receipts.

Army entered the 1932 contest slight favorites, having decisively beaten Yale and Harvard, edging tough Carleton College, and only losing to Pitt, 18–13—a better score than N.D.'s against the Panthers. But the day belonged to the Fighting Irish, rolling over the Kaydets, 21–0. One of Hunk's new assistants, Marchy Schwartz, had changed the passing attack and this accounted for two TDs, including one caught by future Irish head coach Hugh Devore, and the running backs wracked up impressive yardage. In addition, the Irish defense constantly rushed the Army QB and played the rough, tough style preached by Anderson. After the game, some West Point officials complained to President O'Donnell about the "murderous" line rushes but, in the Army locker room, he patiently soothed their feelings.

"Outside the Notre Dame dressing room," according to one reporter, "things were different. Alumni and alumni-by-adoption milled about and fought with stadium guards for a look at the Irish players." Unlike Rockne, Anderson preferred a closed and quiet postgame locker room, only admitting one or two reporters and barring alumni and hangers-on. This led to some harsh exchanges between Hunk and his critics.

Back at Notre Dame, the students were ecstatic, the *Scholastic* headlining "IRISH DAZZLE CADETS; Score on Passes, Fumbles, as Merciless Offense Stuns Army Team and 80,000." Most students also believed that the team would win its season finale at USC, gain revenge for the past year's loss to the Trojans, and have a chance for the national championship. Few voices warned against overconfidence.

> "The biggest outpouring of furs and fur-belows and outdoor fashions of
> the season. That was moviedom's contribution to the biennial Notre
> Dame–Southern California football game in the Los Angeles stadium
> today."
>
> —Rosalind Shaffer,
> wire service fashion reporter, December 11, 1932

In an attempt to imitate the New York reception for the N.D.–Army game, Hollywood movie stars and West Coast VIPs turned out for the Irish visit to Los Angeles. Douglas Fairbanks, Jr., sat on the USC bench; Spencer Tracy and his wife on the Notre Dame side; child star Jackie Cooper brought his uncle and rooted for the Trojans; Loretta Young, a Catholic, cheered for N.D.

In the wake of the successful 1932 Olympics in the city, Los Angeles was enjoying a brief prosperity and the papers reported that "as many spectators as attended any session of the Olympic games will be banked around the gridiron today" in the L.A. Coliseum. The paid attendance was 93,924, the total crowd over 100,000.

The 1932 Trojans were stronger than the previous year's edition, with huge Aaron Rosenberg anchoring the line and "Cotton" Warburton, a deceptive jackrabbit runner, at the back. On the day, the Trojans easily handled the Irish, 13–0, becoming the first school to beat N.D. back-to-back since Nebraska in the early 1920s.

The Trojan QB, Howard Griffin, and "Cotton" Warburton took advantage of a number of breaks and N.D. miscues and combined for a touchdown each half. The USC defense, with Rosenberg leading the rush into the N.D. backfield, snuffed out the Fighting Irish attack. West Coast sportswriters—partly in revenge for Rockne's having tricked them during N.D.'s last visit—played up the Irish miscues and, surprisingly, Arch Ward, on the scene for the *Chicago Tribune,* joined their chorus.

With the headline on his article, "NOTRE DAME IS BEATEN AT OWN GAME BY U.S.C.," Ward abandoned his usual N.D. cheerleader stance and emphasized that, unlike Rockne's "opportunist" teams, Hunk's was "out-opportuned . . . by the Trojans." Moreover, "somebody did a poor job of scouting for Notre Dame. . . . No other Notre Dame team I have seen in the last 14 years would have given a back like Warburton the running opportunities that Coach Anderson's men did today." Ward listed other Notre Dame mistakes and then revealed his real grievance—

Anderson had denied him and his newspaper pals entry to the dressing room after the game, only admitting Warren Brown of the *Chicago Herald-Examiner.*

This incident so enraged Ward that when he returned to Chicago, he barraged Notre Dame officials with letters about it, complaining to President O'Donnell that for major American newspapers "to be told that Warren Brown . . . had the only statement he [Anderson] intended to make was downright insulting." O'Donnell tried to placate him by assigning a C.S.C. priest to investigate the incident and eventually, through personal chats with Ward, he was able to soothe the Chicago sports editor. (After Hunk's firing a year later, Arch Ward resumed his Notre Dame cheerleading activities with increased vigor and volume.)

Another key member of the Notre Dame press network whom Hunk lost was Francis Wallace. Less vituperative in his newspaper coverage at the time than Ward, Wallace later complained: "Under Hunk, *Notre Dame was learning to lose.* The two year Anderson record was 13–4–1, fine at most places, but not at Notre Dame."

Anti–N.D. members of the press also smelled blood. Eddie Geiger, the sports editor of the *Chicago Evening American*—whom Rockne had called "a terrible mug"—predicted "that next season will see 'Hunk' Anderson still a coach at Notre Dame but that the head coach will be somebody other than 'Hunk' Anderson; that the head coach also will be the athletic director. That, of course, means that Jesse Harper will go back to his ranch in Kansas."

A major complaint against Hunk and Harper, articulated by the N.D. cognoscenti, was that the new men lacked Rockne's ability to obtain sympathetic game officials and to school them and the Fighting Irish in clear interpretations of the rules. Neither of Rockne's replacements had the clout or even the willingness to deal with Major John Griffith and other intercollegiate administrators and to make the officiating system work for N.D. or, at the minimum, to neutralize it. A knowledgeable priest complained to President O'Donnell:

> Hunk Anderson is the absolute antithesis of the late Knute Rockne. Knute Rockne absolutely refused a certain man to referee Notre Dame games. Last year that man refereed and Notre Dame lost to Southern California. That man threatened to throw out [team captain] Tom Yarr. Next day, Tom complained and Punk [*sic*] Anderson told him to shut up. The next Saturday, Notre Dame lost to Army.

As a result of Hunk's indifference to the game-officiating system as well as his players' on-field lapses in discipline, for the season, his team received more than twice as many penalties as its opponents—sixty-five to thirty—and over twice as many yards lost on penalties—540 to 245.

On the surface, 1932 seemed a good year for Hunk, his squad ending at 7–2–0. But the crucial penalty numbers were symptomatic of his limitations and a portent of how future won-loss records could reverse. It was one thing to preach "hard, rough football"—Rockne had encouraged him in this endeavor—but the master had always combined Anderson's teaching with on-field discipline and clever control of the refereeing situation. Without the latter components, game officials turned against Hunk's teams and his players became unruly and prone to mental errors. (Anderson's real coaching success came a decade later as line coach of the Chicago Bears; in the mayhem of the wartime NFL, when game officials often acted like pro wrestling refs, his approach proved invaluable to George Halas and his "Monsters of the Midway.")

The 1932 penalty statistics did not particularly trouble the Notre Dame administrators; much more worrisome to them was the financial situation at the end of the football season. N.D.'s share of the home games' receipts was less than $62,500, and only the road contests in major cities saved the season financially. The final gross was about $472,000, but with estimated expenses of $210,000, the net profit was less than $260,000, down almost $138,000 from the previous year and potentially dropping further in 1933 when Notre Dame lost the big paydays at USC and Pitt (it would host them) and also traveled to low-paying Indiana and Carnegie Tech. Only the Army annual at Yankee Stadium promised good gate receipts.

■ ■ ■

"Perhaps no school in the country has so large and devoted and desperate a [football] following as Notre Dame. A good proportion of them, particularly our own alumni, can lose if necessary. Sometimes the others cannot so gracefully disguise their disappointment. . . .

It needs remembering, however—and perhaps the reminder is in place for many of us—*that sport is sport, and not war, or politics, or education, or religion.*"

—President Charles O'Donnell,
in the foreword to the 1932 *Notre Dame Football Review*

After the season, Father O'Donnell articulated the dilemma that dogged his presidency as well as the terms of his immediate predecessors and all of his successors: how to place big-time Fighting Irish football within the context of the University of Notre Dame as a serious academic and religious institution. A poet by profession, he chose his setting and his words carefully—in the N.D. publication most read outside the university and with the perfect adjective to describe fanatical N.D. football rooters, "desperate."

The student newspaper took his cue and, in an editorial addressed to all N.D. undergraduates, chided, "Come on, snap out of it! Why so glum? We lost a football game [at USC] but what of it? We've lost before, and it was a pretty successful season after all. You've all been spoiled. You think that because we are not National Champions, the season was not a success." Rationally, the *Notre Dame Scholastic* and the school president made total sense—but Fighting Irish fans were not rational and many scorned anything less than a championship.

Equally irrational were the Notre Dame haters. Throughout the country, many persons mocked the school to local Catholics and the latter passed on the insults to Father O'Donnell, as they had to every N.D. president since the Fighting Irish had achieved national fame. A woman in Waterloo, Iowa, deplored the "queer ideas and false impressions afloat . . . as to the reasons for the real secret [of] success of Notre Dame men in their far-famed field of sport." She then listed some of the rumors on how the Notre Dame football program cheated. The president's office replied with a standard N.D. formulation: "It is difficult to see how any school of high standing would play Notre Dame if there were any truth in the calumnies you have heard."

Even within the American Catholic community, attacks on Fighting Irish football occurred. In late December 1932, at an alumni banquet of Catholic University of Washington, D.C., a prominent jurist assailed "Notre Dame's football success [because it] has caused people to associate football proficiency with Catholic colleges and lose sight of the fact that our institutions are valuable seats of learning." The assistant to the rector of Catholic University wrote to O'Donnell, apologizing, "Unfortunately, the newspapers played up Judge Collins' talk rather extravagantly, emphasizing" the anti–N.D. comments.

The men in charge of Notre Dame also encountered slurs in the serious press. In 1932, an article in the important weekly *Saturday Review* derided Notre Dame as "a place of no particular intellectual pretensions [that] has enjoyed a great reputation simply because its football team was undefeated." President O'Donnell, in a letter to the editor, disputed the implication that his school lacked "intellectual distinction" and had "a low academic rating," and he listed N.D.'s achievements in various educational fields.

Nevertheless, in a passage that showed his deeper comprehension of the problem, he indicated that the "mistake which [the writer] makes, and he is not alone in this error, is in considering that the news-value of intercollegiate athletics, as estimated by the sports' editors, represents either the university's estimate of their value or the estimate placed upon them by thinking men in general."

The University of Notre Dame, however, had shaken down the thunder —the procreating fame and fortune of big-time college football as well as the destructive charges about cheating and anti-intellectualism. No one, least of all the N.D. administrators, could pretend that the thunderstorm had not occurred, and in the aftermath of Rockne-the-Rainmaker, President O'Donnell could mainly grumble about the weather. (Of his successors, only Father Hesburgh managed to do something about it.)

In early 1933, Father O'Donnell brought the greatest living poet, William Butler Yeats—already a Nobel Prize winner and arguably the greatest poet of the twentieth century—to Notre Dame. The press and public all but ignored the visit. However, any hint of trouble in the Fighting Irish football program used up tons of newsprint for the articles, columns, speculations, queries, editorials, letters from fans, and cartoons on the subject.

Unfortunately for President Charles O'Donnell and his associates in the Golden Dome, the events in Notre Dame football in 1933 resulted in a greater journalistic flood than in any previous year.

33

The Removal of a Vice President and the First Firing of a Notre Dame Head Coach: 1933

"I suppose you read in the paper several days ago of Father Mulcaire's being replaced as Vice President by Father O'Hara. This was quite a surprise to everyone. Everyone is agreed, however, that Father O'Hara could not be surpassed as Vice President and eventually as President."

—Arthur Haley to a friend, July 25, 1933

In the late spring of 1933, President Charles O'Donnell was diagnosed as suffering from inoperable throat cancer and the provincial superior of the C.S.C. order, Father James Burns, decided to move Vice President Mulcaire out of the succession line. A C.S.C. historian later explained that Mulcaire possessed "too sharp a tongue and too liberal an attitude toward alcohol." In late June, Burns informed O'Donnell, undergoing treatment at the Mayo Clinic, that "Father [Matthew] Walsh agrees with me that it will probably be best for Father Mulcaire to be elsewhere than at Notre Dame"; the former presidents did not interfere with the work of their successors but, as leaders of the highest council of their order, they controlled the crucial administrative appointments. Thus they sent Mulcaire to teach at a C.S.C. college in Portland, Oregon, and moved O'Hara into the vice president's office.

Father John O'Hara, the longtime prefect of religion, loved Fighting Irish football and promoted it with evangelical fervor. In his widely distributed *Religious Bulletin*, he had frequently stated, "Notre Dame football is a spiritual service because it is played for the honor and glory of God and of his Blessed Mother. When St. Paul said: 'Whether you eat or drink, or whatsoever else you do, do all for the glory of God,' he included football." Nonetheless, as O'Hara's role in the departure of Joe Savoldi indicated, the priest believed that the purpose of Fighting Irish "victories [was] to acquaint the public with the ideals that dominate" the Catholic school; for him, gridiron wins were not an end in themselves, football victories must aid and never tarnish Notre Dame's religious reputation. His formulation codified the school's approach to college football and, during the next seven years, he made it a key tenet of his administration.

The 1933 changes in the Golden Dome pleased the athletic department, A.D. Jesse Harper remarking to Haley, "I sure was surprised that Father O'Hara was to take Father Mulcaire's place. I am sure he will be a delightful man for us to work with." Nevertheless, difficult days were ahead; as vice president and chair of the faculty board, O'Hara not only inherited the athletic department's financial problems—Haley noted in midsummer that season ticket sales were down by 33 percent from the previous year—but also Hunk Anderson's coaching methods and inability to deal with the public.

Shortly after fall football practice began, O'Hara received a vituperative letter from a Chicago priest complaining that on a recent visit to campus, even though he had "often attended practices with Father Mulcaire and Rockne," Anderson had "issued orders to keep out all [Chicago] priests . . . [because] all the forward pass plays had been stolen last year. . . . Not a very veiled insinuation, eh?" The cleric was so angry at being barred from the practice field that he concluded his letter, "With kind personal regards to you, and sincerest and deepest hopes for a rotten and disastrous season for your alibiing coach and his team."

Father O'Hara replied that he had instructed "the Senior [football] Manager to investigate this," and had discovered that "the Coach had given orders that no one, not even a priest, or a scout attired as a priest, was to be admitted . . . without an introduction from a local [N.D.] priest, willing to vouch for his authenticity." Apparently Hunk was beginning to crack under the pressure; until Marchy Schwartz changed the aerial attack for the Army game, opponents did not need advance notice on the N.D. passing offense. However, with a touch of paranoia—his fears about enemy scouts dressed as priests—he had offended an important visitor.

O'Hara apologized to the Chicago cleric but he encountered a more serious criticism of Hunk's practice field behavior from C.S.C. colleagues. A Notre Dame undergraduate during this period explained,

"There were always groups of priests watching practice and you could see them cringe when Hunk exploded with his salty language at regular intervals. Many of them would be wearing earmuffs although the fall weather was hardly Arctic."

The Notre Dame community and Fighting Irish fans probably would have overlooked Anderson's methods if his teams had continued to win football games. Moreover, prospects for the 1933 season seemed excellent; not only did the press predict a banner year but CBS scheduled national broadcasts of five N.D. games—far better coverage than offered to any other school. On the eve of the opener, Arthur Haley advised a former player, "The team is looking pretty good." Unfortunately for N.D. and Hunk Anderson, this evaluation proved wildly inaccurate.

> "It is an actual fact that [in the opener against Kansas] Coach 'Hunk' Anderson used five quarterbacks and made numerous other substitutions, sending all of them in with instructions which . . . most of them promptly forgot. Each man he sent in had three signals to call. Of the five quarterbacks, three called their first play, two called their first and second, and none called the third. One called the same play three times for a net loss of some 35 yards."
>
> —*Notre Dame Alumnus*, December 1933

Jesse Harper had arranged for the Jayhawks to visit N.D., and although not as weak as Rockne's usual opening opponents, Kansas was hardly a powerhouse—they lost the following week to tiny Tulsa. At Notre Dame, they held the mighty Irish to a 0–0 tie but, as most witnesses agreed, the result was less a triumph for the visitors than a humiliation for N.D. Wire service reporters described Hunk's team as "frustrated, disheartened" and authors of "a masterpiece of mistakes"; the *Chicago Tribune* remarked that "the Irish . . . retired in confusion, demoralized as no Notre Dame eleven has been in years." To compound the shame, as the *Notre Dame Scholastic* pointed out, the team *"failed for the first time since 1901 to win its football opener."*

Accounts of the game sparked angry messages from N.D. fans—"Get Anderson Out," wrote one above a clipping of the AP game report—and jibes from the press—a columnist in the *South Bend Tribune*, usually a pro-N.D. organ, remarked, "This fellow Anderson may be a coach but if he is, I'm ready to accept the post of Ambassador to China." In addition, members of the "Notre Dame family" began to complain to Vice President O'Hara, the most disturbing letter coming from the father of Fighting Irish co-captain Tom "Kitty" Gorman. Proud that his son was "too much of a man to complain and I don't believe that he will thank me for writing this," the father bluntly stated, "There is something radically wrong" with Hunk's coaching, "and I would like to find out what it is." Moreover, Mr. Gorman did not appreciate the fact that during the past seasons his son, although an All-America candidate, "has several times been used as an alibi [by Anderson] for a lost game."

In his reply, O'Hara sidestepped the complaints and informed the father, "I told Coach Anderson at the beginning of the season that, since I know nothing myself about football, I was going to count on him to run the team. It would be a dangerous policy, I believe, for me to indulge in criticism of his actions." O'Hara's position was perfectly rational and would have succeeded during normal times—when the team was winning—but 1933 was unlike any previous season. The N.D. administration refused to acknowledge it but, after the Kansas debacle, the first protracted and agonizing dismissal of a Notre Dame head coach—an important ritual in the future history of Notre Dame sports—had begun.

Notre Dame—Open Letter to Hunk Anderson:
There's no disgrace in failure.
There *is* disgrace in sticking through when one sees that he has not measured up. Of course no one can expect another Rockne—the main builder, the marvel and inspiration—but Rockne pupils all over the country are producing fine teams and results from poorer material than N.D. has . . .
Mr. Anderson himself must see that he has failed and should not ask Notre Dame and its million followers to sacrifice its past, present, and future.

—An irate fan, October 8, 1933

This Fighting Irish rooter also mentioned that he had driven more than "600 miles" to see the Kansas game and that "if the [N.D.] crowd's expressions in the stands mean anything"—loud boos—the faculty athletic board would remove Hunk immediately. In addition, the fan emphasized a major criticism of Anderson's coaching—he was not getting much out of his excellent football material. In the second game of the 1933 season, at Bloomington, Indiana, the coach again proved his critics right.

Against a feeble Hoosier squad that had slipped by Miami of Ohio in its opener—for what proved to be its only victory of the year—N.D. registered a 12–2 win. But the Irish were flat and error prone, Indiana's points resulting from a misplayed run that turned into a safety.

The third game, on the road at Carnegie Tech, was a disaster. Having beaten the Pittsburgh school, 42–0, the previous year, N.D. handed the weak Tartans a 7–0 win. The TD occurred on an Irish miscue and, after the game, one Chicago sportswriter observed that "the Notre Dame team—dejected remnants of the once Fighting Irish—filed off the field" with their heads down. A Pittsburgh friend of O'Hara's told him, "The team's spiritless, colorless, disorganized play against Tech brought tears to the eyes of those of us who have been watching Notre Dame teams since I first saw them in Cap Edwards' day, away back in 1909."

After this defeat, the quantity of O'Hara's mail increased considerably, including letters from graduates complaining that the team's performance was "humiliating to us as well as to you and the faculty, and is hurting the prestige of the school."

Most alumni and Fighting Irish boosters not only condemned Hunk's coaching but suggested alternatives: "If Slip Madigan can do what he has at St. Mary's with only a handful of boys, what could he do at Notre Dame with able assistants and a wealth of material"; and from another fan, "I have always been an admirer of Tom Lieb . . . his [Loyola of Los Angeles] teams have been over the heads of the opposition—colorful—fighting and closely harmonizing—clicking." Slip Madigan was the popular choice but, throughout the fall, Lieb waged a subtle personal campaign for the head coaching job, writing frequently to Father O'Hara for spiritual advice and asking the priest to bless and send him "Our Lady of Victory" medals for his Loyola players to wear during games.

Not all of the letters from Notre Dame supporters demanded a new, high-powered coach. A Catholic physician in New Jersey urged the school authorities to keep Anderson and to use the awful season as a transition to deemphasized football; he offered the example of New York University, which "by the simple expedient of changing from [Rockne's friend, "Chick"] Meehan to Kahn as her coach, de-emphasized the greatly over-emphasized value of football, [and] has placed it *upon the sane level* that it should occupy in the life of a University." A prominent Catholic layman in Saint Louis deplored the fact that "the entire nation seems concerned over whether or not a new coach is to replace Hunk Anderson. . . . I do hope that this wrecking publicity will not get the best of Notre Dame officials. I do most fervently hope that your school is far more interested in giving a good Catholic education to ONE boy, than developing a hundred football stars."

O'Hara appreciated these arguments; even though he did not want N.D. to deemphasize, he commented to a friend, "Personally, I am getting a big kick out of the season. One of these reverses now and then helps to fix in the public mind the fact that Notre Dame exists for something besides football."

The vice president also claimed that "the University officials are in no way affected by the popular hysteria" over the N.D. football situation and "we have tried to maintain our equilibrium in spite of the national howls." But, as the squad continued to lose, he became increasingly disturbed by the uproar. In the 1920s, Father O'Hara had helped promote Notre Dame into the favorite team of millions of American Catholics, but until 1933, he had not encountered the full force of Fighting Irish fanaticism. He had encouraged Catholics to identify completely with the team but he had ignored the other part of the equation—*with fan identification came the illusion of power over their team's destiny.* O'Hara, an authoritarian personality, believed that the fans should accept and never question the Golden Dome's control over Notre Dame football. He prized his coreligionists' loyalty to the team but he failed to realize that they demanded a say in the decisions concerning their beloved Fighting Irish. At the minimum, they wanted the N.D. administrators to hear their voices.

The vice president, however, saw the mass outcry as a challenge to Notre Dame and to the C.S.C.'s authority over every aspect of the university. He believed that the loudest protests came from the worst kind of "synthetic alumni," and he told friends that the "heads of the institution" have "to remain calm in the midst of [this] adverse criticism."

O'Hara also attempted to explain the explosion with, "We don't do much betting on games here and as a consequence we are less concerned than some of the Notre Dame fans on the outside [about the defeats]." His denigration of many fans as disgruntled bettors suggests that he did not understand the authenticity of their anguish—just as they felt triumphant when the Fighting Irish won football games and championships, they experienced a sense of personal defeat and humiliation when the team lost consistently. Furthermore, they felt the losses intensely during the Depression when so many of them were doing so badly economically. O'Hara, however, held to his rationalization, stating, "Some of the small-time gamblers who have lost money on the team have become abusive. An occasional defeat is very valuable if it serves to separate the true from the false friends." (Probably some fans did lose money by betting on Notre Dame but they never mentioned this in their complaints. Almost every plea concerning the 1933 football situation in O'Hara's files seems sincerely written, albeit often with the premise that the main purpose of the University of Notre Dame is to produce winning football teams.)

The fourth game, at home against Pitt, further tested the vice president's resolve. The Panthers were not as strong as in previous seasons but they did not need much to beat N.D., 14–0. Irish errors and a lackluster performance resulted in a game where "Notre Dame was whipped by a vaster margin than the score indicates" (United Press). Even the school's publications turned up the volume on their criticisms, the *Scholastic* leading its game report, "The Pitt Panthers, decisively outplaying the Irish in every department," and the *Alumnus*, "The Pittsburgh game saw a senior back 'go dumb,'" and allow the first TD and then an Irish fumble provided the second. But the most surprising critic of all was Joe Petritz, N.D.'s full-time sports publicity man, writing for public consumption that the players "were not fighting in the traditional Notre Dame style . . . Somehow they just didn't feel up to playing football as it ought to be played. They admit it and wonder at it as much as we do."

For the Notre Dame administrators, an equally disturbing result of the Pitt game—a star attraction on the home schedule—was the small crowd, 16,627, and the paltry payday, $14,445. A businessman friend of O'Hara's underlined the problem for the vice president: "the poor [football] showing that Notre Dame has made up to date will cost the University $150,000 this year . . . no doubt it would take very conservative management to balance the [N.D.] budget" without the usual football receipts; "Now, if you have some other way of getting it [extra income] besides from the football team, then the thought of a winning team should be dismissed from everybody's mind," however, if you do not, change head coaches. With the low attendance and poor receipts from the first home games, and the meager advance sales for the remaining home contests also indicating small crowds, the longtime fears of N.D. officials about the new stadium seemed to be coming true—they could not fill it. Furthermore, a losing Fighting Irish team did not do that well on the road; the payout at Indiana was less than $8,000, and at Carnegie Tech, $23,600. O'Hara, whose academic field was commerce, understood the numbers, and in late October, when President O'Donnell returned from the Mayo Clinic, he discussed them with him.

O'Donnell was well enough to conduct some business and, after the Pitt game, he replied to a letter from trustee and alum A. D. McDonald, the president of the Southern Pacific Railroad: "Doubtless you realize, as do all of the true friends of Notre Dame, that since Rockne's death we have been forced into a position of temporizing. After three seasons of football, that period should come to an end. I cherish the hope that before final decisions are given, there may be an opportunity to talk to you and go over the entire situation."

O'Donnell had to acknowledge his mistake in not searching for the best coaching replacement for Rockne either before or after the 1931 season. He had hoped that Anderson, by winning, would justify his inaction, however, the reverse had occurred and the error had been placed under the intense magnifying glass of the sports world. In addition, because Jesse Harper's second tour at N.D. exactly paralleled Anderson's senior and head coaching time, his future at the school was now in doubt. In late October, President O'Donnell instructed his vice president to poll a number of important Notre Dame alumni about the athletic department situation and to ask specifically whether the positions of coach and athletic director should be recombined; whether Harper should be replaced as A.D., and, if so, by whom; and their choice for head coach— Anderson's remaining was no longer an option. The poll occurred during November, as did the continuing agony of the 1933 football season.

"Up to this time, the Notre Dame boys have lost two games, tied one, and won just one. They have been called a dumb team for Notre Dame. This sounds rather harsh but they talk a blunt language in football. . . .

I suppose the players are wondering whether they are as dumb as they have seemed or are the victims of inferior coaching. It must affect their confidence in themselves and Hunk to read that they have let down Notre Dame so badly as to require one of those massive [athletic department] shakeups."

—Westbrook Pegler, November 4, 1933,
in his pregame Notre Dame–Navy story

Father O'Hara hoped that something could be salvaged from the 1933 season and, on the eve of the Fighting Irish visit to Baltimore to play Navy, he telegraphed the head coach: "TODAY IS FATHER O'DONNELL'S FEAST DAY. . . . HE'S NOT FEELING SO WELL THIS WEEK. . . . CHEER HIM UP WITH A VICTORY." Unfortunately for the N.D. vice president, Westbrook Pegler's analysis of the team's problems proved a better forecast of the game's outcome than O'Hara's request for victory.

Navy had only beaten weak opponents and had been stomped by Pitt 34–6; against N.D., it slogged to a 7–0 win. The Midshipmen in the stands were ecstatic—it marked the academy's first victory in seven meetings with Notre Dame—and, at the final whistle, they and the Navy fans ran onto the field, overwhelming the Baltimore police and firemen trying to protect the goalposts. Notre Dame rooters, including the student body back in Indiana, were shocked; the *Scholastic* called it "THE PROBLEM"—the defeat marked the first time since the very beginning of N.D. football in 1887 that a Notre Dame team had lost three games in a row and the first time that the Fighting Irish had been "held scoreless in three consecutive games."

After the East Coast loss, the public lamentations to O'Hara about Anderson's coaching increased, as did the informed complaints from N.D. insiders to Arthur Haley. Francis Wallace sent a newspaper clipping about a published photo of a Pittsburgh "sports promoter" with "three members of the Notre Dame football team" and the tag line that the promoter "is given credit as having sponsored them at Notre Dame." Wallace sarcastically commented, "The latest favorable publicity. The Carnegie Foundation, etc., might be interested," and he implied that the Harper-Anderson regime was at fault: "One guess as to how all this happened—or is it public information who 'sponsors' all the N.D. players." (A remnant of Rockne's "sponsorship" network survived into the 1930s, contradicting, along with Notre Dame's over one hundred annual "B.R.T." grants to football players, Hunk's exhausted excuse that "almost half of my squad in 1933 paid their own way.")

Haley also corresponded with Frank Leahy, at the time a young assistant at Fordham to Jim Crowley, one of the Four Horsemen; before the Navy game, Haley noted that "this coming Saturday will be taken over by the Notre Dame system of football, with your game with [Slip Madigan's Saint Mary's] Gaels and ours with the Middies," coached by Rip Miller (the former "Mule" was one of the few Rockne men not interested in his mentor's old job, preferring to remain at Annapolis). Leahy took pride in Fordham's successful season but he told Haley, "Very sorry to hear about Notre Dame's poor showing. I say 'poor showing' to you because I really feel that way. To those I don't know well, I search for alibis regarding the football situation there, but in my heart I think it is *a deplorable state of affairs.*"

On the afternoon when N.D. lost to Navy, the Fordham–Saint Mary's game drew almost sixty thousand fans at the Polo Grounds in New York. Both teams played well and were prospects for Rose Bowl invitations; in addition, according to the press and many Fighting Irish supporters, their head coaches were the leading candidates for the Notre Dame job.

Unbeknownst to the people clamoring for Jim Crowley or Slip Madigan, N.D. officials did not rate them highly on account of the former's love of drink and the latter's bitter feuds with his school's administration

—Madigan felt so underpaid that he once kept Saint Mary's share of the gate guarantee from a Fordham game in New York for himself. Similarly, another of the Four Horsemen, Harry Stuhldreher, at the top of some fans' lists because of his success at Villanova, was considered too volatile and loudmouthed by the N.D. decision makers.

Throughout November, other candidates for Hunk's job also emerged. Frank Reese, a former N.D. quarterback coaching at North Carolina State, promised O'Hara that "Notre Dame football will come back as it always has," and added, "The memory of your life [as prefect of religion] has always been an inspiration to me since graduation and I believe all Notre Dame men feel that way." (Ironically, North Carolina State replaced Reese at the end of the season with Hunk Anderson!) From Texas came a telegram to President O'Donnell urging him to hire Jack Chevigny, "WHO HAS PROVEN HIS ABILITY AS AN INSTRUCTOR, A LEADER, AND A [ATHLETIC] DIRECTOR." But Chevigny was too young and had made a poor impression as Hunk's junior coach. A more serious candidate was one of Rockne's "Seven Mules," Noble Kizer, and the following Saturday, the N.D. administrators were able to obtain a firsthand look at him in action when he brought his Purdue Boilermakers into Notre Dame Stadium.

> "[In 1933] the Purdue faithful didn't expect their best player, Duane Purvis, to see any action. The reports all week long gave no indication that Purvis would be available for the Notre Dame game after developing a leg infection. When he underwent surgery on the Wednesday before the game, the entire population of Indiana was certain that Purvis would be lying on a Lafayette [Indiana] hospital bed Saturday."
>
> —Ned Colletti, *Golden Glory:*
> *Notre Dame vs. Purdue*

The Notre Dame community desperately wanted the Fighting Irish to beat Purdue and avoid setting new records for futility: no N.D. football team had ever lost four games in a row, had ever gone scoreless for four games, and had failed to score a single point at home. On game day, the *Scholastic* reviewed N.D.'s dominance of the series but warned that because this was the first meeting in ten years with the Boilermakers: "All the [previous] contests are so far removed from the present era that they bear little [on today's game]."

The main connection to the past were the head coaches, both Rockne products. But Noble Kizer had learned the master's techniques better, not only consistently winning in the Big Ten with the "Notre Dame system" but also with some of his mentor's trickery. The medical reports about Duane Purvis fooled Anderson and he did not prepare his players for the Purdue All-American—Hunk should have noticed that the only doctor listed as treating Purvis, including performing surgery, was the team physician. On game day, Purvis played a superb fifty-eight minutes and notched a TD on a fifty-yard pass-and-run.

The final score was 19–0, and most frustrating for the home fans was their team's inability to score, even though N.D. had the ball on offense near the Boilermaker goal line a number of times. The *Scholastic* despaired that "per custom, they [the Irish] folded up when they penetrated deep into Purdue territory." For the N.D. administrators, the only thing that saved the Purdue visit from total disaster were the trainloads of fans from Lafayette; an estimated seven thousand Boilermaker partisans pushed the attendance to over twenty-seven thousand and gave each school a $22,500 payday. However, Kizer's deception did not please O'Hara and apparently it eliminated him from consideration as the N.D. head coach.

The following week's game at Northwestern also promised decent gate receipts. The Soldier Field matches against the Wildcats were a fading memory, as were the full houses at Dyche Stadium, but in 1933, over thirty-one thousand fans in Evanston provided $28,100 to the visitors. The game also brought a bit of joy to Fighting Irish partisans.

Northwestern was weak, having won once in six games and being shut out in the other five. In a dull contest, the Fighting Irish had a single burst of aggression and turned it into the margin of victory, 7–0. Three Chicago boys on the N.D. team were the difference: "Moose" Krause blocked a punt on the NU ten-yard line, "Kitty" Gorman recovered, and from scrimmage, Andy Pilney ran for the TD. Hunk then ordered his team into a defensive posture and, according to one disgruntled reporter, "During the remainder of the game, Notre Dame played a strictly defensive game to protect its score." Fighting Irish fans were relieved by the result but very unhappy with Hunk's coaching—the victory in no way loosening the rope around his neck.

"In answer to your letter of October 19th regarding a block of thirty tickets for the Southern California [at] Notre Dame game, we will be only too glad to take care of this order of tickets in one group. I am also sure that if you order your tickets now, you will be entirely satisfied with their location."

—Arthur Haley replying to a letter from a Chicago fan
a few weeks before the 1933 USC game.

If Knute Rockne had returned to Notre Dame in 1933, he might not have been totally surprised by the team's performance—he had seen foreshadowings of Anderson's failure as a head coach in the 1926 N.D. loss at Carnegie Tech as well as Hunk's ragged University of Saint Louis teams—however, the quiet surrounding the ticket sale for the Southern Cal visit would have astonished him.

Arthur Haley no longer played an autocratic role, dispensing precious ducats to the chosen few; now he had to hustle like any other salesman in the Dirty Thirties and fawn over potential buyers. He still enjoyed helping the rich and famous—he was pleased to pull thirty tickets for Freeman and Gosden of the hit "Amos & Andy" radio show shortly before the USC game—but he also had to be polite to ordinary applicants.

A crowd of only 25,037 attended the USC contest, providing $34,100 per school and turning one of their major paydays into a financial bust—Southern Cal barely covered its travel expenses. Compounding the N.D. woes was another awful performance by the no-longer-Fighting Irish. As in 1932, the running of "Cotton" Warburton and the line play of Aaron Rosenberg, along with a strong cast of supporting Trojans, smashed Notre Dame, this time 19–0. The L.A. reporters relished the result, one commenting, "At no time during the contest did the Fighting Irish even feebly threaten." Arch Ward, covering his first game of the year at N.D., remarked acidly, "The most popular young men in South Bend tonight were Warburton and Rosenberg, the Jewish guard," and after the game, all the well-wishers and autograph hunters mobbed them, ignoring the hometown players.

Other members of the "Notre Dame family" were even more sarcastic, Arthur Haley telling a friend the next day, "The particular event at which we [the Irish] were so successful was that at no time during the entire home schedule did we pilfer, puncture, or tarnish the enemy's goal line." Not scoring a single point at home was a Notre Dame nadir, one incomprehensible to the sports world as well as to Irish insiders. James Armstrong expressed his bewilderment in the *Alumnus,* albeit with a sense of humor: "The following have been blamed for the defeats of 1933 —Harper, Anderson, the sophomores on the team, the seniors on the team (who nominates the juniors?), the present generation of [N.D.] softies, the new Dining Halls, the students, the alumni, the faculty . . . the natives of South Bend, 3.2 [beer], blondes, the weather, the Notre Dame system *à la* Frankenstein, and as many variations of causes as there have been commentators."

The Frankenstein reference was to the Rockne "Old Boys" who had taken the master's techniques to other schools and, like Rip Miller and

Noble Kizer in 1933, beaten their alma mater with them. However, this pool of former Rockne players also provided the names that Vice President O'Hara kept hearing throughout the month of November as he conducted his poll on the future of the N.D. football program.

> "We believe . . . in selecting one of the successful Notre Dame men for the position at Notre Dame [of A.D. and head football coach] and that certain factors are of equal, if not greater, importance than merely achieving victory. We believe these factors to be:
> 1. The man himself.
> 2. Technical knowledge of football and originality.
> 3. Capacity to teach the game and ability to make the most of available material.
> 4. Ability to work with the University Administration.
> 5. Capacity to handle the Alumni in relation to Athletics.
> 6. Capacity to handle the press.
> 7. Respect and confidence of other coaches and athletic directors . . ."
>
> —Letter to O'Hara from Raymond J. Kelly,
> governor of the Notre Dame Alumni Club of Detroit

The Detroit alum, representing one of the largest groups of N.D. graduates, defined the criteria for the position of Notre Dame football coach and athletic director better than the men in the Golden Dome did in any of their memos or letters. After laying out the seven points—and, in a sense, articulating the job description that Notre Dame would use ever after for A.D.s and coaches—he pushed for his own candidate, Gus Dorais, Rockne's teammate and friend, and the longtime athletic director and head football coach at the University of Detroit.

But Fathers O'Hara and O'Donnell considered Dorais too old and lacking the personality necessary for the N.D. job. They did agree, however, with the Detroit concept of a single person as athletic director and head football coach, not simply to eliminate one salary—although that was a consideration—but to clear the lines of communication between the vice president's office and the athletic department and to make one man answerable for both the operation of the department and of its most important division, Fighting Irish football. (A generation later, after the N.D. intercollegiate athletic program had grown much larger, Father Hesburgh decided to separate the jobs again.)

Francis Wallace, commenting on the 1933 search process, noted: "The job of football coach requires many talents, more so at Notre Dame than any other school; so the personality of the coach becomes an important part of the system." Rockne had set the standard and thus the man in charge of Fighting Irish football had to be affable, energetic, an excellent speaker, clean-living, and smart. "The man himself" was at the top of the Detroit list and this primary point eliminated such leading candidates as Crowley and Kizer, who did not measure up to the personality standards set by the Notre Dame administration. (Similarly, during future searches, many applicants for the job—including volcanic, obscenity-spouting Vince Lombardi in the late 1950s—slammed into this first hurdle.)

In the 1933 competition, the criteria on coaching football, numbers two and three in the Detroit list, were key parts of the job description, but those outside the "Notre Dame family" did not understand the importance of the other points. The press and fans judged the candidates solely in "football terms"—and to replace Hunk, they rated the winningest coaches, Madigan and Crowley, highest—but, for N.D. officials, *even though winning was essential, it was not the only thing.* "Certain [other] factors," as the Detroit alum wrote, "are of equal, if not greater, importance than merely achieving victory." (This attitude informs the rest of N.D. football history, explaining, in part, the hirings of all subsequent head coaches.)

In 1933, various aspects of the other criteria—ability to work with the university administration, alumni, and press—eliminated Madigan, Stuhldreher, and "Clipper" Smith. The final point, on respect and confidence of other coaches and athletic directors, worked against Tom Lieb because of his inexperience and removed Harry Mehre at Georgia, Frank Thomas at Alabama, and Frank Reese at North Carolina State from contention because Notre Dame administrators considered their sleepy southern schools too far out of the college sports loop, still dominated by eastern universities and the Big Ten, with Pacific Coast institutions gaining prestige.

"I do know, however, that you could go farther and do worse than Elmer Layden. Entirely aside from the marked success he has had winning games with his Duquesne material is the very fine character of the man . . . The large number of priests here [in Pittsburgh] who have noted his influence closely since he came here in 1927 can attest to that.

Whoever the new coach is . . . I, for one, hope the new man is a Catholic. Since there are no more Rocknes around, I am confident that you, who know all of them [Rockne's "Old Boys"] so well, will select a real Notre Dame man for the job of leading the team back where it belongs."

—Letter to O'Hara from Pittsburgh sportswriter
Jim Costin, November 17, 1933

Costin was a childhood friend and confidant of the N.D. vice president and his advice played a crucial role in O'Hara's focusing on Elmer Layden as the replacement for Anderson and Harper. Following a glorious football career as one of the Four Horsemen, Layden returned to his native Dubuque, Iowa, to practice law and to coach football at a local Catholic college. A few years later, with Rockne's encouragement and aid, he went to Duquesne as A.D. and football coach and, although working at the number-three school in the area (behind Pitt and Carnegie Tech), he built up his football program through such tactics as recruiting Jewish and black players and scheduling home games at night under arc lights. He moved Duquesne ahead of the Tartans and, in 1933, his team lost to Pitt by only 7–0.

As important to Fathers O'Hara and O'Donnell was Layden's commitment to Catholicism, his activity as a layman, his speaking ability, his smooth public demeanor, his spotless private life, and his general intelligence. On the list of criteria for the ideal Notre Dame coach, he scored very high in all categories, including a talent for dealing with athletic administrators at other schools, even his main competitors. O'Hara subsequently wrote the manager of the Carnegie Tech athletic department, "I should tell you frankly that the fine praise of Elmer Layden given by you . . . on your recent visit here was no small factor in Father O'Donnell's decision."

The N.D. vice president, in his reply to the Detroit alum who submitted the list of seven points, explained the final decision: "Elmer Layden was second choice on most of the recommendations I received. There were plenty of strong arguments advanced for favorite sons, but along with these arguments there was most frequently a recommendation of Elmer."

In late November, before Notre Dame's final game of the season, the Army annual, O'Hara brought the results of the poll and his own recommendation of Layden to O'Donnell and the president confirmed the choice. The vice president then learned that Layden would be in New York to see the N.D.–Army game and he arranged to meet him for dinner on Friday night in Manhattan. The coach later recalled: "Father O'Hara put it straight off at dinner. . . . Would I consider becoming head football coach and athletic director at Notre Dame?" Layden accepted, but because he still had commitments to fulfill at Duquesne and the Fighting Irish had a game the next day, they agreed to sign the contract and make the announcement a week later.

"In the smoldering ashes of the most disastrous season in Notre Dame history was kindled the spark of a great football team at Yankee Stadium yesterday to end Army's dream of national gridiron domination."

—Allison Danzig's lead in the *New York Times* coverage of the N.D.–Army game, December 3, 1933

Notre Dame was not looking forward to the annual visit to Yankee Stadium. In mid-November, Vice President O'Hara told a New York alum, "I suppose I will have to attend the Army game, although I find the crowds quite distressing. The duties of my new job are not at all to my liking but I will have to make the most of the situation." And, for the first time in many years, N.D. did not send its student cheerleaders to New York, asking Army to provide a few of theirs to lead the Fighting Irish fans in the "Victory March" and other well-known school songs.

West Point was in a joyous mood and agreed to the request. Under new coach Gar Davidson the Kaydets had swept through their season, compiling an 8–0 record and outscoring opponents 215 to 13, including a decisive victory over Navy. The entire Cadet Corps came down the Hudson for the Yankee Stadium match and provided the pregame and halftime festivities, one reporter noting that the sellout crowd loved the Army's "marching soldiery, its blaring bands, its parading mule," and the high-ranking officers in the special boxes. The Army show and "the host of notables from every walk of life" in attendance were "testimonial to the appeal of this national game."

For three quarters, the Cadet Corps and Army fans were happy, watching their team control play and move to a 12–0 lead. Then the Fighting Irish rose up, in the words of one of their leaders, halfback Nick Lukats, "giving vent in one final quarter to all the surplus energy that had been stored up for the entire season." Lukats led the first scoring drive of fifty-two yards, repeatedly carrying the ball in short, brutal line plunges, eventually pile-driving over for the TD. Notre Dame made the PAT and trailed 12–7.

Then both defenses dug in and the teams exchanged punts until the Fighting Irish pinned the Kaydets inside their ten-yard line. The Army could not move the ball and had to kick from its end zone. An inexperienced sophomore punter, with N.D. men crashing through his blockers, foolishly attempted to kick rather than take a safety for two points. Notre Dame left end Wayne Millner blocked it cleanly and fell on the ball for a touchdown. Even with the missed PAT, the Fighting Irish were ahead 13–12.

The Notre Dame partisans, including the school's vice president, were ecstatic. O'Hara called the comeback "as thrilling an exhibition of old-time Notre Dame football as anyone would want to see. There were rosaries waving all over the Yankee Stadium when that second touchdown was scored." But time remained for another Army series, the vice president noting, "I turned to Frank Walker [FDR's adviser] with a comment on a play . . . and he replied, 'I can't hear you, I am praying for the game to end.'"

The Fighting Irish hung on and their fans, including many middleaged and older New York ethnics, rushed from the stands, Father O'Hara observing that it was "a cure for lumbago, gout, and sciatica all at once . . . [people] were delirious, and rosaries were waving in every direction." Beyond Yankee Stadium, the Fighting Irish national following also rejoiced, one alum informing the vice president that after the radio broadcast, his wife "cried for half an hour . . . and then sat down and wrote her son [a student] at Notre Dame on the power of prayer." A footnote to this great Fighting Irish victory, one that Rockne would have enjoyed, was that Wayne Millner was Jewish. As the master coach always said, not all Fighting Irish hailed from Ireland.

Another irony about this game observed by the *New York Times* was that at the final gun, Hunk Anderson "was so singled out by the celebrating horde" of N.D. fans wanting to congratulate him that "it became necessary for State troopers to form a cordon around Anderson and escort him from the scene of battle. Anderson was smiling through it all and appeared to be enjoying himself immensely." Another reporter added that "the officers were not taking the Notre Dame coach up Tyburn to the gallows at Holborn, as so many had predicted before the game began. He was on his way to glory"—and congratulations in the N.D. locker room and the alumni banquet that night.

At the end of the radio broadcast, the Notre Dame students listening on campus erupted in celebration, chanting, "We Were Down But We Weren't Out." Then en masse they invaded downtown South Bend, snake-dancing through the streets, disrupting movie theaters and other public places, the victory affirming their belief in the uniqueness of their school's football tradition.

The *Alumnus* subsequently connected the win to "everything that

Notre Dame football has ever stood for . . . Dorais-to-Rockne, Gipp,
the Four Horsemen . . . and all of the other heroes," and it explained
the 1933 team's ability to rise up and the fans' reaction as "the faith that
has kept alive the brilliant spark that is the Notre Dame spirit through
times which have tried the uninitiated." (Later in Notre Dame football
history, during losing periods as bad as 1933, other Fighting Irish teams
have suddenly exploded and defeated national powerhouses; for example,
the 1957 squad, coming off a 2–8 year, ended the record-setting Oklahoma win streak. These upset victories are as central to the Notre Dame
mythos as the championship seasons, proving to the faithful that Fighting
Irish football might be at times on the ground but never under it.)

The New York press in postgame comments were less generous to the
N.D. team than the men on-campus. Richard Vidmer, a rising sportswriting star, focused on the Army kicker's fatal blunder in not downing the
ball for a two-point safety and a 12–9 victory. Damon Runyon sourly
noted that "Notre Dame should have won by three touchdowns at least.
They have the stuff that makes a great team. I picked Notre Dame to
win." And Joe Williams in the *World-Telegram* mocked the hypocrisy of
the New York N.D. alumni and boosters: "Now it appears that 'The
[Loudmouth] Boys' are willing to permit Mr. Anderson to hang around
for another season. It seems that it was all a mistake. Anderson is really a
fine coach."

The following Saturday, the N.D. president's office announced the resignations of Jesse Harper and Hunk Anderson. The draft of the official
statement reveals some interesting crossings-out. In praising Harper's
"very difficult task in carrying on" from his predecessor, Father O'Hara
first wrote, "Knute Rockne was a keen business man *but he had his own
methods,*" then the vice president revised the clause to the less pointed
"but his methods were unique." For Anderson, he began, "It is unfortunate that the public demanded of him more than football coaching,"
underlining Hunk's inability to do more than that task; O'Hara subsequently wiped out the entire sentence, replacing it with the innocuous
"No alumnus of the University was ever more honest and sincere." As
the N.D. administrators put the best face on the dismissals, so did
Harper and Anderson, each pledging permanent affection for Notre
Dame and departing gracefully—Hunk to North Carolina State and
Harper to his ranch in Kansas.

Along with the resignations came the announcement of Layden's assumption of the head coaching and A.D. posts, the *Chicago Tribune* pointing out that "Layden is taking over the biggest, if not the hardest, coaching job in the country." To the press, the new man affirmed, "All I know about football is what Rock taught me," and he promised to return to the true "Notre Dame system." One of the losing candidates, "Clipper" Smith, graciously elaborated on this point: the winner's "fine record at Duquesne" was due to "his fidelity to the Notre Dame system," whereas "the trouble with most of Rockne's men in coaching is that we try to improve on the old system—as a result we have no definite style of play."

> "A prominent topic of conversation among the thirty-three Bishops present was the change in the athletic regime at Notre Dame. I heard from many of them that they were most pleased to know that Notre Dame had found a scholarly cultured gentleman to head the athletic department . . . Even His Excellency, the Apostolic Delegate, voiced his pleasure at [this and] the result of the Army game. I told him that it was considered good form among the members of the hierarchy to attend at least one Notre Dame game each year."
>
> —Father O'Hara in a letter to Notre Dame
> patron James A. Phelan, December 16, 1933

No one was more pleased with the appointment of Elmer Layden— other than the candidate himself—than the N.D. vice president. The Notre Dame community lauded the new man, the press mainly praised the selection, and the alumni and even the boosters seemed pleased by the move. O'Hara wrote his friend Jim Costin, "I am tickled to death that your advanced judgment on Layden has met with such universal approval . . . the reception of Layden's appointment has been so whole-hearted that you have great reason to be satisfied with your recommendation."

Particularly pleasing to the N.D. vice president because he had ambitions to move up in the church hierarchy was the approval of the prelates. Not only did the bishops and the Pope's delegate congratulate him on Notre Dame's choice but so did many high-ranking Catholic educators around the country. However, in replying to one well-wisher, O'Hara offered a caution, paraphrasing pro–N.D. sportswriter Warren Brown's fear "that the over-publicizing of our popular new coach might be as dangerous as the over-publicizing of Sophomore [football prospects] before the season started. He [Brown] commented that Elmer realizes how fickle the mob is, and gave an illustration or two from Layden's own experience."

O'Hara's optimism was also tempered by the end-of-season fiscal results. The Army annual had prevented complete disaster, but even a full
Yankee Stadium brought the total attendance to only 278,258, the lowest
number in a decade. As sobering were the final gross receipts of $297,544
—down $193,000 from the previous year—and, after factoring in the
total expenses, a net profit of only $177,494, down a whopping 66 percent
from the 1929 benchmark. If the first seasons of the Layden regime
continued the slide of the Harper-Anderson era, football profits would
turn to red-inked numbers within two years and the University of Notre
Dame would be in serious financial difficulty.

Father John O'Hara, although a practical man, frequently turned to
prayer. No doubt, at the end of 1933, he made more than one novena for
his beloved university, its football team, and its new coach.

34

O'Hara and Layden
Assume Power: 1934–1936

"Civilization, not simply athletics, was on a spree during that decade [the 1920s]. . . . The athletic organizations didn't pay much attention to price tags during that period. Football gates reached phenomenal proportions and . . . gravy flowed largely in these directions: 1. Salaries of athletic officers; 2. Equipment for teams; 3. Long trips in Pullman cars, with overnight accommodations at swanky country clubs; 4. Huge stadia."

—Address by Vice President John O'Hara
of Notre Dame to the annual convention
of the National Collegiate Athletic Association,
December 29, 1933

In the 1930s, to prevent a resurgence of the college sports reform movement and to co-opt its remaining members, the intercollegiate athletic establishment began to use the previously obscure NCAA as its front organization. At its annual meetings, the association created "study groups" to investigate the problems in college sports, and when these panels eventually reported that widespread abuses did indeed exist in many areas, notably recruiting and subsidization, the NCAA passed such resolutions as: "The Association by its very nature has no police power. It is the responsibility of each individual institution to correct its own shortcomings. The Association's code but points the path to follow." Nevertheless, to appear as reformers, the NCAA promulgated a code of high ideals that rivaled the 1930s constitution of the Soviet Union and, like that document, was a Potemkin Village fronting a multitude of sordid practices.

The point man for the intercollegiate athletic establishment was Major John Griffith, commissioner of the Big Ten. He assumed the presidency of the NCAA in 1933 and while retaining his Big Ten position brought that conference's strategy to the association—a public espousal of the "pure amateur code" and a private wink-and-a-nod to such "bosses" as Fielding Yost with their corrupt football programs. Ignoring the obvious symbolism, Griffith located the NCAA office in the Hotel Sherman in Chicago, an address the association shared with many of the city's crooked politicians.

Because Griffith had a fondness for Notre Dame and knew that he could count on President Charles O'Donnell for a high-minded discourse, he invited the N.D. official to speak at the 1933 convention. O'Donnell accepted, but because his health deteriorated further during the fall, he sent his vice president in his place.

Father O'Hara was as direct and aggressive as O'Donnell was restrained and accommodating. The vice president also took pride in his commerce background and his no-nonsense approach to ledger sheets. No doubt, the delegates to the NCAA convention were surprised to hear the priest condemn their means and methods of livelihood. After listing the financial problems created by the 1920s splurge on college sports, O'Hara criticized "the kiting of [coaches'] salaries" as well as their outside entrepreneurial deals, but he predicted that "popular coaches, like movie stars, [have] passed through the testimonial period, and that particular form of 'goofiness' seems to be waning." He also attacked excessive expenditures on equipment, including "silk pants" for football squads, and the money spent on the "elaborate system of scouting" that sends assistants to "every [single] game played by rivals whom the coach considers important."

In his condemnation of coaches' excesses, O'Hara never mentioned Knute Rockne by name, but his audience, particularly Major John Griffith, must have made the connection and also wondered if the Notre Dame vice president was sending a signal to his new A.D. and head coach, Elmer Layden. The message for the latter became clearer when, at the end of his talk, O'Hara denounced the academic "leniency in favor of athletes" occurring at many schools and argued that because "the world expects more of representative athletes than of many other stu-

dents in their classes," universities "should be very exacting in their demand for sound academic work from athletes." A week later, O'Hara
instituted an N.D. policy requiring Fighting Irish athletes to maintain a
grade average of 77 percent to play intercollegiate sports, whereas regular students only needed 70 percent to pass courses and graduate.

With this speech, Father O'Hara began a new approach to intercollegiate
athletics at Notre Dame. Previous administrators had *reacted to* attacks
on the school's athletic program; Father O'Hara, assertive by nature and
savvy about the uses of publicity, decided to take the moral high ground
and make Notre Dame cleaner in fact as well as in word than all other
universities in big-time college sports. His strategy was simple—on the
ethical heights he would construct "Fortress Notre Dame" and render it
impervious to the charges and rumors that had long plagued the Catholic
school.

Unlike his predecessors, O'Hara did not have to deal with the original
"power coach," Knute Rockne, and he knew that he could control Elmer
Layden. Therefore, in 1934, when the NCAA redid its code and, according to its official history, termed " 'unjustifiable' almost all forms of
recruiting and subsidy except legitimate on-campus employment at standard wage rate and, in the case of recruiting, a coach's reply to an appli-
cant-initiated inquiry," O'Hara not only accepted the new standards but
went them one better—he forbade Layden to leave campus to meet even
legitimate recruits; all prospects had to visit the coach in his athletic
department office. Instead of simply going along with the Big Ten rules
and the NCAA code as his N.D. predecessors had done, O'Hara upped
the ante and challenged other universities to follow the Catholic school's
lead. His action at this time determined the future course of Notre Dame
sports and became the permanent policy of the institution in regard to its
intercollegiate athletic program.

The vice president acted out of religious and pragmatic impulses; for
him, the Fighting Irish represented the Holy Church, thus the athletic
program had to be as pure as "Our Lady on the Dome." If the school
adhered to this mandate, increasing numbers of Catholic families would
send their boys to play for Notre Dame and the Fighting Irish would
achieve on-field success. His predecessors also held these beliefs but,
mainly because of Rockne, had been unable to implement them.

O'Hara's move also locked his successors inside "Fortress Notre
Dame." Even if they had wanted to—and none ever did—they could not
oppose the command to run the cleanest possible athletic program. In

addition, the "Notre Dame family" supported this position and came to take great pride in it; even Fighting Irish fanatics eventually accepted it. Then, insuring its perpetuity, the Notre Dame mythmakers—ignoring or unaware of the irony—turned Rockne into the originator of the totally-clean-program edict. (The policy, however, created one major problem: the outside world was and is often irritated by what former N.D. professor Thomas Strich calls the institution's "holier-than-thou image" in college sports, and in recent years, whenever a stain has appeared on a blue-and-gold uniform, the press and public have magnified it with an intensity never applied to incidents at other schools.)

■ ■ ■

"Last spring these two football enterprises [Notre Dame and USC] felt justified in signing a contract for three years in their football business . . . It is a far cry from the devotion of the fathers who founded Notre Dame and of the earnest men who labored to create a university in Southern California to the three year contract these colleges have signed to exploit their football teams for commercial purposes."

—Henry S. Pritchett,
president emeritus of the Carnegie Foundation,
in an essay for the annual report, February 1934

The longtime antagonist of big-time college sports, in his seventy-sixth year and in retirement in Santa Barbara, could not resist a final shot at the intercollegiate athletic establishment. His short essay, "A Slump in the Football Trade," attacked the whole notion of commercialized college sports and he included a brief swipe at the Fighting Irish and the Trojans.

With President O'Donnell now semiparalyzed, Father O'Hara called a press conference and counterattacked, assuring the world: "Dr. Pritchett stated with a false assumption that highly publicized football is inimical to the intellectual interests of the university. That has not been our experience at Notre Dame. We wish to reiterate at this time that if we ever find it to be the case we will drop football without a moment's hesitation."

In his replies to letter writers, O'Hara was even more assertive, telling an oil company executive, "we have a beautiful front yard [campus quadrangle] that we would not trade for the front yard of any other school. Dr. Pritchett hates to think that we got it the way we did [through football profits] but I would much rather have it that way than to have obtained it out of some of Andy Carnegie's old squeeze plays," that is, union busting and bankrupting competitors.

The N.D. administrator also had an excellent sense of the sporting press and a willingness to use it. Unlike his predecessors, who kept most sportswriters at arm's length, O'Hara knew that because these journalists abhorred reformers, he could win them as allies for his school. He explained to a friend, "I found among sports writers a tendency to regard Dr. Pritchett as a publicity seeker and to meet his charges with a [near] conspiracy of silence . . . Monday, a brief paragraph or two on Pritchett's report; Tuesday, twice as much space given to my reply; Wednesday, something by the sports columnist [in favor of us]. The columnists in Chicago have not even mentioned the report, and I have heard on the side that they omitted the reference in order to kill the story."

O'Hara was so interested in the press coverage of Notre Dame sports that he had the school subscribe to a Chicago clipping service and was soon rewarded with a packet of articles from newspapers commenting favorably on N.D.'s new eligibility rules for its athletes. With his hands-on approach to the press, the N.D. vice president also sought out prominent sportswriters. In October 1934, he wrote Grantland Rice: "I enjoyed that hour with you [in New York] immensely the other night. I hope we may meet often, and at least occasionally at Notre Dame. Our [student] journalists have had the benefits of talks by several sportswriters this fall and I certainly hope that you can join this special staff some time at your convenience." Unlike President O'Donnell, who appreciated writers like Westbrook Pegler at a distance, O'Hara used Rockne's technique of actively courting important journalists.

In addition, O'Hara wanted "some recognition . . . given each year to an outstanding sports writer who has defended Notre Dame." He was too canny to give a public "award" because it "would be misinterpreted as the purchase price of a favorable attitude," but he approved sending invitations "to the [N.D. annual] football banquet" to a number of pro–Notre Dame writers and feting them there.

In his policy toward the sporting press, O'Hara codified a situation that had been building for a number of years. As Notre Dame's School of Journalism turned out more graduates, increasing numbers of them gained prominence in the sports field, and by the mid-1930s, they formed an unofficial network, along with pro–N.D. writers like Grantland Rice, in support of the Fighting Irish. Francis Wallace listed among his fellow alums Bill Fox of the *Indianapolis News*, Arch Ward and George

Strickler of the *Chicago Tribune*, Jim Gallagher, Jim Kearns, and Bill Moloney on other Chicago papers, and the most famous product of N.D. journalism, at the time in Saint Louis but eventually making it to New York and national syndication, Walter "Red" Smith. Wallace acknowledged that he had "never heard of any of them giving their alma mater the worst of it."

O'Hara brought these writers to campus for various occasions and also extended regular invitations to such sportswriting friends of Notre Dame as Warren Brown and Wilfred Smith in Chicago, and Bill Corum, Frank Graham, and Dan Parker in New York.

With the "Aw-Nuts" school of sports journalism literally and metaphorically dead—W. O. McGeehan passed away in 1933 and left few heirs—and Grantland Rice prospering in syndicated columns and magazines as well as on radio and in movie shorts, most of the young pro–N.D. writers were second-generation "Gee-Whizzers." Red Smith was an independent exception, but Arch Ward was more typical, representing, according to his biographer, "Counter-Skepticism, a tighter alliance of sports management and the makers of newspaper publicity than had existed before." (The remaining "Aw-Nuts" writers scattered; some, like Westbrook Pegler, leaving the "sandbox of the newspaper—the Sports Department" for general journalism, others, like Damon Runyon, turning full-time to alternative genres, in his case, short stories.)

Not all 1930s sportswriters loved the Fighting Irish, but a decreasing number attacked them in print. During the regime of vice president and then president John O'Hara, the relationship between the N.D. athletic department and some newspapers became so symbiotic that these journals carried Fighting Irish pregame and game stories written by Joe Petritz, the Notre Dame sports publicity man, as straight news items.

Under O'Hara, the N.D. administration was also willing to use influence to silence writers. In the fall of 1934, Jesse Harper wrote Arthur Haley, "I see by the *South Bend Tribune* that [columnist] Jack Ledden continues to take his dirty cracks at me. I came away [from Notre Dame] and kept my mouth shut and will continue to do so unless a poor sap, like Jack Ledden, keeps up his present tactics." Haley quickly assured Harper that "this matter has been taken care of, and there should be nothing further along this line, for there is absolutely no rime or reason for it."

One midwestern sportswriter who began his career in this period recently recalled: "During O'Hara's reign, the Golden Dome became much more aggressive about rewarding its newspaper friends and shutting out or off its supposed enemies. O'Hara had a real us-versus-them mentality and you were either completely on board or you were in the enemy's camp. Many later N.D. administrators inherited this attitude . . . some of it continues today, they're still very thin-skinned and they're even unhappy with the tame NBC house announcers doing 'Notre Dame Saturday.' It all started with O'Hara."

> "He [O'Hara] decreed that to be eligible for football, a player not only had to pass all of his subjects, he also had to maintain a 77 average, which was seven points above the passing mark. Quite honestly, I [Layden] did not favor this change. When I got word of it, I called in [my administrative assistant] Bob Cahill, who knew his way around the university's record offices, and gave him a list of distinguished alumni of the university. These ranged from bank presidents to railroad presidents. 'Bob, go over and find out just what kind of averages these gentlemen had,' I told him.
>
> I had the notion that if I could show Father O'Hara that some of the best contributors had less than a 77 average, he might relent.
>
> Bob Cahill reported the next day that all the names on my list had averages in the 80's or better. 'And while I was there, Mr. Layden,' he added, 'I checked your average [as an undergraduate] and I might say that you were very lucky that this rule wasn't enforced ten years ago.'"
>
> —Layden in his memoir, *The Elmer Layden Story*

Even before Layden arrived at Notre Dame in early 1934, Vice President O'Hara began to make major changes in the operation of the athletic department. Arthur Haley, still the business manager, wrote a friend that "several things have happened, of which I was more or less fearful." O'Hara, as chairman of the athletic board, instituted "a new set-up" that resulted in the "lessening of authority in the [athletic] director's hands . . . They [the board] plan on handling more of making the schedule and the director is to advise [consult] with them [before taking action] on practically all matters."

O'Hara's reorganization contradicts the central myth about Elmer Layden's term as N.D. athletic director—that he single-handedly built a great football schedule. Although he improved relations with a number of Big Ten schools, he was mainly the Notre Dame contact for scheduling; behind the scenes, the N.D. administration and the faculty athletic board called the shots.

Layden helped perpetuate the myth by claiming, "One of the first games I scheduled after becoming athletic director of Notre Dame was with Ohio State [for a home-and-home in 1935–1936]." In fact, negotiations with OSU began during Jesse Harper's years as A.D. and that school's faculty representative visited Notre Dame in early 1933 to inspect its academic treatment of athletes (such instances of Big Ten condescension toward the Catholic school infuriated O'Hara and led, in part, to his one-upmanship athletic policy). In November 1933, Ohio State agreed to the series, and the edition of the *Chicago Tribune* that headlined "LAYDEN SIGNS CONTRACT AS NOTRE DAME COACH, DIRECTOR" (December 10, 1933) also carried a sidebar, "HARPER'S LAST ACT IS ANNOUNCEMENT OF 1935 SCHEDULE," that included the contest in Columbus.

In addition to controlling scheduling, Father O'Hara also tightened athletic department spending. He began by cutting the salary of the A.D. and coach to $8,000 and by lowering the football assistants' pay to $3,000. The vice president allowed Layden to propose his staff but not only did the faculty athletic board insist on approving the appointments, its chair did the actual hiring. Joe Boland, an N.D. lineman under Rockne, was coaching and doing radio work in Minnesota in January 1934 when, his wife recalled, "a long-distance call came from Father John O'Hara [asking] Joe to serve as line coach." After Boland agreed and hung up the phone, his wife inquired about the salary—Boland's "tremendous grin adjusted to one of startled incredulity that anybody [offered a chance to return to Notre Dame] should bother with such a minor detail as money."

Vice President O'Hara, although authoritarian by nature, preferred to deal with Layden, Boland, and other former N.D. athletes in more subtle ways. He told a Pittsburgh friend: "When Elmer and I were talking over the prospect of his coming to Notre Dame, he said to me, 'You know, I'm a great griper.' I replied, 'You're telling me! Who is there who has ever listened to your griping more than I have.'" And, throughout the 1930s, O'Hara often called on his early relationship as father confessor to Layden to calm his coach and/or to insure that administrative directives were carried out. (O'Hara also served as Layden's protector, and when the priest left N.D. in 1940, the younger man, unshielded, began his final lap at the school.)

In 1934, Layden acknowledged that "Father O'Hara had decided that the advent of a new coach was the right time for some new athletic eligibility rules," but the football man did not like them. In addition to the 77 percent grade rule, O'Hara moved ahead of the Big Ten and the NCAA by limiting an athlete's playing eligibility to eight semesters—sophomore year through a fifth year. Layden pointed out that "transfer students often competed in sports for considerably more than eight semesters, particularly if they were good players," but O'Hara explained that he "wanted [N.D.] to be ahead of the [rules] game for a change" and he imposed an unilateral limit of eight semesters.

The vice president did continue the N.D. on-campus job program for athletes but he insisted that they do actual work, including work in the dining halls. Layden, like his predecessors in the football office, controlled a number of so-called athletic scholarships (grants-for-work) but he could not leave campus to offer them to recruits. His trainer, Scrapiron Young, recalled how two outstanding prospects from Riley High in South Bend—one "a strapping 190-pounder" and the other "a slight 140-pound" lineman—visited the coach in his office: "One glance at the [bigger] boy set off a gleam in the eyes of Elmer Layden. He okayed a scholarship for him immediately. The same was not true for" the other recruit, Joe Kuharich, who had to earn his grant but became an All-American and eventually an N.D. head coach.

O'Hara's restrictions on recruiting did not totally hamper his coach— unofficial Notre Dame "bird dogs" such as Francis Wallace still hunted for football talent and often paid a prospect's train fare to South Bend— but Layden had to compete against rival coaches who courted recruits in the latters' hometowns and front parlors. Nevertheless, according to Layden, the N.D. president warned him: "If I wanted to see a boy [badly enough], I had better make a novena that somebody would bring him to campus to see me."

After working under this restraint for two years, the coach began to quietly dispatch Scrapiron Young to check out the "bird dogs'" best prospects and "to talk with the boy, and perhaps induce him to come to South Bend." Nonetheless, the N.D. head lost a number of future All-Americans because he could not visit them and their families. "Right at the head of the list," he placed Marshall "Biggie" Goldberg, from West Virginia—considered the best Jewish football player in a period with many great ones, including Jay Berwanger, the first Heisman Trophy winner, and Sid Luckman, an eventual Hall of Fame QB.

Layden used his contacts in western Pennsylvania to woo Goldberg, and apparently the running back wished to go to Notre Dame. Francis Wallace related that the player was "assured of a [N.D.] scholarship by an alumnus who was qualified to talk, but Goldberg's father, a businessman, wanted to hear it from the coach . . . [who] wasn't allowed to leave campus." In the end, Jock Sutherland of Pitt won over the father, clinching the deal with a no-work athletic scholarship. Years later, Layden still bemoaned the loss of this prospect: "Can you imagine what it would have meant . . . if Marshall Goldberg had been an All-American at Notre Dame [instead of Pitt]?" According to the N.D. coach, another of the "ones that got away" was 1940 Heisman Trophy winner Tom Harmon of nearby Gary, Indiana. The high school star was interested in Notre Dame but the package offered to him by the University of Michigan proved irresistible and he enrolled in Fielding Yost's athletic program.

Nevertheless, just as Father O'Hara had planned, increasing numbers of Catholic high school football stars came to Notre Dame, and by 1938, the N.D. coach had forty-two captains of parochial high school teams on his Fighting Irish squad. This phenomenon sparked the sports proverb "Notre Dame doesn't recruit, it gathers." Many prospects came without guaranteed jobs on-campus and, according to one of Layden's aides, even though the freshman team was "cannon fodder for the varsity in practice," most youngsters "went into every scrimmage as if their very existence depended on their showing. In many cases it did, they were working to gain Layden's approval and thus insure the coveted scholarships in the years to come."

Layden, like his mentor Rockne, believed in huge squads and, in addition to over 100 freshman team members, he divided the other players into twelve separate units, 132 men in all, most on some sort of "B.R.T." work-grant. The head coach kept the first six teams—the "A" group—with him and his main assistants and he assigned other aides to drill the "B" elevens. However, Layden frequently promoted members of the "B" units to the "A" teams, as well as players up through the "A" ranks. Because he was also demoting athletes, the competition produced rigorous practices and an alert varsity.

> "Elmer humorously remarked [in his speech at the banquet] that he has a two-fold program for Notre Dame. His first move, he said, will be to 'set up a defense against the downtown coaches,' and the other will be to 'get the Bendix Corporation [of South Bend] to take the brakes off our [running] backs.'"
>
> —*Notre Dame Alumnus,* April 1934

Layden's smooth wit and diplomatic demeanor concealed a very tough and ambitious personality. He was always polite to those who could help him but tended to ignore those who could not. Jesse Harper complained to Arthur Haley in April 1934: "I sent him [Layden] a wire of congratulations and also left a letter in the office [in December 1933] giving considerable detail [about the A.D. job], especially in regard to the spring schedule, and he has never taken the time to write even a form letter [in return]."

Layden learned many things from his mentor Rockne, including a hard-nosed, pragmatic attitude. Their correspondence reveals their mutual bond. When Layden was trying to leave his first coaching job at a small Catholic school in Iowa and negotiating with Duquesne, he explained his reasons in terms his coach totally understood: "They [Duquesne] are in bad shape [in football], but very anxious to get ahead. They aim [high]. I know it will not be a bed of roses but I like the idea of trying to build up [a football program]."

Rockne affirmed that Duquesne was "anxious to step out and do things," noting that "if they have a couple of Pittsburgh [money] men behind them, they will probably have enough brains to realize that you have to spend some money to make some money." When Layden accepted the job, Rockne told him, "I believe you are smart in going to Duquesne and they will give you full leeway" in recruiting and subsidization. The school did, but Layden still had to scramble and innovate to compete with his main rivals, Carnegie Tech and Pitt.

While head coach at Duquesne, Layden also discussed the refereeing situation with the master: "One Saturday our shift is illegal and the next it's all right . . . [one official] refused to explain a couple of his rulings, which were wrong according to the rules. So we refused to have him anymore. He, on the other hand, tried to get all the other officials to set down on us but we have overcome any prejudice he may have set up in their minds. It [dealing with refs] surely is a great life!"

Layden thoroughly understood the game official system and, with his diplomatic skills, he manipulated it. Throughout his N.D. years, he employed many of Rockne's and his own favorite officials, and unlike teams of the Hunk Anderson period, his squads did not rack up excessive penalty yardage—he also instilled greater on-field discipline in his players. Even for road games, Layden "worked in" such Rockne pals as J. J. Lipp; after the 1934 USC contest in Los Angeles, Arthur Haley jokingly remarked to Arch Ward: "I have just written Lipp a letter and told him I was surprised that he did not penalize somebody fifteen yards for something or another. That being an official's delight. I am wondering if he really enjoyed himself. Perhaps he forgot his whistle."

"The morale of the team has been restored. It is seldom that the Notre Dame fan is satisfied in defeat, but those 33,000 fans who came away [from the opening game] and saw the 7 to 6 victory by Jack Chevigny's Texas Longhorns went away enthusiastic, proud that Notre Dame, with its back to the wall in the closing minutes of play, struck again and again with the old-time poise and confidence."

—*Notre Dame Alumnus,* November 1934

Unfortunately for Elmer Layden, he had to open his N.D. coaching career against a tough Texas team run by former Notre Dame player and junior coach Jack Chevigny. According to an N.D. insider, Chevigny "had nurtured a grievance" against his alma mater because "he felt he had received a 'bum deal' " during his term as Hunk Anderson's main assistant. Chevigny primed his squad for this game and, in the locker room before the kickoff, he gave what one of his players described as "the greatest speech we had ever heard. We were a bunch of demons when we went out to play Notre Dame."

Texas scored a TD on its first possession and hung on as Layden shuttled in various units—he had never seen most of the Irish in game action. The N.D. coach, recalling how Chevigny as a player had scored a key TD in the famous "Gipper" game, later commented, "Jack went out and won one for Chevigny." Even though the loss marked the first-ever N.D. defeat in a home opener, Fighting Irish fans were pleased by the spirit and alertness of the team.

The second game of the season vividly illustrated the difference between Hunk Anderson's regime and Elmer Layden's. The Purdue Boilermakers visited, and their coach, Noble Kizer, a leading candidate in 1933 for the N.D. job, wanted to prove that his alma mater had erred in choosing Layden over him—also, as one of the Seven Mules, he always resented the fame and fortune heaped upon the Four Horsemen. With essentially the same Purdue starting eleven that had beaten the Irish 19–0 the previous year, Kizer expected an easy time of it. In fact, Layden had his team ready, and the Irish built a three-touchdown lead before Purdue got one back. Final score 18–7, and a campus full of happy fans.

The following week, Layden avenged the previous year's loss to Carnegie Tech by beating the Tartans, 13–0, at Notre Dame. Then his team took on the Wisconsin Badgers—another Big Ten school restored to the schedule by Harper—and mauled them, 19–0, the N.D. coach playing the reserves in the second half.

Fighting Irish fans were beginning to talk about a national championship, but Layden knew that the real test for his crew was the next game, against Pitt in their stadium. He wanted to win for personal as well as professional reasons—he disliked Pitt coach Jock Sutherland and resented the latter's frequent jibes at him—but the 1934 Panthers were deep and tough, having lost only to powerful Minnesota (the Gophers went on to win the national championship). Led by fullback "Izzy" Weinstock, Pitt battered the young Irish line and triumphed, 19–0. After the game, a reporter remarked that, unlike Hunk Anderson and most other coaches, "Layden refused to alibi the defeat," frankly acknowledging Pitt's superiority. The *New York Times* man saw the loss as part of the continuing decline of "the once famed [football] outfit of Notre Dame," but the new coach believed his boys would fight back.

Unfortunately, the next game was in Cleveland against a good Navy squad led by an excellent passing QB, "Buzz" Borries. Notre Dame controlled the contest with its ground game but Navy struck suddenly with two long pass plays, converting them into a field goal and a TD for a 10–6 victory.

The following contest against Northwestern in Evanston revealed another link between Layden and Rockne. Instead of playing strictly defensive football, as Hunk Anderson had ordered the previous year against the Wildcats, N.D. scored the winning TD on a Rockne-like trick play. On a crucial down in an offensive drive, the Irish QB, before taking the snap, suddenly stopped his cadence and turned around, pretending to examine the formation of his backs—meanwhile, during the pause, the center snapped the ball to a running back who spun wide of the startled Wildcats for the touchdown. Northwestern never recovered and the Irish won, 20–7.

> "Tomorrow is the annual gathering of that amazing clan of self-appointed Notre Dame alumni which will whoop and rage and rant and roar through our town [New York] from sunup until long after sundown in honor of a school to which they never went. . . .
>
> There are no self-appointed Colgate or St. Mary's or Tulane or Purdue alumni when those teams come to visit our town. But there is some sweet magic about the name of Notre Dame that annually draws the damndest rabble out of its warrens. There is nothing that the proud old University can do about these boorish sons."
>
> —Paul Gallico, *New York Daily News,*
> November 23, 1934

Elmer Layden realized that the key test of his first campaign—and depending on his grade on it, whether he would have many more seasons at Notre Dame—was the game in Yankee Stadium against a strong Army team. The East Coast N.D. alumni, the Fighting Irish fanatics, and the New York and national media would judge and loudly comment upon his

work. Even though the Notre Dame administrators always downplayed
negative New York reactions, Layden knew that they could not ignore
them completely, particularly because bad reviews could eventually affect the school's largest annual payday.

Army was favored in 1934 and the game attracted the "biggest turnout of fans in the East this season." Eighty-one thousand "jammed the
huge triple-decked Yankee Stadium, overflowed into the aisles and furnished a brilliant, vociferous background . . . for the football battle"
(AP). Paul Gallico estimated that "three-quarters [of the fans were] bawl-
ing at the top of their lungs for Notre Dame du Lac," and, on this day,
they cheered a satisfying Fighting Irish win. They also embraced the new
head coach, some running onto the field after the game to lift him onto
their shoulders.

The press emphasized the point that, in this victory, a symbolic torch
passed from Rockne to Layden because the player scoring the winning
TD was "the last remaining Rockne coached member of the Fighting
Irish" (New York Post). Fullback Dan Hanley of switched-jersey fame
had sat out 1931–1932, but Layden sent him into the Army game as a
substitute and, with the clock running out, Hanley plunged over to secure the 12–6 win.

To complete the season, the team then went to the West Coast to meet
USC. Fortunately for the young coach, the Trojans were in a slump and
entered the contest with a 4–5–1 record. Also luckily for him, because he
had to go into his third-string units to find healthy players, he had an
excellent junior halfback whom he had benched for personal reasons—
his younger brother, Francis "Mike" Layden. Not wanting to show any
favoritism to his sibling, from spring practice on, the head coach had
ignored Mike both on and off the field and had even considered yanking
his athletic scholarship, awarded by Hunk Anderson. But against USC,
he had to play his brother, and Mike responded by scoring the only two
TDs of the contest.

The Notre Dame faithful were content, Arch Ward writing in his
game article for the Chicago Tribune, "There was no discounting the
superiority of Elmer Layden's eleven . . . Notre Dame had the dash,
the zip, and some of the cohesion that marked its last victory on Los
Angeles soil in 1930." Thus, even though Layden's Fighting Irish had
not yet returned to the heights attained by Rockne's great teams, they
were climbing in the right direction and the 6–3 season was an excellent
first stop.

The Notre Dame administration also approved of the job done by the new coach. Father John O'Hara was now president—Father Charles O'Donnell's suffering had ended during the summer and the C.S.C. order had quickly moved the vice president into the top office. O'Hara was pleased with the team's on-field success but he worried about the gate receipts: N.D.'s share of the four home games—$50,000 and change—was about $25,000 less than the past year's, even though the Fighting Irish had won three of the contests. What saved the season financially were the visits to Pittsburgh and Cleveland as well as an even better payout than previous ones in Yankee Stadium. However, the USC game in the Los Angeles Coliseum had produced only $48,000 for N.D., an all-time low from that venue. Nevertheless, the total attendance for the season was 365,000, up almost 77,000 from the previous year, and more important, the football receipts were almost $363,000, an increase of approximately $65,000 over 1933. Less comforting were the profits: after subtracting football and athletic department expenses of almost $193,000, the profit was merely $15,400 more than in 1933.

When he closed the books on Layden's first year as athletic director and football coach, O'Hara acknowledged the younger man's accomplishments, but with the Great Depression continuing, he knew that Notre Dame and college football still faced very difficult economic times.

To complicate O'Hara's problems, in 1934 the civic leaders of New Orleans and Miami established the Sugar Bowl and Orange Bowl games to attract tourists to their cities. After the Fighting Irish wins over Army and USC, representatives of those bowls approached Notre Dame about sending the team to their contests. Promises of large paydays floated about, but the Catholic school, having long ago decided against playing in the Rose Bowl with its guaranteed $150,000 payout, was adamantly against going south to a lesser event. "Just more post-season games," one member of the athletic board remarked, "for us to turn down invitations to. Let's see how long the Big Ten holds out."

■ ■ ■

"The present administration [of Notre Dame] welcomes assistance [in athletic matters from alumni, boosters, and the press]. And yet, all concerned know that there is a limit to this friendly help, and in the last analysis, this University exercises complete independence [in all football matters]. . . . This is as it should be, because Notre Dame, although a

school, is at the same time a family and, as in a family, there is the final
authority in the head. So at Notre Dame, the final authority and accompanying responsibility are vested in the president and the [C.S.C.]
council."

—Vice President Hugh "Pepper" O'Donnell,
addressing the 1935 N.D. football banquet

After being named president of Notre Dame, O'Hara appointed the
longtime N.D. prefect of discipline, Father Hugh "Pepper" O'Donnell,
as his vice president. Pepper was the first former Fighting Irish football
player to reach the highest echelons of his school's administration, and
although he loved the team and the sport, his run-ins with Rockne in the
1920s over the disciplining of athletes foreshadowed his adherence to
O'Hara's tough line on executive control of the athletic department.

In O'Donnell's speech at the football banquet, he offered his version
of O'Hara's hierarchical approach and he elaborated on the "Notre
Dame family" theme; for example, "family that we are, we have never
permitted our ineligible student athletes to have their weaknesses broadcast to the nation and thereby become outcasts on the altar of publicity."
(This policy continues to the present and frustrates a press now interested in spotlighting ineligible and/or disciplined N.D. athletes.)

As vice president and chair of the athletic board, Pepper O'Donnell
carried out O'Hara's mandate and, before the 1935 season, declared that
All-American center Jack Robinson had used up his intercollegiate eligibility because, during a year with the N.D. reserves, he had played a total
of five minutes in a game against a small college.

With Robinson and a number of other starters lost through ineligibil-
ity, graduation, and injury, Elmer Layden, employing Rockne's preseason
pessimistic line, told the press, "Prospects were bad last year, this year
they may be described as worse." Nevertheless, with a huge squad and
excellent players at the "skill" positions, the Fighting Irish whomped
Kansas, 28–7, in the opener, and then took Carnegie Tech, 14–3, in
Pittsburgh.

In the third game, at Wisconsin, N.D. kept the Badgers in their holes,
27–0, and were ready to meet unbeaten Pitt the following week. The
game attracted almost forty thousand spectators to Notre Dame Stadium
and most went home happy because of a last-minute, 9–6, victory. One
journalist reported that the team "played great football reminiscent of
the Rockne era when a Notre Dame team wouldn't be beaten," and
declared this "team as the greatest since Rockne."

The momentum from the last-minute victory continued into the following game, an easy 14–0 win over Navy in Baltimore, and set up the long-awaited match against Ohio State in Columbus. The Buckeyes were extremely strong in 1934, with a huge line—"an almost unbelievable collection of collosi" (New York Times)—and an imaginative offense—three hundred plays from seven basic formations designed by coach Francis Schmidt. Ohio State had breezed through its previous six games and some midwestern sportswriters proclaimed: "Without a doubt the winner [of this game] will go on to an undefeated season and a possible national championship." The pregame hoopla for the first ever meeting between N.D. and OSU helped sell out the huge eighty-one-thousand-seat stadium in Columbus—an achievement in the Depression. The entire Notre Dame student body took special trains to the game but, in the Ohio capital, encountered extremely hostile crowds and anti-Catholic taunts. Moreover, on Friday, when the team went to practice at a small college outside of Columbus, according to one of the players, "there must have been 15,000 people there . . . And of course, they were yelling, 'Catholics, go home.' It didn't shock me, but it kind of made me feel tense and tight."

The match more than lived up to pregame expectations. Allison Danzig began his New York Times story with: "One of the greatest last-ditch rallies in football history toppled the dreaded Scarlet Scourge of Ohio State from its lofty pinnacle today as 81,000 dumbfounded spectators saw Notre Dame score three touchdowns in less than fifteen minutes to gain an almost miraculous 18–13 victory in jammed Buckeye Stadium."

Other reporters also proclaimed the 1935 contest as "thrilling" capped by "an astounding finish": down 13–0 entering the final quarter, the Irish, led by Andy Pilney's running, fought back to a one-point deficit; then, in the final minute, with Pilney hurt and lying on a stretcher on the sidelines, a long desperation pass from Bill Shakespeare to Wayne Millner scored the winning TD.

In 1950, a poll of veteran sportswriters declared this contest "The Greatest College Football Game of the Half-Century," and "Red" Barber, broadcasting the event for WLW of Cincinnati, later told an interviewer that it was "the greatest college football game I ever called. I particularly remember that my Notre Dame student spotter became so excited at the final touchdown that he immediately ran out of the radio booth to join his fellows rushing onto the field to tear down the goalposts. It took forever to find out who had caught the ball for Notre Dame."

The radio coverage of the game—excitable Ted Husing doing the CBS national broadcast—helped make it memorable for countless Americans, particularly the growing legions of Notre Dame fans. A nun in Oregon boasted that she was one of those "pressed around the radio in every live city in the United States" and that she had discovered "the secret behind that surprising, spectacular, last minute victory, the hidden power behind the team"—the millions of prayers offered before and during the game for the Fighting Irish. Near the radio in her convent, she heard a colleague "gamefully bargaining with the Poor Souls whose feast it was. 'One Holy Mass, no two, if they [the Fighting Irish] make it.' Five decades of the beads, ten, fifteen, and so on, up to forty-five . . . Such gambling! Such bargaining of spiritual wealth! Such chiding! Such threatening of all the sweet saints of heaven! What chance, I ask you, had Ohio State against the combined forces of heaven and Notre Dame?"

A C.S.C. sister in Illinois wrote President O'Hara: "Enclosed is a Mass stipend for the Suffering Souls in Purgatory in thanksgiving for the Notre Dame victory over Ohio State." O'Hara, who relished such communications, replied, "Thanks a thousand times for your congratulatory note and for the beautiful spiritual sentiments behind the Masses." One of the Protestant boys said in the huddle near the end of the game, " 'That Hail Mary Play is the best one we've got.' " The official chronicler of Notre Dame football, Joe Doyle, later supplied an ironic footnote to this outpouring of prayers and the great "Hail Mary" TD—"the winning play involved non-Catholics, Shakespeare, a Protestant, throwing to the Jewish Millner."

The ecumenicism of the passing combination was only emphasized in Notre Dame lore a generation later. In 1935, many Catholics, particularly in the Midwest, regarded the Ohio State contest as a struggle against nonbelievers and, as one nun informed O'Hara, at her gathering everyone was asked "to pray for a Notre Dame victory." Moreover, many OSU supporters also saw the game as a religious struggle—as did numerous fans of other N.D. opponents when their teams played the Catholic school. The Columbus zealots, anticipating a victory over the Fighting Irish, began "celebrating Friday night . . . with revelry and riotousness," but, at the final whistle, "filed out of the stadium in abject despair" (Allison Danzig).

"In the 1930s," according to Mary Jo Weaver, a professor of religion at Indiana University, "the custom began in primary and secondary parochial schools, each Friday in the fall, to have the students pray for a

Notre Dame victory the following day. The 1930s wins over mighty Ohio State gave great impetus to this, and when I attended Catholic schools in the 1950s, we continued to pray with special fervor for 'Our Lady's Team.' It was an important part of our 'Holy War' against the Protestant majority in America."

The victory at Columbus also enhanced the football reputation of the Fighting Irish—begun in the Rockne era—as the team that "always won the big ones" (Francis Wallace). The press nicknamed Layden's 1935 squad "The Two Minute Men" because, in their most important games of the season, they came from behind to win or tie in the final two minutes.

Nevertheless, as Rockne knew too well, the week after "a big one" often produced a huge letdown, and the following Saturday, at home against weak Northwestern, N.D. was totally flat. The Wildcats had lost to Ohio State, 28–7, and seemed as tame as during the previous seasons, but NU had a new coach, Lynn "Pappy" Waldorf, embarked on a brilliant career that would include Big Ten and Pac-8 championships. His squad played a smart, determined game and bested the Irish, 14–7, before thirty-five thousand disbelieving fans.

> "Elmer is doing all right with the football team. In two seasons he has brought it from the bottom . . . he has already put over one of the most dramatic performances in the history of the game, the Ohio State conquest, as fine a victory as the Old Master, Rock, ever achieved."
>
> —Francis Wallace, *New York World-Telegram,*
> November 13, 1935

In the buildup in the New York papers for the 1935 N.D.–Army annual, Wallace signaled his approval of Layden's coaching and, after the contest, most East Coast Notre Dame alums and Fighting Irish fanatics agreed. One reporter led his game story: "A wild screaming throng of 80,000 saw in Yankee Stadium a battle which left them gasping for air and limp in their seats at its conclusion . . . After leading 6–0 for 59 minutes of the game, the Army was forced to yield a touchdown," at the very end and settle for a 6–6 tie.

The key moment in the final Fighting Irish drive occurred on another "Hail Mary" pass from Shakespeare to Millner but, instead of catching the ball, the N.D. end was taken out of the play by an Army defender. The field judge ruled pass interference, the Kaydets and their fans howled, but Notre Dame got the ball on the two-yard line. Layden inserted a fourth-unit fullback and he smashed over for the touchdown. N.D. missed the PAT, yet the tie satisfied the Fighting Irish faithful and they looked forward to seeing more Elmer Layden–coached teams at Yankee Stadium.

The next day, the films and photos of the "Hail Mary" play were inconclusive, neither supporting nor disproving the correctness of the pass interference call. But the N.D. cognoscenti praised Layden's ability to work the game official system à la Rockne—disputed calls no longer automatically went against the Irish as they had during Hunk Anderson's years. In fact, this crucial penalty saved the day.

The team returned to Indiana for the season finale against visiting USC. The Trojans were in decline—coach Howard Jones had not adjusted to the new offenses entering the game—and they came east with a 3–4 record. On a frigid day in late November only thirty-eight thousand turned out at Notre Dame Stadium to see the Irish easily handle Southern Cal, 20–13.

Thus, the 1935 Fighting Irish season ended with a 7–1–1 record, but again the home attendance and gate receipts were disappointing. An underused Notre Dame Stadium provided less than $102,000 for the school and forced the Fighting Irish to continue to play a majority of their big games on the road. Though some newspapers, even those with pro–N.D. writers, still called the team the "Ramblers," their travels saved the season financially. The huge crowd at Ohio State put almost $84,000 into the bank for Notre Dame, and the road games with Navy and Army, close to $196,000. The 1935 total gate receipts for N.D. were $408,757, the first time they had been above $400,000 since Rockne's last years. Yet, with athletic department expenses at an estimated $217,000, the profit was below expectations.

Then, in early December, came the temptation of Rose Bowl money. Stanford had triumphed in the West and that school's athletic department, students, and fans wanted their Indians to play the Fighting Irish —in this period, the Pacific Coast champ selected the eastern team. Notre Dame alum and trustee A. D. McDonald, president of the Southern Pacific Railroad, wired his alma mater: "REFUSAL TO ACCEPT INVITATION MIGHT BE MISUNDERSTOOD BY STANFORD AND [COULD] SERIOUSLY JEOPARDIZE POSSIBLE FUTURE GAMES. IF STANFORD CAN IGNORE POSSIBLE CRITICISM OF COMMERCIALISM AND JUSTIFY POST-SEASON GAME, [I] THINK NOTRE DAME HAS EQUALLY GOOD GROUNDS FOR SAME POSITION."

Other Notre Dame alums and fans demanded this rematch of the 1925 Rose Bowl, arguing that it would provide reams of sports publicity, including the angle that the 1925 contest had been Elmer Layden's greatest game as a player, and that the contest would sell out the Rose Bowl, providing the Catholic school a payout of at least $150,000, an enormous sum at the time. For a few days, with N.D. students joining the clamor for the game, Vice President Hugh O'Donnell and the athletic board seriously considered the invitation—after all, the team had not gone West that year—but, in the end, Father O'Hara vetoed the trip.

The Notre Dame president pointed out that playing in a postseason contest not only violated N.D. policy and a ten-year precedent but also, instead of staying ahead of the Big Ten in the rules game—the conference still banned members from participating in postseason events—accepting the Rose Bowl bid would cost the Catholic school the lead. He acknowledged that Notre Dame needed the money (its endowment had dropped below $1 million) and that he had no other way of raising a quick (or even a slow) $150,000 in the depths of the Depression—his requests for grants from the Carnegie Foundation and other educational philanthropies were always rebuffed—but he would not compromise on this issue. He could not continue his "Fortress Notre Dame" strategy on athletics and also send the team to Pasadena.

Aiding O'Hara in his decision was the impending visit to campus of the President of the United States, Franklin D. Roosevelt. This marked the first time in Notre Dame's ninety-three years that the occupant of the White House had visited the school and, symbolically, it indicated approval from the highest level of the nation's government and establishment for the Catholic institution. Father O'Hara and his predecessors in the Golden Dome had worked hard to gain this endorsement and the N.D. president was not about to spoil it by starting a public fracas with Big Ten schools over a postseason football game.

Thus, when FDR visited on December 9, 1935, ostensibly to help Notre Dame observe "Philippine Day," a pet project of the Spanish-speaking O'Hara, and witness an honorary degree to Philippine statesman Carlos Romulo, the N.D. president enjoyed chatting with the U.S. president about various topics, including Fighting Irish football, and was pleased that no sports controversy marred their conversation on this important occasion.

■ ■ ■

"Marshall 'Biggie' Goldberg, 17 year old sophomore from the mountains of West Virginia, solved the great mystery of the Irish, who came to Pittsburgh undefeated and untied.
Slippery as an eel, as fast as lightning, the boy called 'Biggie' because

he is small as compared with other heroes at Pitt, led the furious attack
that turned the South Bend typhoon into a zephyr. The [26–0] defeat
was the worst suffered by Notre Dame since Yale walloped the Irish,
28–0, in 1914."

—Paul Mickelson, AP writer, October 25, 1936

Layden had been correct about Marshall Goldberg; he was the perfect running back for the Rockne system—extremely quick, fast, and
smart, similar to the coach himself as a player as well as the other Horsemen. But Goldberg played for Pitt and Layden was unable to find his
equal among the Fighting Irish, even though the coach listed an astounding total of 183 players on the 1936 N.D. football squad (Layden had six
"A" and eleven "B" units, plus over 120 freshman team members—thus,
over 300 intercollegiate football players in uniform).

Notre Dame began the season at home with an easy win over Carnegie Tech, but the following week against visiting Washington of Saint
Louis, the Irish only squeezed by, 14–7. The fans were uneasy because
most of the eleven starters for the small Missouri school played the entire
sixty minutes and held off wave upon fresh wave—fifty-two players in all
—of the supposedly mighty Fighting Irish.

An unusual matchup for the next game distracted attention from the
team's problems. Wisconsin, under new coach and A.D. Harry Stuhldreher, visited, and this marked the first time one of the Four Horsemen
had coached against his alma mater and another Horseman. Earlier in
the year, Wisconsin had fired Rockne's close friend and business partner,
Doc Meanwell, because of the latter's malfeasance in a number of areas
and had brought in the ambitious Stuhldreher. "Stulie" was rebuilding,
and his Badgers could not compete with Layden's team, losing 27–0. The
following Monday, the very first weekly college football poll appeared,
the AP asking thirty-five writers for their top ten choices. On the strength
of N.D.'s early season victories, the voters placed them seventh, ahead of
their next opponent, Pitt.

This provided the shrewd Jock Sutherland with a perfect prod to
energize his team, and at home to N.D., the Panthers whipped the Irish,
26–0. Vice President O'Donnell ruefully recalled that the last time the
team had suffered a more humiliating defeat—at Yale in 1914—he had
played center.

Layden focused his squad on the next game, the Ohio State visit to
Notre Dame, and fortunately for the coach, the Scarlet were not as
strong as they had been the previous year. The Irish held them to a

safety, winning an extremely hard-fought contest, 7–2. The N.D. offense sputtered for most of the game and, the next week in Baltimore against Navy, stalled completely, the unranked Middies edging Notre Dame 3–0.

That year, the Army annual followed the Navy game. New York N.D. partisans were nervous, Francis Wallace choosing not to criticize but to spur on Layden by pointing out that he had "a unique spot in [N.D. versus] Army tradition" because as a player and as a coach, he had never lost to the Kaydets. A few New York writers were more direct, wondering whether the "Notre Dame system" was becoming obsolete. On the day, however, the Irish were up and a mediocre Army team was down, N.D. pulling away in the second half for a 20–6 victory.

Unlike previous years, in 1936 the Northwestern game came after the Army match, and "Pappy" Waldorf had the Wildcats on top of the Big Ten and high in the national rankings. The contest sold out Notre Dame Stadium—the Ohio State visit had been standing room only—and the *Scholastic* reported that the "railroad companies" filled "twenty special trains" to South Bend for the game. A throng of 52,131 rooters provided Layden's athletic department with its best home payday of the first half of his regime.

Chicago writer Tony Ardizzone later explained that "in this period, with Prohibition repealed, Chicago Fighting Irish fans discovered that Notre Dame was exactly the right train distance from the city to get a nice glow on during the ride to the game, keep it going through the afternoon, and then get really loaded on the trip home. They never had to hassle with the highways—which were still primitive—and they spent an enjoyable day with their drinking buddies, drowning their sorrows if N.D. lost but more often celebrating because they won. The perfect distance of the train ride for drinking turned out to be the key to finally filling Notre Dame Stadium."

Although this overstates the situation—throughout the 1930s, only the best attractions sold out Notre Dame Stadium—home attendance did improve because of the excursion trains, not only from Chicago but also from Detroit, Cleveland, Toledo, and Indianapolis. Moreover, an increasing number of rooters were willing to challenge the two-lane highways twisting through midwestern towns and drive to South Bend. In its coverage of the Northwestern visit, the *Scholastic* noted that "an estimated number of 7,500 cars filled up the parking spaces surrounding the stadium," many with out-of-state licenses.

Fighting Irish fans greatly enjoyed the NU game because their team easily handled the Wildcats, 26–6. Chicago sportswriters praised the precision of Layden's men and the student reporters rejoiced because the Irish had completed their home season with a 5–0 record. Also pleased with the 1936 home season were Fathers O'Hara and O'Donnell. The school's share of the gate receipts at Notre Dame Stadium was $182,000, and that, coupled with over $71,000 at Pitt and $181,000 from the road games against the military academies, pushed the total to approximately $434,000. The following week's contest in the Los Angeles Coliseum added another $71,000 in gate receipts to the N.D. total, allowing the football program to break the half-million-dollar mark for the season and revive memories of Rockne's best years.

On a beautiful, sunny December afternoon, with the Depression beginning to ease in California, over seventy-one thousand people paid to see the visiting Irish play a still-down USC team. They sat through a very strange and, for N.D. rooters, frustrating 13–13 tie. Notre Dame made 19 first downs to the Trojans' one and 411 total yards versus 49. Yet, at key moments, the Irish attack sputtered, only managing two TDs, and the defense lapsed, allowing USC to score. Southern Cal coach Howard Jones admitted, "We were lucky," and Layden remarked, "Sometimes the breaks go your way, and sometimes they don't." However, after the game, one West Coast football expert pointed out that Notre Dame's road record for the season was only 1–2–1 and he questioned whether Layden's adherence to the "Rockne system" made sense.

In the five years since the great coach's death, college football had changed considerably. In the Southwest, "Dutch" Meyer, the head coach at Texas Christian, with "Slingin'" Sammy Baugh at quarterback, had demonstrated the potential of a wide-open air attack. Baugh finished his college career in 1936 with 274 completions for 3,437 yards and forty aerial TDs—higher numbers than the combined passing totals of all the N.D. quarterbacks for all the Rockne years. In addition, on the East Coast, Frank Leahy, line coach at Fordham, was proving with his "Seven Blocks of Granite" that his new kind of line play also won games.

Nevertheless, back at Notre Dame, the fans refused to acknowledge the changing football reality; student reporter Charlie Callahan—later a longtime N.D. sports publicity head—in the season summary for the *Scholastic,* derided those "sportswriters [who] wrote articles on how the famed Notre Dame system was slipping . . . had faltered perceptibly before the advances of time . . . and that the torch which the 'Old Master' had passed on to others was slowly being snuffed out. However, this [1936] team was a club that did come back"—and it proved the detractors of the "Rockne system" wrong.

In retrospect, Callahan's optimism appears Panglossian, but at the time, few fans understood the implications of the new Southwest aerial game and how it would forever change the sport of football. Some traditionalists claimed that TCU won not as a result of Meyer's offense but because of the exceptional athletic ability of six-foot-three, triple-threat Sammy Baugh. However, the TCU coach, nicknamed "The Saturday Fox," clinched his argument by winning the 1938 national championship with Baugh's successor, scrawny, little—five-foot-six—Davey O'Brien as his passing quarterback. By the end of the decade, with more teams switching to aerial offenses and also with Clark Shaughnessy's T formation entering the game, Elmer Layden's faithful adherence to his master's system became increasingly inappropriate.

35

O'Hara and Layden in Power: 1937–1939

"The [end of the] football season is about to release the nation's colleges to the pursuit of education, more or less. Soon the last nickel will be rung up at the gate, the last halfback will receive his [pay]check, and the last alumnus will try to pay off those bets that he can recall. Most of the students have cheered themselves into insensibility long ago."

—Robert Hutchins in the *Saturday Evening Post*,
December 12, 1938

In the late 1930s, the leading advocate for the reform of college sports was Robert Hutchins, the president of the University of Chicago. In frequent public statements, as well as articles for the general reader, he tried to revive the attack on big-time intercollegiate athletics begun by the Carnegie Foundation in the 1920s and rephrase it in contemporary terms. He particularly assailed "the apologists [who] have created a collection of myths to convince the public [to support big-time football]." At the top of his list were coaches, athletic directors, and sportswriters, and he mocked their most cherished beliefs, including their maxim that athletes were ideal role models for young people: "Since this country needs brains more than brawn at the moment, proposing football heroes as models for the rising generation can hardly have a beneficial effect on the national future." (Hutchins's late-1930s barbs are part of the cultural context of the film *Knute Rockne—All American,* notably the scenes where the N.D. coach flays the reformers.)

444

Unlike most critics of college sports, Robert Hutchins had the power to make some changes, at least at his own university, and he began in 1933 by easing out the school's famous coach and A.D., Amos Alonzo Stagg (who moved to the College of the Pacific and coached there until 1946). To replace Stagg, Hutchins hired the bright and articulate Clark Shaughnessy, with Marchy Schwartz as his assistant, but the president refused to allow them to recruit. In addition, the University of Chicago was beginning its innovative "Great Books" curriculum and the faculty would not sanction a Physical Education major—the main academic shelter for athletes at other Big Ten schools. Shaughnessy had to work with real student-athletes, and as a result, the once-mighty Chicago Maroons free-fell to the bottom of the Big Ten, losing by increasingly large scores to conference opponents. In addition, this deemphasis moved Chicago to the margin of the group that it had once led.

Hutchins was an anomaly among university presidents. Many of his peers privately congratulated him for his words and actions but they so feared their powerful coaches, A.D.s, and team boosters that they remained publicly silent on the reform issue. Most college officials also refused to comment when sportswriters, in bed with the athletic establishment, loudly attacked the University of Chicago president.

Typical of the media assaults was a nationally syndicated column by Bill Corum of the Hearst papers; he attributed Hutchins's activity solely to the Maroons' woeful on-field performances and offered the analogy, "I have been going to horse races for twenty years and coming home on the train, it is always the loser who wants to tar and feather the stewards and burn down the track." Such clever propaganda drowned out Hutchins's more cerebral arguments for reform.

One remarkable exception to the media hyperbole for college sports was Paul Gallico, longtime sports editor and columnist of the *New York Daily News*. In a series of articles collected in his 1938 book, *Farewell to Sport*, the former "Gee-Whizzer" repented of thirteen years of helping promote what he now termed "total hypocrisy": "College football today is one of the last great strongholds of genuine old-fashioned American hypocrisy. During Prohibition, naturally, it ran second, but with the coming of repeal and the legalization of betting on horses in most of the states of the union, it easily took the lead."

As a man who played and loved amateur sports, Gallico attacked the charade that big-time college football was a nonprofessional endeavor. Because he knew the sports business from the inside, his scorn bit deeply: "So long as the football player 'working his way through college' will make the pretense of dropping into the boiler-room of the dormitory or gymnasium once a week and waving his hand at the furnace, he may accept whatever stipend the prominent alumnus or the graduate manager of athletics is willing to pay him." But this writer saw the players more as victims—they left college poorly educated—than as beneficiaries of a system that in his years on the sports beat had become so huge and so profitable for the coaches, A.D.s, and the media that it had a momentum of its own and was unstoppable.

On this pessimistic note, Paul Gallico left sports journalism and moved to Europe, spending most of the remainder of his life abroad.

■　■　■

"Once football [at Pitt] threatened to muscle the academic programs out of joint, the [Pitt] administration contends, there was nothing to do except to . . . knead this muscular development back into its proper place . . . Jock Sutherland's resignation came because he could not reconcile himself to the idea that the academic side comes first."

—Francis Wallace, *Saturday Evening Post*,
October 28, 1939

Beginning in the late 1920s, in part because of the pressure to fill its massive new stadium, the University of Pittsburgh sponsored an increasingly professional football team run by ruthless Jock Sutherland. This A.D. and coach not only paid his athletes on a regular salary scale but, in the 1930s, also arranged free off-campus housing and other amenities for them. Playing at Pitt became such a lucrative job that many of the athletes married, and critics began calling the Panthers "The Married Man's Team." Not surprisingly, Sutherland's pros achieved success on the field, including four Rose Bowl appearances.

By 1937, a number of Pitt's regular opponents, chiefly Notre Dame and Navy, that disapproved of Sutherland's methods dropped the Panthers from their future schedules. Then the national accreditation associations threatened to investigate the University of Pittsburgh and possibly decertify its degrees. Reluctantly, the school president instructed Sutherland, his undergraduate fraternity brother at Pitt, to clean up the football program. The students went on strike to protest this deemphasis and local sports fans as well as the press backed the coach. However, the school's board of trustees, realizing that more was at stake than empty seats in the stadium, supported the president. Sutherland, rather than change his methods, departed—he subsequently coached "open professionals" in the NFL.

The NCAA and the college athletic establishment turned the Pitt incident into positive propaganda, friendly sports journals headlining "PITT PURGE SIGNALS END OF GRID HYPOCRISY." But, as the reformers pointed out, purging Pitt—a notorious example of the sins of big-time college football—hardly terminated the corruption pervading the system.

For Notre Dame, dropping the University of Pittsburgh from its schedule was a straightforward process; much more complicated were football relations with another school with obviously subsidized athletes—Ohio State. In 1936, Vice President Hugh O'Donnell asked Major John Griffith of the Big Ten to investigate rumors that OSU athletes were on the state payroll in Columbus. The Big Ten commissioner replied that members of the faculty athletic board at OSU were also concerned that "some of their football players had been subsidized with state jobs, etc.," and after a thorough inquiry, he "found that the boys secured their own [state] jobs through state representatives, state senators, or others who interceded in their behalf."

Griffith admitted, "The fact that most of the boys in question were pretty good football players aroused the suspicion that someone must have recruited a team to enhance the athletic prestige of the state university." But he maintained that the jobs for football players were not part of a master plan: "[when] I submitted all the evidence that I could collect to our special Conference committee, these men have reported that they did not feel that Ohio State had been guilty of any infractions of the Conference rules." The Big Ten commissioner found Notre Dame's complaints unwarranted and requested that the Catholic school keep "this information" about OSU "confidential."

Father Hugh O'Donnell answered Griffith: "Naturally I shall keep the contents confidential, for obvious reasons"—the N.D. administration saw no point in publicly embarrassing the Big Ten and igniting a major dispute, but the vice president and his superior, Father John O'Hara, felt stymied by this flagrant abuse. Because the situation at Ohio State had been covered up and because OSU had a powerful conference and commissioner behind it—as opposed to independent Pitt—the only recourse for the Notre Dame administrators was to quietly stop scheduling football games with the Ohio school. Thus, N.D. made no attempt to renew the home-and-home series with OSU—polite excuses were made for public consumption—and the 1936 Buckeye visit to Notre Dame marked the last football contest between the institutions.

"When he [Father John O'Hara] was Prefect of Religion, he had not
been bothered too much by the suggestion that Notre Dame was a 'football school,' but the unpleasantness of the Pritchett report and the cold
reception [to his request for funds] from [President] Keppel of the Carnegie Foundation were ample reasons for trying to strengthen the intellectual side of Notre Dame."

—Father Thomas McAvoy in his biography,
O'Hara of Notre Dame

Based on his experiences with universities such as Ohio State, President O'Hara believed that a double standard existed in American higher
education: powerful schools like the Big Ten institutions, running corrupt
football programs, had the approval of the national authorities, whereas
Notre Dame, with a clean athletic program, earned their opprobrium
because of its Catholic heritage and Fighting Irish fame. However, rather
than publicly rail against this hypocrisy, he chose a wiser course: make
N.D. unassailable in college sports—his "Fortress Notre Dame" strategy
—and improve it academically.

Not a scholar or an intellectual—he banned many secular publications from the library—the N.D. president sought and followed the advice of Father James Burns, the man who had prodded the school toward
the academic mainstream in the 1920s, and O'Hara moved to upgrade
the faculty and the graduate program. He went to Europe and hired
scholars trying to escape the advancing Nazi threat—nicknamed "Notre
Dame's Foreign Legion," they soon became the leading members of
many N.D. departments. He also appointed a distinguished intellectual,
Father Philip S. Moore, to build up the graduate school. An early result
of these moves was the founding of a number of academic publications at
N.D., including the *Review of Politics,* and the hosting of important academic conferences. In 1938, the French philosopher Jacques Maritain,
the University of Chicago's Mortimer Adler, and other famous guests
attended a week-long meeting on "Political and Social Philosophy."

Nevertheless, more traditional visitors were still important to the
Catholic school. In late 1936, the Papal Secretary of State, Cardinal
Pacelli, came to campus and O'Hara conferred an honorary degree on
the probable next pope (Pacelli became Pius XII). Moreover, O'Hara, for
all his work to improve Notre Dame academically, still considered the
school's religious mission to be paramount. He replied to an inquiry
requesting the names of prominent N.D. grads in the business world:
"Notre Dame's primary purpose is to save souls, not to train men for
material success. One of the brightest and most promising men who ever

went through Notre Dame, Patrick McDonough, has devoted his talents to looking after Irish immigrants at the Port of New York."

In part for this reason and because O'Hara saw the growing anti-Communist crusade as a secular mission, in 1937 he invited J. Edgar Hoover to address the student body. The FBI director pronounced: "There can be no higher ideal for the student of Notre Dame . . . than that he should consecrate his life to the cause and virtue of justice." Hoover, not a Catholic, was so impressed by the conservative political ethos of the school and the gung-ho energy of the students that subsequently he hired many Notre Dame grads as FBI agents.

■ ■ ■

"You will be interested in knowing that a sports-columnist of the *Chicago Tribune* is starting a little high pressure to have the Notre Dame-Navy game played in Chicago in 1937. He stated in his column that the Navy is willing, and that for us to turn down such a proposition would mean a loss of about $100,000 from our own receipts. He is probably aware that we have insisted that the game be played in South Bend."

—President O'Hara to Dr. Howard Savage
of the Carnegie Foundation

The Chicago columnist was Arch Ward, and although O'Hara maintained cordial relations with the former N.D. student, the Notre Dame president detested such outside pressure and, from his hierarchical point of view, felt that Ward had overstepped his place. However, because O'Hara was still trying to obtain funds from the Carnegie Foundation and other educational philanthropies, he used the incident as an example of his school's commitment to a sane football program, even if it meant passing up a significant amount of money.

To gain the approval of the educational mandarins, O'Hara also decided to put a new twist on an old Notre Dame strategy—actively woo the anti–N.D. members of the Big Ten. Unlike some of his predecessors, he did not wish to apply for membership in the conference but he did want to schedule games with the Big Ten leaders. He reasoned that because the national authorities accepted big-time football at those universities, they could not continue to shun Notre Dame if it gained total Big Ten approval.

The Fighting Irish had long played the small schools of the conference—Indiana, Purdue, and Northwestern—and had mid-1930s series with middle-tier Wisconsin and Ohio State—but O'Hara wanted the imprimatur of games with the pacesetters of the era—Illinois, Minnesota, Iowa, and, most of all, the University of Michigan.

Fathers O'Hara and O'Donnell knew all the charges against Fielding Yost's athletic program—although, by the late 1930s, the Wolverine subsidization of athletes was more subdued than in earlier periods—but the N.D. administrators calculated that if the University of Michigan agreed to place Notre Dame on its football schedule, this would be the most visible public sign that the old accusations against the Catholic school were dead.

Elmer Layden was the perfect salesman for this N.D. strategy. First, he convinced Bob Zuppke of Illinois to forget his personal rivalry with Rockne as well as the long-ago Taylorville-Carlinville fiasco and to schedule a home-and-home series to start in 1937. He used similar charm on national champion Minnesota for a series also beginning in 1937, and Iowa for 1939–1940. His greatest triumph, however, was his successful courtship of Fielding Yost of Michigan.

The Notre Dame coach visited Ann Arbor in May 1937 and, upon returning home, effusively thanked Yost for his hospitality. He also sent the Michigan A.D. congratulations on various personal occasions, in one birthday greeting noting that "your contribution to the game and to life should provide a most happy day [of memories]." Yost melted and, in late 1939, agreed to visit the Catholic school.

By chance, Francis Wallace was at his alma mater that day and recalled, "you can imagine my surprise . . . to meet Yost in Layden's office. I accompanied them on a tour of the campus and we finally came to the Rockne Memorial. There's a bust of Rock in the foyer, a grim and fearsome face . . . this was probably the Rockne that Yost had known. Yost stood and looked at Rock for quite a little while. Rock glared back. Layden and I said nothing. This was drama." Then Yost, as he later confirmed to Wallace, silently settled accounts with his longtime antagonist.

This incident ended the hostilities that began in 1909 between Michigan and Notre Dame. Yost had already agreed to resume athletic relations with the Catholic school in "minor sports" such as baseball, and now, when slots opened on his football schedule, in that most publicized area. The Michigan A.D. subsequently committed the Wolverines to a home-and-home with the Fighting Irish starting in 1942. In this way, one of college football's most famous rivalries moved into its modern phase, eventually evolving into the ferocious annual games of the current era.

The N.D. administrators were pleased with Layden's work and allowed him to schedule the 1940 season opener against Amos Alonzo Stagg's College of the Pacific. It was a sentimental tribute to the "Grand Old Man," and to Frank Hering, Notre Dame trustee, a former Stagg player, and early N.D. coach. It was also a signal that Notre Dame did not agree with Robert Hutchins's "total de-emphasis" policy and believed that a big-time college football program had a firm place on its campus.

Elmer Layden, with his diplomatic manners, was also moving to the top of the American Football Coaches' Association and, in 1939, was elected its second vice president—Fritz Crisler, the Michigan coach, was one rung ahead of him. Layden represented his university in a very positive way and, by implementing O'Hara's policies, helped move Notre Dame toward a leadership role in college sports.

President O'Hara realized that the improved external relations would disintegrate if he did not "run a tight ship" at home. Thus, during the summer of 1937, he wrote his football coach, Elmer Layden:

> While I don't want to impose my own views on you in the selection of the [football] recipients of jobs, I have a suggestion to offer which may help you. . . . Cut to the bone on freshmen applicants whose academic record indicates that they are likely to fail in the classroom. You don't want to have charged against your budget men who are not going to make good, and your own experience will indicate that those who have an average that barely admits them are not likely to succeed in their classes.

Earlier that summer, O'Hara had issued a memo stipulating "$158,000 for student employment in the 1937–38 schoolyear. Not more than 50% of this amount is to be allotted to students recommended by the Athletic Association." Layden protested and received an increase, O'Hara informing the A.D. that "no further allowance beyond . . . $90,000 can be granted" to his department. The president then suggested the cut in jobs for freshman recruits—advice that Layden did not want to follow. Nevertheless, at the average annual Notre Dame BRT cost in 1937 of $650, the athletic director had enough money for at least 138 full grants-for-jobs—or many more if he divided the amount into full and partial aid.

Elmer Layden, like all football coaches, disliked cutting grants for

freshman recruits and he took his case to the N.D. athletic board. In
early 1938, they forwarded his argument to Vice President O'Donnell:
"Mr. Layden pointed out that competitive conditions made it difficult for
him to select responsible athletic material and [he] suggested . . . that
he be given 30 freshmen footballers on a job basis each year, and that
they be furnished work sufficient to pay for everything but books and
special fees."

By September 1939, Layden pushed the number of unilateral freshman grants to thirty-three and then he convinced the N.D. administration to allow him to add "five additional freshman football players to the
number already assigned." But Vice President O'Donnell warned the
coach that "it must be distinctly understood that you are not to proceed
[beyond this number]": thirty-eight.

Layden, however, had other ways of getting money to his athletes,
and by the late 1930s, he had reestablished the off-campus and summer
job network. An article in the *Scholastic* began, "If you [employers] need
any graves dug or ice carried or buildings constructed, you might see
Coach Elmer Layden about it. For, after the past summer [1937], the
members of his present Fighting Irish squad are capable of performing
almost any job you can name." With the help of N.D. alums and boosters,
Layden placed many members of his varsity on construction and highway
crews around the Midwest and other players worked as lifeguards at
country clubs and beaches (there was one grave digger). None of this
violated NCAA or Big Ten rules and was standard operating procedure at
all big-time football schools during this era.

Like all coaches, Layden also hoped that after their summer of outdoor work, his players would be in great physical shape for the coming
football season.

> "After a lengthy discussion at the meeting [of the N.D. faculty athletic
> board] last night, it was decided not to commercialize our broadcasting
> rights for the fall [1937] season . . . [our decision] will enable all our
> friends and admirers throughout the country to enjoy each game, and at
> the same time save us the embarrassment that might follow from an
> over-emphasis on the commercialization of football."
>
> —Letter from the Notre Dame faculty board
> in control of athletics to Frank C. Barton,
> New York advertising executive, May 15, 1937

For many years, Notre Dame had allowed radio networks and stations
to broadcast its games for free, mainly to please Fighting Irish fans

around the country and to cement their loyalty. As the broadcasts became increasingly popular, each of the national networks tried to buy exclusive rights to them. In 1937, President O'Hara estimated that the refusal to sell these rights "had cost Notre Dame approximately $1 million" since the broadcasts began (the price of its most expensive campus building project during this era). Moreover, most other universities, including Yale and Harvard, sold their broadcasting rights, and "no other school in the country . . . has the first-come-first-served policy in vogue at Notre Dame"; that is, admit as many radio broadcasters as its stadium facilities could accommodate. As a result, Notre Dame had a far larger radio audience than any other college football team.

This policy, which continued into the 1940s, served N.D. well, enlarging its fan base and aiding student body and football recruiting—many of the young men who grew up listening to Fighting Irish games every Saturday afternoon wanted to attend the school and play for or cheer on "Old Notre Dame." The downside, however, was that the policy contributed to fan expectations for national championships and forced the Irish football coach to work in a fishbowl.

Elmer Layden listed 214 players on his 1937 roster, including five Kellys and five Sullivans. Against Drake in the home opener, he tried various combinations and won, 21–0, but he felt that his first units were not ready for their next game, a visit to the University of Illinois at Champaign-Urbana. Against the Big Ten team directed by Bob Zuppke, in his twenty-fifth year as head coach of the Illini, Layden's squad had to settle for a 0–0 tie in what the *Scholastic* headlined "A DULL BATTLE."

The following contest versus Carnegie Tech in Pittsburgh was neither dull nor rewarding for N.D. The Pittsburgh school had decided to try to match crosstown rival Pitt in football and had hired Jock Sutherland's main assistant, Bill Kern, to upgrade its program. That year, the Tartans surprised the Irish with a 9–7 upset on a late field goal. Most national sportswriters proclaimed the loss as the end of N.D.'s national championship hopes, but the *Scholastic* tried to comfort its readers by quoting the "always unbiased . . . sports savant," Grantland Rice, "on the fact that Notre Dame, with its tough schedule, can consider the winning of sixty percent of its games a highly admirable record."

Nonetheless, according to another report, "there was more gloom on the campus than we've seen in many years . . . even Clashmore Mike added to the ignominy of the footballers." The Irish Terrier mascot "took a 24 hour leave of absence and one and all said that he had taken his life.

He was found pacing the shores of Lake St. Joseph." The next game, at home against a mediocre Navy team, did not alleviate fan anxiety—the Irish squeaked by, 9–7, on a late TD.

The following Saturday was the big game of the year. In their first visit to Minnesota in over a decade, the Fighting Irish faced an extremely tough team coached by Bernie Bierman, a.k.a. the "Hammer of the North." According to one sports historian, Bierman's men were "renowned for their Neanderthal play" and they gave the much lighter N.D. players a physical beating but could only manage to score six points. The Irish marked seven and went home battered but happy.

Unfortunately for Layden, the next opponent was Pitt. Jock Sutherland and his squad—angry because N.D. had canceled future games in the series—wanted to give the Irish a "parting gift." In front of a sellout crowd in Notre Dame Stadium, the Panthers humiliated the Irish, 21–6, Marshall Goldberg again leading Pitt with his passing, running, and even downfield blocking. This loss brought the N.D. record to 3–2–1, with a point total against major opponents of 29 to 43.

Before the following week's trip east for the Army annual, the N.D. administrators began receiving letters from "synthetic alumni" complaining about the Catholic school's supposed "de-emphasis in football." One booster enclosed a newspaper clipping that falsely quoted President O'Hara as stating, "We want no more national championship football teams at Notre Dame," and the incensed fan asked the priest, "How, in the hereafter, can you excuse yourself for having wilfully voided the prayers of thousands and thousands of nuns who sit at their [radios] each Saturday and fervently pray for victory for Old Notre Dame? What about the urchins of New York whose faith in Notre Dame is so great that the Army asked for a police escort" for the Cadet Corps's march to Yankee Stadium to avoid the bricks and bottles thrown by these kids. This fan, an accountant named William O'Toole, ended, "You can become a National Hero, Father, by insisting on winning teams and you may be canonized later."

Even the *Notre Dame Alumnus* was defensive about the "de-emphasis" charges and told its readers that "to place the *blame* for" the team's performance "at the door of the administration for stiffening eligibility requirements" was wrong-headed. But some alums pointed the finger, not at the Golden Dome, but at Elmer Layden, Francis Wallace remarking, "1937, by the usual coaching calendar, should have been Layden's best year, the one in which the first freshmen he recruited became seniors." The 1937 Army team was respectable but not nationally ranked. On a rainy, cold day in New York, with the scalpers outside Yankee Stadium dropping their ticket prices to cost by game time, the Irish slipped by the Kaydets, 7–0. Although gaining thirteen first downs to Army's three, the Notre Dame offense could only sustain one drive for a TD.

The following week at Northwestern was almost a replay of the Army game, N.D. again winning 7–0, with the press commenting on the team's "seldom-scoring offense." Entering the final match of the season—at home against USC—Layden's squad had a 5–2–1 record, whereas their mediocre Trojan opponents stood at 3–3–2. Only 28,900 came to Notre Dame Stadium to watch the dull, 13–6, home team victory. The highlight of the day was the halftime ceremony honoring old-time Irish players— this was Notre Dame's fiftieth year of college football—and the "N.D. family" loudly cheered "the living mementos of the school's glorious football history" (*South Bend News-Times*). The low-scoring 1937 team must have reminded some of the old-timers of their long-ago bruising defensive battles. In eight games against major opponents, Layden's squad managed only 56 points against the opposition's 49, an average game score of approximately 7–6.

Even the 1937 attendance and gate receipt numbers were lower than the previous year's—although mainly because of the administration's decision to move the Navy annual from Cleveland to Notre Dame Stadium. Total attendance dropped to slightly less than 400,000 and gate receipts for N.D. to a bit below the half-million mark. With football expenses at $130,000 and estimated costs for other intercollegiate and intramural sports at about $100,000, the profit from Fighting Irish football was still healthy, albeit on a plateau.

More pleasing to President O'Hara were the presence and speech of one of the guests at the end-of-season football banquet. John T. McGovern, the legal adviser to the Carnegie Foundation, "paid glowing compliment to the football team and the coaches and to Notre Dame, laying particular stress on the faculty [athletic board], which he said must exist [and do outstanding work] to produce such excellent results, yet which is so often overlooked in the analysis of an institution."

As if to emphasize the Catholic school's commitment to a clean program, that same month, because of a "Notre Dame rules infraction," the new captain-elect of the 1938 squad, Alec Shellogg, permanently left school. Pro–N.D. sportswriters and Fighting Irish fans were upset with his departure, along with that of his football-playing twin brother, but the administration would neither relent nor release the details of the Alec Shellogg case.

For President O'Hara, the "Fortress Notre Dame" strategy was paying off and sending clear signals to the outside world as well as internally. He did continue to receive negative comments from "synthetic alumni" about the policy and the team's performance but he kept these communications in a file he labeled "Crank Letters," and he treated them as such.

* * *

"As the Irish came marching through seven straight games this fall . . . the advance has been chronicled too often in terms of Knute Rockne— his spirit, his inspiration, his coaching genius, his hand guiding the boys from 'Valhalla,' and a variety of other vague spiritualistic ties between him and the present crop of Notre Dame football players who were in eighth grade or seventh grade when the great coach died in 1931 . . .

When the [N.D.] teams of the last four years lost games here and there, the team was Elmer Layden's. But when those teams have won major victories, they became by some strange operation, Knute Rockne's."

—James S. Kearns, *Chicago Daily News,*
November 19, 1938

This sportswriter, a Notre Dame alum, in a column asking Fighting Irish fans to be fair to Layden, clearly defined the current coach's problem—he could never move out of his mentor's shadow. Part of Layden's dilemma was self-induced—his faithful adherence to the "Rockne system"—but, as the headline of Kearns's piece argued, "IT'S TIME THE ROCKNE WORSHIPERS GAVE LAYDEN HIS DUE," and the year to do this was 1938.

With another huge squad—173 on the roster—the Fighting Irish overwhelmed Kansas in the home opener, 52–0, the coach shuttling eighty-two players in and out of the game. However, the following week's contest against Georgia Tech in Atlanta underlined Layden's problem with the Rockne memories—the newspapers played up the 1920s history of the series and even the *Notre Dame Scholastic* lead its pregame article: "Fighting the Yellow Jackets from Georgia Tech was an annual pastime during the Rockne era." When the Irish won by only 14–6, most game stories compared that score to the routs recorded during the Rockne period, ignoring the close calls and the Georgia Tech victory in the 1920s.

Fortunately for Layden, the next game was against the University of Illinois, and their head man, Bob Zuppke, had always refused to play a Rockne-coached team. N.D. won at home, 14–6, led by scatback Benny Sheridan. This player, from a small downstate Illinois town near Champaign-Urbana, was one of Layden's recruiting coups; Sheridan planned to enroll in Zuppke's program but his parish priest drove him to Notre Dame and deposited him at the coach's office.

Layden also had a quiet hand in the following week's victory at home over Carnegie Tech, but he could never claim so publicly. The Tartans were nationally ranked entering the contest and fought the Irish to a scoreless tie into the fourth quarter. Then, with Carnegie Tech on offense in its own territory, the Tartan QB asked the referee for the down number and the official indicated "Third down." The Tartans ran an off-tackle play for no gain and went into punt formation; however, the ref informed them that he had erred—they had just used their fourth down and had lost the ball to Notre Dame. Carnegie Tech's long, vehement, and futile protest took them out of the game and N.D. scored on this possession, winning 7–0 (the Tartans' only other loss of the season came in the Sugar Bowl against the national champions, TCU.)

Layden's command of the game officials system had saved the day; in the Carnegie Tech match, the ref made an honest error but a more neutral official and crew might have reversed the decision. However, the N.D. cognoscenti attributed Layden's success in this area to what he had learned from the master, Rockne, and the public innocently pointed to the "Luck of the Irish." More perceptive observers of this game, like Francis Wallace, mainly worried about the coach's "super-conservative [offensive] strategy" and the outcome of the impending Army annual.

In 1938, President Roosevelt ordered West Point to adhere to the three-year eligibility rule and the Kaydets were in decline. Because of the new Army regulation and also to stay ahead of the Big Ten in the rules race, before the Irish trip east, the N.D. faculty athletic board informed Layden that he could take only thirty-six players on his traveling squad.

The newspapers played up the "small squad" angle without explaining the context and New York Fighting Irish fans protested to President O'Hara, worried that this regulation would hurt their beloved team's chances for victory. In addition, one fan complained, "Shocked to read [about] this. Notre Dame, of all schools, gone CHEAP! I feel the Notre Dame football team won't be so popular in New York in the future. There is one thing New Yorkers hate—that is CHEAPNESS."

On Saturday afternoon, in the twenty-fifth year of football between the schools, the Irish rolled to an easy 19–7 victory, Benny Sheridan again leading the attack. When Layden arrived back in Indiana, he sent a memo to President O'Hara: "We should sit down and compare notes as I have a great deal of correspondence [from fans] from last week, some of which are beauties."

But the coach and the team soon had to return to the East Coast, this time to play Navy in Baltimore. Although the Middies by pressuring the White House had reduced Army's strength, they had not improved their own, entering the N.D. game with a mediocre crew. The Irish scored a convincing 15–0 win but again, even neutral sportswriters alluded to Rockne, the AP story beginning, "Notre Dame's greatest football team since the last glorious 1930 model, turned out by Knute Rockne, rolled over hapless, outclassed Navy."

The following week, at home against Minnesota in a sold-out stadium, the team pleased the faithful with a surprisingly easy 19–0 victory. The Gophers had lost previously to a good Northwestern squad and Layden tried to get his players up for the next Saturday's visit to Evanston. In that contest, after a listless opening, the Irish pulled together to slip past the Wildcats, 9–7. This allowed Notre Dame to travel to the West Coast for the season finale against Southern Cal with a ranking of number one in the AP poll.

USC entered the game at number eight and the contest packed the Los Angeles Coliseum. The teams played evenly until late in the first half, when on fourth down deep in Irish territory, the N.D. punter, instead of kicking the ball, tried to run with it and was nailed far short of a first down. The Trojans converted the error into a TD and never looked back, winning 13–0.

After the game, Layden defended his kicker, QB Bob Saggau, stating, "A Notre Dame quarterback is always right. And that is that." In public, the coach rarely complained but, in private, he was a "griper" and, on this occasion, quick to pass the buck to the offending athlete. Chicago sportswriter Warren Brown, close to the N.D. football program, privately compared this side of Layden to the attitude of Eddie Anderson, another ex-Rockne player and the head coach at Iowa in the late 1930s. Anderson, with undermanned squads, always "went to work to get the utmost out of what he had, and there was never a moment in which he wept and moaned for what he had not. I am sorry that I cannot say as much for" Elmer Layden, even though he had great talent at his disposal. Warren Brown and other Notre Dame insiders condemned Layden's not assuming full responsibility for his program and his players' actions.

Unfortunately for the N.D. coach, with the 1938 loss to Southern Cal, his best chance at a national championship slipped away and, after the season, most polls placed the TCU Horned Frogs, with their amazing aerial circus, at number one.

Because the polls still put Notre Dame near the top—fifth in the final AP rankings—Fighting Irish and other football fans clamored for the team to play in a postseason bowl. The loudest and most seductive calls came from Texas, where state leaders wanted to match the Irish against TCU and make their new Cotton Bowl in Dallas the most important postseason contest of the year. Notre Dame alumni in the Southwest joined the chorus, imploring the N.D. administrators to send the team, arguing that Notre Dame's appearance in Texas would greatly help fundraising efforts in the region. President O'Hara was skeptical about this argument, preferring to try to obtain money from the national foundations and philanthropies.

O'Hara also examined the gate receipts—a total of $534,422—noting the increase over the previous year due to the large payout in Los Angeles. For the N.D. president, a long railroad trip to Texas, coming after the recent West Coast journey, would revive the "Rockne Ramblers" image, and he instructed Vice President O'Donnell to write a standard reply to the Texas alums as well as to others calling for trips to New Orleans, Miami, and Pasadena: "years ago the Faculty Board in Control of Athletics legislated against any post-season football games and [it] has consistently refused to rescind its policy. We were literally besieged with requests this year, and refused every one of them. The good reasons for this policy [should] appear obvious to you."

Thus Elmer Layden never had the opportunity of playing his "Rockne system" against "Dutch" Meyer's passing offense, but if the decisive TCU postseason victory over Carnegie Tech was any indication, the old methods would not have triumphed over the new aerial attacks.

■ ■ ■

"Ten years ago Knute Rockne said, 'Prospects are not so good but possibly fair.'

Now Elmer Layden says, 'Prospects look good, but they are not as good as they look.'

Rockne's statement preceded a national championship season . . .

Our personal conviction is that Notre Dame stood last year on the threshold of a return to the good old days . . .

Our personal hunch is that 1939 may very well simulate the 1909, 1919, and 1929 [championship] seasons."

—*Notre Dame Alumnus,*
1939 football preseason article

Starting in the spring of 1939, the ghost of Knute Rockne seemed even more present at Notre Dame than in previous years. The construction of the Rockne Memorial Building was finally completed and the school made elaborate plans for its dedication. The key event occurred on June 3, 1939, with speeches from visiting dignitaries carried coast-to-coast by the Mutual radio network. Elmer Layden also spoke, eloquently stating Rockne's achievement and, in the subtext of the speech, his current burden: "Primarily, what Rock did was not [only] to teach a few hundred men football, but to reach millions through football. The teams of Notre Dame became the teams of the people and Knute Rockne the most popular coach in America." Moreover, those men who learned football from the great coach had an obligation to "perpetuate the lessons of Rockne throughout the ages."

For Elmer Layden, 1939 was the make-or-break campaign. Five years previously, he had reconstructed Fighting Irish football from the collapse of Hunk Anderson's regime and he had returned it to national respectability. Nevertheless, he had never achieved an undefeated season or a clear-cut national championship, and even though most of the Notre Dame faithful liked him personally, they still demanded perfection. Resorting to numerology—1909, 1919, 1929—and other superstitions, many believed that 1939 would be a championship year.

The order from the N.D. administration to play as many Big Ten teams as possible forced Layden into opening the 1939 season, not with the usual second-class opponent, but with the Purdue Boilermakers. Purdue students and fans descended on South Bend with banners imploring "Let's Fill the Old Oaken Bucket with Irish Stew," and their team held N.D. scoreless until the fourth quarter. Then Irish third-string QB Johnny Kelleher kicked a field goal for a 3–0 win. The newspapers gave the coach almost no credit for inserting the player into the game and instead pounced on the angle that Kelleher was the son of Knute Rockne's teammate and pal "Wild Bill" Kelleher.

The second game, at home to Georgia Tech, also invoked Rockne memories and the close (17–14) win did not please the fans. However,

the third contest against visiting SMU was less important for past references than future portents. The Mustangs, although not one of the strongest Southwest teams, featured a passing offense and almost upset N.D.,
losing only 20–19. The Irish scored with their running game but SMU
consistently fought back, notching a last-minute touchdown but failing to
tie because of a missed PAT.

The first road game of the season, against Navy in Cleveland, was
almost a breather for Layden's men, Benny Sheridan having a great day
and leading the Irish to a 14–7 win. The following week in Pittsburgh
against Carnegie Tech was much tougher, a late Tartan miss of a PAT
saving a 7–6 N.D. win. After this contest, Joe Petritz, Notre Dame director of athletic publicity, rhetorically asked in print, "You wouldn't expect
this department to say that Notre Dame has been lucky to win five
football games in 1939 by the [total] margin of 15 points, would you? Nor
shall we."

Elmer Layden admitted: "Last year we got a few touchdowns we
didn't deserve. This year we're giving them back"—the opposition had
scored TDs on Notre Dame errors. Fighting Irish fans were restless and
the national media increasingly interested in the N.D. situation. *Look*
magazine ran a feature in October 1939 with the headline "DOES NOTRE
DAME GET THE FOOTBALL BREAKS?" After opening, "Do Notre Dame teams
live on a diet of four-leaf clovers and rabbits' feet, as many football
followers like to insist," and citing such events as the referee's mistake in
the 1938 victory over Carnegie Tech, the writer—one of Arch Ward's
assistants on the *Chicago Tribune*—decided that the Fighting Irish made
their own luck by following Rockne's dictum: " 'Block, Tackle!' The
words make up the order of the day [at Notre Dame]. At times they seem
to be [heard by the players from] the spirit voice of the departed Knute
Rockne."

The following week's Army annual illustrated another Rockne dictum
—if West Point operated under the three-year eligibility rule, the Fighting Irish could easily beat the Kaydets. The rule, in its second season at
the academy, had depleted the squad, and before the usual full house in
New York, N.D. controlled the game, winning 14–0. In addition, Notre
Dame publications began calling the New York working-class fans "Subway Alumni," moving away from the lowercase pejorative "synthetic
alumni."

For the next game, the team traveled to Iowa and ran into another set
of Rockne maxims, these enforced by Hawkeye head coach and former
Rockne end Eddie Anderson. He had played on his mentor's first teams
and after a successful coaching career at Holy Cross had then moved to

the Big Ten school. Anderson believed in tough Rockne-style football, and he had an extraordinary athlete, Heisman Trophy candidate Niles Kinnick, to lead his undermanned Hawkeyes.

Against Notre Dame in 1939, Kinnick and seven teammates played the entire sixty minutes. Following an Irish fumble on the four-yard line, Kinnick scored Iowa's only TD, and he also dropkicked the PAT. Then, after N.D. got a late touchdown but missed the PAT, Kinnick saved the game with a seventy-two-yard punt from deep in his own territory. Eddie Anderson called the contest "My greatest day in football," and, partly due to this victory over his alma mater, he earned Coach of the Year honors; Kinnick got the Heisman.

To compound Layden's failure at Iowa, Warren Brown pointed out that "many of Anderson's [N.D.] teammates of the early twenties sat on the bench with him when Notre Dame visited Iowa City. That seemed to be regarded in some [N.D.] sectors as downright treason." But, for Brown, it indicated the behind-the-scenes "factional" squabbling in Notre Dame football, with some important alums wanting to get rid of the current coach as soon as possible. The anti-Layden faction never mentioned that Rockne's 1921 team, with Eddie Anderson as captain, had also lost at Iowa.

The following Saturday, the Fighting Irish returned home to face another Big Ten opponent, Northwestern, and they beat the Wildcats, 7–0. The late rally for the TD pleased the almost full house at Notre Dame Stadium but the national sportswriters in attendance wondered how the team would do in the finale against a strong USC squad.

Notre Dame had scored only twelve touchdowns on the season but they entered their final game ranked number seven in the AP polls, Southern Cal at number four. A sellout crowd in Indiana watched an error-plagued contest, the Irish unable to contain the Trojan offense on crucial third downs. The visitors won 20–12, Layden's second straight loss to USC and, according to many Fighting Irish rooters, a very large nail in his coaching coffin.

Peg Boland, wife of his line coach, Joe Boland, tried to dismiss the fan complaints as "the usual rumblings from the second-guessers, 'not enough razzle dazzle,' 'scores not big enough,' and there were those who wanted an unbeaten team. A loss or two, or tie, wasn't Notre Dame's style." But, in terms of her husband's and his boss's coaching futures, she was "whistling past the graveyard."

The Trojans went on to a Rose Bowl victory and number three ranking in the polls, the Irish landing at a generous number thirteen. More relevant was the changing nature of college football and the Pacific Coast coaches' use of the new passing offenses as well as quicker ground attacks, exemplified in 1939 by UCLA's black halfbacks, Kenny Washington and Jackie Robinson (later to break the "color barrier" in major league baseball). The following season, when Clark Shaughnessy installed his T formation at Stanford, Layden's adherence to the "Rockne system" seemed increasingly outdated, even to his backfield coach and former Rockne QB, Chet Grant.

Nevertheless, Notre Dame President John O'Hara, who claimed no expertise in the area of football strategy, was pleased with the 1939 record as well as the gate receipts. Attendance at Notre Dame Stadium had improved considerably, the road games had been sellouts, and the total payout to N.D. had increased to $546,000, providing greater profits because of stable expenses.

Part of these profits would now maintain the Rockne Memorial, the new showpiece of Notre Dame's recreational sports program. In 1939, work also began on another and even more important monument to the great coach—the Hollywood film based on his life. Only a tiny percentage of Americans would ever use the facilities in the Rockne Memorial on the Notre Dame campus but millions of people would see *Knute Rockne—All American* and embrace its idealized view of college sports.

36

Beginning
Knute Rockne—All American: 1939

"I was fascinated with the life story of Knute Rockne. . . . Over lunch in the Warner Brothers commissary [in mid-1938], I began talking up the idea of a movie based on his life and asked some of our writers for pointers on how to write a screenplay about him. I began working on a script and suggested to Pat O'Brien, a fellow Irishman who had become a good friend, that he'd make the perfect Rockne.

Of course, I'd already cast my own part in the movie: George Gipp . . .

Then one day I saw an article in *Variety:* Warner Brothers were going to make a movie based on the life of Knute Rockne starring Pat O'Brien.

When I asked some friends how this had happened they told me I talked too much, that it was a good idea so Warners bought the rights to Rockne's life story."

—Ronald Reagan, *An American Life,* 1990

Many myths surround the genesis of the film *Knute Rockne—All American,* most of them created by men claiming paternity. Former president Ronald Reagan put forth his version in his recent memoir; however, Pat O'Brien asserted in his autobiography that Mark Hellinger, the Broadway producer, had the "great idea for the picture," had cast O'Brien in the leading role, and had pitched "the concept" to Jack Warner. The movie executive liked it immediately, called O'Brien into his office, and offered him the part of the Notre Dame coach. Contrary to these versions, the historical record, especially the correspondence between Warner Brothers and the University of Notre Dame, suggests a very different creation.

Throughout the 1930s, as biographical movies became increasingly popular, a number of people proposed a film on the life of Knute Rockne. Christy Walsh, Rockne's agent, flogged the idea for years, and in early 1938, N.D. alum Vernon Rickard, a small-time Broadway actor, wrote a screenplay based on the coach's life, registered it with the Screen Writers' Guild, and had his agent send it to Paramount Pictures. This studio rejected it and, according to a reliable report, his agent "then submitted the script to Warner Brothers who kept it for about a month and returned it." Later, when Rickard learned of Warners' plans to make the biopic, he asked a prominent N.D. alum, William Cronin, to complain privately to Vice President O'Donnell about Warners' unfair treatment of him.

Arthur Haley, doing PR work for the university at the time, saw this correspondence and wrote Cronin confidentially, "Poor Vernon, unfortunately, is a victim of the old adage about 'putting the cart before the horse.' Before he began writing his Rockne script, he should have conferred with Mrs. Rockne and Mr. Vitus Jones, her legal counselor [because] his theme relates purely to Rockne and football, and I can tell you that neither Mrs. Rockne nor her legal counselor would give permission for this kind of presentation." Moreover, they were now negotiating directly with Warners and that studio intended to use its own scriptwriter.

According to the copyright law of the time, a film company could not portray a deceased person's life without permission of the heirs—for Rockne, his widow, Bonnie—thus Vernon Rickard, although muttering about a lawsuit against Warners, had no case. Whether his script was the genesis of the film is unprovable; he has a better claim than most, but the historical record shows that many people suggested a Rockne biopic, and in late 1938 the idea reached critical mass at Warner Brothers and they launched the project.

■   ■   ■

"I got in touch with my publishers [of my biography of Rockne] about that picture [in the book] to which Mrs. Rockne objected. It was mechanically impossible to take it out of such books as were off the press, but they agreed to delete it from those that followed. This much I wrote her, at once.

This morning she called me up and wanted to know if I couldn't appoint someone to go 'round cutting the picture out of every book,' and again I told her what my publishers had said."

—Warren Brown, author of *Rockne*,
in a letter to Father John W. Cavanaugh, May 1931

Bonnie Rockne, like many widows of famous men, tried to preserve her version of her husband's life and purge all other accounts. She insisted on the "Saint Knute" portrayal, and because she had the copyright law on her side and a tenacious lawyer aiding her, she usually prevailed in her negotiations with Rockne's biographers and with Warner Brothers. She demanded $50,000 from the Hollywood studio "for the privilege of letting them film the story of her famous late husband" (the cost of a new house in South Bend at the time was $4,500). But when the contract was drawn up and the University of Notre Dame had signed its portion— *N.D. refused to accept any money from Warner Brothers*—Bonnie balked at giving her approval until she had seen the script.

After reading the first draft, she instructed her lawyer to inform the movie studio of her objections, primarily that the "picture, as we understood it, was to be an inspiration to young men. Rockne was particularly fond of and spent much time with young men, particularly Boy Scouts. Every young boy was inspired by him." She felt that the script slighted this aspect of her husband's life and she demanded major revisions to include it.

The reasons for Bonnie's insistence on this theme seem to belong to the psychological, not the factual, realm. Indeed, Knute Rockne liked boys, but because he was so busy during his lifetime, he did not spend an inordinate amount of time with his own or with other children. In reality, the N.D. coach was more attentive to his past and present football players—his adult "boys"—than his actual sons or their contemporaries. Possibly Bonnie was unable to deal with this memory and the fact that she had raised their children mainly by herself; even though Rockne had been the often-absent father during his lifetime, she would render him a living presence to his sons and to all other boys in death.

In addition, if she harbored any resentment toward him for so carelessly leaving her a widow with four children, she could expiate some of it by erecting a memorial to him as a perfect father. Moreover, by 1939, it was clear that the three Rockne boys—now adult and teenage—were pale shadows of their father and possibly their mother hoped that the movie would spur them to minimal achievement (in all probability, because the film increased the coach's fame, it added to the already enormous psychological weight they carried as Rockne's sons; none of them made it through Notre Dame academically or succeeded athletically).

In the negotiations with Warner Brothers, Bonnie pushed the "inspiration to young men" theme and because it fit the sentimentality of sports movies of the era, the movie studio accommodated her wishes on this point.

Her other major complaint about the script concerned the absence of any "dignified reference to Rockne as a teacher and his influence in the class room. His ability to teach, his [intellectual] influence on students in the class rooms was equally as great as his influence on the [football] field." She wanted this aspect of his life emphasized in the film; again, she acted out of psychological and social reasons rather than a concern for the facts.

When Bonnie and Knute married she was of the genteel middle class and a recent convert to Catholicism; he had come from rough-and-tumble Logan Square in Chicago and, although a college graduate, he also inhabited the world of semipro football and Hullie & Mike's pool room. She abhorred this part of her husband's life and later tried to expunge it from the historical record, replacing it with, as she insisted to Warners, a portrait of a man of "scholarly attainment . . . a lover of good books . . . a man who loved good pictures, good shows, a scholar." Thus, for the film, she demanded scenes of his faculty career at Notre Dame.

Warners' scriptwriter Robert Buckner willingly accepted her mandate; because he opposed the college sports reformers and wanted to rebut their charges that athletic coaches did not belong in the academy, he emphasized Rockne's teaching career and his work for N.D. chemistry professor Father Julius Nieuwland. Most important of all, the scriptwriter created the legend that Knute Rockne would have been a great chemist if he had not chosen to coach football.

The final word on the accuracy of this depiction belongs to Jesse Harper. When informed of Warners' portrayal of these events, Harper wrote Arthur Haley: "I do not know whether they wish too much accuracy but Rock was hired at Notre Dame primarily as the head track coach and assistant football coach. *Father John Cavanaugh [president at the time] decided to have him teach chemistry [in the N.D. prep school] because he would not have enough to do assisting in football and coaching track. What a change in [Rockne in] twenty-seven years."*

"Warner Bros. will agree with the University not to use the University's name in the picture title and to relate it to the script only in those instances where it is absolutely essential because of the indivisible relationship between Rockne and the University.

[For filming on campus] The University agrees to offer facilities to Warner Bros. without compensation, provided Warner Bros. will in the primary announcements contained in the film, state the fact that the facilities were given without expense and indicate by suitable terminology the fact that the University is not being compensated. . . .

It is also understood that some phase of the script will contain the idea that the University is not a football school, that it has no great endowment fund, and is not a wealthy institution."

—From the preliminary agreement between
the University of Notre Dame and
Warner Brothers, January 10, 1939

The men in the Golden Dome neither sought out Warner Brothers to make the biopic on Rockne nor welcomed the proposal from the film company when it arrived. Because the project smacked of overemphasis of football, they hesitated before cooperating. The deciding factor for President John O'Hara and Vice President Hugh O'Donnell was the Rockne family's precarious financial situation in 1939; because the film project would provide Bonnie with a large sum of cash that she could obtain in no other way, the N.D. administrators extended the university's approval.

Fathers O'Hara and O'Donnell, however, feared that the film would spark public criticism that the Catholic school was totally commercializing its football program as well as profiting from the life and tragic death of the famous coach. Therefore, they refused to accept any money from Warners and stipulated in the contract that N.D.'s assistance "*without compensation*" be made absolutely clear in the foreword to the film.

In addition, they did not want the university's name exploited in any way and they would not allow it in the title nor in most of the picture. Part of their motivation was the negative experience with the last Hollywood movie about N.D., the 1931 piece of fluff *The Spirit of Notre Dame*. Harry Stuhldreher, who had a small part in that picture and was asked to appear in the Warners' one, summed up the general feeling in a letter to the N.D. vice president: "Our experience in the last Notre Dame picture, as Elmer [Layden] will tell you, wasn't any too pleasant. You may remember that [Rockne's agent] Christy Walsh employed sentiment to a great extent to influence us and . . . we [later] learned that the same Christy was being well taken care of financially," whereas the N.D. men involved and the university were exploited. This time, Notre

Dame would deal directly with the film studio and the name of the university would not help sell the movie.

Beyond the basic contract stipulations, the Notre Dame administrators were very accommodating to Warner Brothers—much more so than Bonnie Rockne. They assigned Arthur Haley and Father Eugene Burke as the N.D. liaison men on the project, and after reading the first draft of the script, Burke's main suggestion to Robert Buckner, its author, was that instead of having Father John W. Cavanaugh as the school president who both hired Rockne and eventually gave his funeral eulogy—in reality, Father Charles O'Donnell performed the latter rite—"it might be well to use the fictitious name of a priest." Burke suggested "Casey," but, in the end, the scriptwriter combined the two past presidents into the fictional character of "Father Callahan."

In early June 1939, Notre Dame gave its official "approval of the Warner Brothers' picture *The Spirit of Knute Rockne*" (the first version of the title). Bonnie, however, refused to sign the contract until Warners met her demands on the "inspiration to youth" and "scholar" themes. The men at the studio scrambled to accommodate her and did so by the end of the month.

■   ■   ■

"We [at Warners] feel, as you [the authorities at N.D.] do there, that Spencer Tracy is the ideal choice [to play Rockne]. In fact, this is so obvious to everyone that there is practically no alternative. The picture is much too important from both your viewpoint and ours to take any chance with mis-casting. Rather than do this, we would postpone making the picture until we have the right actor."

—Robert Buckner,
scriptwriter of the Rockne film,
to Arthur Haley, May 9, 1939

Later accounts of the making of the film state that Pat O'Brien had the Rockne role locked up from "Day One." In fact, he was a compromise choice. In early 1939, Arthur Haley informed a producer at Warners that "the name most popular at the university [to play Rockne] seems to be that of Paul Muni," a graduate of New York's Yiddish Theatre who had triumphed in a number of 1930s biopics, notably *The Life of Emile Zola*. However, Pat O'Brien actively campaigned for the Rockne role; he had spoken at the 1937 Notre Dame football banquet and knew some of the school's officials. Thus, in early 1939, when an Indiana Catholic weekly accused him of signing a petition in favor of the Loyalist side in the Spanish Civil War—most Catholics favored General Franco's rebels —O'Brien's secretary informed Arthur Haley that the actor had "absolutely nothing to do with the Spanish petition." Moreover, he "didn't want to sign the German petition [deploring Nazi intervention on Franco's side] either and dodged the issue as long as possible but the studio finally pinned him down and he had to make the concession."

Warner Brothers did not want to cast Paul Muni for the N.D. coach's role and pushed for Spencer Tracy. Notre Dame loved the idea—he had succeeded the previous year as Father Flanagan in *Boys Town.* But one major problem existed; Metro-Goldwyn-Mayer owned Tracy's contract and they refused to lend one of their hottest stars to Warner Brothers for a picture. This prompted Warners to recruit the men at Notre Dame in a campaign to pressure Louis B. Mayer into loaning them Tracy. First, the studio requested that N.D. officials write to Bishop Ryan of Omaha (head of the diocese that included Boys Town) to speak to Mayer; Father Hugh O'Donnell complied, as did Bishop Ryan, but the movie executive would not budge. Next, Haley enlisted Mayor Ed Kelly of Chicago, an N.D. grad; His Honor wrote "My dear L.B.," and pleaded for Tracy to play Rockne. Mayer, one of the toughest moguls in Hollywood, replied, "To let Tracy do what you wish would be a terrible setback [for M.G.M.]—as a matter of fact, my dear Mayor Kelly, I am confident I would not be able to get a confirmation from our New York office on such a request" (Mayer was referring to his bankers in Manhattan).

In midsummer 1939, Robert Buckner informed Haley: "The Spencer Tracy deal appears to be completely cold." However, Warners had a new idea—"The answer is James Cagney." Not only is there "no better actor in the business [but Cagney] is absolute tops as a box-office name [and] even more than Tracy, Cagney possesses Rockne's dynamic personality and drive; they talk alike and think alike. Cagney can play Rockne at 23 years old and Tracy would be much less convincing [as the young Rockne]." Finally, and most important of all: "We have Cagney under contract and he would be readily available."

The arguments for Cagney made sense and probably he would have been superb as the N.D. coach. All that Warners needed was Notre Dame's and Bonnie Rockne's approval—the contracts gave the school and widow veto power over the casting of the Rockne role—and the studio would begin shooting during the fall football season.

Arthur Haley's reply, on behalf of Vice President O'Donnell, was strangely evasive. Rather than directly oppose Cagney, he explained that it was "the thought of the executives here that Pat O'Brien should take the part of Rockne," and the main arguments for this actor were that "he is a family man of high character, and has a large following of Notre Dame people throughout the country."

Warners replied directly to Father Hugh O'Donnell, showing an aggressiveness necessary in the movie business, with its huge risk capital ventures:

> Pat O'Brien possesses only a fractional degree of Cagney's popularity . . . Cagney is now among the first three or four male stars in the industry. Pat is not among the first fifty. The picture's cost has been estimated at $750,000 [a high number for a Hollywood film of the period], with the strong possibility that it may run higher. The studio could not afford the extremely dangerous gamble with Pat. In fact, it is a certainty that neither our sales organization nor the thousands of exhibitors would react favorably to the idea. In effect, it is a simple matter of arithmetic. Cagney would insure the picture's success. O'Brien would not.

Then, to emphasize the point, the Warners' representative added, "If O'Brien is still your verdict after a reconsideration, I feel quite certain that the studio will not make the picture this year, and very possibly [will] abandon the project entirely."

If Warners thought that by "playing hardball" they would force the N.D. administration to yield, they totally miscalculated. Arthur Haley, in a confidential letter to Robert Buckner, explained that for President O'Hara and Vice President O'Donnell the issue was one of religious and political principle—Jimmy Cagney's "support of the Loyalist Cause in the recent [civil] war in Spain" and the "publicity he received" as a result ruled him out completely.

Because the Spanish Catholic church had opposed the Loyalists, some of whose factions had burned churches, most American Catholics ardently supported their Spanish coreligionists and the latter's champion, General Francisco Franco. Therefore, according to Haley, "Father O'Hara and Father O'Donnell do not feel that they can jeopardize the reputation of the university" among American Catholics by allowing Cagney to play Rockne. This decision was final.

Hal Wallis, a top executive at Warners, then informed Notre Dame in mid-August that the studio regretted the school's verdict but "we will keep trying to get someone for the part [of Rockne] who will be, not only an important name for the good of the picture, but one who will also be acceptable to you." Wallis made no mention of Pat O'Brien; obviously this actor did not yet meet Warners' criteria.

Without a leading man, filming could not begin in 1939 as originally planned and, during the fall, the project grew increasingly cold. In late November, Robert Buckner wrote Arthur Haley about the lack of "news on the Rockne picture" and that the scriptwriter was now "working hard on a new picture, *Virginia City*."

As 1939 ended, for many people at Notre Dame the biopic seemed as dead as the old decade. If the men in the Golden Dome had second thoughts on their veto of Cagney, they never revealed them in their memos or correspondence; for them, religious and political principles were paramount and they were prepared to accept the consequences of their actions even if it meant that the Rockne picture would never be made.

37

Filming *Knute Rockne—All American:*
1940

Dear Art:

Just a quick note to tell you that THE LIFE OF KNUTE ROCKNE is finally out of the egg-stage and ready to start chirping.

[Hal] Wallis wants to begin shooting in April or May at the very latest, with Pat O'Brien playing Rockne . . . he [O'Brien] is so anxious to do the part that I think he will give us a swell performance, the best of his career. The idea is to surround him with a first-class cast thruout. . . .

We read the news about Father O'Hara with much interest. Please give our warmest congratulations to them all, especially to Father O'Donnell and Father [John J.] Cavanaugh.

—Robert Buckner to Arthur Haley, January 25, 1940

The Warners' scriptwriter referred to the news that Father John O'Hara would soon become a bishop and his church's "Military Delegate" in charge of all Catholic chaplains and missions in the United States Armed Forces. Upon his departure from Notre Dame in early 1940, the C.S.C. council appointed Father Hugh O'Donnell as acting president and Father John J. Cavanaugh as his second in command. They would now direct N.D.'s dealings with the movie studio.

Why Warners finally accepted Pat O'Brien for the Rockne role is unclear. Possibly, after the Notre Dame–USC game in December 1939, they were reminded of the Catholic school's huge national following and the box-office potential in the Rockne movie, no matter who played the lead, and/or Pat O'Brien's star wattage had increased sufficiently—his recent portrayal of the priest in *Angels with Dirty Faces* had won praise and that film had done well at the box office. When Warners sent their news to Notre Dame, they also included a print of their current hit, *The Fighting 69th*, about an Irish-American regiment in World War I (starring Pat O'Brien).

The movie studio then began to implement the plan to surround O'Brien with a strong supporting cast. Robert Buckner sent Arthur Haley "a few pictures of Donald Woods, whom I think would be excellent for the part of George Gipp." The scriptwriter, who had unusual power on this picture due to his excellent relations with the N.D. administrators, noted: "We have tested three other men for the Gipp part. They are Dennis Morgan, Ronald Regan [*sic*], and Alan Baxter. None of them approximates my idea of Gipp as much as Woods . . . he is in excellent physical condition and handles himself in a football uniform as if he knows what it is all about [he played three years at Cal-Berkeley]. This is something the other three boys whom we have tested have not been able to do. . . . A unified approval of Woods by Notre Dame would be of almost conclusive weight, I am certain."

The N.D. men had no special preference in this matter and were willing to endorse Buckner's choice. However, on the Warner Brothers' lot in California, Ronald Reagan was lobbying hard to land the Gipp role. He buttonholed the executives in charge of the picture to allow him to do another screen test and, for it, he persuaded Pat O'Brien to play Rockne to his Gipp. Because Donald Woods was a less aggressive type, Reagan passed him on the final turn and landed the role.

The future politician immediately began identifying himself with the N.D. football hero and with the school. In the spring of 1940, he spoke at a Notre Dame alumni function in Los Angeles and, according to one observer, "he gave a fine talk. He spoke of how Gipp was his hero when he was a youngster and how several times he had occasion to talk to him in his broadcasts [when he was a radio sports announcer]." Ronald Reagan was only five years old when George Gipp began his Notre Dame playing career, but as Reagan proved during his political career, re-creating events in a dramatic and audience-pleasing way was his forte, and the legend of George Gipp—as opposed to the reality—provided perfect material.

The next major casting decision concerned "Father Callahan," the fictitious Notre Dame president. The studio tried to obtain the excellent
character actor Thomas Mitchell, but he was unavailable, as was the
second choice, Walter Connelly. Warners moved to Donald Crisp but
Arthur Haley, visiting Los Angeles, warned them that Notre Damers
would be unhappy with this actor because "he has a Scotch accent and
rather drawn facial features," unlike the rotund Father John W. Cavanaugh, the president who had hired Rockne. The movie executives nodded politely and placed Crisp, under contract to them, in the part.

No controversy developed over the casting of Gale Page as Bonnie
Rockne. This actress, "very wholesome and fine quality," fulfilled the
studio's criteria for "a feminine, domestic, and maternal" character "vital
to [any film's] success" because of the huge "woman's [movie-going]
audience." The minor roles were quickly cast, and by the middle of
February, the research department at Warners requested from Notre
Dame a long list of photographs—for example, "The old Chicago Post
Office where Rockne worked around 1910"—so that the studio could
design sets "to make the Knute Rockne picture as authentic as possible in
all of its details."

Robert Buckner claimed similar authenticity for his shooting script—
"I have stuck very close to the actual events and dialogue of Rockne's
life"—but neither the N.D. administrators nor Bonnie Rockne agreed.
Because their contracts with Warners allowed them censorship of the
script, during late February N.D. asked for minor—and Bonnie, major—
changes.

Most of Notre Dame's criticisms, articulated by Arthur Haley after con-
sultation with his superiors, concerned factual errors; for example: "The
script should be changed to read 'Congregation of Holy Cross,' which is
[the] correct [name of the order]." But the list also included requests to
soften some of the history; for a scene where a reporter quizzes Rockne
—"I hear Southern Cal and Columbia have asked you to name your own
price [to coach their teams]. Is that right?"—N.D. commented, "We
prefer not to use the name of any particular university, and suggest using
'Several eastern universities.'" These outside-offer incidents were not
Rockne's most glorious moments, and probably the N.D. administrators
preferred to muffle the actual events with a vague and general reference.

They also pointed out many script errors concerning specific football
games and seasons, but generally allowed most to remain to help the

writer—"Rockne really missed [much of] the 1929 season because of illness. For dramatic purposes, however, it is undoubtedly necessary to advance this [to 1928] in order to keep the story moving faster." Thus, in the film, Rockne starts the "Win One for the Gipper" speech from a wheelchair.

N.D.'s other suggestions were minor and easily satisfied; Bonnie Rockne was not nearly as cooperative and her lawyer sent the legal department at Warners an eight-page, single-spaced letter containing a large number of general as well as thirty-seven specific "corrections." Some were basic and others trivial, but they all conformed to Bonnie's vision of "Saint Knute"—"When we contracted with you, [the film] was to be a portrayal of his inspiration to youth and the educational side of his life . : . We believed that Knute Rockne was going to be shown as an educated man, a man of influence, while we really find him wrapped up in some manner, and almost entirely, with a football."

As always, Bonnie acted out of personal needs, not faithfulness to history. She seemed incapable of acknowledging that *Knute Rockne was mainly an athletic coach*—indeed, the prototype of the single-minded coach—and had achieved dominance in his profession through his obsessive devotion to his teams and his sport.

Her criticisms of the shooting script also contained a social-class component: "He was not slouchy, as indicated. He had and loved good clothes." She wanted her Knute upscale and she relentlessly pressed her point of view: "Rockne did not come to Notre Dame [as a young man] with a battered suitcase. It was not fancy, but his father and mother did not let him go away with a battered suitcase, high water pants and turtleneck sweater." On the other hand, his freshman roommate, Gus Dorais, recalled him as a "not very genteel character . . . a very rugged character."

At times, she also protested out of pure self-interest: "Sporting goods story must be out. Make it cigarettes or anything else you wish, but not sporting goods." The scene to which she objected has Rockne receiving a letter from the "Nonsuch Sporting Goods" company, stating, "We have a great proposition that can be worth $10,000 to you. In short, this is the deal—write us a testimonial stating the fact that 'Nonsuch Sporting Goods are the best in the world'—signed Knute Rockne. We figure that your name alone can sell $250,000 worth of our . . ." At this point, according to the stage directions, "Before any more can be read Rockne's hands crumple the letter into a ball and toss it away."

Bonnie approved of the antimaterialistic "Saint Knute." The problem, as Arthur Haley explained to Buckner, was that "Rockne actually did have some equipment named after him, made by the Wilson Western Sporting Goods Company." Because Wilson continued to market part of its Rockne line through the 1930s, Bonnie was receiving royalties from them.

If the widow were not so driven by her psychological and social needs, her actions would seem mainly hypocritical, and as such, the movie company could have bought off her demands. However, she was adamant, and Arthur Haley had to inform Hal Wallis, when he briefly met the producer in Chicago, of the absence of "Mrs. Rockne's O.K." for the shooting script, whereas "the university's release had been sent out." Haley complained, "There really has been nothing I could have done to expedite matters" with Bonnie and her lawyer.

In early March 1940, Hal Wallis wired Notre Dame:

"HAD HOPED TO RECEIVE MRS. ROCKNE'S APPROVAL BY NOW. AM SURE ALL HER OBJECTIONS HAVE BEEN MET WITH. . . . AS YOU KNOW PLANNING PRODUCTION OF THIS MAGNITUDE REQUIRES GREAT DEAL OF PREPARATION AND IN ORDER FOR US TO HAVE PICTURE READY FOR LEADER ON NEXT YEAR'S PROGRAM WE MUST START SOON. . . . WILL YOU PLEASE SEE MRS. ROCKNE AND MR. JONES AND EXPLAIN OUR POSITION AND NECESSITY OF GETTING WORD SOON."

Then, as a sweetener: "WE AGAIN REPEAT OUR INVITATION TO HAVE MRS. ROCKNE COME HERE AS OUR GUEST BEFORE OR DURING FILMING OF PICTURE."

Finally, after Buckner had redone the script to the "Saint Knute" specifications, adding such fictitious scenes as the conversation between President Callahan and the graduating Rockne about whether the young man should become a great chemist or a football coach, her attorney sent the signed approval to Warners. Bonnie was not completely satisfied— her demands for a "Perfect Rockne" would have removed all humanity from the character—but in April 1940, she left South Bend for a vacation in Hollywood courtesy of Warner Brothers.

The movie studio also wanted to reward Haley for his help and to continue his services as N.D.'s liaison man, Buckner writing him, "You can expect a wire from Mr. Wallis almost any day now asking you to come out . . . for $250 a week, living expenses and transportation" (in 1940, Haley earned $4,890 from Notre Dame and $2,695 from Warner Brothers). Once on the coast, he "went Hollywood," Buckner joking with him about Ilona Massey, a beautiful Hungarian actress, and "Dutch" Reagan.

Shooting began on the film at the Warners lot in Burbank, California, in late March 1940. A major problem occurred during the first week—the studio executives disliked director Bill Howard's work and even though he had made a number of important movies and had ingratiated himself with the Notre Dame liaison people, Warners yanked him off the Rockne picture. Into the director's chair went the reliable albeit pedestrian Lloyd Bacon. Arthur Haley, in describing these events to his bosses at N.D., carefully underlined the fact that Bacon had "attended Santa Clara University" that is, he was Catholic and sympathetic to Notre Dame.

Once Bacon took charge, he encountered the problem that Bill Howard had been unable to solve—how to shoot the forty-one-year-old and very middle-aged Pat O'Brien as young Rockne entering Notre Dame. The actor had lost "18 pounds in 3 weeks" to get ready for these scenes but, as Buckner had warned the previous year when lobbying for Jimmy Cagney for the part, few older actors would be convincing as the twenty-three-year-old Rockne. Bacon never solved this problem, and film reviewers later commented on O'Brien's implausibility as an undergraduate, even an overaged one.

After completing the initial phase of the movie—the interior scenes on the Warners' sets replicating Rockne's office, Gipp's hospital room, and so forth—in May the cast and crew traveled to South Bend for exterior shots of the campus as well as the "funeral service in the Notre Dame Cathedral." (The football field scenes were done at Loyola College in Los Angeles during the summer of 1940; in addition, newsreel game footage was later edited into the film.)

The publicity department at Warners wanted to turn the trip to Notre Dame into a major news event and in an interoffice communication laid out its plans: midwestern reporters would meet the actors in Chicago and be taken on a junket to Indiana; there, the "reception at South Bend station, with the entire student body . . . on hand" should be made "even more riotous than the receptions to Rock and his team coming back from a big victory." Next, "Pat [O'Brien] should go direct from [the] station to lay a wreath on the Rockne grave. This will give" the photographers for the "newsreels a chance to cover the reception and the wreath laying ceremony." (In a pre-TV age, Americans could only view news events in the newsreels in movie theaters, and the film studios manipulated the system to create "news" to promote their products.)

The publicist also enthused, "It would be great for the University [of Notre Dame] to name Pat an honorary alumnus, and present him with some scroll to that effect." The writer, with mock irony, added, "Even I hesitate to suggest an honorary degree of some sort [for O'Brien]."

The P.R. man was correct about Notre Dame's not being willing to award Pat O'Brien an honorary degree at this time (it did many years later). Nor would the school allow the student body to be publicity props at the railroad station. Furthermore, Acting Vice President John J. Cavanaugh wrote a sharp letter to Hal Wallis laying out the ground rules for the film crew's activity on campus—"the regular academic functions of the University must continue without interruption. The month of May is one of the most important of the entire school year and we must maintain an atmosphere conducive to serious study while your troupe is at work [here]."

One area where the N.D. administration was amenable concerned football. The publicity memo had suggested:

> If Spring football practice is still on, Pat [O'Brien], in coaching togs and Rockne make-up, should be down on the field with the boys. Good for lots of shots, particularly with Elmer Layden. Maybe the boys would get in uniform for the pictures, even if they're not practicing. In any event, Pat should talk to the football squad and have pictures taken with the players and Layden.
>
> The more Notre Dame trained coaches and great football players of the past who can be on hand, the better. They'll be good for news shots and copy shorts.

Charlie Callahan, doing promotional work for the N.D. athletic department, noted at the bottom of his copy of this memo: "I think this is a great start."

Elmer Layden was not pleased with Warners' plans for the practice field but grudgingly went along with them. His negative premonitions proved correct—not only was the publicity event disruptive to his coaching but it brought the ghost of Rockne to life through O'Brien's impersonation, reminding onlookers as well as the multitude of Fighting Irish fans who saw the scene in the newsreels that *Elmer Layden was no Knute Rockne* and his current squad was a blurred image of the great teams of the past. Previously for Layden, the Rockne ghost had symbolically hovered overhead, but in 1940, the film placed it on his back, hastening the end of his coaching career.

More disturbing to Acting Vice President Cavanaugh than the ballyhoo during the May visit were Warners' ideas for the sales promotion of the movie. A memo "Outlined by Mr. Einfeld," head of publicity for the

studio, laid out a campaign whereby the Catholic school sold the movie
to the public through such devices as "Notre Dame dinners stemming
from South Bend and reaching to every city and town where there
are Notre Dame alumni." Einfeld's definition of N.D. alums extended
to all Fighting Irish fans as well as a majority of American Catholics and "those millions must be swung behind the [Rockne] picture
just as rabidly" as the school's actual graduates—"It's their [the millions of fans'] picture, *just as Notre Dame is their college and their football team.*"

Someone had neglected to inform Warners' publicity head as to who
owned Notre Dame—the C.S.C. order, in legal deed and daily fact. His
words raised red flags for the N.D. administrators—as similar claims had
for their predecessors in the Golden Dome—and the acting vice president wrote Hal Wallis, politely but firmly: "It is our desire that neither
the University nor our Alumni Association be put in the position of 'promoting' the 'Life of Knute Rockne.' Hence, such suggestions as Notre
Dame dinners next fall . . . must not be entertained. . . . We will not
foster the exploitation of Notre Dame relationships" with fellow Catholics or the general public "or of the Alumni Association in advertising"
the movie.

Cavanaugh did not comment on other aspects of the Warners' sales
campaign—for example, "Build-up Pat O'Brien as a great American"—
but the Hollywood cynicism must have displeased him. More distressing
at this time was Warners' attempt to wiggle out of the contract clause
concerning the foreword to the film and its statement that Notre Dame
received no money for its cooperation. The head of the studio's legal
department informed N.D.:

> Mr. [Jack] Warner and [producer] Mr. Wallis . . . are rather disheart-
> ened that the University should insist upon including the words 'without
> compensation' as they feel that the usage of such words will, to a great
> extent, cheapen the picture from the standpoint of public reaction, and
> they do not feel that such words are appropriate in the foreword of a
> picture made for entertainment purposes.

Bonnie Rockne and her lawyer were behind this move, realizing that
if the public learned that *Notre Dame received no money for the picture
but that she had obtained a huge sum,* she would appear greedy. Warners
recognized that this admission in the foreword would indeed "cheapen
the picture from the standpoint of public reaction." Therefore, as their
head lawyer stated, the studio wished "to eliminate the words 'without

compensation' " and, in this way, avoid any suggestion of the widow's profit.

The lawyer included Warners' new version of the foreword. Beginning with two syrupy paragraphs about Rockne's "dedication to the Youth of America," the third and final one read: "This picture has been made with the permission and valuable assistance of his widow, Bonnie Skiles Rockne, together with the cooperation of the University of Notre Dame." In heavy black pen, Cavanaugh crossed out the last clause and wrote: "Gratitude is expressed to the University of Notre Dame, which without compensation, has cooperated."

Warners pressed on, Bonnie Rockne on its side, and because the movie was almost in the can and she was due to receive the bulk of her money, Arthur Haley informed the studio, "The University advises that if there is some better wording which you might have to suggest, but which would still impart this idea [of no compensation], it would be satisfactory." Warners' new formula was: "Appreciation is expressed to the University of Notre Dame for its gratuitous cooperation." Possibly the N.D. administrators were tired of the haggling or they believed that the average American moviegoer's vocabulary included a secondary meaning of the word *gratuitous,* but surprisingly, they accepted this sentence. Another explanation is that N.D. had already clashed with Warners over the use of the school's name in the title of the film and now faced a fight over the final title; rather than skirmish on many fronts, the N.D. authorities focused on the most important one—keeping "Notre Dame" off the theatre marquees and out of the advertising campaign.

Hal Wallis had long pushed for *Knute Rockne of Notre Dame,* arguing that it "seems such a 'natural' [and] has so much more general appeal than just *The Spirit of Knute Rockne* or *The Life of Knute Rockne.* It ties him in with your great institution and recalls to his millions of followers and admirers the association of many years." But the N.D. administration held its ground, Haley informing Wallis that "the authorities of the university do not believe they can change their decision concerning the title, as covered by the contract."

By the summer of 1940, the studio bosses had hit upon *Knute Rockne—All American,* Robert Buckner telling Arthur Haley, confidentially, "I think it [this title] is terrible, I think it is cheap in every sense of the word. . . . Of course," with the United States probably entering World War II, "it is obvious what the studio hopes will be read into the word 'All American.' . . . I hate to see the hard work which we poured into it [the film] now handicapped by a cheap, jingoistic, flag-waving, opportunistic title!"

Haley showed Buckner's letter to Cavanaugh; the N.D. administrator agreed with the scriptwriter's comments and also disliked the title because, as Haley informed Jack Warner, *Knute Rockne—All American* "definitely tags it as a football picture, a title that might be given to some great football player, such as *Red Grange—All American*" but provokes "much dissatisfaction here at the University." Haley suggested the two-word title *Knute Rockne,* pointing to the recent success of the biopic *Lillian Russell.*

Jack Warner, like his fellow movie magnate Louis B. Mayer, was neither polite by nature nor concerned about Notre Dame not wanting to be labeled "a football school." His studio had lived up to its contractual obligations—"Notre Dame" would not appear on the marquees or advertising—and he informed Haley, "We here at the studio have come to the conclusion that no matter what thought you have of Knute Rockne, he will still be known for his association with the great game of football." Warners had already placed the title on the prints of the movie and they soon announced it to the press.

In mid July, the studio "sneak previewed" the picture in a small California town and, as Jack Warner informed N.D., "it was amazingly [well] received by the audience." Robert Buckner noted: "The entire sequence of Gipp was one of the highlights of the picture. When he died I don't believe there was a dry eye in the theatre. 90% of the preview cards . . . commented on Reagan's performance." Warners decided to emphasize the scene in its publicity campaign and, subsequently, the deathbed request transcended the film, "Win One for the Gipper" becoming Ronald Reagan's most famous movie speech and his political slogan.

In late July, Warners sent a print of *Knute Rockne—All American* to Notre Dame, but the campus reaction to the initial showing was more muted than the one at the California sneak preview. Arthur Haley informed Robert Buckner: "Everyone here last night really did like the picture very much, but I did not find anyone using the word 'great.' The story was well done, but . . . it lacks some finishing touches in direction . . . I think there were several opportunities missed. In Gipp's death scene, Reagan really does fine, but I think Pat misses a little direction in work. . . . On the whole, the picture is very good and I am sure will do great business."

By the end of the summer of 1940, the Notre Dame administrators were tiring of the Rockne commemorative festivities. They had not initiated the film project and had not enjoyed the constant negotiations with

Warners and Bonnie Rockne. They detested the studio's reneging on parts of the contract as well as its plans for the university to promote the film. The movie, with a title they disliked, was due for fall release, and even though they agreed to participate in a South Bend premiere, they privately looked forward to the day when all the Rockne memorials were in place. The recreation building had been completed in 1939 and, by the end of 1940, the movie, *Knute Rockne—All American,* would have come and gone.

Fathers Hugh O'Donnell and John J. Cavanaugh, the relatively young and very energetic men in charge of the Catholic school, preferred a Rockne ghost permanently fixed in stone and celluloid, not a "living presence" to disrupt their plans for the future. With the country coming out of the Depression and probably entering World War II, the N.D. administrators faced very different circumstances than their predecessors had encountered. They regarded their regime as beginning a new period in Notre Dame history. Nevertheless, many elements from the past would not die, notably the debate on the overemphasis of college football and N.D.'s relationship with the Big Ten conference.

38

The End of the Rockne Era: 1940

"The University [of Chicago] believes in athletics and in a comprehensive program of physical education for all students. It believes its particular interests and conditions are such that its students now derive no special benefit from intercollegiate football."

> —The opening of the statement by the University of Chicago's
> board of trustees and President Robert Hutchins
> announcing the school's exit from Big Ten football,
> December 21, 1939

The final season of Big Ten football for the University of Chicago was an on-field disaster, with the Maroons losing to opponents such as Michigan and Ohio State by 85–0 and 61–0, and only besting totally deemphasized Wabash and Oberlin. Francis Wallace wrote that the Chicago "boys shouldn't be asked to break their hearts against Grade A competition." At the end of the season, when President Hutchins requested that the school's trustees abolish the intercollegiate football program, they responded quickly and affirmatively.

Predictably, most sportswriters howled in outrage, denouncing Hutchins as a "betrayer of youth" and even a Communist, Arch Ward noting in the *Chicago Tribune* that "there is nothing new about the Maroons' policy . . . There's a school down in Arkansas called Commonwealth College which never has had a football team—it was founded by and is operated by Communists." Ironically, after the announcement, Hutchins received a private wire from the head of the University of Arkansas, the home of Razorback football; President J. William Fulbright telegraphed: "SINCERE CONGRATULATIONS ON YOUR COURAGEOUS DEFENSE OF THE UNIVERSITY AND ITS TRUE FUNCTION"—but Fulbright, later a distinguished U.S. senator, did nothing to curtail his school's big-time football program.

Unlike the sports journalists, many editorial page writers applauded Hutchins's stand against "the hypocrisy of present intercollegiate football," and in the Midwest, some wondered why other Big Ten schools did not follow Chicago's lead. However, the conference commissioner, Major John Griffith, launched an immediate counteroffensive, even prevailing upon the other nine schools to cancel scheduled events with Chicago's teams in "minor" sports—Hutchins believed that these activities were student based and he wanted to continue intercollegiate competition in them. Griffith conducted an unrelenting campaign against Hutchins in particular and deemphasis in general; eventually, the University of Chicago, a founding member of the conference, resigned and the Big Ten remained at nine until Michigan State entered in 1949.

"A genial and knowing gentleman, Father John O'Hara of Notre Dame, was invited to join the anvil chorus [condemning Chicago's dropping of football, but O'Hara refused] . . . The good father knows his way around. He had the exact opposite of the job that confronted Hutchins. Father O'Hara had the task of making Notre Dame known as an educational institution rather than a football team.

In the opinion of many educational authorities, O'Hara's achievement has been a brilliant one. He isn't the demigod that Knute Rockne was, but kids who graduate from his school now can look for jobs without degrees in tackling, blocking, passing, and kicking as major recommendations."

—*Chicago Times*, January 18, 1940

When Father John O'Hara left Notre Dame in early 1940, shortly after this statement in the *Chicago Times*, his departure marked the end of a three-decade cycle for him and his beloved school. He had arrived as a young student in 1909 and, as he said in his farewell address in 1940: "During thirty-one years' residence here I was impelled by a natural curiosity to see everything going on." He had lived through and contributed to the major physical and academic construction of his

university and also to the creation of Fighting Irish football, particularly
its religious component. His exit not only signaled the end of a crucial
phase in the evolution of his school but also in its intercollegiate sports
history.

The year Father John O'Hara departed, his protégé, Elmer Layden,
also completed his N.D. career, rounding out the "Rockne Era" in Notre
Dame football. This cycle began almost three decades previously when
Jesse Harper brought the "shift" to N.D. and used Rockne as a key
player and then as an assistant. Subsequently, in the 1920s, as the great
coach perfected his methods, the Fighting Irish, particularly the Four
Horsemen, achieved amazing success and fame. In the 1930s, however,
the "Notre Dame system" declined in effectiveness, especially in
Layden's final years.

For Elmer Layden, the football world was changing not only because of
on-field tactics but, at N.D., because of the men now in charge of the
school; Fathers Hugh O'Donnell and John J. Cavanaugh had launched a
new internal strategy. The vice president wrote to Layden on July 3,
1940:

> You will recall a conversation that you and I had with Father [Hugh]
> O'Donnell in which he asked that the number of the football squad
> returning here in the fall should be reduced to 60. I recall this to your
> attention so that there will be no misunderstanding.
>
> A second point you and I discussed at length some weeks ago [was]
> the matter of reducing employment to athletes. You will recall that in this
> meeting, which we had together, the objective was to reduce from 117 to
> 80 or 90 the jobs for football players.

A major part of President O'Hara's legacy to N.D. was his "Fortress
Notre Dame" policy and his formulation that if the school capitalized on
its unique strengths, foremost among them its ability to recruit and edu-
cate the best Catholic football prospects in America, Fighting Irish football would be highly successful and profitable.

In the summer of 1940, the C.S.C. Council confirmed Father Hugh
O'Donnell as N.D. president and Father John J. Cavanaugh as vice president and chair of the faculty athletic board. President Hugh "Pepper"
O'Donnell described himself as an "old, broken-down center"; having
played on the small tight varsities of 1914–1915, he never understood
why Rockne in his later coaching career and then Hunk Anderson and

Elmer Layden needed mammoth squads. Father John J. Cavanaugh, a highly intelligent and well-informed football fan, shared this concern. Both men also believed that the N.D. head coach was the beneficiary of the highest quality of football recruits in the country and that quality, not quantity, produced winning teams.

Thus, in the spring of 1940, the new N.D. administrators decided to reduce the varsity to sixty players and the freshman team to a little less than that number. Moreover, they enforced this reduction by cutting the number of jobs for football players and, for the first time in memory, shrank the percentage of athletes employed by the university to less than half of all student workers. By the following spring, the administration allocated 40 percent of the employment money to the athletic department and only 18.5 percent of student jobs to athletes.

Layden protested this policy but, as a product of Notre Dame's hierarchical system, he knew that he could not overturn an official edict. Unfortunately for his future at the school, he manifested his unhappiness by becoming uncooperative in a number of minor areas, including his work on the film *Knute Rockne—All American*.

Warners needed Layden's approval for the use of his name in the movie and they also wanted him to appear in the final scenes. Father Hugh O'Donnell had generously assured the studio that he would obtain the coach's signature as well as the permissions of the other Horsemen and former Notre Dame players mentioned in the film. Most of the signed releases arrived promptly but Layden held out, explaining to Arthur Haley that he disliked "the scenes concerning the Four Horsemen . . . and I don't feel that cooperation should go to the extent that a picture connected with Rockne and Notre Dame should necessarily place me in an ill light when I am located at the University"—the "ill light" was the script's clear implication that no successor could measure up to Knute Rockne.

The current N.D. coach also disapproved of granting "Stuhldreher the final words in what is evidently a closing or climax scene." Then, revealing his intense rivalry with his famous cohorts, he added, "Consideration of Fordham [where Crowley was coaching] and Wisconsin [Stuhldreher's employer] does not fit in with my idea of cooperation in the picture."

Layden, with surprising stubbornness, refused to sign, provoking a Warners' executive to write to Father John J. Cavanaugh that without the "release, it would mean the elimination of the 'Four Horsemen' from the story and this I consider would work a great hardship on the picture. . . . I presume that you have talked to Mr. Layden."

A few weeks later, Warners wired Cavanaugh: "DEEPLY EMBARRASSED TO TROUBLE YOU ABOUT THE LAYDEN RELEASE. WANT TO SHOOT FOUR HORSEMEN SEQUENCE [IN STUDIO] STARTING MONDAY. . . . IT IS IMPORTANT THAT WE GET SOME EXPRESSION FROM MR. LAYDEN AS SOON AS POSSIBLE." All of the other Horsemen and former players had signed, but the N.D. vice president had to inform Hal Wallis: "I have talked to Elmer about his part in the picture. . . . I tried to make it clear that he would be given prominence at the end of the picture in accordance with his position as the man who is carrying on Rockne's tradition here on campus. But he sees the matter in a different light, and after having talked to him again today, I cannot see much change in his attitude from the first times we talked about the matter [months ago]."

Layden believed that the movie company was trying to exploit him, not only monetarily—they offered him no money for the use of his name and time—but also professionally. The film placed him totally in Rockne's shadow, not giving him his proper due as an individual or as a football coach.

The vice president found Layden's position irritating, but President Hugh "Pepper" O'Donnell took the coach's obstinacy as a personal insult —he had guaranteed delivery of the release. After another month of refusals, Layden finally signed, but this incident contributed to his demise as Notre Dame A.D. and football coach. In addition, it confirmed for the men now in charge of the school that a new athletic policy was needed, one paying obeisance to, but not directly "carrying on Rockne's tradition here on campus."

Mr. E. L. Bach
Executive Secretary
Association of Commerce
South Bend, Indiana

Dear Mr. Bach:
We [Warner Brothers] are presently of the opinion that South Bend should, by all means, have the world premiere of "The Spirit of Knute Rockne." We will make every effort to bring this about. . . .

Cordially yours,
S. Charles Einfeld
Director of Advertising and Publicity

As the Notre Dame administrators had discovered during their initial dealings with Warner Brothers, many elements of the production of *Knute Rockne—All American* were beyond the school's control. During the summer of 1940, they learned similar lessons concerning the selling of the film. Neither President O'Donnell nor Vice President Cavanaugh wanted N.D. involved in the sales or advertising campaign, but they had not reckoned on South Bend's nor their students' enthusiasm for the picture. On its own initiative, the local chamber of commerce persuaded Warners to hold the world premiere in South Bend and to create appropriate hoopla for the occasion, while the boys on campus pressed for a role in these events.

The N.D. administrators refused to permit the movie company to use the school's facilities for the premiere but they did agree to the introduction of the film's principal actors during halftime of the 1940 home opener against the College of the Pacific. On the Friday night before that game, the movie festivities began with a national broadcast of Kate Smith's radio program from Adams High School in South Bend. Appearing with Kate to plug the Rockne film were Pat O'Brien, Ronald Reagan, Gale Page, and others. Later that night, at the Palais Royale Theatre in downtown South Bend, the movie stars came on stage before the showing of the film. Outside, a huge crowd, including many Notre Dame students, cheered their entrance into the theater and listened to the stage ceremony over loudspeakers.

President Hugh O'Donnell was not in a good mood during the weekend events and he was uncomfortable entertaining the visiting celebrities. He later fired off a ferocious memo to Arthur Haley: "Who had the consummate nerve to charge this [the president's] office with $20.90 for chicken and ham sandwiches, coffee and Coca-Cola, for service to guests of the president at the College of the Pacific game . . . it was always my understanding that the stadium concessionaire furnished refreshments to guests of the president at all home games" as part of the school's contract with the concessionaire, no matter how many extra guests were present.

Vice President Cavanaugh, a smoother, more politic personality, made small talk with the visiting dignitaries, including a son of President Roosevelt and such newspaper luminaries as William Randolph Hearst, Jr., and Ed Sullivan. He also agreed, when pressed by the Notre Dame students, to allow multiple showings of the film on campus throughout the weekend. But Fathers O'Donnell and Cavanaugh were relieved when the movie promotion ended and their school returned to its normal autumn routine—academics, religious services, classes, interhall and Fighting Irish football.

"[I must] emphasize my disapproval of the course we have pursued [in football] for seven years [from 1934 through 1940] . . . seven years in a fog of evasion, compromise, and non-commitment. . . .

But let the present trend continue—right now, Notre Dame's popularity, in my opinion, is in the exact balance—and we may experience a crash from which it will take a long time to recover."

—Assistant Coach Chet Grant, in a private evaluation of Elmer
Layden's work for Vice President John J. Cavanaugh

During the ballyhoo for *Knute Rockne—All American,* Elmer Layden refused to comment on the film or its brief portrayal of him, pleading the demands of "football business." Privately, he worried about the constant reminders of Rockne and the increasingly oppressive task of trying to equal his mentor's achievements. Because of the mandate from the new N.D. administration, Layden began the 1940 campaign with a smaller squad than for any previous year of his regime. He was fortunate that his team faced a number of weak early season visitors, beginning with Amos Alonzo Stagg's College of the Pacific and a totally deemphasized Carnegie Tech (the scaled-down Pitt program had embarrassed the Tartans into abandoning their big-time ambitions). The Irish won these games 25–7 and 61–0 but sandwiched in between was a 26–20 squeaker at home over a mediocre Georgia Tech squad.

Layden's luck continued in the fourth game, a visit to the not-so-Fighting Illini, in a down period and with their fans demanding the ouster of Bob Zuppke because of his "out-moded football." N.D. won easily, 26–0—and Illinois ended the season at 1–7, losing all its Big Ten games.

The Irish faced a similar situation the following week in the Army annual. As a result of the three-year eligibility rule, the Cadets were feeble, already having lost to Cornell 45–0 and Lafayette 19–0, and notching only one victory, over tiny Williams by a point. Yet, on a sparkling autumn day in New York, the Army "pushed" the Irish "all over Yankee Stadium, outdoing them in everything but the scoring." N.D. marked the only TD of the game on an intercepted pass, sneaking by, 7–0. "Thus did Notre Dame gain her 20th victory of the series over" what most sportswriters proclaimed "the weakest Army team in history" (United Press report).

The usual set of New York "glitterati" attended the game, among them Ambassador Joseph P. Kennedy and some of his family. But one enterprising reporter walked through the crowd "to locate the 'typical' fan in the stands." He found a man from Los Angeles, who "never went to college, had no particular interest in collegiate sport, but traveled" six thousand miles round-trip to see his favorite annual event, Army versus Notre Dame.

The following Saturday against an average Navy squad, the Irish won 13–7. Layden's team, with a highly deceptive 6–0 record, entered its next game, at home against Iowa, as strong favorites. Hawkeye coach Eddie Anderson had lost his star, Niles Kinnick, and his undermanned squad came to N.D. after four consecutive defeats, including one to weak Indiana.

Using only fifteen players in the game, Anderson clearly outcoached Layden and his team beat his alma mater's, 7–0. One retired Chicago gambler recalls this contest as his greatest betting coup:

> I was sure that Elmer had totally lost it as a coach and the Iowa game was the set-up that every bettor dreams of finding. I knew that Eddie Anderson's team would win and I went all over Chicagoland plunging on them, getting nice odds at first from the Irish lovers but later taking whatever I could get. By kickoff, I had put down every dime I had and could beg and borrow. . . . Listening to the game, my heart was in my friggin' mouth until Notre Dame fumbled in the fourth quarter and Iowa finally scored. I won over $60,000, that would be at least a half-million today.

The professional gambler added a postscript: "I was so convinced of Layden's failure that I left most of my winnings with the bookies and put it on Northwestern for the next N.D. game. I hit that one too but the payoff wasn't as good as on Iowa. Still, I totaled over one hundred grand. One friggin' million today. Oh, how I loved 1940 and the end of Elmer Layden. His worst football season and my alltime best. My son's middle name is Elmer in honor of him."

After the loss to Iowa, Notre Dame was still the favorite to beat Northwestern. Coach "Pappy" Waldorf was between excellent teams (the phenomenal quarterback Otto Graham joined his varsity in 1941), but in that year's contest in Evanston, the Wildcats toyed with Layden's squad, winning easily, 20–0. In the postmortems, Arch Ward tried to defend his favorite team: "Now let's have a talk about Notre Dame. Frankly there isn't much to discuss. The Irish are coming up to their final contest with a record of six victories and two defeats . . . Still our mail has been cluttered with abuse directed at Elmer Layden and his inability to keep his players at top peak."

The N.D. coach also had increasing problems with his school's new administrators regarding the athletic director aspect of his job. Fathers O'Donnell and Cavanaugh wanted to crack down on the consumption of alcohol in the stands at home games, and after the Iowa visit the vice president wrote to Layden about this problem. Layden lamely replied: "We enclose with our tickets a note which asks people not to bring liquor into our stadium. We do not, however, announce over the loudspeaker that drinking is prohibited. . . . I do not know how we can control it except to constantly urge our patrons to desist." The administration preferred more aggressive tactics, such as guards at the gates searching patrons, but with the home season over, they postponed taking action on this problem.

The 1940 finale was against USC in Los Angeles. Not surprisingly, Notre Dame received many requests from the people at Warner Brothers for tickets, Arthur Haley happily accommodating them. Before a huge crowd in the L.A. Coliseum against a Trojan team with a 3–3–1 record, the Irish slipped by, 10–6. Near the end of the contest, Elmer Layden showed that the strain of the season and being Notre Dame head coach was getting to him; uncharacteristically, he ran onto the field to protest a pass interference call against his team, screaming at the officials, then verbally blasting the Southern Cal coach, Howard Jones, as well as the school's athletic director.

After the game, when the N.D. head asked the player accused of the foul, Bernie Crimmins, whether the game official had erred, Crimmins admitted that he had committed interference. Layden immediately apologized to the officials and the USC men but this incident stands as a sad symbol of his final coaching appearance.

There are two important footnotes to Elmer Layden's last game: his USC coaching opponent and Rockne's longtime friend, Howard Jones, also never coached again, dying of a heart attack after the season and completing a cycle that started at the beginning of Rockne's football career; then, the following year, in a move representative of the difference between Layden's abilities and his successor's, Frank Leahy transformed Bernie Crimmins from a second-string fullback to an All-American right guard.

"Three things might happen soon:
1. You [Vice President John J. Cavanaugh] might bring Leahy in and make a clean sweep of the coaching staff.
(a) In this event, you might leave Layden in the athletic directorship or
(b) you might bring in W[arren] Brown or someone else to be athletic director.

2. You might preserve the status quo indefinitely.

3. You might preserve the status quo now with the ultimate purpose of bringing in Leahy or someone else. . . ."

—Chet Grant, in a private communication
to Vice President John J. Cavanaugh, January 5, 1941

After the 1940 season, Notre Dame assistant coach Chet Grant went on a fact-finding trip to New Orleans to scout the performance of Frank Leahy's underdog Boston College team against top-ranked Tennessee in the Sugar Bowl. Grant, a former Rockne quarterback and a future historian of N.D. football, loved his school and its Fighting Irish tradition, placing his loyalty above even personal considerations. He indicated to Vice President Cavanaugh: "Any coaching change which eliminates Layden must eliminate me. [Moreover] In view of my connection with this inquiry, I couldn't stay on even if invited."

Most of Grant's lengthy report to Cavanaugh focused on Frank Leahy, whom he found as "smooth as silk, he's [also] as forceful as the circumstances dictate. He extends the velvet glove but you can feel the steel underneath." In addition, according to Grant, an astute football analyst, Leahy was on the cutting edge of the coaching profession and, in a clinic, his "presentation was not only well-organized but delivered with beautiful lucidity—you will realize the contrast" to Elmer Layden.

As important for Grant, Leahy's assistant coaches and players sincerely respected him and "Boston College outsmarted, outcharged, outstayed probably the best team in the country [Tennessee] in as well-played a game as ever I saw. Boston College showed me things I didn't think could be done . . . In short, to repeat, the man has everything. Maybe the report sounds too good to be true, but remember, there was a Rockne once, why can't there be a Leahy?" Finally, Grant appealed to Cavanaugh personally: "I became convinced that Leahy is a coach of destiny. . . . *The guy is there, John—believe me, he is there.*"

Grant understood that the hiring of Leahy meant the end of his own N.D. coaching career—he admitted to the vice president: "Heaven knows that would be an economic blow to my folks," whom he supported financially—but he refused to "pull punches." Chet Grant's obsessive honesty and love of Fighting Irish football prevailed, and his document stands as an extraordinary comment on the Layden regime as well as the correct prediction of the Leahy future.

O'Donnell and Cavanaugh accepted Grant's recommendation and began a series of moves that ended with the hiring of Frank Leahy. However, because the administrators filed away Chet Grant's confidential report, journalists at the time and subsequent commentators were unaware of its crucial role in Notre Dame football history. The official story of Layden's departure, told often by the coach himself, was that in early 1941, after completing his Notre Dame contract—signed five years previously with President O'Hara—the new administrators offered him only a one-year extension. Instead of accepting, he chose "more money, more security, [and] a better life for my family," and through his friend Arch Ward he obtained the position of commissioner of the National Football League at $20,000 a year.

In March 1941, when Layden left his alma mater, Fathers O'Donnell and Cavanaugh saw no point in contradicting his story and they issued a polite statement "congratulating him on his new appointment and wishing him success in his new position." However, that same month, after Cavanaugh had signed Frank Leahy as the school's new A.D. and football coach, the vice president placed in his files a newspaper clipping headlined "IRISH SOUGHT LEAHY BEFORE LAYDEN QUIT," with the underlined sentence, "This report is borne out somewhat by Leahy's own admission that he was sought out for the job long before Layden had indicated he would resign."

Whether Cavanaugh requested silence from Leahy on this aspect of his hiring is unknown. The two men, as well as their superior, President Hugh O'Donnell, were not interested in the past, only the future, and they looked toward it when Frank Leahy assumed his athletic department duties at Notre Dame in the spring of 1941.

39

The End of the Creation of Notre Dame Football: 1941

"Notre Dame's net athletic revenue, made public for the first time today in a precedent-breaking move, will approximate $211,915.45 for the 1940–1941 schoolyear.

The figure was announced by Rev. John J. Cavanaugh, vice-president of the University and chairman of the faculty board in control of athletics, in connection with his mid-year report to the Rev. J. Hugh O'Donnell, C.S.C., [N.D.] president, in an effort to dispel the popular notion that Notre Dame makes 'a million dollars a year' on the gridiron."

—N.D. press release, March 28, 1941

In a move that would have shocked their predecessors in the Golden Dome, the new administrators embarked upon a "sunshine" policy on athletic department finances and, after the 1940 football season, released the final numbers—receipts of $524,483, expenses of $312,568, and a much smaller profit than the world believed. Even during the previous regime, when *Time* magazine reported that Notre Dame garnered "millions a year" from Fighting Irish football, President O'Hara had refused to disclose the actual figures. But, as Vice President Cavanaugh pointed out in his press release, "Notre Dame is not a wealthy school" and its "total endowment is less than $2 million. As of 1940, there were 134 colleges and universities in the United States with endowments of more than $2 million" (immediately after the University of Chicago dropped football, President Hutchins raised $8 million for his school's fund, putting it over the $100 million mark).

Cavanaugh, after placing the football profits within the context of the institution's finances, then gave a clear signal that N.D.'s main priority was to raise money for "proposed laboratories, for research, for the development of the graduate school, for scholarships to brilliant but needy students." Most of all, the new administration wanted to counter the image of Notre Dame as a "football factory" and to shift public attention to its academic mission.

The vice president admitted, however, that the "current athletic revenue is typical of the past 15 years. Athletic profits represent about half of the $7 million spent for additions to and improvements in the physical plant of the school." Thus, for the new men in the Golden Dome, Fighting Irish football had again "shaken down the thunder"—the destructive charges to which they felt impelled to respond as well as the procreating rain of football profits that helped build and sustain the school through the 1920s and the Great Depression.

Later, in an internal move that also set an important precedent, the Notre Dame administration articulated the school's intercollegiate athletic policy. The "Memorandum of the Conference on August 3, 1942, Between Father O'Donnell, President of the University, and Mr. Frank Leahy, Director of Athletics" began with the long view: "The athletic prestige of Notre Dame is the fruit of the labors of many men and of innumerable sacrifices made in the hundred years of the University's existence," and the document pledged absolute adherence to the school's "Constitution for Intercollegiate Athletics." Furthermore, "victories or winning teams are to be sought only in accordance with the Constitution, policies, practices, and the principles of true sportsmanship." Then, unlike other schools with high-minded but vague athletic policies, the memo articulated a long list of *specific* points for Notre Dame's A.D. and coaches to follow, including detailed restrictions on recruiting and the number of days for football practice.

This Notre Dame president, like his predecessors, warily eyed the two-edged sword of Fighting Irish football fame. When the school's program stayed within the prescribed rules, it performed "an apostolate for the working of incalculable good." However, if coaches ever deviated because of a desire to win at all costs, they would bring immeasurable harm upon "Our Lady's School."

Nowhere in the memorandum does the name Knute Rockne appear. The participants in this conference had known him well but they did not want his memory haunting their offices. Since the release of *Knute Rockne—All American,* the Notre Dame athletic department had issued an official biography that closed the loop on the great coach's life—it followed the movie scene-by-scene, never deviating from the mainly fictional portrait concocted by Bonnie Rockne, Robert Buckner, and John B. Kennedy, including the latter's "Win One for the Gipper" speech.

For naive viewers, the film "brought Rockne to life," giving the illusion that *this was Rockne in life.* However, many people who had worked with him, including Father Hugh O'Donnell and Frank Leahy, privately acknowledged the film's inaccuracies and fictions. But *Knute Rockne—All American* did bind the coach to one place and one time and, in 1941, his successors at Notre Dame preferred him that way—as a celluloid and stone statue, invoked when needed but not a "living presence" to interfere with current and future operations.

Frank Leahy became a master of the Rockne reference, claiming many connections to the "Rockne system" but, in fact, mainly using his mentor's psychological techniques and not the on-field strategies. Leahy, like his teacher, was able to build upon, not slavishly repeat, the past and thus succeed in the present. He proved that when he discarded the "Notre Dame Shift" in favor of the T formation and went on to achieve a coaching record almost equal to Rockne's—Leahy came close to Rockne's phenomenal winning percentage and his teams rarely played the early-season patsies.

When the new coach assumed office at his alma mater, a Boston columnist, Bill Cunningham, who knew him well during his Boston College days, traveled to Notre Dame to survey the situation. He began by asserting, "Maybe, instead of a football story, it's really the story of the United States of America, in its current physical crisis [on the eve of World War] reflected in a football mirror."

Notre Dame football, like many businesses, as well as the country, had entered its mature phase and, as Cunningham indicated, "no football machine, no business firm, no nation, no way of life can live in a highly competitive world on nothing more tangible nor more active than former glory and the veneration of a hallowed name, now resting in peace." For Notre Dame football, as well as mature businesses and nations, he continued, "somebody virile and vital must take over, meet the new with the new, think faster than the fastest, hit harder than the hardest, stay alert, remain alive, keep everlastingly punching." According to this writer, Frank Leahy was the perfect coach for the Fighting Irish in 1941.

Thus the hiring of Frank Leahy drew a clear line between the past and the future of Notre Dame football. During the "Rockne Era," the enterprise had grown from a small, disorganized pastime to a huge thriving business. Many men, most of all the great coach, had contributed to its creation. By 1941, Fighting Irish football had achieved maturity. Frank Leahy's task was to sustain and enhance its fully created state.

Epilogue

Frank Leahy won five unanimous or nearly unanimous national football championships, compiling an 87–11–9 record, including four consecutive undefeated seasons. He did it through a combination of perfectionism, innovation, smarts, and ruthlessness. He recruited ferociously— harvesting the Catholic parochial school feeder system to perfection— trained his players mercilessly—they called his main assistant coach "Captain Bligh"—and he beat his opponents in any way possible.

But he made one major public mistake: in his final season he violated Notre Dame football tradition, arousing the anger of the Fighting Irish faithful and the scorn of N.D.-haters and the national press. Needing extra time-outs in a close game against Iowa on November 21, 1953, he instructed a player to fake injuries to stop the clock. The player did this perfectly and Notre Dame scored as a result, avoiding defeat. The headline writers called Leahy's last team the "Fainting Irish," and the administrators in the Golden Dome received letters from fans decrying the tactic as unworthy of the Catholic institution as well as from anti-N.D. individuals mocking the school and its football history.

At this point, Father Theodore Hesburgh was in the second year of his Notre Dame presidency. Father John J. Cavanaugh, N.D.'s chief administrator from 1946 to 1952, had groomed him for the office and, in the same way that Cavanaugh had carried out and enlarged upon the

academic and athletic policies begun by presidents O'Hara and Hugh
O'Donnell, Hesburgh followed his predecessors.

By late 1953, the youthful Hesburgh and his vice president, Father
Edmund Joyce, had already clashed with Frank Leahy over a number of
issues, and the coach's health had also been impaired by his
workaholicism. The administrators asked him to retire. Leahy left and
twenty-five-year-old Terry Brennan was given the most difficult job in
college football.

In his first two years, Brennan's teams were 9–1 and 8–2 but then
they slipped to 2–8, and Fighting Irish fans became restive. Because
Father Hesburgh had started to transform the school into a modern
university, critics charged that he also wanted to "de-emphasize football."
In fact, he was merely acting appropriately as president of Notre Dame,
attempting—with greater vigor, intelligence, and determination than any
of his predecessors—to emphasize the academic side of the institution
but still preserve its athletic heritage. Therefore, after the team struggled
to a 6–4 record in 1958, Fathers Hesburgh and Joyce replaced Brennan
with former N.D. player and NFL coach Joe Kuharich. The national
press condemned the "firing" of Brennan, N.D. adversaries mocked the
transition, and even some Fighting Irish fans claimed great shame. All
held Notre Dame to a standard imposed on no other university.

In a sense, the Catholic school had oversold its myths and allowed the
fiction of Knute Rockne's innocent purity to become the reality of Notre
Dame football for many Americans. The Kuharich years were an on-field
disaster, but President Hesburgh was focused on implementing his
academic plans; then, in 1964, he and Father Joyce brought in Ara
Parseghian, the first non–Notre Dame graduate to head the football
program since Jesse Harper. Such stalwarts as Francis Wallace
interpreted this hiring through the lens of N.D. history, pointing out that
Parseghian, like Harper, was a Protestant but that he had a French
mother like Father Sorin and would "wake up the echoes."

More to the point, Parseghian was young, ambitious, and extremely
well organized: he achieved an .836 winning percentage in eleven
seasons. But, like Leahy, he is now remembered by many for a single
event that violated Notre Dame football history—the tie against
Michigan State in 1966. Rather than attempting to win the game with a
late desperation play, he allowed his team to sit on the ball and preserve
a tie. The national press jibed—"TIE ONE FOR THE GIPPER"—the N.D.-
haters jeered, and many Fighting Irish fans felt ashamed. No one
condemned the Michigan State coach for also playing conservatively;

Parseghian's sin was that he had broken faith with the past, with Rockne's edict to fight to the final whistle.

The modern period of Notre Dame football often appears to an observer as a drama written long ago, with actors playing entirely scripted parts. The head Notre Dame football coach must be personable—Dan Devine's failing in the late 1970s—he must win consistently—Gerry Faust's downfall in the 1980s—and he must handle the immense pressure of the job—Lou Holtz's task at present. In addition, Fighting Irish fanatics are as demanding as ever, anti-N.D. people as hostile, and the media spotlight never dims. Meanwhile the "Notre Dame family" of administrators, faculty, students, and alumni continue to participate in the drama with mixed emotions—they enjoy the excitement of Notre Dame Saturdays but they detest those times, such as the end of a head coach's regime, when football overshadows all other aspects of their beloved school.

In an interview for this book with Robert Schmuhl, an N.D. faculty member and alum, I mentioned philosopher Michael Novak's comment that the University of Notre Dame's crowning achievement, its great gift to America, was Fighting Irish football. Schmuhl replied: "I hope that his occupying a chair [of philosophy] here when he made that remark also signifies Notre Dame as a place that takes the mind seriously."

Notre Dame has long valued the mind as well as the body. Since the Greeks defined the dichotomy between the two, no institution has systematically achieved excellence in both. But the University of Notre Dame has engaged this conundrum more seriously than has any other school in the world, and Notre Dame's struggle with its athletic culture and its academic aspirations will likely continue well into the next century.

Notes

The following notes reference all quoted material and financial figures in the book and also add further explanations to some of the comments in the text. For the citations of documents in the University of Notre Dame Archives (hereafter cited as UNDA), I have followed their cataloging code. The first letter in their code stands for: U for university records; P for printed materials; and M for microfilm.

The UNDA codes used in the notes to identify records sources are:

UADR for University Athletic Director's Records, ca. 1909–1929
UABM for University Athletic Business Manager, ca. 1900–1940
UPWC for University President John W. Cavanaugh, 1905–1919
UPBU for University President James Burns, 1919–1922
UPWL for University President Matthew Walsh, 1922–1928
UPCO for University President Charles L. O'Donnell, 1928–1934
UPOH for University President John F. O'Hara 1934–1940
UPHO for University President J. Hugh O'Donnell, 1940–1946
UPCC for University President John J. Cavanaugh, 1946–1952
UPHS for University President Theodore Hesburgh, 1952–1987
UVMU for University Vice President Michael Mulcaire, 1928–1933
UVOH for University Vice President John F. O'Hara, 1933–1934
UVOC for University Vice Presidents J. Hugh O'Donnell and John J. Cavanaugh, 1934–1946
UVMR for University Vice President John Murphy, 1946–1949
UVHS for University Executive Vice President Theodore Hesburgh, 1949–1952
UVJO for University Executive Vice President Edmund Joyce, 1952–1987

UDIS for University Department of Information Services
UDSS for University Director of Student Studies
UATH for University Athletics Collection
MPRR for University Registrar's Records

Thus, the source of the quote in the text by Notre Dame President John W. Cavanaugh to football coach Frank Longman concerning Gus Dorais, from a letter dated March 22, 1910, in Father Cavanaugh's papers, is UPWC, 180/9 (box number 180, folder number 9). In those instances where the Notre Dame Archives has not designated a box and folder number for a document, they requested that I cite their code for the papers, the folder title, and the date—for example, the financial figures for the home games of the 1911 football season are in the University Athletic Business Manager's papers (UABM, "Financial Reports of Games: Football 1911–17" folder).

After the first mention, frequently cited non–Notre Dame Archives sources are given in shortened form throughout the Notes section. Full information on these sources can be found in the Bibliography beginning on page 613. The notes follow the order of material presented in each chapter. However, those references marked clearly in the text, particularly quotes from newspapers with clearly marked datelines, are not repeated here. Finally, unless otherwise noted, the text is my interpretation of the primary and secondary sources; in no way is the University of Notre Dame Archives or any other possessor of primary or secondary material responsible for my particular interpretations. Where emphasis has been added to the text it is so indicated in the Notes.

PREFACE

Father Frank Cavanaugh's quote from Wells Twombley, *Shake Down the Thunder: The Critical Biography of Notre Dame's Frank Leahy,* Radnor, Pa., 1974, is on page 66.

The athletic department papers in the subbasement of the Hesburgh Library were kept with an uncataloged jumble of books, films, and memorabilia, all under the grandiose title of "International Sports & Games Collection." The only writer who ever mentioned the papers was Michael Steele in his *Knute Rockne: A Bio-Bibliography,* Westport, Conn., 1983, page 305, but the contents of Rockne's files totally contradict—factually as well as interpretatively—this author's portrait of the N.D. coach. Considering the mouse poop and disintegrated paper that spilled out when I opened the boxes, it was obvious that no researcher had ever examined the vast majority of Rockne's correspondence or the letters of the N.D. athletic department business office.

INTRODUCTION

Except for the ABC-TV story, all of the material in the Introduction is discussed in greater detail in the main text of the book. The reader can find the specific topics in the Index and turn to them as well as to their notes.

Keith Jackson appears to have based his story of the scheduling of the first Notre Dame–USC game on the memories of longtime Southern California athletic department manager Gwynn Wilson (UATH "Arnold Eddy Reminiscences"). Wilson stressed that it was his wife whom Bonnie Rockne liked—other biographers of the coach claim that it was the wife of USC coach Howard Jones—and Wilson says that he told Rockne that "the guarantees can be $20,000 or $100,000 or anything in between." According to Wilson, "Rock said $20,000 would be enough," and according to Keith Jackson, President Matthew Walsh of Notre Dame agreed to that amount. Unfortunately for this version, Rockne would not have called $20,000 "fluttering"—it was well below average for offers to the Fighting Irish in this period—and the coach never mentioned Bonnie Rockne or anyone else's wife in his letter to Paul J. Schissler, 9 December 1925, concerning the scheduling of the game (UADR 19/67). In addition, no one on the Notre Dame side of the story, including Bonnie Rockne, ever told the Marion Wilson anecdote during their lifetimes.

I. "What Though the Odds Be Great or Small": 1789–1918

1. L'UNIVERSITE DE NOTRE DAME DU LAC AND THE NINETEENTH CENTURY

Because of his recent novels, Father Andrew Greeley is a controversial figure among American Catholics; however, in a previous manifestation as a professor of sociology, he did important work on Catholic higher education. The opening quote is from his *From Backwater to Mainstream: A Profile of Catholic Higher Education*, New York, 1969, page 5, and the later quote by him is on page 21 of that book.

For the background on Catholic higher education, I used a number of works and sources, including *Adapting to America: Catholics, Jesuits, and Higher Education in the Twentieth Century* by William P. Leahy, S.J., Washington, D.C., 1992; *The Academic Man in the Catholic College* by John D. Donovan, New York, 1964; *American Catholicism* by John Tracy Ellis, second edition, Chicago, 1969; *The Survival of American Innocence: Catholicism in an Era of Disillusionment, 1920–1940* by William M. Halsey, Notre Dame, Ind., 1980; and Garry Wills's *Bare Ruined Choirs: Doubt, Prophecy, and Radical Religion*, New York, 1971 (the quote in the text is on pages 23–24 in that work). The statistics on the survival rate of Catholic schools are in Edward J. Power, *Catholic Higher Education: A History*, New York, 1972. A superb but unpublished work is the Ph.D. dissertation *The University of Notre Dame, 1919–1933: An Administrative History* by Notre Dame graduate Rev. David Joseph Arthur, The University of Michigan, 1973. In addition, a very long taped interview on 13 April 1991 with Indiana University professor of religion Mary Jo Weaver (a Notre

Dame Ph.D.) provided much useful information; Professor Weaver also answered many follow-up questions.

The standard work on American higher education is *The American College and University: A History* by Frederick Rudolph, New York, 1962; the comment by the first president of the University of Chicago is on page 352 of that work. Professor Rudolph's *Curriculum: A History of American Undergraduate Courses of Study Since 1636*, San Francisco, 1977, also provided important background information, as did *Academic Freedom in the Age of the College* by Richard Hofstadter, New York, 1955; *The American College and American Culture* by Oscar and Mary Handlin, New York, 1970; and *The Emergence of the American University* by Laurence Veysey, Chicago, 1974. For the histories of specific universities, I used *Pioneers: A History of the Johns Hopkins University* by Hugh Hawkins, Ithaca, New York, 1960; *The Launching of a University* [Johns Hopkins] by Daniel Coit Gilman, New York, 1969; *Harper's University: The Beginnings—A History of the University of Chicago* by Richard J. Storr, Chicago, 1966; and *The University of Illinois, 1867–1894: An Intellectual and Cultural History* by Winton Solberg, Urbana, Ill., 1968.

Of the histories of the University of Notre Dame, one stands out: *The University of Notre Dame: A Portrait of Its History and Campus* by Thomas Schlereth, Notre Dame, Ind., 1976; the first quote from that work is on page 28. Of the other histories of Notre Dame, Rev. Arthur J. Hope's *Notre Dame: One Hundred Years*, Notre Dame, 1948, is useful, and two books by Francis Wallace, *Notre Dame: Its People and Its Legends*, New York, 1969, and *The Notre Dame Story*, New York, 1949, contain interesting anecdotes. From the latter book comes the Father Sorin quote on the disobedience of the Irish, page 53. After Father Sorin, every president from 1874 to the present has been of full or partial Irish extraction, including Father Hesburgh, who is half German and half Irish.

The *South Bend Tribune* headline on the Notre Dame fire is in Schlereth, page 55; Father Sorin's reaction to the fire is on page 57; and Schlereth's summation of Sorin's character is on page 32.

2. THE ORIGINS OF NOTRE DAME'S ATHLETIC CULTURE

The quote from the president of Cornell is in Rudolph, *The American College and University*, pages 373–74. The best histories of American sports in the nineteenth century are Benjamin Rader's *American Sports: From the Age of Folk Games to the Age of Spectators*, Englewood Cliffs, N.J., 1983, and Ronald Smith's *Sports and Freedom: The Rise of Big-time College Sports*, New York, 1988. For part of the background on boxing in the nineteenth century, see Randy Roberts, *Papa Jack: Jack Johnson and the Era of White Hopes*, New York, 1983; also informative was a lecture by Roberts, "A Sporting People: The Culture of Irish-American Sports," given at the University of Notre Dame, 10 October 1991. The scholar and novelist Thomas Flanagan provided information about Fenians in America in an interview, 2 March 1991, and his novel, *Tenants of Time*, New York, 1988, depicts them movingly and in detail.

During the 1880s, Anson's Cubs won five National League pennants; he was one of the true fathers of twentieth-century baseball—in negative as well as positive terms. He helped professionalize the sport and establish better playing conditions but he abhorred black players and was active in bringing segregation to organized base-ball. For a discussion of Anson's racism see *A Hard Road to Glory: A History of the African-American Athlete 1619–1918* by Arthur Ashe, New York, 1988, page 74, and *Only the Ball Was White* by Robert Peterson, Englewood Cliffs, N.J., 1970, pages 29–30.

The famous 1929 document from the Carnegie Foundation, often miscalled a report, was part of a regular series of bulletins on problems in American higher education. *Carnegie Foundation Bulletin Number Twenty-Three: American College Athletics* was published by the foundation in New York in 1929, the main author was Howard J. Savage. The quote about the "boilermaker" appears on page 29; the athletic teams of Purdue University supposedly gained their "Boilermakers" nick-name when the team manager, in the 1890s, enlisted a number of boilermakers from the Monon Railroad Shops in Lafayette, Indiana—across the Wabash River from the university—to strengthen a weak Purdue team.

In the current age of NCAA image building, Purdue disavows this provenance of its nickname and claims that in an early game against Wabash College, the latter's students mocked the Purdue players and fans as being as "rough as boilermakers" and that the nickname pleased the Purdue people and they kept it (see "100 Years of Purdue Football" by Jim Russell in *1987 Purdue Football Media Guide*). The sani-tized version seems farfetched and the boilermakers-enlisted-as-players truer to the nature of nineteenth-century college football. When I was a student at Purdue a generation ago, university publications acknowledged the use of actual boilermakers on the team as the source of the nickname.

The stories about Fielding Yost are in Smith, page 139, and Rader, pages 139–40. Even Notre Dame, not yet involved in big-time football, participated in the spirit of the era; Chet Grant, former N.D. player, coach, and sports historian, noted in his *Before Rockne at Notre Dame: Impression and Reminiscence,* South Bend, Ind., 1978, page 37, that there were "members of the 1890s teams [whose] academic status remains a mystery. . . . Certainly they were not tramp athletes in the errant sense of the term. Rather, they were community-spirited citizens of South Bend, let's say, who loved to play football and had no prejudice against rubbing elbows with higher educa-tion."

The *Notre Dame Scholastic,* the student newspaper for many years, was a weekly. At the end of each school year it was bound into a volume with its pages numbered consecutively. However, in September 1931, it stopped the practice of consecutive numbering and changed to weekly numbering. To help readers locate references in pre-1931 *Scholastics,* the year and page number are given; for 1931 issues and after, the week and page are given. For the quote about the 1899 "contest with Lake Forest," see page 119 of the 1899–1900 volume.

The standard histories of Notre Dame football are filled with errors and mislead-ing tales; rather than use them, I have gone directly to the newspapers of the time, including the *Notre Dame Scholastic* and the school's excellent yearbook, *The Dome.*

These contemporary sources also provide more accurate football statistics than do the later histories, which tend to perpetuate common mistakes.

The quote from the 1905–1906 *Dome* is in an article, "Athletics of the Past," anon., no pagination. The comment about N.D.'s "masculine atmosphere" is in Wallace, *Notre Dame Story*, page 29, and the discussion of N.D.'s ecumenicism is in James Armstrong, *Onward to Victory: A Chronicle of the Alumni of the University of Notre Dame du Lac,* Notre Dame, Ind., 1974, page 16 (Armstrong was the longtime secretary of the Notre Dame Alumni Association). Father Morrissey's comment is in Hope, page 279.

The *Scholastic*'s "Are you out for the Varsity?" is in the 1906–1907 volume, page 32. The 1899–1900 volume contains the quote about the 1899 game against Stagg's powerhouse, page 88; the one about the N.D. game at Ann Arbor, page 120; and the "rooters" for the home game against Indiana, page 136. Frank Hering later became an ardent Notre Dame alumnus and South Bend civic leader; he is also credited with being the originator of Mother's Day. Armstrong discusses his career on page 88 of *Onward to Victory.*

3. CATHOLIC VERSUS AMERICAN HIGHER EDUCATION

The Greeley quote is in *From Backwater to Mainstream,* page 13; the discussion of Catholic higher education under Pope Pius X and his condemnation of modernism is in Arthur, page 46. The complaint by Father Zahm about N.D. as "a large boarding school for elementary students" is in *Academic Development [of the] University of Notre Dame: Past, Present, and Future* by Father Philip S. Moore, a C.S.C. priest, privately printed, 1960, pages 9–10, available through the University of Notre Dame libraries. This study provides excellent information on the school's curriculum in the first part of the century.

The quote from Frederick Rudolph on elective courses is in *The American College and University,* page 305; he also discusses at length the new phenomenon of "Academic Man." John Dos Passos sketched a brilliant portrait of Thorstein Veblen in *The Big Money,* New York, 1933 (see NAL reprint, 1991, pages 113–22).

The quote from the N.D. student about "student-teacher relationships" is in Wallace, *Notre Dame Story*, page 91; the Armstrong quote on Father Crumley is in *Onward to Victory,* page 161. Ronald Smith's *Sports and Freedom* provides information on early attempts to regulate intercollegiate athletics as well as Michigan's departure from the Western Conference; the organization of that group is in *A History of the Intercollegiate Conference* by Carl Voltmer, New York, 1935, pages 2–8; and the information on Notre Dame's first athletic constitution is in Hope, page 278. The official title of the University of Michigan's trustees was "Regents": to avoid confusion, I use the term "trustees" in its generic sense—those people to whom the university is "entrusted" by the state or private corporation that owns the school, whether they are called "regents," "overseers," or one of their other official titles, including "trustees."

4. THE ORIGIN OF "THE NOTRE DAME VICTORY MARCH"

Ring Lardner's comment about the Western Conference's opposition to Catholic Notre Dame was in his "Wake of the News" column in the *Chicago Tribune*, reprinted in the *Notre Dame Scholastic*, 1913–1914, page 379. Lardner was from Niles, Michigan, close to Notre Dame, worked in South Bend as a young reporter, and was a lifelong Notre Dame fan; Jonathan Yardley wrote an excellent biography of him, *Ring: A Biography of Ring Lardner*, New York, 1977.

For the *Scholastic*'s front-page poem, see the 1913–1914 volume, page 161. Chet Grant made the comment on "no eggheads" at Notre Dame in *Before Rockne*, page 86, and he quoted the lines from Shuster on page 33. The popular N.D. expression about the "mile of land between the University and the city of South Bend" appears in many places, including Christy Walsh's *Intercollegiate Football: A Complete Pictorial and Statistical Review from 1869 to 1934*, New York, 1934, in "History," page 348, an article on Notre Dame by Joe Petritz. For more on American campus life, see Calvin Lee, *The Campus Scene: 1900–1970*, New York, 1970. The origin of the N.D. cheer "He's a man" is obscure, although Grant dates it before 1910, page 64.

The *Scholastic*'s 1912 comment on interhall football is on page 17; the following year, Lambert Sullivan of the *Chicago Daily News* discussed the charges against N.D.'s interhall program at length, reprinted in the *Scholastic*, 1913–1914, page 378. Chet Grant quotes the 1901 *South Bend Tribune* report on the Indiana game on page 43; the 1913 *Scholastic* comment on the home game against South Dakota is on page 63, and the *Dome*'s description of the crowd greeting the team returning from Yale is on page 150 of the 1914–1915 edition. The *Dome*'s photos of head cheerleader Joe Gargan are in the 1915–1916 volume, page 194.

Beano Cook discussed the N.D. "Victory March" in Richard Whittingham's *Saturday Afternoon: College Football and the Men Who Made the Day*, New York, 1985, page 212, and also notes its popularity in terms of other American favorites. In *Notre Dame* and *The Notre Dame Story*, Francis Wallace gives the standard stories on the origins of the "Victory March." John Shea told the Sorin Hall version to James E. Murphy for the latter's article, "Notre Dame Victory March," *Notre Dame*, spring 1960, page 16; however, in an unpublished article by Robert O'Brien, John Shea said that the march was also composed in Massachusetts (UDIS 30/14).

Michael Shea's "very amateurish" comment was in the *Scholastic*, 25 October 1935, page 10. The passages from Michael's undergraduate poems quoted in the text appeared in the *Scholastic* in the volume for 1903–1904, pages 1 and 137; in the volume for 1904–1905, page 21; and John's couplet was in the 1905–1906 volume, page 265. The words in the eulogy to Rev. Michael Shea are in the *Scholastic*, 20 September 1940, page 15.

5. NOTRE DAME SPORTS: 1900–1912

Chet Grant's comment on Notre Dame baseball is in *Before Rockne*, page 69. Notre Dame's turn-of-the-century baseball schedules are listed in the Contents sections of most of the *Scholastics* in this era. The subject of the school's alumni in big-league baseball was discussed in *The Dome*, 1915–1916, page 238, and by Armstrong in *Onward to Victory*, page 87—on the latter list is Roger Bresnahan, although there is some dispute as to whether he actually attended N.D. or merely claimed it. The modern *Notre Dame Baseball* guide, Notre Dame, Ind., 1991, page 43, claims that Lou Sockalexis, an American Indian who attended N.D. briefly in 1897 and went on to play for the Cleveland club of the American League, was the main reason the team's nickname became the "Indians."

The letter by Frank C. Longman to James L. Hope, 3 September 1910, about Don Hamilton and summer baseball is in UNDA (UADR 1/61). The item about the Notre Dame versus the American College of Medicine and Surgery game is in the 1905–1906 *Scholastic*, page 134; the story about coach Pat O'Dea playing for the opposition is in that paper, 1901–1902, page 68. O'Dea totally disappeared after the 1903 season, only to turn up thirty years later in California, living under the assumed name of Charles J. Mitchell. By 1934, with Notre Dame football a national phenomenon, he was pleased to claim his early association with the program; see " 'Pat O'Dea' is Pat O'Dea Says the Judge," *Notre Dame Alumnus,* December 1934, page 59.

In an article in *A Treasury of Notre Dame Football*, edited by Gene Schoor, New York, 1962, page 13, Louis "Red" Salmon (N.D.'s first All-American) wrote that Father Morrissey, the president of the school at the time, dismissed Pat O'Dea after the 1901 season and did away with coaches for the following two years. Mike Bonifer and Larry Weaver, in *Out of Bounds: An Anecdotal History of Notre Dame Football,* Blue Earth, Minn., 1978, page 21, relate the story of the 1930s publicists. Farragher as ghost coach is also confirmed by the *Scholastic* for these years: in all of the articles about the football team no mention is ever made of Coach Farragher—the main spokesman for the team is Captain Salmon or the student managers; however, when Notre Dame plays other teams, their coaches are identified; for example Pat O'Dea coaches the Missouri Osteopaths when N.D. plays them in 1903. Thus Farragher found the perfect way to avoid the public hue and cry that has come to surround football coaches at Notre Dame and he even skipped the hiring and firing press conferences.

During the 1900s, the football schedules are listed in the Contents sections of the *Scholastic*, as are articles about the team. The comment in that paper about the mediocre 1905 season is in the 1905–1906 volume, page 556. Tom Barry's remark about moving west to practice law is in the 1907–1908 *Scholastic*, page 180. Allan Dwan's description is in *We Remember Rockne*, edited by John D. McCallum and Paul Castner, Huntington, Ind., 1975, page 36.

The *Scholastic* quoted the remark of the Detroit journalist in the 1909–1910 volume, page 158, and on that page and the following ones, it ran the excerpts and cartoons from various newspapers; Walter Camp's comment was on page 159, and Yost's on page 186; the description of the Miami of Ohio crowd on page 175, and the article by the Chicago writer, Daniel J. F. Sullivan of the *Chicago Inter-Ocean*, stating that N.D. deserved to be national champs was reprinted on page 191. The 11

December 1909 issue of the student weekly was devoted to the victorious season. For the photo of the 1909 team see the photo insert in this book.

The *Detroit News* report on Michigan's cancellation of its 1910 game with Notre Dame is reprinted in the 1910–1911 volume of the *Scholastic,* page 160. For Longman's letter, 3 September 1910, to James Hope about prospects for the coming year, see UADR 1/61, and for President John W. Cavanaugh's letter to Longman on 22 March 1910, see UPWC 180/09 "Lof-Lop" 1908–1910. Joe Collins made his comments about how other schools recruited the 1909 team in a letter to Rockne, 31 January 1922 (UADR 9/208).

See the *Detroit News* for the comments on Yost's cancellation of the 1910 game; the *Scholastic* explained the situation of the Whitman players in the 1910–1911 volume, pages 143–44; the standard histories of Notre Dame football have various garbled versions of these events.

On page 33 of the text, James L. Hope's letter to Vice President Matthew J. Walsh, 23 July 1911, is in UADR 2/10. For the 1911 exchange of letters between Marquette and Notre Dame see John J. O'Connor to Vice President Walsh, 28 August 1911 (UADR 2/16), and John J. O'Connor to John P. Murphy, 27 September 1911 (UADR 2/16). The financial figures for the home games of the 1911 football season are in UABM, folder "Financial Reports of Games: Football 1911–17." The final figures for the 1911 football season are in a memo from Jesse Harper to President John W. Cavanaugh, 29 May 1916 (UPWC 36/9).

For the letter from the N.D. student manager to Glenn "Pop" Warner, 12 December 1911, see UADR 2/28; for Warner's reply to John P. Murphy, 25 February 1912, see UADR 2/28. The satiric poem on Walter Camp appeared in the 1912–1913 *Scholastic,* page 187.

An outstanding study of Warner's days with the Carlisle Indians is Jack Newcombe's *The Best of the Athletic Boys: The White Man's Impact on Jim Thorpe,* Garden City, N.Y., 1975. In 1914, a congressional committee investigated Carlisle; Warner did not like the reforms that it imposed upon the school, and in February 1915 he jumped jobs to Pitt, see Newcombe on this, pages 241–42, as well as Tom Perrin, *Football; A College History,* Jefferson, N.C., 1987, page 83. In addition, contrary to legend, Warner helped Thorpe and other athletes play summer professional baseball. When Thorpe's professionalism became controversial and he was stripped of his 1912 Olympic medals, the coach pretended to know nothing about it; the 1951 movie *Jim Thorpe—All American,* starring Burt Lancaster, perpetuates the myth, absolving Warner of any complicity in Thorpe's summer pro baseball career. That the most popular form of little league football is named after one of the early buccaneers of college sports is ironic.

On page 35 of the text, for the source of Jesse Harper's starting salary see the memo from Harper to President John W. Cavanaugh, 29 May 1916 (UPWC 36/9 and UPBU 43/"Athletics" folder); Father Joseph Burke's letter to Harper is in UADR 3/58.

6. JESSE HARPER: 1913 AND THE FIRST ARMY GAME

The three full-length scripts of *Knute Rockne—All American* are in UABM *Knute Rockne—All American* Series/"Knute Rockne—All American* scripts"; they were written by Robert Buckner of Warner Brothers and dated 15 May 1939, 20 January 1940, and 11 March 1940. The quotes in this chapter are from the 11 March 1940 version and the film. Because, in delivering their lines, the actors sometimes deviated from the script, there are slight variations from script to film; I have followed the script for the stage directions and the film—the original, uncut, pre-TV version—for the words.

The Index to the *Notre Dame Scholastic* during this period listed the baseball schedules as well as articles about the eastern trips; see the 1912–1913 volume, page 352, for the spring 1913 games. The revenue and profit from that trip are in UADR 2/153.

Harper's initial contact with West Point, 18 December 1912, and H. F. Loomis's reply for Army, 17 March 1913, are in UADR 3/21. The best history of the N.D.–Army series is *Army vs. Notre Dame: The Big Game 1913–1947*, New York, 1948, by Jim Beach and Daniel Moore; they provide excellent game descriptions, statistics, and discussions of attendance and guarantees. Elmer Oliphant's career at Purdue and West Point is described in *Army vs. Navy*, New York, 1965 and *Gridiron Grenadiers: The Story of West Point Football*, New York, 1948, both by Jack Clary, and, for the Purdue part, *The Big Nine: The Story of Football in the Western Conference* by Howard Roberts, New York, 1948. Harper's comment on being forced to obtain a national schedule is in Ken Rappoport, *Wake Up the Echoes*, Huntsville, Ala., 1975, page 61.

On page 38 of the text, N.D. Vice President Walsh's comments to Harper came in letters on 7 February 1913, 22 March 1913, and 25 March 1913 (UADR 3/87).

The description of Rockne's injury in the Ohio Northern game is in the 1913–1914 *Scholastic*, page 47, and the "GRIDIRON GOSSIP" item, page 79. Jesse Harper's comments on his early use of the forward pass is in Allison Danzig, *Oh, How They Played the Game*, New York, 1971, page 233; the quote from *St. Louis Post-Dispatch* sports editor Ed Wray is in Danzig, page 179.

On page 39 of the text, the comments about Jesse Harper training Dorais and Rockne to use the forward pass were made by "Cap" Edwards in a letter to N.D. President John W. Cavanaugh on 14 September 1931 (CJWC *Autobiography of Knute Rockne* series/"Edwards" folder). In the 1920s, Eddie Cochems confirmed his claim in a letter to Chick Meehan, NYU football coach: "You probably know that I am credited with being the father of the forward pass. In fact, Rockne got the basis of his style of play from the one I used at St. Louis University." The NYU coach forwarded Cochems's letter to Rockne on 10 September 1928; and the latter replied to Meehan, 18 September 1928: "Confidentially I guess Cochems must have been a good coach in his day but he went a little loco mentally, it is sad to say" (UADR 16/42).

Rader, *American Sports*, has a good explanation of how the new rules facilitated the use of the forward pass and Camp's objections, pages 143–44. Rockne made his comment about the forward pass being the "sweetest thing" in after-dinner speeches throughout the 1920s; his amanuensis, Francis Wallace, quoted it in *O'Reilly of Notre Dame*, New York, 1931, page 37. The Delos Lovelace quote from *Rockne of Notre Dame*, New York, 1931, is on page 57.

The 1913–1914 *Scholastic* ran many pages of sportswriters' comments on the N.D. victory over Army; the Chicago reporter's remarks are on page 109. The weekly also increased its coverage of N.D. football with much longer pregame and postgame stories; on page 141, it mentioned Harper's use of bottled water from Notre Dame. The claim that Rockne did this first is in Eugene "Scrapiron" Young, *With Rockne at Notre Dame*, New York, 1951, page 8. Harper's scheduling success in 1913 and subsequent years also contradicts the legend that Rockne, as Notre Dame coach and A.D., began the school's national schedules.

The comments of the nationally syndicated writer Harvey Woodruff on N.D.'s problems with the Western Conference were reprinted in the 1913–1914 *Scholastic*, page 142. The comment by the historian Edward Wakin about the meaning of N.D.'s victory over Army in 1913 is in *The Catholic Campus*, New York, 1963, page 60.

On page 42 of the text, the football profit ($1,364) is in UPWC 36/"Athletics" folder. The net deficit for 1913–1914, as well as the coaches' salaries, is in a memo from Jesse Harper to President John W. Cavanaugh, 29 May 1916 (UPWC 36/9).

Jesse Harper's remarks on N.D.'s bid for membership in the Western Conference were in the *South Bend Tribune*, 2 December 1913; that newspaper discussed the conference's refusal on 8 December and 9 December 1913. Amos Alonzo Stagg was the main opponent, and Chicago newspapers in the winter of 1913–1914 carried various articles about his opposition; the *Chicago Inter-Ocean* on 12 March 1914 noted, "From the feeling which now exists Notre Dame is tabooed from ever gaining admission." The N.D. student reporter's reaction and the jibe about Northwestern and Indiana were in the 1913–1914 *Dome*, page 241.

On page 42 of the text, the reaction of the N.D. administrators involved in this and previous applications to the conference is in a letter from Rev. Thos. A. Lahey and Professor J. E. McCarthy to Rev. Geo. Finnigan, 18 March 1926 (UVMU 2/74).

7. JESSE HARPER: 1914 AND THE FINANCES OF COLLEGE FOOTBALL

The Walter Eckersall letter to Jesse Harper, 30 March 1914, is in UADR 4/8. The quote from the officer in charge of athletics at West Point, Dan J. Sultan, is in his letter to Jesse Harper, 11 December 1913 (UADR 4/3), and the $700 guarantee from Yale is in UADR 4/69.

Glenn "Pop" Warner's demand of half the gate for the N.D.–Carlisle game is in UADR 4/11: in this document, dated 1 December 1914, Warner's settlement is 50 percent, no doubt according to the pregame agreement. Stagg's letter about the refusal to allow the teams to stage the game at the University of Chicago's field is in UADR 4/8. Because Carlisle, Haskell, and similar institutions called themselves "Indian" schools, it would be a historical anachronism to apply the current "Native American" tag to them. In the same way that sports historians employ the term

"Negro Leagues" for the segregated baseball leagues during the first half of this century, using Carlisle Indians, Haskell Indians, and so forth seems most efficient. The quote from Paul Gallico is in his *Farewell to Sport,* New York, 1938, page 13.

Harper wrote Walter Eckersall about officiating and promoting the Carlisle game on 26 June 1914 (UADR 4/50), and Eckersall replied on 28 June 1914 (UADR 4/8). The Army veto of Eckersall for the 1913 game came on 26 September 1913 (UADR 3/21). Harper wrote Otto Engel of the *Chicago Tribune* about working as "head linesman" for the N.D.–Haskell game on 28 September 1914 (UADR 4/150); he wrote Harvey Woodruff of that paper about McEvoy of the *Record-Herald* and sent along fourteen complimentary tickets on 10 November 1914 (UADR 4/164).

On page 45 of the text, Jesse Harper's barrage of McEvoy came in letters on 9 November 1914, and he sent complimentary tickets and his request to Lambert Sullivan of the *Chicago Daily News* on 10 November 1914 (UADR 4/161). For examples of Harper's notes to depot masters, see his letter to Mr. Rafferty, Indianapolis, 6 November 1914 (UADR 4/8), and his "Dear Sir" letter to Notre Dame alumni, 6 November 1914 (UADR 4/8).

Harper wrote to Warner about having the players wear numbers on 29 October 1914 (UADR 4/8), and the roster information from Carlisle was sent by Hugh R. Miller on 5 November 1914 to William J. McAssey (UADR 4/8). Among other Carlisle trades listed were blacksmith, painter, tailor, and plumber.

On page 46 of the text, the settlement statement for the Carlisle game of 1 December 1914 is in UADR 4/11. McEvoy did his job and the Chicago press carried a full complement of stories during the week before the game. Walter Eckersall was particularly effusive in his postgame article in the *Chicago Tribune* of 15 November 1914. The officiating situation during this period was deplorable; an athletic administrator at Northwestern University, Fred J. Murphy, complained to a colleague at the University of Wisconsin, Edward J. Samp, that "new officials either try to 'get by' by doing nothing, or strive to please at the expense of better judgment. Quite a few do not know the rules. Many know the rules but do not have the courage to speak out" 30 October 1917 (UADR 5/231).

Harper's letter to a friend, Chester Slemmans, 29 September 1914, about betting on the N.D.–Yale game is in UADR 4/161. An excellent study of the early days of semipro and professional football in the Midwest is Emil Klosinski's *Pro Football in the Days of Rockne,* New York, 1970; on pages 34–37, he discusses Rockne's work with the 1914 South Bend Silver Edges and the betting surrounding their game with the Fort Wayne Friars. Notre Dame's suspension of five of its athletes was in the *South Bend Tribune* and *South Bend News-Times,* 17 November 1914; the school never named the athletes, nor do internal records turn up their names. Among other writers, Hunk Anderson, in his memoir *Notre Dame, Chicago Bears, and Hunk,* with Emil Klosinski, Oviedo, Fla, 1976, discusses the tradition of college players in this era betting in winner-take-all pots, p. 41–42. The poem about "Yale's goat" is in Joseph Doyle, *Fighting Irish: A Century of Notre Dame Football,* Charlottesville, Va., 1987, p. 82, and Scrapiron Young, page 58; the *Scholastic*'s comments about the loss as well as the *Boston Post* report are in the 1914–1915 volume, page 92, and its remark after the loss to Army is in page 141. Walter Eckersall's puff in the *Chicago Tribune* appeared on 15 November 1914.

On page 47 of the text, Harper's letter to the manager at Yale, 8 December 1914, and the reply from Geo. Carrington of Yale, 12 December 1914, are in UADR 4/198; the Michigan turndown by P. G. Bartleme, 7 December 1914, is in UADR 4/179. Jesse Harper's letter to M. S. Stedman at Syracuse, 30 November 1914 is in UADR 4/190. The letter from the business manager of the Polo Grounds in New York, 29 October 1914; Harper's reply, 3 November 1914; and the letter to Harper from the "New York Base-Ball Club," 6 November 1914, are in UADR 4/140.

The 1914 football revenue is in UPWC 36/"Athletics" folder; the exact football receipts were $16,285, the total Athletic Association deficit for the year was $8,235, and the final loss after student fees was $977. Harper wrote President Cavanaugh on 29 May 1916 (UPWC 36/"Athletics" folder), questioning "whether all my salary or only a part is charged to the athletic association."

8. JESSE HARPER: 1915–1917 AND THE JOB OF ATHLETIC DIRECTOR

Frank G. Menke's letter to Jesse Harper, 15 November 1915, and the latter's reply, 20 November 1915, are in UADR 5/77. For the N.D. athletic director's letter to the Haskell Institute's Mr. Venne concerning Eckersall, 27 April 1915, see UADR 4/175; and for his letter to Otto Engel, 20 September 1915, see UADR 4/183. The *Austin American* game description is in the 26 November 1915, edition of that paper. Chet Grant's comment on a Notre Dame "athletic scholarship" is in *Before Rockne,* page 149.

On page 50 of the text, Jesse Harper's letters to Dudley Pearson on 25 January 1915, 17 February 1915, and 13 April 1915 are in UADR 4/183. The *Scholastic* and the *Dome* followed his career, and the latter publication summed it up in the 1919–1920 volume, page 216. The *Indianapolis News,* 1 October 1919, discussed his entrepreneurial activities.

The letter from the Iowa high school fullback, William H. Johnson, to Harper on 22 June 1917 is in UADR 6/42. The N.D. coach's initial letter to Earl "Curly" Lambeau, 18 January 1917; Lambeau's reply, 17 February 1917; and Harper's response, 9 March 1917 are in UADR 6/44. Lambeau's subsequent career is documented in *The Green Bay Packers* by Chuck Johnson, New York, 1961, and in a fine article, "Packerland" by Herbert Warren Wind, the *New Yorker,* 8 December 1962. Hunk Anderson's remark about "proselyting in Harper's day" is in his memoir, *Notre Dame, Chicago Bears, and Hunk,* with Emil Klosinski, Oviedo, Fla., 1976, page 101. For more on Warner see Newcombe, *The Best of the Athletic Boys.*

On page 51 of the text, the Nebraska reporter, C. S. Sherman, complained to Harper on 3 December 1916, and the coach's strong reply came on 5 December 1916; Guy Reed, the Nebraska manager of athletics, wrote to Harper on 15 December 1915, and the latter replied 20 December 1915; this correspondence is in UADR 5/110. The Nebraska manager mistakenly used the past tense—"were"—when he should have employed the present—"are."

Joseph "Chief" Meyer wrote to Harper on 2 March 1915 (UADR 5/73), and his return to N.D. is in the *Dome*, 1915–1916 volume, pages 221–222; the captain of this team was "Jake" Kline, subsequently N.D. baseball coach for many decades. Harper's letter of recommendation for Mal Elward was to John Griffith, 30 January 1916 (UADR 5/63), and for Hugh O'Donnell to Charles Howard Mills, 8 April 1916 (UADR 5/79).

Jesse Harper's letters to Harvard's manager of athletics, Fred Moore, 15 November 1915, and 6 December 1915, as well as the Harvard telegram to Harper, 7 December 1915, are in UADR 5/103. The quote about Alfred Morales is in Bonifer and Weaver, *Out of Bounds,* page 32.

Chet Grant's description of assistant coach Rockne's pregame talk is in CJWC 12/ "16 Add Rockne stories" folder. Harper attempted to obtain the head coaching job at Wabash for Rockne in a letter to Harley Ristine, 30 January 1915 (UADR 4/154). Harper's coaching in the 1916 Army game was criticized in the *New York World,* 5 November 1915, and *New York Sun,* 6 November 1916.

On page 54 of the text, the Nebraska athletic manager's prediction about the 1916 crowd is in a letter from Guy Reed to Harper, 15 December 1915 (UADR 5/110); the payout figures from the game came in a letter from Williams to Harper, 10 January 1916 (UADR 5/110), that was misdated by the letter writer as 1915. The N.D. athletic department profit for 1915–1916 is in UPWC 36/"Athletics" folder. For 1915–1916, "Student Tickets" were $8,010, and the total department deficit was $5,504.

The New York newspaper that criticized Notre Dame in 1917 because of its helmets was the *Commercial Advertiser,* reprinted in the *Scholastic,* 1917–1918 volume, page 175. For the student weekly's comment after the Wisconsin game see page 62.

The high and low in football receipts for Jesse Harper's years is in UPWC 36/ "Athletics" folder.

9. JESSE HARPER'S ASSISTANT: KNUTE ROCKNE

For a full discussion of Bonnie Rockne's role in the making of the film about her husband, see chapter 37; she held up production during the spring of 1940 until Warner Brothers added this scene of Rockne-as-Potential-Scientist.

Jesse Harper's comment about President Cavanaugh's hiring of Rockne came in a letter to Arthur Haley, 21 April 1940 (UABM *Knute Rockne—All American* series/ "H" folder). During the 1920s, as Rockne became famous, an occasional sportswriter would mention his background in pharmacy and chemistry. In late 1924, H. G. Walker, the editor of the trade magazine *The Chemical Bulletin,* asked the coach to write "an article . . . on 'Why I Left Chemistry.'" Rockne did not reply, and on 4 February 1925, the editor asked again; this time, on 6 February 1925, the coach promised "a little article on 'Why I Left Chemistry.'" However, he failed to deliver, and on 29 June 1925, Walker implored him, "Please do not disappoint us on this." On 14 July 1925, Rockne noted: "I am busy with a number of summer schools in football" and never sent the article. This correspondence is in UADR 21/22. Rockne never showed the slightest desire to return to academic work in science; nowhere else in his extant files—over 14,500 letters, notes, and other materials, from 1918 until his death—is there a mention of his career in chemistry.

Many writers have documented Rockne's pre–Notre Dame life; however, most wrote after the coach's tragic death and were influenced by the hagiographies of "Saint Knute." A more authentic biography appeared in the *Chicago Evening American* from 12 to 19 December 1929. Jimmy Corcoran, a reporter close to the coach, interviewed Rockne's mother and sisters as well as many of his early schoolmates and provided important details about why Rockne originally went to N.D.

Charles "Gus" Dorais's memories of his freshman roommate came in a letter to former President Cavanaugh, 12 June 1931 (CJWC, *Autobiography of Knute Rockne* Series/"Statement of Charles Dorais" folder). Rockne's participation in semipro and professional football during his student years is discussed in Klosinski, *Pro Football*, page 38; the comment on his coaching is on page 40; the types of players he liked, page 30; and the *South Bend Tribune* item is reprinted on page 35. Collegians usually played under the names of Smith, Jones, and Brown, but the South Bend teams, because of the large Polish community in the city, had a clever variation on the usual anonymous names. For Stan Cofall, N.D. quarterback and captain, they used the name Kowalski—the Polish equivalent of Smith (see Klosinski, page 66).

On page 57 of the text, the letter of the Ohio man, R. H. Jamison, who reminisced to Father John W. Cavanaugh on 27 May 1931, about how he met Rockne "on his way to Canton" is in CJWC, *Autobiography of Knute Rockne* Series/"Reminiscences of Rockne, B–K" folder. At the top of this letter, Father Cavanaugh wrote "Pranks at College." The recollection of Rockne having the "pool table concession" is in a letter to Cavanaugh from Jimy [*sic*] Hayes Jr., 24 July 1931 (CJWC, *Autobiography of Knute Rockne* Series/"Reminiscences of Rockne, B–K" folder). Jesse Harper's comments about the offensive "shift" and Captain Rockne's help with it are in a letter to President Cavanaugh, 4 June 1931 (CJWC, *Autobiography of Knute Rockne* Series/ "Reminiscences of Rockne, B–K" folder).

On page 58 of the text, Harper wrote to W. O. Hamilton, the athletic director at Kansas, on 8 January 1915 (UADR 4/154), and President Cavanaugh wrote to Hamilton on 30 January 1915 (UPWC 41/"Knute Rockne" folder). For Harper's letter to his Wabash friend, Harley Ristine, 30 January 1915, and his letter to Clyde Williams, athletic director at Iowa State, 15 March 1915, see UADR 4/154. Rockne's raise to $1,500 was discussed by Harper in a letter to Cavanaugh, 1 December 1915 (UPBU 43/"Athletics" folder).

On page 59 of the text, the letter from Bill Kelleher to Cavanaugh, 27 May 1931 is in CJWC, *Autobiography of Knute Rockne* Series/"Reminiscences of Rockne, B–K" folder; and Chet Grant's account of Rockne's bet on the 1916 Nebraska game and his comment about "the ruthless side" of the famous coach is in CJWC, *Autobiography of Knute Rockne* Series/"Statement of Chet Grant" folder, emphasis added.

For Jesse Harper's testimony on how Rockne turned adversity "to his advantage," see his letter to Cavanaugh, 4 June 1931 (CJWC, *Autobiography of Knute Rockne*

Series/"Reminiscences of Rockne, B–K" folder). Cavanaugh's long comment about the change of coaching regime from Jesse Harper to Knute Rockne in 1918 is in CJWC *Autobiography of Knute Rockne* Series/"Autobiography Mss. and Notes #2" folder.

The *Scholastic*'s congratulations to "Coaches Harper and Rockne" after the 1915 Nebraska game is in the 1915–1916 volume, page 125; and the *South Bend News-Times* article, "ROCKNE TO STAY AT NOTRE DAME," appeared on 3 February 1917. Harper's explanation for leaving N.D. in 1918 was told by his son and is from Rappoport, *Wake Up the Echoes,* page 69.

On page 62 of the text concerning the Western Conference rebuff of Harper, typical of the excuses from the faculty representatives was that of Prof. Paige of Minnesota in a letter to Harper, 2 November 1917: "The question of the advisability of enlarging the Conference and the admission of members is a Conference question and not one to be viewed as it may affect individual schools."

Enthusiastic endorsement of Rockne's promotion is in the *Scholastic*'s 1917–1918 volume, page 322, and in *The Dome* for that year, page 184.

II. Shaking Down the Thunder: 1918–1931

10. CATHOLIC VERSUS AMERICAN HIGHER EDUCATION IN THE 1920S

The opening quote is from Leahy, page 36, as are the statistics on enrollment in Catholic higher education. Donovan, *The Academic Man in the Catholic College,* and Arthur's Ph.D. dissertation about Notre Dame in this era also supply important information. An interesting sidelight to the problems in Catholic higher education is the history of the Newman Clubs: originally an attempt to provide Catholics attending non-Catholic schools with a connection to their religion, they became very controversial within the church because many clergy felt that the clubs encouraged Catholic students to move from the parochial system to the secular one. As a result, in this period, funding for the Newman Clubs was cut back.

Schlereth, *The University of Notre Dame,* describes President Burns's impact, as does Moore, *Academic Development.* Arthur quotes Burns's desire to make Notre Dame the "Yale of the West," page 114; Arthur also discusses the North Central Association criteria, page 118, and the grant application to the General Education Board of the Rockefeller Foundation, pages 121 and following. Notre Dame first approached this foundation in 1917; President Cavanaugh, with Burns assisting him, made preliminary inquiries, but because of the war and the foundation's skepticism about Catholic schools, nothing occurred until Burns's effort in 1921. Armstrong, *Onward to Victory,* discusses the bolstering of the N.D. alumni association under Presidents Burns and Walsh in the 1920s and gives the final tally of the campaign, page 203. For Father John McGinn's comparison of the fund-raising drive to football and Rockne's help in the campaign, see the *Scholastic,* 1920–1921 volume, page 507.

The quote from Notre Dame Associate Vice President Richard W. Conklin was taken from an interview on 12 March 1991. Father Byrne informed President Walsh that N.D. was spending only "$2.56 per student for books, periodicals, and binding" in a memo dated 3 August 1926 (UPWL "By" folder). Father Walsh wanted to rectify this situation because he knew that his school could not claim academic seriousness or begin to grant graduate degrees without a decent library. Rev. George Shuster's famous article, "Have We [Catholics Produced] Any Scholars?" appeared in *America*, 15 August 1925; the quote is on page 419.

11. THE GROWTH OF THE ATHLETIC CULTURE

James Wechsler quoted Rockne in his *Revolt on Campus*, New York, 1935, page 43. Again, Schlereth and Arthur are the best sources on Notre Dame's post–World War I growth; the latter historian provided the quote, page 377. David Edward Schlaver's unpublished Ph.D. dissertation, *The Notre Dame Ethos: Student Life in a Catholic Residential University*, University of Michigan, 1979, also has useful background information on this period. Many issues of the 1918–1919 *Scholastic* ran the ad soliciting applications, often on the back cover.

Moore, *Academic Development*, discusses N.D.'s establishing a School of Education, pages 29–31. An excellent unpublished Ph.D. dissertation by Robin Lester, *The Rise, Decline, and Fall of Intercollegiate Football at the University of Chicago, 1890–1940*, Chicago, 1974, reveals how Big Ten schools set up Physical Education curriculums and often used them to shelter intercollegiate athletes, pages 310 and following.

On page 73 of the text, Rockne's comment on the split between coaches and "physical educators" is in a letter to Frederick Rand Rogers, 24 May 1928 (UADR 18/124). Rockne mocked degrees in PE to his former player, Eugene Oberst, 15 May 1929 (UADR 17/35). Father Vincent Mooney complained to President Charles L. O'Donnell about the football coach's PE work on 17 May 1929 (UPCO 6/20). Even in the modern era, some big-time college coaches claim that they are primarily "teachers" and demand—in addition to all their supplementary income deals from their universities—an academic appointment. In 1983, even though he has no graduate degrees, basketball coach Bob Knight asked to be made a full professor of health, physical education, and recreation at Indiana University, Bloomington; his school complied.

On page 75 of the text, Rockne's boast to college president E. C. Higbe, 26 March 1928, about "the best intramural program" is in (UADR 12/129). Eugene "Scrapiron" Young's remarks on intramural sports at N.D. are in *With Rockne*, page 83. The interhall football schedule for 1920–1921 is in the *Scholastic*, page 16. Young made the comment that "the varsity athletes set the customs," *With Rockne*, page 82, and Harry Stuhldreher's praise of his fellow students is in *Knute Rockne*, page 97. Francis Wallace told the story of his mentor coming "into his office, pink-faced with outrage" in *Notre Dame Story*, pages 156–57, and in *Knute Rockne*, pages 130–31.

President John W. Cavanaugh's comment about campus traditions is in *The Dome*, 1923–1924, page 363. Schlereth, *The University of Notre Dame*, discusses Professor Vincent Fagan's songwriting on page 142. Rockne made his observation about school spirit in many after-dinner talks in the 1920s; it was included in his *Autobiography of*

Knute K. Rockne, New York, 1931, page 110. The *Scholastic's* praise of the N.D. student fans at Indianapolis is in the 1919–1920 volume, page 106; of the events in the gym for the Nebraska away game, page 62. Schlereth discusses the "Gridgraphie" and supplies excellent photos of the student rooters in this period. The *Scholastic* poems with the titles cited in the text are in the 1919–1920 volume, page 165.

12. THE ORIGIN OF THE "FIGHTING IRISH" NICKNAME

The quote from Francis Wallace's *O'Reilly of Notre Dame,* New York, 1931, appears on page 11; Doyle tells the Northwestern story on page 35, and Bonifer and Weaver tell the Pete Vaughan one on page 27. The 1904 *Scholastic* quote is on page 99; the *Detroit Free Press* report is in its N.D.–Michigan game story, November 7, 1909; and the quote from the 1913–1914 *Dome* is on page 340. Father Arthur Barry O'Neill discussed the anti–Notre Dame epithets (in his article "The Fighting Irish," *Notre Dame Alumnus,* 1923, page 105), as does Arthur, page 311.

The *New York Times* headlined a story for the N.D.–Army encounter, 29 October 1920, with "ARMY IN GOOD SHAPE FOR HOOSIERS' GAME." Rockne's "Whose ear" anecdote is in his *Autobiography,* page 88, ascribing its conception to the first N.D.–Army contest in 1913. This is one of many unattributed origins of the word; for a full discussion of the many possible origins see *Webster's Word Histories,* Springfield, Mass., 1990, pages 224–26.

Another geographic 1920s nickname for the Notre Dame football team was the awkward "Indianans": the *New York Herald-Tribune,* October 18, 1924, headlined "INDIANANS SLIGHT FAVORITES [over Army]." The Midwest papers did not call Notre Dame the "Hoosiers" or "Indianans" because of their extensive coverage of the Western Conference and its Indiana University Hoosiers.

On page 80 of the text, President Burns's disapproval of the "Fighting Irish" term came in a letter to Frank Egan, 30 September 1920 (UPBU "E #2" folder). For the controversy over the nickname in the 1919–1920 *Scholastic,* see pages 78–80 and 119; President Burns's welcome for Eamon De Valera is on page 58, and the comment after the Army game is on page 130.

Francis Wallace discussed his role in the "Fighting Irish" nickname on a number of occasions, at greatest length in his *Notre Dame Story,* pages 141–43. A search of New York newspapers in the 1920s substantiates Wallace's account, including his brief attempt to use the "Blue Comets"—see the *New York Evening Post,* 26 October 1925. The quote from the *New York World* occurred 14 November 1926.

On page 82 of the text, President Matthew Walsh's reply to Herbert Bayard Swope, 6 October 1928, is in UPWL "Su-Sy #3 of 13" folder. Harry Stuhldreher's comment is in *Knute Rockne,* page 124. Delos Lovelace, among others, gives the statistic on Rockne's monogram winners with Irish family names, *Rockne of Notre Dame,* page 148.

The 1924–1925 volume of the *Scholastic* carried the story "Irish Terrier Joins Irish," page 8. Rockne also had an Irish terrier: his friend Edward "Copper" Lynch gave it to him: see Rockne to Lynch, 13 March 1925, and the latter's reply, 17 March

1925 (UADR 15/17). At one time in the 1920s, the team also adopted a feline, see "Notre Dame Mascot Is Black Kilkenny Cat," *New York Sun,* 11 November 1927. The *Scholastic* discussed "Clashmore Mike" on 28 October 1933, page 19. Bonifer and Weaver use the "University of Notre Game," page 16.

13. ROCKNE AT GROUND ZERO: 1918–1919

Chet Grant's assessment of Rockne is in CJWC, *Autobiography of Knute Rockne* Series/"Statement of Chet Grant" folder). This 1931 statement seems more authentic than Grant's later comments in his self-appointed role as official historian of N.D. football. Rockne's salary figure is from UPBU "ND President Burns" folder "A"; this document is for the following year, 1919–1920—no figure is available for 1918–1919 but my assumption is that $3,500 was the salary. This document and the "Memorandum for Father Burns" attached to it are cited in Arthur, page 103; the writer of the memo argued that "the salaries of Rockne and Dorais are questions not of faculty expense but of athletics. These men bring in considerably more than we pay out for them. Good athletic men are invariably high priced." Dorais, Rockne's assistant, was hired for 1919–1920 at $2,000.

The story of Rockne's pro football encounter with Jim Thorpe appears in many places, most authoritatively in Richard Whittingham, *What a Game They Played,* New York, 1984, page 13. When he was an assistant coach, Rockne was in better shape and played regularly for Massillon; an Ohio man, F. A. Lambert, wrote to Harper on 17 January 1918: "I have become quite well acquainted with many of your stars at Canton, Massillon, and Youngstown these past two seasons where I officiated regularly. These men are: Rockne, your Asst., . . ." (UADR 5/232). Warren Brown described the dire 1918 situation in "Rockne's Early Coaching Days," *Chicago Herald-Examiner,* 7 April 1931. Only an inquiry from Andy Smith, the new football coach at the University of California, looked promising: the previous fall, Smith had proposed a Notre Dame trip to Berkeley for a 1918 or 1919 Thanksgiving game with a guarantee of $3,000 and a possible higher payout; see Smith to Jesse Harper, 6 October 1917 (UADR 5/217). Probably because of wartime travel restrictions, Rockne could not pursue Smith's offer.

The *New York Times* headline and comment appeared 31 December 1917. Hunk Anderson discussed Rockne's "athletic scholarships" in his memoir, pages 20–25. For the *Scholastic's* description of the team's hasty trip to Wabash, see the 1918–1919 volume, page 77; its account of the injury to Gipp in the Michigan State Aggies game is on page 109; the mud at Nebraska story is on page 140. The *Indianapolis Star,* 24 November 1918, described the N.D.–Purdue game in detail; the profit of $358 is in Wallace, *Knute Rockne,* page 73, and the Nebraska payout of about $4,000 after expenses is on pages 72–73.

Rockne's letter to Heze Clark, 31 July 1919, is in UADR 6/62; the guarantee at Purdue was only $1,000 (UABM "Contracts—Football—P"), but the Morningside one was stated as $2,500 in J. M. Saunderson to Rockne, 29 November 1919 (UADR 6/86). The *Detroit Free Press* item appeared in a column by Ralston Goss, 3 December 1919; Rockne's comment about his early scheduling problems is in Harry Stuhl-dreher, *Knute Rockne,* page 272. Francis Wallace, *Knute Rockne,* pages 73–74, quotes the "Financial Reports of the Notre Dame Athletic Association" for the year 1918–1919; the original of this document is now lost, but Wallace's numbers seem very accurate and the Purdue and Nebraska profits are based upon his figures.

For the totals on the 1918 season see UPBU Statement of Athletic Account 1918/19 and 1919/20/"Athletics" folder. The *Scholastic*'s summary of Rockne's initial campaign is on page 155.

On page 88 of the text, Rockne's form letter to prominent South Bend citizens, 30 September 1919 (UADR 6/58) began: "The Notre Dame football team travels from coast to coast." In fact, by 1919, the N.D. team had been only as far west as Nebraska; Rockne might have been thinking of Andy Smith's proposal of a game in Berkeley when he wrote the line. He often exaggerated to make a point, especially when trying to convince his audience to do something he wanted it to do—win a football game, buy season tickets, or purchase a product he was promoting. Francis Wallace described Rockne's ticket-selling practices in *Notre Dame Story,* page 168, and the South Bend papers frequently referred to his presence downtown. The 1919–1920 volume of the *Scholastic,* page 47, noted the purchase of one hundred season tickets by Studebaker.

On page 90 of the text, Walter Eckersall's letter to Rockne, 5 October 1919, is in UADR 6/68. A vivid example of the "shenanigans" taking place in college football in this era is provided in a letter to Rockne from J. W. Graves of Dallas, 10 November 1919 (UADR 6/69):

> I have just seen in an afternoon paper that your team is scheduled to play Henry Kendall College at Tulsa on Thanksgiving Day, for $4,000. . . . I want to caution you . . . to be very sure about your officials, including the time-keeper. Unofficially I held a watch on a game between Kendall and the Haskell Indians in 1915. . . . The actual playing time of the last quarter was 37 minutes, and it ended as soon as Kendall made a touchdown making the score 7 to 3 in Kendall's favor. The Kendall players are not responsible for this, but those moneyed men in Tulsa bet heavily on the game, and like many outside bettors they will do anything to win that they can get away with, and think it legitimate. I want to see the best team win, of course, but I want to see your team get a square deal.

Rockne never scheduled a game with Kendall but he was very aware of the mine field in college football at the time.

On page 90 of the text, Eckersall's letter to Rockne, 11 November 1919, about his "All-Western team" is in UADR 6/68. Chet Grant's comment that the coach "was a finder, not a founder" is in his *Before Rockne,* page 2. The letter to "Mr. Rockney" from Richard Guy, 20 September 1919, is in UADR 6/69. The 1919–1920 *Scholastic* discussed the football roster in detail on pages 15–16; because Lambeau needed financial help and/or an on-campus job to attend N.D.—see his pleading letter to

Rockne, 6 January 1919 (UADR 6/44)—but did not measure up to the quality of the service returnees and recruits, Rockne did not renew his "athletic scholarship."

The *Scholastic*'s enthusiasm for the freshman team is on page 171. Stanley Cofall recommended a number of players, some of whom Rockne took and others he did not; see Cofall's letter to the coach, 5 May 1919 (UADR 6/36). The letter from John Shea (of N.D. "Victory March" fame), 9 September 1919, is in UADR 6/96. Paul Castner revealed his "athletic scholarship" in *We Remember Rockne*, pages 18–20.

Klosinski, *Pro Football in the Days of Rockne*, discussed the 1919 team's semipro excursions on pages 79–85. Red Grange's description of George Trafton is in *Biographical Dictionary of American Sports*, edited by David L. Porter, New York, 1987, page 601.

On page 93 of the text, the source of Charlie Bachman's comment to Rockne about the "Trafton case," 9 January 1919 [1920] is in UADR 6/90, and the coach's later letter to Trafton, 6 December 1929, is in UADR 20/52.

The quote from the "Football Prospects" article in the 1919–1920 *Scholastic* is on page 15. Rockne missed the opening game against Kalamazoo, his assistant, Gus Dorais, later related:

Rock had a notion he wanted to scout Nebraska. . . . He left me in charge. He said that instead of direct passes, everything would be handled by the quarterback. At the third quarter the score was nothing and nothing. I sent in a new man and said, "Play as you practiced." In the last quarter we got two touchdowns. When Rock came back he wanted to know why I did not follow instructions. I said, "I believe if I had we would not have made anything."

The source for this is Dorais to former President Cavanaugh (CJWC, *Autobiography of Knute Rockne* Series/"Statement of Charles Dorais" folder). This is an example of the tension between the two former roommates; after the 1919 season, Dorais left and Rockne hired Walter Halas—the brother of George "Papa Bear" Halas—as his assistant. The *Scholastic*'s comment about the crowds for practice is in the 1919–1920 volume, page 15.

On page 94 of the text, Walter Eckersall's private comment to Rockne, 5 October 1919, is in UADR 6/68. The profits from the 1919 Nebraska and Indiana games are in Francis Wallace, *Knute Rockne*, pages 73–74. The *Scholastic*'s comment on the N.D. fans at the Army game is on page 126; the editorial, "A Stadium for Notre Dame," is on page 139; and the billing for the Purdue game is on page 157. The *Lafayette* (Indiana) *Journal* warned Purdue fans on 21 November 1919.

On page 95 of the text, Rockne's remark about not giving pep talks to this squad of war vets is in CJWC, *Autobiography of Knute Rockne* Series/"Statement of Chet Grant" folder. For the final polls see Perrin, page 102.

Jesse Harper wrote his plaintive letter to Rockne on 10 April 1919 (UADR 6/40). Harper's advice about obtaining a raise is in a letter to Rockne, 6 December 1919 (UADR 6/40); the availability of the Kansas job and the congratulations on the "financial report" are in the same letter. For Rockne's raise to $5,000, see UPBU 43/

"Athletics" folder. The inquiry about the Cornell job came from A. R. Coffin to Rockne, 17 December 1919 (UADR 9/200).

On page 97 of the text, the Athletic Report for 1919–1920 is in UPBU 43/"Athletics" folder.

14. ROCKNE'S ROCKET—FIRST VERSION: 1920

For Charlie Bachman's letter to Rockne, 9 December 1919, see UADR 6/90. The Northwestern authorities obviously knew that Bachman had played at Notre Dame but, as he wrote Rockne in the previously cited letter, his strategy throughout was to appear disinterested: "I didn't advise him [Lee] one way or the other [about Notre Dame], this for policy sake because I believe that my [supposed] indifference in the matter will get quicker results." The last time that Notre Dame had played the Chicago school was in 1903, long before the Big Ten had taken its 1920s shape and rules.

On page 99 of the text, the reply from the Harvard man, Fred Moore, 5 December 1919, is in UADR 6/73; the Syracuse letters to Rockne were from Geo. B. Thurston, 9 October 1919 and 7 December 1919, and from W. A. Smith, 13 December 1919, all in UADR 6/96. Theo. Bellemont wrote from the University of Texas, 30 December 1919 (UADR 6/97); J. R. Townsend from Wabash, 15 December 1919 (UADR 6/99); and William McNamara from Georgetown, 3 December 1919 (UADR 6/69).

The complaint from the Marquette Athletic Association to Rockne came on 23 December 1919 (UADR 6/83). The *Scholastic* noted the "assured success" of N.D. Homecoming in special block type in the 1920–1921 volume, page 47. Chet Grant's comment about his age when he returned to N.D. is in an interview that he did with Steele, page 248; for his observation about Rockne's two units see CJWC, *Autobiography of Knute Rockne* Series/"Statement of Chet Grant" folder). The *Scholastic*'s report on the 1920 Kalamazoo game is on page 46, and the Western Michigan visit is on page 62.

On page 100 of the text, for Chet Grant's story about his problems with Gipp in the Nebraska game, see CJWC, *Autobiography of Knute Rockne* Series/"Statement of Chet Grant" folder. In this same contest, Gipp and his cohorts also tried an old sandlot trick: the quarterback pretended to be hurt and, according to the *Scholastic*, page 78: "Nebraska's eleven, intent on the anguished expressions on [QB] Brandy's face, were dazed as Brandy hurled the ball to the waiting Gipp and the entire Notre Dame backfield swept down the field unmolested." The referee did not allow the touchdown.

The 1920–1921 *Dome* carried brief but highly descriptive game summaries; see it for the Kalamazoo game and the "Gold and Blue" term for the team at Valparaiso, no page numbers.

Grant's recollection of the 1920 Army game is in CJWC, *Autobiography of Knute Rockne* Series/"Statement of Chet Grant" folder. Ring Lardner's comment is in Beach and Moore, page 49; the *New York Times* report appeared 31 October 1920;

and the *Scholastic* gave the details of the Homecoming preparations and ticket prices on page 95, and of the event on page 125.

Grant's comments on the IU game in Indianapolis are in CJWC, *Autobiography of Knute Rockne* Series/"Statement of Chet Grant" folder. For the pregame sellout in Evanston, see the *Chicago Tribune,* 16 December 1920; the comment about the church "dignitaries" was in the *Scholastic,* page 143, and the game description was on page 159. Walter Eckersall refereed the contest and puffed it in the *Chicago Tribune,* 18 November 1920. Grantland Rice applauded Gipp in the *New York Tribune,* 2 December 1920; the comments on Rockne by Army's head coach, C. D. Daly, were published by the *Scholastic,* page 170, and the weekly's own praise is on the same page.

On page 103 of the text, the 1920 receipts from football and other 1920–1921 financial figures are in UPBU 43/"Athletics" folder. The quote is from Klosinski, page 96.

15. GEORGE GIPP'S FIVE SEASONS AT NOTRE DAME

George Gekas's anecdotal biography, *The Life and Times of George Gipp,* South Bend, 1987, relates the story of Gipp's post–high school employment on page 29; that book provides some of the other details in the text. Another biography, *One for the Gipper: George Gipp, Knute Rockne, and Notre Dame,* by Patrick Chelland, Chicago, 1973, also contains accurate information. Rockne, or more probably the ghostwriter of his *Autobiography,* John B. Kennedy, made the error about Gipp's father, page 225.

On page 105 of the text, Gipp's letter to Father Matthew Schumacher, N.D. Director of Studies, 21 March 1916; Schumacher's two replies of 28 March 1916 and one of 5 April 1916; and a letter from Gipp to Schumacher, 3 April 1916, are in UDSS "George Gipp" folder. Jim Beach, in a well-researched article, "Gipp," *Fireside Book of Football,* New York, 1964, discusses Gipp's financial problems upon arrival at Notre Dame, page 37; and Wallace, *Knute Rockne,* mentions the athlete's "private job plan," page 86. Exactly when Gipp moved off-campus is unclear: almost all the biographers agree that he lived in the Oliver Hotel during 1918–1920 and that he was at Notre Dame for only six weeks during the fall of 1917 and lived the remainder of that year in downtown South Bend. Probably he spent his freshman year in Brownson Hall, although some of his classmates later recalled him being absent much of the time; Chelland, page 86, says that he "quit waiting table at Brownson Hall after only one semester."

On page 106 of the text, for Rockne's statement to John Heisman, 1 April 1929, see UADR 13/64. The coach's comment about Gipp and the illustration of a pool player at night are in *Collier's* magazine, 22 November 1930, page 15. For the transcript of Gipp's academic record, see "George Gipp Transcript" (MPRR). Notre Dame Professor of History Robert Burns offered his well-informed observations on Gipp's academic career in an interview, 11 November 1991.

On Gipp's transcript, "S.A.T.C." is stamped for his third year, implying that he was in the Student Army Training Corps. However, his best friend, Hunk Anderson, wrote in his memoir: "Ojay Larson and I signed up for the program, but Gipp was rejected" (page 24). In any event, S.A.T.C. students took regular courses and final exams, and this notation does not explain Gipp's blank year—during which he played varsity football. Hunk Anderson talked about Gipp's dismissal and the recruiting by other schools in his memoir, page 52; Chelland adds details about Yost and Pop Warner, page 137.

On page 107 of the text, for the petition from the South Bend citizens, see UPBU 43/"Miscellanous" folder. The autobiographical article signed by Rockne, *Collier's,* 22 November 1930, page 15, promulgated the story about the faculty exam for Gipp— probably it appeared because the Carnegie Foundation in 1929 was so critical of "football factories" and their lax academic rules for athletes. Francis Wallace is the source of the story of the exam by President Burns; he first told this tale in the early 1950s, the time of another reform movement in college sports, and by his *Notre Dame People,* page 139, he had polished it. Further discrediting the oral exam legends are the discrepancies in dates: Rockne places his version in 1919 and Wallace dates his September 1920, whereas Gipp was readmitted in late April 1920 and played baseball for N.D. in May 1920.

The actual reason for Gipp's expulsion is not entirely clear. Some historians claim that Notre Dame expelled him for frequenting the Tokyo Dance Hall in South Bend (Professor Burns favors this explanation). However, since Gipp spent most of his time in this and similar spots in the city, it is hard to understand why this infraction of the N.D. rules would be the specific cause of his expulsion. The academic reason—too many class cuts—seems more probable because the Notre Dame faculty was growing increasingly restive with the behavior of some of Rockne's athletes and President Burns supported their academic aspirations and criticisms of the athletes.

The telegram from Army to Gipp is in Beach, page 41; the stories about other schools recruiting Gipp are in Beach—the University of Detroit—page 41; and Twombly—the University of Michigan—page 125. Star end Bernie Kirk stayed in Ann Arbor, increasing Rockne's enmity toward Fielding Yost; in describing the previous year's N.D. victory over the Michigan (State) Aggies, the *Scholastic* noted: "Notre Dame's nationally famed 'Gipp to Kirk' aerial attack was the feature of the game," page 141.

The *Scholastic's* comment on Rockne reacquiring Gipp is in the 1920–1921 volume, page 30. Klosinski, *Pro Football,* discusses Gipp's lack of practice at Notre Dame on page 80, and Chet Grant confirmed this in CJWC, *Autobiography of Knute Rockne* Series/"Statement of Chet Grant" folder. Grant explained the coach's behavior with: "Rockne recognized Gipp's greatness. Perhaps it was a case of genius recognizing genius and permitting it a latitude which narrower minds would have shrunk from" (CJWC, *Autobiography of Knute Rockne* Series/"Statement of Chet Grant" folder), and in the same reminiscence, told the story of Gipp's maneuver in the 1920 Army game.

Chelland outlines Gipp's pool playing prowess on page 107, and the *South Bend Tribune,* 21 May 1920, carried the story of Gipp's "100-point pocket billiards match."

Hunk Anderson, in his memoir, called his friend "a Rembrandt with a cue stick," page 41, and amplified on his card sharking, page 41. Gipp's description of himself as "the finest free-lance gambler ever to attend Notre Dame" is in "Was 'the Gipper' Really for Real? You Can Bet He Was," by James A. Cox, *Smithsonian Magazine,* December 1985, page 133; Gekas tells the Indiana game story on page 12; Hunk Anderson, in his memoir, talks about the winner-take-all pot at the Army game on pages 41–42; and Chelland quotes eyewitnesses for the halftime talk on page 166.

Moe Aranson offered his story about Gipp's fatal illness in an interview for this book, 24 June 1991; Jim Beach quotes Grover Malone, page 42.

On page 111 of the text, President Burns wrote to Rev. Joseph A. Paquet, 14 December 1920 (UPBU "P" folder), and President Walsh to Professor Frank W. Cavanaugh, 1 May 1923 (UPWL "Caa-Cap" folder). Rockne, however, was less certain of the conversion: in a 25 March 1926 letter to R. K. Hanson, he remarked, "here are the crooks of the whole matter, confidentially. George Gipp was supposed to have been baptized a Catholic before his death. Whether this was so or not, I do not know. At any rate, I understand the family were very much put out. These are the facts as I know them" (UADR 13/23).

Chelland relates the story of Father Pat Haggerty on page 192. Gipp's sister Dorothy wrote to Iris Trippeer, 29 December 1920 (UATH "Gipp letters to Trippeer" folder). In an article in the *Los Angeles Times,* 23 November 1982, Iris Trippeer discussed her relationship with Gipp and called herself his "fiancée." Thomas Schlereth, however, in his outstanding history of Notre Dame described Gipp as a "womanizer, laconic, aloof, troubled young man who became a tragic hero," page 144.

On page 111 of the text, the comment by Bill Howard, the original director of *Knute Rockne—All American,* is in a letter from Arthur Haley to N.D. Vice President John J. Cavanaugh, 12 April 1940 (UABM *Knute Rockne—All American* Series/"Rev. John J. Cavanaugh" folder). Cavanaugh's reply to Haley, 22 April 1940, is in the same folder.

The Gipp conversion scene in the film is less obvious than Howard wanted. As directed by his replacement, Lloyd Bacon, the fictitious Father Callahan of Notre Dame, dressed in full religious vestments, stands next to Gipp's bed and reads from a prayer book. Gipp's eyes are closed, his head upon the pillow. After Father Callahan prays, he says "Amen" and mournfully leaves. The message to Catholic viewers is that Gipp either converted earlier on this occasion or previous to it, otherwise the priest could not conduct what N.D. alum Michael Steele terms "the church's last rites," page 196.

On page 112 of the text, the letter from President Matthew Walsh to Dr. C. H. Johnson, 10 January 1923, is in UPWL 46/40. Father Arthur Hope's comments are in his history of N.D., page 353. The *Scholastic* ran the eulogies to Gipp in the 1920–1921 volume, pages 209 and following and *The Dome*'s statement is in the 1920–1921 volume, no page number.

The $4,500 figure "for doctors, bills, hospital bills, personal debts" was specified by Rockne in a letter to Joseph P. O'Rourke on 22 November 1928 (UADR 17/93).

The coach also pointed out: "[the] story you mention was given out by Fielding Yost, the coach of Michigan, who has always been very anti–Notre Dame. It was absolutely without foundation in any shape, manner or form . . . It is not true and is like many of the other stories that Mr. Yost sends out."

Grantland Rice wrote in the *New York Herald-Tribune,* 2 April 1926: "A leading Western Conference coach [Fielding Yost] has written that he will be one of a group to pay back to George Gipp's father and mother money they should never have been asked to pay at such crushing sacrifice."

On page 113 of the text, the football fan in New Jersey, Edward Brady, wrote to Rockne, 27 November 1925, and the coach replied, 7 December 1925 (UADR 8/14).

16. THE ROCKET CRASHES—ROCKNE'S MIRACULOUS ESCAPE: 1921

The letter from Harry Costello of the *Detroit News* to Rockne, 22 January 1921, is in UADR 10/22. Few journalists–game officials considered their practices corrupt; however, Harry Costello gave a signal when, in his inducement to Rockne that he would speak to Walter Camp, he underlined the word *confidential* five times. But for the most part, the sportswriters were inside the system and reluctant to change it.

Major Philip Hayes's telegram to Rockne, 6 December 1920, is in UADR 6/60. The *New York Times,* 27 October 1920, described how the Polo Grounds had been enlarged to hold forty thousand and subheaded: "New Stands Being Built for Army-Navy Game"; the next day that paper carried an article on the coming Rutgers-Nebraska match in New York.

On 19 December 1920, William P. Garrison of Rutgers sent Rockne a telegram about a New York City game (UADR 6/95). The payment to Eckersall for the Rutgers game is in UADR 6/95; Costello pushed himself for the Army–Notre Dame assignment (UADR 6/60); Garrison of Rutgers wrote Rockne, 17 August 1921, about the official indicted for "notorious malfeasance" (UADR 6/95); and Costello sought the extra games in a letter to Rockne, 22 March 1921 (UADR 6/62).

Rockne's notice "TO THE 'OLD BOYS' " was on the front page of the *Scholastic,* 1 October 1921. Although Rockne's signature is below this letter, the prose is so vivid and similar to Francis Wallace's signed pieces in the *Scholastic* during this period— and so uncharacteristic of Rockne's usually turgid prose—and because Francis Wallace was his press assistant at the time, the inevitable conclusion is that the young Wallace wrote it, Rockne looked it over, and it went out over the coach's name.

The *Scholastic* carried full game accounts in the 1921–1922 volume; Chet Grant's comment on the Iowa contest is in CJWC, *Autobiography of Knute Rockne* Series/ "Statement of Chet Grant" folder; Francis Wallace told the anecdote about the trip home in *Notre Dame Story,* page 173. Ned Colletti, in *Golden Glory: Notre Dame vs. Purdue,* New York, 1983, pages 62–63, described Hunk's performance in the Purdue game; the *Scholastic* laid out the plans for the Homecoming weekend, page 64; and Armstrong, *Onward to Victory,* lauded the success, page 200.

On page 117 of the text, Chet Grant's story about the 1921 game against Indiana is in CJWC, *Autobiography of Knute Rockne* Series/"Statement of Chet Grant" folder; because Grant wrote this account in 1931, three years after the "Gipper" speech occurred and one year after Rockne's *Autobiography* memorialized it in its famous form, probably if Rockne had used the dying request during the 1921 talk, Grant would have mentioned it.

The *Scholastic's* headline and story about the long 1921 trip is on page 111; the *New York Times* carried its report on the N.D.–Army game, 6 November 1921, and on the Rutgers game, 9 December 1921. The profit from the eastern trip is in UVMU 2/51. For Joe Byrne, Jr.'s, letter to Rockne, 15 November 1921, see UADR 6/61; the letter from the prominent Iowan, Mrs. Raymond Wright, to President Burns, 12 October 1921, and the latter's reply, 18 October 1921, are in UPBU "W" #6 folder.

On page 119 of the text, the almost $1,600 loss for the home game against the Haskell Indians is in UVMU 2/51, and the net profit for N.D. in 1921 is from the same source. The *Scholastic* carried the item about Rockne scouting at Marquette; Pat O'Brien, *We Remember Rockne,* mentioned playing in this game, page 132.

The *Chicago Tribune,* 29 January 1922, carried the Associated Press report on the Taylorville-Carlinville game. The details of the game are from the newspapers of the time; see the *Chicago Tribune,* the *Chicago Evening American,* and the *Chicago Daily News* for the week beginning 27 January 1922. They ran daily articles on the story, often starting them on the front page; the *New York Times* picked up the story 28 January 1922 and followed it for its duration. In addition, later comments by various participants are useful: Francis Wallace discussed it in a *Scribner's* magazine article, "The Hypocrisy of Football Reform," November 1927, page 572, and in *Notre Dame Story,* pages 184–85; and Joey Sternaman, the University of Illinois star who beat the N.D. ringers, gave an account in *What a Game They Played,* page 5. The Taylorville QB was a nonuniversity athlete, Charlie Dressen, future manager of the Brooklyn Dodgers.

The writers of "The Wake of the News" column in the *Chicago Tribune* admitted that they had received phone calls from "down state" about the university affiliations of the players, 1 February 1922. The Taylorville coach, Grover Hoover, made his comments about Rockne's knowledge of the game in the *Chicago Evening American,* 2 February 1922; the N.D. coach replied in that paper the next day. There are many anecdotes of Rockne's lunches at Hullie & Mike's; in a typical friendly postscript to a letter, Stan Cofall added, "Best regards to Mike and Hullie," 5 May 1919 (UADR 6/ 36). Midwest newspapers started carrying the news of the college athletes in the Green Bay Packers' season finale on 7 December 1921; the *South Bend News-Times* picked it up on 8 December 1921, and even the *Scholastic* discussed it shortly after in an editorial, "Keeping the Slate Clean," page 216. Klosinski, *Pro Football,* gives Hunk Anderson's version of events on page 106, and coauthors the account in Hunk's memoir, pages 36–37.

In the extensive writings on Rockne, the events of late 1921 and early 1922 are almost always ignored or glossed over. One biographer, Jerry Brondfield, *Rockne: The Coach, the Man, the Legend,* New York, 1976, does furnish a vivid narrative of these events but he supplies no footnotes and commits many errors; he confuses the revelation in early December about the Green Bay Packers' incident with the public disclosure of the Illinois game almost two months later, thus his chronology makes no sense.

The American Professional Football Association (the forerunner of the NFL) responded to the Green Bay Packers incident and similar ones in this period by cleaning up its act. The day after the Illinois–Notre Dame story broke, it expelled the Green Bay Packers for using college players and it established a rule against this practice, demanding "a deposit of $1,000 by each club to guarantee observation of this rule." The press release announcing this also added the note that "George Halas, with Decateur Staleys last fall, was granted a franchise for the Chicago Bears," *Chicago Tribune,* 29 January 1922.

The 1922 N.D. game against the University of Wisconsin was announced in the *Chicago American,* 3 December 1921, but the next day in the *Chicago Tribune,* Walter Eckersall, after talking to Rockne, hedged on this contest. Undoubtedly the news of the Packers' Milwaukee game put pressure on nearby Madison for the Big Ten school to back out; the game soon disappeared from the announcements of Wisconsin's and Notre Dame's 1922 schedule.

On page 121 of the text, the Rose Bowl committee member was Seward A. Simons, a prominent L.A. attorney, and he wrote to Rockne, 14 December 1921 (UADR 6/96). His roundabout, overly polite prose leads him to the contradiction, "the rumor of the professionalism of some of your players, who I see have been properly disciplined." Why would Notre Dame discipline the players if the report of them playing pro football were only a "rumor"?

As early as mid-November a group in Tacoma, Washington, had proposed a postseason game there, Kenneth W. Hood to Rockne, 18 November 1921 (UADR 6/97). The late-November victories over Marquette and the Michigan Aggies propelled N.D. into the Rose Bowl picture, and on 1 December 1921, Joe Byrne, Jr., informed Rockne that Cal's Andy Smith, the coach of the host team, had been "won over [and] was willing to play Notre Dame" (UADR 9/17). The *Chicago Tribune,* 29 November 1921, headlined an article "NOTRE DAME ONLY FOE LEFT FOR COAST TEAM."

After the wire services carried the news of the Green Bay Packers' fiasco, the Rose Bowl bid evaporated. However, N.D. alum Leo Ward in a letter to Rockne, 7 December 1921 (UADR 21/63), thought that the San Diego Chamber of Commerce would invite N.D. to play a late-December game in its city against Centre College of Kentucky—the "Praying Colonels" had upset mighty Harvard that season and were unbeaten and unscored upon. But Centre refused to play Notre Dame, again because of the professionalism charges.

An amazing element about these events is that subsequently, the Rockne hagiographers turned the situation 180 degrees and used it to reflect glory upon the coach. Steele says: "The incident reveals a new facet of Rockne's character: he canceled his team's chances to play in the Rose Bowl that year on the grounds that his team was 'ethically tarnished,' " page 172. He quotes Brondfield on the latter remark and adds, "Clearly Brondfield has done his homework well"[!].

On page 122 of the text, the letter to Rockne from Charlie Bachman, 9 December

1921, is in UADR 6/79; for Joe Byrne, Jr.'s, letter to Rockne, 15 November 1921, see UADR 6/61; for the unsolicited outside offers to Rockne, see A. R. Tiffany, University of Oregon, 15 January 1921 (UADR 6/93), and Wm. A. Reid, Colgate University, 29 November 1921 (UADR 6/62). The article in the *Chicago Tribune* about Rockne "considering" the Northwestern job appeared on 7 December 1921.

The telegram from Byron Kanaley to Rockne, 7 December 1921, is in UADR 6/78; and Kanaley's special-delivery letter to President Burns, 7 December 1921, is in UPBU 44/"K #5" folder. For Kanaley's "Dear Knute" letter, 7 December 1921, see UPBU 43/"K #5" folder; in it, the alum warned the coach that Northwestern "is a school entirely without traditions—practically without college sentiment—and with practically no athletic background." Kanaley contrasted this to Notre Dame's rich athletic culture and advised Rockne, "It is doubtful if Northwestern can be pulled out of the athletic cellar by anyone."

For the Iowa State telegram to Rockne from C. W. Mayser, 8 December 1921, see UADR 6/81; the University of Cincinnati one from Boyd C. Chambers, 8 December 1921 (UADR 6/62); and the one from the alum of the University of Minnesota, R. S. McIntyre, 10 December 1921 (UADR 6/81). The latter telegram—like almost all telegrams of the period—has no punctuation (it cost extra). I have supplied the period after "coach" and the question marks after "post" and "terms." Only with this punctuation does the telegram make sense.

On page 123 of the text, the letter informing Minnesota that the coach was "seriously considering" Northwestern is a copy of one sent to Dr. L. J. Cooke, Manager of Athletics, University of Minnesota, 21 December 1921 (UADR 6/81), and is unsigned. No doubt, the writer was a friend of Rockne's—the copy was sent to him— and became unattached from the cover letter. The invitation from University of Minnesota President L. W. Coffman to Rockne, 22 December 1921, is in UADR 6/81. If Notre Dame had not met Rockne's 1921 demands and he had gone to and succeeded at Minnesota, today he would be enshrined in football mythology as "Knute of the North Country" (so much for the historical inevitably of Rockne at Notre Dame).

There are no direct documents on the late 1921 signing of Rockne by President Burns, however, in a letter from President Walsh to A.D. McDonald almost two years later, 21 November 1923, Walsh remarked, "Rockne has fixed his relations with Notre Dame by signing a gentlemen's agreement to remain here for the remainder of his days. This agreement was made here with Father Burns, two years ago, but the matter was not given much publicity" (UPWL "McDonald" folder). As for the 1921 raise in salary, Harry "Red" Miller, a former N.D. football captain and very active in alumni affairs, in a letter to President Walsh, 29 November 1922, estimated the coach's current salary at $7,500 a year (UPWL "Mi #14" folder). Miller also urged Walsh to raise Rockne to $10,000, and the alum mentioned that the coach had received an offer of $10,000 from Washington and Jefferson, an aspiring football power at the time.

Rockne's friends also played the outside offer game; Charlie Bachman, 9 December 1921, requested his aid after the 1921 season (UADR 6/79):

I know that my salary will be boosted considerably if such offers [from other schools] are forthcoming and for this reason I am soliciting your services in putting me in touch with other schools who are in search of a coach for next year. I am not thinking of leaving the [Kansas State] Aggies, but could stand a raise in "the kitty."

After Rockne dropped out of contention at Northwestern, the *Chicago Tribune* floated the rumor "Purple May Ask Bachman Back to Coach Eleven," 18 January 1922.

On page 124 of the text, the 8 January 1922 letter from Jesse Harper to Rockne is in UADR 13/31; Father Carey's note to President Burns, 11 January 1922, is in UPBU 43/"Athletics" folder. The *Chicago Tribune* ran the front-page headline "ILLINOIS BARS NINE ATHLETES FOR 'PRO' GAME," 29 January 1922; Bob Zuppke's comments appeared in that paper the previous day; Amos Alonzo Stagg's in the *Chicago Evening America*, 7 February 1922; and Father Carey's in the *Chicago Tribune*, 31 January 1922. Johnny Mohardt confessed playing for the Racine team in the *Chicago Daily News*, 3 February 1922.

On page 125 of the text, the letter from Joe Byrne, Jr., to Rockne is only dated "Tuesday"—thus probably 31 January or 7 February 1922 (UADR 9/17). Amos Alonzo Stagg made many comments about this game in 1922 and succeeding years; the quotes in the text are from the *Chicago Evening America*, 7 February 1922; the *New York Times*, 21 November 1923; and *What a Game They Played*, pages 27–28.

Former N.D. player Joe Collins wrote to Rockne, 31 January 1922 (UADR 9/208). Rockne's tip to "Professor French, chairman of the Conference" is referred to in a letter to Professor O. F. Long of Northwestern, 14 February 1922 (UADR 6/80). The comment of one of the N.D. athletes involved in the Carlinville fiasco is in Wallace's *Scribner's* article, page 572. Rockne never wrote about his reaction to the Carlinville-Taylorville incident, but in the *Scribner's* article, Wallace, the coach's amanuensis at this time, remarked:

> The coach, having been a player, is intimately acquainted with the workings of the [supposedly] amateur system and is vividly aware of the injustice it frequently visits upon the boys who make it [big-time football] possible. There is a close bond of sympathy between the mentor and his men. They understand each other. Neither believes that a bit of help from the usual sources is criminal. They bow to expediency. The athlete matriculates for a four year course in deception and the coach learns to shout mightily at the faculty revival meetings [on the need for reform].

Frank Hering complained to Indiana University about the sudden transfer to that school in January 1922 of two young N.D. athletes. Hering was paying their tuition at Notre Dame—he saw nothing wrong with this—and on 21 February 1922 he urged President William Lowe Bryan of IU to investigate "the sources of the funds that at the present time are helping them to meet expenses that five months ago they could not meet." Hering added, "It seems to me little short of wonderful" that two well-paying jobs in Bloomington, where work was so scarce, "should conveniently appear just as these two young men changed institutions." Hering sent copies of his letter to President Burns as well as to Rockne (UPBU "H" folder).

On page 126 of the text, the 4 February 1922 letter from President Burns to Byron Kanaley is in UPBU 43/"K #4" folder.

17. BUILDING A BETTER ROCKET: 1922

Various histories of college sports discuss the attempts at reform in the aftermath of the Taylorville-Carlinville affair; for the Big Ten and NCAA points of view, see Kenneth L. (Tug) Wilson and Jerry Brondfield, *The Big Ten,* Englewood Cliffs, N.J., 1967, pages 185–91; and Jack Falla, *NCAA: The Voice of College Sports: A Diamond Anniversary History, 1906–1981,* Mission, Kan., 1981, page 128, for the quote in the text, emphasis added.

On page 128 of the text, the 24 July 1922 letter from Harry Costello of the *Detroit News* to Rockne is in UADR 10/22; the listing of Costello as "Umpire" for the 1922 Notre Dame–Army game is in Beach and Moore, page 77; and J. J. Lipski grumbled to Rockne, 23 August 1922 (UADR 6/80).

On page 129 of the text, the letter from Rev. Joseph Burke of the Faculty Board of Control of Athletics to Rockne, 27 September 1922, is in UADR 6/58. Burke began by noting the existence of the Eligibility Committee of the board: the seven players involved were two starters, Forrest "Fod" Cotton and Paul Castner; two backups, Noble Kizer and Paul McNulty; and two reserves, Russ Arndt and Bernie Coughlin. Only Rex Enright, who played in subsequent years, did not suit up in 1922.

A typical inquiry from a Catholic school to the N.D. coach came from a Creighton alumni official, H. M. Baldridge, 5 June 1922 (UADR 6/61): "I have heard of your disapproval of Jesuit colleges playing each other but I wish you would give us a try." Did he know that Notre Dame was not a Jesuit school? An important N.D. alum, F. Henry Wurzer, on 15 December 1922, begged Rockne for an away game against the University of Detroit, adding: "We have enough dagos in Detroit that we will have to get the Pope to write for us" (UPWL "Wu-Wy #6" folder). President Walsh replied, 27 December 1922, "I had to smile at your reference to outside influence in the direction of our athletic plans. . . . Even the Holy Father himself would hardly be able to fix the itinerary of the Fighting Irish" (UPWL "Wu-Wy #6" folder).

The *Scholastic's* summary of the athletic board's work is in the 1922–1923 volume, page 310; Francis Wallace's passage about Rockne's ongoing "feud with the professors" is in *Notre Dame Story,* pages 158–59. The first passage from Wallace's roman à clef *Huddle,* New York, 1931, is on page 97; the previous passage in the book stated:

> Barney Mack had no illusions about football. He appreciated its commercial faults; but he loved the game and taught it as hard as his boys played it. It

brought him an increasingly profitable return, mostly from by-products, and it offered a constant challenge to his wits.

He liked the big stuff too; and although he recognized the futility of most of it, he read the papers—and liked the applause.

Wallace believed that he had "apotheosized" his mentor in *Huddle* and was surprised at Rockne's dislike for the book, *Notre Dame Story*, page 82. When the novel came out, the *Notre Dame Alumnus* praised it, December 1930, page 150, commenting: "In Barney Mack, Frank [Wallace] has put all of his knowledge of and admiration for Knute Rockne. . . . Mack's talks and phrases at New Dominion smack strongly of the authorship of the Old Man [Rockne]."

The *Huddle* passage beginning "You're a gladiator" is on pages 94–95. The *Notre Dame Alumnus*, 1922–1923 volume, listed the coaching jobs for Rockne's "boys," pages 23 and 47. Hunk Anderson related the story of his first job with Rockne, page 54, and the demand by Stagg and Yost, pages 69–70. Bob Zuppke often told the story about visiting Notre Dame; the quote here is from Elmer Layden's memoir, *It Was a Different Game: The Elmer Layden Story*, with Ed Snyder, Englewood Cliffs, N.J., 1969, pages 20–21. The incident at the 1921 Army game concerning the "Notre Dame shift" is in Beach and Moore, page 65; Rockne referred to it on 1 December 1921 when he wrote Capt. M. B. Ridgway (photocopy, UADR 6/60): "I am very glad we are playing again next year despite a slight mishap Major Daley and I had [in this year's game]." In the same letter, he asked Army to raise the guarantee to $3,000, but Army later refused.

Harry Stuhldreher described his coach's perfectionism in *Knute Rockne*, pages 156–58 and 198–99. Adam Walsh's comments are in Danzig, page 281. Rockne's "bird dog" in Los Angeles, Leo Ward, attended the 1922 Rose Bowl game between California and Ohio State and informed the coach, 3 January 1922 (UADR 21/63):

> One great difference between the style of play employed by both of the teams and the way N.D. plays is that they are both terribly slow in getting off their plays. N.D. would have got in three plays [to their one]. . . . I would say that N.D. could have beaten Calif. by as large a score as Calif. beat Ohio [State, 28–0].

On page 133 of the text, Rockne's letter to E. K. Hall, chair of the Rules Committee, 28 February 1927, is in UADR 13/10. Jim Phelan, at the time head coach at the University of Missouri, praised Rockne's "system," quoted in the 1920–1921 *Scholastic*, page 172. Walter Turnbull's article appeared in the *New York Herald*, 26 October 1922; the comment in *Scholastic*'s "Football Number" was on page 293; and the *Chicago Tribune*'s preseason pronouncement appeared on 31 January 1922. Wallace describes the first Notre Dame "Spring Game" in *Notre Dame Story*, page 201; Rockne's sarcasm about the departing war vets is in Beach and Moore, page 68.

On page 134 of the text, the total profit from the openers of $811 and the $3,547 after the first four games are in UVMU 2/51. For John J. Cavanaugh's article about the Purdue trip, see the 1922–1923 *Scholastic,* page 51; Rockne's locker room talk before the Georgia Tech game was related by Jim Crowley in the film *Wake Up the Echoes,* 1986, produced by NFL Films and RPR Productions; and by Brondfield, pages 5–6.

On page 135 of the text, for the source of the attendance at the Georgia Tech game, see UADR 12/34; and for the profit for this game as well as the Indiana and West Point contests, see UVMU 2/51. The *Scholastic's* headline for the Homecoming game is on page 199; the first issue of the *Notre Dame Alumnus* describes the Homecoming festivities in detail. An indication of the festivities during football weekends in South Bend in the 1920s came in a long letter from a Protestant minister, probably a Prohibitionist, to President Walsh, 21 November 1924 (UPWL "Ti-To #5" folder), complaining that he had "never before seen as many men drunk" as at the Oliver Hotel and in South Bend after the Nebraska game in 1924: "Liquor was in evidence on every hand . . . it seemed to be participated in by both Notre Dame and Nebraska students as well as outside friends and followers."

Ed Sullivan's praise was in the *New York Mail,* 13 November 1922. The *Scholastic's* "Meeting the Team" after the Army game is on page 242, and the front-page tribute to Paul Castner is on page 263; he was later called the "Fifth Horseman" because he would have been a member of the famed backfield except for his career-ending injury.

On page 137 of the text, the profit from the Carnegie Tech game is in UVMU 2/51; the *Notre Dame Alumnus* described the crowd at Pittsburgh in the 1923–1924 volume, page 89; the *Dome* commented on the team's travel in its 1922–1923 volume, page 243.

For the profit from the final games and the season net profit, see UVMU 2/51; for the *Scholastic's* praise of Rockne, page 295.

18. ON THE LAUNCH PAD: 1923

Brondfield's quote is in his *Rockne,* page 180. A typical letter to Walsh came from John F. Shea (of N.D. "Victory March" fame), 23 November 1923 (UPWL "Sh #12" folder); Walsh's comments about Army and Dartmouth are in his reply to Shea, 25 November 1923 (UPWL "Sh #12" folder). The Princeton guarantee is in UABM "Contracts, Football—P" folder. The *Scholastic* carried an article about the football banquet at the Oliver Hotel, 1922–1923 volume, page 331.

On page 139 of the text, for the source of Harry Costello's letter to Rockne, 2 February 1923, see UADR 10/22. Elmer Layden told the story of riding "back to the hotel in a cab with Eckersall and Rock" in his memoir, page 26.

On page 139 of the text, for a typical plea from the southern California N.D. alumni see the letter from Joseph Scott to President Walsh, 4 October 1923 (UPWL "Scott, Joseph" folder); Father McGinn's letter to Walsh, 30 October 1923, and Walsh's reply, 31 October 1923 (UPWL "McE-McK #12" folder). The trustee of the University of Toledo, Elizabeth Pilliod Rundell, wrote to Walsh, undated in 1923

(UPWL "RO #9" folder), and the N.D. president replied, 17 December 1923 (UPWL "RO #9" folder).

The 1922–1923 lineman from Fordham was George Vegarra. Wallace quoted the player, years later and a member of the coach's fan club, as claiming that Rockne alone ended his intercollegiate athletic career, in *Knute Rockne,* pages 155–56. However, considering the internal politics between the faculty board and Rockne and the coverage of Vegarra's background in the New York press at the time of the Army game—when Fathers Walsh, Burns, and McGinn were in New York—probably the order to terminate came from the faculty board, not the coach. Wallace refers to an article in the *New York Sun,* but the much more widely read *New York World* had Vegarra in a subhead and wrote about his Fordham career, 9 October 1923. The editorial in the *Notre Dame Alumnus* appeared in the 1923–1924 volume, page 38; and the quote from the Carnegie Foundation Bulletin 23 is from page 225.

On page 141 of the text, the letter to President Walsh from Chicago alum Thomas Shaughnessy, 8 February 1923, is in UPWL "Sh #15" folder; Walsh replied 14 April 1923 (UPWL "Sh #15" folder). Shaughnessy continued his recruiting efforts and, a year later, Father McBride wrote Rockne about two of Shaughnessy's "protégés": "the best I could do was offer them an allowance of two hundred dollars [off N.D. fees]"; however, their patron "claims that he had the boys refuse offers which would take care of their entire expenses" and wanted more for them. To resolve the dispute, McBride asked the coach to "send me a note whether they are worthy of better consideration than we have been giving them." Nevertheless, in the same note, 29 August 1924 (UADR 15/150), the administrator told the coach that two of his blue-chip recruits "have not credits sufficient for entrance so they will have to spend another year in St. Edward's," a C.S.C. prep college in Texas.

Elmer Layden discussed N.D.'s recruiting of him in his memoir, pages 12–13; for the Big Ten's 1923 ban on subsidizing athletes, see Voltmer, pages 68–69. Earl "Curly" Lambeau's letter to Rockne concerning Jim Crowley, 4 May 1921, is in UADR 6/80. On 10 March 1923 (UADR 14/116), Lambeau wrote apologetically to Rockne, referring to the 1921 fiasco where three N.D. players suited up for Lambeau's Packers—"No doubt you will be surprised to hear from me"—but he went on to recommend Tom "Red" Hearden, a Green Bay high school phenom. The N.D. coach, in a letter to John V. Diener, another friend in Green Bay, 4 June 1925 (UADR 10/94), also requested, "I wish that either you or Curly Lambeau would write me regarding the couple of men you have in mind. Have Curly write me very frankly regarding their qualifications, etc." Rockne, ever the pragmatist, took Lambeau's recommendations—Hearden became an outstanding varsity player as well as co-captain of the 1926 team.

Francis Wallace discussed the recruiting of the Four Horsemen and Seven Mules at length in *Knute Rockne,* pages 110–111; Frank Hering's letter to President Burns about Noble Kizer, 6 July 1921, is in UPBU "H" folder; Leo Ward's recommendation to Rockne of Adam Walsh, 3 January 1921, is in UADR 21/63. For the 1923–1924 *Dome* quote on freshman recruits, see page 276 and Johnny "Blood" McNally's story in *What a Game They Played,* pages 31–32. In Mary Stuhldreher's memoir, *Many a*

Saturday Afternoon, New York, 1964, she revealed the hurried process in which her husband wrote his book about Rockne with her help and that of *Saturday Evening Post* ghostwriter Pete Martin, page 90. Harry Stuhldreher, *Knute Rockne,* discusses the Cedar Point, Ohio, tradition, page 137; and in a letter to Harry Stuhldreher at Cedar Point, 15 August 1924, Rockne wrote: "Don't let the [Notre Dame] men on the Beach work too hard but have them in fair shape" (UADR 20/25). Adam Walsh explained Rockne's South Bend job assistance program in *Oh, How They Played the Game,* pages 278–79. The coach's remark to a recruit in Francis Wallace's *Huddle* is on pages 10–11; the athletes' comment, page 22; and the line about the "golden dome," page 11.

The coach's instructions to his press assistant are in Wallace's *O'Reilly of Notre Dame,* pages 207–208; throughout his nonfiction books on Rockne and Notre Dame, Wallace discussed his apprenticeship with his mentor. An excellent biography of Arch Ward, *Arch: A Promoter, Not a Poet, the Story of Arch Ward* by Thomas Littlewood, Ames, Iowa, 1990, describes the young Ward's work for Rockne; the quote about "Archie's job" at Notre Dame and ever after is on page 25, as is Rockne's line about being noticed in New York. The quotes from Wallace about Rockne's concept of journalism are in his *Knute Rockne,* pages 152 and 147. Wallace graduated from Notre Dame in 1923; he wrote a parting note to his mentor, 2 January 1924 (UADR 21/23): "I will leave Monday to try my luck down there [in New York City] and if I land, please consider me for anything I can do in the publicity field in New York." That fall, he did advance publicity work for the team's eastern games and also sent back reports to the *Notre Dame Daily.*

On page 146 of the text, the 1923 contract between the United States Military Academy and Notre Dame is in UABM "Contracts, Football—T, U, V" folder, and N.D.'s profit of $19,400 is in UVMU 2/51. In a letter to Rockne, 21 May 1923 (UADR 9/17), Byrne outlined his plan for the team to stay at the Westchester-Biltmore Hotel and to practice on its polo field; this worked so well that it became the N.D. pregame billet in New York for many years.

The New York buildup of the N.D.–Army game in 1923 began on Tuesday, 9 October, in the *World* and the *Brooklyn Eagle,* and continued with increasing volume until Saturday, 13 October 1923. The *New York Herald* reported on Byrne's ticket-selling, 10 October 1923; the *New York Telegram's* description of the exhausted Army players appeared 14 October 1923; and Harry Stuhldreher, *Knute Rockne,* told the story about the taunting of the Army stars, pages 284–85.

On page 147 of the text, Vice President Irving explained to J. P. McAvoy, 17 October 1923 (UPWL "McA-McD #19" folder) about the team returning to Notre Dame. Frank McCabe in the *New York World,* 19 October 1923, remarked about Rockne having "his men out for practice"; and the same day, Vernon Van Ness in the *New York Evening Telegram* noted that "for Notre Dame this game is a major affair." On the Sunday after the game, 21 October 1923, the *New York World* headlined "NOTRE DAME BURIES THE PRINCETON ELEVEN" and it described the Tigers' "most crushing reverse." For the references on the social history surrounding this game, see the notes for Chapter 19: "Notre Dame versus Klandiana: 1924." The *Notre Dame Daily* described the student reaction to the Princeton game, 23 October 1923, and quoted Indiana state senator Bob Proctor in that issue.

On page 149 of the text, the letter to Rockne from Henry A. Sullivan, 5 January 1924, is in UADR 19/35. For the low payout from the Princeton game and the net profit from the Georgia Tech contest, see UVMU 2/51. The *Notre Dame Daily* announced the extensive Homecoming program, 3 November 1923; Rockne's letter to the Nebraska student newspaper was reprinted by the *Notre Dame Daily*, 15 December 1923.

On page 150 of the text, the payout at Nebraska is in UVMU 2/51, as are the gate receipts for the Butler, Carnegie Tech, and St. Louis University games. The note to Rockne warning him about the St. Louis players is a copy of a letter to the athletic director, University of Missouri, 25 August 1923, and is signed "THE ATHLETIC INVESTIGATING COMMITTEE." It was probably forwarded to Rockne by a friend and the cover letter later separated from it (UADR 16/90).

The final football profit of $69,093 for 1923 is in UVMU 2/51. The line at the bottom of the statement—"$3,454.69 Commission"—is exactly 5 percent of net profit; apparently this was Rockne's commission for the successful year. This arrangement gave rise to the frequent charge that Rockne made a personal commission from his football team's games (see page 309 of the text). However, in the long-term contract that he signed the following winter, no commission clause existed, nor do the subsequent annual football financial statements for his regime contain the commission note and figure. In the 1920s, a college coach receiving a commission from his team's profits seemed radical and unacceptable, but in the modern era it is an increasingly standard practice, see Sperber, *College Sports Inc.*, pages 194–95.

The "Song in Honor of Rock" is quoted in the *Notre Dame Alumnus*, 1923–1924 volume, page 109; it was written by Princeton and Western Reserve graduates; however, the N.D. alums obviously enjoyed it and the *Alumnus* printed it proudly. Jethrow Kyles, formerly of the International Sports and Games Collection at N.D., offered the opinion on Rockne sharing the prejudices of his time, 8 August 1991. That magazine noted Rockne's winter speaking tour and his standard talk on page 108. Notre Dame historian Father Arthur Hope discussed President Walsh's guidance in his history of Notre Dame, page 386; Arch Ward offered his comments in his obituary on Rockne, *Chicago Tribune*, 1 April 1931. The coach's after-dinner anecdote on how, in 1923, Notre Dame inexplicably went "cake-eater" is retold in many places, among them his *Autobiography*, pages 187–90; probably his ghostwriter, John B. Kennedy, cobbled together this version from the various printed sources. Francis Wallace related his role in the original composition in *Knute Rockne*, pages 130–32; however, Wallace quotes the version that mocks Northwestern, whereas in the original, reprinted in the 1923–1924 *Dome*, page 371, Nebraska is the opponent. Wallace probably heard the NU one so often that he became confused; Rockne changed from Nebraska to NU after the Notre Dame administration broke off football relations with Nebraska and he wanted to resume them.

In both versions and his after-dinner talks, Rockne's standard description of future "Fighting Irish" players included: "Hanging from their necks were pendants, lavalliere type." One wonders what he would have thought of current Notre Dame football players, many with gold chains around their necks and jeweled earrings in pierced earlobes! If they won football games and national titles for him, no doubt he would have hugged them in celebration.

Bonifer and Weaver, in *Out of Bounds,* relate the story of the halftime show in Soldier Field and also quote from the "effete easterners" speech, pages 50–51. Benjamin Rader, in *American Sports,* provides an analysis of the Christian "manliness" movement and supplies excellent references.

On page 152 of the text, the quotes from Father J. C. McGinn to President Walsh, 30 October 1923, are in UPWL "McE-McK #12" folder, emphasis added. In addition, Father McGinn warned: "I can't see what is going to become of us if assurances and promises as I have quoted in this letter are repudiated. Of course you understand that I don't hold the University responsible, nor the Faculty Board, for these promises of Rockne's."

On page 153 of the text, Rockne's complaints to influential alumni and the conference in New York are described in another letter to Walsh from McGinn, 19 December 1923 (UVMU 2/49). The coach's demands for a newly constituted athletic board are in a copy of a letter from Father McGinn to President Walsh, 21 December 1923 (UVMU 2/61). The *Notre Dame Daily* announced the administrative changes, 28 January 1924, and the Iowa overture to Rockne was in that paper, 25 March 1924. Howard Roberts, in *The Big Nine,* discussed Howard Jones's problems at Iowa, page 126.

On page 154 of the text, the Iowa alum, King Thompson, made the charge in a newspaper dispatch, "Rockne Once Broke Contract with Iowa, Says Hawkeye Alum," datelined 15 December 1924; no newspaper identifiable but clipped and placed in President Walsh's files (UPWL 53/10). Two years later, 21 May 1926, the secretary of the athletic board, Professor J. E. McCarthy, told Ray Eichenlaub, an important alum and a former teammate of the N.D. coach's, that "Rock had absolutely signed a contract with the University of Iowa" (UVMU 2/48).

McDonald described his efforts on Rockne's behalf in a letter to the coach, 21 March 1924; a letter to Walsh from McDonald, 18 March 1924; and to Walsh from McDonald, 21 March 1924, all in (UVMU 2/49). Rockne's contract, 25 March 1924, is in UPWL 53/10 "Rockne—Columbia Incident" folder), as is his announcement to the press. The coach's demand for "the reorganization of athletic affairs" is in UVMU 2/49).

On page 155 of the text, for President Walsh's letter to McDonald, 5 April 1924, about "The new constitution," see UPWL "McDonald, Angus, Trustee NYC #3" folder. For Walsh's appointments to the athletic board, see the *Notre Dame Alumnus,* 1924–1925 volume, pages 8–10. That magazine rejoiced on Rockne's signing in the 1923–1924 volume, page 219.

19. NOTRE DAME VERSUS KLANDIANA: 1924

Father Hope's comment is in his history of Notre Dame, page 445; he also discusses Father John O'Hara's role in the Albany excursion, page 446, and O'Hara's connection between religion and football at Notre Dame, page 447 and following. Father Thomas McAvoy, C.S.C., wrote a biography, *Father O'Hara of Notre Dame: The Cardinal-Archbishop of Philadelphia*, Notre Dame, Ind., 1967, that provides many of the details used in this chapter of the text, especially those concerning O'Hara's Religious Bulletins. Francis Wallace outlines the N.D. prefect of religion's role at the 1923 N.D.–Army game in *Notre Dame Story*, page 229; the headline "ELSIE JANIS TO KICK OFF" was in the *New York World*, 10 October 1923. The newspaper was not interested in the religious angle but, as the subhead explained, the fact that she "Will Be First Woman to Start [a] Football Game." O'Hara's line about "timid freshmen" is in his essay "Religion and the Student Body," *Notre Dame Alumnus*, March 1923, page 41. Father Hope, page 300, described the spontaneous exhibitions of faith; Schlaver summed up: "Thus football was used to promote the cause of religion and to inculcate a masculine image in the Notre Dame student," page 90.

The quote from the *Atlantic Monthly*, May 1928, is in "Gentlemen from Indiana" by Morton Harrison, pages 670–80. It is a look back at the heyday of the Klan in Indiana; apparently the North Manchester incident occurred in 1924. There are many histories of the 1920s, ranging from Frederick Allen's *Only Yesterday: An Informal History of the 1920s*, New York, 1931, written immediately after the decade, to the retrospective, *The Culture of the Twenties* by Loren Baritz, Indianapolis, 1970, and *Babbitts and Bohemians* by Elizabeth Stevenson, New York, 1967. In addition, historians have written many specific books and articles on this fascinating era and the events that led up to it: of particular use for the study of Notre Dame football were *The Irish in America: Emigration, Assimilation and Impact*, edited by J. P. Drudy, Cambridge, Eng., 1985; *From Paddy to Studs: Irish-American Communities in the Turn of the Century Era, 1880 to 1920*, edited by Timothy J. Meagher, New York, 1986; *Al Smith and His America* by Oscar Handlin, New York, 1958; *The First Hurrah: A Biography of Al Smith* by Richard O'Connor, New York, 1970; and *A Catholic Runs for President* by Edmund A. Moore, New York, 1956. On the phenomenon of the Ku Klux Klan, Wyn Craig Wade wrote *The Fiery Cross: The Ku Klux Klan in America*, New York, 1988; and on its Indiana manifestation, M. William Lutholtz did an excellent recent study, *Grand Dragon: D. C. Stephenson and the Ku Klux Klan in Indiana*, West Lafayette, Ind., 1991. The overview of the 1920s offered in this chapter of the text is my understanding of the period based on the documents of the time and the subsequent histories.

In the 1920s, the mainstream of American Jewry began to embrace Zionism and only small amounts of money went overseas; as for Catholics, the American Catholic church needed all the money it could raise from its adherents to keep the parish and parochial school system going. These facts had little impact on the prejudices of anti-Semites and anti-Catholics.

Lutholtz outlines the Klan's plans for Valparaiso on page 76, and the events in South Bend on pages 140–44. Various Notre Dame histories offer versions of the events: Armstrong, page 244; Hope, pages 372–78; and Bonifer and Weaver, pages 41–42 (the source of the quote about Hullie & Mike's). President Walsh's speech to the students is quoted extensively in Hope, pages 376–77.

On page 160 of the text, the Walsh letter to concerned citizen George Rickerby, 9 June 1924, is in UPWL "Rh-Ri #5" folder. A recent PBS documentary in the American Experience series, "Knute Rockne and His Fightin' Irish," claimed that Rockne helped convince the students massed in South Bend to return peaceably to Notre Dame. No newspaper or other account at the time placed Rockne at this gathering and, usually at this time of year, he had left Notre Dame to attend to his increasingly lucrative businesses in New York and elsewhere. The documentary film, produced by Larry Hott of Florentine Films, offered absolutely no reference for this or any other assertion in the voiceover narration; however, the announcer—in a resonant and authoritative voice—made this and many other questionable pronouncements appear absolutely true. Such is the wonder of film.

On pages 160–61 of the text, President Walsh's letter to a colleague, Father Charles O'Donnell, 11 October 1924, is in UPWL "O'Donnell, Charles L., Rev. C.S.C." folder. Lutholtz, page 107, discussed Stephenson's relations with Watson. The letter to Father John W. Cavanaugh from Senator James E. Watson, on United States Senate stationery, 26 March 1925; the note to Rockne from Cavanaugh, 30 March 1925; the reply to Cavanaugh from Rockne, 2 April 1925; the letter to Rockne on White House stationery, 31 March 1925 (from Everett Sanders, secretary to the president); and the reply to Sanders from Rockne, 6 April 1925, are all in UADR 21/86.

Edmund Moore quotes Methodist Bishop Adna W. Leonard on page 21, and he describes the 1924 convention on page 23 and following. Oscar Handlin explains Smith's appeal on page 83 and following.

20. BLAST-OFF: 1924

Francis Wallace's description of New York in the fall of 1924 appeared in the *Scholastic*, 1924–1925 volume, page 185. Benjamin Rader has an informative chapter on the meaning of college football to "The Sons of the Elite," pages 70–86.

On page 164 of the text, Joe Byrne, Jr.'s, plans are in a letter to Rockne, 9 September 1924 (UADR 9/18), and the letter from Warren Nolan to Hugh O'Donnell, 25 August 1924, is in UADR 17/51. The *Times* man who offered his services "as a press representative" for the N.D.–Army game was James Harrison in a letter to Rockne, 16 September 1924 (UADR 16/136). Rockne replied, 18 September 1924 (UADR 16/136).

The *New York Telegram*'s comment on the crowd appeared in its Saturday postgame edition, 18 October 1924, and the *Times*'s observation on 19 October 1924. Adam Walsh told how he nicknamed his linemates and himself many times; one detailed version of this story as well as his entire N.D. career is in *Oh, How They Played the Game*, page 274 and following.

Grantland Rice's Four Horsemen lead appeared in the *New York Herald-Tribune*,

19 October 1924; see the *New York Daily News* on the same day for its non–Notre Dame coverage. The payouts from the Army and Princeton games are in UABM "Semi-Annual Financial Statements—Football 1924–30," and the contract with Princeton is in UABM "Contracts-Football-P." The *New York Sun* announced its Gridgraphie featured game on 25 October 1924. After the Notre Dame games in the East, Rockne received many letters from fans suggesting various plays for him to use in future games. A typical one came from Broadway actor Harry Bloomfield; the N.D. coach replied, 21 November 1924 (UADR 8/3), with an edge to his words, "Your play is the play which has probably been used in football for over thirty years."

Terri Wenzel offered her observation in a telephone interview for this book, 12 October 1991. For the fall of 1924, the *Notre Dame Alumnus* increased its coverage of the football team and discussed the additions to Cartier Field, November 1924, page 40 and following; and the Rockne testimonial, December 1924, page 73.

On page 167 of the text, J. M. Cleary of WGN wrote to Rockne on 24 September 1924, and the coach replied on 26 September 1924 (UADR 9/68); Rockne's comments about the victory over Nebraska were made to Chet Wynne, 17 November 1924 (UADR 21/183). Jack Fishman offered his comment in a discourse on Chicago in the 1920s, 6 June 1961. The *Chicago Tribune* carried articles on Tuesday and Wednesday before the Notre Dame–Northwestern game, 18 and 19 November 1924, about the sellout. The fifty-fifty split with Northwestern as well as the costs of moving the game from Evanston to Grant Park (Soldier Field) are in the settlement statement (UADR 16/198), and the payout for this game and the Carnegie Tech one are in UABM "Semi-Annual Financial Statements—Football 1924–30." Avery Brundage's praise of N.D. was noted in the *Notre Dame Alumnus,* December 1924, page 74.

On pages 168–69 of the text, President Walsh's explanation to Father Matthew Schumacher, 7 October 1924, about the Rose Bowl game is in UPWL "Schumacher, Matthew Rev. C.S.C." folder. Among the West Coast alums lobbying for the trip to the Rose Bowl was Leo Ward in a letter to President Walsh, 27 October 1924 (UPWL "War-Waz #3" folder). The histories of the Rose Bowl offer various versions of Notre Dame's 1924 participation, all written without access to the N.D. documents: Rube Samuelson, *The Rose Bowl Game,* Garden City, N.Y., 1951, pages 67–76; and Herb Michelson and Dave Newhouse, *Rose Bowl Football Since 1902,* New York, 1977, pages 54–65.

On page 169 of the text, for the letter to President Walsh from West Coast alum A. D. McDonald, 18 October 1924, see UPWL "McDonald, Angus, Trustee NYC #3" folder. USC coach "Gus" Henderson sent his telegram to Rockne on 3 November 1924 (UADR 13/66); Leo Ward complained to Rockne that "Notre Dame pulled an awful 'Brodie,'" 8 December 1924 (UADR 21/63). The Rose Bowl payout is in UABM, "Financial Reports of Games: Football" folder. Layden discussed the Rose Bowl trip and game in his memoir, pages 30–34. The *Notre Dame Alumnus* wrote about the trip in great detail and provided the quotes in the text, January 1925, pages 106–8 and 116–18.

The letter to Rockne from Father Matthew Schumacher, president of St. Edward's College in Texas, 24 November 1924, is in UADR 19/42; the coach's notes to Slip Madigan, 13 and 14, December 1924, are in UADR 15/110; and the copy of the telegram about Herbert Fleishacker from Paul Shoup to A. D. McDonald, 12 December 1924, is in UADR 18/179.

21. THE FOUR HORSEMEN—GRANTLAND RICE VERSUS REALITY

The quote from Robert Lipsyte's *Sports World*, New York, 1975, is on page 170; Lipsyte added, "Without the aid and abetment of sportswriters . . . college football would never have been able to grow into America's grandest monument to national hypocrisy." This book and Robert W. McChesney's article, "Media Made Sport: A History of Sports Coverage in the United States," in *Media, Sports and Society*, edited by Lawrence A. Wenner, Newbury Park, Cal., 1989, supplied much of the background for this chapter. In addition, the memoirs of such sportswriters of the period as Paul Gallico (*The Golden People*, Garden City, N.Y., 1965, and *Farewell to Sport*) and the memories of others in *No Cheering from the Press Box*, collected and edited by Jerome Holtzman, New York, 1974, were extremely informative, as were the biographies of Herbert Bayard Swope (*The World of Swope* by E. J. Kahn, New York, 1965) and Westbrook Pegler (*Fair Enough* by Finis Farr, New Rochelle, N.Y., 1975).

The New York Times editorial on the Klan and N.D. football was reprinted by the *Notre Dame Alumnus*, December 1923, page 72. The Carnegie Foundation's Bulletin No. 23 contained a chapter titled "The Press and College Athletics," pages 266–90; the quote on the "overstressing of athletics" is on pages 266–67, and the one on coaches transcending their teams, made by E. K. Hall, is on page 275. The Carnegie Foundation surveyed the actual column inches devoted to sports in a number of important papers around the United States in the years 1913, 1920, and 1927; it charted the explosion in coverage, especially for intercollegiate athletics.

Paul Gallico offered his mea culpa in *The Golden People*, page 27, whereas Grantland Rice maintained his wonderment in *Sport's Golden Age*, edited by Allison Danzig and Peter Brandwein, New York, 1948, page 6. The *New York Herald-Tribune* carried W. O. McGeehan's observation about the "average reader," 22 October 1924.

On page 176 of the text, the sports editor of the *Omaha* (Nebraska) *World-Herald*, Frederick Ware, wrote to Rockne, 9 October 1925 (UADR 21/70). Grantland Rice's lead for his 1923 N.D.–Army game article appeared in the *New York Herald-Tribune*, 14 October 1923, and for the 1922 game, reprinted from the *Knickerbocker Press* in the *Scholastic*, 1922–1923 volume, page 277. Rice's *The Tumult and the Shouting*, New York, appeared in 1954; his comments about Middlebury were in the *New York Herald-Tribune*, 15 October 1923. One of Rice's self-serving legends is that he conceived the Four Horsemen nickname while standing on the sidelines of the 1923 Ebbets Field game. However, nowhere in his newspaper articles on that event or on the N.D. eastern trip of that year does he employ or even imply a horse metaphor. He first told the anecdote about the Brooklyn conception years later and polished it for his *Tumult and the Shouting,* page 178. It seems very ex post facto and, considering Rice's talent for fantasy, doubtful at best.

On page 178 of the text, Rockne's observation about the 1924 team made to Tom Johnson, 8 October 1924, is in UADR 13/165. Harry Stuhldreher's remarks about his injury are in his *Knute Rockne,* pages 174–75. George Strickler told his story about *The Four Horsemen of the Apocalypse* to Jerome Holtzman, pages 146–47. Rice's lead ran on the front page of the Sunday *New York Herald-Tribune,* 19 October 1924. Grantland Rice put the attendance at fifty-five thousand in his Four Horsemen lead, however, other newspaper accounts as well as the authoritative Beach and Moore book indicate a crowd of at least sixty thousand. As a result of Rice's probably errone-ous estimation, most sports historians as well as the current N.D. athletic department use his number—although the latter in its football media guide fudges with "c55,000."

The game reports of the *New York World* and the *New York Times* appeared on 19 October 1924; the *New York Post* and *New York Sun* comments on 20 October 1924. Strickler's subsequent comments are in Holtzman, page 148; Jim Crowley's and Don Miller's are in Rappoport, page 134. Rice's lead for the Columbia-Williams game was in the *New York Herald-Tribune,* 25 October 1924. Red Smith's comments are in the *Red Smith Reader,* edited by Dave Anderson, New York, 1982, page 261.

On page 181 of the text, New York newspaper executive Warren Nolan wrote to Al Ryan about Rice going "crazy" (UABM 16/141). The *Scholastic* reprinted Fox's poem, page 315, and many other hosannas to the Four Horsemen; Eckersall's Rose Bowl story appeared in the *Chicago Tribune,* 2 January 1925. Mary Stuhldreher discussed her husband's life as one of the Four Horsemen, page 233. See page 338 of the text for the evaluation of Rice on the 1930 backfield. Elmer Layden's remarks are in his memoir on pages 4–5.

22. ROCKNE THREATENS TO JUMP SHIP: 1925

The opening quotes are from the Annual Report of the Carnegie Foundation for the Advancement of Teaching, New York, 1924, pages 35–37. Wilson and Brondfield outline the Big Ten's 1920s reforms on pages 153–54, and the new stadiums on pages 192–93.

Rockne's letter to G. B. Clippinger, 9 February 1925, about stadium construction is in UADR 9/183; Father Hope discusses President Walsh's commitment to build "needed dormitories" etc. on page 361, and the *Notre Dame Alumnus* featured it, January 1926, page 106. The financial figures on 1924–1925 are in UVMU 2/51. For further information on the finances of college sports as well as the many myths that burden all discussions of the topic, see my previous book, *College Sports Inc.* A typical early example of the problem was provided by Georgetown University coach Lou Little in a 27 September 1928 letter to Rockne (UADR 14/160), explaining how his school had overexpanded its football program and that he needed a good payday game with N.D.: "The situation we now face is financial embarrassment, this bad predicament being due to the fact we sacrificed financial return for an athletic prestige."

President Walsh quoted and commented upon the newspaper article about the convict to Joseph Scott, 19 December 1924 (UPWL "President #2" folder). The *Notre Dame Alumnus*'s comment on football publicity came March 1925, page 167. Among the typical inquiries to N.D. authorities and the replies are the letter to Rockne from Andrew L. Boerner, 25 November 1924, and Rockne's answer, 9 December 1924 (UADR 8/4); and the letter to Rockne from W. T. Gorman, 1 November 1924, and the coach's reply, 5 November 1924 (UADR 12/3).

Father Hope outlined the composition of the athletic board on page 388, and the *Notre Dame Alumnus* discussed all the appointments and the 1924 constitution, October 1925, pages 8–10.

On page 186 of the text, for Walsh's letter to Father Finigan, 23 September 1925, see UVMU 2/61; and for Rockne's ideas on an "Alumni Advisory Committee," see his letter to Byron Kanaley, 28 May 1925 (UADR 14/31). The Rockne letter to Amos Santweir, 4 June 1925, is in UADR 19/55, and the letter from the University of Wisconsin alum, Edward J. Samp, 2 December 1924, is in UADR 21/156. The telegram to Rockne from Warren Bovard, the USC comptroller, 15 January 1925; the two-page telegram to Rockne from Warren Bovard, 16 January 1925; and Rockne's reply to Warren Bovard about "sweating blood," 4 June 1925, are all in UADR 8/179. Bovard noted on 27 January 1925: "It has seemed to me almost a crime for your [Athletic] Board to hold you to a contract if Mrs. Rockne is well and happy here [in southern California] and not in South Bend" (UADR 8/179). Apparently, Bonnie Rockne wanted to move to a more hospitable climate.

Rockne's letter to the sports editor of the *Cleveland* (Ohio) *News*, Ed Bang, 18 February 1925, is in UADR 8/72; his letter to Tom Keady, 2 April 1925 (UADR 14/41), mentioned the "7500 miles of travel." An indication of how, by 1925, the N.D. faculty board had control of the scheduling occurred in an exchange between Rockne and the athletic director of the University of Texas for a game in Austin that Rockne wanted to schedule: "Our faculty board just at present is rather hot against traveling and after sizing up the situation I do not believe it is wise to approach them on the Texas trip until near the end of the season": L. Theo Bellmont to Rockne, 29 September 1925, Rockne reply 2 October 1925 (UADR 8/128). The N.D. coach never liked this situation, later telling a friend, "No coach worth his salt is going to stand any interference by the faculty members of athletic boards with his schedule making," McCready Huston, *Salesman from the Sidelines: Being the Business Career of Knute Rockne*, New York, 1932, page 79.

On page 188 of the text, for an example of Rockne's standard reply, see his letter to L. F. Eick, 21 November 1924 (UADR 11/40). In the correspondence on the refusal to play Holy Cross (UADR 9/18) are a letter to Rockne from C. A. O'Donnell, 4 November 1925; Rockne's reply, 24 November 1925; a telegram to Rockne from Joe Byrne, Jr., 17 November 1925; and a letter to Rockne from Byrne, undated (but internal evidence points to 19 November 1924). Father John A. MacNamara wrote the N.D. coach about Holy Cross's jealousy, no date, and Rockne replied on 30 January 1925 (UADR 15/108).

In the 1920s, Georgetown University hired a smart young coach, Lou Little, to build up its football program, and the Jesuit school tried for a number of years to obtain a game with N.D. Georgetown even enlisted the chairman of the Notre Dame lay board of trustees to plead its case, but the N.D. authorities would not yield. Rockne referred to the Georgetown "pressure" in his letter to Father John A. MacNamara; also see Lou Little's letter to Rockne, 29 October 1925, and Rockne's reply, 3 November 1925 (UADR 14/159); the letter to E. A. Saunders from N. F. Brady, 3 December 1924; Saunders's reply to N. F. Brady, 4 December 1924; and Rockne to Saunders, 15 December 1924, all in UADR 19/57. Georgetown did not give up easily: Lou Little wrote to Rockne, 27 September 1928; Rockne replied, 11 October 1928 (UADR 14/160). An important Georgetown alum also tried, James K. Finn to Rockne, 25 July 1928; Rockne answered on 6 September 1928 (UADR 11/106). Notre Dame also vetoed games against other Catholic schools, including Catholic University in Washington, where many N.D. administrators and faculty had gained their doctorates: see the letter to Rockne from Charles Moran, 7 October 1924, and Rockne's reply, 10 October 1924 (UADR 9/165). Also see the Creighton, Loyola of New Orleans, and Boston College requests and turndowns: Creighton letter to Rockne from A. A. Schabinger, 17 November 1924 (UADR 10/48); Loyola of New Orleans letter to Rockne from R. J. Ducote, 11 September 1924, and Rockne reply, 30 October 1924 (UADR 15/8); Boston College requests from F. A. Reynolds on 6 October 1926 and 6 December 1927, and Rockne replies on 12 October 1926 and 12 December 1927 (UADR 18/86).

Notre Dame also received requests from important citizens in various localities requesting games in their municipal stadiums. John Ruckelhaus wrote to Rockne, 3 December 1925, on behalf of "the most influential men of our city" for a game against Butler in Indianapolis but, probably because of Klandiana, the board instructed the coach to refuse, 7 December 1925 (UADR 18/134). Notre Dame never played in that city after 1921.

President Walsh's statement about postseason games came in a letter to Bishop Lillis, 12 June 1925 (UVMU 2/48). Arthur commented on the results of the bowl game ban, page 340. For Rockne's explanation of how USC got on the schedule, see his letter to Paul J. Schissler, 9 December 1925 (UADR 19/67); although no record exists of the guarantee offered by Southern California, the assumption that it was higher than the going rate of the time—Rockne called it "fluttering," using 1920s slang meaning to take a high risk (or "flutter") on a financial investment—puts it in the $75,000 range.

For Major John Griffith's contractual letter to Rockne, 3 March 1925, see UADR 12/81; the football contract with Minnesota, 12 December 1925 (UABM "Contracts —Football—M" folder); the letter from Griffith congratulating Rockne on the 1924 season, 9 January 1925 (UADR 12/80). Griffith sent the names of prospective attendees to Rockne on 10 May 1925 (UADR 12/80), and had done so in the past, 16 May 1923 (UADR 16/51). Alice Griffith asked Rockne for an ad, 30 January 1929, and the coach answered, 22 March 1929 (UADR 12/88). As for Rockne's professional relationship with Griffith, apparently the Big Ten commissioner would try to pay the coach for his articles for the *Athletic Journal* but Rockne would refuse; for example, on 26 September 1926 Griffith wrote Rockne: "Thanks for the article. I wish you would let me pay for it as suggested in my other letters" (UADR 12/83).

On page 191 of the text, Griffith told Rockne about the faculty reps, 6 February 1925, and Rockne reacted, 9 February 1925; Rockne arranged the Chicago meeting, 2 February 1925 (UADR 12/80). The letters from Fred Gardner to Rockne, 7 November 1924, and Rockne's reply, 15 December 1924, are in UADR 12/33. Walter Eckersall thanked the N.D. coach, 16 December 1924 (UADR 11/67), and pestered Rockne about an assignment for the 1925 N.D.–Army game in a telegram, 17 January 1925 (UADR 11/67). In the Rose Bowl game, Eckersall, the head linesman, made an extremely controversial call. Late in the game, with the score at 20–10 and Stanford trying to push the ball over the N.D. line on an Ernie Nevers plunge, "Eck" signaled a Stanford TD. However, when the referee came over, "Eck" changed his call; Notre Dame held, and instead of the score's being 20–17, the Irish remained in control of the lead and then, with Layden's TD on an interception, put the game away at 27–10. The question became: did "Eck" signal the TD as an automatic reflex and then change his call to help Rockne, or was he simply overruled by the referee, Ed Thorp of La Salle? Stanford fans long felt that the game officials had robbed them. See Samuelson's book and Michelson and Newhouse's for detailed accounts.

On page 192 of the text, among the other friends Rockne hired was J. J. Lipski, 11 March 1925 (UADR 14/157). Lipski worked the Beloit and Carnegie Tech games in 1925; he later changed his name to "Lipp" and appears on game rosters with that name. Rockne wrote to Milton Ghee, 13 February 1925, and the journalist replied on 2 February 1925 and 24 March 1925 (UADR 12/42).

Being totally inside the hiring-of-officials system, Rockne saw nothing wrong with his actions, in fact, he felt that he was less aggressive about hiring his favorites than were some of his rival coaches. On 13 April 1925 (UADR 14/43), he wrote one of his regular referees, Nick Kearns, who had been vetoed by the coach of Carnegie Tech, Judge Wally Steffen: "These men like Steffen, Page [coach at Indiana], Bedzek [coach at Penn State], and Walker [coach at Drury College] for some reason are always objecting to officials. I have more trouble with these men than I do with all the hundreds of coaches combined with whom I deal."

Rockne sometimes sent Commissioner Griffith inside information, particularly on such enemies as Fielding Yost of the University of Michigan. On 25 May 1927, Griffith referred to a story Rockne had told him about real estate in Detroit that has "been sold over and over to help out Michigan athletes"—they pocketed the phony commissions (UADR 12/84). Griffith included the copy of a smarmy letter that he wrote to Yost, 25 May 1927, apologizing for even asking whether these charges were true (UADR 12/84). The Big Ten commissioner was the proverbial fox guarding the henhouse—unlike the Carnegie investigators, he rarely found anything amiss in Big Ten athletic programs.

On page 193 of the text, for Bill "Stub" Allison's letter to Rockne requesting betting advice, 6 November 1925, and the coach's answer, 21 November 1925, see UADR 7/121. The Carnegie Foundation warned about gambling in its 1924 Annual Report, and the *New York Times* featured this warning on 10 March 1924. Rockne's comment about N.D. fans betting on the Army game came in a letter to Colonel H. J. Koehler, 29 October 1925 (UADR 20/106). The quote from a typical Rockne column was in the *New York World*, 29 October 1927. Rockne had a low toleration for many fans, telling a "Mr. H. W. Lever," 18 August 1925, who sent in a diagrammed play for the Fighting Irish to use: "I believe that the play looks very good on paper but would look very ridiculous on the field" (UADR 14/102).

Rockne's comment to Frank Wallace, 18 August 1925, is in UADR 21/24; Rockne explained Christy Walsh's luncheon in a letter to Harry Atwell, 13 February 1925 (UADR 7/149). The N.D. coach sent his effusive thanks to Rice, 24 August 1925, and his inside information to Rice for the latter's All-America team, 10 November 1925 (UADR 18/89). Rice's game story of the Penn-Yale game was in the 18 October 1925 *New York Herald-Tribune*, opposite the N.D.–Army game story.

On page 196 of the text, Rockne's go-ahead on editing to Hughie Fullerton, 29 September 1924, is in UADR 11/171. In his memoir, *Adios to Ghosts*, New York, 1937, Christy Walsh explained his methods, and Paul Gallico condemned them in *Golden People*, page 28. The *Chicago Tribune*, 15 December 1925, characterized Christy Walsh's operation as "the syndicate which sells certain articles" by coaches Rockne, Warner, and Yost, *"which are known as their writings."* Of course, the *Tribune* did not subscribe to Walsh's service and lost readers to those papers that did.

Rockne's letter to Frank Wallace, 18 August 1925, is in UADR 21/24; these lines are a particularly authentic example of Rockne's prose because, unlike most of his typed letters, they do not have his secretary Ruth Falkner's initials at the bottom. She was more literate than her boss and cleaned up his prose and/or took his dictation and changed his speech into written phrases.

On page 196 of the text, his admission to C. S. "Cy" Sherman, 18 December 1925, about his lack of cleverness in English is in UADR 23/3. Rockne's postgame article on the N.D.–Army game was in the *New York World*, 17 and 18 October 1925.

There are basically two separate canons of Rockne writings: those works clearly authored by him and those that were ghost-edited or ghostwritten. In the former category are his awful novel *The Four Winners*, New York, 1925, and his casual articles for small magazines like Griffith's *Athletic Journal;* these works are easy to identify because of Rockne's turgid prose style and shaky grasp of sentence and paragraph construction. The ghosted Rockne writings are usually his well-paid work for Christy Walsh, especially the postgame articles and the pieces in national magazines such as *Liberty* and *Collier's*. His *Autobiography*, ghosted by John B. Kennedy, appeared originally in the latter magazine in the issues from 1 November through 6 December 1930.

Internal analysis is the best indication of ghostly typewriters: crisp style, tight dialogue, well-constructed paragraphs, and transitions characterize these pieces. I base my judgments not only on many years as a professional writer but on more than twenty-five years of teaching English and having to deal with plagiarism—the best detection of the latter crime is internal analysis, a comparison of the person's actual writing style versus the final polished product. Fortunately, the archival material on Rockne provides the writing sleuth with evidence of his prose style versus the ghosted printed pieces.

On page 197 of the text, Colonel H. J. Koehler's letter to Rockne, 26 October 1925, is in UADR 20/106; the N.D. coach's comments on the first three games of the season came in a letter to C. Wilbur White, 12 October 1925 (UADR 20/172). Rockne had the foresight in 1924 to anticipate his difficulties in building the 1925 team, and he told a fellow athletic director, A. A. Schabinger, 17 December 1925 (UADR 10/48), that because "we play West Point in New York the Saturday following, [it] makes it imperative that I schedule a rather easy game at home on the 9th of October [1925]." This turned out to be the Beloit contest, won by N.D. 19–3.

The *New York Times*'s prediction was in its 17 October 1925 edition. Rockne's former player, Joe Brandy, wrote him about the "ten tickets" on 2 October 1925, and the coach replied on 6 October 1925 (UADR 8/183). Rockne wrote Ed Barrow, manager of Yankee Stadium, on 27 October 1925 (UADR 8/87). In 1925, Rockne still sent large blocks of seats to his friend Joe Byrne, Jr., to dispense among Notre Dame alumni, informing him on 21 September 1925 (UADR 9/19): "I have written Ed Barrow at the Yankee [Stadium] to let you have 3000 reserved seats and 500 box seats."

Rockne's attitude toward scalping tickets was characteristically pragmatic. He did not want N.D. alums massively doing it in New York or Chicago because it embarrassed the school and led to hard questions by the faculty athletic board to the athletic director, in charge of ticket selling. But when friends scalped a few ducats on the side, he joked about it. Eugene "Scrapiron" Young related the story in *With Rockne*, pages 124–25, of how, one Saturday in Pittsburgh, the N.D. coach sent him out to deliver four tickets to "some bigwig steel mill owner," and to sell them for " 'All you can.' " Young "asked for and received $100 per ducat" and later, Rockne told him:

"Give me twenty dollars [face value of the tickets], and keep the rest."

"You mean," Young asked him, "I can keep three hundred and eighty bucks?"

It was Rock who now looked startled. "[Why not,] You got four hundred dollars . . . and without a gun!"

On page 198 of the text, Joe Byrne, Jr., wrote to President Walsh, 20 November 1925 (UPWL "Joseph M. Byrne" folder); the settlement check from Yankee Stadium, the payday at Minnesota, the payout from the game against Northwestern, and the net profit from football for the 1925 season are in UABM "Semi-Annual Financial Statements—Football 1924–30." Even important alums complained that they could not obtain the number of tickets and location of seats that they wanted; six weeks before the Northwestern game, 11 October 1925, Byron Kanaley, a member of the N.D. lay board of trustees, wrote Rockne: "The situation surrounding the Northwestern tickets seems to be getting more aggravating" (UADR 14/30). Rockne's letter to S. B. Robinson, a longtime local patron, 6 November 1925, is in UADR 18/45. Arthur discusses President Walsh's handling of ticket requests to his office on pages 317–18.

On page 200 of the text, for the letter from Father H. Ryder to Father George Finigan, 10 December 1925, see UVMU 2/65. Bonifer and Weaver describe N.D. visits to Nebraska, page 40; and Dan Young, in *We Remember Rockne,* recalled the epithets, page 40.

For Rockne's correspondence with the Nebraska newspapermen about the slanders spread at Illinois, see the coach's letters to Frederick Ware, 7 October 1925 and 13 October 1925 (UADR 21/70), and to C. S. "Cy" Sherman, 7 October 1925 (UADR 23/3). Sherman made the remark about Gipp, 14 October 1925, and the N.D. coach replied, 20 October 1925 (UADR 23/3). The full-page ad with the headline "BEAT NOTRE DAME" appeared in the *Lincoln* (Nebraska) *State Journal,* 22 November 1925.

On page 201 of the text, C.S.C. priest Joseph J. Boyle described the crowd at the game to Rev. George Finigan, 10 December 1925 (UVMU 2/65). The *Nebraska Alumnus* commented on the game and "The Notre Dame Break," January 1926, pages 13–16. The publisher of the *South Bend News-Times,* J. M. Stephenson, sent a copy of the letter he had written to Mayor F. C. Zehring of Lincoln, Nebraska, 8 December 1925, to Notre Dame (UVMU 2/65). The profit from the 1925 Nebraska game as fifth highest of the year is calculated by including the heavy travel expenses to Lincoln (UABM "Semi-Annual Financial Statements—Football 1924–30").

On page 202 of the text, the secretary of the athletic board, J. E. McCarthy, informed President Walsh, 29 November 1925, of his group's "opinion" (UPWL "McA-McD #14" folder). Rockne's statement appeared in the *Lincoln* (Nebraska) *State Journal,* 10 December 1925. The supervisor of Catholic schools in Nebraska, Rev. D. B. O'Connor, wrote to Rockne, 19 December 1925 (UADR 17/15). Anti–Notre Dame fan Herbert G. Esden wrote to Harvey Woodruff of the *Chicago Tribune,* 26 October 1926, and Rockne excoriated Esden, 11 November 1926 (UADR 21/59). Rockne received Esden's letter from Arch Ward, who wrote across the top, "Coach: Please keep source of this letter confidential." This is a good example of how, during this period and for years later, many sportswriters were in bed with the coaches whom they covered and publicized.

The Cornhuskers: Nebraska Football by David Israel, Chicago, 1975, discusses the new stadium in Lincoln in the 1920s, pages 69–70. Rockne was never happy about the break with Nebraska and later tried to resume football relations with the school; see his letters to C. S. "Cy" Sherman, 28 January 1927, 7 April 1927, 29 September 1927, and 10 November 1927 (UADR 23/5).

On page 203 of the text, Joe Byrne, Jr.'s, letter to President Walsh, 16 December 1925, is in UPWL 53/10. The Columbia athletic manager, Robert W. Watt, wrote to Rockne, 23 January 1923 (UADR 20/160). The *New York Daily News*'s "Biggest Boner" article appeared 3 January 1926. Francis Wallace's version of the Columbia signing is in *Knute Rockne,* page 208, and he also refers to President Walsh's poker playing; Grantland Rice's column was in the *New York Herald-Tribune,* 11 December

1925. The story of Rockne's conversion is told by many authors, in greatest detail by Brondfield, *Rockne,* pages 163–67.

On page 204 of the text, Joe Byrne, Jr.'s account of Rockne's reaction to the newspaper headline is in a letter to President Walsh, 16 December 1925 (UPWL 53/10). In this letter, Byrne, referring to a telephone call between the N.D. president and Rockne, congratulated Walsh for his calm during this crisis: "If you had told him [Rockne] over the phone on Friday night [when the news broke] that Notre Dame was through with him [Rockne], I would not have been surprised, and it is a great satisfaction to know that such good sense and fair dealing was displayed by you in such a trying situation." It was probably this or a later telephone call from President Walsh to Rockne that Wallace quoted.

Rockne's comment that he "took a man's word" was made to Ivan Gaddis, 17 December 1925 (UADR 12/14); the coach condemned the press to D. R. Connell, 17 December 1925 (UADR 10/12). The Associated Press sent out Knapp's statement nationwide, among the hundreds of papers that ran it was the *New Orleans Times Picayune,* 12 December 1925. Brondfield, *Rockne,* repeats the hagiographers' version of events, pages 192–95. The coach made his statement to the *Chicago Tribune,* 15 December 1925.

On page 205 of the text, President Walsh's memorandum with Rockne, 18 December 1925, is in UPWL 53/10. Joe Byrne, Jr.'s, letter to Walsh, 14 December 1925, about the press taking a "poke at our old friend Rock," is in UPWL 53/10; the specific writer to whom Byrne referred was Ed Hughes of the *New York Evening Telegram,* and he made his "glistening coat of whitewash" crack on 20 December 1925. Westbrook Pegler called Rockne "a hick on Broadway" in the *Chicago Tribune,* 16 December 1925. That same year, Rockne told Colonel H. J. Koehler, 29 October 1925 (UADR 20/106): "I do not know Westbrook Pegler and have never met him but you can say to anyone you want to that the article [he wrote about me] is a rotten lie." Their feud would simmer throughout the 1920s. According to Francis Wallace, even Joe Byrne, Jr., took a shot at the famous coach: "After it was all over, Rock and Joe Byrne were walking in the rain. A few bits of paper were floating down the gutter. 'Don't sign any of those,' Byrne ordered" (*Knute Rockne,* page 222).

On page 206 of the text, C. S. "Cy" Sherman advised Rockne not to buy "the Brooklyn bridge," 15 December 1925 (UADR 23/3). The 1925–1926 volume of the *Dome* printed the headlines and photos on page 370. Rockne complained about his work being "an open book" to Lawrence Perry, 21 December 1925 (UADR 17/156), and he told L. V. Novak, 2 January 1926, about the "changed matters" in the N.D. athletic department (UADR 17/2). Father Carey's report is in UVMU 2/40.

Because such key documents as the secret memorandum have not interested writers on Rockne, they have floated other explanations for his fiasco with Columbia. A popular one is that Rockne suffered a "nervous breakdown" from the pressure of continuous work over the years and that he was not "mentally balanced" in late 1925. Arch Ward first retailed this story in the *Chicago Tribune,* 19 December 1925, and the Rockne hagiographers repeated versions of it. However, the coach's extensive correspondence during this period shows absolutely no signs of mental deterioration.

He was, however, embarrassed by the events, and possibly for that reason and/or because he wanted to get away from Notre Dame and the daily reminders of his diminished powers after the Columbia episode, he accepted Joe Byrne, Jr.'s, invitation to accompany him to Europe in early 1926; he enjoyed the ocean voyages and his visit to the Continent.

A few years later, when Lou Little moved from Georgetown to Columbia, Rockne, on 24 December 1929, congratulated him and noted, "I was interested in watching your selection of schools, Lou, and I think if anybody can put this Columbia thing over you can and if they are paying you the money that the papers say, more power to you." Little went on to a long happy career at the Ivy school, eventually being nicknamed "Columbia Lou" (UADR 14/160).

23. ANTI-AIRCRAFT FIRE FROM THE BIG TEN: 1926

For the source of the opening quote by Rockne to Jesse Harper, 17 March 1926, see UADR 13/32; for the comments of Father Crumley and the letter to Rev. George Finigan, 18 March 1926, see UVMU 2/74; for the Carnegie Foundation's correspondence with Notre Dame, Howard Savage's letter to Rockne, 29 March 1926, and Rockne's reply, 8 April 1926, see UADR 19/26; and for President Walsh's letter to Savage, 27 September 1926, see UPWL "sa #4" folder.

Rockne pointed out to the Carnegie Foundation that "proselyting [recruiting] by alumni" was a key problem area; aware that this was the Big Ten's greatest weakness, he wryly noted, "there is still too much hypocrisy in its discussion." The Savage letter to Rockne, 29 March 1926, and Rockne's reply, 8 April 1926, are in UADR 19/62.

Throughout 1926, Rockne tried to maintain a low profile on reform issues. When his former press assistant George Strickler, now with the *Chicago American,* asked him about the proposal to abolish scouting of future opponents, he wired back: "Better to scout openly and honorably the football games than to have teams use bootlegged information. There is enough hypocrisy to college athletics now without adding to it. Please do not use my name." Telegram to Rockne from Strickler, 14 October 1926; telegram to Strickler from Rockne, 14 October 1926 (UADR 20/19).

On pages 208–9 of the text, the source of Harper's correspondence with Rockne about N.D.'s admission bid to the Big Ten is UADR 13/32: letter to Rockne, 7 April 1926; Rockne reply, 8 April 1926; Harper letter to Rockne, 7 May 1926; Rockne letter to Harper, 20 May 1926; Harper letter to Rockne, 27 May 1926; Rockne letter to Harper, 3 June 1926 and 14 June 1926. The Notre Dame proposal to the Big Ten, 25 May 1926, is in UADR 21/106.

On page 209 of the text, the details of McCarthy's intrigue against Rockne are in Ray Eichenlaub's letter to President Walsh, 21 May 1926 (UVMU 2/48). Walsh's reply to Eichenlaub, 26 May 1926, was typical of his behind-the-scenes control and his ability to pave over dissent (UPWL "Ei-En" folder). He assured the alum that the complaints against Rockne were in the past and that the coach and N.D. were proceeding with a clean "slate." Of course, he had the secret memorandum signed by

Rockne after the Columbia fiasco in his drawer; in addition, Walsh told the alum not to mention McCarthy's visit to anyone.

On page 209 of the text, Rockne's letter to Griffith, 24 September 1926; Griffith's reply, 25 September 1926; Rockne's reply, 27 September 1926; and Rockne's long explanation, 24 November 1926, are in UADR 12/83. Other Rockne letters on this position were to John R. Flynn, 8 September 1926 (UADR 11/149), and to Ralph Jones, 24 September 1926 (UADR 13/170).

Rockne's communication with Griffith about officiating choices, 26 February 1926, is in UADR 12/82. In this letter, Griffith also stated, "If any of these are not entirely satisfactory, let me know and I will see that the change is made." Normally Rockne would have vetoed Morton of Michigan, but not in 1926. For Griffith's letters to Rockne on 27 October 1926, 29 October 1926, and 3 November 1926, see UADR 12/83. Rockne complained about the ninety-five yards in penalties in a letter to Fred Dawson, 12 March 1927 (UADR 10/40); he made his "Big Ten suckhole" comment to Griffith on 5 November 1926 (UADR 12/83).

Fielding Yost vilified Notre Dame for many years; even a flattering biography, *Fielding Yost's Legacy to the University of Michigan* by John R. Behee, Ann Arbor, 1971, page 203, quotes him as writing to John Griffith in late December 1926:

> I was in Battle Creek at the Battle Creek College football banquet and found that they have played Bronson [*sic*] Hall, of Notre Dame, in one of their football games. . . . In other words, they [N.D.] are without restriction, they have competition for all their teams, hall teams, freshmen teams and second teams—they can play as long as they like and can be absent from college two weeks, and so far as I know, never have a man ineligible scholastically that was a good varsity man. In other words, we are furnishing all the funds and prestige to help maintain the institution athletically in the course it is pursuing.

Considering Notre Dame's restrictions on its teams in 1926, Yost's comments illustrate the depth of his hatred for the Catholic school. Moreover, his concluding remark makes no sense—possibly he meant that if N.D. had been admitted to the Big Ten, the conference would have furnished "all the funds . . ." Yet N.D., like all Big Ten schools, would have been required to pay its own way. Finally, the bigotry of Fielding Yost, like all irrational prejudice before and since, was nonsense.

On page 210 of the text, the wire service inquiry to Rockne was from Tim J. O'Connell, 14 November 1926 (UADR 17/14). Rockne replied to O'Connell on 20 November 1926 (UADR 17/14). The *Minnesota Daily,* the student paper at the University of Minnesota, endorsed N.D.'s bid on 20 November 1926. Rockne's reply to the Minnesota student journalist E. M. Carlin, 22 November 1926, is in UADR 9/42. An excellent articulation of the fans' opposition to N.D.'s joining the Big Ten came from a lawyer in Iowa, Richard G. Swift, 10 November 1926 (UADR 19/23).

The November attack on Notre Dame by Stagg and Yost appeared in, among other newspapers, the *Chicago Evening Post,* 10 November 1926. The Chicago coach and A.D. was Notre Dame's other implacable antagonist throughout the 1920s. In a

letter to Father Michael Mulcaire, at the time Notre Dame vice president, an important N.D. alum wrote, "I had represented the *Chicago Tribune* at Notre Dame for
four years and Stagg was always harping on [N.D.'s cheating, claiming that N.D. had
a prep school and trained players for years] prior to . . . playing on the varsity, [but]
no one ever saw anything but Stagg, and no one ever presented any evidence to
substantiate Stagg's charges" (copy of Ambrose O'Connell to Mulcaire, 30 March
1929, UVMU 2/44). In fact, President Burns ended the prep school in 1921.

On page 210 of the text, Rockne's angry note to a Chicago sportswriter, Harvey
Woodruff, 18 November 1926, is in UADR 21/176. McCarthy's comments about the
conference meeting are in Arthur, page 342, based on C.S.C. papers, as is McCarthy
to Finigan, 30 November 1926.

Rockne's comment on Fielding Yost's religious prejudices came in a letter to Pat
Malloy, 22 April 1929 (UADR 15/120). For more on Christy Walsh's activities, see his
Adios to Ghosts. Rockne never forgave Michigan for its insults to him and Notre
Dame; in the spring of 1927, when he learned that Morton was assigned to work the
Colorado (Denver campus) game against Iowa the following season, he spontaneously
wrote to Colorado coach Fred Dawson: "You will pardon my intrusion but I notice
that Morton is working one of your Big Ten games next fall," and he warned the
coach to watch this official carefully because his "kind of officiating shows that you
might not get . . . a fair break" (12 March 1927, UADR 10/40). At other times, he
openly rooted against the Wolverines; in the fall of 1927 he casually remarked to
"Doc" Spears, coach at Minnesota, "I certainly hope you take Michigan Saturday
with a big score" (17 November 1927, UADR 16/90). The 1929 Carnegie Foundation
report contains an excellent index that leads directly to its criticisms of Big Ten
athletic programs.

On page 212 of the text, the correspondence on the refusal to play in "Cubs Park"
is in a telegram to Rockne from Frank Carson, 23 September 1926, and a Rockne
telegram to Carson, 24 September 1926 (UADR 9/48). For McCarthy's comment on
Father Carroll, 16 August 1926, see UPWL "McA-McD, #9" folder. Rockne's remarks about the Minnesota game are in his letter to John Neeson, 7 October 1926
(UADR 16/169), and the payout at Minnesota is in UABM "Semi-Annual Financial
Statements—Football, 1924–30" folder.

Francis Wallace's comments about Rockne's system are from *Huddle*, page 120.
Rockne's defense of his shift appeared in the *New York World*, 12 November 1926.
Stuhldreher's observations are in his *Knute Rockne*, page 113. For all of Rockne's
public disclaimers that his varsity football players were just ordinary Notre Dame
students, increasingly they were a special breed, recruited and trained to play college
football at the highest possible level. The previous year, the sports editor of the
Dayton (Ohio) *Journal*, had complained that one of the N.D. interhall teams scheduled to play in nearby Middletown, Ohio, had been falsely advertised as a Fighting
Irish unit; Rockne replied, 27 October 1925 (UADR 10/85): "These boys on the
Walsh Hall team are a *bunch of amateurs* with but very little ability and they are just
as they are advertised—the Walsh Hall Team" (emphasis added).

The sellouts for the 1926 Northwestern and Army games were discussed in detail in Chicago and New York newspapers during the days preceding the October 23 and November 13 contests, particularly see the *Chicago Tribune* and the *New York Herald-Tribune*. Rockne criticized the Chicago alums in letters to Daniel J. O'Connor, 12 October 1926 (UADR 17/47), and Thomas J. Shaughnessy, 20 October 1926 (UADR 19/93). For the scalpers' price in Chicago see the *Chicago Tribune*, 22 October 1926. The payout for N.D. in Evanston is in UABM "Semi-Annual Financial Statements—Football, 1924–30" folder.

On page 215 of the text, Rockne's letter to Gerald Craugh on 2 November 1926 is in UADR 10/43; Rockne also noted in this letter: "There is only one way to pack the bowl [stadium] full of people and that is to have a good football team and I have been working my head off along that line."

For the controversy between N.D. officials and the New York alums concerning the ticket allotment for the 1926 Notre Dame–Army game, see President Walsh to John Balfe, 25 September 1926, and John Balfe to Rev. Geo. Finigan, 21 June 1926 (UADR 8/68); Rockne to E. G. Barrow, 29 September 1926 (UADR 8/88); and Rockne to Rev. P. J. Carroll, 19 October 1926 (UADR 9/156). The quote from the *New York World* is in the 13 November 1926 edition; McCready Huston wrote about the scalpers in Grand Central Station, page 72.

The New York Yankee employee whom Ed Barrow sent with the tickets to South Bend was Paul Krichell, at the time a young scout with the team (E. B. Barrow letter to Rockne, 26 October 1926, UADR 8/90). Krichell discovered such players as Lou Gehrig and Phil Rizzuto and, at a tryout camp, he converted "Whitey" Ford from a first baseman to a pitcher.

Notre Dame was also asked by John T. Balfe in a letter to Rev. George Finigan, 21 June 1926, to distribute seats to alumni from other institutions—almost two thousand to other Catholic alumni groups in New York, fifteen hundred to "Local [New York] Clubs of Big Ten" schools; and seven hundred to Ivy alumni groups—the upscale status of the fans at Notre Dame–Army games continuing throughout the 1920s (UADR 8/68).

For the correspondence with Rockne about tickets for sportswriters, see Al Nagel to Rockne, 3 November 1926, and Rockne to Nagel, c/o Byrne, 5 November 1926 (UADR 9/23). The telegram from Harry M. Stevens to Rockne, 28 October 1926, and the reply, 28 October 1926, are in UADR 19/26.

Allison Danzig's comment was in the *New York Times,* 12 November 1926; Paul Gallico's remarks as well as the *New York Daily News*'s betting chart were in the 13 November 1926 edition of that paper. The N.D. football team's itinerary was in the *New York Sun,* 12 November 1926.

On page 216 of the text, the note from Walter Eckersall was dated 3 November 1926; Rockne replied, 6 November 1926: "Dear Eckie, I am enclosing one ticket for the game in New York as per your note. We will be at the Hotel Vanderbilt and if you will drop around there about 12:00 o'clock we will be very glad to haul you out as usual" (UADR 11/67).

The *New York Daily News*'s use of the "Irish" nickname occurred on 14 November 1926, and its article on Flanagan's family background appeared on 15 November

1926. Grantland Rice flogged his "Horseman" metaphor in the *New York Herald-Tribune,* 14 November 1926. Newspapers of the 1920s, including the *Notre Dame Scholastic,* spelled Christy Flanagan's first name with a *y.* For some reason, such current historians of N.D. football as Joe Doyle spell it "Christie." Flanagan's schoolmates' choice, as well as his own—he signed "Christy" on his article "Speaking of a Genuine Thrill" (N.D. *Scholastic,* 1926 edition, page 250)—seems most accurate.

Rice's request to Rockne for his *Collier's* magazine All-America team, 14 November 1926, and the coach's reply 16 November 1926, are in UADR 18/89. The N.D. coach had agreed to select an "All-America" team for Christy Walsh's syndicate but privately he supplied Rice with names for the latter's competing *Collier's* magazine team. The New York writer assured Rockne that the information "will be treated in a confidential manner" with no one learning of the coach's contribution. Rice asked Rockne to wire him at his private magazine, *The American Golfer,* not his newspaper, the *New York Herald-Tribune.* In an age when reading telegrams addressed to other people, especially famous ones, was standard office procedure, Rice used his magazine as his private mail drop; see Rice to Rockne, 29 October 1926, and Rockne to Rice, 2 November 1926 (UADR 18/89).

Joe Vila's article about Rockne's downfield blocking appeared in the *New York Sun,* 15 November 1926. The term for downfield blocking in the 1920s was "interference"; because, in football terminology, this came to have a different and negative meaning, I have used "downfield blocking" in the text. However, the earlier meaning is still found in such colloquial expressions as "running interference" for someone. The Frank Leahy comment on Rockne's coaching technique is in, among other places, Twombley, page 71.

On page 218 of the text, Christy Walsh's letter to Rockne, 27 March 1926, about attending the Army-Navy game at Chicago is in UADR 21/40. Francis Wallace wrote his comment in the *New York Post,* 15 November 1926. Christy Walsh outlined his arrangements for Rockne in Chicago in letters to the coach on 9 October 1926 (UADR 21/45) and 18 October 1926 (UADR 21/44). Walsh's request concerning the early editions is in a copy of a letter to Walsh from W. W. Waymarch of the *Des Moines Register* that the agent sent to Rockne (UADR 21/45). Christy Walsh articulated his worries about the plan on 18 August 1926; Rockne dismissed his worries on 3 August 1926 (UADR 21/43). The N.D. coach complained about Judge Walter Steffen to Nick Kearns, 13 April 1925 (UADR 14/43).

Steffen's pregame quote is from Francis Wallace's *Knute Rockne,* page 198. The best account of the Carnegie Tech game and Hunk Anderson's coaching is in the *Notre Dame Scholastic,* 1926–1927, pages 345–46; the *New York Herald-Tribune* stories appeared on 28 November 1926, W. B. Hanna writing the N.D. one. Contemporary sports historians Bill Cromartie and Jody Brown made their comment in *The Glamor Game,* Nashville, Tenn., 1989, page 8. The *Chicago Tribune's* game story appeared 28 November 1926. The 1926 poll results are in Perrin, *Football,* page 127; the quote is in Doyle, *Fighting Irish,* page 82, and also in Scrapiron Young's *With Rockne,* pages 85–86.

On page 220 of the text, Christy Walsh's request for Rockne to be as conspicuous as possible in Chicago came in two letters on 18 November 1926 (UADR 21/45); see also his "Promotion Ad No. 2," reproduced in the photo insert and in UADR 21/44. The Rockne–Christy Walsh correspondence for 1926 contains many surprises—the foremost being Walsh's honesty about the problems facing Rockne if he missed the Carnegie Tech game. In a letter to Rockne on 18 August 1926, Walsh conveyed a warning from "Pop" Warner before the season not to take Steffen's team too lightly (UADR 21/43). However, considering the N.D. coach's rivalry with Warner, probably Rockne thought that his competitor was trying to scare him away from the Army-Navy game—after all, Stanford was scheduled to play that afternoon and Warner was not planning to coach his team.

After the coach's death in 1931, such hagiographers as Scrapiron Young concocted the "scouting Navy" story, twisting the fact that earlier in the 1926 season Rockne had skipped the N.D.–Indiana game to scout Army (but for the following week's— not the following year's—game). The volume of "Saint Knute" propaganda and the silence of his enemies, who chose "not to speak badly of the dead," helped cover up the real reasons for the N.D. coach's absence in Pittsburgh. By the time of Steele's *Knute Rockne,* the story was in concrete: "For the 1926 game with Carnegie Tech, Rockne decided to go to Chicago to scout a new opponent for 1927, Navy, who was then playing Army at Soldier Field."

The journey to the USC game is described at length in Francis Wallace's *O'Reilly of Notre Dame* and in Cromartie and Brown; the headline "N.D. DEFEAT DE-TRACTS . . ." appeared in the *Chicago Tribune,* 28 November 1926. The Sunday editions, 5 December 1926, of the *Chicago Tribune* and *Los Angeles Times* provided excellent game stories, as did the *Notre Dame Scholastic,* 1926–1927, page 374. In the spring of 1927, the *Scholastic* bid farewell to "Arthur Parisien, the tiny quarter-back whose ambidextrous passes . . ." page 458. He transferred to Boston University (he was from Haverville, Massachusetts) but later returned to N.D. as an assistant coach.

The first N.D.–USC game was the beginning of Rockne's friendship with Ben Frank of the Ambassador Hotel in Los Angeles. In addition, after the game, the coach attended a ball in Los Angeles for the "Hebrew Sheltering & Home" of that city: see B. Rosenburg telegram to Rockne, 12 November 1926, and Rockne reply, 18 November 1926 (UADR 18/50). Rockne had many Jewish friends—he was particularly close to Bernard "Buck" Hennes of Chicago, an N.D. grad. The coach was a Judeophile, often speaking before Jewish groups and for Jewish causes, and also recruiting Jewish players for the Fighting Irish.

The payouts for the USC and Army games, and other football receipts, are in UABM "Semi-Annual Financial Statements—Football, 1924–30" folder. For the postseason game turndown referred to on page 222 of the text, see Rockne telegram to Al Cusick, 22 November 1926 (UADR 10/74). The Calvin Coolidge quote is in *Familiar Quotations: John Bartlett,* sixteenth edition; Justin Kaplan, general editor; Boston, 1991, page 614. For Rockne's contract, see UPWL 53/10 "Rockne—Columbia Incident" folder. The N.D. coach's disclaimers about inventing various football strategies occurred frequently, a typical one in a letter to Walter Eckersall of the

Chicago Tribune. After hiring "Eckie" for the 1925 Army game and a number of other contests that year, the newspaperman reciprocated, in part by informing Rockne on 2 October 1925: "We are doing a series of articles on Big 10 coaches but I told the powers that be here such a series would not be complete without a word or two about you." Eckersall asked Rockne for some facts about his coaching career and the N.D. mentor replied, 6 October 1925, with a modesty at odds with Rockne's later hagiographers: "I don't claim to have originated [offensive formation] stuff that was being used by Stagg, Warner and others 15 years before I began coaching" (UADR 11/67).

In 1926, Walter Eckersall kept up his usual barrage to try to obtain refereeing assignments from Rockne, writing him, 16 November 1926, about 1927 games: "In picking your officials for next fall, I wish you would get busy as soon as possible. I am not so keen for this conference business and would like to be in your Army, Navy and Southern California games." Rockne replied, 17 November 1926, that he could have all three games (UADR 11/67).

24. KNUTE K. ROCKNE INC.

Grantland Rice wrote to Rockne, 2 March 1925 (UADR 18/89); Rockne's friend, Harry Costello, advised him to play Walsh off other newspaper syndicates, 20 February 1923 (UADR 10/22); William Abbott wrote to Rockne, 13 December 1923 (UADR 7/100); for Bill Roper's problems with Princeton, see the letter to William Abbott from Henry M. Snevily, 13 December 1923 (UADR 7/100). Christy Walsh offered his self-justification in *Adios to Ghosts,* pages 14–15. The best biography of Babe Ruth is Robert Creamer's *Babe: The Legend Comes to Life,* New York, 1974.

The figures on Christy Walsh's payments to Rockne in 1924 and 1925 are in UADR 21/40; Rockne disclosed the figures on his book, *Coaching,* in a letter to Glenn "Pop" Warner, 18 February 1927 (UADR 21/72). The *Notre Dame Scholastic,* 1925–1926 volume, reprinted William Abbott's profile on Rockne, pages 377–78; the N.D. coach received a letter from a writer, Herbert R. Mayes, 17 November 1927, doing a biography of Horatio Alger, Jr., and asking for his opinion on the series; Rockne replied, 1 December 1927: "As a boy I read the Horatio Alger works. . . . They created a fine impression and stimulated ambition" (UADR 15/38). Rockne's story so came to exemplify the American immigrant saga that a half century later, *Life* magazine, in its Special Bicentennial Issue, proclaimed him, along with Andrew Carnegie and Albert Einstein, one of the three greatest immigrants in the nation's history.

On page 225 of the text, Rockne's letter to W. E. "Doc" Meanwell, 1 September 1927, is in UADR 16/37. Rockne's escalating income from his coaching schools can be charted in his correspondence: in a letter to him from J. W. Tasker, 10 October 1923, the agreed fee "for a three weeks coaching school" at the College of William and Mary was $500 (UADR 22/58); on 8 November 1924, M. Ellwood Smith of Oregon State proposed $1,000 for less than two weeks' work (UADR 22/56); and Rockne told W. E. Meanwell, 27 October 1925, that he had been offered $1,500 for ten days at Oregon State in 1926 (UADR 16/34). Rockne informed John Callahan, 27 April 1927, of the N.D. salary for the athletic department's business manager, and mentioned that secretary Ruth Faulkner was at $1,800 (UADR 9/36). Various historians of Notre Dame football mention his coaching schools but seem unaware of or unwilling to divulge how much money he made from them: Joe Doyle, page 81; Brondfield in his biography, *Rockne,* acknowledges that the coach "held seven or eight each summer" but suggests that he was doing it simply to spread his football gospel, pages 214–15; and Jim Crowley, in *We Remember Rockne,* said that Rockne "was coaching as many as 5,000 high school coaches a year," page 96. My calculation for Rockne's maximum annual revenue from the coaching schools was computed by multiplying the total number of students at his schools by his $25-per-student fee, adding in his income from the short stints, and subtracting Meanwell's cut plus probable expenses.

Rockne mentioned his 1925 enrollment in a letter to J. T. Peppard, 6 June 1925 (UADR 11/6); the coach discussed his arrangement for his students to gain "two semester hours" of Notre Dame credit in a letter to L. B. Maplesdon, 26 August 1927 (UADR 15/124). Rockne made his comment about *"the school"* in a letter to Bill "Stub" Allison, 2 April 1925 (UADR 7/120). Rockne had many revenue-producing ideas that were ahead of his time; in a letter, 13 February 1925, to John F. Meagher, who was helping out with a coaching school in Texas, Rockne asked, "see if you cannot get one of the sporting goods houses to donate three of their basket balls and three of their footballs to be used as an advertisement in the school" (UADR 22/51). When the N.D. coach went with Wilson in 1926, he arranged this for all of his schools.

Rockne's correspondence files are filled with letters to and from his coaching school partner, W. E. "Doc" Meanwell, concerning their business operation. In addition, various pamphlets for their schools survive; a typical one is the sixteen-page glossy brochure for the 1927 school held at Southern Methodist University (PATH, Rockne Series/"Summer Coaching Schools & Camps" folder). "Doc" Meanwell was an ambiguous character; throughout his career at Wisconsin he was accused of various irregularities, and in 1936, as athletic director, he went before the school's board of regents on charges that he had given football players whiskey as a stimulant before games and a relaxant after (*Detroit News,* 29 January 1936). This incident ended his Big Ten career.

Rockne stated his "usual fee . . . $2,000" in a letter to T. W. Thordarson, 10 September 1928 (UADR 16/145). Rockne begged off some of the schools in a letter to W. E. Meanwell, 10 December 1927 (UADR 16/38); he informed the Camp Rockne prospective parent, Cecilia A. Knox, 31 May 1928, about his absences (UADR 22/45); and his partner Frank Hayes wrote to him, 30 April 1925 (UADR 22/37).

Rockne wrote R. H. Blackwell, 24 February 1928, about the application from Texas College (UADR 22/119). The other correspondence for this section of the text is: Dean H. D. English to Rockne, 26 January 1928; Ruth Faulkner to Dean H. D. English, 9 February 1928; R. N. Blackwell to Rockne, 21 February 1928 (UADR 22/119); and Rockne to Sol Butler, sporting editor, the *Chicago Bee,* 11 May 1926

(UADR 8/44). Another "coach in a Negro school," S. E. Williams, wrote to Culver Academy, 20 April 1925, about attending the Rockne-Meanwell "coaching school" there; a copy of the "refusal to accept your [Williams's] application" by C. C. Chambers of Culver, 22 April 1925, was sent to Rockne; Chambers also sent a copy to Rockne of his letter to W. E. Meanwell, 22 April 1925, stating that "the situation here at the Academy makes it necessary to refuse to accept applications from negroes to attend this [summer coaching] school." Rockne had the last word on 28 April 1925, writing Chambers that "I can only say that you took the only action possible for you to take." All of the letters concerning S. E. Williams are in UADR 22/48.

Not all schools shared Notre Dame's policies in this period. Rockne received a letter from the Sisters of the Blessed Sacrament of Xavier University in New Orleans, 23 June 1926, asking whether they could send two of their "colored" students, who would "assist in the coaching work next fall," to his coaching school on the Notre Dame campus; on 28 June 1926, Rockne's secretary forwarded the inquiry to him— he was doing a coaching school session in Oregon—and upon her letter he scrawled "No KKR" (UADR 22/97).

Rockne did employ a black trainer at N.D.; however, there are very few references to him in his correspondence. In a letter to H. G. Fischer, a salesman for a sports medicine firm, 8 July 1926 (UADR 11/108), Rockne related:

> Soon after you saw me I saw our colored trainer and shook him up very strongly for his carelessness in allowing liquids to gather on top of [the] cabinet machine, causing a short circuit. Shortly after that while I was gone, Dr. Clough was here and convinced Smith, our trainer, that the trouble was not with him but in the machine and offered to exchange it.

But Rockne did give the trainer a positive letter of recommendation, 22 November 1926 (UADR 19/10). G. W. Cox wrote to Rockne for the "Southern Teachers' Agency," 13 August 1926; Rockne answered Cox on 21 August 1926 (UADR 9/98). Z. G. Clevenger wrote to Rockne, 5 February 1920 (UADR 6/79), and 24 January 1925 (UADR 13/129). The head of Holy Trinity High School, Brother Theophilus, appealed to President Walsh for aid, 29 March 1923 (UPWL "Th #6" folder). James Armstrong's calculations on the number of Notre Dame men coaching are in *Onward to Victory*, page 261, and he based them on an article in the *Notre Dame Alumnus*, January 1926, pages 76–78. Foy Roberson, the North Carolina booster, wrote to Rockne, 19 October 1927, and the coach responded, 26 October 1927 (UADR 18/107); the president of the University of Wyoming, E. G. Crane, wrote to Rockne, 29 March 1927, and Rockne replied, 4 April 1927 (UADR 21/14); the letter to Rockne from the bishop of Sioux Falls, Rev. Bernard J. Mahoney, is dated 30 February 1928 (UADR 15/24).

Rockne wrote to Chet Wynne, 18 February 1927 and 21 November 1927 (UADR 21/184). James Phelan at Purdue asked Rockne for the favor, 26 October 1927, and the coach came through for him, 3 November 1927 (UADR 17/165). After Rockne's death and with the increasing professionalization of college coaching, the rest of the intercollegiate athletic world caught up with Notre Dame in the placement of ex-players into coaching. In the modern era, with no particular college functioning as "the cradle of coaches," only a few former N.D. players, like the alums of other schools, hold head coaching jobs. The Rockne files contain many letters from Basil Stanley, the 1917 team member, and to him, as well as Rockne comments about him to others; see Rockne to Stanley, 2 February 1925 (UADR 19/165–72), and Rockne to Pop Warner about Stanley, 10 May 1928 (UADR 21/73).

Pittsburgh banker H. A. Davis wrote to Rockne, 17 August 1925, and the coach replied to Davis, 24 August 1925 (UADR 10/84). Rockne wrote to Stuhldreher, 26 March 1926 (UADR 20/25). The Rockne hagiographers—portraying the N.D. coach as a leading reformer of the era—have spread the tale that he was against pro foot-ball; see Steele, page 218. As always, the sanctified Rockne is far from the real pragmatist, and in Steele's case, the biographer based his judgment on comments in a Rockne article by ghostwriter John B. Kennedy.

The letter from Jesse Harper to Rockne, 19 February 1925, and Rockne's replies, 25 February 1925 and 11 March 1925, are in UADR 13/31. Rockne wrote to Profes-sor O. F. Long of Northwestern, 24 February 1925 (UADR 16/200).

Francis Wallace commented on and quoted from the Westbrook Pegler column in *Knute Rockne,* page 10. Probably part of Rockne's feud with Pegler occurred because after the initial hostility in 1925, the N.D. coach tried to court him, in 1927 even hunting up tickets to the Army game for the journalist's mother (Pegler was covering the Yale-Princeton match) and giving him a special interview before the Navy contest; see Pegler telegram to Rockne, 8 November 1927, and Rockne's reply, 9 November 1927; Pegler telegram to Rockne, 12 October 1927, and Rockne's reply, 13 October 1927 (UADR 17/141). But the acerbic Pegler was not a man easily charmed, and he simply took what he wanted from people and went his own way. However, when Rockne became ill in 1929, Pegler did send him a warm get-well telegram; see page 315 of the text.

Chet Grant's comments are in CJWC, *Autobiography of Knute Rockne* Series "Statement of Chet Grant" folder, emphasis added. The quote from Francis Wallace's *Huddle* is on pages 222–23, and the ones from Huston, *Salesman from the Sidelines,* are on pages vii and 8. The quote from Rockne's contract with the Wilson Athletic Equipment Company, 17 May 1927, and his remuneration from it are in UADR 21/145. See the letters from G. H. Adams of Draper-Maynard to Rockne, 2 June 1925 (UADR 11/1), and 27 October 1926 (UADR 11/2); the telegram to Rockne from "WILSON WESTERN SPORTING GOODS CO.," 10 May 1926, about mar-keting his ball on the West Coast, is in UADR 21/145; the copy of a letter to Rockne from L. B. Icely, president of Wilson, 10 February 1928, about the Rockne-Cadet line, is in UADR 21/135. Ruth Faulkner sent "several sheets of Mr. Rockne's letter-head" to W. L. Robb of Wilson, 16 January 1928; W. L. Robb informed Rockne about the stationery, 26 January 1928, and sent the advertising letter on a facsimile of University of Notre Dame Athletic Association stationery, 24 January 1928 (UADR 21/137).

Christy Walsh wrote Rockne about meeting Al Smith and Mayor Jimmy Walker,

31 March 1926 (UADR 21/40), and the agent asked Rockne to endorse Babe Ruth's Health Service, 19 October 1926; the coach agreed, 21 October 1926 (UADR 21/44). Barbasol Shaving Cream ran its Rockne ad in most issues of *Collier's* magazine during the fall of 1929. The example of Rockne's form letter to prospective buyers of his Olympic Tour package was sent to John H. McCormick, 23 February 1928 (UADR 22/137); Rockne's pal Jay Wyatt joked about "the story of the Bootleggers" to the coach, 28 March 1928 (UADR 22/137); and the coach wrote to Pop Warner, 10 May 1928 (UADR 19/145).

Rockne told "Curly" Byrd, 30 October 1928, about the Havana excursion (UADR 21/73); Byrd was head football coach at the University of Maryland and eventually became his school's president, fulfilling the dream of many athletic administrators of running their universities.

The hagiographers have paved over the reality of Rockne's entrepreneurial spirit and success: portraying him as selfless and unconcerned with personal wealth, even such a writer as Francis Wallace said: "Rock was a wonderful businessman for Notre Dame and all of football, but like many another genius a poor one for himself" (*Notre Dame Story*, page 237). In fact, excluding the ticket requests to Notre Dame games, the bulk of Rockne's correspondence files concerns his personal business deals and reveals the full extent of his attention to these matters as well as his success at supplementing his N.D. salary.

For the letter from Rockne, 28 December 1927, to Arthur J. Kennedy, see UADR 14/6. Harry Stuhldreher's comment is in his *Knute Rockne*, page 312; the telegram to Rockne from Father Olson, St. Mary's Church, 16 January 1928, and Ruth Faulkner's reply, 23 January 1928, are in UADR 14/137. Rockne wrote to Francis Wallace, 3 November 1927 (UADR 21/26).

W. Colston Leigh wrote to the N.D. coach, 7 December 1927 (UADR 14/139), and Rockne mentioned his standard titles to W. Colston Leigh, 1 March 1927 (UADR 14/137). W. Colston Leigh proposed the $400 figure to Rockne, 10 December 1927 (UADR 14/139). Leigh raised his offer, 19 March 1928; Rockne articulated President Walsh's objections in a letter to W. Colston Leigh, 22 March 1928 (UADR 14/141).

Francis Wallace's *Knute Rockne* contains the story that, in 1927, the N.D. coach received "Five hundred dollars for opening the [Chicago] Auto Show" and was both amazed and pleased, exclaiming, "Five hundred dollars for a twenty-minute talk. Hmmm!" Wallace termed this "Rockne's discovery of the Wonderful World of Easy Money" (page 251).

The letter from Rockne to Harry J. Allen, 14 November 1928, is in UADR 7/82, and Ruth Faulkner told Moray Eby, 28 February 1929, about her boss's travels (UADR 11/65). A. R. Erskine sent C. C. Hanch's letter to Rockne, 3 October 1929, and Rockne replied, 9 October 1929 (UADR 11/92). McCready Huston quotes Rockne's standard opening for his Studebaker sales talk in his chapter "The Typical Rockne Sales Address" (see page 95 for the quote in the text). Frank Leahy informed Wells Twombley about how much the coach earned from Studebaker in Twombley, page 148; Paul Castner, who worked for Studebaker during this period, discussed

Rockne's remuneration in *We Remember Rockne,* pages 172–73; these accounts differ a bit but both mention $10,000. Paul "Bear" Bryant of Alabama was the first post-Rockne college coach to hit six figures in annual income, but to measure Rockne's pioneering accomplishment, consider the fact that John Wooden never made more than $25,000 a year from UCLA after winning NCAA men's basketball championships in the 1960s and 1970s (*College Sports Inc.,* page 152).

McCready Huston quotes from Rockne's standard Studebaker speech, pages 96–97, mentions "football applied to life" on page 88, and tells how the firm "handled Rockne" on page 118. Ruth Faulkner conveyed her boss's turndown, 28 February 1929, to the coach and A.D. at Coe College, Moray Eby, a close enough friend that Rockne gave him a coveted game on the 1927 schedule (UADR 11/65). The obituary notice of Bob Nesbitt appeared in the *Terre Haute* (Indiana) *Star,* 2 April 1931. Robert Harron, in his *Rockne: Idol of American Football,* New York, 1931, referred to the $50,000 in vaudeville, pages 122–23.

On page 239 of the text, Homer Hogan of KYN asked Rockne to broadcast the 1928 game, 16 November 1928, and Rockne sent his bill to Hogan, 17 December 1928 (UADR 13/91). Rockne referred George W. Buck to Christy Walsh, 4 September 1929 (UADR 8/31); Delos Lovelace mentioned the radio contract "worth $30,000" on page 185. The *Notre Dame Scholastic* noted Rockne's new brokerage office in the 1930–1931 volume, page 186.

The stage directions from *Knute Rockne—All American* are based on the final shooting script (UABM *Knute Rockne—All American* Series/19 March 1940 script), and the dialogue is taken from the film. Rockne told the president of Notre Dame, Father Charles L. O'Donnell, that Universal Pictures had offered him $50,000 to play the role of the football coach; see page 351 of the text. Elmer Layden commented about Rockne's acting in his memoir, page 78. President Charles O'Donnell wrote to Carl Laemmle, Jr., the head of Universal Pictures, 28 September 1931 (UPCO 8/79).

One exception to the myth of Rockne as an innocent idealist is the portrayal of the coach by the Catholic writer Eugene C. Kennedy. His novel *Father's Day,* Garden City, N.Y., 1981, opens:

> Rockne, I always thought, was a noisy bastard, a brass band of a man forever crowding you and winking inside at his own tricks . . . he was cunning too . . . Such men don't have the time for grand introspective journeys. The world of action was the place for [them].

25. ANTI-AIRCRAFT FIRE FROM THE COLLEGE SPORTS REFORMERS: 1927

Rockne's run-in with O'Donnell in 1925 occurred because of quarterback Eddie Scharer, Harry Stuhldreher's replacement. Bill Hayes, a contractor in Saint Louis, sponsored Scharer at Notre Dame; on 25 July 1925, Hayes complained to Rockne about Father Hugh "Pepper" O'Donnell's expelling Scharer for breaches of discipline, and Hayes enclosed a copy of O'Donnell's letter to the athlete (UADR 12/117).

Apparently Rockne complained to O'Donnell, and although no copy of the letter exists, the priest told the coach, 4 August 1925: "You must have been beside yourself when you wrote such a letter. . . . I do want you to know that I am thoroughly displeased with your characterization of the members of the Committee who recommended such action in this case" (UADR 17/56).

Rockne was at a coaching school in Texas and he wrote Al Ryan, N.D. athletic department business manager, 5 August 1925, that on "things such as sharer's [*sic*] case we get a lot of dogma and authority. I don't know whether or not I care to return [to Notre Dame] if things are going to run along these lines. I cannot and will not be responsible for the stupid decisions of committees." Then, in a line that could have been his motto, he summed up: "I believe in results and when they can't be had the hell with it." Ryan tried to calm the coach, and on 10 August 1925, wrote, "hope you understand the pompousness of J. Hugh [O'Donnell] well enough not to pay too much attention to it" (UADR 18/139).

The final letter in the file is to Scharer in Saint Louis, 19 August 1925 (UADR 18/162), and it informs him: "I have seen the President and . . . it looks very good but sit tight and say nothing." The letter is a carbon copy and, like all of Rockne's carbons, without a pen signature; at the bottom, the writer called himself "Yours in the Bond." The contents are very characteristic of Rockne's letters of advice to his players, especially such lines as "Bill [Hayes?] tells me you are in great shape and have been taking wonderful care of yourself. You must do this, Eddie, and you will have to cut out your kid tricks." Scharer played in 1925.

On page 242 of the text, Father Joseph Boyle wrote to Rockne about his experiences as "a missionary," 2 December 1927 (UADR 8/11). The head of a Washington press syndicate, Frederic William Wile, wrote to President Walsh, 17 October 1927; Walsh replied, 2 November 1927; and Wile telegraphed Walsh, 7 November 1927 (UPWL "Wile #1" folder).

Voltmer, *A History of the Intercollegiate Conference,* discusses the proceedings and regulations of the Big Ten's "Committee of Sixty," pages 69–71. Rockne expounded on the problems in college sports to Frederic Ware, 13 October 1925 (UADR 21/70). Francis Wallace's article, "The Hypocrisy of College Football Reform," appeared in *Scribner's,* November 1927, pages 568–73, and the quote in the text is on page 571; Wallace outlined his mentor's role in its composition in *Notre Dame Story,* page 19. Wallace wrote Rockne, 16 April 1927, about the article, and on 21 April 1927, Rockne replied: "I would like very much to look over your manuscript for Scribner's and I have some information for you that might be interesting" (UADR 21/25). Wallace asked President Walsh for a comment, 26 October 192[7] (UPWL "Wal-Wag #2" folder).

The letter to Rockne from Lou Little of Georgetown, 6 April 1927, and Rockne's acceptance, 14 April 1927, are in UADR 14/159. Rockne wrote to Rip Miller about the prospect, 11 September 1928 (UADR 16/66). Charlie Bachman recommended two "Indian" players to Rockne, 2 February 1927, and the N.D. coach answered Bachman, 8 February 1927 (UADR 8/55), emphasis added. Rockne made his comment about Yost's personal jealousy to Glenn "Pop" Warner, 22 March 1927 (UADR

21/72). In the same letter, he mentioned the hiring of Haskell coach Dick Hanley by Northwestern and noted: "Fielding H. Yost was very much provoked at [this] appointment . . . and at a recent meeting in front of a lot of Athletic Directors he took occasion to pan you [Warner] very severely," presumably because of Warner's tricks at Carlisle involving Indian players and also at Stanford. "He also took Tad Jones [of Yale] and myself to task rather severely." Rockne also complained about Yost's opposition to the "Notre Dame shift," telling Colonel H. J. Koehler of West Point, 25 February 1927: "Mr. Yost is certainly very bitter against it, but for selfishness I think he takes the cake" (UADR 20/107).

On page 246 of the text, Rockne wrote to Florian Trares, 31 May 1928, replying to a letter from Trares, 26 May 1928 (UADR 20/52). Rockne answered Frank "Bodie" Andrews, 25 August 1926, in response to Andrews's recommendation of "a boy out here named John Murphy," 20 August 1926 (UADR 7/142). Wallace discussed his "bird-dogging" in *Notre Dame Story*, page 250, and used a comic code in a letter to Rockne, 26 January [1927] (UADR 21/25).

The quote from McCready Huston is on pages xii–xiii. For Ruth Faulkner's report to Father P. J. Carroll, 7 December 1926, see UADR 9/156. Frank Leahy told Wells Twombly about Rockne's red-shirting, in Twombly, page 62; when he coached at Notre Dame, Leahy used a similar system. Frank Carideo recalled spring practices in *We Remember Rockne*, page 152. On page 248 of the text, Rockne wrote the coach at St. Viator College, S. J. McAllister, 24 September 1928 (UADR 19/50). The statistics on the 1927 varsity are from a Rockne letter to Rev. Otis Moore, 3 December 1927, in which the coach says: "Of our first thirty-three boys seven of them are Protestant" (UADR 15/90), and a listing of the roster is in the *Notre Dame Alumnus*, October 1927, page 58.

To some observers, including Frank Leahy, who won a starting berth in 1929, the attrition system was cruel; however, few Fighting Irish hopefuls complained about their failure to grab the varsity brass ring, and many later bragged about their brush with Rockne's greatness. For some of them, trying out for Knute Rockne was superior to actually playing college football for another head man. In later years, as the coach's mystique grew, these Notre Dame alums became the most rabid supporters of his legend and of their alma mater's football teams.

An interesting example of Notre Dame's attraction for Catholic football players and the conflicts this raised with Rockne's "boys" coaching at other schools occurred during the fall of 1926. Chet Wynne at Creighton wrote his old coach (in September 1926): "Gordon Diesing my only quarterback informed me that he was leaving for Notre Dame," and also "Bertoglio from Butte [Montana] . . . If you don't mind I would like to have him back too." Rockne replied, 16 September 1926, that through a mix-up, the quarterback was admitted to N.D. but the other boy was not allowed in and the N.D. coach would try to send both back to Creighton (UADR 21/184).

By all accounts, Rockne could remember most of his players' names and skill levels. In addition, each summer he sent letters to many of his players telling them what he expected of them in the fall and how to prepare for the coming season.

On page 249 of the text, Rockne wrote about the "kind of" players he wanted for his system in a letter to A. A. Scott, 21 January 1927, and he referred to Scott's scouting and that of "old Red [Leo Ward]," another of his regular "bird dogs" (UADR 18/169).

For the Carnegie Foundation's comments on Notre Dame and the Big Ten schools, see the excellent index to "Bulletin 23"; for the quotes in the text on the recruiting systems, see pages 228, 236, and 238. In 1929, Frank Hering, an important N.D. alum, sent the new Notre Dame president, Father Charles O'Donnell, some of his "reflections" on big-time college football, 23 November 192[9] (UPCO 4/38) and also included a clipping from the *Chicago Herald-American,* 21 November 1929, in which the writer explained the subsidization system in the Big Ten, noting: "Northwestern, Purdue, Indiana, long weak in football, have in the last five years made determined efforts to secure athletes, with what results all who follow football know"; that is, excellent recent seasons. He then listed various star athletes and their supposed deals, adding, "Only Major Griffith knows the facts, and he won't tell."

The Carnegie Foundation's "Bulletin 23" defined subsidies on pages 240 and following. All athletic scholarships in this era and until the 1960s went to males, mainly football and basketball players—thus, the male pronoun for athletic scholarship holders. The Carnegie investigators did not cite Iowa for recruiting violations—however, the year that their report appeared, the Big Ten not only cited the school for massive misdemeanors but expelled it from the conference. In addition, the Carnegie report did not cite Illinois, however, a 1920s football team manager at the school, Paul Strohm, Sr., explained in detail to this writer how the fraternities recruited and sponsored players, and the Chicago papers frequently hinted at this.

On page 251 of the text, Rockne wrote to Edward D. Kelly, the alum with a high school "phenom," 21 February 1927; Kelly had written him, 17 February 1927 (UADR 14/3). Rockne sent the note to Rev. Patrick McBride about Frank Carideo, 17 September 1927 (UADR 15/150); John McMullan wrote Rockne about the New Orleans prospect, 26 August 1927, and Rockne replied to McMullan, 31 August 1927 (UADR 16/21), emphasis added. The N.D. coach wrote "Chile" Walsh, 4 August 1926 (UADR 21/39), and told John Wallace about his job, 9 August 1926 (UADR 21/30). Rockne wrote Chicago alderman George Maypole about John Bachman, 15 September 1927 (UADR 15/145), and about "Chunky" Murrin, 26 January 1928 (UADR 15/146). Frank Hayes offered the "phony" job in a letter to Rockne, 2 February 1927; the coach answered Hayes, 4 February 1927 (UADR 15/53). Rockne wrote to John P. Murphy, 1 February 1928; Murphy asked for tickets in a letter to Rockne, 5 October 1928, and the coach complied, 8 October 1928 (UADR 16/124).

Carnegie "Bulletin 23" discussed jobs at Notre Dame on page 264; Voltmer's study of the Big Ten detailed the "easy 'no work' jobs," pages 62–63. Rockne's letter to Chicago alderman George Maypole, 8 February 1927, is in UADR 15/145. Carnegie "Bulletin 23" had an excellent chapter, "The Recruiting and Subsidizing of Athletes," pages 224–66, that detailed the many abuses in these areas.

On page 254 of the text, Neil M. Fleming, Penn State athletic department manager, informed Rockne about his school's reform, 8 September 1927, and the N.D. coach answered Fleming, 20 September 1927 (UADR 17/148). Rockne wrote Rev.

Emiel DeWulf about players changing to earlier classes on 9 October 1928 (UADR 10/92).

Unlike the case at some of N.D.'s football rivals, no elaborate academic double standard for athletes existed at Notre Dame (USC and Georgia Tech were guilty of this). However, the N.D. coach was allowed some maneuverability in special cases: in 1928, when Father Thomas Steiner conducted the annual audit on eligibility for the athletic board, he ruled that seven football players had not made sufficient grades to play the next fall, 21 June 1928 (UADR 11/79). Rockne's secretary telegraphed the news and the players' names to her boss at his coaching summer school in Oregon, 21 June 1928; the list included two starters, John Niemic and John Chevigny, both important offensive players (UADR 11/79).

No record exists of the negotiations between Rockne and the Notre Dame administration on this issue, but the results are documented: three of the ineligibles never played a down for Notre Dame; one sat out the following season and subsequently suited up; the three others took summer school and played on the varsity in the fall—Niemic and Chevigny becoming heroes in the "Win One for the Gipper" upset over Army.

Wisconsin basketball coach W. E. "Doc" Meanwell, wrote to Rockne about Cavosie, 15 September 1927; the N.D. coach answered Meanwell, 17 September 1927 (UADR 16/37). Rockne told Paul Danculovic about his "weakness," 11 August 1926 (UADR 10/79), and the coach appealed to Rev. C. C. Miltner, 17 February 1927, on Danculovic's behalf (UADR 15/73). Father Hugh O'Donnell informed Danculovic of the end of his N.D. career, 5 August 1927, and sent a copy of the letter to Rockne (UADR 10/79). Rockne telegraphed Harry Mehre about the athlete, 7 September 1928 (UADR 16/47), and Danculovic thanked Rockne, 19 September 1928 (UADR 10/79). Both Cavosie and Danculovic were high-profile players, and their careers, including their departures from various schools, were followed by the press at the time.

Rockne wrote to Gus Dorais about the Detroit game against St. Louis, 7 November 1928, in response to Dorais's letter to Rockne, 4 November [1928] (UADR 10/193). Rockne wrote to G. A. Bisset, 8 November 1927, about the N.D. ban on "Charity [exhibitions] and games of this sort" (UADR 7/183). Rockne wrote to SMU athletic department business manager R. N. Blackwell, 25 April 1927 (UADR 19/136), about Notre Dame's refusal to play a postseason game. The N.D. coach asked his colleague at Minnesota, C. W. "Doc" Spears, 17 March 1927, to continue the series (UADR 16/90). The alums who wrote letters to Professor J. E. McCarthy in opposition to joining a new conference were John P. Murphy, 17 October 1927, and Frank Hering, 13 October 1927 (UVMU 2/61). President Walsh added his comment, 2 November 1927, in a letter to Frederic Wile (UPWL "Wile #1" folder). Edward "Moose" Krause talked about Rockne's hiring of refs in a telephone interview, 8 August 1991.

On page 258 of the text, Frank Birch wrote about the USC protest of his and Wyatt's work in a letter to Rockne, 15 July 1927; the N.D. coach informed Birch of the USC veto, 19 July 1927 (UADR 8/150). Birch asked Rockne for the following year's USC game, 19 December 1927, and Rockne told Birch that he would recommend him, 29 December 1927 (UADR 8/151).

On page 259 of the text, Big Ten commissioner Griffith asked Rockne for his advertising copy, 2 March 1927 (UADR 12/84), and on 29 November 1927 asked for "a short endorsement" of the *Athletic Journal,* Rockne sending his endorsement to Griffith, 3 December 1927 (UADR 12/84). Rockne wrote to the man at Michigan Agricultural, Ralph C. Huston, 18 January 1927 (UADR 17/67).

On page 259 of the text, the Big Ten Commissioner wrote Rockne about Walter Eckersall's game officiating assignments, 28 January 1927, and the coach replied, 31 January 1927 (UADR 12/84). Rockne notified Griffith about "Eckie and Lipp" doing a scrimmage, 17 September 1927, and the coach wrote Eckersall about his tickets, 28 September 1927 (UADR 12/85). Eckersall asked Rockne about "fresh dope," 13 March 1927 (UADR 11/67). Rockne's selection of Eckersall as head linesman, 20 September 1927, is in UADR 11/68, and his offer of $250 for publicity, 17 November 1927, is in UADR 11/68.

The Carnegie Foundation investigators noted "the newspaper publicity accorded to many coaches" in "Bulletin 23," page 184. N.D. ticket manager Art Haley told Ambrose O'Connell about the Chicago ticket sale, 30 November 1927 (UABM General Correspondence "0 1927" folder).

When "Eck" later wrote Rockne about payment for the publicity work, 6 December 1927 (UADR 11/68), he noted: "I did all that I possibly could on this sheet," the *Chicago Tribune;* and the N.D. coach replied, "The check for publicity should have reached you before now—I want you . . . to smoke up our Navy game [in Chicago] next fall if you care to." In the same letter, Rockne mentioned: "I am telling Griffith to hold up Army and Navy dates" next year to slot you as a game official, in addition to your other N.D. officiating assignments.

The Notre Dame alum with the childhood memory of "special cars for N.D. rooters and . . . bootleggers coming down the aisles" did not wish to be identified— he felt that anything that reflected negatively on his school, including the mention of the bootleggers, would bring criticism upon him by fellow alumni. However, a letter in the N.D. Archives very much backs up his story: Father J. P. Carroll wrote to Edward Gould, 2 November 1927, about drinking on the excursion trains (UVMU 2/48):

I have been informed that at the Detroit [away] game with Detroit University certain members of your [N.D. alumni] party on the train were given cards admitting them to the confidence of a well-known bootlegger. It is also quoted that you sold tickets to the Detroit–Notre Dame game at $6 a ticket [$2 above our price]. Finally, this week there comes information that in the train you are sponsoring to New York "licker" concessions have already been handed out. . . .

I know that the University would be very much aggrieved if in any excursions conducted by Notre Dame men, anything should happen unworthy of the traditions and reputation of the school. I am asking you, therefore, on every occasion when you assume responsibility for conducting Alumni trips, to make sure and guard the good name of your Alma Mater.

The *Notre Dame Alumnus* noted the crowd for the Coe game, November 1927, page 176. Rockne worried about the Detroit game in a letter to Joe Byrne, Jr., 5 October 1927 (UADR 9/25). Colonel J. P. O'Neill boasted to President Walsh about Baltimore, 4 December 1923 UADR 17/23. Westbrook Pegler covered the Navy game for the *Chicago Tribune,* 15 October 1927. Crowd statistics and game accounts are from the newspapers of the day, particularly the *Chicago Tribune,* the *New York Herald-Tribune,* and the *Notre Dame Scholastic.* Bronko Nagurski's comment about the 1927 game is in Wilson and Brondfield, page 156; he also said, "I don't think I ever forgave Fred [Hovde] until he became a Rhodes Scholar and later president of Purdue, and I figured I should be proud just to know him."

Grantland Rice wired Rockne for his All-America picks, 7 November 1927, and the coach replied, 8 November 1927 (UADR 18/89). N.D. Vice President P. J. Carroll commented about the Notre Dame–Army annual to General M. B. Stewart, 15 March 1927 (UPWL "St #3" folder); President Walsh told John P. Carroll, 4 August 1927, about his new ticket policy (UPWL "Caq-Caz" folder); Walsh turned down the ticket request of Ned Welch of the *New York Morning Telegraph,* 1 November 1927 (UPWL "Weh-Wem" folder). New York Justice Ernest L. Hammer wrote to Rockne, 19 October 1927, the N.D. coach replied, 27 October 1927 (UADR 13/15). Rockne was sarcastic about the N.D. alums to John Neeson, 26 October 1927 (UADR 16/170), and sent the tickets to "Rupe" Mills, 21 October 1927 (UADR 16/79). *Time Magazine* put Rockne on its cover, 7 November 1927.

On page 264 of the text, Rockne wrote to Herbert Bayard Swope of the *New York World,* 2 November 1927 (UADR 20/40). The *New York Sun* described the ticket demand, 10 November 1927; the *New York Daily News* ran its poem the same day, and announced its award for its "Pick 'Em" contest, 7 November 1927. The origin and meaning of the term "Subway Alumni" is difficult to pin down. In reading the New York papers of the era, this researcher discovered that the first writer who used it consistently was Paul Gallico in the *New York Daily News.* Other sportswriters, especially Grantland Rice, later took credit for originating the term, and some sports historians believe that it referred to Notre Dame fans who read newspaper articles about the Fighting Irish while riding the subways to work, hence the change from "Strap-hanging Alumni" to "Subway Alumni."

On page 265 of the text, Rockne was pessimistic about the Army game in a letter to Joe Byrne, Jr., 30 September 1927 (UADR 9/25). The *New York World,* 1 January 1927, carried an article, "Army Recruiting Football Stars for 1927," that is, those who had played out their eligibility elsewhere. Beach and Moore discuss this on pages 104–105, and Clary discusses the Army-Navy controversy throughout his chapters on the 1920s. New York journalist Paul Webster made his comment about Army men who "have played so much football" in the *New York World,* 12 November 1927. The *New York Daily News* ran the headline "KAYDET VETERANS . . ." on 8 November 1927, and remarked on N.D.'s green uniforms on 11 November 1927; the *New York World* discussed Rockne's "punishing" workout, 9 November 1927, and noted, 13 November 1927: "Rockne changed the players' numbers—it only deceived the people who paid 50 cents for a program." The game stories referred to in the text appeared in their newspapers, 13 November 1927; the *New York Times* also ran a feature on the "notables" in attendance that Sunday. Paul Gallico remarked on N.D.'s "incognito" in the *New York Daily News,* 15 November 1927; Walter Eckersall's article was in the *Chicago Tribune,* 13 November 1927.

On page 266 of the text, "Eck" offered his private thoughts about the Army game to Rockne, 14 November 1927 (UADR 11/86). The *Notre Dame Alumnus* commented on the Chicago city council and the USC game, September 1927, page 26. The *New York Daily News*'s predictions appeared on 19 November 1927, and the comments about the win over Drake were in the *Chicago Tribune,* 20 November 1927.

On page 267 of the text, Harvey Woodruff of the *Chicago Tribune* wrote to Rockne about tickets, 3 November 1927; the coach replied, 15 November 1927 (UADR 21/177). Rockne sent the seats for Colonel McCormick to Don Maxwell, 22 November 1927 (UADR 15/141). New York sportswriter W. B. Hanna observed the crowd spectacle for the *New York Herald-Tribune,* 27 November 1927; the *Chicago Tribune* headline ("RECORD CROWD"), photos, and stories appeared the same day. Including thousands of free passes, the crowd topped 120,000. The umpire who made the controversial decision during the USC–Notre Dame game was John Schommer. The usually calm and polite Howard Jones told a wire service, "I got this fellow John Schommer out of a hole once before on a blocked punt in the Michigan game [at Iowa in 1923]. I couldn't vouch for him again." The story was carried by the *Denver Post,* 30 November 1927, and Rockne made his comment about N.D.'s being "not in any way involved in the misunderstanding" in a letter to the editor of that newspaper, 28 December 1927 (UADR 10/151). An interesting postscript to the controversy occurred on 6 January 1928, when Griffith wrote Rockne about the N.D. coach's game officials for the 1928 season. John Schommer, who had never been a Rockne selection, now became one. The Big Ten commissioner noted, "since I did not know that you wanted Schommer, we had him down to umpire the Purdue-Northwestern game. . . . [I] will do what I can about Schommer if you insist" (UADR 12/86).

The final numbers for the 1927 Notre Dame football season are in UABM "Semi-Annual Financial Statements—Football 1924–30" folder. Rockne wrote Byron Kanaley, 28 December 1927, about the low income at home (UADR 14/31). The *Notre Dame Alumnus* carried the complaint about "the inadequacy of Cartier Field," November 1927, page 90. Minnesota ended the series, in part, because of the conference reform movement, but it also disliked the small payday at Cartier Field—for the 1927 game, Rockne thanked Dr. C. W. Spears of Minnesota, 11 November 1926, for assuming "the financial sacrifice which is necessary when coming to play at South Bend" (UADR 16/90).

Rockne wrote his letter of resignation to President Walsh, 28 November 1927 (UPWL 53/10). In *Knute Rockne,* Brondfield quotes the coach's desire for "a first class setting," page 181. Arthur paraphrases the argument by the members of the

C.S.C. order who preferred "the homey confines of Cartier Field," page 289; Francis Wallace quotes the N.D. official in *Knute Rockne,* page 209.

On page 269 of the text, Rockne explained the problems in Soldier Field to Commander Jonas Ingram of the Naval Academy, 17 December 1928 (UADR 20/118). The *New York Herald-Tribune* headlined "NOTRE DAME TO BUILD $800,000 STADIUM" on 17 November 1927. President Walsh's addendum is in UPWL "Stadium" #2 folder. Frank Hering, secretary of the committees, distributed it. The *Notre Dame Alumnus* discussed the stadium project in an article, "Stadium Proposed by Local Alumni Club," November 1927, pages 89–91. Arthur described President Walsh's objections and explained the committee's work, pages 288 and following; Francis Wallace explained President O'Donnell's role in the stadium construction in *Notre Dame People,* pages 154–55; McCready Huston paraphrased Rockne's arguments in his chapter "The Stadium, a Business Problem." Father Charles O'Donnell spoke to the *New York Times* about the stadium, 13 February 1929, and Arthur quotes his comments to the Provincial Council of the C.S.C., page 291.

Rockne wrote to P. P. Evans of the Osborn Engineering Company of Cleveland, Ohio, 23 October 1928 (UADR 11/96), and told R. N. Blackwell about the Osborn contract, 28 November 1929 (UADR 8/163). McCready Huston commented on "Notre Dame's stadium speculation," page 71.

26. AL SMITH AND "WIN ONE FOR THE GIPPER": 1928

Major John Griffith asked Rockne to support Hoover, 20 September 1928 (UADR 12/87); in *The First Hurrah,* Richard O'Connor commented on the "virulence" of the Republican campaign; also see Oscar Handlin's *Al Smith* and Edmund A. Moore's *A Catholic Runs for President* for details on the 1928 election. H. L. Mencken's observations on "the extent of bigotry" were in his column in the *Baltimore Evening Sun,* 5 November 1928, and the fears of the populace concerning Smith were discussed by Marion Elizabeth Rodgers in *The Impossible Mr. Mencken,* New York, 1991, pages 290–91. Father Andrew Greeley described the "Paddy" cartoon in his *The Irish Americans: The Rise to Money and Power,* New York, 1981, page 174; and Richard O'Connor mentioned the mockery of the Smiths as Maggie and Jiggs, page 210.

On pages 274–75 of the text, Rockne wrote to Griffith, 22 September 1928, about "the Smith people" (UADR 12/87). The coach complained to Charles A. Dean, in charge of an athletic magazine, 30 January 1928 (UADR 10/144); Rockne received a telegram from Millard E. Tydings of the Democratic national committee, 13 September 1928, and answered, 15 September 1928 (UADR 10/149). Tydings, later a distinguished U.S. senator, asked Rockne to address a national radio audience on the topic "Governor Smith—The Inspiration of America's Youth." Father Charles O'Donnell wrote Rockne about the electoral campaign, 7 September 1928 (UPCO 7/63), emphasis added. The *Notre Dame Alumnus* praised Smith in March 1929, page 196.

On page 276 of the text, Glenn Thistlethwaite consoled Rockne, 25 October 1928 (UADR 21/158); the N.D. coach wrote to George Strickler, 26 September 1928 (UADR 20/19). The *Chicago Tribune* commented on the Loyola opener, 30 September 1928, and the *Notre Dame Scholastic* on the loss to Wisconsin, 1928–1929 volume, page 118. Rockne sent tickets to Tom Barry of the *Herald Examiner*, 9 October 1928 (UADR 8/95); to Don Maxwell, *Chicago Tribune*, 3 October 1928; to the sports editor of the *American*, Ed Geiger, 3 October 1928; to the unnamed sports editor of the *Daily News*, 3 October 1928; to "Mr. Foley" of the *Journal*, 3 October 1928; and to the unnamed sports editor of the *Evening Post*, 3 October 1928 (all in UADR 20/120).

On page 277 of the text, Walter Eckersall reminded Rockne of their deal, 28 October 1928; Rockne answered Eckersall, 2 November 1928 (UADR 11/86). Eckersall's paper, the *Chicago Tribune*, headlined "BIGGEST CROWD IN FOOTBALL HISTORY," 14 October 1928. Rockne wrote to Ernest B. Cozens of the University of Pennsylvania, 18 October 1928 (UADR 17/154). The *Chicago Tribune* reporter talked about "a great Tech machine," 21 October 1928. Rockne complained about his team's lack of killer instinct to Sam Hill, 23 October 1928 (UADR 13/85). Not only did the *Atlanta Journal*'s "Fuzzy" Woodruff attack Rockne's coaching but he mocked the N.D. uniforms, the subhead on his article of 21 October 1928 blaring: "Irishmen Wore Silken Trousers." Probably this offended Rockne's "machismo," and he sent a letter to "Editor, Atlanta Journal," 9 November 1928 (UADR 7/96).

On page 278 of the text, Rockne wrote his friend, W. A. Draper, 24 October 1928, about sneaking "up on someone" (UADR 11/8). Francis Wallace's comment in the *New York Daily News* appeared 3 November 1928, and the next day a reporter for the *New York Herald-Tribune* commented on the unimpressive "display."

On page 279 of the text, Arthur Haley, the N.D. ticket manager, told Vincent A. McNally, 13 July 1928, and Ambrose O'Connell, 21 November 1928, about the demand for the Army game (UABM "General Correspondence Series," "Mc" and "O" 1928–29 folders). Grantland Rice offered his comment on "Psychology" in the *New York Herald-Tribune*, 4 November 1928. During this period, Rice was syndicated in the *South Bend Tribune*, and Rockne praised his work in a letter to the writer, 20 October 1927 (UADR 18/89).

Psychology Professor Coleman Griffith wrote to Rockne, 9 December 1924, and the coach replied, 13 December 1924 (UADR 13/122), emphasis added. Paul Castner commented on Rockne's speechmaking in *We Remember Rockne*, page 27; former N.D. president John W. Cavanaugh touched on the coach's showmanship in his postscript to Rockne's *Autobiography*, page 260; Father Arthur Hope on the same subject, page 424; and Jim Crowley on his coach's "lies" in Rappoport, page 80. Paul Gallico wrote about his visit to the N.D. training camp in the *New York Daily News*, 10 November 1928.

For the letter from Rockne to Nebraska journalist C. S. "Cy" Sherman, 5 March 1928, Rockne referred to a letter from Sherman, 29 February 1928, both in UADR 23/5, emphasis added. Of all the Rockne lines in his correspondence that surprised this researcher, his remark about Frank Wallace was the most astounding. That the coach could so callously sell out a person whom he mentored and who loved him so much was a side of Rockne's personality that was shocking. Fortunately, Wallace probably never read this letter.

Francis Wallace wrote about Gipp in the *New York Daily News,* 8 November 1928; W. O. McGeehan wrote his praise in the *New York Herald-Tribune,* 9 November 1928. John Davies's *The Legend of Hobey Baker,* Boston, 1966, explained that athlete's extraordinary mystique. Rockne wrote about "traditions" in *Coaching,* page 144.

On page 283 of the text, Rockne wrote to Walter Eckersall, 23 October 1928 (UADR 11/68). Grantland Rice's fabrication about the "Friday night before the game" meeting with Rockne is in his *The Tumult and the Shouting,* pages 182–83. In the *Atlanta Journal,* 11 November 1928, O. R. Keeler noted the "visitor from the east . . . I mean Grantland Rice. I was sitting with him in the press box. He watched the performance of Georgia Tech like a man hypnotized."

The editor of Rockne's *Autobiography* placed the "Gipper" story at the very end of the memoir as the ultimate moment in the coach's career (page 236). Wallace mentioned Rockne's displeasure with him in *Notre Dame,* page 251; Rappoport offered the remark about Gipp's more probable last words; and Steele quotes interviews with Chet Grant and Paul Castner about Gipp's never referring to himself as "the Gipper," page 23.

Ted Twomey gave his recollection in McCallum and Castner, pages 61–63. Years later, Frank Leahy repeated the *Collier's* version of the "Gipper" speech almost word-for-word for Wells Twombley, page 120; and other players on the 1928 team also used it as their rendition of Rockne's original speech. Considering the players' turbulent emotions during this game and the difficulty in such situations of remembering speeches verbatim, as well as their faith in their beloved coach's veracity, that the version in the *Autobiography* and the movie became theirs is not surprising. No doubt, the vividness of the Hollywood re-creation of the speech as well as its frequent recital at Notre Dame reunions by actor Pat O'Brien and others reinforced their belief in its accuracy. Nevertheless, the fact remains that there is absolutely no trace of this version until it appeared in the ghostwritten article in *Collier's* more than two years after the event, 22 November 1930, page 64.

The New York papers, particularly the *Herald-Tribune* and the *World,* offered the best accounts of the game in their 11 November 1928 editions. Ed Healy gave his recollection in *We Remember Rockne,* pages 63–64; Westbrook Pegler wrote about the game for the *Chicago Tribune,* 11 November 1928; Beach and Moore described Cagle's departure from the game, page 118.

On page 287 of the text, the *New York World* headlined "WEST POINT AN INCH FROM GOAL LINE AS FINAL WHISTLE BLOWS IN STADIUM," 11 November 1928, and wired Rockne about "THE SITUATION," [13] November 1928; Rockne telegraphed back, 14 November 1928 (UADR 7/93). He sent his telegram to Francis Wallace, 13 November 1928 (UADR 21/28). That writer quoted Eckersall in the *New York Daily News,* 14 November 1928. *New York World* columnist James S. Collins, 12 November 1928, believed that Army would have scored.

The *Notre Dame Scholastic* headlined and wrote about the loss to Carnegie Tech in the 1928–1929 volume, page 313; Rockne discussed the dangers of "keying up" a team in his letter to Professor Coleman Griffith, 13 December 1924 (UADR 13/122).

Francis Wallace wrote about the "PSYCHOLOGICAL EDGE" in the *New York Daily News*, 15 November 1928; and the *Chicago Tribune*'s Arch Ward wrote about the game, 18 November 1928.

On page 288 of the text, Rockne wrote to Paul Hoffman, 25 November 1928, about the Carnegie Tech game (UADR 12/133); the coach told Grantland Rice about the Tartans' QB, 21 November 1928, and added: "The football coaches, as a whole, all feel very grateful to you, Grant, for the very constructive way in which you write" (UADR 18/89). The coverage of college sports has changed since the Rockne-Rice era, but there are still many sportswriters, particularly in college towns, who only write "constructively" about the coaches they cover.

The quote from Francis Wallace's *O'Reilly of Notre Dame* is on page 71. Many papers carried the United Press dispatch about Rockne's son, 1 December 1928, including the *Chicago Tribune* in its next-day edition. That paper ran the story of the pregame sellout, 1 December 1928.

Joe Gargan wrote Rockne in an undated letter, probably November 1928 (UADR 12/24); the coach explained the situation to Joe Byrne, Jr., 23 November 1928 (UADR 9/27). Rockne never claimed to be the originator of the character-building remark in the text here, or, in Wallace's version: "When a coach wins, he wins; when he loses, he builds character," *Notre Dame Story*, page 121. This coaches' maxim became popular in the 1920s and the quote in the text here is from Delos Lovelace, who says that the N.D. coach "very probably . . . remembered the wisecrack which exploded at a dinner of football coaches," page 187.

W. O. McGeehan commented on the "Wandering Irish," 13 November 1928, and on the "Pullmans," 19 November 1928, in the *New York Herald-Tribune*. Christy Walsh said that "Bill McGeehan" was the only writer who refused all offers to ghost-write for him, page 45.

On page 290 of the text, McGeehan wired Rockne about visiting Notre Dame, 13 November 1928, and the coach replied, 14 November 1928 (UADR 16/7). McGeehan wrote about the N.D. profits from football in the *New York Herald-Tribune*, 17 November 1928, and continued his favorable commentary on Notre Dame, 19 November 1928 and 22 November 1928; he had defined the "assistant alumni," 16 November 1928. Paul Gallico's "LET US OVEREMPHASIZE" appeared in the *New York Daily News*, 12 November 1928. The *Notre Dame Alumnus* reprinted the *South Bend Tribune* editorial, January 1929, pages 139–40.

N.D. Vice President Rev. P. J. Carroll wrote to Rockne, 16 July 1928 (UVMU 2/40). Rockne was sympathetic to Nebraska's entreaties for a resumption of football relations: see his letters to C. S. "Cy" Sherman, 1 June 1927 and 20 October 1927 (UADR 23/5); and to George W. Holmes, 25 September 1928 (UADR 13/96). Rockne sarcastically referred to the athletic board in a letter to Charles "Gus" Dorais, 29 September 1928 (UADR 10/192), and the N.D. coach wrote about the athletic board's criticism of him to George "Potsy" Clark, the A.D. at Butler University—the school where Cavosie ended up—11 October 1928. Rockne told R. N. Blackwell, 7 November 1928, about the "beautiful gates" (UADR 8/157); the 1928 football receipts are in UABM "Semi-Annual Financial Statements—Football 1924–30" folder.

On page 293 of the text, Leo Ward wrote to Rockne, 20 November 1928, about the Jesuit College job, and the coach replied, 26 November 1928 (UADR 21/66). Francis Wallace quotes Lynn St. John, Ohio State athletic director, in *Knute Rockne,* page 221. Toledo sportswriter Kenneth S. Conn wrote to Rockne, 1 November 1927 (UADR 10/11). President Charles O'Donnell's files contain a newspaper clipping of late December 1928 headlined "ROCKNE SOUGHT BY OHIO STATE" (UPCO 3/73), and W. O. McGeehan discussed the OSU situation in the *New York Herald-Tribune,* 22 November 1928. For President O'Donnell's petition to the Provincial Council, see Arthur, page 291. Francis Wallace quotes the Ohio State official in *Notre Dame Story,* page 170. Rockne told C. S. "Cy" Sherman, 4 January 1929, about his "situation" (UADR 23/6).

Francis Wallace's accounts of the Ohio State offer to Rockne are the most accurate on record. Not only did he have many contacts at OSU and among its alumni—his hometown of Bellaire, Ohio, was not far from Columbus—but his reportorial skills insure a high degree of accuracy. The same cannot be said for other writers on Rockne: Jerry Brondfield, in *Rockne,* pages 225–26, discusses the OSU episode at length and includes a nonreferenced conversation between Rockne and Notre Dame President Matthew Walsh about whether the coach should take the offer or not. Unfortunately for the accuracy of this account, when the conversation supposedly occurred, in December 1928, Walsh was no longer president and was on a sabbatical in Europe—Father Charles O'Donnell had assumed the office in September. The brazenness and laziness of such authors as Brondfield is rather astounding.

27. ROCKNE ATTACKS THE COLLEGE SPORTS REFORMERS: 1929

Frank Leahy's comment on Rockne's recruiting is in Twombley, page 126. Rockne wrote Jesse Harper about the new "proselyting," 4 January 1929 (UADR 13/36); he informed Don Hamilton of his "plans," 3 January 1929, and suggested a meeting of key alums, 4 January 1929; Hamilton asked Rockne about letters to prospects, 16 January 1929, and the coach replied, 23 January 1929. Hamilton told Rockne, 26 January 1929, about requesting a meeting with President O'Donnell. These Rockne-Hamilton letters are in UADR 13/14.

President O'Donnell wrote to Hamilton, 28 January 1929 (UPCO 3/135). Rockne grumbled about "the old time chiseling" to Roger Kiley, 9 April 1929 (UADR 14/170), and wrote to John Neeson about the alumni recruiting, 13 September 1929 (UADR 16/171). Henry Dockweiler told Rockne, 10 May 1929, about Vejar's recruitment (UADR 10/171); a copy of the letter from Larry Vejar to Henry Dockweiler, undated but probably fall 1929, is in UADR 10/172. Henry Dockweiler informed Rockne about Vejar's complaint, 10 October 1929, and the N.D. coach replied with the crack about USC, 14 October 1929 (UADR 10/172).

On page 298 of the text, Frank Wallace wrote to Rockne, undated but probably summer 1929, and the coach replied, 6 August 1929 (UADR 21/29); Wallace reported about "Stulie," 5 February 1929 (UADR 21/28). Rockne wrote to John Neeson of Philadelphia, 18 December 1929 (UADR 16/172). Detroit alum Louis P. Malone complained to Rockne, 17 April 1929, and the coach responded, 17 April 1929 (UADR 15/16). Rockne wrote to Monroe H. Loeb, 29 May 1929, about the transfer rule (UADR 14/107); Harry Mehre told him about Gellis, 5 July 1929, and the N.D. coach expressed interest, 19 July 1929 (UADR 16/47). Rockne wrote to Joe Byrne, Jr., about Gellis, 29 July 1929 (UADR 9/29); he told Isaac Landman, 7 December 1929, about Gellis's job, and also named Gellis, Zoss, Herwit, and Goldstein as Jewish, plus Marchy Schwartz as half Jewish (UADR 19/1). Joe Petritz, a former N.D. student and the school's first full-time Director of Sports Publicity, informed the *Western Catholic*, 26 December 1930, that "Martin Brill is of German-Jewish descent and Clarence ["Manny"] Kaplan . . . is Jewish." In addition, Sam Goldstein's nephew, Robert, recounted his uncle's experiences at Notre Dame in an interview, 20 December 1992.

Jim Silver informed Rockne about Joe Medwick, 28 December 1929, and the coach replied, 30 December 1929 (UADR 19/1). Rockne wrote to Al Feeney about the two recruits, 20 March 1929 (UADR 11/133), and commented on them to A. A. Kutch, 3 October 1929 (UADR 14/26). He asked George Maypole to help Vezie, 28 May 1929 (UADR 15/146), and wrote Toledo alum Frank R. Lockard, 18 February 1929 (UADR 14/106).

On page 300 of the text, Rockne sent a "night letter of June 28 [1929]" asking the President to look into "the scholastic rating" of the athlete; O'Donnell ruled negatively, 1 July 1929, and offered his comment (UADR 17/149). O'Donnell sent his poetry to Harriet Monroe, 15 December 1928 (UPCO 6/22), and invited Westbrook Pegler to Notre Dame, 12 March 1929 (UPCO 6/145). N.D. President Charles O'Donnell wrote to Rev. Joseph Burke, 17 December 1929 (UPCO 1/66), and asked Rockne to mention N.D.'s academic achievements, 26 April 1929 (UADR 17/49). The quote from O'Donnell's speech is in the *New York Times*, 13 February 1929.

On page 302 of the text, Rockne complained to journalist C. S. "Cy" Sherman, 22 March 1929 (UADR 23/6); the coach sent his telegram to President Charles O'Donnell, 1 July 1929, and his long letter, 4 July 1929 (UPCO 7/63). Francis Wallace's roman à clef *Huddle* repeats Rockne's complaint about his opponents on the Notre Dame faculty: ". . . his constant struggle with a group of second-grade faculty men who carped about his false eminence and disproportionate salary. Barney [Rockne] considered them among life's failures" (page 98).

Rockne wrote to Wallace, 23 July 1929 (UADR 21/29); in his instructions to Wallace for the *Saturday Evening Post* article—it appeared on 28 September 1929— the coach underlined Yost's hypocrisy concerning the "over-commercialization" of college football:

And mention Michigan as being a great money maker. They played the Marines some years ago and kept all the receipts and in playing the Navy when the game was in Ann Arbor, Michigan, kept all the receipts, and when the return game was supposed to be played at Annapolis [and] was transferred to Baltimore [Municipal Stadium], Michigan got half the receipts. High finance by Yost!

Rockne referred to the standard agreements whereby the home team either paid the visitor a guarantee or split the receipts fifty-fifty.

Rockne wrote to Jesse Harper, 7 January 1928 (UADR 13/34). Pete Vaughan, coach at Wabash, complained to Rockne, 10 March 1927, and Rockne replied, 14 April 1927 (UADR 20/141). The N.D. coach commented on "highbrow" Wabash to W. O. Davies, 19 September 1928 (UADR 10/83).

On page 304 of the text, John Griffith mentioned their private discussions in a letter to the coach, 17 September 1927 (UADR 12/85); the Big Ten commissioner sent Rockne a copy of a memorandum to "Director of Athletics of the Western Conference" expressing Griffith's fears of a coaches' revolt, 3 January 1928, Rockne disagreed, 23 January 1928 (UADR 12/86); and commented about Yost to Jesse Harper, 7 January 1928 (UADR 13/34). McCready Huston explained Rockne's position, page 48. The *Washington Evening Star* commented on Rockne's talk, 4 February 1929.

The quote from Abbé Dimant is in the Carnegie Foundation's "Bulletin 23," page xiv. Henry S. Pritchett offered his strong criticisms on pages xii and xiv; see the excellent index in that book for references in my text to specific schools and abuses. The sad part about the Carnegie report on college sports is that its criticisms are still valid—and unanswered—in the 1990s. American higher education is as far from squaring the circle of big-time college sports versus the academic institutions that house them as it was seventy years ago. But I wrote an entire book on this issue, *College Sports Inc.: The Athletic Department vs the University*, and will not repeat the arguments here.

The *New York Times* featured the Carnegie study, 25 October 1929, and stayed with the story for the following week. The *Chicago Tribune* ran articles on it, 24 October 1929; that paper had William Howard Taft's opinion, 25 October 1929; the man-in-the-street's, 27 October 1929; and Westbrook Pegler's, 25 October 1929. W. O. McGeehan wrote consecutive columns for the *New York Herald-Tribune* on the study, 15 and 16 November 1929; defended Notre Dame, 24 November 1929; and ran more letters pro-and-con his position, 9 December 1929.

On page 309 of the text, Rockne wrote to John Neeson, 10 December 1929, about the "effort . . . to discredit Notre Dame" and "the story on the fancy salary" (UADR 16/172). Newspaper clippings about a revival of football relations with Michigan are in President Charles O'Donnell's files (UPCO 8/125). By 1929, Fielding Yost no longer coached Michigan but was the athletic director; he scheduled the games and, by all accounts, interfered in the coaching. Bob Zuppke was still coaching at Illinois.

On page 309 of the text, Rockne replied to an inquiry from H. J. McGuire, 31 December 1929, about Yost's hostility to N.D. (UADR 15/55). The *Chicago Tribune* reported on the new alignment in the Big Ten, 3 December 1929, and the *New York Times* carried the story on Rockne not finding football "COMMERCIALIZED ENOUGH," 17 December 1930. The *Notre Dame Scholastic*, 1930–1931 volume, also had more of Rockne's opinions on this subject, page 366. The Rockne speeches in the film after the dialogue quoted in the text make the filmmakers' isolationism

explicit: "In many parts of Europe and elsewhere in the world, this spirit has manifested itself in continuous wars and revolutions . . . But we have tried to make
competitive sports act as a safer outlet for this spirit of combat. And I believe we have
succeeded." The script then states: "A spontaneous burst of applause from the spectators and press greets Knute's credo of sport" (UABM *Knute Rockne—All American*
Series/"*Knute Rockne—All American* Script 1940/0120" folder).

On page 311 of the text, the *Notre Dame Alumnus* ran its editorial on the
Carnegie findings in November 1929, page 83; President Charles O'Donnell responded to the study in an article in that magazine, January 1930, pages 67–69.
Rockne wrote to Paul Schissler, 1 October 1929; the "acid test" comment is also in
this letter (UADR 19/72). In the *Chicago Tribune*, Edward Burns jibed about the
N.D. performance at Indiana, 6 October 1929; George Strickler wrote Rockne about
Griffith's move, 18 April 1929, and the N.D. coach offered "to use you as an official,"
23 April 1929 (UADR 20/19); Frank Haggerty of the *Chicago Daily News* wrote the
coach, 17 January 1929, and Rockne replied, 23 January 1929 (UADR 13/4); Donald
Hamilton wrote Rockne, 17 December 1929 (UADR 13/14); Griffith informed
Rockne about Eckersall's illness, 1 October 1929 (UADR 12/89). James D. Whalen
wrote about Eckersall's demise in *Biographical Dictionary of American Sports*, page
159.

The United Press report on Rockne's incapacity was in the *Chicago Tribune*, 11
October 1929; McCready Huston discussed Rockne's "chart of play," page 69.
Rockne sent a night letter to Tom Lieb, 11 October 1929 (UADR 14/154). Westbrook
Pegler wrote about Rockne's telephone call and the Navy game, 13 October 1929;
Milton Mayer did the satire in the *Chicago Evening Post*, 16 October 1929.

Art West reported to President Charles O'Donnell on the meeting with the *Chicago Evening Post* editor, 25 October 1929 (UPCO 3/73). Rockne wrote to George L.
Little, A.D. at Wisconsin, 19 March 1929 (UADR 21/155), and to Tom Barry, Notre
Dame Club of Chicago, 20 September 1929 (UADR 8/95). Rockne's correspondence
files, as well as those of N.D. athletic department business manager Arthur Haley,
bulge with requests for seats for the games at Soldier Field in 1929.

An unnamed Madison, Wisconsin, reporter sent a "Special" to the *Chicago
Tribune*, 16 October 1929, about Lieb's knowledge of Notre Dame. Grantland Rice's
proclamation was in the *New York Herald-Tribune*, 21 October 1929; Rockne
thanked Rice, 22 October 1929 (UADR 18/90). Rockne's speech at the Carnegie
Tech game is in Wallace, *Knute Rockne*, pages 227–28; Warren Brown told Rockne
about Steffen's plan [28 October 1929] (UADR 8/206); Westbrook Pegler wired
Rockne, 30 October 1929 (UADR 17/141). The *New York Herald-Tribune* discussed
the coach's medical problem and his doctor's report, 30 October 1929; by this season,
that paper as well as the *New York Times* and the *Chicago Tribune* carried very full
game reports on all Notre Dame contests.

On page 316 of the text, Rockne wrote to Rice before the USC game, 30 October
1929 (UADR 18/90); Rockne replied to the ticket request of Charles W. Dunkley, a
sports editor with the Associated Press, 1 November 1929 (UADR 11/25). The *Chicago Tribune* carried Arch Ward's report of the huge bonfire, 15 November 1929;

Harvey Woodruff's game story, 17 November 1929; and, on the same day, Don Maxwell's account of the locker room speeches. In the *Chicago Daily News*, William S. Forman mocked Rockne "in a wheel chair," 18 November 1929, and the letters from fans who complained to the *Chicago Daily News*, 21 November 1929, are in UADR 9/173.

The *Notre Dame Alumnus* printed "Savoldi's Keed" in December 1929, page 119; the *Chicago Tribune* ran the dig about Savoldi's intelligence on 21 October 1929, and the *New York Herald-Tribune* published W. O. McGeehan's column about Rockne's coaching on 26 November 1929. The *New York Sun* and the *Chicago Tribune* reported on the ticket situation before the N.D.–Army game, 27 November 1929.

On page 319 of the text, President Charles O'Donnell turned down the ticket request of Rev. James H. Griffin, the president of Villanova, 10 October 1929 (UPCO 3/123); O'Donnell wrote to E. J. Tracy, 31 October 1929 (UPCO 8/45), and to Rev. Michael Shea, 22 November 1929 (UPCO 7/137). Elmer Oliphant asked Rockne for tickets, 26 October 1929, and the coach replied, 28 October 1929 (UADR 17/20). Rockne sent seats to Ring Lardner, 26 November 1929 (UADR 14/120), and told Al Nagel about the tickets for Byrne and other friends, 21 November 1929 (UADR 16/151). John Kiernan thanked Rockne for the tickets, 25 November 1929 (UADR 14/9); Allison Danzig asked for tickets, 22 October 1929 (UADR 10/81); and Rockne complained to Paul Gallico, 31 October 1929 (UADR 11/175). The N.D. coach had billeted the team in New York at the Vanderbilt Hotel—his friend, Tom O'Malley, was a manager there—but, as he wrote O'Malley on 23 September 1929 (UADR 17/89):

> Our President, Father Charles O'Donnell, has been taken in and wined and dined by the manager of the McAlpin Hotel and I have received orders to let the team stop there at the time of the Army game and there is nothing I can do about it. But rest assured I shall be very critical and we hope to be with you the year after if not sooner.

The *New York Herald-Tribune* and other New York papers carried stories on the ticket situation from 24 to 30 November 1929; the *Daily News* offered its "First prize . . ." on 22 November 1929, and Noel Busch in that paper discussed the "speakeasies," 26 November 1929. The *Herald-Tribune* reported on the game day drinking, 1 December 1929. The temperature during the 1929 Army game was fourteen degrees, and the wind a brisk thirty-five miles per hour; today's calculations for wind-chill factor put that temperature well below zero.

On page 320 of the text, Rockne wrote to Grantland Rice, 20 November 1929 (UADR 18/90). The *New York Times* reported on the coach's telephone call to the team and the radio broadcast, 1 December 1929; the *Chicago Tribune* carried Rockne's warning about Army, 1 December 1929; Paul Gallico in the *New York Daily News* predicted an Army victory because of "Biff" Jones's departure, 30 November 1929, and analyzed "Red" Cagle's fatal error, 2 December 1929; and the *New York Herald-Tribune* wrote about the welcome in South Bend, 3 December 1929.

Columnist George Trevor of the *New York Sun* discussed the N.D. strategy, 2 December 1929, and wrote Rockne, undated but probably the first week of December 1929; Rockne replied, 11 December 1929 (UADR 20/89). The *New York World* headlined "ROCKNE TO REFUSE POST-SEASON GAME," 26 November 1929, and followed this story, as did other papers, after the victory over Army; the press did not understand the long-standing Notre Dame administrative ban on postseason games.

On page 321 of the text, N.D. alum Angus McDonald conveyed the Rose Bowl's interest in Notre Dame and the message of the chairman of its Football Committee, L. B. Henry, to Vice President Mulcaire, 5 December 1929 (UADR 15/166). President Charles O'Donnell wrote to Rev. James J. Mertz about "the never ceasing requests," 21 November 1928 (UPCO 8/136). President Charles O'Donnell discussed the misconceptions about N.D.'s football profits in his address at the annual football banquet, 4 December 1929, and the *Notre Dame Alumnus* carried his salient points, January 1930, page 140. In the Notre Dame Archives, no game-by-game financial breakdown for the 1929 season exists. The numbers quoted in the text are from the folder labeled "Recapitulation All Sports, July 1st, 1929 to July 1st, 1930" (UVMU 2/52), and the "Gain" from football is clearly marked at $541,840.92. If that number is subtracted from the bank deposits from all sports—and football accounted for 99 percent of the gain—the sum of $208,282 is arrived at. Because the campaign to finance the new stadium occurred during this period, my assumption is that the main source of this money, as well as the $223,353 of other athletic department deposits between January 1, 1930, and June 30, 1930, was from the sale of ten-year leases on box seats of the stadium. Unfortunately, not enough documentation exists to track this completely and some financial sheets seem to contradict other ones.

Rockne's comment about "playing in our own stadium" was in the *New York Herald-Tribune,* 1 December 1929. Rockne sent his "Holiday Greeting" to Grantland Rice, 24 December 1929 (UADR 18/90).

28. ROCKNE'S LAST AND GREATEST ROCKET: 1930

Frank Wallace wrote to President Charles O'Donnell, 15 July 1930 (UPCO 8/68); Howard Savage wrote to President Charles O'Donnell on behalf of the Carnegie Foundation, 17 June 1930; O'Donnell answered, 23 July 1930; Savage wrote, 29 July 1930; and the N.D. president replied, 4 August 1930 (UPCO 8/69). O'Donnell informed Wallace of N.D.'s position, 14 August 1930 (UPCO 8/68).

President Charles O'Donnell approved Rockne's projects, 22 March 1930 (UPCO 7/60); the coach wrote John Neeson of Philadelphia, 18 December 1929 (UADR 16/172). New York alumni official Eddie Byrne communicated with Arthur Haley, 2 July 1930, and the latter replied 24 July 1930 (UABM General Correspondence Series "B" folder). Rockne told Art Haley, 31 March 1930: "West Point will want one entire side, twenty or thirty thousand tickets, so I guess we are kind of up against it with them." However, as a master strategist, he suggested beginning Army's block of seats at "the goal line at the south and working north, which would give us all of the tickets around the [opposite] turn, and making them take some of the bad seats." Because the Soldier Field officials knew and liked Rockne, they accepted his seating plan, giving N.D. the entire "west side" (UABM General Correspondence Series "Knute Rockne" folder). Nevertheless the ticket demand for Army's first game against Notre Dame in the Middle West far exceeded the school's block of forty thousand seats. The June 1930 *Notre Dame Alumnus* announced: "FOOTBALL TICKETS—IMPORTANT CHANGES! Alumni Whose Dues are Paid Only Ones to Receive Preference; Tickets for Army Game Limited to Four in Preferred Section" (page 305).

Notre Dame Law School Dean Clarence Manion discussed the conflicts between Mulcaire and Rockne in McCallum and Castner, pages 7–8; Scrapiron Young related the story of his hiring in *With Rockne,* pages 111–13, and raved about his "training room," page 12; Thomas Schlereth discussed the $15,400 for football uniforms, page 147. Hunk Anderson explained his St. Louis University experience and his N.D. salary in his memoir, page 78; the *Notre Dame Alumnus* mentioned Tom Lieb's three-year contract with Loyola of Los Angeles, February 1930, page 172, and Rockne's coaching staff, October 1930, page 53. The remark about the Jesuits was made by an older N.D. alum in an interview for this book, 12 November 1991. Like many Notre Dame alumni, he requested anonymity on his comments about his alma mater and his church, explaining: "It's important to me to be under the tent at the reunions and home games"—each class has its own large tent set up for these occasions—"and some of my classmates are fanatical about not saying anything negative about our school and our church."

On page 327 of the text, "Manny" Vezie remarked to Arthur Haley, 29 February 1940; Morrie Starrett to Haley about Tommy Yarr, undated but pre–September 1930; Frank Hering to Haley, 23 May 1930 (UABM General Correspondence Series "Manfred Vezie," "S," and "H" folders)—the Hering awards continue to the present, except the players now receive medals, not cash, as in the donor's day. Reverend Mulcaire wrote to Rockne, 21 January 1930 (UVMU 2/39), and Haley informed John O'Brien about fall work positions, 15 August 1930 (UABM General Correspondence Series "O" folder). Wells Twombley discussed Frank Leahy's 1930 summer job, page 134; Earl Walsh informed Rockne about Leahy's financial situation, 9 February 1928, and the coach responded, 22 February 1928 (UADR 21/49). Twombley explained Leahy's ambitions and quoted him, page 94.

John B. Kennedy did an interview article on Rockne and the Fighting Irish, "The Halfback of Notre Dame," for *Collier's,* 19 November 1927—the bantering style and superficial content point to his future work for the coach. Kennedy wrote to Rockne about the *Mentor* piece, 3 July 1929, and the coach replied, 19 July 1929; the ghost-writer sent the manuscript, 28 August 1929, and Rockne approved it, 12 September 1929 (UADR 14/57).

Father John W. Cavanaugh's correspondence with A. H. Hepburn is in CJVC *Autobiography of Knute Rockne* Series, "Bobbs-Merrill" folder. The Bobbs-Merrill editor first wrote to Cavanaugh about Kennedy, 19 October 1931; Hepburn noted Bonnie Rockne's elusiveness and informed Cavanaugh about Kennedy pressing his case, 4 November 1931; in this letter, Hepburn has a typo, "article" for "articles"—all parties, including Cavanaugh, acknowledge that Kennedy worked on the entire

Collier's series, eight articles in all. The editor alerted the former N.D. president as to future acknowledgments on the authorship, 7 November 1931; Cavanaugh replied angrily, 13 November 1931.

The disappearance of the Kennedy-Rockne 1930 correspondence as well as Kennedy's letters to Hepburn makes the coach's exact relationship with the ghost-writer somewhat difficult to reconstruct. However, important documents remain, among them some typed chapters—including "The Four Horsemen" (CJVC *Autobiography of Knute Rockne* Series, "Unedited Typescript Draft of Chapters 1–3 of *Collier's* "Autobiography" folder)—of the work. At the top of the first page—in handwriting that matches John B. Kennedy's—is the note: "Preliminary copy (not Rockne's revision)." Attached to the document is a typed one-sentence revision and a note in Rockne's writing: "Rush" (that is, back to Kennedy). Comparing this manuscript with the final printed version in *Collier's* and in the *Autobiography* reveals almost no changes from the typed manuscript to the printed form—hence the conclusion that Rockne made minimal changes to this chapter and probably to the other ones as well.

In Father Cavanaugh's letter of 13 November 1931, he discussed Kennedy's visit to Notre Dame during 1930 and Rockne's "retailing" of anecdotes to him; Cavanaugh again implied that the coach did not write the text: "Rockne's conversation was as good as the writing in the Autobiography." Nevertheless, Cavanaugh rejected Bobbs-Merrill's solution on the future acknowledgment to Kennedy.

Finally, this issue becomes a question of what constitutes authorship. Celebrities have long employed ghostwriters—Rockne's friend and agent Christy Walsh made a lucrative living by matching the two parties and selling the resulting texts. For many years, the ghosts remained invisible, then, in the 1960s, some celebrities agreed to acknowledge the writer's role with "As told to" tag lines. In the 1990s, this has been replaced by "with"—short for "with the help of" (for example, *The Fighting Spirit* by Lou Holtz with John Heisler, New York, 1990).

None of this would be important to the Rockne *Autobiography* except for the claim of his hagiographers that the coach, as a "scholar," wrote every word printed under his name. In fact, it appears that John B. Kennedy wrote most of the words that appear on the printed pages of the coach's autobiography, with many passages as his version of the coach's stories and speeches. Because he worked in a pre–tape recorder age, his versions are not verbatim and some of them so contradict the factual record that they constitute Kennedy's fictional accounts.

A final irony on the authorship issue: if, in a Notre Dame English class during Rockne's era or subsequent ones, a student named John offered to write an essay assignment for fellow student Kenneth and then, after they discussed the paper, John wrote it, Ken loosely edited it *and submitted it for credit under his own name*, Ken would have clearly committed plagiarism and, if discovered, would have been expelled. Moreover, the excuse that Ken's conversation was as good as the writing would have encountered an extremely hostile response from the Notre Dame authorities.

Francis Wallace commented on the *Autobiography* in *Knute Rockne,* pages

28–29. Haley wrote to Rockne about the *Official* [Notre Dame] *Football Review,* 21 February 1930 (UABM General Correspondence Series "Knute Rockne" folder); Edward Burns mentioned *Collier's* offer of "twelve grand for eight magazine articles" in the *Chicago Tribune,* 2 November 1930; and the *Autobiography* contains a passage on "the faculty must run the institution," page 107.

James Armstrong commented on naming the stadium, page 277; Hope discussed its financing, page 403; N.D. fan Edna Larkin complained to Arthur Haley, 6 October 1930; Chicago papers as well as Notre Dame publications carried ads for football excursions throughout the fall of 1930 and for many years after; and photographer Lester E. McDermott wrote to Haley, 13 October 1930 (UABM General Correspondence Series "L" and "M" folders).

The *Notre Dame Alumnus's* encomium to Gipp appeared in October 1930, pages 62 and following; President Charles O'Donnell's address is in that issue, pages 39–42, and the poem to Gipp is on page 46. The various quotes from Rev. John O'Hara to N.D. President Charles O'Donnell about the Savoldi case, 11 November 1930, are in UPCO 7/124; Francis Wallace pointed out Joe's blunder in *Knute Rockne,* page 238; and McCready Huston discussed the South Bend press's reaction, pages 9–14. In McCallum and Castner, Dan Halpin recalled the coach writing out a personal check for Savoldi, page 163; *The Tablet* praised the school's actions, 22 November 1930; the letter to the *Pittsburgh Catholic* appeared 10 January 1931; and Arch Ward criticized the N.D. faculty in the *Chicago Tribune,* 18 November 1930.

On page 336 of the text, President Charles O'Donnell wrote to Rev. Joseph Burke, 21 November 1930 (UPCO 7/123). The Chicago and New York papers covered Notre Dame football in great detail in 1930; with their statistical charts on each game, they listed the officials. The *Chicago Tribune* headlined "ROCKNE VIEWS GAME WITH USUAL ALARM," 16 October 1930, and Irving Vaughan in that paper noted the absence of a "Son of Erin" in the backfield, 19 October 1930. Francis Wallace commented on Pitt's new stadium in *Knute Rockne,* page 234, and wrote a novel, *Stadium,* New York, 1931, about it. An unbylined *Chicago Tribune* reporter invoked the "echoes," 26 October 1930; that paper carried the remarks of the president of Purdue University, 8 November 1930, and the next day headlined "BRILL GOES HOME TO SCORE 3 TOUCHDOWNS AGAINST PENN." Lovelace quotes an undated Rice comment in the *New York Sun* on the N.D. backfield, and Rockne remarked on Marchy Schwartz's "Jewish blood" to the *San Francisco Call,* 8 December 1930; the N.D. alum who remarked about Hunk Anderson and the Jesuits also commented on the 1930 backfield, 12 November 1991.

The *Chicago Tribune* put the NU–Notre Dame agreement to move the 1930 game to Soldier Field for "poor relief" on the front page, 14 November 1930; the official reasons for the Big Ten's refusal emerged in that paper, 5 December 1930; the *Chicago Tribune's* game-day stories, including Westbrook Pegler's article, appeared on 23 November 1930. Frank Carideo proclaimed it "my greatest football game" in a book of that title, New York, 1949, pages 78–79.

The letter to the "University of Notre Dame" from F. J. Oelerich, 19 November 1930; the one from a state senator of Illinois, Frank A. McCarthy to Art Haley, 3

October 1930, requesting tickets for the "Governor's office" on down, over "one hundred tickets for the State officials and members of the Legislature"; and "Rig" Sackley, class of 1917, to Haley about Chicago "pols" getting seats, 18 November 1930 are in UABM General Correspondence Series "O," "M," and "S" folders. The *Chicago Tribune* mentioned the barrage on Rockne, 27 November 1930, and Haley predicted a crowd of 125,000 to that paper, 26 November 1930; that same day, Paul Gallico remarked on the "pre-contest festivities" in the *New York Daily News;* he commented on the game for his paper, 1 December 1930. Westbrook Pegler described the scene for the *Chicago Tribune,* 1 December 1930, and that same day, the *New York Times* described the crowd melee. At the end of the game, because Army kicker Chuck Broshous was small, only a reserve, used the old-fashioned dropkicking method, and the ball was extremely slippery, "Red" Blaik believed that a surprise pass play would tie the score—it was many years before the two-point pass-or-run PAT came into college football. When Blaik ran the team during World War II and its aftermath, Army dominated college football—with help from draft boards around the country.

Paul Gallico's "Retreat from Moscow" column appeared in the *New York Daily News,* 2 December 1930; Beach and Moore describe the locker room scene and its aftermath, page 133. Francis Wallace related the details of the trip west in his paper, 2 and 3 December 1930, and told the story of the Hanley-O'Connor switch in *Notre Dame Story,* pages 261–62. Warren Brown commented on Rockne's "gamble" in his memoir, *Win, Lose, or Draw,* New York, 1947, page 139. The *Chicago Tribune* carried the AP report on the team's arrival in L.A., 6 December 1930; the *New York Herald-Tribune* ran the story about the Cal-Berkeley accusations against USC, 19 November 1930; and Bill Henry of the *Los Angeles Times* criticized Rockne, 7 December 1930.

On page 344 of the text, Rev. Joseph Burke wrote to President Charles O'Donnell about the USC game, 17 December 1930 (UPCO 1/65); Rev. Robert Shuler's sermon was in the *Los Angeles Record,* 8 December 1930; Scrapiron Young described the trip home, pages 145–47; the *Notre Dame Alumnus* proclaimed "Gangway for God" in December 1930, page 1; Cromartie and Brown noted the popularity of Notre Dame and Rockne, page 42. The *Chicago Tribune* covered the "Loop" welcome and the return to South Bend, 11 December 1930; the *Notre Dame Scholastic* described the local reception in the 1930–1931 volume, pages 330 and following, and quoted Warner on page 330 and Meehan on page 345. The *Los Angeles Times* carried the AP report about the rowdy students in South Bend, 12 December 1930.

The 1930 football financial figures are in UVMU 2/52. The *Notre Dame Alumnus* printed President O'Donnell's warning, January 1930, page 140; the 1930 home attendance figures are based on the current Notre Dame football media guide, and their numbers for this period tend to be quite accurate, corresponding to the newspaper and other contemporary accounts. The Carnegie Foundation issued its post–1930 season warning in "Bulletin 26," pages 8 and following. The *Notre Dame Alumnus* described the Erskine Award and the New York ceremony in January 1931, pages

169–70. Rockne wrote to Maurice "Doc" Keady about Rupe Mills's death, 5 August 1929 (UADR 14/40).

29. THE DEATH OF REFORM AND ROCKNE: 1931

Rockne wrote to President Charles O'Donnell, 10 March 1931 (UPCO 7/61). The *Chicago Tribune* covered Loyola of Chicago's abolition of football, 5 December 1930; A. H. Whitten wrote his editorial in the *Illinois High School Athlete*, January 1931, page 8; President Charles O'Donnell wrote to prominent N.D. alum Frederic Wile, 17 January 1931 (UPCO 8/96). The *New York Times* featured the Carnegie update, 15 June 1931; for material in the text from Carnegie Foundation "Bulletin 26," see its excellent index of topics and specific schools, emphasis added.

On page 350 of the text, for the quote from the *Notre Dame Alumnus*, October 1931, see page 14. In McCallum and Castner, Paul Castner related the story of the coach's last argument with the faculty athletic board and Father Mulcaire, page 74; for Rockne's last letter to President Charles O'Donnell, 30 March 1931 (see UPCO 7/59), emphasis added; the Delos Lovelace quote, page 206; the AP headline appeared in many papers, including the *Kansas City Star,* 1 April 1931; William Allen White's obituary was reprinted in many places, including Wallace, *Knute Rockne,* pages 258–59, this work also contains former president Cavanaugh's statement, page 257. John McCallum's comment is in McCallum and Castner, page 206; and in *The Glory of Notre Dame,* edited by Frederic Katz, New York, 1971, Jack Newcombe supplies many details about the reaction to the coach's death, pages 57 and following.

On page 353 of the text, the legend about the rosary is in many sources; the Notre Dame Archives possesses a comic book that narrates it, "The Spirit of Notre Dame," *Timeless Topix Comic Books,* November 1944, page 4, (PNDP 3320-5-1). Byron Kanaley wrote President O'Donnell, 2 April 1931 (UPCO 4/130). The *Notre Dame Alumnus* devoted a special issue to Rockne's death, May 1931; editor James Armstrong collected many of the telegrams and notes of condolence sent to Notre Dame and to Bonnie Rockne and republished them. The quotes of the following persons are in the Rockne memorial issue of the magazine: Etta Eckersall, Joe Savoldi, Major John Griffith, Grantland Rice, Herbert Hoover, Ambassador H. H. Bachke on behalf of the king of Norway, Babe Ruth, Lou Gehrig, Jack Dempsey (did a ghostwriter at Christy Walsh's agency pen the three sportsmen's almost identical wires?), Lou Little, Raymond C. Eubanks, the unnamed Youngstown (Ohio) journalist, the Norden Lodge of Tacoma, and the B'Nai B'Rith of South Bend. Many years later, President Richard Nixon began the P.R. trick of associating himself and his faltering presidency with victorious teams, coaches, and athletes, and every subsequent chief executive has continued the practice.

John Kieran wrote his obituary in the *New York Times,* 1 April 1931, and Will Rogers's column was widely syndicated to such papers as the *Fort Wayne* (Indiana) *Journal-Gazette,* 1 April 1931. Rogers began another article on Rockne with the following bizarre lead: "When your [the readers'] Grandchildren are sitting around some Penal Institution at recreation time, they will talk of the time away back, when their parents and Grandparents used to tell about a certain man [Rockne]" (*Fort Wayne* (Indiana) *Journal-Gazette,* 30 April 1931). Grantland Rice's doggerel poem was reprinted in the program of the Twelfth Civic Testimonial Banquet for the football team, 7 December 1931 (PATH, Football Series, "Annual Banquet" folder). The editorials in the *New York Herald-Tribune* and the *South Bend News-Times* appeared on 1 April 1931.

The complete text of President Charles O'Donnell's funeral oration is in the *Notre Dame Alumnus,* May 1931, pages 299–300; James Armstrong's comments, as well as those of Right Rev. Francis Clement Kelley, the bishop of Oklahoma, are also in that issue, emphasis added. In *Knute Rockne,* Wallace quotes Westbrook Pegler, page 266, and Fielding Yost and Amos Alonzo Stagg, page 260. John Tunis wrote scathingly about Rockne and the Fighting Irish in the *New York Evening Post,* 24 November 1930, and predicted Rockne's canonization in "The Great God Football" in *Harper's Magazine,* November 1928, page 744. Bill Cunningham wrote his anti–Notre Dame article in the *Boston Post,* 6 October 1925; his pro-Rockne obituary appeared on 1 April 1931.

President Charles O'Donnell's foreword to Warren Brown's *Rockne,* Chicago, 1931, is on pages 9–10. Warner Brothers executive Bryan Foy wrote Arthur Haley, 23 January 1939, "As quickly as possible please mail out a couple of copies of the autobiography of Knute Rockne"; later that year, 22 June 1939, Haley sent screenwriter Robert Buckner the special issue of the *Alumnus* (UABM *Knute Rockne—All American* Series/"Foy" and "Buckner" folders), and in their correspondence they discuss the film's use of the Brown and Stuhldreher works. The *Notre Dame Alumnus,* May 1931, contains Christy Walsh's "Happy Landings," page 301; James Armstrong's comments on the coach's final journey, page 293; and Armstrong's editorial, page 319. For the promotional article on "The Spirit of Notre Dame," see the *Notre Dame Alumnus,* October 1931, pages 13–14.

III. *"Rally Sons of Notre Dame": 1932–1941*

30. IN THE DEPRESSION: 1931–1941

The line "Rally sons of Notre Dame" is from one of the less well-known verses of the N.D. "Victory March." There are many excellent books on the financial Depression that began in 1929, including John Kenneth Galbraith's classic *The Great Crash: 1929,* Boston, 1961; William Klingaman's *1929: The Year of the Great Crash,* New York, 1989; Robert S. McElvaine's *The Great Depression America: 1929–1941,* New York, 1984; in addition, Studs Terkel did an excellent oral history, *Hard Times: An Oral History of the Great Depression,* New York, 1970. The background for this chapter and many of its details are from these books, as well as from works cited in them.

President Charles O'Donnell wrote to Chicago banker Byron Kanaley, 2 January 1932 (UPCO 4/127); Voltmer noted the Big Ten's athletic problems, page 37; and historian William Klingaman commented on the "loss of confidence" in an interview in *USA Today,* 14 January 1992. Ambrose O'Connell wrote to Art Haley, 5 February

1931 (UABM General Correspondence Series "O" folder), and the 1931 editorial in the *Notre Dame Scholastic* appeared on 24 February 1931, page 15. An interesting insight on the difference between the 1920s and 1930s was offered by Hugh Hefner, founder of the *Playboy* empire, in an interview in *USA Today,* 16 November 1992: "Raised in the Depression, I always felt I was there the day after the party, that being the Roaring '20s. So for me the party became a symbol, a remembrance of the past and a reaction to . . . socio-political repression."

The quote from Father William P. Leahy is on page 55; he discussed the 1930s trend in Jesuit education on pages 48 and following, and the statistics on approved graduate programs at Catholic schools on page 42; Father Andrew Greeley, in his sociologist phase, analyzed the enrollment patterns of American Catholics in *The Irish Americans,* page 117; Thomas Schlereth outlined Notre Dame's enrollment in the 1930s, page 169; and Father Arthur Hope explained N.D.'s finances, contacts in Washington, and student ethos during that decade, pages 458 and following. The *Notre Dame Scholastic* profiled William E. Miller's undergraduate student activities on 28 September 1934, page 1; Ed "Moose" Krause offered his recollections in a telephone interview, 8 August 1991. Arthur gives the results of Father O'Hara's Religious Surveys, pages 387 and following; and Thomas Strich recalled his undergraduate days in his memoir, *My Notre Dame,* Notre Dame, Ind., 1991, page 136.

The letter from "Gus" Dorais to Father John O'Hara, 3 February 1934, is in UVOH 2/9; President Walsh wrote to Rev. S. J. Kelly, 14 July 1922 (UPWL "Kea-Kem" #9 folder); and Father O'Hara wrote to Guy Stuart Mills, 7 March 1934 (UPOH "Admissions Towards Blacks" folder). The *Notre Dame Alumnus* gave the demographics of the N.D. student body in April 1931, page 274; Father Leonard Carrico wrote to Dorais, 6 February 1934 (UVOH 2/9), and O'Hara wrote Dorais, 20 February 1934 (UVOH 2/9). Wilson and Brondfield discuss the integration of Big Ten athletics; see their index for specific schools and athletes. In addition, the Indiana University Archives supplied information concerning African-Americans on that school's football rosters, 16 April 1993. Elmer Layden discussed the enlightened policy of Duquesne University, pages 55–63.

31. AFTER ROCKNE IN 1931

Francis Wallace asked the post-Rockne questions in *Knute Rockne,* page 272; Major John Griffith turned down the Notre Dame offer in a letter to President Charles O'Donnell, 20 April 1931, (UPCO 3/123); O'Donnell replied, 22 April 1931 (UPCO 3/123); and Arthur discussed the N.D. administration's moves at this time, page 330.

Jesse Harper praised Rockne in a letter to him, November [1927], (UADR 13/33). John Neeson, president of the N.D. alumni association, wrote to Haley, 17 April 1931, and the latter replied, 6 May 1931; Haley told Jesse Harper about Ruth Faulkner, 18 June 1931 (UABM Correspondence Series "Neeson" and "Harper" folders). She asked President Charles O'Donnell for a reference, 14 August 1931, his secretary replying affirmatively, 19 August 1931 (UPCO 3/22).

On page 373 of the text, Harper instructed Haley about the football managers' stationery, 15 June 1931 (UABM Correspondence Series "Harper" folder). Dan Halpin, a student manager at this time, told his anecdote to Bonifer and Weaver, page 66; Vice President Mulcaire wrote to the chairman of the Board of Athletics, Oregon State University, 2 October 1931 (UVMU 1/46); Paul Schissler complained to Harper, 10 June 1931 (UVMU 2/41); and Harper wrote to Mulcaire, 19 June 1931 (UVMU 2/41).

For Hunk Anderson's quote, see Rappoport, *Wake Up the Echoes,* page 167; Francis Wallace on Rockne's complicating the succession process, *Knute Rockne,* page 191; and Hunk Anderson on his expectations, page 99. Francis Wallace discussed the appointments in *From Rockne to Parseghian,* page 29; President Charles O'Donnell's announcement is in *A Treasury of Notre Dame Football,* page 101. Anderson related his version of his initial conversations with Harper and Mulcaire in his memoir, pages 100–101.

Rockne sent the N.D. administration his "scholarship list," 12 January 1931 (UVMU 2/39); the 1932 figures are in "Classification of Services" memo [1932] (UVMU 4/20) and "B.R.T. Report," 20 January 1932 (UVMU 4/21)—a comparison of the names of students on the B.R.T. list with the school's 1932–1933 intercollegiate athletic rosters reveals that almost all of the forty-eight names on the main list played football or another sport or worked in the athletic department training room. F. W. Lloyd informed Rev. M. A. Mulcaire about the 1933 numbers, 20 April 1933 (UVMU 4/22); and, 15 February 1934, Lloyd wrote to Elmer Layden about the athletic scholarship situation during the final season of Hunk's regime (UVOH 2/43). The figures on B.R.T. per student and the B.R.T. totals for the athletic department are per semester, thus the total for an academic year would be approximately double these.

Francis Wallace described Anderson's personality and weaknesses in *Autumn Madness,* New York, 1937, pages 100–104, and in *Notre Dame Story,* pages 188–91. Arthur Haley told Christy Walsh about Anderson's trip to the Mayo Clinic, 23 June 1931 (UABM General Correspondence Series/"Walsh" folder); and Reverend Mulcaire wrote to Jesse Harper about Hunk's illness, 10 July 1931 (UVMU 2/41). Anderson grumbled about his problems with Chevigny in his memoir, page 110.

The *Chicago Tribune* wondered about N.D. without Rockne, 3 October 1931. The payout to Notre Dame for the Indiana and other games of this season are in UPCO 8/130 ("Financial Report, N.D. Athletic Association, July 1st, 1931 to July 1st, 1932"). President O'Donnell explained his school's agreement for the NU game to Owen D. Young, 18 September 1931 (UPCO 6/68); the *Chicago Tribune,* 10 October 1931, carried "Tug" Wilson's plea, and the *Chicago Evening Post* carried the AP report about the Drake game, 18 October 1931.

On page 379 of the text, Haley wrote to Harper, 19 December 1931 (UABM Correspondence Series/"Jesse Harper" folder); N.D. actually earned $27,867 from the Pitt game and $20,496 from the Penn visit, as well as $27,001 at Carnegie Tech (UPCO 8/130, "Financial Report, N.D. Athletic Association, July 1st, 1931 to July 1st, 1932"). Westbrook Pegler's comments were in the *Chicago Tribune,* 15 November 1931; Walter Winchell's "blind item" was in many newspapers, including the *Baltimore Sun,* 17 November 1931. President Charles O'Donnell's secretary replied on his behalf to R. A. Coleman about the Winchell item, 19 November 1931; Coleman had written to O'Donnell, 18 November 1931 (UPCO 3/71).

The game stories on the 1931 Notre Dame–USC contest were generally excellent, particularly those in the *Los Angeles Times*, 22 November 1931; Hunk Anderson gave his "sportsmanship" explanation to Joe Doyle, who appears to have believed him (see page 97); Francis Wallace described the blunders in *From Rockne to Parseghian*, pages 41–42. Westbrook Pegler's pregame comment on the N.D.–Army contest was in the *Chicago Tribune*, 28 November 1931.

Arthur Haley informed John Neeson about the ticket situation, 21 October 1931; Christy Walsh begged Haley for extra tickets, 23 November 1931, and the latter complied, 25 November 1931 (UABM Correspondence Series/"Neeson" and "Walsh" folders); one fan wrote about Mayor Jimmy Walker's demand for "80,000 seats" and her request of five: "Gee! Won't that be a shock to 'hizzoner' when he finds out he can only have 79,995 ducats" (Grace V. Murphy to Haley, 1 September 1931 [UABM General Correspondence Series/"M" folder]). The *Chicago Tribune* carried reports on the Army's 1931 ticket-selling problems, the "gala occasion," and Westbrook Pegler's evaluation of Army as a "nice, earnest lot," 28 November 1931; that day's edition of the *New York Times* mentioned the scalpers. The *New York Times*, 29 November 1931, discussed the fans' expectations; Beach and Moore have the story about the N.D. signals, page 140; and the *New York Herald-Tribune*, 29 November 1931, described the postgame scene. The *Notre Dame Scholastic* defended Hunk, 4 December 1931, page 19; the payout to N.D. for the Army game and the final financial figures for the season are in UPCO 8/130.

President Charles O'Donnell's announcement of the Rockne Memorial and the school's fund-raising plans were published in the *Notre Dame Alumnus*, June 1931, page 361; and there was an update in the *Notre Dame Scholastic*, 16 October 1931, page 15. Northwestern president Walter Dill Scott wrote to President Charles O'Donnell, 27 August 1931, in reply to O'Donnell's refusal, 25 August 1931 (UPCO 6/68); O'Donnell turned down Ray Graham's suggestion on the alumni versus New York Giants game, 16 November 1931 (UPCO 3/69); and the N.D. president wrote to Hugh O'Donnell about soliciting Timmins, one of the richest men in Canada, 23 November 1931 (UPCO 6/74). Arthur discusses the contribution buckets plan, the student and alumni campaigns, their failures, and the eventual success, pages 154–55.

32. THE DEMAND FOR PERFECTION: 1932

The editorial in the *Notre Dame Scholastic*, 7 October 1932, was on page 19; President Charles O'Donnell wrote to John Neeson, the N.D. alumni association head, 11 February 1932 (UPCO 6/52); Arthur Haley wrote Jesse Harper about the ticket situation, 27 June 1932 (UABM Correspondence Series/"Harper" folder), and the latter replied, 30 June 1932 (UABM Correspondence Series "Harper" folder).

On page 389 of the text, the attendance figures are based on the current N.D. football media guide; the gross receipts are in UPCO 9/87. Harper began the policy of only four games a season in Notre Dame Stadium and this continued every year, with an occasional exception, until 1953. The *Notre Dame Alumnus* discussed the "Point-a-Minute" expectations, November 1932, page 46. Jock Sutherland was a protégé of Pop Warner's and later in the 1930s the details of his recruiting and subsidization system emerged; Francis Wallace discussed it in the *Saturday Evening Post*, 28 October 1939, and indicated that in 1932, Sutherland's players were paid $650 and that due to the deflation of the dollar because of the Depression: "They found themselves comparatively well-to-do. Some of them married [on the salary]. Others grouped together in apartments and lived in comparative opulence" (page 51). The *Chicago Tribune* carried the story about "Panicky" N.D., 30 October 1932, and the *Indianapolis Star* of that date carried the AP report.

The priest in Pittsburgh, Rev. Eugene Kozar, wrote to President Charles O'Donnell, 1 November 1932, and the latter replied, 4 November 1932 (UPCO 3/66). The *Notre Dame Scholastic's* cartoon and editorial appeared 4 December 1932, page 18; Jesse Harper commented on the "rumors" to the *South Bend Tribune*, 2 November 1932. President Charles O'Donnell, 31 October 1932, received the angry letter about Harper, signed "Just an old grad," but the writer's knowledge of the inside of the N.D. situation indicates that he was probably an alumnus of the school (UPCO 8/126); Rev. Mulcaire informed the chairman of the Board of Athletics, Oregon State University, 2 October 1931, about Harper's scheduling the home-and-home with Kansas (UVMU 1/46); Arch Ward wrote to President O'Donnell, 3 November 1932, and the latter answered, 4 November 1932 (UPCO 8/84); Haley replied to Ward's letter of 18 October 1932 and invited Ward to stay with him, 22 October 1932 (UABM Correspondence Series/"W" folder).

Francis Wallace wrote about the NU game in the *New York Daily News*, 13 November 1932; the gross receipts for the NU and Navy games are in UPCO 9/87. Sportswriter Wilfrid Smith of the *Chicago Tribune* criticized N.D.'s play in Cleveland, 19 November 1932. Hugh O'Donnell of the *New York Times* paraphrased and transmitted the message from FDR's private secretary to Arthur Haley, 15 November 1932; Congressman Emanuel Cellar wired Haley, 1 November 1932, and the latter replied the same day; Stephen J. Donahue, secretary to the cardinal, wrote to President Charles O'Donnell, 11 November 1932 (UABM General Correspondence Series "O," "C," and "D" folders).

Beach and Moore describe the scene on the way to Yankee Stadium, page 144, and the Army protests, page 148; the *New York Times* discussed the scalping, the radio coverage, and devoted many columns and photos to the "Celebrities at the Game"—FDR did not attend but Governor-elect Herbert H. Lehman smiled for the cameras, 27 November 1932; on an inner page of its sports section, the *Times* headlined "POWERFUL OFFENSIVE LED BY [SID] LUCKMAN ENABLES ERASMUS HALL TO TRIUMPH AGAIN." Westbrook Pegler offered his observations in the *Chicago Tribune*, 27 November 1932; the *New York Herald-Tribune* described the postgame scenes, 27 November 1932; and the *Notre Dame Scholastic* headlined the victory, 2 December 1932, page 20.

Rosalind Shaffer's report, a feature on the movie stars in attendance, and Arch Ward's angry article were carried by the *Chicago Tribune*, 11 December 1932; on the same day, the *Los Angeles Times* also ran multipage coverage of the N.D.–USC game. Arch Ward complained to President Charles O'Donnell, 9 January 1933, and the latter replied, 11 January 1933 (UPCO 8/84); Littlewood discusses the aftermath of the episode, page 64.

Francis Wallace later complained about Anderson's coaching in *From Rockne to Parseghian*, page 48 and following; Rockne called Eddie Geiger "a terrible mug" in a letter to Arthur Haley, 26 February 1930 (UABM General Series "Knute Rockne" folder); Geiger predicted the demise of Anderson in the *Chicago Evening American*, 20 December 1932; Rev. Eugene Kozar complained to President Charles O'Donnell about the coach, whom he called "Punk" Anderson, and his handling of officials, 1 November 1932 (UPCO 3/66). The year-end statistics are in *The Notre Dame Football Scrapbook*, Richard M. Cohen, et al., Indianapolis, 1977, page 82. Anderson discussed his success with the Bears in his memoir, pages 121–52.

On page 396 of the text, the final gross receipts are in UPCO 9/87. The financial documents in the Notre Dame Archives for the 1932 season reveal only the school's share of gross receipts from football games; the estimated expenses and net profit are based on the previous year's and the fact that expenses, especially with the extra travel in 1932 to southern California, could not have shrunk appreciably.

A final draft of President Charles O'Donnell's message for the 1932 *Notre Dame Football Review* is in UPCO 3/65, my emphasis added; the *Notre Dame Scholastic* editorialized on 6 December 1932, page 4; the woman in Iowa, Katherine C. Bohan, wrote to President Charles O'Donnell, 28 November 1932, and his secretary replied for him, 30 November 1932 (UPCO 3/65); the official of Catholic University, Rev. Maurice S. Sheehy, wrote to President Charles O'Donnell, 7 January 1933, and enclosed a newspaper clipping—dateline and origin not included—quoting Judge Collins's speech (UPCO 3/64). The *Notre Dame Alumnus* covered the *Saturday Review* controversy and reprinted President Charles O'Donnell's letter to the editor, April–May 1932, pages 168–69; the alumni magazine was sympathetic to the president's position, and in an editorial, December 1931, page 77, had said:

> Supremacy [in football] requires its price. It produces an artificial glamour. The public becomes hyper-critical. . . . Professional sports, business concerns, crime, and society can pay this price.
>
> Universities cannot and continue their proper academic tenor. [With the football championships] Notre Dame was losing, in the public eye, that perspective which its status as a leading educational institution should command.

33. THE REMOVAL OF A VICE PRESIDENT AND THE FIRST FIRING OF A NOTRE DAME HEAD COACH: 1933

For the *Notre Dame Alumnus*'s comment on the Kansas game, see December 1933, page 75. Arthur Haley wrote to his friend Anthony Kegowicz, 25 July 1933 (UABM General Correspondence Series/"K" folder); Arthur explained about Mulcaire's weaknesses, page 413; and Rev. James Burns wrote to President Charles O'Donnell,

29 June 1933 (UPCO 1/67). The quote from Father O'Hara was in his Religious Bulletin, 8 October 1929 (PNDP 83-Re-1b); see also Rev. McAvoy's biography of O'Hara, pages 103–114, which sums up: "above all this admixture of education and football was the religious spirit of Notre Dame, manipulated by Father John O'Hara."

On page 400 of the text, Jesse Harper wrote to Haley, 21 July 1933; Haley replied, 24 July 1933 (UABM Correspondence Series/"Harper" folder). Rev. John P. Griffin complained to O'Hara, 3 October 1933, and the latter responded, 4 October 1933 (UVOH 1/32). The N.D. undergraduate is quoted in Emil Klosinski, page 174; Arthur Haley was optimistic about the opener in a letter to Frank Leahy, 6 October 1933 (UABM General Correspondence Series/"L" folder).

One fan sent a copy of the AP report on the opener that had been clipped from the *Minneapolis Journal*, 8 October 1933, and scrawled across the top: "Get Anderson Out" (UABM General Correspondence Series/"Miscellaneous . . . 1933" folder); the *Chicago Tribune* game story appeared 8 October 1933, and the *Notre Dame Scholastic*'s comments, 13 October 1933, page 10; the sarcastic column in the *South Bend Tribune*, 5 October 1933. John C. Gorman, the father of co-captain Tom "Kitty" Gorman, wrote to O'Hara, 12 October 1933, and the vice president replied, 17 October 1933 (UVOH 1/32). Irate fan V. Alba sent his "Open Letter to Hunk Anderson," 8 October 1933 (UABM General Correspondence Series/"A" folder).

The *Chicago Tribune* carried the N.D.–Indiana game report, 15 October 1933, and on the front page of its sports section featured a photo of "Jesse Babb, Indiana's diminutive Negro ball toter"; according to the Indiana University Archives, in a written communication dated 15 February 1993, Babb subsequently "was not listed in registrar's graduation lists" and did not earn a degree from IU (*plus ça change*). French Lane covered the N.D.–Carnegie Tech game for the *Chicago Tribune*, 22 October 1933.

O'Hara's Pittsburgh friend, Jim Costin, told him about the team's performance, 17 November 1933 (UVOH 1/9); old grad C. J. Pope complained to O'Hara, 22 October 1933 (UVOH 1/70). Rabid fan Jim T. [illegible name] addressed his letter to "Notre Dame" and did not date it; he added: "It's a disgrace to [the] memory of Rockne to all continuance of what we saw yesterday" (UABM General Correspondence Series/"Miscellaneous . . . 1933" folder). Dr. John F. Fahey endorsed Lieb in a letter to "Moderator of Athletics" at Notre Dame, 24 October 1933 (UABM General Correspondence Series/"F" folder); Tom Lieb wrote to Father O'Hara in 1933 on 5 October, 17 October, 19 October, and 23 October (UVOH 1/47); Dr. Leo J. Ward called for deemphasis in a letter to "Board of Athletic Control," 22 October 1933 (UABM General Correspondence Series/"W" folder).

On page 403 of the text, Thomas M. Murphy wrote about Catholic education to President Charles O'Donnell, 4 November 1933; O'Hara answered for O'Donnell, 6 November 1933, and in his reply gave the "popular hysteria" disclaimer (UVOH 1/55); O'Hara wrote to Richard B. Swift, 3 November 1933, noting the "kick out of the season," the need "to remain calm," and the "small-time gamblers" (UVOH 1/79); O'Hara mentioned "equilibrium" to Robert Donovan, 14 November 1933 (UVOH 1/19); and O'Hara remarked to Arthur J. Lea Mond, 30 October 1933, about the "betting" (UVOH 1/47). Lea Mond, an N.D. alum, was a columnist for the *New York Morning-Telegraph,* and he sent a column to Father O'Hara, 26 October 1933, commenting that Anderson's "selection . . . was considered a poor one from the start" mainly because of his unimaginative play-calling and his lack of "the vocal polish that a successful modern coach should have . . . the one factor that made Rockne the beloved man of millions." When these inadequacies combined with his inability to win games and the fact that "he cannot run a Notre Dame team without internal dissension," the time had come for him to resign.

The *Chicago Tribune* carried the critical comments on the N.D. team in its story about the Pitt game, 29 October 1933; the *Notre Dame Scholastic*'s blast appeared, 3 November 1933, page 10; and Joe Petritz's remarks were in the *Notre Dame Alumnus,* November 1933, page 54. The payouts from Pitt, Indiana, and Carnegie Tech are in UVOC 6/6. O'Hara's businessman friend G. L. Rathel wrote to him, 24 October 1933 (UVOH 1/76); President Charles O'Donnell answered A. D. McDonald, 30 October 1933 (UPCO 5/131); Westbrook Pegler's comments were in the *Chicago Tribune,* 4 November 1933; O'Hara telegraphed Anderson, 3 November 1933 (UVOH 1/1); and the *Indianapolis Star* had a full account of the N.D.–Navy game and the postgame scene, 5 November 1933. The *Notre Dame Scholastic* discussed the ramifications for N.D. football history before the Navy game, 3 November 1933, page 11, and after it, 10 November 1933, page 11.

On page 407 of the text, Wallace wrote to Haley, 7 November 1933: compounding the screw-up, apparently this booster was a professional gambler, because Wallace added, "In these days of increasing gambling on football games, I wonder if it is wise to have one of 'the boys' hanging around" the football program (UABM General Correspondence Series/"W" folder); Anderson's exhausted excuse is in his memoir, page 112.

Frank Leahy wrote to Haley, undated but probably late October 1933 (emphasis added), and Haley replied, 1 November 1933 (UABM General Correspondence Series/"L" folder); the *New York World-Telegram* featured the Fordham–St. Mary's game, 5 November 1933. Jim Crowley was well-known for his love of drinking, when he began as head coach at Michigan Agricultural, Rockne warned him, 3 September 1929: "you and Carberry [Crowley's assistant and a former Rockne player] stay absolutely on the wagon in Lansing and East Lansing. That is just about as good advice as I can give you" (UADR 10/58). In *Biographical Dictionary,* James D. Whalen outlined Madigan's disputes with St. Mary's, noting that the school finally fired him when he "deposited St. Mary's' $100,000 share of the 1939 Fordham game receipts into his personal bank account" (page 379).

Frank Reese wrote to O'Hara, 5 November 1933 (UVOH 1/76), and T. R. McKeever sent the telegram from Texas to President Charles O'Donnell, 27 November 1933 (UVOH 1/59). Ned Colletti, tells the Duane Purvis story and has a detailed game account, page 75; the *Chicago Tribune* carried reports of Purvis's medical problems, 8 November 1933; the *Notre Dame Scholastic* reviewed the N.D.–Purdue series, 10 November 1933, page 10; and the following week despaired about the N.D. performance, 17 November 1933, page 10. The payouts from the Purdue, Northwestern, and USC games are in UVOC 6/6. The news report on the Northwestern game is in the *Notre Dame Scrapbook,* reprinted from an unidentified newspaper, page 84; Arch Ward discussed the Chicago connection of the N.D. players in the *Chicago Tribune,* 19 November 1933.

On page 409 of the text, Haley wrote to Chicago fan J. Patrick Lannan, 24 October 1933 (UABM General Correspondence Series/"L" folder); Freeman Gosden asked Haley for tickets, 6 November 1933, and Haley replied the same day (UABM General Correspondence Series/"A" folder); John Gallagher of the *Los Angeles Times,* 26 November 1933, commented on the N.D. feeble attack; the same day in the *Chicago Tribune,* Arch Ward took his shots. Arthur Haley wrote to John Neeson, 26 November 1933 (UABM Correspondence Series/"Neeson" folder); and James Armstrong in the *Notre Dame Alumnus* expressed his bewilderment, December 1933, page 74.

Raymond J. Kelly, governor of the Notre Dame Alumni Club of Detroit, wrote to O'Hara, 5 December 1933 (UVOH 1/18); Francis Wallace commented on the qualities needed to coach at his alma mater in *Notre Dame Story,* page 98; *Vince: A Personal Biography of Vince Lombardi* by Michael O'Brien, New York, 1987, discusses the great coach's interest in the N.D. job and that, in 1958, after the dismissal of Terry Brennan, "Lombardi applied and claimed they never even acknowledged his letter," page 124. Lombardi certainly did not meet the criteria for the "Notre Dame type of coach."

Pittsburgh sportswriter Jim Costin wrote to O'Hara, November 17, 1933 (UVOH 1/9); the best source for Elmer Layden's career and lifestyle is his generally accurate memoir; O'Hara wrote to the manager of the Carnegie Tech athletic department, Clarence Overend, 14 December 1933 (UVOH 1/66); and the N.D. vice president replied to Detroit alum Raymond J. Kelly, 13 December 1933 (UVOH 1/18). Layden told the story of the dinner with O'Hara in his memoir, pages 86–87. O'Hara complained to New York alum John Balfe, 13 November 1933, about not wanting to go to the Army game (UVOH 1/5).

The *New York Times* explained about the N.D. cheerleaders and extensively covered the pregame and halftime festivities, 3 December 1933. Nick Lukats's comment is in *Intercollegiate Football,* edited by Christy Walsh, page 357; Beach and Moore describe the winning play in great detail, pages 154–55; O'Hara told Bishop Ralph L. Hayes about the final minutes of the game, 5 December 1933 (UVOH 1/36); the N.D. vice president related the "cure for lumbago" and the alum's wife's story to Monsignor John P. Durham, 6 December 1933 (UVOH 1/18).

The *New York Times* reported on the reception for Anderson after the game and also carried an AP report about the student celebration in South Bend, 3 December 1933; Caswell Adams in the *New York Herald-Tribune* used the Tyburn metaphor, 3 December 1933; the *Notre Dame Scholastic* featured the campus reaction as well as various newspaper columnists' comments, including Damon Runyon's, 8 November 1933, page 10; and the *Notre Dame Alumnus* connected the triumph to the football history, December 1933, page 80. For an account of the Oklahoma–Notre Dame game of 1957, see Whittingham, *Saturday Afternoon,* page 196 and following.

Richard Vidmer commented in the *New York Herald-Tribune,* 3 December 1933, and Joe Williams in the *World-Telegram,* 4 December 1933. Although the draft of the official statement on the resignations of Harper and Anderson is in N.D. President Charles O'Donnell's files (UPCO 4/6), the handwriting is O'Hara's, emphasis added. The *Chicago Tribune* covered the A.D.'s and coach's resignations and Layden's assumption of power, 8–10 December 1933; the *Notre Dame Alumnus* had Anderson's statement, January 1934, page 117.

Father O'Hara wrote to Notre Dame patron James A. Phelan, 16 December 1933 (UVOH 1/69), and to his friend Jim Costin, 14 December 1933 (UVOH 1/8); O'Hara offered a caution to Rev. Maurice Sheehy, 18 December 1933 (UVOH 1/78). The final financial figures for 1933 are in UVOC 6/6; the expenses are in URPT 13/0.

Hunk Anderson holds the distinction of being the first head football coach fired— as the sports world understands that term—by Notre Dame: Shorty Longman left by mutual agreement after the 1910 season, John Marks wandered away in 1912, none of their predecessors were "fired" in the modern sense; that is, Hunk would have continued if he had been able to. In fact, fewer resemblances exist between the pre– Harper-Rockne era at Notre Dame and the football situation twenty years later than do between the early 1930s and the present.

34. O'HARA AND LAYDEN ASSUME POWER: 1934–1936

The *Notre Dame Alumnus* carried the text of Father John O'Hara's address to the NCAA, January 1934, pp. 107–8; the official history of the NCAA by Jack Falla outlines the association's activity in the 1930s, pages 129–131. In his letter to Griffith, 13 October 1933, O'Donnell accepted the invitation (UPCO 3/122), and O'Hara informed Griffith, 22 December 1933, that he would speak in place of the N.D. president (UVOH 1/35). McAvoy discusses O'Hara's policy on N.D. football, especially in reaction to the Pritchett attack, pages 139–40, and Arthur does the same, page 326. Professor Strich remarked on the "holier-than-thou image," page 136.

Henry S. Pritchett's short essay, "A Slump in the Football Trade," and his comments about Notre Dame appeared in the Carnegie Foundation's Annual Report, February 1934, pages 32–33. The *New York Times* carried O'Hara's reply, 20 February 1934; O'Hara's letter to oil company executive Lucien P. Locke, 24 February 1934, is in UVOH 2/40; O'Hara wrote Joseph Greeley about the press's reaction to Pritchett's remarks and also how N.D. could benefit from friendly sportswriters, 26 February 1934 (UVOH 2/23). The packet from the clipping service referred to in the text is in UVOC 4/49. O'Hara massaged Grantland Rice's gargantuan ego, 25 October 1934 (UPOH "Rh-Rog" 1934–35 folder).

Francis Wallace listed his fellow alums on the N.D. network in *Notre Dame Story,* pages 47 and 154–55; in his memoir, Layden paid homage to the Chicago and New York sportswriting friends of Notre Dame, page 173; Littlewood commented on Arch Ward's "Counter-Skepticism," page 204; Finis Farr traced Westbrook Pegler's transition from sports to punditry, page 103 and following. During the Layden years, N.D. alum Bill Fox's *Indianapolis News* was particularly flagrant in reprinting Joe Petritz's handouts as news stories; after the latter's one-time attack on Hunk Anderson in 1933, Petritz returned to regular flackery for the duration of the 1930s.

In the long history of attempts to reform college sports, only one element has changed—the press. During the recent reform attempt of the late 1980s through the early 1990s, not all members of the press sided with the athletic establishment, and the investigative reports and commentary from these sportswriters provided an alternative albeit minor voice against the voluminous propaganda spewing from athletic departments, the NCAA, and the electronic media.

On page 424 of the text, Jesse Harper's letter to Arthur Haley, 19 September 1934, and Haley's reply, 5 October 1934, are in UABM Correspondence Series/ "Harper" folder. The midwestern sportswriter who began his career during the 1930s made his comments in an interview, 30 November 1992. He requested anonymity, explaining:

> My wife is Catholic and, wouldn't you know it, my only son went there [N.D.] and he's so proud of being a "Domer." Anyway, I was mainly a baseball writer and tried to stay clear of college football. I much preferred being in a warm, dry newspaper office on a fall Saturday "pulling scores" off the wires than out at Notre Dame Stadium or in the Big Ten trying to identify the dumb oxen wallowing in the mud, the rain whipping into the pressbox. You can't believe how rickety most of them were. Also I hated the football coaches and the alums and all the rah-rah horseshit. . . . At the time I didn't care what the N.D. athletic department thought of me and I sure as hell don't now but because of my wife and son, I don't want to go on the record saying anything against their sacred Notre Dame. This "Notre Dame family" stuff is for real and they kick you out too. I worry that my kid would choose the Dome over me.

Layden's anecdote about the "77 average" is in his memoir, pages 95–96; Haley wrote to John Neeson about the changes in the athletic department, 10 January 1934 (UABM Correspondence Series/"Neeson" folder); Layden's claim about the Ohio State series is in his memoir, page 104; Vice President Mulcaire sent B. L. Stradley of Ohio State invitational telegrams, 16 February and 21 February 1933 (UVMU 2/45), and then after the visit, Mulcaire dispatched "reports on class absences, employment to athletes, and a list of the professors in the Department of Physical Education, as you requested," 7 March 1933 (UVMU 2/45). The football salaries for Layden and his assistants are in UABM Correspondence Series "Frank Lloyd" folder. Peg Boland told the story of O'Hara's phone call to her husband in *Joe Boland–Notre Dame Man*, Hammond, Ind., 1962, page 10. Father O'Hara informed Dr. Leo D. O'Donnell of his awareness of Layden as a "griper," 19 December 1933 (UVOH 1/66).

Layden discussed O'Hara's reforms in his memoir, pages 96–97, O'Hara's advice about making "a novena," page 131, Marshall Goldberg, page 132, and Tom Harmon, page 133; Scrapiron Young related the anecdote about the South Bend recruits in his memoir, page 208, his out-of-town recruiting, pages 224–25, and how players competed for varsity spots, page 222; Young, when not apologizing for his idol, Knute Rockne, is usually reliable. Francis Wallace offered his Goldberg anecdote in *From Rockne to Parseghian*, page 64; *Glory of Notre Dame* lists the Catholic high school captains on the 1938 team, page 60; and the *Notre Dame Alumnus* explained Layden's "A" and "B" system, November 1934, page 43.

The *Notre Dame Alumnus* quoted Layden's speech, April 1934, page 198; Jesse Harper complained to Haley, 16 April 1934 (UABM Correspondence Series "Harper" folder); and Layden wrote to Rockne about the Duquesne job, undated but probably February 1927 (UADR 14/126). Another of Rockne's "old boys," Mal Elward, was also in contention for the Duquesne job and the coach told him that the school was "anxious to step out" (UADR 11/86). Rockne advised Layden that he was "smart in going to Duquesne," 2 March 1927 (UADR 14/127), and Layden discussed the refereeing situation with his mentor, 15 November 1927 (UADR 14/127). Arthur Haley commented to Arch Ward about J. J. Lipp, 17 December 1934 (UABM General Correspondence Series "W" folder).

The *Notre Dame Alumnus* remarked on the Texas opener, November 1934, page 43; Scrapiron Young revealed in his memoir how Chevigny "had nurtured a grievance," page 187; Texas player J. Neils Thompson told the story about Chevigny's locker room talk in *The College Game*, edited by Don Campbell, Indianapolis, 1974, page 180; and Layden in his memoir remarked on Chevigny winning one for himself, page 100. The *Notre Dame Alumnus* remarked on Kizer's "Mule" grievance, October 1934, page 13, and Ned Colletti provides a good account of the N.D.-Purdue game, pages 79–81; the *Chicago Tribune* covered the Notre Dame home games against Carnegie Tech and Wisconsin in detail, 21 October and 28 October 1934; the *Indianapolis News* commented on Layden's refusal to alibi after the loss to Pitt, 4 November 1934; most accounts of the N.D.-Navy game praise "Buzz" Borries's play: see Wayne K. Otto in the *Chicago Herald-Examiner*, 11 November 1934; all the accounts of the NU-N.D. game mention the "hocus-pocus play"—termed that in the *Notre Dame Alumnus*, December 1934, page 63.

Alvin Gould of the AP proclaimed the N.D.-Army game, "the biggest turnout," the *Indianapolis Star* carried his article, 25 November 1934, and on the same day, the *New York Post*, among other papers, played up the Dan Hanley angle. The best account of Layden's relations with his younger brother and the latter's play in the 1934 USC game is in *The Glamor Game*, pages 71–75; and Arch Ward's game story in the *Chicago Tribune* appeared 9 December 1934.

On page 433 of the text, the football receipts from 1934 are in UVOC 6/6, and the end-of-school-year profits and expenses are in URPT 13/Correspondence Series "Frank Lloyd" folder). The faculty athletic board turndown of the bowl bids was discussed by Dean Clarence Manion, a longtime member, in his "Newsletter," January 1962, no pagination. The new bowls later became important to Notre Dame in an indirect way; they helped build the coaching reputation of Frank Leahy—particularly after his Boston College team scored an upset victory in the 1940 Sugar Bowl—and positioned him as the leading candidate to succeed Layden.

Vice President Hugh "Pepper" O'Donnell's address at the 1935 N.D. football banquet is in the *Notre Dame Alumnus*, February 1936, pages 123–24; that magazine discussed the new rules with a headline that President O'Hara must have liked, "NEW ELIGIBILITY RULES PLACE N.D. IN FRONT," January 1935, page 81, and it outlined the Jack Robinson case as well as Elmer Layden's prediction for the season, October 1935, page 15. As usual, the Chicago papers covered Notre Dame games in exhaustive detail and wire service journalist Gene Vaslett praised the team after the Pitt game, reprinted in the *Notre Dame Football Scrapbook,* page 89. One of the few negative incidents involving Layden and the referees occurred at Pitt in 1935 when his great antagonist Jock Sutherland unilaterally named the officials. One penalty so enraged Layden that, for one of the few times in his coaching career, he lost his famous "cool" and rushed onto the field and argued toe-to-toe with the official; unfortunately for Layden, the AP ran a photo of this argument on its wire.

Allison Danzig of the *New York Times* described the Ohio State "collosi," 2 November 1935, and the next day his game story included the description of the "despair" in Columbus; a young Jerry Brondfield proclaimed that the winner could win "a possible national championship," *Notre Dame Scholastic,* 1 November 1935, page 15. The story of the anti-Catholic crowd at practice is in Rappoport, page 192; Elmer Layden talked about the scene in Columbus in his memoir (op. cit.), p. 106; "Red" Barber related his experience in a telephone interview for this book, 16 June 1991; and the nun in Oregon, Sister M. Helen, narrated her experiences in an article, "The Power Behind the Team," for the *Notre Dame Alumnus,* March 1936, page 156 and following.

On page 436 of the text, Sister Mary Benigna sent President O'Hara a "Mass stipend" and mentioned the prayers at her gathering "for a Notre Dame victory," 4 November 1935, and O'Hara replied, 9 November 1935 (UPOH 62/"Fan Letters Football Games" folder); Joe Doyle supplied the ironic footnote, page 104; Bill Shakespeare was nicknamed "The Merchant of Menace" and, according to class-mates, did not do well in English classes. Professor Mary Jo Weaver told the story in the text and many other wonderful anecdotes in an interview for this book, 11 April 1991.

Francis Wallace commented on N.D. always winning "the big ones" in *From Rockne to Parseghian,* page 67; the *Notre Dame Alumnus* in its season review played up the "The Two Minute Men" angle, December 1935, page 66 and following; even the *Notre Dame Scholastic* was not too downcast by the loss to Northwestern, 8 November 1935, page 11 and following. Lynn Waldorf had coached successfully at small-time Oklahoma City and Kansas State but the Northwestern job in 1935 was his entrance into the "Big Show." He later won a conference championship with the Wildcats and, in the 1940s, three Pac-8 titles with Cal-Berkeley; one biographer noted that his great achievement was winning at "several traditional coaching grave-yards," *Biographical Dictionary,* page 627.

Arch Gott in the *Notre Dame Scholastic* described the crowd at Yankee Stadium, 22 November 1935, page 19; Beach and Moore examine the game and particularly the controversial N.D. pass play in great detail, pages 165–77; the gross gate receipts for the season are in UVOC 6/6, and the estimated expenses are in UVOC 5/53.

On page 438 of the text, A. D. McDonald wired Layden, 25 November [1935] (UVOC 4/49). The *Notre Dame Scholastic* discussed the possible Rose Bowl trip, 29 November 1935, page 10 and following; Father Hope outlined the end of 1935 and the visit by President Franklin D. Roosevelt, page 161 and following, as did McAvoy, page 146 and following.

The Paul Mickelson quote about Marshall Goldberg was in the *Indianapolis Star,* 25 October 1936; the *Notre Dame Alumnus* listed all 183 players on the football squad, October 1936, page 12 and following, and critiqued the opening games, November 1936, page 63 and following; the *Notre Dame Scholastic* did a pregame feature on the coaching careers of the Four Horsemen, 16 October 1936, page 19, and that paper lamented the loss at Pitt, leading its article "Sadly deficient in all departments . . . the Notre Dame football team . . ." 30 October 1936, page 17; the Chicago papers continued to cover N.D. games and the New York journals pointed to the annual clash with Army. Francis Wallace supported Layden in the *New York World-Telegram,* 13 November 1936, and Paul Webster in the *New York Evening Post* wondered about the "Notre Dame system," 14 November 1936; Beach and Moore describe the game on pages 177–84.

The *Notre Dame Scholastic* reported "Crowds Come from Distant Corners to See Contest" against Northwestern, 27 November 1936, page 18; Chicago writer Tony Ardizzone offered his insight on the excursion trains in an interview for this book, 20 April 1992; the *Chicago Tribune* and *Chicago Herald & American* sportswriters praised the N.D. attack in their game stories, 22 November 1936.

On page 442 of the text, the school's share of the 1936 gate receipts are in UVOC 6/6; the *Los Angeles Times* carried full game stories, statistics, and the coaches' comments after the N.D.–USC match, 6 December 1936; Braven Dyer in that edition wondered about Layden's adherence to the "Rockne system"—Dyer's career continued for many decades, reaching its nadir when he was punched out by Angels' pitcher "Bo" Belinsky.

In *Football: A College History,* Tom Perrin discussed the passing attack introduced by "Dutch" Meyer and "Slingin'" Sammy Baugh, pages 172–73, and Leahy's "Seven Blocks of Granite," page 171. Articles in *Biographical Dictionary* explain Baugh's career, pages 29–31; Meyer's, pages 391–92; and O'Brien's, pages 443–44. Charlie Callahan defended the "Notre Dame system" in the *Scholastic,* 11 December 1936, page 19.

35. O'HARA AND LAYDEN IN POWER: 1937–1939

Robert Hutchins offered his comments in his article, "Gate Receipts and Glory," *Saturday Evening Post,* 12 December 1938, page 23 and following; Robin Lester's excellent unpublished Ph.D. dissertation, "The Rise, Decline, and Fall of Intercollegiate Football at the University of Chicago, 1890–1940," details Hutchins's moves throughout the 1930s; in addition the *University of Chicago* [Alumni] *Magazine* tracked the events month-by-month and ran many letters from alumni on both sides of the deemphasis issue. A subsequent myth has sprung up that Hutchins suddenly decided to pull Chicago out of the Big Ten one day in 1940 and got immediate permission from the trustees of the school. In fact, Chicago's detachment from the Big Ten was a long-term process that began in the late 1920s and did not end formally until 1946.

Bill Corum's column appeared in the Hearst flagship paper, the *New York Journal-American,* 30 November 1938; according to this writer, Hutchins's arguments were based solely on the "passé and dated" Carnegie Report—the sole result of that investigation was that "it frightened some of our higher institutions of learning into a state of temporary purity—a condition from which they happily recovered quickly." Thus, even some of the bedmates of the athletic establishment openly acknowledged the widespread corruption in college sports.

Paul Gallico's *Farewell to Sport* is well worth reading, with many of his insights and arguments as true today as when he wrote them in the 1930s; the quotes in the text are on pages 208 and 109. Francis Wallace's long exposé, "Test Case at Pitt—The Facts About College Football Play for Pay," appeared in the *Saturday Evening Post,* 28 October 1939, page 14 and following, and 4 November 1939, page 12 and following. The headline "PITT PURGE SIGNALS END OF GRID HYPOCRISY" appeared in *Collyer's Eye & Baseball World,* 18 March 1939, page 1.

On page 447 of the text, Major John Griffith wrote to Rev. Hugh O'Donnell, 8 January 1936, and the latter replied, 20 January 1936 (UVOC 4/50); a Notre Dame–Ohio State game is scheduled for 1995. The quote from Father McAvoy's biography of O'Hara is on page 157, and the subsequent pages in that work supply many details of Father O'Hara's presidency; Professor Thomas Strich also discusses this period, pages 26–29; the *Notre Dame Alumnus* reported the visit of Cardinal Pacelli, November 1936, page 1; O'Hara replied to J. R. Nulty's inquiry requesting the names of prominent N.D. grads in the business world, 28 December 1933 (UVOH 2/55).

The *Notre Dame Scholastic* covered J. Edgar Hoover's address to the student body, 15 January 1937, page 5; in *Onward to Victory,* James Armstrong later affirmed that "Notre Dame alumni were welcome in the FBI, numbering at one time 102 agents," page 307. President O'Hara wrote to Dr. Howard Savage, 22 May 1935 (UPOH 64/"S-Schl" folder). Elmer Layden discusses his diplomacy with former Big Ten foes in his memoir, pages 124–26; Layden's communications with Yost are in the Bentley Historical Library at the University of Michigan, Fielding Harris Yost Collection, Box 36, "Notre Dame 1910–45" folder; the birthday greeting from Layden to Yost came in a telegram, 29 April 1939. Francis Wallace told the story of Yost's visit to his alma mater in *Notre Dame Story,* page 208; Yost had agreed to resume athletic relations in minor sports in late 1937—the *South Bend Tribune,* 2 December 1937, featured the story of the resumption of athletic relations between the schools. In addition, the *Notre Dame Scholastic,* 10 December 1937, carried an article titled "Relations Resumed with Michigan," page 15. Yost visited Notre Dame on the occasion of the N.D.-Purdue game in 1939 and reporters were amazed at his presence (*South Bend Tribune,* 1 October 1939).

Layden told the story of how he scheduled the 1940 season opener against Amos Alonzo Stagg's College of the Pacific in his memoir, pages 126–27. On page 451 of the text, at the top of President O'Hara's letter to Layden about the "recipients of jobs," there is "c.c. [Vice President] Father [Hugh] O'Donnell" and "c.c. [Comptroller] Mr. Lloyd," 19 August 1937 (UVOC 6/6); F. W. Lloyd sent a copy of O'Hara's memo and the "Local Council" of the C.S.C.'s "budget allotment" for athletes to Rev. Hugh O'Donnell, 24 July 1937 (UVOC 6/6); the average yearly cost—tuition and room and board—at Notre Dame in 1937 was $700.

F. W. Lloyd wrote on behalf of the N.D. athletic board to Father Hugh O'Donnell about Layden's protest, 25 January 1938 (UVOC 4/50); E. J. Murray, N.D. supervisor of student employment, wrote to Layden about the thirty-three jobs, 8 September 1939, and Rev. Hugh O'Donnell informed Layden of the increase, 11 September 1939 (UVOC 5/7); the article in the *Notre Dame Scholastic* about the summer jobs appeared 24 September, 1937, page 15 and following.

On page 452 of the text, J. E. McCarthy of the Notre Dame Faculty Board in Control of Athletics wrote to Frank C. Barton, 15 May 1937 (UVOC 6/52). President O'Hara's estimate of the loss from refusing to sell the broadcasting rights was in an article in the *South Bend News-Times*, 18 May 1937; the complete 1937 football roster is in the *Notre Dame Alumnus*, October 1937, page 8 and following; the *Notre Dame Scholastic* commented on the Illinois game, 15 October 1937, page 17; Francis Wallace explained Carnegie Tech's coaching move in the *Saturday Evening Post*, 4 November 1939, page 12; the *Notre Dame Scholastic* quoted Grantland Rice, 22 October 1937, page 18; the Clashmore Mike story was in the *Notre Dame Alumnus*, November 1937, page 43; Tom Perrin referred to the "Neanderthal play" of Minnesota, page 175; the Chicago papers and the wire services covered all N.D. games in detail, many using "PITT CRUSHES IRISH" as their headline, *Chicago Tribune*, 7 November 1937.

Irate fan W. H. O'Toole wrote to President O'Hara, 22 October 1937 (UPOH 73/ "Crank Letters" folder); the fan mentioned the "police escort to the Polo Grounds," however, N.D. had only played Army there in 1924, and the 1930s New York newspapers carried accounts of how the Cadet Corps got off the train from West Point at 125th Street and marched from there to Yankee Stadium in the Bronx. The "urchins" would gather in Hells' Kitchen on the West Side and travel uptown to Harlem, "greeting" the Cadet Corps along the route of its march.

The *Notre Dame Alumnus* commented on the "stiffening eligibility requirements," November 1937, page 42; Francis Wallace remarked about Layden and "the usual coaching calendar" in *From Rockne to Parseghian*, page 77; see the *New York Herald-Tribune* and the *New York Times* 12 November 1937, for the pregame articles on the N.D.–Army game, and see their editions of the next day for comprehensive coverage of the event; the *Notre Dame Scholastic* reporter remarked on the team's "seldom-scoring offense," 26 November 1937, page 19; the *South Bend News-Times* wrote up the N.D.–USC game, 28 November 1937.

On page 455 of the text, for the gross gate receipts, $495,445, and the estimated football expenses for 1937–1938, see UVOC 6/6. That file also contains documents on the estimated expense for varsity basketball, $22,805, and a communication to Layden, 11 January 1937, that put the "Expense listed in budget" for track at

$19,470; baseball, $9,095; tennis, $2,042; golf, $1,747; and fencing, $1,065 (UVOC 4/50). The C.S.C. Council cut the amounts, but even with the cuts and the normal costs of intramural sports, the number in the text is probably a low estimate. The speech of John T. McGovern was covered by the *Notre Dame Alumnus,* February 1938, page 1; the *Chicago Times* headlined the departure of captain-elect Alec Shellogg, 30 January 1938.

The *Notre Dame Alumnus* listed the 1938 roster, October 1938, page 14 and following; the *Notre Dame Scholastic* commented on the Kansas opener and the coming Georgia Tech game, 7 October 1938, page 15; Beach and Moore tell the Benny Sheridan recruiting story, page 198; Sheridan ended up as a beer distributor in Bloomington, Indiana. There are many accounts of the controversy at the 1938 N.D.–Carnegie Tech game; the *Indianapolis Star* carried the wire service stories, 23 October 1938; that same day the *Chicago Tribune* had its reports, and the *Pittsburgh Press* predictably saw it from a Carnegie Tech point of view; Francis Wallace discussed it and Layden's strategy in *From Rockne to Parseghian,* pages 78–79. Beach and Moore explain the Army decline and the 1938 game on pages 191–200.

On page 457 of the text, the N.D. faculty athletic board informed Layden about the traveling squad, 4 October 1938 (UVOC 5/7). New York fan E. T. Collins complained to President O'Hara, 27 October 1938, and Layden wrote to O'Hara about the "beauties," 1 November 1938 (UPOH 77/"Athletic Office Layden 1937–39" folder). The *Indianapolis Star* carried Paul Mickelson's AP story, 6 November 1938, the *Chicago Tribune* featured the N.D.–Minnesota game, 13 November 1938, and the N.D.-Northwestern contest, 20 November 1938; and the *Los Angeles Times* did its usual excellent job on the N.D.–USC game and got Layden's quote on Saggau, 4 December 1938.

Chicago sportswriter Warren Brown wrote to Rev. J. Hugh O'Donnell, undated but apparently March 1941, after Layden's resignation from N.D. (UPHO 88/ "Layden Resignation" folder); Brown's comparison between Eddie Anderson and Layden came in a letter in which he proposed Anderson as Layden's replacement. In his columns in the *Chicago Herald & American* during Layden's last years, Brown frequently complained about the coach's not getting the most out of the extraordinary football talent on the Notre Dame campus.

In 1938, the "Frank G. Dickenson System," named after and run by an old friend of Rockne's at the University of Illinois, put the Fighting Irish on top. Dickenson heavily weighted his rankings toward midwestern teams; the AP poll was the most accurate in this period and, in 1938, their final ratings put N.D. fifth, Minnesota tenth, Michigan sixteenth, and Northwestern seventeenth, and no other midwestern team in the top twenty.

On page 459 of the text, the 1938 gross gate receipts are in UVOC 6/6; Vice President O'Donnell wrote to Clyde E. Broussard of Texas, 29 November 1938 (UVOC 4/50).

The *Notre Dame Alumnus's* 1939 football preseason article appeared October 1939, page 15 and following, and that magazine covered the dedication of the Rockne Memorial building, including Layden's speech, June 1939, page 209 and following.

Ned Colletti described the N.D.–Purdue game, pages 82–83; and the *Chicago Daily News,* among other papers, played up the Kelleher angle, 1 October 1939. The AP report on the N.D.–SMU game noted that Notre Dame "backed into" the win, *Notre Dame Scrapbook,* page 99, but its story on the win over Navy was more positive, *Indianapolis Star,* 22 October 1939. Joe Petritz asked his rhetorical question and Layden gave his explanation in the *Notre Dame Alumnus,* November 1939, page 52; *Look Magazine* ran its feature on N.D. by Irving Vaughan, October 1939, page 30 and following; the *New York Times* and *New York Herald-Tribune* covered the N.D.– Army annual with a bit less enthusiasm than previously, 4 and 5 November 1939; and the *Notre Dame Alumnus* used the "Subway Alumni" term, December 1939, page 80. Tom Perrin describes the N.D.–Iowa game in a chapter appropriately titled "End of an Era," page 195 and following, and Eddie Anderson gave his version of events in *My Greatest Day in Football,* pages 8–11.

Warren Brown wrote to Rev. J. Hugh O'Donnell about Anderson's N.D. team- mates on his bench, undated (UPHO 88/"Layden Resignation" folder); Brown won- dered about N.D.'s coming game with USC in the *Chicago Herald & American,* 19 November 1939; the *Los Angeles Times* writers were very uncharitable to Layden's attack, 26 November 1939; and Peg Boland tried to dismiss the fan complaints, page 14. Tom Perrin described the UCLA offense, pages 189–90. The gross gate receipts for 1939 are in UVOC 6/6.

36. BEGINNING *KNUTE ROCKNE—ALL AMERICAN*: 1939

For the quote from Ronald Reagan, *An American Life,* New York, 1990, see pages 90–91; Pat O'Brien asserted his claim in *The Wind at My Back: The Life and Times of Pat O'Brien,* Garden City, N.Y., 1964, page 239. Ronald Reagan published his first version of the genesis of the film in his memoir, *Where's the Rest of Me?,* with Richard G. Hubler, New York, 1965. The story there is essentially the same as in his later memoir; however, in the 1965 book, he included an anecdote that offers an insight into his sense of history and his preference for the dramatic tale over the facts. Reagan commented, page 94:

> As in every picture based on real-life exploits, [in Rockne's life] truth was stranger than fiction. There were scenes that couldn't be photographed be- cause an audience wouldn't accept the truth, or it would appear too melodra- matic. For instance, it is told that Jack Chevigny, who carried the last touchdown over the goal in that game and then was carried off the field himself with a broken leg, looked up from the stretcher and said, "That's the last one I can get you, Gipper."

Ronald Reagan told this "inside" story often on the banquet circuit; in historical fact, before approximately eighty thousand witnesses on 10 November 1928, Jack Chevigny scored the tying, not the winning, touchdown, and after his TD, Chevigny did not break his leg or suffer any other injury but played for the remaining sixteen minutes of the game, making a number of key plays that helped set up Johnny O'Brien's winning TD. Probably the running back with the broken leg watching from the stretcher is Reagan's interpolation of Andy Pilney in this situation at the end of the 1935 Notre Dame–Ohio State game.

On page 465 of the text, William F. Cronin wrote to Rev. J. Hugh O'Donnell about Rickard's script, 31 December 1938 (UVOC 8/56); Arthur Haley wrote Cronin, 14 January 1939; Haley also told Cronin the day before, "Frankly, the idea came for the picture following the Cavalcade of America Broadcast put on by Du Pont in the early part of December [1938]" (UABM *Knute Rockne—All American* Series/"C" folder). Whether Haley actually believed this or was just trying to defuse the Rickard claim is impossible to tell. However, the writer of that radio broadcast, John H. Driscoll, later noted, "Naturally, I was thrilled after the broadcast when Warner Brothers bought my radio script for their picture *Knute Rockne—All American*. The film did use several of its scenes, but none of the scenes can be shown when the picture is shown on television [because this would infringe the broadcast's copyright]"; Driscoll's statement is undated (UATH "Radio Script of America's Knute Rockne" folder).

Warners did not have the foresight to include possible future TV showings in its purchase-of-rights contract. This is the reason the "Win One for the Gipper" scene was cut from many TV showings of the film—not for any nefarious political purpose, as some Reaganites charged. However, because in the "Win One for the Gipper" scene Driscoll followed the *Autobiography* closely, and in those scenes, the film reproduced that work almost word for word, it is amazing that when TV showings of this scene became an issue, the owners of Warner Brothers' film library never challenged Driscoll's copyright in court. According to the copyright law in the 1930s, the Cavalcade of America Broadcast sold something that it did not own—scenes from the *Autobiography of Knute Rockne*. Thus, the person who really lost out on royalty payments for the "Win One for the Gipper" scene was its author, John B. Kennedy.

Finally, although some of Driscoll's heirs assert that the radio broadcast was the genesis of the film, this ignores the reality of Hollywood in the 1930s and the many earlier proposals for a Rockne biopic. It was standard business practice for movie studios making biopics to purchase a wide range of copyrights from various holders of them as a routine, preemptive measure to insure against any possible future legal claims against the film companies. No doubt, Warners bought the radio script by Driscoll as part of this strategy.

On pages 465–66 of the text, Warren Brown wrote to Father John W. Cavanaugh, undated but probably May 1931 (CJWC, *Autobiography of Knute Rockne* Series/ "Letters Received Concerning Rockne Books, Memorials" folder). It is impossible to ascertain exactly which photo of Rockne provoked Bonnie's anger—they are all standard shots. Because the copyright law at the time made no distinction between public and private figures, Bonnie Rockne "owned" her husband's life and name. Under 1990s copyright law and current court interpretations of the First Amendment, a public figure and his or her heirs no longer enjoy such exclusive rights, and a film company can portray the life and use the name in any way it wants; the only protected material is copyrighted and/or published speeches, letters, and so on. Thus, a film company could now make a biopic about Knute Rockne without obtaining permission from his heirs, and scholars may write about him under the "fair use" doctrine.

Haley wrote William Cronin about "the handsome stipend that will accrue to Mrs. Rockne and her children [from the sale of her rights to Warners]," and stated: "obviously the University will cooperate in any worthwhile undertaking that will rebound financially to her and her children," 14 January 1939 (UABM *Knute Rockne—All American* Series/"C" folder). Sheilah Graham ran a trade item: "Mrs. Knute Rockne is demanding $50,000 from Warner Brothers," 21 February 1939, *Hollywood Reporter*.

On page 466 of the text, Bonnie Rockne's lawyer wrote to Warner Brothers about the themes in the film, 12 June 1939; he listed the scholarly attributes that Bonnie wanted in the picture in a letter to Warners, 16 February 1940 (UABM *Knute Rockne —All American* Series/"Vitus G. Jones" folder). The eldest son, Billy, had a very troubled life, including involvement in a shooting incident in which he was critically injured; he never attended Notre Dame and died at the age of forty-four, *South Bend Tribune*, 8 November 1960; the other sons entered Notre Dame but failed to graduate and also have had wandering, difficult lives.

Jesse Harper wrote Arthur Haley, 21 April 1940 (UABM *Knute Rockne—All American* Series/"H" folder), emphasis added. Haley, as the N.D. point man on the project, had written Harper to gain his permission for the film to use his name in "a scene where 'Rock' accepts employment to teach chemistry and assist you in coaching," 17 April 1940 (UABM *Knute Rockne—All American* Series/"H" folder). Harper, who harbored no resentments toward Notre Dame, signed the release and added, "I surely hope the picture will be a big success." In a postscript, he elaborated on the historical point: "The deal for Rockne's services at Notre Dame was made entirely by Father Cavanaugh and myself. At that time the President consulted no one of the [C.S.C.] order."

Bonnie Rockne and her attorney insisted to Warners on her point of view: "Mrs. Rockne and myself will never be satisfied with this picture unless you develop the intellectual side of Rockne. If Rockne had not devoted his life to coaching, wherein he became famous, but had devoted it to chemistry, he would be an equally noted scientist," 16 February 1940 (UABM *Knute Rockne—All American* Series/"Vitus G. Jones" folder). Warners tried to accommodate her and asked Haley for more information on former chemistry professor Nieuwland. Haley wrote a fellow N.D. official, Tom Barry, 9 April 1940: "They are thinking seriously of writing another scene for Father Nieuwland, which will enhance the educational value of the picture" (UABM *Knute Rockne—All American* Series/"B" folder). Warners subsequently added the scene where Father Callahan, the fictitious president of Notre Dame, and Rockne discuss whether the recent graduate should become a chemist or a football coach. Of course, the real Rockne faced no such dilemma—he loved athletics and desperately wanted to coach after graduating from N.D.

The preliminary agreement between the University of Notre Dame and Warner Brothers, 10 and 11 January 1939, is in UABM *Knute Rockne—All American* Series/

"Contracts" folder, emphasis added. Harry Stuhldreher wrote to Rev. John J. Cavanaugh, 11 April 1940 (UVOC 8/57). Arthur Haley informed Buckner of Father Burke's suggestions, 2 May 1939, and the Notre Dame approval, 6 June 1939 (UABM *Knute Rockne—All American* Series/"Buckner" folder); Bonnie's objections are in her lawyer's letter to Warner Brothers, 12 June 1939 (UABM *Knute Rockne—All American* Series/"Vitus G. Jones" folder).

The scriptwriter wrote to Arthur Haley about Spencer Tracy, 9 May 1939 (UABM *Knute Rockne—All American* Series/"Buckner" folder); Haley wrote to the Warners producer about Paul Muni, 24 February 1939 (UABM *Knute Rockne—All American* Series/"Bryan Foy" folder). Confusing the issue on the casting of the film is the fact that in Warners' first announcement of the movie in late 1938, they listed O'Brien in the Rockne role and Reagan as George Gipp. The studio did this because these actors were under contract to them and it was standard Hollywood procedure to announce "contract players" in the initial cast. Buckner explained this to Haley—"the item you saw in the [*Hollywood*] *Reporter* about Pat O'Brien playing the life of Rockne is nothing more than a publicity handout. The casting has not yet been discussed, and I am pretty sure that Mr. Wallis will try to get the best man for the job [that is, not Pat O'Brien]," 20 March 1939 (UABM *Knute Rockne—All-American* Series/"Buckner" folder).

On page 470 of the text, Pat O'Brien's secretary, Wallace Fitzsimmons, wrote to Arthur Haley, 23 February 1939 (UABM *Knute Rockne—All American* Series/"Pat O'Brien" folder). Buckner requested that N.D. officials write to Bishop Ryan of Omaha in a letter to Haley, 9 May 1939, and Buckner mentioned O'Donnell's letter to Bishop Ryan to Haley, 25 May 1939 (UABM *Knute Rockne—All American* Series/ "Buckner" folder). Arthur Haley informed Bryan Foy, 15 June 1939, that he and the scriptwriter had visited Mayor Kelly of Chicago (UABM *Knute Rockne—All American* Series/"Bryan Foy" folder); copies of Mayor Kelly's letter to Louis B. Mayer, 20 June 1939, and Mayer's reply to Kelly, 3 July 1939, are in UABM *Knute Rockne—All American* Series/"Edward J. Kelly/Louis B. Mayer" folder).

The scriptwriter's letter to Haley about Jimmy Cagney, 11 July 1939; Haley's cool reply, 24 July 1939; a copy of Buckner's explanation to Rev. J. Hugh O'Donnell of Warners' position on Cagney versus O'Brien, 26 July 1939; and Haley's explanation to Buckner of the veto of Cagney, 2 August 1939, are all in UABM *Knute Rockne—All American* Series/"Buckner" folder). The Spanish Civil War was one of the most complicated and confusing events in modern history. For Americans, the terms "Loyalists" and "Republicans" usually suggest conservative groups, whereas "Rebels" denotes the left. However, the Spanish Civil War began with a rebellion of army officers, led by General Francisco Franco, against the Spanish Republican government. Franco was backed by the Spanish Catholic church and later aided by Hitler and Mussolini—his forces were usually called the "Rebels" or "Nationalists." Defending the government were the moderate liberal to extreme left political parties in Spain and similar groups abroad, including the International Communist Party and the Soviet Union. People on the government side were called the "Republicans" or "Loyalists"; that is, they were loyal to the Republic.

The war became a rallying point for various political groups in the Western world, and many people, usually idealistic but often merely naive, went to Spain either to aid the Republic or to fight for the Rebels. In addition, many writers traveled to Spain to participate in the events; my first book, *And I Remember Spain,* New York, 1974, collects works from authors across the political spectrum. No one writer or political group had an option on the truth and many sincere people fought and died on both sides of the war.

On page 471 of the text, Hal Wallis wrote to Haley, 11 August 1939 (UABM *Knute Rockne—All American* Series/"Wallis" folder). The scriptwriter informed Haley about the lack of "news on the Rockne picture," 21 November 1939 (UABM *Knute Rockne—All American* Series/"Buckner" folder).

37. FILMING *KNUTE ROCKNE—ALL AMERICAN:* 1940

Robert Buckner wrote to Arthur Haley about the production start, 25 January 1940, and his preference for Donald Woods, 28 February 1940 (UABM *Knute Rockne—All American* Series/"Buckner" folder). Anne Edwards, in *Early Reagan,* New York, 1987, documented Reagan's campaign for the Gipp role and Pat O'Brien's help, pages 206–7; Haley told his assistant, Herb Jones, about Reagan's talk, 16 April 1940 (UABM *Knute Rockne—All American* Series/"Herb Jones" folder). Haley wrote to Rev. J. Hugh O'Donnell about the casting of Donald Crisp and Gale Page, 20 March 1940 (UABM *Knute Rockne—All American* Series/"O" folder), and the scriptwriter commented on the "woman's audience" in a letter to Haley, 26 April 1939 (UABM *Knute Rockne—All American* Series/"Buckner" folder).

Herman Lissauer, head of the "Research Department" at Warners, wrote to Haley, 19 February 1940 (UABM *Knute Rockne—All American* Series/"L" folder). Buckner made his claims about the script's authenticity to Haley, 26 April 1939 (UABM *Knute Rockne—All American* Series/"Buckner" folder). In this letter, he did acknowledge dramatic license in Rockne's relationship to the Carnegie Foundation investigation:

In 1928 or so when there was the famous "over-emphasis" investigation in football by the Carnegie Foundation, I believe there arose a very serious threat to the existence of football itself in American schools. I am sure you remember this period and Rockne's attitude toward the subject, of which we have record. For purposes of picture making, I telescoped this investigation to a scene of a hearing held in New York by a committee of American educators. Rockne comes to this hearing of his own volition and defends the game of football to which he has devoted his life. . . . It is a very dramatic scene and I know it will play well.

The dialogue which I put into Rockne's mouth in this scene is taken entirely from his own statements, but at various times in his life. . . . It is probably the most dramatic single scene in the entire screenplay, which is why I am so anxious for it to be retained. There is nothing in it that will antagonize

anyone, and it answers what you may remember as our greatest problem—
[with the film]—the creation of [real drama through] a definite menace to the
[Rockne] story.

Buckner's remarks contain various contradictions: in his fervor to defend college
football from the reformers, he seems a genuine zealot; however, in his comment
"There is nothing in it [the scene] that will antagonize anyone," he renders the
reformers invisible and trivializes the debate. Yet, in the end, his career ambitions
dominate—he wants to use the scene as the dramatic highlight of the film and, not
incidentally, to showcase his writing talent. However, because Buckner based his
script mainly on the coach's *Autobiography,* many of the mock-courtroom speeches
in the film are lifted from that work and belong more to the pen of John B. Kennedy
than to Knute K. Rockne.

The scriptwriter also preludes the scene by having the fictitious president of
Notre Dame, Father Callahan, urge Rockne to go to New York and defend himself
and his fellow coaches against the charges of the reformers. If the Carnegie Foundation had held public hearings, it is inconceivable that President Matthew Walsh or his
successor, President Charles O'Donnell, would have encouraged Rockne to speak
against the reformers. Considering their cooperation with the Carnegie Foundation
and their desire to get along with as well as obtain grants from the educational
mandarins, if these N.D. administrators had found out that Rockne intended to attack
the reformers at a high-profile public hearing, they would have forbidden him from
making the trip.

On page 475 of the text, Haley wrote Warners' lawyer, 21 February 1940 (UABM
Knute Rockne—All American Series/"Obringer" folder). The question by the reporter
in the script is in UABM *Knute Rockne—All American* Series/"Script–1940/0120"
folder). Bonnie's lawyer, Vitus G. Jones, wrote to Warner Bros. Pictures, Inc., 16
February 1940 (UABM *Knute Rockne—All American* Series/"Vitus G. Jones" folder).
Dorais's comment is in CJWC *Autobiography of Knute Rockne* Series/"Statement by
Charles Dorais" folder), and the scene with the sporting goods company is in UABM
Knute Rockne—All American Series/"Script–1940/0120" folder). Haley explained the
problem with the sporting goods reference to the scriptwriter, 16 February 1940
(UABM *Knute Rockne—All American* Series/"Buckner" folder).

Haley told James E. Coston that he had informed Hal Wallis about the absence of
"Mrs. Rockne's O.K.," 29 February 1940 (UABM *Knute Rockne—All American* Se-
ries/"James E. Coston" folder). Wallis telegraphed to Notre Dame, 4 March 1940
(UABM *Knute Rockne—All American* Series/"Wallis" folder), and Vitus E. Jones and
Bonnie Rockne sent their signed approval to Warner Bros., 15 March 1940 (UABM
Knute Rockne—All American Series/"Vitus E. Jones" folder). The scriptwriter told
Haley about the Hollywood trip, 13 February 1940 (UABM *Knute Rockne—All
American* Series/"Buckner" folder), and Haley's 1940 earnings are in Haley's per-
sonal papers, CHAL "1940 Income Tax Return" folder. Buckner joked to Haley
about Hollywood, undated (UABM *Knute Rockne—All American* Series/"Buckner"

folder). Bonnie's departure for Hollywood was covered by the Midwest press, including the *Chicago Herald-American*, 3 April 1940.

On page 478 of the text, Arthur Haley discussed Bill Howard's problems and Bacon's background in a letter to Vice President John J. Cavanaugh, 16 April 1940 (UABM *Knute Rockne—All American* Series/"Rev. John J. Cavanaugh" folder). Arthur Haley told Rev. J. Hugh O'Donnell about O'Brien's losing weight, 20 March 1940 (UABM *Knute Rockne—All American* Series/"O" folder). A list of scenes to be shot in Indiana, dated 22 April 1940, is in UABM *Knute Rockne—All American* Series/"Miscellaneous Documents" folder). The Warners' "Inter-Office Communication" was circulated and written by Bill Rice of the studio's publicity department, 24 April 1940 (UABM *Knute Rockne—All American* Series/"Joseph Petritz" folder). The *New York Times* had an article on Warners' use of the field at Loyola of Los Angeles and the shooting of the football scenes, 21 July 1940.

Father John C. Cavanaugh wrote to Hal Wallis, 30 April 1940 (UVOC 8/58). The memo "Outlined by Mr. Einfeld," 19 March 1940, was apparently written by Bill Rice (UVOC 5/58), emphasis added. The Warners' lawyer wrote to Haley, enclosing the new Foreword, upon which Cavanaugh crossed out the last clause, 18 June 1940; Arthur Haley informed Obringer of the university's compromise, 26 June 1940; and Haley telegraphed N.D.'s acceptance to the lawyer, 12 July 1940, emphasis added, all in UABM *Knute Rockne—All American* Series/"Obringer" folder).

Hal Wallis suggested the film title to Haley, 8 February 1940, and Haley replied negatively, 16 February 1940 (UABM *Knute Rockne—All American* Series/"Wallis" folder). The scriptwriter discussed the new and final title in a letter to Haley, 9 July 1940 (UABM *Knute Rockne—All American* Series/"Buckner" folder); Rev. John J. Cavanaugh wrote to Haley about the new title, 13 July 1940 (UVOC 8/57); and Haley informed Jack Warner of the dissatisfaction with the new title, 16 July 1940 (UABM *Knute Rockne—All American* Series/"Jack Warner" folder). Haley suggested the two-word title, 16 July 1940 (UABM *Knute Rockne—All American* Series/"Robert Buckner" folder). Jack Warner gave Haley the studio's final decision on the title, 17 July 1940, and informed Rev. J. Hugh O'Donnell about the sneak preview, 12 July 1940 (UABM *Knute Rockne—All American* Series/"Jack Warner" folder).

On page 482 of the text, Buckner told Rev. John J. Cavanaugh about the audience reception, 12 July 1940 (UVOC 8/57), and Arthur Haley informed Robert Buckner about the initial Notre Dame reaction, 23 July 1940 (UABM *Knute Rockne—All American* Series/"Buckner" folder).

38. THE END OF THE ROCKNE ERA: 1940

The statement by the University of Chicago's Board of Trustees and President Robert Hutchins was carried by the *New York Times*, 22 December 1939. Robin Lester has an excellent analysis of the events leading up to the decision, page 246 and following; he begins by quoting an epigram by Thorstein Veblen—big-time college football "has the same relation to physical culture that bull-fighting has to agriculture." Francis Wallace commented about the Chicago "boys" in his "Pigskin Preview" article in the

Saturday Evening Post, 23 September 1939, page 35; Arch Ward red-baited Hutchins in the *Chicago Tribune,* 15 January 1940; and Lester quoted the telegram from J. William Fulbright, page 268. The *Milwaukee Journal* editorial page, 15 January 1940, was typical of the pro-Hutchins reaction. The Chicago sportswriters sided with Major John Griffith and played up his anti-Hutchins moves, see the *Chicago Daily News,* 22 and 23 December 1939; the *Chicago Herald-American,* 22 December 1939 and 22 April 1940; and the *Chicago Tribune,* 19, 22, and 29 April 1940. Ironically, the University of Chicago was the only Big Ten conference member at the time with squads in all thirteen "minor" sports.

The *Notre Dame Alumnus* featured Father John O'Hara's "Farewell to the Students," February 1940, pages 114–15, and a lengthy portrait of Father J. Hugh O'Donnell that same issue, page 115. Rev. John J. Cavanaugh wrote to Elmer Layden, 3 July 1940 (UVOC 5/7); for the employment of Notre Dame students in the 1940–1941 and 1941–1942 academic years, see UVOC 5/12.

Father Hugh O'Donnell's commitment to obtaining the releases was discussed by Buckner in a letter to Haley, 26 February 1940 (UABM *Knute Rockne—All-American* Series/"Buckner" folder); the original agreement between the studio and Notre Dame obligated the school to this process, 10 January 1939 (UABM *Knute Rockne—All American* Series/"Contracts" folder). Layden complained to Haley, 29 March 1940 (UABM *Knute Rockne—All American* Series/"Layden" folder). Rev. John J. Cavanaugh asked Haley, 10 April 1940: "Have you received from Elmer his written permission?" and Warners' executive Robert Fellows protested to Rev. John J. Cavanaugh about Layden's intransigence, 11 April 1940 (UABM *Knute Rockne—All American* Series/"Rev. John J. Cavanaugh" folder). Wallis wired Cavanaugh, 24 April 1940, and telegraphed about Crowley's release, 25 April 1940; the N.D. vice president told Wallis about Layden's continuing refusal, 27 April 1940 (UVOC 8/57). Haley informed Warners of Layden's "signed release," given the previous day, 20 May 1940 (UABM *Knute Rockne—All American* Series/"Robert Fellows" folder).

S. Charles Einfeld wrote E. L. Bach, 13 June 1939 (UABM *Knute Rockne—All American* Series/"Charles Einfeld" folder). The *Notre Dame Scholastic* wrote about the plans for the film premiere, 4 October 1940, page 7; and the *South Bend Tribune* covered the events, including with a special pullout, 4, 5, and 6 October 1940. President J. Hugh O'Donnell wrote to Haley, 20 November 1940 (UPHO 81/"1940–41 Athletics" folder).

The long private communication from Chet Grant to Vice President John J. Cavanaugh, 5 January 1941, is in UPHO 88/19a. Someone tore Grant's signature from the letter—probably to protect his confidentiality—but every piece of factual internal evidence indicates his authorship; for example, the writer states that losing his assistant's job would be "an economic blow to my folks"—Grant, the only bachelor on Layden's staff at the time, lived with and supported his parents. In addition, Grant's inimitable writing style—he worked as a professional sportswriter before and after his coaching stint at N.D. with Layden—including his verbosity and grammatical quirks, is identical to his signed pieces of this period, especially his newsletter about Notre Dame football, "Under the Hat." Moreover, none of Layden's other assistants had his writing ability or this style. Thus, only Chet Grant could have authored this report.

During the 1940 season, the Chicago papers, especially the *Chicago Tribune,* continued full coverage of Notre Dame football, with lengthy game reports for the College of the Pacific opener, 6 October 1940; the Georgia Tech game, 13 October 1940; the demolition of Carnegie Tech, 20 October 1940; and the visit to the University of Illinois, with extra coverage from their regular reporters on the Illini beat, 27 October 1940. The New York papers covered the Army annual; their sportswriters were surprised at the N.D. showing an reported that on 3 November 1940; the UPI report is in the *Notre Dame Scrapbook,* page 101. Beach and Moore reported on the fans, including the "typical" one in Los Angeles, page 217. The eastern papers continued with extensive coverage for the following week's game in Baltimore against Navy, see the *Washington Star,* 10 November 1940.

The sentence dropped from the text of the Chicago gambler's speech was, "My wife had just given birth and I even took the money she put aside for the hospital bill and the baby's furniture and laid it down." The retired gambler spoke in an interview for this book, 18 March 1992, but requested anonymity:

Look, I made a lot of money gambling over the years and never declared much of it to the IRS. If you read the tax laws, you'll know that there is no statute of limitations on unpaid taxes, they can come after you any time, no matter how long ago it was [that the unpaid taxes occurred] and collect, plus you've got to pay their friggin' interest too. So what kind of schmuck do you take me for if I let you print my name? You're lucky I'm telling you the story. By the way, I'm still making money at the track and trying to pay as little taxes on it as possible. It's not as easy to hide it as it used to be.

After the loss at Northwestern, Arch Ward tried to defend his favorite team in the *Chicago Tribune,* 4 December 1940; and James Kearns in the *Chicago Daily News,* 3 December 1940, was equally defensive about N.D. Layden wrote to Rev. John J. Cavanaugh about the drinking in the stands, 26 November 1940 (UVOC 5/7); Layden's final N.D. game and the incident with the official were covered extensively by the newspapers, especially the *Los Angeles Times,* 8 December 1940, and Cromartie and Brown, pages 110–113. Among the Warners people asking for tickets to the N.D.–USC game was attorney R. J. Obringer, who had always placed his client's interest far ahead of Notre Dame's; Haley promised to accommodate his request for four tickets, 21 October 1940 (UABM *Knute Rockne—All American* Series/"Roy J. Obringer" folder).

Layden gave the official story of his departure in his memoir, pages 135–41, with the quote in the text on pages 135–36. The *Notre Dame Scholastic* carried the Golden Dome's statement on Layden's leaving, 7 February 1940, page 12; the newspaper clipping headlined "IRISH SOUGHT LEAHY BEFORE LAYDEN QUIT" is in UVOC 5/10.

39. THE END OF THE CREATION OF NOTRE DAME FOOTBALL: 1941

For the N.D. press release from Rev. John J. Cavanaugh, 28 March 1941, see UVOC 6/6; the memo of the conference between President J. Hugh O'Donnell and Frank Leahy, 3 August 1942, is in UVOC 5/12. The N.D. athletic department publicity handout with Director of Sports Publicity Charles M. Callahan's name at the top is in UABM *Knute Rockne—All American* Series/"Background Rockne" folder. Among other passages in the document is: "After graduation, Rock remained at Notre Dame as a graduate assistant in chemistry. In accepting the post, he attached the stipulation that he be allowed to assist Jess Harper in coaching the football team."

Boston columnist Bill Cunningham published his column in the *Boston Herald*, 3 June 1941.

EPILOGUE

Frank Leahy's main assistant was Joe "Captain Bligh" McArdle. In *From Rockne to Parseghian,* Francis Wallace traces Notre Dame football history from his mentor to Parseghian and discusses the "Fainting Irish" game, pages 156–157. N.D. player Frank Varrichione feigned injuries in the last minute of the first half and his team scored; he did it again near the end of the game and the Irish scored again, gaining a 14–14 tie. Because of the limited time-out rule during this period, every big-time college football team had a fake injury play and designated "actors." Leahy could never understand the fuss that the press and public made after Notre Dame used a tactic employed by almost every other major team in the country. Wallace's comments on Parseghian's ancestry are on page 231.

Michael Novak's *Joy of Sports: End Zones, Bases, Basket, Balls, and the Consecration of the American Spirit,* New York, 1976, is one of the few books written by an intellectual that is unabashedly pro big-time sports. He discusses Notre Dame football on pages 35–39. The interview with Professor Robert Schmuhl took place 13 March 1991.

Bibliography

Allen, Frederick. *Only Yesterday: An Informal History of the 1920s.* New York, 1931.

Anderson, Dave, ed. *Red Smith Reader.* New York, 1982.

Anderson, Heartley "Hunk," with Klosinski, Emil. *Notre Dame, Chicago Bears, and Hunk.* Oviedo, Fla., 1976.

Armstrong, James. *Onward to Victory: A Chronicle of the Alumni of the University of Notre Dame du Lac.* Notre Dame, Ind., 1974.

Arthur, Rev. David Joseph. "The University of Notre Dame, 1919–1933: An Administrative History." Ph.D. dissertation, University of Michigan, 1973.

Ashe, Arthur. *A Hard Road to Glory: A History of the African-American Athlete 1619–1918.* New York, 1988.

Autobiography of Knute K. Rockne, The. Authorship in dispute, probably John B. Kennedy. Indianapolis, 1931.

Baritz, Loren. *The Culture of the Twenties.* Indianapolis, 1970.

Beach, Jim, and Moore, Daniel. *Army vs. Notre Dame: The Big Game 1913–1947.* New York, 1948.

Behee, John R. *Fielding Yost's Legacy to the University of Michigan.* Ann Arbor, 1971.

Boland, Peg, ed. *Joe Boland—Notre Dame Man.* Hammond, Ind., 1962.

Bonifer, Mike, and Weaver, Larry. *Out of Bounds: An Anecdotal History of Notre Dame Football.* Blue Earth, Minn., 1978.

Brondfield, Jerry. *Rockne: The Coach, The Man, The Legend.* New York, 1976.

Brown, Warren. *Rockne.* Chicago, 1931.

———. *Win, Lose, or Draw.* New York, 1947.

Campbell, Don, ed. *The College Game.* Indianapolis, 1974.

Carnegie Foundation, *Carnegie Foundation, Bulletin Number Twenty-Three: American College Athletics.* New York, 1929, main author, Howard J. Savage.

Chelland, Patrick. *One for the Gipper: George Gipp, Knute Rockne, and Notre Dame.* Chicago, 1973.

Clary, Jack. *Army vs. Navy.* New York, 1965.

———. *Gridiron Grenadiers: The Story of West Point Football.* New York, 1948.

Cohen, Richard M., et al., eds. *The Notre Dame Football Scrapbook.* Indianapolis, 1977.

Colletti, Ned. *Golden Glory: Notre Dame vs Purdue.* New York, 1983.

Creamer, Robert. *Babe: The Legend Comes to Life.* New York, 1974.

Cromartie, Bill, and Brown, Jody. *The Glamor Game.* Nashville, Tenn., 1989.

Danzig, Allison, ed. *Oh, How They Played the Game.* New York, 1971.

———, and Brandwein, Peter, eds. *Sports Golden Age,* New York, 1948.

Davies, John. *The Legend of Hobey Baker.* Boston, 1966.

Donovan, John D. *The Academic Man in the Catholic College.* New York, 1964.

Dos Passos, John. *The Big Money.* New York, 1931 (reprinted 1991).

Doyle, Joseph. *Fighting Irish: A Century of Notre Dame Football.* Charlottesville, Va., 1987.

Drudy, J. P., ed. *The Irish in America: Emigration, Assimilation and Impact.* Cambridge, England, 1985.

Edwards, Anne. *Early Reagan.* New York, 1987.

Ellis, John Tracy. *American Catholicism,* 2nd ed. Chicago, 1969.

Falla, Jack. *NCAA: The Voice of College Sports: A Diamond Anniversary History, 1906–1981,* Mission, Kans., 1981.

Farr, Finis. *Fair Enough: A Biography of Westbrook Pegler.* New Rochelle, N.Y., 1975.

Flanagan, Thomas. *Tenants of Time.* New York, 1988.

Galbraith, John Kenneth. *The Great Crash: 1929.* Boston, 1961.

Gilman, Daniel Coit. *The Launching of a University* [Johns Hopkins]. New York, 1969.

Greeley, Rev. Andrew. *From Backwater to Mainstream: A Profile of Catholic Higher Education.* New York, 1969.

———. *The Irish Americans: The Rise to Money and Power.* New York, 1981.

Gallico, Paul. *Farewell to Sport.* New York, 1938.

———. *The Golden People.* Garden City, N.Y., 1965.

Gekas, George. *The Life and Times of George Gipp.* South Bend, Ind., 1987.

Goodman, Murray, and Lewin, Leonard, eds. *My Greatest Day in Football.* New York, 1938.

Grant, Chet. *Before Rockne at Notre Dame: Impression and Reminiscence.* South Bend, Ind., 1978.

Halsey, William M. *The Survival of American Innocence: Catholicism in an Era of Disillusionment, 1920–1940.* Notre Dame, Ind., 1980.

Handlin, Oscar. *Al Smith and His America.* New York, 1958.

———, and Handlin, Mary. *The American College and American Culture.* New York, 1970.

Harron, Robert. *Rockne: Idol of American Football.* New York, 1931.

Hawkins, Hugh. *Pioneers: A History of the Johns Hopkins University.* Ithaca, N.Y., 1960.

Hofstadter, Richard. *Academic Freedom in the Age of the College.* New York, 1955.

Holtz, Lou, with Heisler, John. *The Fighting Spirit.* New York, 1990.

Holtzman, Jerome, ed. *No Cheering from the Press Box.* New York, 1974.

Hope, Rev. Arthur J. *Notre Dame: One Hundred Years.* Notre Dame, Ind., 1948.

Huston, McCready. *Salesman from the Sidelines: Being the Business Career of Knute Rockne.* New York, 1932.

Israel, David. *The Cornhuskers: Nebraska Football.* Chicago, 1975.

Johnson, Chuck. *The Green Bay Packers.* New York, 1961.

Kahn, E. J. *The World of Swope.* New York, 1965.

Kaplan, Justin, ed. *Familiar Quotations: John Bartlett,* 16th ed. Boston, 1991.

Katz, Frederic, ed. *The Glory of Notre Dame.* New York, 1971.

Kennedy, Eugene C. *Father's Day.* Garden City, N.Y., 1981.

Klingaman, William. *1929: The Year of the Great Crash.* New York, 1989.

Klosinski, Emil. *Pro Football in the Days of Rockne.* New York, 1970.

Layden, Elmer, with Snyder, Ed. *It Was a Different Game: The Elmer Layden Story.* Englewood Cliffs, N.J., 1969.

Leahy, Rev. William P. *Adapting to America: Catholics, Jesuits, and Higher Education in the Twentieth Century.* Washington, D.C., 1992.

Lee, Calvin. *The Campus Scene: 1900–1970.* New York, 1970.

Lester, Robin. "The Rise, Decline, and Fall of Intercollegiate Football at the University of Chicago, 1890–1940." Ph.D. dissertation, University of Chicago, 1974.

Lipsyte, Robert. *SportsWorld.* New York, 1975.

Littlewood, Thomas. *Arch: A Promoter, Not a Poet: The Story of Arch Ward.* Ames, Iowa, 1990.

Lovelace, Delos. *Rockne of Notre Dame.* New York, 1931.

Lutholtz, M. William. *Grand Dragon: D. C. Stephenson and the Ku Klux Klan in Indiana.* West Lafayette, Ind., 1991.

McAvoy, Rev. Thomas. *Father O'Hara of Notre Dame: The Cardinal-Archbishop of Philadelphia.* Notre Dame, Ind., 1967.

McCallum, John D., and Castner, Paul. *We Remember Rockne.* Huntington, Ind., 1975.

McElvaine, Robert S. *The Great Depression America: 1929–1941.* New York, 1984.

Meagher, Timothy J., ed. *From Paddy to Studs: Irish-American Communities in the Turn of the Century Era, 1880 to 1920.* New York, 1986.

Michelson, Herb, and Newhouse, Dave. *Rose Bowl Football Since 1902.* New York, 1977.

Moore, Edmund A. *A Catholic Runs for President.* New York, 1956.

Moore, Rev. Philip S. *Academic Development [of the] University of Notre Dame: Past, Present, and Future.* Privately printed, Notre Dame, Ind., 1960.

Newcombe, Jack. *The Best of the Athletic Boys: The White Man's Impact on Jim Thorpe.* Garden City, N.Y., 1975.

———, ed. *Fireside Book of Football.* New York, 1964.

O'Brien, Michael. *Vince: A Personal Biography of Vince Lombardi*. New York, 1987.

O'Brien, Pat. *The Wind at My Back: The Life and Times of Pat O'Brien*. Garden City, N.Y., 1964.

O'Connor, Richard. *The First Hurrah: A Biography of Al Smith*. New York, 1970.

Perrin, Tom. *Football: A College History*. Jefferson, N.C., 1987.

Peterson, Robert. *Only the Ball Was White*, Englewood Cliffs, N.J., 1970.

Porter, David L., ed. *Biographical Dictionary of American Sports*. New York, 1987.

Power, Edward J. *Catholic Higher Education: A History*. New York, 1972.

Rader, Benjamin. *American Sports: From the Age of Folk Games to the Age of Spectators*. Englewood Cliffs, N.J., 1983.

Rappoport, Ken. *Wake Up the Echoes*. Huntsville, Ala., 1975.

Reagan, Ronald. *An American Life*. New York, 1990.

———, with Hubler, Richard G. *Where's the Rest of Me?* New York, 1965.

Rice, Grantland. *The Tumult and the Shouting*. New York, 1954.

Roberts, Howard. *The Big Nine: The Story of Football in the Western Conference*. New York, 1948.

Roberts, Randy. *Papa Jack: Jack Johnson and the Era of White Hopes*. New York, 1983.

Rockne, Knute. *Coaching*. New York, 1925.

———. *The Four Winners*. New York, 1925.

Rodgers, Marion Elizabeth, ed. *The Impossible Mr. Mencken*. New York, 1991.

Rudolph, Frederick. *The American College and University: A History*. New York, 1962.

———. *Curriculum: A History of American Undergraduate Courses of Study Since 1636*. San Francisco, 1977.

Samuelson, Rube. *The Rose Bowl Game*. Garden City, N.Y., 1951.

Schlaver, Edward. *The Notre Dame Ethos: Student Life in a Catholic Residential University*. Ph.D. dissertation, University of Michigan, 1979.

Schlereth, Thomas. *The University of Notre Dame: A Portrait of Its History and Campus*. Notre Dame, Ind., 1976.

Schoor, Gene. *A Treasury of Notre Dame Football*. New York, 1962.

Solberg, Winton. *The University of Illinois, 1867–1894: An Intellectual and Cultural History*. Urbana, Ill., 1968.

Smith, Ronald. *Sports and Freedom: The Rise of Big-time College Sports*. New York, 1988.

Sperber, Murray, ed. *And I Remember Spain*. New York, 1974.

———. *College Sports Inc.: The Athletic Department vs the University*. New York, 1990.

Steele, Michael. *Knute Rockne: A Bio-Bibliography*. Westport, Conn., 1983.

Stevenson, Elizabeth. *Babbitts and Bohemians*. New York, 1967.

Storr, Richard J. *Harper's University: The Beginnings—A History of the University of Chicago*. Chicago, 1966.

Strich, Thomas. *My Notre Dame*. Notre Dame, Ind., 1991.

Stuhldreher, Harry. *Knute Rockne: Man Builder*. New York, 1931.

Stuhldreher, Mary. *Many a Saturday Afternoon.* New York, 1964.

Terkel, Studs, ed. *Hard Times: An Oral History of the Great Depression.* New York, 1970.

Twombley, Wells. *Shake Down the Thunder: The Critical Biography of Notre Dame's Frank Leahy.* Radnor, Pa., 1974.

Veysey, Laurence. *The Emergence of the American University.* Chicago, 1974.

Voltmer, Carl. *A History of the Intercollegiate Conference.* New York, 1935.

Wade, Wyn Craig. *The Fiery Cross: The Ku Klux Klan in America.* New York, 1988.

Edward Wakin, *The Catholic Campus.* New York, 1963.

Wallace, Francis. *Autumn Madness.* New York, 1937.

———. *Huddle.* New York, 1931.

———. *From Rockne to Parseghian.* New York, 1966.

———. *Knute Rockne.* New York, 1960.

———. *Notre Dame: Its People and Its Legends.* New York, 1969.

———. *The Notre Dame Story.* New York, 1949.

———. *O'Reilly of Notre Dame.* New York, 1931.

———. *Stadium.* New York, 1931.

Walsh, Christy. *Adios to Ghosts.* New York, 1937.

———. *Intercollegiate Football: A Complete Pictorial and Statistical Review from 1869 to 1934.* New York, 1934.

Wechsler, James. *Revolt on Campus.* New York, 1935.

Whittingham, Richard. *Saturday Afternoon: College Football and the Men Who Made the Day.* New York, 1985.

Wills, Garry. *Bare Ruined Choirs: Doubt, Prophecy, and Radical Religion.* New York, 1971.

Wilson, Kenneth L. (Tug), and Brondfield, Jerry. *The Big Ten.* Englewood Cliffs, N.J., 1967.

Yardley, Jonathan. *Ring: A Biography of Ring Lardner.* New York, 1977.

Young, Eugene "Scrapiron." *With Rockne at Notre Dame.* New York, 1951.

Index